THE LAST NEW DEALER

by

MILLARD GRIMES

PAGE PUBLISHING, INC.
Conneaut Lake, PA

First originally published by Page Publishing 2020

ISBN 978-1-68456-192-6 (pbk)
ISBN 978-1-68456-193-3 (digital)

Printed in the United States of America

Contents

Dedication

To who else but Charlotte Sheridan Grimes, my wife and invaluable companion for more than 60 years; and to my grandchildren Lauren, Forrest, Sheridan and Stephen, who I hope will take ideas in this book into the 22nd century.

Prologue

A RAINY NIGHT IN GEORGIA

> *It seems to me that we are most completely, most*
> *loudly, most proudly American around Election*
> *Day. Because it is then that we can assert our-*
> *selves—voters and candidates alike. We can assert*
> *the most glorious, the most encouraging fact in all*
> *the world today—the fact that democracy is alive—*
> *and going strong.*
> —*Franklin D. Roosevelt, campaign*
> *address in Boston, October 30, 1940*

The rain began falling when he was about ten minutes out of the Atlanta City limits. Soon the windshield wipers were fighting a losing battle with the huge raindrops coming out of an ominously black night.

But Thomas Alexander Franklin pressed ahead. In all his sixty-one years, he'd never been in a serious auto accident, either as a driver or a passenger. He had left Atlanta with $7 million in cash, checks, and notes in his coat and had already deposited $4 million in three banks along the way, leaving him $3 million tucked in his inside coat pockets. Home was just one hundred miles away, and he meant to get there soon. In his sturdy 1988 Lincoln Town Car, he felt virtually invulnerable.

The night became darker, and the rain got harder. His aging eyes, tired from the four days of negotiating the sale of his newspaper group, strained to make out the lights on the other side of the interstate highway.

Briefly he considered trying to pull over to let the worst of the traffic pass, but he actually couldn't make out the sides of the pavement. Then suddenly he felt the wheels begin to lose traction, and he did all the things you were told not to do. He tried to apply the brakes to regain control, but instead the wheels slid sideways and then out of control his car crossed the median. He could see the headlights of a car coming from the other direction as his car swerved into the wrong lane. There was a collision, and his head jerked forward, hitting the windshield as the seat belt caught the rest of his body.

Instinctively, he reached for the heavy envelope of checks in his coat pocket. It was still there, still dry although rain was pelting through the broken window, still as secure as an envelope could be in a broken car on a dark rainy night with its driver slipping into unconsciousness. Thoughts kept racing through his mind of his plans, how he would use the money from the sale of his newspaper group to finance his candidacy for president of the United States of America, of all the ideas he had written about in hundreds of newspaper columns and editorials and the additional ideas he'd found in the dozens of books he'd studied in the past few months.

In the distance, Franklin heard sirens coming closer then a voice loudly asking if he was all right. A flash of lightning revealed a middle-aged man trying unsuccessfully to open the smashed car door. The sirens came closer. "Are you all right?" the man asked again.

"Not really," Franklin managed to say, "but I think I'm alive." The sirens stopped, and Franklin sensed two men lifting him from the wreck and felt the hard rain on his face and arms. One man was taking his pulse, while the other tried to stop the flow of blood from his forehead. He vaguely thought about the envelope and hoped the men who were trying to save his life wouldn't discover that it contained nearly $4 million in checks and notes.

"He's alive," the EMT taking his pulse announced. Then Franklin lost consciousness for a very long time.

Chapter One

New Hampshire Autumn

Let us never forget that government is ourselves and not an alien power over us. The ultimate rulers of our democracy are not a President and senators and congressmen and government officials but the voters of this country.
—Franklin D. Roosevelt, July 8, 1938

Indian summer had stayed late that year in New Hampshire. The leaves were brighter, the mountain panorama more striking; the tourist season promised to be a good one. Thomas Alexander Franklin was sitting back and enjoying the scenery. He had a driver, Jack Hardy, who was capable and familiar with New Hampshire roads. They'd met earlier that day at the Manchester airport and rented a 1988 Lincoln Town Car, the same model Franklin drove and had found comfortable for long trips, reliable, and except for one terrible experience in the rain, very safe.

Hardy, a lanky, amiable employee of Jody Powell's high-powered political relations firm in Washington, had gotten his early experience as a driver for Jimmy Carter in the 1976 presidential campaign and again in the 1980 campaign.

"So Jody tells me you're planning to run in the Democratic presidential primary here," Hardy said.

"That's right," Franklin replied. "It seems like a good year."

"He also said you've never run for or been elected to a political office."

"Well, that is one of my good points," Franklin said. "Politicians seem to be out of favor this year, but I personally admire politicians. Without them, we wouldn't have a democracy. I've thought about this for a long time. After all, Carter was a long shot."

Hardy sounded skeptical. "Yeah, he was a long shot, but he had been governor of Georgia. You sound like a no-shot. But hey, I'm glad to get the job. It's been a slow year for Democratic candidates."

"Are you a Democrat?" Franklin asked.

"Am I a Democrat?" Hardy exclaimed. "I was the only white man in Hickory, North Carolina, who voted for George McGovern in 1972."

"That's strong," Franklin agreed. "I voted for Nixon that year, even wrote editorials in his favor. I really believed in my vote, but in addition, the publisher would have fired me if I'd written in favor of McGovern. Actually, I was a bona fide Republican in those years, but I also was one of the first editors to write that Nixon knew all about the Watergate break-in. It just seemed logical that he did. You recall his campaign manager, John Mitchell, resigned a week after it happened. That was the tip-off. Nixon had to have known. He should've fessed up then, and it would have all blown over, and he would've been reelected easily, but maybe with a few less than the forty-nine states he actually carried."

"But you still voted for him?"

"Well, I actually voted against the demonstrators against the Vietnam War and the students who were taking over college presidents' offices and the people who seemed to have lost faith in the democratic process. Chaos has never produced a good government, and I sense some of that in the air today, but so far without the visible chaos we had in 1972."

"You've got a point," Hardy said. "That kind of sentiment hurt Carter when he ran for reelection in 1980. There was still that feeling that Democrats had let the demonstrators take over the country in those days and that Nixon, no matter what his mistakes and law breaking, had put things back in order."

"I even felt that way," Franklin admitted. "God forgive me, I voted for Reagan in 1980, but he had the wrong answers, and the nation will suffer from his policies for years if they aren't changed by the next administration. The federal government must be restored to its historic role as the answer, not the problem."

Hardy nodded in accord. "That's good," he said. "I never heard Carter put it quite that way. He was usually attacking the government, which was the popular thing to do in 1976, and from what I see, it's still the popular thing to do."

"Well, I'm not going to do that. I'm going to tell people this is still the greatest nation in history, and that's because of its government, which might not be perfect but is still the best one ever conceived and, in 1992, has the chance to be even better and stronger."

"My father would have agreed with that, for sure," Hardy said. "He was one of the original CCC boys in 1933."

"No kidding," exclaimed Franklin. "That's great. The Civilian Conservation Corps was the very first New Deal program approved by Congress after Roosevelt became president. It was the model for much of the rest of the New Deal."

"My dad used to talk about it when I was growing up," Hardy explained. He was only seventeen when he enrolled that first summer. "He said he weighed about 130 pounds, and when he got out six months later, he weighed 180 and was in the best shape of his life."

"The CCC was an idea Roosevelt had while he was governor of New York, and he decided to move on it immediately after getting the bank crisis settled," Franklin said. "CCC was a subject that excited him. He wanted to get people to work. Most Americans don't know that the CCC was also the origin of the environmental movement. On March 14, 1933, Roosevelt outlined the plan which put an army of unemployed young men to work in the nation's countryside, saving the forests and reducing the dust storms then sweeping the Midwest. He turned the project over to Louis Howe, his longest and most faithful assistant, who had guided his early political career and stood by Roosevelt during his years recovering from polio.

"Roosevelt sent the CCC plan to Congress, asking for the funds to launch the Corps. Congress was in a mood to act in that first week of the Roosevelt administration although some cabinet members thought it might be dangerous to put hundreds of young men in the woods, and organized labor leaders were wary of the idea of the government paying one dollar a day to the CCC workers. One witness told a House Senate committee, 'This program smacks of Fascism and Communism. It would legalize a form of forced labor.'

"But with the US in the grip of the worst economic crisis in its history, the bill was approved by Congress on March 31, just two weeks after being introduced. The idea was to pay its recruits thirty dollars a month, of which twenty dollars was to be sent home to their families, many of whom no longer had a wage-earning adult. The CCC member kept ten dollars a month for spending money, with his food and housing provided by the government.

"Within four months, 300,000 previously unemployed young men had been enrolled and were working in the countryside. They planted trees, dug ditches, created dams, built bridges, cleared beaches and old battlefields, and did much more to reclaim and develop resources that had been neglected for years, and while they revived the land, they developed themselves as your father did. One man said he felt like he owned the land he rescued. 'I wanted to go back when trees I planted had grown large and look at them,' he said. The CCC workers also met young men from all parts of the nation and learned that they were not alone in their troubles or their hopes. During the CCC's existence, more than 2.5 million members passed through the camps, earning money for the first time, helping families, and giving the nation an idea of how the federal government could help alleviate the economic crisis.

"Many of the CCC officers came from the regular Army, and one of the most successful was a colonel named George Catlett Marshall, who organized seventeen camps and later, of course, was a military leader in World War II.

"The CCC was one of the most successful New Deal programs and remained close to President Roosevelt's heart. He wanted to make it a permanent program, but World War II came along, and there was also growing opposition to the CCC from labor unions and private companies, which finally did it in. But your father can be proud that he helped build a legacy for preservation and purification of the land. Today's forests and streams are a legacy of the CCC."

"You're right, and my father knew it," Hardy agreed. "The CCC made him a real man and taught him skills he used in making furniture until the day he died."

"As I mentioned," Franklin continued, "the CCC pioneered the environmental movement and not a minute too soon. In the movie and book *The Grapes of Wrath*, John Steinbeck dramatically depicted conditions doing the great dust storms and how they destroyed the farms in the Plains states, forcing many people to move to California where they still struggled to survive. But on the plains, conditions were improving due to the efforts of those young CCC recruits, plus Roosevelt felt that the trees they planted would provide a shelter belt against the impact of the wind and dust along a stretch where the dust storms came in. Critics ridiculed his plan—as they did so many—by saying if God couldn't grow trees in the Great Plains, there was no reason to think the New Deal could."

"But under the leadership of Ferdinand Silco, a career forest ranger, the Forest Service continued the job the CCC started and, in the next few years, planted more than two million trees, which became a barrier to future dust bowls."

"I'm impressed," Hardy commented. "How do you know all this?"

"I've read a lot and have a trick memory that recalls a lot of trivia even when it can't remember phone numbers. Also, I was born in 1930, a few weeks after the Great Depression started. So I lived through the Depression as a child in LaGrange, just thirty miles from Warm Springs, where President Roosevelt often visited for treatment of his crippled legs.

"I remember vividly the day Roosevelt came to visit LaGrange when I was six years old, and we got out of school to join the crowd along the streets as his big car passed, his head thrown back, and waving his hat to us. That was 1936, probably the peak of his popularity although the people in Georgia revered him for years. Many homes had pictures and newspaper clippings of him in their living rooms. So from my childhood years, I followed Roosevelt's presidency and saw firsthand the improvements from the New Deal.

"My family had moved from Newnan to LaGrange, about thirty miles away, when my father lost his job in 1930, the first year of the Depression. I was only a year old, and in retrospect I consider it a fortunate event in my life because LaGrange was a great place to grow up during the 1930s. My family didn't have much money, but we never thought of ourselves as poor. My father got another job as a traveling salesman for a grocery produce company. I think he made about twenty dollars a week, and I've always joked that we were so poor we could hardly afford a maid. But we did because you could get a good maid for two dollars a week plus a couple of meals a day. During my growing up years, we always had a maid, which meant there were regular meals, the beds were made, and the small houses we lived in were clean and neat. My mother was always a semi-invalid, and some days she never got out of bed, but her sickness was never diagnosed.

"When I was ten, we moved to Columbus, about fifty miles down the road but still close to Warm Springs. Roosevelt served as president from when I was three until I was fifteen. In a way, my generation thought he was supposed to be president forever, and it was a jolt when he suddenly died."

"That was in the final weeks of World War II, wasn't it?" Hardy interjected.

"Yes, on April 12, 1945. Germany surrendered a few weeks later, and Hitler killed himself. It was such a tragedy that Roosevelt didn't live to see the success of the great Allied war effort he did so much to create, with an incredible leap forward for the nation in industrial production and overall workforce. It was an odd coincidence that Roosevelt became president and Adolf Hitler took power in Germany the same month in 1933, and both died in the same month, twelve years later, and those were arguably the most tragic but important twelve years in history. They were also the years I was growing up, mainly removed from the world tragedy but absorbing the changes and the peculiar fear and exhilaration of being alive in such a time."

"By the way, my directions say we're going to Wolfeboro, New Hampshire, which I've never heard of," Hardy said. "It's scarcely a dot on the map. Why in God's name are we going to Wolfeboro, New Hampshire?"

"You mean you didn't go through Wolfeboro in those two campaigns with Carter?"

"I thought we went through every town in New Hampshire, but I don't remember Wolfeboro."

"Well, it's the only place in New Hampshire where I've ever spent a night. So I thought I'd go back and renew old acquaintance."

"So do you know anybody there?"

"Actually not. My wife and I were on one of those autumn bus tours with about thirty other Georgians, and I mainly talked and ate with them while in Wolfeboro. I don't think I even met the manager of the inn."

"You don't sound like a very good politician. Carter would have shaken hands with everyone from the manager to the maid and cook."

"Different kinds of campaigns win elections, especially today," Franklin said. "One reason I'm running is to find out if a president— or any political candidate—can win without being marketed like a bar of soap or a bottle of beer and become a parody of who he really is or who he'll be if elected. There's too much of that today. A candidate should not be created by an ad agency with all his statements poll-tested by so-called consultants who are using the same arguments and TV spots they use for candidates from Maine to California."

Hardy had heard all that before.

"By the way, who will be writing your stuff?" he asked.

"In the early going, I guess I will. That's basically what I've done since I was sixteen, write newspaper editorials, and when you think about it, that's a useful background for a president."

Hardy chuckled. "Only losers have time to write their own stuff. A candidate has to be the front man, propped up by consultants and writers, and then if you should catch on, the media will seize on every word and twist it into whatever fits in a one-column headline or can be spit out in a thirty-second TV spot. I gather from what Jody is paying me for this job that you don't have a lot of money."

Franklin smiled. "On the scale of what most campaigns spend today, I don't. But the cost of campaigns is scandalous. Every candidate, from a city council member to president, promises to cut wasteful spending but then in their campaign they spend money recklessly and needlessly, and the voters don't seem to notice the contradiction. They usually elect the campaign spend-thrift.

"I'm trying to find out if you can win a campaign without so many consultants and TV commercials. Wolfeboro, by the way, is the county seat of Carroll County and has one of the oldest weekly newspapers in New Hampshire, *The Granite State News*, which is also the county legal organ. On the downside, Carroll has the smallest population of New Hampshire's ten counties."

Hardy shook his head and looked skeptical. "I've driven for about twenty candidates," he muttered. "All of them thought they were going to win and had peculiar ideas about how, including Carter, but you are one of the strangest...but also one of the smartest sounding. Carter never told me as much history as you have in just thirty miles."

"We're on a quixotic venture," Franklin said, "and you never know the exact way to where you're going."

"What kind of adventure?"

"Quixotic. It's a reference to Don Quixote, the fictional hero who charged at windmills with his lance because he thought they were dragons."

"Did he ever kill one?"

"I don't know. I never read the book, not even the Classic Comics version."

"So you're not an intellectual?"

"No, I'm a newspaperman. I didn't have time to be an intellectual. Newspaper people know a little about a lot of things but not a lot about anything. But they are curious, so they keep looking. By the way, did your father serve in World War II?"

16

"He sure did. Four years, from North Africa to the Normandy invasion. He didn't talk about it much, but he won several medals and came out a captain. He never encouraged me to join the Army."

"The former CCC boys were the hard-core of the US military service that won the war," Franklin said. "They'd had the training and discipline that prepared them for military service, which other draftees lacked, and also the physical attributes. That was another valuable legacy of the CCC. Boys like your father who were in their teens were just the age to be soldiers, sailors, and airmen in World War II, and they were much better prepared and were examples for the younger recruits who came in during the war, who had never been on a camping trip or fired a gun or even worked hard in their lives."

"Are you going to say that in your campaign?"

"Probably. People need to be reminded of what the CCC meant to the country and how it was a part of the New Deal and, in fact, provided the model for its future. There are still leaves today that need to be raked and too many young people who can't find useful employment."

"There's a fork in the road ahead and the sign seems to point toward Wolfeboro," Hardy observed.

"Well, as Yogi Berra is supposed to have said, when you come to a fork in the road, take it."

Franklin glanced out the window. He knew they were passing by Lake Winnipesaukee, the largest lake in New Hampshire and the reason Franklin's group came that way in 1985 and spent the night in Wolfeboro.

Hardy drove into Wolfeboro and found Endicott Street, which the newspaper directory listed as the location of the Granite State News. New Hampshire had long been identified as the Granite State, although granite was now down the list of its assets. Franklin prided himself on being able to find the newspaper office in any town he passed through. It was usually on the town square no matter how small the square. The Granite State News office proved to be just off the square, which had the courthouse and not much else.

Franklin and Hardy went inside. The building had one large front room, which apparently included the whole operation. The familiar odor of cold-type chemicals was a sign that the composition and makeup of the paper was also done in the room. There appeared to be two compugraphic machines and three typewriters on one large table along the side of the wall. To Franklin, it was a familiar scene and a familiar smell. Ink and metal had lost their prominence on newspapers as linotype machines were replaced by photographic typesetting, and the actual printing of the paper was often done at a central plant removed from the actual newspaper office.

In his publishing career, Franklin had been a pioneer in introducing offset printing, or cold type as it was commonly known, in both Georgia and Alabama. He had titled his book on Georgia newspapers, written and compiled from 1983 to 1985, *The Last Linotype*, as by then most newspapers no longer used linotype machines, which had been the workhorses of the industry since their introduction in 1884 and had freed editors and printers from the grueling task of composing every sentence in a page by hand, the same way Benjamin Franklin did in the early 1700s.

They were greeted by the only person who still seemed to be on duty, a pleasant gentleman in his early sixties. "I want to place an ad," Franklin told him. "Can you handle that?"

"I can always handle an ad," the man replied, as he eyed Franklin suspiciously. "You sound like you might be from Georgia. I met a lot of Georgians when Jimmy Carter was running for president in 1976 and 1980."

"You're right, I'm a Georgian, and my friend here worked for Carter in his two campaigns. I've got the material for the ad right here," Franklin said, pulling several sheets of paper from his briefcase. "I'd like a three-column-by-ten-inch ad on page 3, if possible. I want to run it for ten weeks. How much would that be?"

"Well, what are you advertising?"

"Myself. I'm planning to be a candidate in the Democratic presidential primary in February."

The Granite State News employee didn't look especially surprised. "A political ad?" he sniffed. "That will be payment in advance."

"I understand," Franklin said. "I'm a newspaper publisher myself, have been for forty years. I'm Thomas Alexander Franklin, and this is Jack Hardy. We are starting the campaign right here in Carroll County, New Hampshire, and you're the first person we've talked to about it."

"Well, I guess I should appreciate that. I'm Andy Burkhart, I've been at the newspaper about forty years myself, starting as a lino-type operator and doing about every job in the building, till I finally became editor and publisher about twenty years ago. If I might ask, why are you thinking about running in the primary?"

"I feel the country needs a good newspaper editor as president, don't you? I've written editorials about nearly every policy problem that the US has faced and have operated thirty newspaper businesses that involved selling, manufacturing, and dispensing information, not to mention supervising various staffs of people ranging from contrary reporters to surly production types and carriers who always thought the paper was late getting to them."

"Well, I can identify with that," Burkhart said.

"So can every other editor and publisher in New Hampshire, and I'm planning to base my campaign on newspaper advertising. That's no longer fashionable among so-called political consultants, of course, and it has upset me for years that millions of dollars in political advertising go into TV and mail-outs and only a pittance to newspapers, even though every candidate from dogcatcher to president comes to the office with news releases they want published free."

Burkhart smiled. "You got that right," he agreed. "Here in New Hampshire, we get all that in spades every four years, but not many dollars."

"I've also got some ideas and issues that other candidates aren't discussing, and this election in 1992 is the time when they must be discussed. The world has changed just in the past few months. The Soviet Union is dissolving, the Cold War is over after more than fifty years, and the US must decide how to proceed in a world without its longtime adversary, not to mention that the US economy is faltering as the middle class keeps shrinking; the rich get richer, and the poor get poorer."

Burkhart shook his head slowly. "Well, sounds like you've got a campaign speech already in mind, but it sounds vaguely familiar."

"It won't be," Franklin assured him. "It'll be different because I'm planning to say the answer to our problems is not a weaker federal government, as Ronald Reagan and George Bush have preached, but a stronger government, which has been the answer to our problems ever since Benjamin Franklin came up with the idea in 1754 and which the other founding fathers believed when they composed the Constitution in 1787."

"Well, let me see the ad," Burkhart said.

"I've made a rough layout, but you can adjust it. 'Let's reduce the UNFAIREST tax of all,' the headline read. 'If you work every day for a salary, you are taxed 7 percent on the first dollar you earn. The payroll tax takes 7 percent of that first dollar and a like amount from your employer. But the richest Americans don't pay the payroll tax on the thousands of dollars they earn above $60,000 a year. That's right! The lowest wage earners in the US are paying the maximum percentage of payroll tax every payday, while the highest wage earners pay all of their payroll tax in the first few paydays of the year.

'My first goal will be to CUT the payroll tax to 4 percent a week and extend it to all earned incomes, which will bring in more money but shift the burden from the lowest wage earners to the highest. This will provide tax relief to 90 percent of workers as well as cutting the tax expense for the majority of small business owners, who don't have many employees making more than $60,000 a year.

'Watch this space in *The Granite State News* each week for Thomas Franklin's plans to shift the burden of taxation from middle-class incomes to wealthier Americans. Franklin plans to be a candidate for the Democratic presidential nomination on February 16, 1992, and if the people of New Hampshire respond to his ideas of a stronger but fairer national government, he will carry that message to the rest of the nation.'

"Here's a photo of me to run with the ad," Franklin said. "Not too big, maybe about one column by three inches, with those capitalized words in larger type and color if possible. It should fit in a three-column-by-ten-inch ad. So what's the price?"

Burkhart eyed him quizzically. "I'd say about two dollars an inch or sixty dollars a week for ten weeks, and I'll throw in some red and blue color. I haven't had a lot of political ads from national candidates."

"That's something I hope to change not just for you but for all newspapers."

"That'll be in advance, of course," Burkhart added.

"I understand," Franklin said, pulling out an envelope with several bills in it. "Here's $600, when can you have the ad composed and ready for me to proofread?"

"How about tomorrow afternoon at three?"

"Okay, we'll be staying the night here. I'd like to proof the ad and send it to other newspapers. Are there any others here in Carroll County?"

"Well, there is this free daily, *The Conway Daily Sun*, which claims about nine thousand circulation, and another weekly in North Conway, called the *Mt. Washington Valley Mountain Ear*, which supposedly covers several counties. But *The Granite State News* is the oldest paper in Carroll and is the legal organ, which means most of the lawyers and officials read it, and there are a lot of local officials since we have four townships. The *Conway Daily Sun* has a press, which in fact is where we're printed."

"Okay, here's the ad copy," Franklin said, handing him the sheets.

Franklin and Hardy drove to the motel they'd spotted nearby. It looked fairly large and had a restaurant. "Let's settle in and get some dinner," Franklin suggested, "and plan tomorrow's schedule."

"You're on a leisurely pace, compared to Carter," Hardy said. "It was always rush, rush. Carter was a stickler for being on time. Once when Jody and I were traveling with him, we were a little late getting to an airport, and Carter had the plane take off without us."

"We're just getting started and don't want to burn out," Franklin said. "We've got a chance to cultivate some roots here in Wolfeboro. It's small but my plan is to concentrate on New Hampshire's 222 townships and then its 10 counties, because New Hampshire is the ball game for this candidacy. In 1976, Carter had won the Iowa

Caucus, but it was his victory in the New Hampshire primary that caught the nation's attention and put him in the lead position among the other candidates that he never lost. Early momentum is essential, especially if no other candidate has jumped ahead."

"You've figured this plan for a long time, haven't you?" Hardy asked.

"Yes. As I mentioned, 1992 is a pivotal year for many reasons, and the Democratic field has no major candidate as long as Cuomo doesn't enter. If he does, he's the guy who should win! See this scar on my head. It's fading, but this is where I hit my head in an auto accident several months ago. I was laid up for weeks and had a lot of time to read and study my campaign plan. I'd just sold the newspaper company I owned and had more than $7 million to fund a campaign or invest. I decided what I really wanted to do was try and make a difference. I'd been writing editorials and making speeches for years and never saw that it made much difference. As we editors used to say, writing editorials was like dropping a rock in a well and listening for a splash but never hearing it. Political candidates can make a difference, which is why we need them, only better ones."

"Have you ever been elected to anything?"

"I was president of a PTA years ago, but it wasn't exactly a contested position. I was elected president of the Georgia and Alabama press associations and actually lived in Alabama while I was president of the Georgia association. But I've never even run in a political election, much less been elected, but I've been involved, shall we say."

"I've been involved too, but not as a candidate," Hardy said. "I've driven for more than ten candidates since Carter's two campaigns."

"Were any of them winners?" Franklin wanted to know.

"Yeah, one congressman. The others lost. Politics is a tough game, and losing was hard to take. The worst loss to me by far was Carter's reelection campaign in 1980. That was bad."

They checked in the motel and joined each other in the restaurant. It was surprisingly large, probably for the tourist groups that came through and wanted to eat together.

Neither of them had eaten since breakfast at their respective airports. A waitress asked for their order. Franklin had always had respect for waitresses. They were usually hardworking, friendly, and didn't make much money. This one was relatively young, no more than twenty, he'd guess, and looked to be nearly six feet tall. But she was definitely not the friendly type. Her face was a mask barren of expression. Her uniform was straight and plain, providing little hint of her figure.

They both ordered hamburger steaks. "I'll take some french fries with mine," Franklin added.

"We don't serve french fries any longer," the waitress said. "Will freedom fries be okay?"

"What are freedom fries?" Franklin asked, thinking they may be some northern version of french fries.

"They are the same as french fries," she replied, "but we now list them as freedom fries because the French wouldn't help the US in the war against Saddam Hussein."

Franklin glanced at the menu. Listed with the steaks were freedom fries. "Some places in Georgia have made that change since the Gulf War," Hardy explained.

"Actually, I've noticed," Franklin admitted. "I just didn't realize French-phobia had reached New England. By the way, one of my campaign themes will be opposition to wars, even wars like the Gulf War."

Hardy frowned. "That war was very popular," he noted. "President Bush's approval ratings are off the charts. The US won big and proved to the world how strong we really are. It was the victory everybody has wanted since Vietnam."

"That's right," said Franklin. "All those are reasons why it should have never been fought. I'm not saying that Saddam wasn't the main reason for the war, but I editorialized against it, and if you recall, the Senate voted by just two votes to go to war. Most Democrats voted against it."

"That wasn't a smart political move, the people loved the war."

"I know, and that's the problem. Successful wars are always popular and even some that aren't successful. Saddam had his country and most of his army destroyed, but he's still in power and is more popular in Iraq than before the war. Bush and his generals were all hailed as heroes, and Bush was virtually conceded the 1992 election. That's why the best-known Democrats aren't candidates this year. They're waiting for 1996 and missing what could be the most important election in recent history, and I mean that. If we truly want to do away with wars, we have to diminish their popularity. We need to praise and give medals to peacemakers and elect those who keep peace. It's actually an effort some years to find a recipient for the Nobel Peace Prize *even* when there is a good one, such as Jimmy Carter has been ever since the Camp David Accords between Israel and Egypt. The prize that year went to Sadat, who was deserving, and Begin, who did everything he could to sabotage the agreement. Carter still hasn't gotten the Nobel despite his efforts through the Carter Center to promote peace in many ways. Sadat was assassinated for his role as a peacemaker."

"You almost sound like a pacifist," Hardy remarked.

"This is just between you and me, but the fact is that we've got to stop glorifying war if we ever expect to stop wars. Combined with all the profit war produces for weapons makers, it is a tempting option for military leaders, many of whom need war to make themselves relevant."

They ate quietly, and the waitress returned to gather the dishes. Her long arms could reach every corner of the table. The restaurant had cleared somewhat, so Franklin tried to engage the waitress in conversation. "You don't really hold it against the French for not helping us against Saddam, do you?" he asked.

She looked bothered but finally answered, "Not especially, but the manager changed the menu and told us to call french fries freedom fries and that was that."

"Let me tell you a little story about French soldiers," Franklin said. "Germany invaded Belgium and France in August 1914, and within twenty days, German armies had driven across France to within ten miles of Paris and seemed to be on the verge of conquering France—as they did twenty-three years later. The French armies had retreated steadily before superior armament and numbers. Then suddenly at the Marne River, just outside Paris, they turned and halted the German advance, and within days the German troops were in retreat.

"The German general Alexander von Kluck wrote later, 'The reason for our failure and retreat that transcends all other was the extraordinary attitude of the French soldiers to so suddenly recover. That men will let themselves stand and be killed is a well-known thing and is counted on in every plan of battle. But that men who have retreated for twenty days, sleeping on the ground and are half-dead from fatigue, should be able to take up their rifles and attack when the bugle sounds, is a thing on which we never counted. It was a possibility not studied in our war academy.'"

"So why didn't they send troops to Iraq?" the waitress asked.

Franklin looked thoughtful for a moment. Finally, he said, "During World War I, the death toll for the French was one for every twenty-eight people, the highest of any country, including Germany. I guess their children and grandchildren decided a two-bit dictator like Saddam wasn't worth another French life."

The waitress looked impressed, which was her first change of expression. "Well, thanks for the history lesson. Is that in place of a tip?"

"No." Franklin chuckled. "Lessons are too cheap to replace a tip, and that was philosophy more than history. By the way, what's your name?"

She hesitated but finally said, "Susie, Susie Schultz."

"I've been a newspaper man for fifty years and am just naturally curious," Franklin explained. "I hope you don't mind. Everybody is a potential story."

Her manner changed suddenly, back to the blank expression, almost angry. "Do you think there's a story in me?"

"Absolutely," Franklin said.

"You're right," she said with a frown, "but people around here know the story, and I sure as hell don't want to talk about it."

She picked up the check and quickly walked away.

"Odd girl," Hardy commented.

"But interesting," Franklin added. "There's more to her than meets the eye, which admittedly isn't much, but she has a three-letter high school athletic sweater hanging on the rack and wears an honor society ring. I have a notion about her."

"Very observant. I don't know what kind of politician you are, but you must be a first-rate reporter."

"Let's have a drink and talk some more," Franklin suggested as he walked toward the small bar in the lobby.

Franklin ordered a glass of White Zinfandel wine, which was all he ever drank. Hardy hesitated and finally asked if he could have a milkshake. "I have to be careful," he explained. "Jody probably didn't tell you I'm a recovering alcoholic."

"How recovered?" Franklin asked with a concerned expression.

"Pretty recovered. I haven't had a drink in six months, but I'm still feeling my way."

"What happened? You said you drove for Carter in 1976 and 1980."

"Yeah, that was the high point of my life, but like many of us in the Carter camp, I didn't handle the 1980 landslide defeat very well. Jody and Hamilton kept getting me driving jobs, but in the next few years, if you recall, Democrats had a tough time. In 1982, the people I drove for went down to defeat again, even in the state and county races. There are no hiding places for a Democrat in the South today. So I went back to being a mechanic, a pretty good one, which I'd been before Jody picked me up for the 1976 campaign. But it was a tough adjustment. I'd been away from home a lot during the campaigns, and my wife had found someone else. She asked for a divorce and got our two kids.

"I wandered around doing odd jobs and then went on binges, which I'd never done in the past. One binge landed me in jail. Jody got me out and offered to put me back on the road. This is my first assignment. He said he thought you might be good for me even if neither of us felt you have a chance to win. He said Carter had been reading your columns and editorials since he was a peanut farmer in Plains, and the family's daily newspaper was *The Columbus Enquirer* when you were the editor."

"Well, I appreciate the confidence—not in my chances as a candidate, which admittedly are dubious, but in being a useful companion when you need one."

"We're going to have a Quixotic time," Hardy said, "and might even slay a dragon or two. What's the schedule tomorrow? I've already got us a room at the inn for tonight."

"Good, let's get some rest, and I'm going to work up another ad we'll take to the daily paper in LaConia, which I think is on the other side of Lake Winnipesaukee, not too far but it's in Belknap County, which will give us two counties covered. Then we'll come back and go to that daily in North Conway."

The next morning, they crossed the lake, the one Franklin's Georgia tour group crossed in October 1982. He remembered the day well because when they got off the boat after the two-hour ride, there were newsboys selling extras, which told of the assassination of Anwar Sadat while he was watching a parade in Egypt. The assassins had gotten revenge on Sadat for supporting peace with Israel. They were described as terrorists but were never executed. In fact, many Arabs considered them heroes, which is not unusual for many murderers, whether of one man or hundreds.

Franklin remembered grimly that was one moment when he realized editorials were so weak and meaningless in the real world.

The newspaper in LaConia was a paid daily, with an audited circulation of 12,500. Belknap County had a population of 39,000 which was even higher during tourist season due to the lake. The building for the newspaper had a large front room. There were about ten employees, all with small computers. Franklin was impressed. Computers were just starting to replace compugraphic machines at newspapers. Some large newspapers were still using hot-type equipment because of union rules.

He went to the office indicated for advertising and picked up a rate card. "I'd like to run an ad," he told the young man who greeted him. Like Burkhart in Wolfeboro, the salesman was surprised and pleased that it was a political ad. The price was higher of course, but Franklin still stipulated ten weeks with color on page 3. He handed the rep a folder with his photo and a short bio. "The copy for the ad will be sent to you in the morning from *The Granite State News*," Franklin told him.

"You're running the same ad there, it's a small weekly. We've got three times the circulation."

"I know, but in a different county. I'm planning to be in every small paper in New Hampshire and some dailies."

The ad rep looked over the ad skeptically. "So you're really serious about running in the presidential primary?" he asked. "I don't see any political offices on this resume."

"I'm going to see what kind of response I get in New Hampshire before I officially announce, but I'm serious, as that money in your hand shows."

"Say, let me get our political reporter over here for an interview. You at least sound interesting."

Franklin hadn't counted on that, but the offer pleased him. "Sure," he said, "that would be great. This will be my first interview. If I run, or win the primary, *The LaConia News* will have a scoop."

A young lady with a pad and pencil in hand came over and asked Franklin and Hardy to sit at a table. The newsroom buzzed with activity, but in the day of computers, it was quiet compared to the newsroom of Franklin's early years in the business, when newsrooms were a cacophony of sounds, from teletype machines to telephones to air-conditioning.

"I'm Connie, so why are you thinking about running for president?" she asked. "I always ask that first," she explained, "because we get a lot of candidates for president through New Hampshire and a lot of them stumble on that question sort of like Ted Kennedy did in that TV interview with Roger Mudd in 1980."

Pretty sharp girl, Franklin thought, but he was glad to get the question because he had pondered the answer a lot. "I want to run because I'm tired of every candidate, Democrat and Republican, tearing down the United States federal government, which is the fairest and most enduring government that democracy had ever created, and if someone doesn't start saying that, we could lose it. Look what just happened to the Soviet Union, a dictatorship, which is dissolving for many reasons, but a major reason is that the people lost confidence in the flawed and corrupt structure of the government, and even in a dictatorship, that loss of confidence finally went too far. To hear many of our leaders, you'd think the US government is weak and ineffective, and that's not true, either today or in the past.

"President Ronald Reagan set that tone when he said, 'The federal government is not the answer, government is the problem.' That was a terrible message to send the people of the very nation he was trying to govern. I hear politicians say, 'I love my country, but I hate my government.' That isn't possible. The country and the government and people together make up what we call a democracy, and that is a message I want to stress."

"Well, that's certainly different," Connie commented, "but people don't like to be told that. One of my first interviews was with Jimmy Carter when he was running for president in 1976, and we didn't think he had a chance, he told me he was running against Washington. He stressed an anti-government message and won. So did Reagan and President Bush, although it's hard for Bush to do that this year since he's been president or vice president for twelve years."

"It's fashionable to blame government and especially so-called big government. It's been fashionable for years, but it's a myth that needs to be questioned and exposed for the damage it does to our politics and ultimately to the nation. The truth is that the United States is the strongest, richest, and greatest nation in the history of the world, and in 1992 it has suddenly become an even more towering power, which presents so many opportunities but also immense challenges that can't be met with outmoded Cold War solutions and certainly not with miniature hot wars like Iraq, which undermine our creditability and destroy what little progress has been made in so-called third world countries."

"Are you talking about the action Bush took to rescue Kuwait from Saddam Hussein?" Connie asked in dismay.

"That requires more detail to explain, but I plan to be talking about the Bush foreign policy as well as the Bush-Reagan supply-side economic policies, which are shredding the US middle class and further impoverishing poorer Americans."

Connie looked at her notes. "Wow," she exclaimed, "none of the candidates I've interviewed had this much to say."

"Have you interviewed Paul Tsongas this year?" Franklin asked.

"He hasn't been through LaConia yet. You're the first candidate we've seen, but I'm sure all of them will be coming later. It's just so small. In fact, why are you here so early?"

"That's a long story, but I'm glad I came. I've published several small daily newspapers in Georgia, which were about the size of LaConia. You say you interviewed Carter? That was sixteen years ago."

"I know, I was just out of college. I never expected to be here this long, but I got married to a local guy, and I get to do all the good stories, too many of them some of the time. Let me get a little more background on you so I can convince the editor you're worth devoting space to and not just a crackpot candidate like several others who have actually announced, including one from Alabama."

"I know that fellow. He's run for office in Alabama for years. He was terribly scarred in World War II, but he made a fortune in real estate and keeps running for office. One year he made the runoff for lieutenant governor, but that was years ago."

"So you were a publisher and editor in Georgia and Alabama for forty years?"

"I started as an eighteen-dollars-a-week copyboy on my hometown paper in Columbus, Georgia, when I was sixteen. I moved up to proofreader, which I highly recommend to any aspiring journalist—we all need to be good proofreaders. With time out for college and a few career adventures, I worked with the Columbus newspaper for twenty years, becoming editor when I was just thirty-two. I also started a weekly newspaper in neighboring Phenix City, Alabama, during those years and for a few months was editor of a small daily, about the size of the LaConia paper. But I always wanted to be a publisher as well as an editor, so at thirty-eight, I got a group of investors together to buy a small daily in a nearby university town. We bought it for $1 million, which was considered a lot of money for a four-thousand-circulation, five-day daily but we sold it for $7 million nine years later, and that gave me a start as a group newspaper publisher."

Connie looked wide-eyed. "That's every reporter's dream."

"It's not as good as it dreams," Franklin said, "but I can't complain. In all, my company owned and operated about thirty newspapers during the next thirty years, including several dailies and then two statewide magazines. I liked putting them out personally, which got very demanding, so I sold everything a few months ago and decided to get into politics, where the real power is. Now, let's see if you can get an article about my candidacy in the LaConia paper."

"Sure," Connie said, "and I'll put this story on the wire. It just might attract attention, especially when I add that you're going to base your campaign on newspaper advertising."

Chapter Two

UNCOVERING A STAR

*History proves that dictatorships do not grow out of
strong and successful governments, but out of weak
and helpless ones. The only sure bulwark of continuing liberty is a government strong enough to maintain its sovereign control.*
—Franklin D. Roosevelt, April 14, 1938

As Franklin and Hardy walked toward the door, Franklin
noticed several framed front pages about notable events in
LaConia's recent history. That was a practice Franklin had
followed at his papers. One front page he spotted had a large headline about LaConia High winning the girls' state basketball championship in 1988. There was a photo of the team's starting five players.
One of them looked familiar. "Look," he told Hardy. "See that girl
in the middle of that basketball team, who does she remind you of?"

Hardy looked closer. "Can't say she reminds me of anyone."

Franklin scanned the cutline, which did not include the names
of the players. "You've got a pretty good paper here," he told Connie,
the reporter, "but you should always identify local people in photos."

Connie joined him and peered at the photo. "I don't remember them all," she admitted, "but the tall one in the middle is Susie
Slutz…uh, I mean Schultz. She was the state tournament MVP in her
junior year but had a bad senior year, and then she just disappeared."

"What was that you called her, Susie Slutz?"

"Sorry, I didn't mean to. That was a slang name you heard a lot after her senior year. I don't know the whole story, but our sports editor, Tim Smith, does if you're interested."

"I am," Franklin said. "I think I can tell you where she is."

Tim Smith was at a desk nearby shuffling through wire copy and looking worried. "I'm an old sports editor," Franklin told him, introducing himself, "and my friend here drove for Jimmy Carter in his two presidential campaigns. Have you got time to talk a minute?"

"Sure," Tim said. "Deadline's not for thirty minutes."

Franklin smiled. "You'll make it," he said. "The game's not till Friday night, is it?"

"Today's edition goes to press in thirty minutes," Tim informed him, "but let me get this headline written and I'll talk to you."

The scene was familiar to Franklin and also the feeling of tension he'd faced many times through the years of an approaching deadline. It had left him with a feeling of apprehension that had never fully gone away. The clock moving relentlessly, the carriers waiting impatiently for the papers to deliver.

Tim came over. "You were asking about the girls' basketball photo on the wall? That was our state championship team in 1988. We put the final game on the front page. It was the first state championship in our high school's history."

"The girl in the middle. I think I know her."

"That's a surprise," Tim said. "She was the most valuable player that championship year but played poorly in her senior year, and after the season, she sort of disappeared, and I've never heard of her again."

"Well, have you looked?" Franklin asked.

"Yeah, sort of, but we knew her story and decided she wanted to be left alone. In the finals that year, the team was leading for the championship again, but she had not played well. I was at the game. In the final minutes, needing just two points to win, Susie managed to get down the court in the clear. A perfect pass was thrown to her near the goal for the winning shot, but Susie stumbled reaching for it and fell. The ball went out of bounds as the game ended, and the other team won. Susie was out there on the floor, crying as her teammates gathered around her, while the coach kept screaming at her for missing the pass. We were told the next day that she had dropped out of school and gone to live somewhere else. She was the best girls' player LaConia ever had."

"Do you have another picture of her, maybe an individual head shot?"

Tim shuffled through his picture file. "Here, here's the game program of that 1988 team with pretty good pictures of all the members. That's Susie on the left."

Franklin nodded. "That's the waitress at the motel we're staying at in Wolfeboro," he exclaimed. "Her hair's different now, but that's her face. She's just twenty-nine miles away."

Tim frowned. "Wolfeboro is in another county and not a very big place," he said. "In fact, I don't think I've ever been through there."

"Wasn't she close to anyone in LaConia?"

"Not really. Now that I think of it, she lived in Carroll County and transferred to LaConia to play basketball when she was a freshman. Her family never lived here. But if you want to find out about her, I'm sure the high school principal could tell you. After what happened in that last game, she left a bad image in Laconia."

"What did happen?"

"It turned out Susie was pregnant the entire season. She was tall and didn't show, so the coach let her keep on playing because even pregnant she was a deadly shot for most of the season. But then she missed that winning shot for the championship, and her condition came to light. She was carried to the doctor after the game, and the baby was dead. The school suspended her before graduation, which was the policy in those days for girls who got pregnant...and as I said, she disappeared."

"She told me she had a story," Franklin recalled, "and it needs a better ending. She's bitter, but there's still something about her that reminds you she was once an all-star. Is the high school near here?"

"Just down the street," Tim indicated.

"Come on," Franklin said to Hardy. "Let's stop by the school on the way back to Wolfeboro."

The principal of the school was very cooperative, although he seemed embarrassed that he hadn't kept up with Susie Shultz. "She was an outstanding student as well as an athlete," the principal related, "a little weak in math and science, but straight As in English, history, and typing. She was so good that in her senior year she was a part-time secretary in the school office. I wasn't principal when her problems arose after the basketball season, but I agreed with the decision to suspend her. You have to realize Susie was the best-known female student at the school her last two years. For her to become pregnant was a terrible example for girls who did not have near as much to lose. I was among the teachers who carried her to the hospital after she fell in the final game. She'd injured her leg, and as you know, the infant was dead in her womb. She agreed she needed to leave the school. I think she moved to Maine for about two years and lived with an aunt…then I don't know."

"So she was a good student?"

"Among the best," the principal replied. "In fact, if you know where she can be found, I've still got a plaque she never picked up which named her the outstanding student-athlete at LaConia. It was to be presented at graduation, but she wasn't there and actually never graduated, so the plaque was just stored away, but I've got it."

"I think I know where she is," Franklin assured him, "and it would mean a great deal to me—and to her I'm sure—if you'd let me give the plaque to her."

The principal agreed and retrieved the plaque from a closet. "Let me hear about Susie. I really should have looked her up earlier, but her situation really upset the entire community at the time, what with the basketball championship loss and the shock of her condition for the entire season."

"I understand," Franklin muttered, but he really didn't. He needed to learn more from Susie herself, whom he only knew as a surly waitress who had listened patiently to his defense of the French during World War I.

"What do you know about that?" Hardy commented as they left. "I knew you were a good reporter, but what kind of candidate are you going to be?"

"One that tells unfashionable truths," he replied. "Let's go back to the Granite State News office in Wolfeboro."

During the drive, Hardy asked Franklin about growing up during the Great Depression.

"It wasn't really all that bad, depending on where you lived. I was in a medium-sized Southern town, which was a good place to be in the thirties. I was born a week after the stock market crash, and my father lost his job. That turned out to be a break for me because the family—I was the only child—had to move thirty miles down the road from Newnan to LaGrange, which was a larger town, with about eighteen thousand people.

"Most importantly, LaGrange was a textile mill company town, and by 1930, it had a city water system, indoor plumbing in most houses, a movie theater, paved streets, and a thriving downtown with two department stores, drug stores, and cafés. Not many places in Georgia could claim all those conveniences. We never thought we were poor. The poor people were the ones who lived in what was called the mill village, where most of the mill workers lived. My family rented a small house just a block off the main street. You could walk to town, to the church, the theater, and the school. My father had a company car, but it wasn't used much, mainly on occasional trips to Columbus and Heard County, where my uncle and aunts lived.

"What I remember most about childhood is there were lots of children my age in the neighborhood, and we played outside a lot. There was no television then, of course, and radio was just becoming widespread. Most families in the South had been relatively poor for a long time, and they hardly noticed the Depression the way people in the cities did. My mother was a semi-invalid who hardly ever left her bed. She complained of heart trouble, and doctors made regular visits to our house.

"As I grew older, I could walk nearly everywhere I needed to go. A dollar a week bought a ten-cent magazine or book, a ten-cent ticket to the Saturday movie matinee, plus a nickel bag of popcorn, a bag of lemon drops at the so-called ten-cent store, with a dime left over for another movie. I went to school with the children of a few well-off families in LaGrange. Most of the mill workers' children went to another white school, and of course, the black children had a separate school. In fact, although about a third of the population was black, or colored as we called them in those days, I don't remember ever seeing many blacks, except our maid. They not only weren't at the school, they weren't at the church or the theater, and I seldom even noticed many on the downtown streets. People outside the South don't realize how segregated it was in those days or how much segregation determined our activities and our views of the world. We were poor, I guess, but not as poor as the blacks, or most of the mill workers.

"In LaGrange, we had indoor plumbing, electricity, ice delivered daily for the icebox, access to stores which had most items sold in larger cities. We did have to build fires with coal and wood, which was our main inconvenience. But just a mile away outside the city limits, houses still didn't have electricity or running water. The city was like another world."

"From what I heard from my parents, Hickory was that way," Hardy said. "My father was in the Army in World War II and got a job at the furniture factory afterwards. He never used his GI Bill benefits for college, but he made a good living all his life, and I sure don't remember being poor."

"That's not to say there weren't a lot of people in Georgia and North Carolina in financial distress. Many families had always been farmers and lived from good harvest to bad ones and sometimes worse," Franklin said.

"A book called *Georgia During the Great Depression* includes some depressing figures. The textile mills provided jobs and sometimes houses for its workers, but the wages were far below wages in other states. The highest-paid mill worker was a loom fixer, always a male, at an average of twenty-two dollars a week, lower than the wage for the same job ten years earlier. Female weavers averaged twelve dollars a week and pay in such places as saw mills, and foundries was twenty to thirty cents an hour.

"The workweek was fifty-five to sixty hours with no overtime, of course. Unions had no place in Georgia and other Southern states, for a variety of reasons, mainly the reluctance of workers to trust so-called outsiders or the government. In fact, when the New Deal finally began trying to improve conditions, Georgia's governor Gene Talmadge was one of the fiercest critics, even though President Roosevelt was a part-time resident of Georgia and owned and operated a farm and business in Meriwether County. Talmadge called unemployed workers *chiselers* and *bums* who would rather live off the government than work. His opposition views are actually still echoed by opponents of federal programs today, such as food stamps.

"Talmadge was first and foremost totally opposed to any programs he thought might improve life for Negroes either as workers or as potential voters. He opposed the National Recovery Administration Act because it required road contractors to pay at least forty cents an hour. Talmadge finally had the state take over all the road building and pay lower wages. The battle resulted in Talmadge having to declare martial law in part of the state and the loss of all federal funds for Georgia roads.

"But the state's voters, still suspicious of the federal government, reelected him as governor in 1935. He rewarded them by refusing to let Georgians participate in the Social Security program, adopted for the nation that year, providing old-age pensions and unemployment benefits, subjects I might say are also still debated in 1992.

"A tornado struck the city of Gainesville in 1936 and changed some Georgia minds. About two hundred were killed, and property damage was estimated at $5 million. Talmadge reluctantly accepted federal funds to help out.

"The state constitution limited a governor to two consecutive two-year terms, so Talmadge ran against Richard Russell for the US Senate in 1936. Russell had been elected to a term as governor in 1931 at the age of just twenty-nine, Georgia's youngest governor ever and moved on to a seat in the US Senate when a vacancy occurred two years later. He was a strong supporter of the New Deal policies, and that became the basis of Talmadge's attack on him in the campaign.

"Roosevelt was running for reelection to a second term as president that year and Talmadge was one of his loudest critics in the entire country, which was saying something.

"Talmadge's popular applause line was 'The New Deal is a combination of wet-nursing, frenzied financing, downright Communism and plain damn foolishness.'

"Talmadge pledged to abolish the income tax, kill the Social Security program, and the minimum wage bill then being debated in Congress. His solution for people applying for federal welfare was to 'line them up against the wall and give them a dose of castor oil.' He even alluded to Roosevelt's crippled legs by saying, 'The nation needs a president who can work in the sun fourteen hours a day and walk a two-by-four plank.'

"In 1936, Georgia still enforced the poll tax, which was a fee for voting, mainly to keep Negroes from voting, but the tax also kept many poorer whites from voting. So Georgians who decided elections were mainly more affluent whites, but they liked what Roosevelt was doing. In the election that year, Roosevelt received 61 percent of the national popular votes. He carried forty-six of the then forty-eight states, including Georgia by a 7–1 margin. His landslide swept Russell to an easy victory over Talmadge after Talmadge had won four previous statewide elections. It also produced a US Democratic majority in the US Senate of 76 to 16, and a New Deal governor for Georgia in E. D. Rivers.

"That year was the high tide of the New Deal, and also of progressive policies in the US. But listen to this passage from a Talmadge speech. If you took out the crudity, it could be given by most Republicans in 1992. They've cleaned up the language but the spirit of Talmadge's opposition to the New Deal was widespread then, and to an extent it still is. It's called by a fancier name today, such as supply-side economics, but the spirit is still a recommendation of castor oil for the poor, the chiselers and bums, as Talmadge called them."

"Are you going to say all that in your campaign?" Hardy asked.

"I plan to. It's the unvarnished truth, but did you ever hear Jimmy Carter say it, or any of the candidates running this year. Rivers, as governor, pushed through what he called a little new deal, which created a department of public welfare, provided free textbooks for all school children, a mandatory seven-month school year, a public health system, and the Rural Electricity Authority, which eventually turned on the lights for the more than 70 percent of rural residents who previously had no electricity.

"Like Talmadge and all Georgia politicians at that time, Rivers was a segregationist, but Talmadge still looked on the federal government as the one that sent General Sherman and his Army marching through Georgia sixty-five years earlier, and Rivers saw the government as a means of salvation for a state in which too many people still lived in third world conditions.

"His programs left the state in deep financial debt because the legislature wouldn't raise taxes to support the reforms and changes, but among Southern governors of that day, he was the one who laid a foundation for his state to move into the twentieth century, and that's a major reason Georgia is still considered the commercial center of the southeast."

"I never heard of Rivers," Hardy admitted.

"Well, he was never elected to another political office," Franklin said.

"Free textbooks were a particularly timely development for me. I was just entering the second grade and had to buy all my first-grade books—several of which I still have—but I never had to buy another textbook. Alabama didn't get free textbooks until 1965."

"What happened to Talmadge?"

"He was elected governor two more times, and then his son, Herman, who you know, was elected governor twice and a US Senator for nearly forty years. Herman, to his credit, was one of the senators who wrote the food stamp program. His father wouldn't have approved, and a lot of Republicans still fight it.

"During the Depression, per capita income in Georgia was $204 compared to $595 for the nation, as a whole. Nobody except the mill owners were making much money. The New Deal and then World

War II were about to change that. At the same time, the US was changing from a mainly agricultural economy to an industrial one. Many people forget or never recognized the two great transitions taking place in the 1920s and '30s. By luck and insight, the Roosevelt Administration did. New Deal programs provided the means and the funding for the federal government to help the states, including the Southern states, which were the poorest and were the most affected by the demise of farms."

"Are you going to say all this in your campaign?" Hardy asked.

"I plan to."

Hardy looked impressed. "Maybe you're not such a no-shot after all."

At the Granite State News, they found Burkhart and the ad proof. Franklin read it over and then asked if they could insert a small box at the bottom. It would say, "If you agree with this idea for cutting the payroll tax from 7.5 percent to 3 percent and extend it to all earned income, please check this box and mail it to the Granite State News, Box 170 in Wolfeboro."

"I wouldn't count on a lot of response," Burkhart said. "The senders will have to supply the stamp."

"Well, it's a start. Now I need you to send a copy of this ad to the ad manager at the LaConia Citizen and tell me how I can get it in the other weeklies in New Hampshire."

"We've got an association," Burkhart said. "I was president a few years ago and worked out a plan for statewide advertising, charging each paper an inch-rate based on the price for a full page."

"That's similar to what we had in Georgia, but not for the daily papers. Let's try all the weeklies on these first ads."

Burkhart smiled broadly. "This will be the most political advertising they've had in years. It should get attention, from the publishers if no one else."

"Okay, I've got another ad for next week," Franklin said, opening his briefcase. "This one is about what I feel is the most important issue of all in this year's election. It overshadows any other political considerations the candidates are talking about, and it is simply this: 'Is the American way of selecting government officials still viable and accepted, and can it continue to function in a society as free as the United States? If the answer is no or even maybe—and if you take seriously what many politicians say, a no answer is not unreasonable—then all the other issues are relatively unimportant.

"I keep hearing the 'system is broken,' 'the nation is bankrupt,' 'the government no longer listens to the people.' Those are the messages consistently sent to the voters by many candidates, magnified by the news media, especially talk radio. Its negative views of the way we decide our government virtually goes unchallenged and has actually become dominant in many circles. It is time someone said a good word for the US political system and the political process.

"It's a short step from where we are today to a complete loss of confidence in the entire elective process, which despite its faults is based on the principle of individual citizens participating in the selection of their political leaders, peaceful transfer of power in government, and the free expression of views through the most extensive communication system ever devised.

"Do we still honor and support this system, given to us by the Constitution and endorsed by 250 years of success? Or would the people prefer a government which invokes the name of liberty and freedom in vain and in essence is another tyranny?

"None of our presidents, past, present or in the foreseeable future, have been as evil as the media portray them. They may be wrongheaded in some ideas, but none of them have been dictatorial or so inept that the national stability was in danger of crumbling. But if enough Americans become convinced that the political process is irrevocably damaged, when people lose faith in all the major party candidates and the parties themselves, then the nation and government are truly in peril. We have seen just recently how the Soviet Union, tyrannical as it was, collapsed when its tyrannized people lost faith, as they should have. Is the United States immune to that kind of collapse? Among the several lessons the Vietnam War taught us was it is hard to conduct a war when it is on display on television screens every night. Can the political process survive similar exposure?

"The US becomes more balkanized every day. It has never been easy to hold the reins of a nation as diverse, free, and argumentative as the US. The Founding Fathers faced similar divisions with a much-smaller population, but they still found compromises despite the odds against compromise in a loose confederation of thirteen scattered and quarrelsome colonies, with no heritage of cooperation.

"The very essence of democracy, of course, is respect and assimilation of diverse views, minority as well as majority, and that process has served the nation well. The US, with the emphasis on *united*, has become the most powerful governmental entity in history and today in 1992 is on the threshold of the opportunity to extend its success to even more of the world.

"So the basic question of this election is, Do enough Americans still believe the system serves them well? Are they willing to tolerate the occasional disappointments and lapses which the election system entails, along with its successes?

"The alternative is the loss of an elected government which can deal with the force of tyranny on one hand and anarchy on the other, and when the choice becomes tyranny or anarchy, people always choose tyranny in the long run.

"Turmoil and ugliness in the political conventions and vicious campaigns make me wince at the paleness of Jimmy Carter and Gerald Ford or the shrillness of Reagan's narrow-gauged supporters. But then I think of the dark alleys where political leaders are selected in many countries, or the relentless firing squads in Iran and earlier in Cuba, and of the awful slaughter in Cambodia and African countries, and the terrorism which is the controlling power in many places, I appreciate the one vote every American has and how vital that one vote is to the fragile freedom we all take for granted and how thankful I am for the men and women willing to seek public office, from the worse candidates to the best. They are all part of democracy's foundation, and they deserve our respect, if not always our vote."

Burkhart had taken notes along with the typed copy Franklin provided. "That'll make a pretty lengthy ad," he observed.

"Well, run it in smaller type and make the ad a little larger. It's a message I want to get before as many people as possible."

Burkhart shook his head. "It'll puzzle some of them, but I see what you're driving at. I'll get it together and get it in as many weekly papers as possible. Of course, you didn't mention the massive national debt or the welfare cheats who are living off the government. They're what a lot of voters in Carroll County talk about."

"What about you?" Franklin asked.

"I just listen to the talk at the civic clubs and cafés and church. A lot of people are hurting financially, and they don't like to see the government wasting money."

"We'll get to them," Franklin said. "How do you usually vote, Democratic or Republican?"

"Well, usually Republican," Burkhart said, "but I'm flexible. One year I wrote editorials in favor of Nixon for one newspaper and in favor of Kennedy for another one."

Franklin smiled. "A man after my own heart," he said. "I did that one year. Get that ad ready, we're going to visit a young lady."

It was lunchtime, so Franklin and Hardy returned to the motel restaurant. It was crowded, and Susie and two other waitresses were serving. She came over, her face still as an expressionless mask, but Franklin noticed a slight difference in her eyes. "Have you got another history lesson for me?" she asked.

"As a matter of fact, I have, but first bring us a couple of daily specials with hamburger steak."

"You want french fries with those?" Susie asked with a slight smile tugging at her lips.

"Of course." Franklin nodded.

He watched her walk away and for the first time recognized the slight swagger of success that good athletes always retain.

"Why are you so interested in that girl?" Hardy asked.

"Because she's a winner who has become a loser in her mind, but I have a notion that deep down she may still be a winner. Some of my best friends in Georgia are Waffle House waitresses."

"Sounds like a possible voter base," Hardy commented.

"Absolutely, and what would we do without waitresses and fast-order cooks?"

"Fix our own breakfast?" Hardy offered.

Franklin frowned. "That's the difference in service and effort, and the American economy today is built on the people's love of service, in a dozen different ways, from dining to entertainment to travel to whatever."

After they finished their meal and Susie was clearing the dishes, Franklin asked if she would take a few minutes to talk with them. She looked around and saw the restaurant cleared of its morning crowd. "Okay," she said. "In fact, I had something I wanted to tell you."

"Well, first, let me give you this," Franklin said, producing the plaque the principal had given him. "This is something you should have had three years ago, but bad communication on both sides kept you from getting it." The plaque read, "To Susan Anne Schultz, as the outstanding student-athlete at LaConia High School in the year 1988."

Susie looked puzzled at first and then grasped the plaque to her breast. "I can't believe it," she exclaimed. "This is the honor I expected so much as a junior, but I made better grades as a senior."

"It was to be presented to you at graduation, but you never went back to the school," Franklin explained. "The sports editor and the principal in LaConia told us your whole story, and I offered to bring the plaque to you. It's about time you got it."

Tears appeared in Susie's eyes, and her frozen expression altered slightly. "Why did you do all this?" she asked.

"I don't exactly know, except I thought there was an all-star under that dismal face you put on as a waitress, and I couldn't understand it. Isn't it time you realize that whatever happened in the past, you're still an all-star, and it's time to move on to the next game?"

Susie put the plaque on the table and stared at it. "What I wanted to tell you was that history lesson…that philosophy lesson… you gave me the other night got me to thinking. I was like the French Army that was defeated and kept retreating mile after mile, with nothing to fight for, and I decided there was nothing to do but what they did, stop and fight back."

Franklin and Hardy exchanged glances. "You had a notion," Hardy said.

"I'm off duty in ten minutes if you'll wait. I'll tell you my whole story. You like stories, you said."

When she returned, the three of them got a back table. "I've never talked to anyone outside my family about this, but I owe you something for bringing that plaque to me," she said. "After that last game, I was taken to the hospital, but the baby had died. You can imagine how I felt. The coach was not very understanding. She was more upset that she'd lost the championship, and she blamed me for playing the entire season while I knew I was pregnant. I'd discovered it about two months before the season started, and I didn't want to admit it and let the team down, so I played, but I was sick on many game days and couldn't focus on the game. It cost us several wins during the season, but I kept telling the coach I just had a lingering case of flu.

"The school suspended me after the final game, and I was so ashamed I never went back. I'd been living with my mother in Conway, but I moved to live with an aunt in Bar Harbor, Maine, far enough away that I never saw any people from LaConia and Conway except my mother. I got a job at a restaurant in Bar Harbor during the tourist season and learned a lot in four months about being a waitress. I stayed for another year and a half before coming back to Conway and getting the job at the inn."

"Could I ask what happened in the early part of your senior year?" Franklin said gently.

"I was crazy," she said, tears coming to her eyes. "This boy and I had known each other for years, and we started dating in high school. He was a football star, and I was the star basketball player, and I guess we just got too physical a couple of nights."

"It happens," Franklin told her. "What happened to him?"

"I've never seen him since that last game. He moved away too. So that's the story. It's taken me a long time to get over it, but now I'm finally at a crossroads. You've been a great help."

Franklin patted her on the arm, and suddenly she smiled a big, broad smile that lit up the room like a Christmas tree had been turned on.

"What a great smile," Franklin said. "I've got an idea. How about talking to us at breakfast tomorrow? We've got to see an editor about an ad."

As they drove back to The Granite News office, Hardy looked at Franklin with an appreciative expression. "Incredible," he commented. "But a slow way to get votes."

Burkhart had the ad ready, and Franklin read it over and made suggestions. The size had to be enlarged to get in all the type and the box.

"I've made some calls, and I think I can get these ads in at least thirty weeklies and a couple of small dailies for a reasonable price," Burkhart said.

"What's reasonable?"

"About two dollars an inch for each paper you run the entire twenty weeks, and you supply the copy, paid in advance."

"That sounds fair. I need a list of the papers you're talking to, and then we can figure out how to proceed." He pulled out some one-hundred-dollar bills and gave them to Burkhart. "See that image on the bills. That's Benjamin Franklin, the first real journalist in America and my favorite Founding Father."

"Is he an ancestor of yours?"

"Who knows? Actually, Franklin had no direct descendants, but he had a great-great-uncle named Thomas, and I think that's where my family got the name. I never knew."

Franklin looked at the ad again. "What's essential is to get across the ideas that the US is still the best government men have conceived, and our politicians are not buffoons or thieves. The US has never elected a real scoundrel as president or a man who didn't accept the procedures for changing governments. The only two presidents who faced impeachment were Andrew Johnson and, of course, most recently Nixon. But both of them accepted the system, and the system worked.

"Now faith has faltered in several long-term pillars of society, such as the church, the schools, the industrial complex as so many workers are being laid off, and the military, despite the success of the skirmish against Iraq. Faith must not falter in a freely elected government not only the best in history but the one that is the example all nations look to for guidance. Admittedly the Watergate trials and the

Vietnam War were difficult challenges, but they were nothing like the Civil War or the Great Depression or World War II."

"I get the message," Burkhart said. "Let me put some color on those words. Red, blue, and of course, white in between."

"What are you doing tonight?" Franklin asked.

"Nothing special."

"How about meeting Hardy and I about seven at the restaurant in the inn and I'll buy you dinner and we'll look at some other information you come up with and the papers we can get the ad in."

"Is he a story too?" Hardy wanted to know.

"I think so," Franklin says, "and he knows a lot about New Hampshire."

Chapter Three

BUILDING A TEAM

*The primary concern of any Government domi-
nated by the humane ideals of democracy is the simple principle that in a land of vast resources no one
should be permitted to starve.*
—Franklin D. Roosevelt, June 28, 1934

They sat at a table in the back of the restaurant to get a degree
of privacy. "I've been reading your newspaper and some of
your local editorials," Franklin told Burkhart. "You're pretty
good! How long have you been on the news side?"

"Well, almost the entire forty years I've been with the newspaper. I had an English degree from New Hampshire U, and I sort
of took over news coverage when the editor left. The publisher was
mainly a linotype operator, and it wasn't long before he let me run
the whole operation. When he retired thirty years ago, he sold me
the newspaper for $500 and some yearly payments. It wasn't doing
a lot of business, but it was enough for me and a couple of helpers.
The Granite State News always got the legal advertising and was the
newspaper most Carroll County residents grew up with. Actually,
while I'm still the editor and publisher, I sold the newspaper a year
ago to the group that operates the daily in Berlin, which covers most
of Northern New Hampshire."

"I bought and sold about forty newspapers in my career, but I loved every one of them, and I liked putting them together and improving them," Franklin commented. "I worked regularly for ten years on the first paper my company owned, a daily in Alabama. But after that one, I never lived where we had a newspaper. I did get to know all of the communities, however, and visited each office two or three times a month."

"Sounds interesting," Burkhart said.

"It was in a way, but you never leave many footprints unless you lived there. For instance, I bet you have plenty of footprints in Carroll County."

"I know the people, and as I said, I was president of the New Hampshire Press Association and got acquainted with most of the editors and publishers in the state."

"Have you met any of the other candidates running for president this year?"

"I know Tsongas fairly well. He's from just across the border in Massachusetts, and he's been traveling in New Hampshire since the first of the year. He's a nice guy, but there is not much enthusiasm among Democrats for another Greek from Massachusetts," he said, referring to the 1988 Democratic candidate Michael Dukakis.

"Tsongas is the only announced candidate right now," Franklin noted, "but it looks as if Bill Clinton, the governor of Arkansas, will be announcing soon. I've read Tsongas's book and some of his speeches. He sounds as if he should be running on the Republican ticket. His economic policy is nothing but warmed-over supply-side economics which has just made the rich richer and reduced the middle class to its weakest growth since the Great Depression. It'll be a pleasure to run against him."

"He's well-known and pretty popular in some parts of the state, but you know more about him than I do. I've heard Clinton speak a couple of times, and he's impressive, but the rumors about him and the ladies are known all the way to New Hampshire."

"The other candidates I've heard mentioned are US Senator Bob Kerrey of Nebraska, Senator Tom Harkin of Iowa, Governor

Doug Wilder of Virginia, and possibly Jerry Brown of California, who ran against Carter in 1976."

"I've heard those names too," Burkhart said, "but none of them have been in New Hampshire yet. After your newspaper ads, I'd say you'll be as well-known in the state as any of them, or even as Jimmy Carter when he ran in 1976. I'd have to say though that Carter started early and ran hard and had his whole family and a bunch of Georgians called the Peanut Brigade that called on about every Democratic family in the state. Carter won with personal contact. Most people in New Hampshire were Republicans then and probably still are. Any Democrat will have a hard time against President Bush."

"I realize that," Franklin admitted. "My idea is to use Carter's strategy to some extent. He knew he was not as well-known nationally so he planned from the beginning to run hard in New Hampshire and felt if he could win or lead here, the first primary, that it would give him name recognition and momentum to rise above the others. There wasn't a surefire leader, just like this year. The only Democrat who could come in and have a clear advantage is New York governor Mario Cuomo. In fact, if he decided to run, I'll drop my campaign, such as it is, and support him."

"Carter felt that way about Ted Kennedy," Hardy interjected, "although he would say he hoped Kennedy ran because he thought he'd beat him, which he did four years later, of course. He never liked Kennedy, and I don't think Kennedy ever liked him, one reason that Carter lost in 1980."

"How would you like a job?" Franklin asked Burkhart.

"I thought you'd never ask. I'm on borrowed time at the Granite News because they want to bring in a younger publisher. I'll even come cheap."

"*Economical* is the right word, and that's the kind of employees I'm looking for. All my big money is tied up in Jack Hardy here," he said with a smile. "Just kidding, Jack's sort of a consultant, as well as a driver."

The three of them talked for two hours on various aspects of campaigning and memories of past campaigns. About nine o'clock,

Susie joined them at Franklin's invitation. "I'm off duty now," she said. "And you three look as if you've found a lot to talk about."

"Susie," Franklin said, "the principal in LaConia said you were one of the best typists in school. Is that right?"

"I was fast and pretty accurate and was always a good proof-reader on the letters written by the principal."

"Have you ever been interested in politics?"

"Very much," Susie said. "I was a youth volunteer for the Robert Dole campaign for four months in 1988, passing out material, writing letters, and organizing young people at the schools we played in basketball. I became a real Bob Dole fan and was very disappointed when he lost to George Bush in the Republican primary that spring. I haven't followed politics much since then, until now, of course. Are you really serious about being a candidate?"

"I'm becoming more serious every minute," Franklin said. "How much do you average in a week here?"

"About one hundred dollars."

"I'll double that if you join the campaign as a typist and chief bottle washer."

Susie looked startled but not really surprised. A bond had been building between them. "I'll have to talk to my boss and my mother, but they'll both say take it."

"You sure make quick hiring decisions," Hardy said. "I suppose you're going on notions again."

Franklin looked at the small group. "Let's join hands," Franklin said. "You three are the start of my presidential campaign committee. Remember that, and when we win the nomination, we'll look back on this night at the inn in Wolfeboro, New Hampshire, as a historic site."

Franklin returned to his room and immediately put through a call to his wife, Jean, at their home in Georgia. A call home was a faithful habit he kept every night of the many nights he had been traveling to the scattered newspapers he operated in the past thirty years. He always wanted to know how Jean and their three children were getting along and to tell her of the day's events. The conversation also calmed him down from whatever trials and tribulations had arisen during the day.

They had been married for almost forty years and had survived tough financial periods as well as unusual living conditions. For many of the years, both of their mothers and Jean's grandmother had lived with them, an arrangement which amazed their friends who said their own marriages would not have survived. Tom gave most of the credit to Jean.

They had met at a church social in Columbus. Both were college graduates and had been in the workforce for several years. They had had several relationships but nothing serious through their college and work years. They were both only children, nearly the same age, and had grown up during the worst years of the Great Depression. As noted, Tom's mother had been a semi-invalid throughout his childhood years and still was. She had lived with her sisters until moving in with Tom and Jean. Jean's mother still worked regularly and looked after the grandmother, who was a total invalid by then.

Franklin was a news editor on the afternoon paper, and Jean was a home economist for the power company when they got together at a fish camp church party. Their relationship developed slowly, but neither of them ever dated anyone else after that night.

They married on a fall Sunday afternoon because Franklin had to work on the newspaper's Sunday edition on Saturday. They paid for their own wedding, which was impressive for people of limited means, and they honeymooned in New Orleans, on a newspaper advertising trade-out.

In many respects, they became the model atomic family of the 1950s, husband, wife and three children, a son, Tim, then daughter, April, and eight years later another daughter, Lara.

Jean continued to work for several years, while a maid helped look after the children, her grandmother, and Franklin's mother.

He worked long hours at the newspaper, overseeing the layout and news selection for the afternoon edition. He also began writing editorials and weekly columns for no extra pay. His diligence didn't go unnoticed, and when the editor of the Columbus morning paper died suddenly, Franklin was named associate editor and later editor.

Among the morning Enquirer's readers at the time were peanut farmer Jimmy Carter in Plains, about sixty miles from Columbus; George C. Wallace of Clanton, Alabama, about sixty miles on the other side of Columbus; Fob James of Opelika, Alabama, twenty-five miles west of Columbus; and Howard Callaway of Pine Mountain, Georgia, twenty-five miles north of Columbus.

All four were elected governor of their states, although Callaway never served due to the peculiar voting system in Georgia. Wallace served for five terms, counting one in which he ran his wife because he could not succeed himself. Tragically, she died in office.

James, whom Franklin knew best and traveled with during his campaign for governor, served one term as a Democrat and was elected to a second term ten years later as a Republican.

At the time Franklin became editor of the Columbus morning newspaper, the ownership always sent an editor to cover the national political conventions, which was how Franklin happened to attend the 1964 Republican convention in San Francisco and the 1968 convention in Miami. The conventions were rare treats, and he never got over the political bug he caught from them. The 1964 convention had nominated Barry Goldwater, whom Franklin enthusiastically endorsed and supported. Goldwater carried Columbus and Georgia, the first time Georgia had not voted for a Democrat for president in its history, but Goldwater lost every state outside the South except Arizona, his home state.

In 1968, Franklin and his newspaper were strong supporters of the Vietnam commitment, as nearly all the US troops in Vietnam had passed through nearby Fort Benning. In fact, Franklin, as editor, dispatched a reporter to Vietnam seven times from 1965 to 1968. The reporter happened to be Charlie Black, who had been a soldier in both World War II and the Korean War, and carried a rifle while covering the war in Vietnam. Charlie became something of a legend in the media corps and was written up in *Newsweek* magazine for his bravery in following troops into battle to interview them while making only $150 a week. When the publisher read the article, he was proud but embarrassed and ordered Franklin to give Black an immediate raise—to $160 a week.

Franklin had left the Columbus papers twice, once to start a weekly newspaper in neighboring Phenix City, Alabama, the so-called sin city, which was placed under control of the United States National Guard the previous year, following the assassination of Albert Patterson, who had been elected the state attorney general. Patterson campaigned on a pledge to clean up the gambling and other corruption which controlled both the city and county governments. Following Patterson's assassination in a downtown parking lot, Alabama's governor ordered the National Guard to take over all city and county law enforcement positions, including mayor and county commissioners. It is believed to be the only time a state has ever so completely taken control of a city and county in the United States. The guardsmen raided nightclubs and barrooms and destroyed the gambling equipment. A special prosecutor, judge, and grand jury were assembled from other counties to try, usually convict, and sentence dozens of culprits, including elected officials.

The county district attorney, the chief deputy sheriff, and the incumbent state attorney general were all charged with assassinating Patterson. Only the deputy sheriff was tried and found guilty. He died in prison seven years later. The district attorney was tried and acquitted, and the state attorney general was never tried due to an alleged mental condition.

It was an exciting time for Franklin, who was then laying out the front page for the afternoon paper, *The Ledger*, which won the Pulitzer Prize for Community Service that year, still the only second Georgia newspaper to earn that most prestigious Pulitzer. Franklin was very modest about his role, saying *The Ledger* won the Pulitzer for "overplaying" the Phenix City story, which was true, but it was a remarkable story from start to finish.

Phenix City had two small weekly newspapers at the time, but hardly anyone read them or even knew they existed. So Franklin launched another one when he was twenty-four years old, renting an office in the same building where Albert Patterson had an office on the night he left it and walked down the stairs to meet his death in the adjoining parking lot.

But Franklin couldn't adjust to the weekly routine after years of the discipline a daily forced on you, not to mention the excitement. He sold his interest in the Phenix City weekly and went back to the Columbus Ledger. So he put his dream of being a publisher on the shelf for several years until the chance came to organize a group of investors to buy the small daily in nearby Opelika, Alabama. In the next twenty years, he followed many paths and came to many crossroads, usually taking the road "less traveled by" until finally arriving back in Athens, where he had gone to college, and then in the Atlanta lawyer's office, where he picked up $7 million for his last newspapers and was using the money to pursue another path less traveled by, which he felt his experience had prepared him for.

Jean's voice came on the phone. He told her about the events of the past few days and got news of their children. Son Tim was married and working at a daily in the group Franklin had sold. Daughter April was a kindergarten teacher, married and the mother of his first grandchild. Lara was working on a magazine the company still operated in Athens.

"You had a lot of wild ideas that worked out," Jean remarked, "but this one is the most outrageous."

"I'm feeling my way slowly, making contacts and reaching out. In a few weeks, we should find out how impossible…or maybe how possible. All the other candidates have been elected officials, but they also have handicaps."

Jean recalled the trip that had carried them through Wolfeboro. "I still remember the other people on the tour bus," she said, "and how beautiful New Hampshire was in the autumn."

"It's even better this year," Tom said. "The leaves are lingering longer, and it's still warm."

"I'm thinking of you," Jean said, "but this sounds as if you are going to be a long time gone." The longest they'd ever been separated were the weeks when he covered the two national political conventions. "Hold tight," he told her. "If we can get my recognition percentage above 5 percent, I'll have a chance to be in a candidate TV debate in four weeks."

Jean sounded worried. "Will that mean you're committed?"

"We'll see. I'm counting on newspaper ads to nudge me past 5 percent recognition, and if they don't, I guess it will prove that newspaper ads don't work in political campaigns. But I've got a good message if people read them, and I think in rural New Hampshire people read weekly newspapers."

By early the following week, Burkhart had rented an office in Wolfeboro and had a few signs printed. He and Susie had officially come to work, and Susie was getting the office together. With Burkhart's help, Franklin had designed a four-piece card with a return stamp to send to all the addresses on the *Granite News* subscription list. The card contained questions on one side about the ads that had been run. "Do you support cutting the payroll tax by 4 percent, and extending it to incomes above $60,000 a year?" was the first question with "Yes" or "No" or "Not sure" boxes. The other questions were "Do you like the US form of government?" "Do you support the NAFTA treaty which will make it easier for US companies to move to Mexico?"

That last question was obviously slanted, but Franklin thought it was fair because he definitely felt that was the end objective and effect of NAFTA. He also knew that the New Hampshire economy was going through one of the worst employment slumps in its history, which was unusual and was hitting middle class jobs as well as lower-paying ones.

Franklin gathered the group together for a strategy meeting. He felt some nuts and bolts were in place, but he could tell by the way Hardy looked that he'd never worked on a campaign this haphazard and he'd seen some bad ones.

New Hampshire was the forty-fourth smallest state geographically and also forty-fourth in population. It had only 10 counties, compared to Georgia's 159; 13 incorporated cities, but 222 townships, which were called little republics because each town's residents would hold an annual meeting in which those attending took part in decisions on how their township was run. They would elect three selectmen to approve budgets and vote on other local issues. The process was one of the purest forms of democracy in the world, but Franklin wondered how anything ever got done. He was often discouraged at how the largest democracy in the world was getting anything done.

Fortunately, Burkhart was familiar with the system and knew his way around the state. So Franklin, Hardy, and Burkhart set out on the first week's travel, while Susie stayed in the office, sent out cards, and other information for brochures.

Franklin outlined a four-week schedule during which they would visit all the counties and most cities, and as many of the townships as they happened across. It was an ambitious goal but one he felt no other candidate would undertake. Burkhart had compiled a list of the selectmen in the towns, with a fair amount of their phone numbers.

In the first few days, they traveled to Ossippee, Sandwich, North Conway, Restone, Jackson, and Mt. Washington, passing by Mt. Washington itself, the tallest mountain in New Hampshire at 6,280 feet, and nearby Mt. Adams, at 5,780 feet. The scenery was invigorating, and Hardy and Burkhart provided interesting travelogues. They visited several other cities and towns and talked to leaders in at least six or seven on the first day. Franklin also talked to several small weekly publishers, keeping the conversation short and placing ads in several larger weeklies.

Burkhart called back to the office, where a phone had been installed, and told Susie to have more pamphlets printed. They were giving out pamphlets at a steady clip to anyone who seemed willing to look at one, and especially any township selectmen they ran across.

They reached Berlin by late afternoon, a city of about twenty thousand with a daily newspaper, one on which Franklin splurged and paid three dollars a column inch for ads. The Berlin newspaper had a stated circulation of fourteen thousand, the largest in the northern area of the state.

They found a comfortable inn with a large dining area and bar and decided to spend the night.

After dinner, the three of them sat around in the bar and discussed the other candidates. The candidate they heard the most about was Paul Tsongas. He had started campaigning in January 1991 and had been to many of the places they visited. He was fairly well-known because he lived in Lowell, Massachusetts, on the New Hampshire border. But looking at his eighty-six-page brochure, "A Call to Economic Arms," Franklin was more and more convinced that Tsongas should be running on the Republican ticket.

"He's the most vulnerable candidate on the issues," he told Hardy and Burkhart. Tsongas preached that "the federal budget is heading for disaster and must be frozen, with no new federal spending, no middle-class tax cuts, no tax credits for having children, and a sharp increase in the gasoline tax." The only tax cut Tsongas suggested was incentives to investors in large and small companies.

"This is incredible," Franklin remarked. "Everything he recommends I'm solidly against and so are most Democrats. These are steps that would make the economy worse, especially for lower income Americans. He's making a case for supply-side economics with a vengeance, tougher than President Bush or Reagan want. He's not only vulnerable, he's dangerous."

Burkhart demurred slightly. "Some people like that message of hardship to get the budget in balance," he pointed out. "They also admire Tsongas for running after his battle with cancer."

"I'd say most of them are Republicans at heart," Franklin said. "My main message is going to be that the government should be spending more to get us out of this recession, not less, and certainly not taxing gasoline, the price of which brought on the high inflation in the 1980s."

Burkhart sighed. "Well, if that's what you believe, you are going to have a hard sale to the folks in New Hampshire. A lot of them think the government already spends too much."

"That's what I'm going to be selling," Franklin persisted, "and if people don't buy it, they can vote for a Republican—or for Tsongas, which would be the same thing. Look at what he writes in his book, 'The Cold War is over, and Japan won.' How ridiculous is that? Japan wasn't even in that war. During most of those years, the Japanese had no defense budget because the US provided its defense. Its economy got a huge boost from rebuilding its cities and industries destroyed in World War II.

"Not only did the US win the Cold War, it was the greatest victory we ever had, but for some reason, we didn't celebrate it. There were no parades, no medals given out. Instead we forfeited our chance to promote peace to the entire world by stomping out a lightweight third world bully with a display of all the technological weapons we didn't get to use in the Cold War. The victory in the Cold War was mainly a victory without bloodshed and destruction or body bags coming home, and it was by far our greater victory."

Hardy looked impressed; Burkhart looked depressed. "That's not exactly what people around here feel," he offered. "They think the US couldn't let that third world bully Saddam Hussein defy the US."

"I know that," Franklin admitted. "That's the oldest reason in history for going to war and why wars are so popular and frequent. But we have a chance today—as the strongest nation militarily, economically, and in every other way, with no equal adversary left in the field—to alter history, and the opportunity is now in 1992 while Russia is weak and its future uncertain and before China gets its act together. That's why this election is so important. And I might add, it's why I want to win in New Hampshire, with the right message and an honest road forward."

"That's a good speech," Hardy said. "I never heard Carter make a better one, but can you make it in front of more than two people?"

Franklin smiled. "I'm not sure," he said. "I made dozens of speeches when I was editor of the Columbus paper and was president of the Georgia and Alabama press associations. But I always held back on the passion and conviction. I think the issues in this campaign will give me the emotion." He looked at Burkhart. "What do you say, Charlie?"

"I've been a Democrat and I've been a Republican. You sound like a confirmed Democrat, and that's the primary you're planning to run in, so I think I can go along with that," he said.

"Okay, Tsongas is the easiest opponent we've found. The hardest I'd say is going to be Bob Kerrey, the senator from Nebraska, who is expected to announce September thirtieth."

On paper, Kerrey did look like the most formable candidate in the field. He was forty-seven, barely older than Clinton at forty-six, but he had been governor of Nebraska for one term and was in his third year as a US senator. Most important, Kerrey had served in the Vietnam War, as a Navy Seal, winning the Congressional Medal of Honor, after losing part of his leg in battle. He had come back home and started a chain of restaurants which made him wealthy in just a few years and proved his ability as a businessman. He won the governorship in his first political race in 1984 and easily won the Senate seat in 1988. He seemed the "dream candidate." Franklin also admired Kerrey because he had opposed the war in Iraq, and because of his service in Vietnam, no one could accuse him of being a pacifist. "I decided it was desirable to beat Bush at the end of the Iraq War," Kerrey stated, even though Bush's approval rating had climbed above 80 percent in the enthusiasm the victory had aroused. "It was unquestionably a marvelous military effort," Kerrey observed, "but somehow it struck the heart of the citizenry in a frenetic way I didn't like."

As someone who had been in combat, Kerrey's word had special meaning to Franklin, but on a closer examination of Kerrey's positions, Franklin realized he wasn't the fire-in-stomach New Deal Democrat to lead the nation into the next century. Kerrey's Senate record was mainly on agriculture issues affecting Nebraska; he supported the NAFTA treaty and other free trade legislation and was in line with other conservative tendencies of Nebraska.

On the personal level, Kerrey was divorced and had a relationship with the actress Debra Winger, who lived with him at the governor's mansion during his term, which apparently didn't bother the conservative voters of Nebraska. He was obviously the candidate with the most upside, but he wasn't sure this was the year. "Maybe I should wait until 1996," he reportedly told his campaign manager. "Hell no," the manager said. "If you can't beat this field with raw talent, you're not going to beat the next group."

Then there was Arkansas governor Bill Clinton, who was showing surprising strength in the early polls and had won an informal straw vote in a Florida convention that summer.

Hardy knew Clinton fairly well from earlier campaigns. "He has charisma and is a real crowd pleaser," Hardy said. "Great one-on-one campaigner, and his wife is a definite asset, smarter than he is actually and more dedicated. He has a lot of connections from his work as chairman of the Democrat Leadership Conference, a group of mainly conservative Democrats formed to move the party toward the center, or even slightly to the right, and Clinton's campaign reflects that sentiment, which has appeal in New Hampshire."

But Clinton also suffered from a variety of handicaps. He had come within a day of announcing for president in 1988, when he was only forty-one, and had backed off only because of his reputation in Arkansas for womanizing. After inviting dozens of Friends of Bill, as they were called, to Little Rock for the announcement, he told them he had decided not to run.

Instead, he was given the chance to introduce the 1988 nominee Michael Dukakis at the Democratic Convention in Atlanta. Franklin had been present that night covering the convention for his daily papers in suburban Atlanta. Clinton's speech, reportedly written for him by the Dukakis campaign, was long and lifeless with the biggest applause coming when Clinton said, "In closing." His reputation as an excellent speaker suffered, especially when Dukakis followed with the best speech of his career, one that transformed him from "Dukakis the technocrat to Dukakis the poet," as Franklin wrote in his newspaper the next day.

Clinton managed to overcome that reversal by playing the saxophone on the Johnny Carson show a few nights later, after Johnny joked that Clinton was being suggested as a prescription for insomnia. Clinton had played the saxophone in high school bands and still had a nice touch.

"He's vulnerable," Franklin concluded. "There's too much smoke in his past for something not to catch fire with him under scrutiny."

Doug Wilder, the governor of Virginia, was also a candidate, but Burkhart thought he wouldn't last to the primary. "It's simple but it's true," he said. "Wilder's black, and only 3 percent of New Hampshire voters are black."

Harkin, a veteran senator from Iowa, was expected to easily win his home state caucus a week before the New Hampshire primary. He was an unabashed liberal, but in speeches to Democratic meetings in other states earlier in the year, Clinton had been judged the most impressive candidate. Harkin made points with labor groups, but they seemed to be his only strong supporters.

Jerry Brown, the former two-term governor of California, was a late entry. He'd run for president twice before in 1976 and 1980 but had been out of elective office for ten years after losing a bid for the US Senate in California. Later he became chairman of the state's Democratic Party, which meant he primarily went around asking for money. He didn't like that and was persuaded by two consultants to enter the 1992 presidential primary. He had little organization and was short of funds. Neither Burkhart or Hardy, who knew him from the 1976 candidacy against Carter, gave him much credence. He was still stuck with his nickname as Governor Moonbeam because of some peculiar habits. He had never married and declined to live at the governor's mansion during his two terms.

With many Democrats still hoping Mario Cuomo would enter the race before the December 23 deadline, Bob Kerrey looked like the class of the field.

"At least these other candidates have campaign staffs and have been elected to something," Hardy said glumly. "What have we got except us and Susie back at the office, hopefully getting together pamphlets, which should have been ready weeks ago?"

"How many townships have we been in?" Franklin asked.

"Sixteen, by my count, and a few cities. So we've only got about two hundred to go."

"Okay, let's get some pamphlets sent to Berlin tomorrow, and we'll split up with Burkhart taking some and you and I will take some. In the next two weeks, our goal will be to hit the rest of the cities and about one hundred townships, and that should put me on track for at least 5 percent of the votes in the telephone polls and a chance to be in the first debate of all the candidates in mid-October, just about the time most voters start paying attention."

Hardy and Burkhart briefly looked cheerful. "It could happen," Burkhart said. "I remember in 1964 Henry Cabot Lodge didn't even come to New Hampshire, and he beat both Goldwater and Rockefeller."

"That was a real fluke, so was 1968, when Senator Gene McCarthy almost beat President Johnson in the primary and even more of a fluke that he was considered a winner even though Johnson actually got the most votes as a write-in candidate."

"You're right, but you are the darkest horse that has ever run. No election wins, no campaign staff, no name recognition, no geographic base. If you get any votes, it'll be a big story," Hardy said.

"You've been with too many losers," Franklin told him.

They split up in the little town of Lancaster. Burkhart rented a car and headed back south while Franklin and Hardy proceeded north to Colebrook. Both towns were small, but they found at least four or five people who agreed to take their pamphlets, pass them out, and announce their visit at the next town meeting. They also identified a few bona fide Democrats who said they'd consider voting for Franklin if he became a candidate. They got their name and address and phone number.

Franklin looked at his map. "We're just a few miles from Dixville Notch," he said. "That's one place I want to be sure and visit. Dixville Notch is one of the towns in New Hampshire that is allowed to cast votes just after midnight on Primary Day and have them counted and reported first in the state. The total vote in Dixville Notch is usually about a dozen."

When Franklin was wire editor in Columbus, he remembered getting that early Dixville Notch result on Election Day and running it as a news flash on the afternoon front page.

Predictably, Dixville Notch turned out to be the smallest place they'd visited. But a few people were on its one street, and there was a building labeled Election Hall, which Franklin and Hardy decided was the place to go. It was small with a couple of tables and chairs plus a voting booth. A woman inside greeted them, and they told her what their business was. "You've come to the right place," she said. "This is where the first votes in the primary and general election are cast. Don't know why exactly but it's a tradition here in Dixville Notch. Every voter in the precinct comes to this building from around midnight, and by 12:30 a.m., all of the votes are cast and counted and all the voters checked off as having voted. The results are sent to state headquarters, and they send them to the Associated Press."

The woman agreed to call some friends as they waited. The Election Hall was old and in need of repairs, which the woman assured them were in the plans. Soon, a crowd of about twenty more residents from Dixville Notch and its surrounding communities had gathered. At least two of them were selectmen from their towns. They agreed to hear a short presentation by Franklin.

He went over with them the same points he'd made in presentations in the other cities and towns.

He was for reducing the payroll tax to 3 percent and levying it on all earned income, not just the first $60,000 a worker earned. He explained this would be an unprecedented transfer of taxation from the lowest-paid workers to the highest-paid ones in the country.

He also promised to work for a more progressive income tax scale, which the 1986 tax revision had moved downward instead of upward with the result of taxing middle incomes by as high a percentage as top incomes and, in one incomprehensible case, by a higher percentage than the next highest bracket.

He opposed the NAFTA trade act because it would encourage United States companies to move their plants and jobs to Mexico and probably encourage more immigration of Mexicans into the United States as their farm jobs were lost.

He would support cooperating with Russia to assure its continued moving away from Communism and possibly becoming a reliable United States ally in promoting peace and stability in the rest of the world. "We did that with Germany and Japan," Franklin pointed out. "And a lot more blood had been spilled and a lot more hate was present on both sides. In the Cold War, Americans and Russians never came to direct combat against each other. We have many grounds for cooperation as the two dominant nuclear powers and are in position to show the way to a lasting peace."

He also promised to maintain the federal government's commitment to assuring a strong and prosperous nation for all its people.

"Basically, that's my message," Franklin concluded, "and I'll be happy to accept any questions."

The group had listened attentively. One man asked a question. It was one Franklin had heard often before. "What about this big budget deficit and all the people on welfare? They're breaking this country."

"Well, not really," Franklin gently explained. "As a percent of the total US Domestic Product, the deficit is lower than it's been for most of this century, and it would be lower if the country was not in this economic slump, which is the worst since the Great Depression. Welfare, as you call it, mainly consists of two programs. One is food stamps, which provides farmers another market for their products and is often the difference in failure or survival for their farms. Food stamps go to the customers of grocery stores who in the past couldn't afford groceries, so the farmers and large and small grocers are helped, and not least, people who sometimes went hungry are now able to get food. It's a relatively small investment of government funds with a good return to several sectors.

"The other so-called welfare program is assistance to single mothers who have no reliable income. These are not people who don't want to work or who get pregnant to get a welfare check. They are people in real need through circumstances beyond their control. The richest nation in history should not do less than support its least fortunate families, and those families spend every cent they get at the stores in their communities, thus helping keep those stores in business, just as food stamps do."

"Well," said one man, "a lot of folks in New Hampshire are having trouble finding work, and then they see other folks not working and buying steaks at the grocery store and big TV sets."

"Who are those people?" Franklin asked skeptically. "I know this is a tough economic time in New Hampshire, which has traditionally been prosperous, but we can turn this economy around by repealing most of that 1986 tax bill, which killed the second home market, and by stemming the loss of jobs in such once-thriving industries as leather goods, and getting money into the hands of the people who do most of the buying in this state. The US has always fared best with a demand-side economy, not a supply-side economy, which has been tried for the past fifteen years. Look at my pamphlets, they repeat the points I'm making and offer a way out of this economic slump."

There was light applause from the small crowd, and most of the people came by to shake hands with Franklin. "I'm going to count on Dixville Notch to give me a head start on election night. Tell your friends and relatives about me, and if a pollster calls you, please tell them to include my name among the candidates invited to the TV debates. I bet I'm the first candidate to visit Dixville Notch this year, and I'll be back, so don't forget me."

As they left, Hardy looked at Franklin with a new appreciation. "That was good," he said. "You're getting better, and I could tell you were making a connection. At some of these stops, it seemed like we weren't meeting any real people. Today we did."

"Thanks. Let's visit more towns this afternoon. I feel I'm making an impression."

"Yeah, but on how many people. These other candidates will soon be all over TV and in the bigger cities."

"You're right, and our last stop tonight will be in Concord, the state capital. Is that big enough for you?"

The trip to Concord was mainly on Interstate 93 and more than one hundred miles with several stops Franklin planned in Plymouth and Franklin, one of the many towns in the country with his family name.

"You were telling me about life during the Great Depression the last time we were riding along and how the New Deal made a noticeable difference," Hardy reminded him. "My father had told me some, but he wasn't a big talker."

"Well, he was certainly a pioneer," Franklin said. "The CCC was the wedge that cleared the way for many New Deal programs. It set the example for government intervention in the private sector and for direct public help to people without work. That idea was not easy for Americans to accept. There was still the powerful appeal of self-reliance and the lone gunman who rode into a town and cleaned out all the bad guys by himself. Democrats, as well as Republicans, believed in that image, and in the myth that the United States had been built by individual effort without much help from the government. That was actually never the case, but the New Deal was at first seen as an attack on that prevailing wisdom. Despite the economic hole the nation was in, the myth was still powerful and persuasive, even among the poorest. It was also powerful in some respects on the man who was elected to change it and create the New Deal, Franklin Roosevelt himself.

"Roosevelt was from a background that was the very model of the aristocracy, an epithet that followed him all his career. He was called a traitor to his class. Actually, one of his ancestors had been a passenger on the *Mayflower*, and both of his parents were from prominent and well-to-do families, his mother, Sara Delano, even more than his father. Roosevelt grew up as a member of the Hudson River elite, went to Groton, the nation's most prominent prep school, to Harvard, where he was editor of the *Harvard Law Review*, and he was married to the niece of the US president at the time.

"The ethos of the American fortress of beliefs his administration assaulted was strong and deep in his background. During his campaign for president in 1932, he even promised to balance the federal budget and criticized Herbert Hoover for spending more money than the government took in. He also promised not to raise taxes.

"All of that ran counter to what he actually did, but it was not because he abandoned his principles but because he quickly recognized how critical the nation's problems were and how many people were suffering. Ironically, one of his main advisers in the early days of his administration was one of the most conservative congressmen, especially on federal spending. That was Lewis Douglas of Arizona, one of two advisers who met with Roosevelt each morning and whom he had appointed director of the budget. Biographers have said Roosevelt was strongly impressed by Douglas and once described him as the most valuable find among the cabinet members.

"In the first weeks of the New Deal, Roosevelt supported a so-called Economy Act which Douglas prepared, slashing pensions to war veterans among other things. Douglas appealed to Roosevelt's innate thrifty side, which led him to say during the '32 campaign that an overspending nation, like an overspending family, is on its way to bankruptcy.

"Roosevelt also had other supporters who were advocates of 'a balanced budget,' among them Bernard Baruch, a Wall Street investment millionaire from South Carolina who remained one of his best friends and advisers throughout his years as president. Baruch was said to own 60 congressmen.

"At the time, nearly a quarter of federal expenditures went for pensions to military veterans. Douglas considered those benefits the appropriate place to start cutting. He also included sharp reductions in pay to federal workers. In a speech, Roosevelt praised veterans for what they'd done in the past to preserve the nation and said now they "must enlist in a war on selfishness and extravagance, enemies with whom we never concluded an armistice."

"It was a speech many of his enemies would echo in future years and could have been lifted from any Republican speech in 1992, but Roosevelt was at the peak of his popularity in 1933, and a compliant Congress approved the Economy Bill, which many Democrats supported reluctantly and some not at all.

"Fortunately for Roosevelt, and ultimately for the nation, his other chief adviser was Raymond Moley, who had coined the term 'New Deal' and fashioned its principles after the Economy Bill was out of the way. Roosevelt felt he had mollified the more conservative elements in society, and he turned to farm legislation, also close to his heart. Agriculture was in a long decline and required a revolutionary approach, plus ample funding. In this endeavor, Roosevelt was strongly supported by Henry Wallace, his secretary of agriculture, and by Frances Perkins, secretary of labor, the first woman to serve in a president's cabinet.

"Soon, forced to make a choice between fiscal conservatism and rampant evidence of families suffering, in a national economy struggling to recover from economic conditions brought on by unrestrained capitalism, Roosevelt moved away from Douglas's influence and pursued the various ideas and programs that promoted economic growth and stability, not only in the 1930s, but in all the years since.

"Moley, a college professor, who later turned against Roosevelt, was an invaluable contributor to those early New Deal programs. First, of course, they included the CCC, popular partly because it was relatively inexpensive. People like your father were paid a dollar a day, or about thirty dollars a month, but the CCC helped thousands of young men get off the streets and become good citizens and contributors to a better nation and countryside.

"Then came the Banking Act, which prohibited banks from using depositors' money on risky speculations; the Securities and Exchange Commission, to regulate stock market practices; the Tennessee Valley Authority (TVA), which provided federal funds to develop water resources; the Federal Deposit Insurance Corporation, which insured bank deposits up to a certain amount; and then the Public Works Administration (PWA), which provided immediate help to the unemployed and was the chief reason for the 1933–34 economic recovery.

"The PWA was fortunate to find a leader named Harry Hopkins, who was one of the most valuable leaders in the New Deal. Hopkins had a background in social work. He also was an indefatigable worker who brooked as little interference as possible. He came to Washington on May 11, 1933, after the New Deal had laid the groundwork for the recovery effort. Unemployment had just reached an 'all-time high,' according to the Commerce Department, and the national per capita income had dropped 50 percent since the end of 1929.

"Hopkins found a desk in a hallway and sat down and went to work. What did he do? He sent federal funds to states and cities that had simply run out of money. In the first two hours, Hopkins dispensed more than $5 million—a lot of money in 1933—and handed out an additional $2 million to the states by June 3. Neither Hopkins nor Roosevelt believed in what they called the dole, and so all the federal relief funds were based on jobs in the PWA, which handled extensive construction projects and other work that needed doing but which states lacked funds to pay for.

"When criticized, Hopkins replied, 'Are these workers hobos, are they unemployable? No, they are carpenters, bricklayers, artisans, architects, engineers, clerks, even doctors and ministers. Some of the best people in the country are on these relief rolls, and now they are getting paying jobs.' Nevertheless, the massive federal spending set many people's teeth on edge, including Lewis Douglas, who realized he had lost his effort to hold spending down. He soon resigned.

"When people told Hopkins the economy would work its way back for the unemployed in the long run, he made his famous remark: 'People don't eat in the long run, they eat every day.'

"Frances Perkins described Hopkins' work 'as taking the edge off human misery.'

"Moley had a further interpretation of the departure from the past that the New Deal was taking. 'You realize,' he told Roosevelt, 'that we are taking an enormous step away from the philosophy of *laissez-faire*,' which basically required the government to let the free market set its course.

"'If that philosophy hadn't proven to be bankrupt, Herbert Hoover would be sitting here right now, instead of me," Roosevelt replied. "I have never felt so sure of anything in my life as the soundness of this approach." The Hudson River Valley politician had been converted, and the third American revolution proceeded. It is the revolution that created the modern nation we have today.

Hardy slowed down as they entered the town of Plymouth. After a visit to its weekly paper, they stopped at a coffee shop on the square. "By the way," Franklin said, "I talked to Burkhart on the phone, and he's set up an appointment with the state Democratic chairman for me in the morning in Concord, so we'll spend the night there."

"I was wondering," Hardy said. "That's progress."

They stopped at the Wayfarer, the largest motel in Concord and a popular hangout for politicians and officials. After dinner, they found their way to the bar, which Hardy remembered from his two campaigns with Jimmy Carter. It was karaoke night, and an elderly gentleman was playing a harmonica and leading the crowd in a few songs. The bar crowd spilled over into the adjoining halls.

"Can you sing?" Franklin asked Hardy.

"It's not one of my long suits," he replied.

"Okay, I'll do the singing then," Franklin said. He asked the harmonica player if he could play "The Gambler" by Kenny Rogers. "Easy," he said, "and I know the words."

He and Franklin finally got into sync by the first chorus: "You got to know when to hold 'em, know when to fold 'em, know when to walk away and know when to run. Don't count your money while you're sitting at the table, there'll be time enough for counting, when the dealing's done."

The crowd quickly picked up the chant and seemed to appreciate Franklin's singing efforts. So did the harmonica player who joined in. "Don't count your money while you're sitting at the table. There'll be time enough for counting, when the dealing's done."

Soon the whole room was singing, and people were coming in from the halls. "How about Lucille?" Franklin called to the harmonica player.

"I got it," he said and started playing.

"You picked a fine time to leave me, Lucille, with four hungry children and a crop in the field, I've had some bad times, been through some sad times, but this time the hurting won't heal, you picked a fine time to leave me, Lucille."

Franklin was excited. He had thought those Kenny Rogers songs, just a few years past being huge hits, would appeal to the crowd, and they did. After the singing ended, Franklin asked for the floor. "I'm so glad to be with you all tonight," he said. "It's that time in New Hampshire when presidential candidates are always dropping by, and I want you to know that I'm one of them. My name is Thomas A. Franklin, the *A* as in Alexander Hamilton, and I'm planning to be a candidate in the Democratic primary in February. You'll be hearing more from me, but I hope you'll keep the name in mind."

"You sound like a Southerner!" one patron shouted.

"In fact, a Georgian, who lived sixty miles from Jimmy Carter, but don't hold that against me."

"You don't talk exactly like Carter did," the patron said. "I met him and even voted for him, but I regretted it."

"Sorry about that," Franklin said. "Carter and I don't sound alike even though we were practically neighbors, but he was a country boy, and I grew up in a small city, and in the 1930s, that made all the difference. The fellow with me was a driver for Carter and now he's helping me. And I hope all you will tell your relatives and friends that I plan to be on the ballot and need their votes. Let's sing one more chorus of 'The Gambler' and then I've got another announcement."

Everybody joined in and "when the gambler, he broke even," Franklin applauded them and told them he thought it was legal for a politician to pick up the bar bill for the singing, which he intended to do.

This was greeted by cheers and laughter, and the bartender looked pleased. Several people came by to shake hands with Franklin, and a few even wished him luck. Several told him to come back to the bar every Wednesday night when the crowd was largest.

The bar bill was about $300, which Franklin considered a pretty useful campaign investment. "We probably reached more voters tonight than we did in any of those little towns," Hardy said. "Probably made more friends."

"Don't count the votes while we're sitting at the table," Franklin hummed. "There'll be time enough for counting when the voting's done."

At the hotel, he called Jean to relate the day's happenings. They recalled their tour of New England again and seeing the Old Man of the Mountain, a rock formation on Cannon Mountain that looks like the side of an old man's face. It had become such a popular tourist attraction that the State used Cannon Mountain as a symbol in its advertising. Profile Mountain, as it was also called, was made famous in the 1800s by the writer Nathaniel Hawthorne, who used it in his short story *The Great Stone Face*. Franklin and Hardy had passed by it that day, and Franklin was distressed to hear that rock experts expected the formation would soon crumble due to erosion, and the old man's face would be no more. Franklin made it a point to promise in every speech that if elected president, he would exert every effort to preserve Profile Mountain, which had become such an important attraction for New Hampshire's economy.

In Concord they easily found the office where they were to meet Burkhart and the state Democratic chairman. It was right on the square across from the state capitol building. There was ample parking, which was certainly not true around Georgia's capitol building in downtown Atlanta.

A good-looking woman always caught Franklin's eye, and while he didn't exactly have a wandering eye, he did have an appreciative eye, and as they walked toward the chairman's office, a strikingly attractive woman was walking toward them with Charlie Burkhart. Almost with a start, Franklin realized she was Susan Schultz. Her hair, previously always wrapped in a bun on the back of her head, was now hanging down around her shoulders, streaked with strands of gold that caught the early autumn sunlight. She had on a short-sleeve dress that revealed her long and well-shaped arms and shoulders, plus a surprisingly ample bosom that had been hidden by the frumpy waitressing uniform. Her athletic figure and legs also benefited from the dress, but most striking was the smile that had replaced the stoic expression she had worn as a waitress.

"You look beautiful," Franklin greeted her. Hardy enthusiastically endorsed the compliment.

"I got some new clothes and hairdo with that salary you gave me," Susie said, "and it's made a difference when I go around passing out pamphlets. Most people are glad to see me and accept the pamphlets, and a lot of them even read them. I've given out hundreds in Carroll and Belknap Counties and to tourists at the Lake and in the White Mountains."

"That's great," Franklin exclaimed. "Tourists often read on the bus or at night, and that'll get my name into other states."

"I brought Susie because I thought she'd be an asset when we talk to the chairman," Burkhart said, "and she's become a real fan of yours."

Franklin smiled. A pretty girl always helped, especially with old politicians. The chairman, Arthur Underwood, was not old. He looked about forty, and he greeted them with the reserve of a man who already had enough on his plate.

"What makes you want to run for president?" he asked pointedly.

Franklin reviewed the main reasons, which were that 1992 was a crucial year for the nation and the world to lay a foundation for enduring peace, and he hadn't heard any of the candidates emphasizing that. In fact, they had hardly mentioned that the United States had won its greatest victory with the breakup of the Soviet Union. "Also, something has to be done at the national level to revive the economy, and the ideas I hear from Paul Tsongas sound like more of the medicine we've been taking for twelve years, which is supply-side economics that directs more money to the well-off in hopes that a little will trickle down to the poor. It hasn't worked, not now or in the past."

Underwood frowned. "Tsongas is the most popular candidate right now," he pointed out. "A lot of voters think he's got the right medicine."

"They're probably closet Republicans, which Tsongas sounds like. He needs to switch parties or get out of the Democratic primary," Franklin retorted.

"A lot of people are waiting to see if Mario Cuomo gets in. If he does, I think he'll carry the state," Underwood replied with a hopeful smile.

"I hear he's got problems with his state legislature in New York and is waiting to see how his budget is treated before making a decision," Franklin commented. "He should have run in 1988. He probably would have won, including in the general election. Something held him back then, and the odds are longer this year."

"We've already got a better field than most people think," Underwood said. "Bob Kerrey is a dream candidate, handsome, a wounded Vietnam veteran, a former governor and current senator. Tom Harkin is popular with the labor people. Bill Clinton seems to have the best organization and has made a good impression with his early speeches. He's won the 'expectations' election and has that great consulting team behind him."

"They're overrated," Franklin said. "They ran Zell Miller's campaign in Georgia. Miller should've won by twice the margin. He'd been lieutenant governor for sixteen years and still struggled."

Underwood glanced at his notes. "Then there's Jerry Brown, whose name is well-known, and he was a governor of California. In fact, there are a lot of people who'll be on the ballot, like Charles Wood, that guy from Alabama, Lenora Fulani, Tom Laughlin, Larry Agran, and a few others…including you, I guess."

"How do you get in the TV debates is what I want to know," Franklin told him emphatically. "I recognize the odds."

"I think the latest standard is that a candidate with 5 percent of the votes in at least two recognized state polls taken in mid-October will make the debates. Right now, Tsongas, Clinton, Kerrey, Harkin, and Brown are the only qualifiers. You aren't mentioned."

Franklin looked at his clean calendar. "First big debate is in mid-October," he pointed out. "This is the last week in September. "I think I've a fair chance of getting to that 5 percent in three weeks. We're visiting every township in the state and advertising in a lot of weekly newspapers."

"Good luck with that," Underwood said. "TV advertising is the only way to get your name known widely, and the only way to win, I might add."

"I'll remember that," Franklin said. "You've been a great help in pointing out the obstacles. Could you give us a list of all the county Democratic chairmen and how to reach them?"

"Sure," Underwood said, punching his computer. "The important ones are in the southern part of the state. About 70 percent of the voters live in the cities of Concord, Manchester, Nashua, and Portsmouth. The pickings are slim in the rest of the state, and most of them are Republicans."

"I've talked to a lot of voters in the past few days, and they are still looking for a candidate," Susie piped up, "and one who is not a politician."

"They probably just want to talk with a pretty girl." Underwood smiled.

"Have you read any of Franklin's ads?" she asked, producing a pamphlet and handing it to him. It contained a full text of his first ad on cutting the payroll tax by 4 percent.

Underwood scanned the ad. "Not bad," he commented, "but wouldn't extending the tax to salaries over $60,000 a year be an increase on those folks?"

"Well, you have to figure they could get the 4 percent cut on their first $60,000 a year," Franklin explained. "How many people in New Hampshire make more than $120,000 a year, which would be the first amount to feel the increase."

"All the rich ones do," Underwood answered. "And they look forward to that first check without a Social Security deduction."

"I'd say 95 percent of the people will have more money in their paychecks under this plan, and they are the ones who need it. The others got big tax cuts under the Reagan administration."

Underwood looked at Susie again. "Did you say your name is Susan Schultz?" he asked. "I think I've heard of you."

Susie froze up but then told him, "I was an all-state basketball player 1987 and 1988."

"That's right," Underwood exclaimed. "I saw you play here in the state tournament in 1987. You had a great night."

"Yeah, I remember that game. It was the semifinals, and I scored thirty-five points. But the player guarding me was only five feet, six inches and I was already five feet, ten inches."

"You stood out," Underwood said, "not just as a player, but as the team leader. You've changed a lot since then."

"I've changed a lot in the past three weeks," Susie said.

Underwood told them he'd be in touch about the debates but said he didn't want too many candidates on stage, and there were already five certain ones.

"Well, he softened up some after Susie came in," Hardy said as they left.

"I told you I had a notion about her. While we are up this way, there's a place down I-73 near Salem I'd like to visit," Franklin told him.

The place was called Mystery Hill, and it was a maze of elaborate buildings, or their remnants, which a resident of Derry had preserved and established as a site very much like the famous Stonehenge in Great Britain. They were a network of tunnels, sacrificial tables, and rock drawings that date the ruins as old as two thousand years.

Mystery Hill had not become a regular tourist stop, but Franklin found it intriguing and wanted to call people's attention to it. He and Hardy found a lot of rocks at Mystery Hill but not many visitors, Hardy complained. Franklin felt referring to it in talks would prove he'd been just about everywhere in the state.

Franklin decided they should establish an office in Concord and work out of the Wayfarer for several days, so they drove back to Wolfeboro to gather their clothes and check out. They found Burkhart at the small office, and he had good news.

"I've got you a speaking engagement at a civic club in Conway," he reported. "Also, we are getting a few replies from that first ad and have sent out the card with a lot of cards coming back and a few replies on the ads. It's not many, but people are noticing."

Susie was going through the mail.

"Great comments on some of them," she called out. "They like the idea of cutting the payroll tax, and surprisingly, most of them agree with you that it's time for people to stop attacking the government and politicians in general."

"The Conway club has a spot open on September thirtieth," Burkhart told him. "It's a luncheon meeting and the club has about thirty members. I was a member for years and know these folks. They are pretty conservative and Republican, but that area has been hit hard by the downturn. It can't be a strictly political speech by the club's rules, but you can talk about your ideas."

"That's fine," Franklin said. "One speech should lead to more and also some publicity."

Picking up pamphlets, Franklin and Hardy hit the road again. There were still more than 150 townships to visit although Franklin had decided they wouldn't find them all. As he viewed the population statistics he recognized that they needed to start concentration on the southern part of the state around Manchester, Concord, Nashua, and

Portsmouth. There were plenty of weekly papers there as well as the larger dailies. On this day, however, they took a road less traveled to Rochester, Gossville, Suncook, and back to Concord.

"You were telling me about growing up in the Great Depression years and how the New Deal made things better," Hardy reminded him. "I've got the tape recorder on, so why don't you follow up on that."

"Well, as I said, the CCC your father joined as a boy was a trendsetter, but there was still a lot of resistance to direct government money to individuals, even by Roosevelt himself. The breakthrough guy was Harry Hopkins, who also believed strongly in a role for states and communities. That early money he gave out was in the form of grants which the states had to match. When they pleaded poverty, Hopkins had to improvise. He mainly was determined to establish the concept that the federal government had a responsibility for the welfare of all citizens, not just the business community, which he felt would be bolstered if consumers had more jobs and consequently more money to spend. He was the ultimate demand-side economist before the term was even coined.

"The PWA only lasted two years, but it was the biggest public works program that had ever existed in the US. It transformed the New Deal to a job-providing machine, which was exactly what the country needed. The jobs were low-paid, but I can recall many workers in my hometown who couldn't get a job at the textile mills who got one from the PWA even though it paid even less. Still, it was a job.

"By 1934, the PWA had created 4 million jobs and, along with the CCC, had broken the back of the Depression. It built sewer systems, replaced dilapidated housing, built playgrounds and swimming pools, helped fund efforts for eradication of ticks and malaria, which were serious health problems, especially in Southern states, some of which resisted the help, including Talmadge's Georgia.

"But Hopkins wanted more money to establish a broader role for the PWA. So what happened in 1934, the PWA became the WPA, Work Projects Administration, which in the next eight years, 1934–1942, created 8.5 million more jobs, constructed more than 830,000 schools, 800 airports, 960 sewage plants, and 650,000 miles of roads, and perhaps most important taught 2 million people to read.

"In short, the WPA, under the direction of Hopkins with funding mainly from the federal government created the world's first truly modern nation, lifting many of its people out of the Depression and laying the foundation for the great nation that was to emerge in later years.

"In 1965, long after the WPA had faded from most Americans' memories, a *New York Times* article quoted a former tenant farmer from North Carolina who had gotten a job from WPA as saying, 'There ain't no other nation in the world that had enough sense to think of the WPA.'

"Not everyone agreed with him in the 1930s. Hopkins was always being accused of 'wasting money' and 'paying people to rake leaves, a common complaint about the CCC, which had proven patently false and was even more false in the case of the WPA. Hopkins lashed back. 'The Republican national chairman has accused me of playing politics because I am sheltering the destitute, feeding the hungry, clothing the naked, regardless of their sex, age, creed, or place of residency. If that be politics, then I plead guilty and decline to get into an argument. Hunger is not a subject for debate.'

"But of course, in a sense, it is the debate we've been having ever since. Some Americans are just not inclined to the charitable instincts of the New Deal, and Roosevelt probably understood that better than his more ambitious associates, such as Hopkins and Frances Perkins. He was only the third Democrat to become president since the Civil War and the first, Grover Cleveland, had been more conservative than Republicans of his day.

'Federal aid in any form encourages the expectations of a paternal core in the federal government and weakens the sturdiness of our national character,' Cleveland declared.

"His policies reflected his philosophy. He vetoed many pension bills for Civil War veterans and fought with the railroad companies on federal funds the government had given them to encourage the building of railroads from coast to coast through the thinly settled western states from the east to California. He opposed labor unions or any legislation that might be considered inflationary. In fact, Cleveland was the perfect model for later Republicans, including those who fought the New Deal, and still do," Franklin pointed out.

Cleveland received the most popular votes for president in 1888, mainly due to getting almost all the votes in the Southern states but was denied reelection when Benjamin Harrison won the most electoral votes. Cleveland won his second term in 1892 by out-polling Harrison in both the electoral vote and the popular vote. The economy caught up with Cleveland in his second term, and his policies were not popular during the Depression that followed.

"It was twenty years before another Democrat was elected. Woodrow Wilson won in a three-way race in 1912," Franklin concluded.

"I didn't realize what a tough time Roosevelt's policies had in those early years," Hardy commented.

"And they still do. Supply economics and Reaganomics were in large measure a rejection of New Deal principles, and the nation is reaping the disabling results. So is the world, for that matter. Parsimony in the federal government has never worked for long, but Bush is still popular, and Paul Tsongas is a twentieth century example of a Grover Cleveland Democrat and the other Democratic candidates are not seeing the resemblance as clearly as they should. Nothing is so powerful as a myth believed."

"You know you may not be such a no-shot candidate after all. You've got the smartest sumbitch I've ever seen as your main adviser."

"Who's that?" Franklin asked.

"Thomas Alexander Franklin," Hardy answered enthusiastically.

Chapter Four

NOT SUCH A NO-SHOT

*Government has a final responsibility for the
well-being of its citizens. If private cooperative effort
fails to provide work for willing hands those suffering hardship have a right to call upon the government for aid. And a government worthy of the name
must make a fitting response.*
   —Franklin D. Roosevelt, January 3, 1938

They were entering Concord by then, and Franklin decided
to try an ad in the Concord daily, which he knew would
be expensive but would reach a lot of state government
employees. The price was six dollars a column inch, so he took a half
page for three weeks and ran the ad about cutting the payroll tax with
references to the phone number the campaign now had and the PO
boxes, as well as a plea to mention his name if called by a pollster.

He and Hardy returned to the hotel, and he began working on
the speech to the club in North Conway. He figured it would be the
most important speech he had ever made. If he got a good reception,
he'd about decided to officially announce he was running in early
October.

Hardy and Susie went with Franklin and Burkhart to the
club meeting, which was in the large motel dining room in North
Conway. He went around and introduced himself to the club officers

and other members. He'd done that dozens of times at civic clubs throughout Georgia and Alabama. The men (and they were all men of course in those days) looked about the same as the ones in the south. They were mostly middle-aged businessmen, doctors or lawyers, and a few teachers.

They were mildly friendly, a bit suspicious, and conveyed an air of having met a lot of people coming through town running for president. Franklin wanted to begin with a joke, but he neglected to think of a good one, so he reviewed his ideas from the newspaper column, pointing out that he had been a small businessman for forty-five years and had owned and edited forty newspapers and had been president of the press associations in both Georgia and Alabama. He stressed that he felt that with the end of the Cold War, the United States had a historic opportunity to lead the world toward an unprecedented era of peace, but first it needed to strengthen its own economy by abandoning supply-economics and improving living conditions for the poorer elements of society.

"The United States is the oldest and purest democracy ever created," he stressed firmly. "No other country has achieved its degree of individual freedom in conjunction with general civil stability. England is often cited as another example, but England is actually still a kingdom with the Queen as its highest public image. The United States has only the president, both as its governmental leader, its civic leader, and to an extent its cultural leader. He embodies the images and responsibilities that the prime minister and Queen embody in England, and for 250 years, except for the four years of the Civil War, the United States has hung together and thrived while dozens of nations have tried democracy and fallen either to tyranny or anarchy. That is still true in too much of the world and even in the US, there are many who would prefer to try out one of those alternatives. I love my country, but I also love my government because the government is what makes our country the greatest in history and must set the example for the rest of the world. The government is not great because of the nation. The nation is great because of its government."

His small support group led a polite round of applause, but he sensed his words had stirred no strong positive emotions and perhaps some negative ones.

Franklin invited questions, hoping there would be a few.

He inwardly groaned when the first question was, "What about all these welfare cheats who are living off the government and driving up our taxes. You didn't say a thing about them."

"Do you know any people like that?" Franklin asked as gently as he could.

"Yeah," the man answered. "My ex-son-in-law. He won't even try to get a job."

The crowd laughed and Franklin suppressed a smile.

"As I said, I've been a small businessman for many years, and what I always wanted was more customers rather than lower taxes. What's wrong today is that too many Americans don't have enough money to make discretionary purchases or to take tours of New Hampshire. The nation needs to get more money into their hands instead of paying CEOs six-figure salaries or overrewarding stockbrokers who shuffle papers but don't make anything except deals when they sell their company's stock to another for millions of dollars."

"You aren't against people getting rich, are you?" one man spoke up. "That sounds socialistic."

"No, I made a lot of those deals myself. I'm for the kind of nation we had in the years after World War II, when the rich got richer but the United States developed the most prosperous middle class of any nation ever. Was there anything wrong with that?"

"Another point you made," said a member, "sounded like you think the US should sidle up to Russia and become friends with that bunch of Communists. Is that what you said?"

"I definitely think we need to try and be friends with Russia," Franklin said. "It still has the second-largest arsenal of nuclear weapons in the world with less control of them than they had before the breakup of the Soviet Union. In some ways, a weaker Russia is more dangerous than a strong one. What's new and encouraging is that we have a chance to forge a relationship with them that puts the two most powerful nuclear arsenals together so that small-time villains like Hussein won't think they can play us off against each other."

"That's a bitter pill to swallow after all those Ruskies did to us. Do you really think we can trust them?"

"We don't have to trust them," Franklin said defiantly. "The US is still by far the most powerful nation militarily, and Russia is on the verge of national bankruptcy and possible chaos. China is a greater danger but is weak economically. The US can afford to trust any nation as long as we have a dominant military and a strong consumer economy. No other nation comes close to us on either count, especially Russia in its present condition. Before the Cold War, Russia and the US had been allies in both world wars, and even during the Cold War, US and Russia military forces never clashed directly or killed each other's military. A hundred years ago, Russia sold us Alaska, which was one of the great bargains of history. Russia suffered the worst loss of human life of any nation in both world wars, holding off the Germans in each war until the US came to the rescue of the Allied forces. Our casualties were as low as they were because thousands of Russians died fighting the Germans at Stalingrad, Ukraine, and Leningrad. That's not to say they shouldn't be watched carefully, but the record shows the two can get along with each other."

Nobody applauded, not even Hardy or Burkhart. Susie started to but thought better of it. The resentment against Russia and Communists still ran strong, and Franklin realized it. But reconciliation and an effort for durable peace was one of his main themes. If people couldn't accept that, he wouldn't get anywhere.

Another member changed the subject. "A lot of folks I talk to think homosexuals are getting too much influence, especially in Vermont and Massachusetts, and it's becoming a serious issue."

"I've been asked what I thought about homosexuals in the military, and I stressed that it was an issue for the joint chiefs of staff and defense officials to handle. The services also have hundreds of officers that deal with the troops, and their first consideration is to make sure they are prepared for battle and other vital duties. I strongly support the chiefs of staff and senate chairmen in the current policy."

That response drew the most favorable applause of the day.

Several members came by to speak with Franklin, most of them complimentary of his delivery and a few saying he sounded better than Jimmy Carter had. They did not mention any of the other 1992 candidates.

Franklin was not satisfied with himself. He'd talked too much about reconciling with Russia and hadn't talked enough about fixing the economy, but he'd gotten through the speech, and it was a landmark in the campaign.

When they returned to the office, there was a call from a Democratic leader in Concord who'd read his ad in the Concord paper. He wanted Franklin to speak the following week to a large civic club in Concord. Franklin agreed. "I'll do better," he told his little group. "He said the talk shouldn't be directly about my candidacy, and that will be good. I'll give them a history lesson."

Susie smiled brilliantly, which had become her habit, and her smile brightened the entire office. "Here's some more returns on the post card," she reported. "I think we should send out another batch, maybe around Concord."

"Good idea," Franklin said. He later looked at the checkbook and was pleased that most of the $6 million was still unspent. He decided to spend more before the time of the debate.

That evening, he and Hardy had dinner at the Wayfarer and then moved to the bar, which was crowded. They recognized a few patrons from their previous visit, but most of them were different. It was Friday night. At one table, Franklin spotted three familiar faces. They were Bill Clinton's brain trust, James Carville, David Begala, and George Stepanopolous. Carville got up and greeted him. They had met a few times during the Zell Miller campaign for governor in Georgia. Carville looked nothing like a campaign consultant. In fact, he looked nothing like anyone Franklin had ever seen before.

"Is this where you are campaigning?" Carville asked. "In a bar?"

"There are a lot of people here," Franklin replied, wincing slightly. "How's Mr. Clinton doing?"

"Just fine. He's picked up strength in every poll, gaining on Tsongas and pulling away from Kerrey and Harkin. I don't see your name coming up yet. Governor Miller is puzzled as to why you're running, and he's also disappointed since he thinks all good Georgians should be working for Clinton."

"I know," Franklin admitted. "I've talked to him briefly. I'm just testing the waters. New Hampshire is a nice place to be in September."

"I heard you got a lot of money when you sold your newspapers. How long do you think that'll last? We're about to start a statewide TV blitz."

"There's only one station in New Hampshire," Franklin noted.

"The Boston stations cover most of the state, and they are expensive," Carville replied, "and then there's the cable services."

"Have you been to Dixville Notch yet?" Hardy suddenly interjected.

Carville looked momentarily puzzled. "Not yet," he said, "but that's on the itinerary."

"We've been," Hardy informed him. "Got the place wrapped up."

Carville laughed. "Well, that's about twelve votes, which gives you a starting base."

At that moment one of the patrons recognized Franklin and clapped him on the back. "Hey, let's sing a chorus of 'The Gambler,'" he said. Nearby was the old man with the harmonica. He began playing the song, and soon the whole crowd got into it. Franklin realized at least a third of them had been present the first night. He joined enthusiastically on the third chorus, and even Clinton's consultants joined in. One man recognized Carville. "Hey," he called. "Mr. Franklin bought drinks on the house the other night, how about Mr. Clinton picking up the bill tonight."

Carville and Begala looked uncomfortable. Franklin quickly said, "I'm not an official candidate yet, so I'll pick up the check again, but you folks got to keep singing a chorus of 'The Gambler' every night and mention my name—Thomas Alexander Franklin."

He smiled at Carville, who looked impressed. "I'll get Clinton to come here and play the saxophone. That'll overshadow all this," he said.

It had been another good night for Franklin at the Wayfarer and created a slight feeling of optimism in him. Hardy was even more impressed. "Did you see that expression on Carville and Begala's faces when the crowd started singing?"

"But Clinton's got Carville and Begala," Franklin said, "and to the media, that means Clinton has won the early round, which was to hire the hottest consulting firm."

Meeting them had been a test, because Franklin was easily impressed by successful people. Carville had earned a large reputation by helping a Democratic candidate defeat Bush's attorney general for a Senate seat in Pennsylvania. Franklin still didn't find him impressive. Zell Miller had been in four successful statewide races, and his runoff opponent for governor was the black mayor of Atlanta, who had never been in a statewide race. Miller was heavily favored.

Carville's unusual looks had gotten him the nickname of Serpent Head, but he preferred Ragin Cajin, which referred to his Louisiana roots and his explosive personality. What Franklin found especially repugnant was his profane language, freely uttered in private conservation.

Franklin was more impressed with his partner, Paul Begala, who was a speechwriter and a convincing personality.

As they left, Hardy commented, "They aren't taking you seriously."

"That's right, and that's good," Franklin replied. "I need to fly under the radar until the debate, just so I get enough support to be in the debate. I think a speech in Concord will do that, and I've got a few more ideas. So don't count the votes…till the dealing's done."

Chapter Five

THE MOST IMPORTANT FOUNDER

*Governments can err, Presidents do make mistakes.
But better the occasional faults of a Government
that lives in a spirit of charity than the consistent
omissions of a Government frozen in the ice of its
own indifference.*

—*Franklin D. Roosevelt, speech
accepting renomination as president,
Philadelphia, June 27, 1936*

Franklin decided to make the Concord speech about the
Founding Fathers and the Constitution, especially one
Founding Father, Benjamin Franklin, whom he'd decided
was the most important one and, for good measure, was from New
England, Boston to be exact, although he was usually thought of as
being from Philadelphia.

Franklin, Hardy, and Susie and Charlie all went to the speech
in Concord. Franklin was pleased to see several reporters there and
two TV units.

Franklin opened with some personal information and stressed
his experience in the business world and in writing and analyzing hundreds of topics as an editorial writer through the years. He

explained that the United States had evolved into history's greatest nation because of its unity over a large land mass, "from sea to shining sea," and how the central government, set up by the Founding Fathers, had held this huge diverse collection of often quarreling states together as one nation.

Many Founding Fathers contributed to this ultimate creation, but Benjamin Franklin was the most important. As early as 1753, when each of the thirteen British colonies had separate governments beholden to England, Franklin was one of three commissioners from Pennsylvania appointed to confer with Indian leaders, who controlled most of the land beyond the western borders of the colonies. The colonies were jammed against the Atlantic coast from Maine to Georgia.

The Indians proposed a plan that would keep English settlers from moving past the Appalachian Mountains and would help them fight French settlers who were also moving into the Ohio Valley. It was also about this time that Franklin was appointed to head the Postal Service in the colonies, which led to the first home delivery mail system and gave Franklin a chance to travel extensively in all the colonies. He was already one of the best-known Americans because of his scientific achievements, including the invention of the lightning rod. He had retired from his printing and newspaper ventures by this time, but his work in electricity was recognized in academic and scientific circles as comparable to Isaac Newton's in the previous century. In the 1750s, Franklin devoted himself to his inventive nature, with the development of a wood-burning stove that could be built so that heat and smoke was channeled to a chimney and the heat into the room.

But in 1752, he came up with his most useful invention, the lightning rod, which eventually tamed one of the most destructive elements of nature at the time. Unfortunately for Franklin's later reputation, the painting of him flying a kite to prove his theories on lightning became the image many Americans remember best but which diminished his true importance. At the time, however, his feat of taming lightning made him world-famous, and the lightning rod proved one of the most valuable inventions for saving lives and preventing fires. The French statesman Turgot later described Franklin as "that man who snatched lightning from the skies and scepters from kings."

In 1753, Franklin's interests turned from his inventions to the future of the colonies. He was one of the first to realize that the colonies would thrive only through unity, and he detected little evidence of unity. As the French pressed their attacks into the western areas, Franklin wrote an editorial in his newspaper, *The Gazette*, which linked French success to the disunity of the British colonies. Accompanying the editorial was what is believed to be the first editorial cartoon in the country and became one of the most influential. It depicted a snake cut into thirteen separate pieces, all separated from the snake's head, with each piece bearing the name of one of the thirteen colonies. The caption read, "Join or Die."

It was a cartoon that has served the nation well, not only in colonial times, but throughout its history, as unity was the key factor in its growth and progress.

"Growing up in Georgia, I always realized Georgia owed its freedoms and stability to the fact that it was in the same nation as New Hampshire, just as New Hampshire is a great place partly because it is in the same nation as Georgia," Franklin told his audiences.

Ben Franklin could not have envisioned how important unity would be in the centuries ahead, but he had an idea, and he promoted it as early as 1753. He sketched out a plan for colonial cooperation among the colonies, with a number of delegates selected in proportion to the taxes the colony paid to the general or national treasury. A single governor would be appointed by the King of England. Money would be raised from a tax on liquor, which for many years was the major source of government revenue. Franklin's rough draft for the new government, which was called federalism, would eventually be the basis for the United States Constitution.

Several colonies sent delegates to a meeting in Albany. They liked the plan and voted to send it to all the colonies for each colony's evaluation and also a copy to the English Parliament. Not surprisingly, the Albany Plan was rejected by every colony on the basis that it transferred too much of their power to a central government. The

English Parliament rejected it because it shifted too much authority to the colonies. Looking back, near the end of his life, Franklin believed that the acceptance of the Albany Plan might have prevented the Revolution and left England and the colonies unified, as it is with Canada. He was probably wrong on that conclusion, but his foresight in seeking unity was phenomenal.

"I'd like to stress that although my surname is Franklin, I make no claim nor have any evidence that any of my family are direct descendants of Benjamin Franklin. I've never even been able to trace my ancestors back three or four generations, but Ben Franklin did have a great-great-great-uncle named Thomas, but my first name was from Thomas Jefferson, whom my grandfather admired for standing up for states' rights. My middle name, of which I was prouder, is for Alexander Hamilton, arguably the strongest supporter at the constitutional convention of a strong central government.

"That ultimate group of Founding Fathers who assembled in Philadelphia in the summer of 1787 had been sent to revise the Articles of Confederation, which the thirteen colonies approved at the end of the Revolutionary War, but which had proved totally inadequate for an expanding country trying to stabilize itself with thirteen separate governments.

"Franklin, eighty-two, was the senior member, still holding to his idea of unity which he had outlined thirty years earlier. The other delegates, however, were mainly there to defend the authority of their individual states. As the convention proceeded, the concept of federalism, a strong central government, became the central issue and the eventual goal.

"Hamilton, a young delegate, supported by Franklin, the oldest, made the decisive argument. Nations without a central government are an awful spectacle, Hamilton declared. His solution was that the greatest possible source of power should be given to the federal or central government.

"Thomas Jefferson, who was in France as the American ambassador at the time, was not present for the debates at the Constitutional Convention, but he wrote to his colleague, James Madison, that he was 'well-disposed to granting the general government authority to induce the states to cooperate in meeting American obligations to foreign creditors.'

"So in the beginning, Jefferson was an advocate of a strong central government, and ironically, as president, he made the most important decision toward assuring that strong government when he approved the Louisiana Purchase, more than doubling the geographic size of the country and making a central government even more crucial and powerful.

"So the first great revolution in US history was against the control of England, but it went further, establishing a unique democracy such as the world had never known and providing that democracy with a government which has endured to become the strongest, most prosperous country in history."

Franklin paused briefly and then added, "It is that government and that nation which our generation must preserve and nurture, and it is certainly not deserving of the attacks made on it by people like presidential candidates who are actually seeking to lead it. I love my country, but I also love my government, and I respect the worst of its politicians because they are the raw material, however flawed, that makes democratic government possible."

The applause was stronger than for his other speeches, although the message had been similar, which is that the central government must be maintained and made stronger, not weaker nor abandoned to the supply-side economists, as Paul Tsongas seemed to advocate.

Many members of the crowd came to speak with Franklin, several saying they hadn't realized how important Ben Franklin had been in determining the shape of the government. They had mainly thought of him as an old man flying a kite, that unfortunate image of his best-known painting.

Susie was a popular figure among the crowd, passing out pamphlets, copies of the speech, and being friendly and charming. Franklin couldn't believe she was the same woman who waited his table just a few weeks earlier. She had become the person he detected behind that glum mask, and she was very attractive now. Franklin knew a pretty woman was always an asset when dealing with a room full of middle-aged men.

A reporter from the Concord Daily Monitor came by and asked if he could have an interview with Franklin after the meeting. Franklin said he'd be delighted. The reporter was about twenty-five, he guessed, and seemed bright. His name was Jay Barry. Franklin and the reporter found a quiet corner of the room. "So you're saying the federal government is the answer, not the problem?" Barry began.

"Absolutely," Franklin stressed. "As I said in the speech, a strong authority was the goal of most of the Founding Fathers from the earliest colonial days. George Washington complained bitterly during the Revolutionary War that he couldn't get guns or rations for his soldiers, not to mention their small paychecks because individual states had not been providing sufficient funds.

"When a flood or a hurricane or some other natural disaster strikes a state today, where is the first place a governor calls for help? It's Washington, and no matter how critical that governor has been of the government, he knows that's the most likely source of immediate assistance."

"That's different from what the people have been hearing from most politicians," Barry commented.

"But it's the truth, and we must begin to create that realization. I see too many of these signs that say, 'I love my country, but I hate my government.' That's wrongheaded. The government is why the country is great. There is no other country in history that trusts its people so completely to select its governmental leaders, at all levels. Only in the United States is every citizen promised one vote in the process, and it's one vote more than people nearly everywhere else have. The process can be messy, and the outcome is not always perfect, such as the electoral college, but it has produced the nation we have today, and not many Americans would settle for any other."

Barry smiled. "I'm convinced," he said, "but a lot of New Hampshire voters are going to be skeptical. Now you've proposed cutting the payroll tax to 3 percent and raising the tax limit on the annual amount of salary on which its paid, right?"

"Yes, that would be the largest shift in taxation from lower-wage earners to higher earners in recent history. It's fairer, and with the highest salaries climbing higher every year and by larger percentages than ever, it would bring in more revenue to the government and make Social Security and Medicare more financially stable for the long run. That's crucial for the future, of course, and that is the first bill I'd propose."

"A caller to Rush Limbaugh recently asked him what people did before the nation had social security," Barry mentioned.

"I heard that, and Rush, rather uncharacteristically, bluntly answered, they died, which in large measure was true. In the 1930s, the average lifetime of Americans was in the sixties, and that has risen dramatically in the years since to more than eighty today, and people who once worked longer, or more likely farmed all their working lives, did not live for years after their working days were over. Social Security—and Medicare—were adopted just in time to meet the needs of the longer lifetimes, and they have been the most effective means of reducing poverty ever devised."

"But what about the huge national debt that is crushing economic incentive and keeps rising to the point we can never pay it off."

"The national debt is not really a big problem. It's a political issue both parties use for their own purposes. The Republicans stress it because they don't want any more government programs. The Democrats use it because they don't want Republicans to cut taxes on the rich any further. The stock market keeps rising, and the general economy usually ignores the debt. The reason for the high inflation in the 1970s and '80s was almost completely caused by the rise in the price of oil and gasoline. For years in the US, gasoline cost about twenty to thirty cents a gallon. Our whole economy was based on low-priced gas, from manufacturing to tourism to agriculture to airlines. Then in the space of eight years, oil prices rocketed and gasoline went to over two dollars a gallon by 1980. There were many reasons, but the national debt was not one of them. Arab nations, which have so much of the oil reserve decided to stop selling their oil for two dollars a barrel and raised their prices to more than twenty dollars a barrel although the price of production of oil in those countries stayed at two cents a barrel. Then the Iranian Revolution and its aftermath cut off one of our main sources of oil, which temporarily led to a shortage.

"Jimmy Carter was the president who decontrolled oil prices in the US, and President Reagan continued decontrol, and the price of a gallon began to fall. At the same time, Carter appointed Paul Volker as Federal Reserve chairman with the task of bringing down inflation, which Volker did, by ruthlessly raising interest rates banks had to pay the Federal Reserve for their money. He decreased inflation, but a deep recession was the price the people had to pay."

Barry looked up from his notes and changed the tape on his recorder. "Tell me some personal stuff," he said. "You are a newspaper man, I believe."

"Started work as a copyboy at sixteen, when I was a junior in high school and have never made a dollar in any other business since. The newspaper business is exciting, but the pay is low and always has been. I was lucky to get out of the hard part of journalism and into the publishing part when I was relatively young. I started a weekly newspaper when I was twenty-four with a $2,000 loan. Didn't like the weekly routine so went back to a daily and became editor at thirty-two when the former editor died suddenly. I've got a brief biography here in my briefcase, which I'll give you and save you some time."

Barry looked impressed. "I've been here four years," he said, "and I'm still a reporter and up to about $150 a week."

"Well, as we used to tell reporters when they asked for a raise, 'You mean you want to have all this fun and get paid as well?'

"When they complained that they made less than linotype operators, we'd ask, 'Do you want to be a linotype operator?' Most didn't, and sadly today there are no linotype operators. They have been replaced by cold type, which is almost exclusively performed by lower-wage women. A woman linotype operator was as rare in my early days on newspapers as a male composing room worker is today.

"I liked putting a daily newspaper together, deciding which stories were the most important, and writing the headlines. Headlines were the best part of newspapers, and still are. I thought the headline captured the reader's attention and was the most important part of the job, plus, of course, rewriting leads on stories so they made sense.

"I became a so-called makeup editor fairly early in my career and then an editor and publisher, so I was not a news reporter for very long, and as editor and publisher, I usually covered mainly big football games. I was a frustrated sportswriter but couldn't afford to be because the pay was so low. Low pay was a mistake newspapers made and still make and one reason they are losing circulation today."

Barry shook his hand. "I think this can make a good story," he said, "probably on the second front page tomorrow. I'll also put it on the AP wire."

"Thanks," Franklin said. "I haven't seen much about any of the candidates in the papers and very much would like to be in that first debate."

Charlie and Susie had gone back to Wolfeboro, so Franklin decided, since they had rooms in Concord, that he and Hardy should visit more cities and townships in that area. For the rest of the day, they went west on I-89 to Lebanon, a fairly long drive. Franklin intended to take a page ad in the daily newspaper. It claimed a circulation of twelve thousand, which served the counties along part of the border with Vermont. He also left ads with several weeklies in the area. Franklin always made a point of trying to meet both the publisher and editor. He felt that even if the newspaper ads didn't reach many voters, they would be seen by the editor and publisher who were usually leaders in the community.

During the drive, Hardy asked him to talk more about growing up during the Depression years. "Well, I was a child most of those years," Franklin reminded him, "and a fairly sheltered one. When I was four, a doctor diagnosed me with a hernia and told my mother to have me wear a truss, as they were called in those days, which was supposed to keep your intestines from falling into your balls. He also told her not to let me lift anything heavy or play hard. She took the advice very seriously, and it affected me more mentally than physically. I wasn't exactly a wallflower, but I hesitated to join in any roughhouse games. I guess I was too cautious. In later life I've been told I'm still so cautious that I always look both ways when crossing one-way streets. The first time I rode a Ferris wheel was the last time, and I'm still a white-knuckled airplane passenger."

"I guess you read a lot."

"Yeah. The first thing I remember reading faithfully were the comic strips in the daily newspaper in LaGrange and the big Sunday color comics section in the Atlanta newspaper we took, which was the Atlanta Georgian, a Hearst newspaper. It had the best comic section, including Alex Raymond's Flash Gordon. Then there were the so-called Big Little Books, which were published from 1932 to 1949. They were fat short books that were reprints of newspaper comic strips. They were all 424 pages, with a comic strip panel facing a written page of dialogue and text. These books were graphic and easy to read, and they cost just a dime. I'm sure they introduced many Depression-era children to reading.

"Then, there were the movies, the most important entertainment of the decade. In those days, about 60 million movie tickets were sold every week in a country of only 130 million people. Today, theaters are lucky to get a million admissions a week but movies were just a dime in the 1930s and range up to $10 now. There were also a lot more movies and a lot more theaters, or picture shows as we called them. Nearly every town of any size had its own theater, which was often its pride and joy. Although LaGrange was relatively small, with 18,000 people, it had three theaters when I was growing up.

"The largest and best theater was only two blocks from where I lived, so I could walk there easily and by myself. I always went to the ten thirty Saturday matinee, especially aimed at kids, and I usually attended at least one other movie during the week. The big Saturday morning matinee included a cartoon, a sixty-minute western, and then the regular Saturday movie. But without question, the favorite part for the young audience came between the western movie and the feature. That was the serial or chapter play, which was a twenty-minute episode which ran for twelve to fifteen Saturdays. Serials had been part of movies since their beginning with the 'Perils of Pauline' the most famous of the nontalking, but they really took off with the start of talking serials in 1930. The first talking serial was 'The Indians Are Coming,' a prophetic title, since the Indians kept coming in one form or another until 1956, with 'Blazing the Overland Trail,' the last serial.

"Their heyday was my own moviegoing years as a child from 1936 to 1943, and they left an impression on me and millions of other Depression-era kids that was a cultural phenomenon that still lingers. Several serials became Saturday morning fare on TV, and most of the rest became available on VCRs in the 1980s, finding a surprising audience of old fans and some new ones.

"It's hard to explain the compulsive cheers and shouts of joy in the theaters that broke out when the screen showed the opening credits of a serial. The serial gimmick was to leave the heroes or heroines in grave danger of death at the end of each chapter, only to have them miraculously escape at the opening of the next chapter, often too miraculously.

"The serials were cheaply and quickly produced and the only big star to emerge from them was John Wayne, who was in some ten serials during the 1930s before becoming one of the biggest box office stars of all on the big screen, with his starring role in *Stagecoach* in 1939. His acting never seemed to change, which to me was bad.

"The serials left a legacy that carried over in television and such recent popular films as the Indiana Jones and Star Wars series, which clearly had roots in the serials of the 1930s. Perhaps the most popular early serials were a trio starring Larry 'Buster' Crabbe as Flash Gordon and made with more investment of time and money.

"My own favorites, however, were those that featured an unknown villain, whose identity was hidden until the last chapter while a number of suspects were scattered through the twelve or fifteen chapters.

"The first serial I remember seeing was 'The Clutching Hand,' when I was about six. I saw it again on the VCR, fifty-five years later, and it still had an electric appeal, but actually it was really bad, overall, and even the unmasking of the Clutching Hand in the final chapter was so poorly handled that you still weren't sure who he was. The acting was beyond awful in most serials, and they were mainly a series of fistfights that seemed to have little or no relevance. It is a wonder that all the boys of that time did not constantly engage in fights. Some did, but I never had a fistfight and found them somewhat boring in the serials, even though I loved the overall product. Why? Serials had an excitement in their music, constant action, and the occasional mystery.

"Actually, I spent most of my time playing in the backyard and streets with the many other kids my age in that particular neighborhood. All of us went to the same school, which was also in easy walking distance, and most of us to the same church. They were all white, of course, and mostly from middle-income families. I'd guess, even me, although my father never made more than twenty-five dollars a week. Middle income was a lot less money in those days."

"So, you had a happy childhood and upbringing?"

"That's always been my story, and I'm sticking to it," Franklin said. "But it is a story recalled through a haze of good and bad memories. I lived with my father, mother, and often my grandmother, who looked after me and was probably the main influence on me as a child. My father and I weren't really close, and although I didn't realize it at the time, he was obviously an alcoholic. Many nights he did not come home until after I was in bed. I'd keep anxiously listening for his car until I finally drifted to sleep. When I woke up, I'd hurry to the window to see if his car was there…and on not a few mornings it wasn't there. He'd never come home. Those experiences left a scar that bothers me to this very day, when I can't stand for one of the children to be out beyond their expected time, and if they are, I get that same feeling of anxiety I had about my father as a child."

"Wait a minute," said Hardy. "You never told me that your father was an alcoholic. You did say your mother was a neurotic semi-invalid who seldom left the house."

"Well, she was never diagnosed with anything but nerves. She would have these panic attacks and cry that she couldn't get her breath and she was dying. Usually I was the only one there to help her through those spells, and I've had to deal with panic spells myself in my adulthood, especially on newspaper deadlines."

"I'm surprised," Hardy said. "You seem calm and collected, never losing your temper or even getting really excited."

"That comes from meeting all those deadlines. I stayed calm most of the time no matter how I felt inside. It was about the only way to get through when everyone was looking to you for what to do next. The carriers impatiently waiting for the paper so they wouldn't be delivering them in darkness, the composing room waiting to build pages according to your layouts and cut stories that wouldn't fit their assigned spaces, so you had to cut them, hopefully leaving the best parts. Reporters were rushing to finish up late-breaking stories, while you scanned the teletype machine for any last-minute national or international news of interest. I had this idea that we needed to get as much last-minute news as possible in the afternoon daily, ahead of four outside dailies coming into the Opelika-Auburn area. It was a very competitive market but good experience, I believe, for a candidate for president. I haven't had a bad panic attack in ten years, but the worry is always there."

They had reached the outskirts of Concord by then and decided to have dinner at an outlying motel. It turned out to be an inspired choice. After dinner, they visited the bar, which was not as large as the Wayfarer's but had a good crowd that night. Franklin asked the desk clerk about the nature of the patrons. "Mostly visitors to the capital on political business from all over state," he said. "They're elected officials, city, county, and township and of course lobbyists."

Franklin felt that they had struck gold. He and Hardy both nursed two glasses of rosé wine, Hardy very carefully. After a few minutes, Franklin asked the three-person band to play and sing "The Gambler." He soon had the crowd singing along on the chorus.

Franklin then introduced himself and said the night's drinks were on him. The crowd applauded and seemed appreciative. Most of them apparently were on tight travel budgets. Franklin asked if he could make a few remarks and was greeted with cheers. Some of the patrons had actually seen his ads in their weekly newspapers; plus, they hoped for another round of free drinks.

Franklin kept his remarks short and, he hoped, sharp. He said he planned to be on the presidential primary ballot in February, that he was running as a New Deal Democrat; he would seek to cut the payroll tax, would oppose the NAFTA bill support better relations with a non-Communist Russia, and work to keep its nuclear arsenal in the safest hands; he'd seek repeal of the 1986 tax revision bill making the personal income tax more progressive, restoring the tax break for second homes, and simplifying the tax return forms.

"Ask the other candidates about their positions on these issues," Franklin told the crowd. "I've given you mine, and I'd appreciate if you mention my name when you get back home and tell any pollsters to at least put my name on their list of candidates."

"That was a pretty good night," Franklin said as they left. "Did Carter ever have a night like that?"

"Well, not exactly. He had a structured schedule and advance men getting up crowds. I do recall we had some very small crowds in 1976, but we didn't just go into a place like this with no advance notice. It's kind of interesting, but you're not seeing many people."

"Well, as I told you, we are on a quixotic adventure."

"I once heard adventure described as discomfort viewed from a distance."

"Hey, that's good," Franklin exclaimed. "Adventure is discomfort viewed from a distance. I've heard that too, but I can't recall where or who said it."

"Well, I'll say this adventure has at least been pretty comfortable," Hardy said.

Franklin glanced at his calendar. "Just three weeks until that first debate. Do you think we're making progress?"

"Hard to say. The other candidates haven't been much in evidence. Tsongas is the only one many people have mentioned."

"That's right, and on the issues, he's the weakest. I don't agree with anything he's advocated, and I still think he should be running in the Republican primary, which I'm going to keep saying."

When Franklin arrived at his room, he had a phone call from Susie with very good news. A labor union leader in Manchester who'd read the story about his speech in the Concord paper wanted Franklin to speak at a union meeting that week. She said she'd accepted, and Franklin told her great. He was proud of her initiative and marveled again at what a great notion he'd had about the tall, dour waitress he'd first encountered.

The union meeting speech was set for October 8, a week before the first debate, leaving time for an effect on the polls, if he did well. In Wolfeboro, his small campaign contingent met to plan the immediate strategy. A few replies were still dribbling in from the ads, mostly positive. Franklin told them he had to get ads in more papers during the next week, and they needed to cover some of the townships they hadn't visited. Burkhart had encouraging reports from his friends in the media business, especially weekly editors. They looked at a map. The task was daunting. Franklin decided that he and Hardy would go to Manchester, where he could work on the speech to the Labor Union during the day.

They visited the towns between Manchester, Nashua, and Keene. He planned an ad in the Nashua paper and several of the weeklies. He'd been told Nashua was a Democratic stronghold. Burkhart and Susie would begin to work along the Maine border on the very short ocean coast around Portsmouth. New Hampshire had the shortest coastline of any state, but it was an important stretch. Portsmouth was the state's fourth-largest city and the oldest, with nearly thirty thousand permanent residents, and was near Durham, the site of the University of New Hampshire's main campus. "We'll visit there before the first debate," he told Hardy. "I need academic exposure."

He and Hardy left in the trusty Lincoln for Manchester, the largest city in New Hampshire. "By the way," Hardy mentioned, "when are we going to start a fund-raising program?"

Franklin frowned. That was not a task he looked on fondly. He'd checked the account and was pleased to see they had only spent about $500,000 of the $6 million, mostly on advance payments for newspaper ads. He'd allocated another $500,000 for that in the next week. He didn't want to be stingy before the early October polls were reported.

They got a room at a nice motel in Manchester. "This week could be decisive," Franklin observed. "We have a chance to lay good groundwork in Manchester and Nashua."

That evening they visited the bar in their motel and did the Gambler routine, plus picking up the bar bill, which was becoming a major campaign expenditure. But the results were again encouraging.

Few of the patrons had even heard of Franklin, but they knew his name after he picked up the bill. Many of them were Republicans, and the Democrats sounded undecided or were leaning toward Tsongas or Clinton. Franklin was surprised he didn't hear Kerrey's name more often.

He made his regular call home that night and also called Burkhart, who reported requests for speeches in North Conway and Berlin and another one in Concord from a club president who'd met Franklin at the Wayfarer.

In the week remaining before the speech to the union meeting, Franklin and Hardy visited at least twenty more townships and placed ads in several weeklies and the daily paper in Keene. He told Burkhart to place ads in weeklies around LaConia and Plymouth.

By the day of the speech, he'd polished up what he felt was a blatant appeal to union members, a group he's had very little contact with in Georgia and Alabama. He'd never had a union shop at one of his newspapers, and his experience with unions had mainly been unpleasant. At his first newspaper job in Columbus, the printers' union was on strike, and he had to cross a picket line every day during his time as a copyboy and into his early days as a reporter. The strike went on for several years in fact, and the company effectively locked out the union workers and replaced the printers with what were called scabs. He never saw any violence, and as the makeup editor, he worked closely with the scabs on a daily basis. Most of them were several years older than he was and often resisted his insistence on making changes once the type was in place. There was also a strict rule that an editor could not actually touch the type. If by some chance an editor did touch the type, the printer would dump the whole tray, and it would have to be reset.

His other experience with a union was in Opelika, which had recently become the site of the largest tire-producing plant in Alabama, which was one reason Franklin decided it would be a good opportunity for a better daily newspaper. But with the tire manufacturer came a strong union, which constantly threatened to go out on strike and finally did—for nearly six weeks. Franklin was just getting the daily going, and construction of a large shopping mall had been announced for a location in the adjoining city of Auburn. Franklin was obviously not happy with a strike by the area's largest employer, and his critical editorials earned him a visit from the union leaders. He stayed genial during their meeting, and they weren't too militant. Most of them had never had as good salaries as the rubber plant paid, and working conditions were much better than at the textile plants, which had been the main source of jobs in previous years.

Franklin appreciated the role unions played in raising pay generally and helping build a middle class, which among other benefits could buy more items advertised in the newspapers he operated through the years. Plus, he was sincerely opposed to the NAFTA treaty, which was the main issue with the unions in 1991.

Hardy, Burkhart, and Susie all went with him to the union hall in Manchester, with plenty of pamphlets and copies of columns to pass out. He thought they made it look as if he really had a campaign organization although they were all there was.

The Union Hall was full, with what Franklin estimated to be about four hundred to five hundred, mostly men. He opened by saying how much he appreciated the opportunity to meet and speak with them and briefly introduced himself as a Roosevelt Democrat who planned to be on the presidential primary ballot in February. "It depends a lot on people like you," he told them. "I'm counting on the voters of New Hampshire to let me know if I should keep on running.

"My first pledge is to reduce the payroll tax to 3 percent by extending it to all earned income, not just the first $60,000 a year, which includes the first dollar people earn and the last dollar most of them earn in any year. This plan will actually increase the total amount collected for future social security payments and for Medicare by taxing the highest incomes in the nation instead of just the lowest. It should give everyone here a full 4 percent increase in their paychecks."

He went on to explain how the United States got its start when the thirteen scattered colonies had united and worked together for the good and prosperity of all and how the expansion of the nation through the Louisiana Purchase and other progressive steps created the basis for a federal or central government that was strong enough to assure its security and determine a course that was best for all the states, not just northern or southern or the old and the new, the large or the small but all of them. Only a strong authority could have achieved that, Franklin said emphatically, and only a strong government could have waged a four-year civil war to assure that the nation continued to be united, with freedom redeemed and reaffirmed for all its people.

"That was the second American Revolution, and then the third revolution was the coming of the New Deal, which rescued most Americans from the economic depths caused by uncontrolled capitalism and ended economic slavery as the Civil War had ended racial slavery."

A round of applause greeted that last and emotional statement, as Franklin rose above his normally reserved demeanor. "This third revolution," he continued, created the modern United States that arose from the Great Depression and then the most powerful military power in history, mostly with union labor, that achieved victory over nations which had spent years preparing for war. The United States was challenged to prepare in just months, and its workers, its military, and both men and women built the Arsenal of Democracy, as President Roosevelt described it, and delivered the world from one of the most dangerous threats it had ever faced.

"That victorious effort produced the broadest, most prosperous middle class in history, and unions played a decisive role in its creation. Today we need an extension of that third revolution to assure that the prosperity of all Americans continues, not just for the richest, but also for the poorest, and most importantly for that great middle class, which emerged in the United States of the 1940s through the 1970s but sadly has seen its upward progress stall in the past fifteen years, and we all know the reasons. Supply economics, or trickle-down economics, or Reaganomics, or by whatever name it is called does not work, and it never has except for the richest top percent."

He received a louder applause, which seemed to give him renewed fervor. "This trend must not be continued, and in fact, it must be reversed, and a most crucial step in reversing it is to defeat this so-called NAFTA treaty."

That brought the crowd to its feet, applauding, as Franklin continued, "A doctor's first commandment in treating a patient is 'Do no harm.' In treating our economy, NAFTA is harm, and I've seen nothing that argues otherwise."

This statement brought another round of applause. "Let us send to our legislative leaders a message that they 'do no harm,'" Franklin repeated loudly. "I have heard of US companies who are planning to move their plants to Mexico for lower wages and looser regulations. I've heard of no Mexican companies planning to move their plants to the United States. What you do hear from Mexico is fear that the largest employer in their country, which is agriculture, will not be able to compete with US farm products, which will result in many displaced farmworkers seeking to cross the border and come to the US. NAFTA is a bill that threatens both economies, with any promise of benefits based on schemes unlikely to succeed.

"We already have trade relations with Mexico and Canada. NAFTA is designed only to make it easier for companies to cut their costs in the US. by reducing their workforce and lowering salaries for their hourly workers and transferring the money to the executives at the top who shuffle papers in air-conditioned offices."

By now Franklin had captured his audience. "I strongly disagree with Mr. Tsongas on his economic policies. They are nothing but warmed-over supply-side economics, and we know that a warmed-over cup of porridge is worse than the original.

"Mr. Tsongas is a good and courageous man who has apparently conquered the worst threat to health a human can encounter, but he should be running on the Republican ticket, if at all, and with their vote on February 18, the voters of New Hampshire have the opportunity to rebuke his policies in their infancy and send an early message to other states that the people of New Hampshire have had enough of trickle-down economics, which never seem to trickle far below the last executive in the boardroom."

There was another round of applause and calls of "Right on."

"I realize that Mr. Tsongas is from a neighboring state, which may be why he is leading in the early polling, but if you read his booklet and listen to what he says, you will see that his policies are influenced more by the several business boards he now serves on rather than the needs of people struggling to make ends meet, even here in New Hampshire, which has usually avoided the worst of the national recessions. But not this one. You can see it in the many second homes for sale, in the decline of the leather goods industry, the empty plants in Manchester. The country doesn't need more supply-side policies. It needs a demand-side economy, which helps the producer and the consumers by generating the money both must have to succeed."

By now Franklin had raised his voice to a pitch his small contingent of staff members had never heard. It was less apologetic, less tinged with his Southern accent.

"Yet," he continued, "among the contenders for the Democratic presidential nomination, Paul Tsongas is a dedicated supporter of NAFTA, Bill Clinton favors it in his wishy-washy way, and Bob Kerrey says little about it. Only Tom Harkin is clearly against NAFTA, and I commend Senator Harkin for his position. I know that many of you support Senator Harkin, and I only ask that you give me some consideration. In Iowa, many of Harkin's own constituents were surprised that he offered for president, and his criticism of US treatment of prisoners in Vietnam certainly gave aid and comfort to opponents of the US commitment to fight the Communist takeover of South Vietnam. Harkin served his nation well as a naval officer, but as many of you may recall, he went to Vietnam as a congressional aide and took photographs of what he called chicken pens that the US military was using to hold enemy prisoners. His photos were published in *Life* magazine, but military officials denied prisoners were being mistreated and that so-called chicken pens were better than the usual housing. Other US congressional visitors disagreed with Harkin, and the net result of Harkin's charges simply added more ammunition for discrediting the US mission.

"Concerning Vietnam, let's clear up a persistent myth. The US did not lose the Vietnam War. Our troops left in early 1973 with the Communist forces pushed back across the border, into North Vietnam and the Viet Cong rebels in South Vietnam scattered and minimized. US soldiers in Vietnam not only didn't lose the war, they never lost a major battle. My friend and colleague Charlie Black went to Vietnam seven times as a reporter, and he was also a soldier and reporter in World War II and Korea, and he said US troops in Vietnam were the finest and best trained of any he'd seen in any of the three wars. Charlie was invited to speak at the Pentagon and to congressional committees to elaborate on his reports, which mainly were interviews with the soldiers from all over the nation.

"Let no one forget the Americans who fought and died there. They were on a noble mission, and they did not die in vain. Vietnam was a pivotal confrontation in the Cold War, and the United States demonstrated its determination to oppose Communism with arms if necessary, and while we did not save South Vietnam, the example of US willingness to fight for its beliefs undoubtedly influenced other nations in the Far East to resist Communism. Indonesia, for example, the fifth most-populous country in the world, was on the verge of falling under Communist control, and other nations—Burma, Thailand, even India—needed assurance in their own struggles against both Chinese and Soviet influence. The US gave them that assurance with its stand in Vietnam.

"The ultimate victory against the Soviet Union in the Cold War was significantly influenced by the American troops who were called to fight for freedom in the jungles of Vietnam, and we should not forget them, and especially we should recognize that they played a role in the ultimate victory of the Cold War and in bringing the opportunity for durable peace throughout the world in the years to come. It is an opportunity which the US must not shirk whether from ignorance or for lack of will.

"President Bush says we have more will than wallet, but the fact is we have more wallet than any nation in history as was just demonstrated a few months ago in Iraq, which was the greatest display of military capability ever seen. The nation is justly proud of the military personnel who carried it out and of the industrial complex which made it possible. The Iraqi operation showed we have the wallet when we have the will. So let us not be told that the US lacks the wallet to enforce peace as well as war. Let us not be told it lacks the will to finance the revenue-sharing plan with cities and counties that promote worthwhile projects and need federal funding to help with them. One such project was a new library in my hometown at the time. Its city library consisted of a single room in the City Hall for a city of thirty thousand, and through Richard Nixon's revenue sharing program, we built a two-story library building with a conference room, space for thousands of books, and a small museum. It transformed the city. That is a very small example of the projects built in the 1970s and 1980s, but it shows how local communities working with and through the federal government can prosper and provide their citizens with the attributes they deserve in the late twentieth century. Let no one tell you we do not have the will to do that and to rebuild US cities as we are committed to rebuild Baghdad with US taxpayer money."

The applause was more generous, and there were more shouts of "Right on." Franklin glanced at his watch. He did not want to go on too long, but he felt the thrill of emotion he hadn't gotten at any other speech.

"Before I leave the subject of NAFTA," he said, "let me repeat that only Tom Harkin and I have definitely come out in opposition. Here's what Bill Clinton states in his pamphlet: 'I support the North America Free Trade Agreement so long as it is fair to American workers and farmers, protects the environment, and observes decent labor standards.' But what kind of convoluted statement is that? We know that none of those conditions are even being considered. They are the reasons so many industries support NAFTA...so they can move to Mexico and have cheaper labor, less regulation, and manufacture goods they can then sell in the US at cheaper prices than manufacturers who stay in the US."

Franklin closed with that and took a few questions, most of which were predictably friendly. "Why haven't we heard about you?" one man asked. "You sound like the candidate we've been waiting for."

"That's right," Franklin exclaimed. "The candidate you and a lot of Americans have been waiting for. Please tell your friends and relatives to mention my name to any pollsters."

Another man had an even better idea. "Our local union is having a meeting in Nashua Sunday afternoon. Would it be possible for you to give that same speech to them?"

"Glad to," Franklin said. That was just two days away but in the same week of the last polls before the debate. Hardy got the details. "We haven't even been to Nashua," Hardy said. It's supposed to be the most Democratic city in New Hampshire."

"I know," Franklin said. "That's why I'm excited. A talk there can give us the basis for a real organization."

Chapter Six

THE FIRST DEBATE

Democracy is not a static thing. It is an everlasting march.

—*Franklin D. Roosevelt, address in Los Angeles, October 1, 1935*

S eptember was splendor but October in New Hampshire was even better.

Although he didn't especially identify with the description, Franklin had always liked fantasy and science fiction writer Ray Bradbury's tribute to October in his book of short stories *The October Country.*

"That country where it is always turning late in the year…where the hills are fog and the rivers are mist…where noons pass quickly, but dusks and twilights linger and midnights stay… That country made up mainly of cellars, coal bins, attics and pantries faced away from the sun…whose people think autumn thoughts…whose footsteps at night on lonely streets sound like soft rain."

On the trip back to Wolfeboro, Franklin reminisced some more about growing up during the Depression. "Because kids didn't have TV, they actually had to read more, and there were dozens of books aimed at children. I told you about the Big Little Books, but there were also series of children's books such as the Bobbsey Twins, the Nancy Drew mysteries, Tom Swift, boy inventor, Uncle Wiggley, for younger readers, and a new book about the Land of Oz was published every year in the 1930s."

"Was that the same Oz where Dorothy went to find the wizard?"

"Absolutely. Most people only know about Oz from the 1939 movie, but the first Oz book was published in 1900, written by L. Frank Baum. It was so successful that he wrote twelve more Oz books before his death in 1920. After that, Ruth Plumly Thompson continued the series and wrote an Oz book every year until 1939, making thirty-two in all. They were regular-size hardcover books and cost more than $1.50, which made them a special gift for birthdays and Christmas. But I read my first Oz books in ten condensed versions published in the late 1930s, which cost only 15 cents apiece. They were my favorite books, and I began getting the full-size editions for my main Christmas gift in 1939. They were brilliantly illustrated and Ruth Thompson followed the Baum model of creating interesting odd characters and fascinating places for the characters to visit in each of the books. She was actually a better writer than Baum, and her plots were better. Some of her titles which I got were *The Purple Prince of Oz*, *Pirates in Oz*, *The Gnome King of Oz*, *Ozoplaning with the Wizard of Oz*. During the 1930s, an Oz book by Thompson was published each year, but none of her books were made into a movie, and they were actually hard to find for sale or in libraries. Oz fans had the Wizard, which was a classic, but most of the Thompson books would have made great movies."

Back in Wolfeboro, Franklin was pleased to find Burkhart and Susie keeping the office going with more pamphlets distributed and more contacts made. There were several requests for speeches, and a reporter from the *Boston Globe* had called about an interview. The *Globe* had a tie-in with the *New York Times*, and Franklin felt that a good interview would run in both newspapers, giving him his first national exposure. There was also a request for an interview on the only statewide TV station in New Hampshire.

For his talk in Nashua, Franklin took Susie with him. Susie wore a sleeveless yellow blouse and a blue skirt which showed off her shapely bosom and long lithe legs, topped off with the dazzling smile she now flashed regularly. Franklin could tell Susie's appearance put an audience in the mood for a rousing speech, which he proceeded to give.

By now, the other Democratic candidates were more active in New Hampshire, and the TV commentator and columnist Pat Buchanan was running against President Bush in the Republican primary. His candidacy was definitely getting attention, and Franklin decided that was an asset for him—another newspaperman who'd never held an elected office running against the incumbent president. Buchanan's message was strongly conservative, antigovernment, and antispending.

Bush, whose approval ratings had soared to record highs following the Iraqi War, were slipping even before Buchanan decided to make his run. Mario Cuomo was still the first choice of many Democrats and had promised to make a final decision by December 21, which was the deadline to enter the New Hampshire primary.

By mid-October, Franklin had spent twenty-five days in New Hampshire, slightly more than Tsongas, who had started nearly a year earlier. Tsongas was still running well, but his message of austerity, while popular with the media and Republicans, was a tough sell for most Democrats. He liked to proclaim that he was not Santa Claus, and as proof, he recited the popular Democratic policies he was against, such as Clinton's middle-class tax cut and no increase in the minimum wage; he was pro NAFTA and was the only Democrat in the field opposed to the so-called strike-breaker replacement bill, which after NAFTA was the first priority for labor.

Franklin made sure to express his support for that bill in his talk to the Nashua union. He had overlooked it in Manchester and, in truth, was not that sold on it. But once more he got a good reception and a few questions. One was if he had ever had a union at one of his newspapers. Franklin had to admit that he hadn't but felt one reason was that he respected his employees, gave Christmas bonuses, and urged his employees to respect each other. Another reason was that in the small to medium-sized communities where he owned newspapers, there weren't that many good jobs, even during the best of times, and some of the best were on his newspapers.

Susie smiled at him as they left. "You slipped by that question nicely," she said, "and the speech was a three-pointer."

"Did you ever travel with the Dole campaign?" Franklin asked.

"No, I mainly worked at the offices but did hear him make a few speeches. I also remember meeting Jimmy Carter. It's an odd coincidence that Mr. Hardy worked for him and is now working for you."

"It can be a small world," Franklin agreed. "A month ago, who'd have believed you'd be working for me, and I've got to say, I don't know where I'd be without you."

"It's been great," Susie exclaimed. "It's given me a whole new life, actually a reason to live after I was so depressed for months, even years. That was foolish of me, I know, but you have to understand, I was the best-known girl at my high school, an all-state basketball player, all-A student, and suddenly, virtually an outcast...plus I actually wanted the baby."

Franklin looked at her solemnly. "I understand," he said. "Just remember, I always thought you looked like an all-star. It showed in your eyes."

They drove back to Wolfeboro and met with the others to plan the following week before the first debate. The critical phone polling was going on throughout the state. Tsongas was expected to lead the polls, with Bill Clinton coming up fast. Harkin had his supporters, but Kerrey seemed stalled. One factor that had hurt him was his emphasis on health-care insurance for all US workers—and then it was revealed that Kerrey did not provide health insurance for the employees in his restaurant chain. Franklin was strong on that point. He had always offered a health-care plan to all full-time workers, and for years the company paid the entire premium for the employees and half the premium for a family. Franklin looked on it as an employee benefit that was tax deductible to the company and as important to the employee as a pay raise.

Earlier in the month, Franklin had called a former reporter of his who now worked in Little Rock, Arkansas, and asked him to do a little investigating into all the rumors about Clinton's womanizing. Franklin couldn't believe there wasn't some fire from so much smoke. The reporter, an editor on a Little Rock daily, called him that night with his findings. "Keep pounding on Tsongas as an undercover Republican. I've seen a couple of your speeches on AP, believe it or not. As for Clinton, my advice is not to worry about him before the primary. Several shoes are going to drop on him that will make Gary Hart's 1988 shenanigans look like a prom party kiss. You can count on it. Clinton has skated on thin ice for years, and it's about to crack."

Franklin had counted on that. In his planning, he'd always thought Clinton was vulnerable to a scandal. He hadn't expected it would be so easy to expose Tsongas as a closet Republican, and he was surprised that none of the other Democratic candidates hadn't come down harder on him. Although he had never met Tsongas or even heard him speak, Franklin was beginning to have a definite dislike for him, almost a fear that if his message found acceptance among Democrats that it would doom the nation to a prolonged period of so-called supply-side economics, with both parties in the thrall of a philosophy that not only retarded growth and economic recovery in the United States but would also discourage the expenditures for the United States to lead the post–Cold War world in the role as a peacemaker.

In some respects, Tsongas was worse than the Republicans. In his booklet, distributed throughout New Hampshire, Tsongas had written, "The Cold War is over, and Japan won." That statement was so ridiculous that Franklin found it hard to believe anyone took it seriously, much less a man running for president. Japan had not even been a participant in the Cold War, and to depict it as a winner was an insult to the thousands of Americans who fought and died fighting the Japanese in World War II.

Tsongas had continued, "America is wasting its future by consuming too much. The federal budget is heading for disaster and has to be frozen, with no new spending. We're going to have to get this budget in balance. So no tax credits for having children, no middle-class tax cuts, no drain on the Treasury. You cap expenditures, and there needs to be a sharp increase in gasoline taxes."

All those points ran counter to what Franklin had advocated and written about during the past few years and which he saw as the main faults of Republican economic policies. He was especially shocked by a call for higher gasoline taxes, which hit the poorest Americans the hardest and which had devastated the airline and trucking industries, not to mention tourism during the 1970s. Tsongas was turning his back on all the party's traditions and was in direct opposition to the New Deal. But he appealed to a strain of puritanism in the American psyche to which a call for sacrifice still resonated, even though it mainly asked for sacrifices from middle- and lower-income Americans, not from those who had benefited so lavishly from the tax cuts of the 1980s. *Fortune* magazine's annual list of millionaires in 1991 had found more of them than ever, with more total income than ever, mainly due to the tax cuts and the rising stock market. But the consumer economy was falling, along with the number of middle-class jobs.

Until he read Tsongas's booklet *A Call to Economic Arms*, Franklin had not realized what a retrograde Democrat Tsongas really was. He just thought he was no Santa Claus but discovered he was Scrooge at his worst.

Clinton with his natural charm plus strong financial support from Arkansas supporters and the experience of six successful campaigns for governor was a close second to Tsongas in unofficial polling.

Franklin felt a poll to be released later that week by the daily paper in Keene would be the most influential and accurate reading of the state's electorate. It had been conducted for several elections and enjoyed some prestige in the state. He had been sure to place an ad schedule in the Keene newspaper.

On Monday, he and Hardy made visits to ten small towns in the Portsmouth area before returning to Concord, where he was to meet with the reporter from the *Boston Globe*. Franklin was always wary of big-city reporters.

The *Globe* reporter was a middle-aged, almost wizened-looking man named John Lawrence. He quickly told Franklin that the first campaign he covered was Kennedy-Nixon in 1960. "Well, I'm no John Kennedy," Franklin smiled, "but then I'm no Richard Nixon either."

Franklin wasn't sure Lawrence appreciated his attempt at humor.

"Just why are you running?" he asked bluntly.

Franklin explained that he thought 1992 was a pivotal year in history, and he hadn't heard the other candidates emphasize the opportunities and challenges the United States faced in a post-Cold War world with Russia and also with Cuba and even Iraq; he also felt the nation had to abandon its allegiance to supply-side economics and return to the policies of the New Deal and the Great Society.

"So you think the federal government should be larger, not smaller?" Lawrence asked. He had his tape recorder running.

"It needs to be large enough to meet its responsibilities to the American people and as the leader not only of the Free World but the entire world," Franklin replied. "This year presents a unique opportunity if we seize it. And the needs on the domestic level have gone lacking for nearly twenty years."

"What about the huge financial deficit we already have? Can the US afford any larger deficit?"

"If history is any judge, then it can. The deficit is a paper tiger, mainly used for political purposes. The US has had financial challenges ever since the Revolutionary War, when there was a lot less money around. The most dramatic example was the Louisiana Purchase. Thomas Jefferson was president, and certainly no friend of stronger central government, but he recognized that only a powerful central government with access to money from all the states could be capable of making such a deal. France wanted to sell and needed cash for the Napoleonic Wars. Jefferson saw the opportunity to more than double the land mass of the country for a price of only $15 million, a large sum in 1803, but a real bargain for 828,000 square miles from which all or parts of fifteen future states were formed. The purchase immediately moved the United States into the league of great nations. At the time, the brand-new country was one of the poorest in the world, but Jefferson and the other leaders decided to gamble."

"Where did they get the $15 million?" Lawrence asked.

"In what would become the good old American way, they borrowed it—from English and Dutch bankers who were anxious to see France removed from the New World. There was opposition to Jefferson's decision, of course, mainly from the Federalists, who saw the addition of so much land, with the potential of many new people, different in background and nationality, as a threat to the original thirteen states, but Jefferson believed that mostly more Englishmen and European immigrants would move into the new states, which, of course, is what happened. The purchase also violated a constitutional provision against acquisition of additional property, but Jefferson got around that by making the Louisiana Purchase a treaty, which was subsequently ratified by Congress. The debt of $15 million was paid off in fifteen years, and the US became bigger in square miles than all of Europe except for Russia."

Lawrence looked impressed. "How'd you know all that?"

"Well, it's in the encyclopedia, among other places. It was a crucial step in the making of America, part of the Revolutionary period, in fact, and Jefferson set the example for Lincoln, the Roosevelts, and others to follow in finding ways to move forward."

"So you aren't worried about the national debt?"

"It needs to be noticed, but it should not overshadow the fact that we are the richest nation in history, not one of the poorest, as we were when the Louisiana Purchase was made. The debt will take care of itself as it always has if the nation moves ahead with the right investments and the right actions to help other nations improve their living conditions and become better customers for American products.

"When other nations ask us for help today, we mainly send them planes, bombs, and ammunition, which is what their rulers want, but what their people want—and need—are toilets and plumbing equipment and stoves and washing machines. Most deaths in third world countries are from lack of proper health and sanitation facilities. Iraq was one of the few countries that had moved toward the twentieth century, and now it has lost much of its modern conveniences that will take years to restore."

"That's all well and good," Lawrence said, "but what about this recession in the US and especially in New Hampshire?"

"My first commitment in this campaign is to reduce the payroll tax from 7.5 to 3 percent, giving every wage earner a tax cut on the first dollar they make. It'll be made up by levying the payroll tax on all earned income, which is the fairest way in any case, a flat tax as the Republican candidates like Steve Forbes have been advocating and a transfer of millions of dollars from the lowest earners in the country to the highest earners. I think we should then look at repealing the 1986 tax bill and making the entire system more progressive as it was during the best economic years the nation ever experienced."

"Can I quote you on all this?" Lawrence asked. "Some of that is pretty unfashionable and unpopular."

"Check out what Tsongas is saying. That's what should be unpopular. He wants the poor and middle class to keep biting bullets while the rich get sirloin steaks."

"That's a good quote," Lawrence said. He looked over the pamphlets Franklin had given him. "So you are a sold-out millionaire publisher, huh?"

"At present, yes, but I'm going through the money fast in this campaign, and I've always reinvested it, mostly in other newspapers or magazines. I like buying them and improving them. The money comes later if you succeed."

"How many people do you have on staff now, and how much money has the campaign spent?"

"Not many, and not much. I've mainly spent on newspaper advertising, and here's a packet of those ads for you to read. I'm planning to run some TV ads but not many. This is a low-budget campaign, and I realize I'm a long shot candidate, but I bet I've been in more New Hampshire townships than any other candidate, and I've spoken to two large union groups this week. Don't know if they'll endorse me, but if they do, that'll give me a boost in the polls I need to get into the debates."

"You're different, I'll say that," Lawrence admitted. "I covered Jimmy Carter when he ran in 1976 and 1980. He surprised us, but I always thought he was kind of phony. You actually sound more legitimate, but I'm not sure voters are any more ready for another Southerner from Georgia than they are a Greek from Massachusetts."

"Do you think your article will be picked up by the *New York Times*?" Franklin asked.

"It could make the front page on a light news day," Lawrence promised. "You're an interesting story."

Burkhart was friends with an editor on the Keene *Sentinel*. He called him Wednesday morning to see if he could get an early reading on the statewide poll. The editor gave it to him since it was coming out that afternoon. Burkhart read the figures and was ecstatic. He got Franklin, Hardy, and Susie on a conference call from the Concord office. "Franklin got 6 percent in the poll," he told them right off, "which means he'll be in the debate. Figures for the other candidates were 28 percent for Tsongas, 23 percent for Clinton, 20 percent for Kerrey, 19 percent for Harkin, and 5 percent Brown, and 7 percent all others."

Six candidates were to be in the debate, which put Franklin clearly in with a percent above Brown. Franklin could hardly believe it. He'd cleared the first hurdle of his campaign plan after just six weeks.

He assigned Burkhart to handle arrangements for the debate, which was scheduled for an hour on WNHT, New Hampshire's only statewide TV station. "We're in the game," Hardy exulted, "and I think you've got some good pitches, if you can get them across."

After consultations with representatives of all the candidates, the debate was set for two hours, 3:00 to 5:00 p.m. on Sunday. That didn't give Franklin much time to prepare. He knew he couldn't just wing it, so he made an attempt to figure out what the questions would be. The moderators were to be four news people from state newspapers and radio stations. Surprisingly one of the questioners was Roy Riley, who had covered Franklin's first speech and once worked for Burkhart. "Is that a break?" Franklin asked Burkhart.

"Absolutely," Burkhart assured him. "Roy is up on the issues and won't be asking silly questions."

Franklin spent the rest of the week traveling in the small towns of the Nashua area and placed another quarter page ad in the Nashua paper and also in the Keene *Sentinel*, both of which were reasonably priced. He'd gotten surprising response from the article the Nashua paper had carried earlier in the week.

On Friday, the interview with John Lawrence ran in the *Boston Globe* and the *New York Times*, although not on the front page, but combined with his appearance among the candidates who would be in the debate, he had gained significant recognition. A call to his wife found that the Georgia newspapers had picked up some of the stories, and she was getting calls from friends and relatives on what this was all about. Was Thomas Franklin really running for president? Even Governor Zell Miller had called and left his number.

Franklin decided that was a call he should return, which he did when he and Hardy got back to the hotel in Concord. Zell's distinctive North Georgia twang came on the phone. Although he was a college professor who'd written three books and was arguably one of the smartest men ever to be governor of Georgia, Miller still sounded like the mountain man from Young Harris, which he was.

"What's this about you being on a list of candidates for president in the New Hampshire primary?" he barked.

"I meant to talk to you about that," Franklin answered hesitantly. "But I thought you'd laugh at the idea, and I wouldn't have blamed you. I actually didn't talk to anybody in Georgia about it except family. I wanted to explore the chances in New Hampshire first, and can you believe I'm in the first debate, with 6 percent of the voters mentioning me in a poll."

"What made you do a fool thing like that?" Miller asked. "You met Governor Clinton at that reception last summer, and I thought you liked him? You know that I'm in his corner and am going to push the Georgia primary up a week in March to give him a boost before Super Tuesday. I helped him get Carville and David Begala as his consultants. He's in a strong position to win, and he's the man the Democrats need to run for president in 1992. You'll only muddy the waters, although I can't see you getting many votes. Bill and his team will sweep the primaries, starting with New Hampshire. You must have gotten too much money for those South Atlanta newspapers and it went to your head."

Franklin and Miller had been casual acquaintances for many years, and he had supported Miller with both money and editorials in 1990. He'd also been to the governor's mansion several times in the past year, including the meeting with Clinton. At sixty-one, Miller was old for a Georgia governor and had served four terms as lieutenant governor. He was actually someone Franklin felt might be a plausible presidential candidate himself, but he'd stepped aside for Clinton, whom Franklin was becoming more convinced than ever shouldn't be the candidate, much less a president.

"Try to catch the debate on Sunday at 3:00 p.m.," he suggested to Miller. "I'll send you a VCR copy, and I'm sure Clinton will. I'd appreciate you calling and let me know what you think. This is a flawed field of candidates, including me and Clinton, but if Cuomo stays out, one of this field will be the candidate."

"You're crazy, but I'll watch the debate," Miller said and hung up. Franklin could tell Miller was unhappy with him, and he knew Miller was not the only Georgian who was going to be a tough convert.

On the afternoon of the debate, the candidates all arrived at the station with a varying number of assistants. Franklin brought Hardy, Burkhart, and Susie and hoped no one knew they were his whole staff. Bill Clinton was the tallest candidate at six foot, two inches and the dominating personality. Paul Tsongas was a slight man, somewhat laid-back; Bob Kerrey was not as impressive as Franklin expected; Tom Harkin was a natural politician, friendly but somewhat boisterous; Jerry Brown was brash and seemed to be anxious to find attention.

Franklin himself was trying not to seem too impressed by the array of better-known candidates. He'd always been slightly in awe of successful people in any field, and it was a trait that restrained him in interviews or meetings despite efforts to repress the feeling or his discovery through the years that most of them were just like him, confident in some ways, uncertain in others.

The candidates and interviewers chatted briefly and discussed the rules of the debate. The studio was not large, but because this was the first official debate of the 1992 campaign, there were a number of media people present, including TV crews from three national networks, as well as the host station.

The chief moderator, a reporter from the *Manchester Union Leader*, got the program underway by introducing the candidates and asking each for a brief statement.

Franklin said he had been a journalist and a small businessman since he was in college, had been involved and interested in politics all that time, written hundreds of editorials and articles on politics and politicians, plus speeches for several candidates, had been president of the Georgia and Alabama Press Associations, and felt all that prepared him to be a candidate although he had never sought or been elected to a political office.

The other candidates reviewed their credentials: Tsongas, a former US senator from Massachusetts; Clinton, elected governor of Arkansas six times; Tom Harkin, a three-term US senator from Iowa; Jerry Brown, a two-term governor of California and currently chairman of the state Democratic party; Robert "Bob" Kerrey, a wounded Vietnam veteran, governor of Nebraska, now in his first term as a US senator from Nebraska, politicians all, who'd braved the election process and won the approval of the voters. For a brief moment, Franklin wondered what he was doing there.

He had planted one question with John Lawrence. It was not a favorable question in particular, but it was one he wanted asked.

The debate proceeded with a series of predictable questions and rather turgid answers from the candidates. Tsongas danced around two questions about his support for nuclear power, which he knew was unpopular in New Hampshire. On other questions, he stuck to his insistence that he wasn't Santa Claus and would demand sacrifices from the people in order to balance the federal budget and prevent economic disaster.

Senator Kerrey had an elaborate plan for national health insurance, which he said would be his first goal; Clinton emphasized his middle-class tax cut and said he would seek a plan to improve the job market; Jerry Brown kept trying to get his 911 number on the air, which people could call and make a contribution to his campaign, although the moderator had specifically asked that no money solicitation should be made during the debate. Brown also said the whole political system had been corrupted, and only by accepting small contributions could it be cleansed. Almost as an afterthought, he said he supported a national sales tax to replace the entire tax system currently in place.

Harkin stayed on the fashionable Democratic formula of more federal spending and tax increases for the rich, with tax cuts for the poor. Oddly, he opposed Clinton's middle-class tax reduction.

Franklin was the last candidate to be asked a direct question. He tried not to look offended that he'd almost been left out. But the question was the one he'd given to John Lawrence.

"Mr. Franklin," he said, "while most candidates are saying the federal government has too much power and needs to reduce its spending, you have called for a stronger federal government role, with presumably more tax revenues to support it. Does that express your views correctly? Do you believe in a stronger federal government with more spending?"

"Yes," Franklin answered. "I believe we need a government strong enough that when a natural disaster such as a flood or hurricane hits a state, that the governor can immediately call Washington and get a promise that federal help is on the way. A federal government strong enough that when your Social Security check doesn't arrive, you can call and they'll tell you the check is in the mail. A federal government that the Founding Fathers created from thirteen scattered, quarrelling colonies that was strong enough to demand and ensure their liberty from the British by force of arms and a few years later was bold enough to borrow enough money to make the Louisiana Purchase, ensuring the great nation of today that developed from sea to sea; strong enough to maintain its overall unity, even at the cost of a terrible Civil War; and strong enough to lift the nation from a severe economic depression and then rescue the world from an onslaught by modern barbarians. Yes, I believe in a strong federal government able to run the most successful and prosperous nation on the globe…and I believe in it for the best of all possible reasons…because it is true."

Franklin's lengthy answer had rung the overtime bell, but the effect on the small audience was electric.

There was enthusiastic applause, and the impact was mirrored on their faces.

Tsongas shook his head and quickly said, "Mr. Franklin admits he's not a politician, and his arguments prove it. They would doom the US as an economic power."

Clinton recognized what had happened. "None of us need a lesson in how the US became a great nation," he exclaimed. "We need solutions on how to keep it a great nation."

"One way is to call my 911 number and make a contribution," Brown interjected.

Harkin said he agreed with much of what Franklin said but achieving any of it would require an experienced, capable politician who knew the obstacles.

Kerrey took another question and didn't comment. But Franklin had changed the atmosphere in the debate and provided a dramatic sound bite for the TV and newspaper accounts: "I believe it for the best of all possible reasons…because it is true." After the debate ended, James Carville walked over to Franklin and gave him a twisted smile. "You planted that question, didn't you?"

"Why would I plant a question that made me admit I want a stronger federal government?" Franklin said innocently. "That's not exactly a popular position in New Hampshire or the country."

"People don't like the federal government in general, but they like it in particular," Carville said, "and you reminded them of some of the particulars."

"Maybe they need reminding," Franklin said. "That's part of what my campaign is about."

The small crowd of media types were mingling with the candidates and their aides. Susie, in one of her most fetching outfits, a black sweater and red skirt, was a center of attraction. The female media types were curious as to how she had such a prominent role at so young an age. Susie stammered a bit but in general managed to impress them with her knowledge of the issues, on which she had prepared many pamphlets. Charlie played the New Hampshire country editor which he was and reminisced with Jerry Brown about the Carter campaigns in 1976 and 1980.

Overall the debate had been a success in elevating Franklin and his small group to a higher level of importance. Franklin wasn't sure how that would play out. He was mainly ignored by the other candidates to that point. But instinctively he realized that he would need more help to carry the campaign to its next level.

That evening as they heard mostly encouraging reports on the debate, Franklin began signing blank checks. One was to Burkhart, and Franklin told him to rent some more space at the Wolfeboro location and then to find twice as much office space in Concord. "You might also get us an office in Nashua," he suggested.

The next morning Franklin put in a call to Jody Powell. He'd known Jody casually during Jody's days as Carter's press secretary, and his best friend from college had become one of Powell's assistants at the White House. Today, twelve years after Carter's landslide loss to Reagan for reelection to a second term. Powell was a public affairs power player in Washington. He had generally been considered the brightest card in Carter's deck of players although he was from Vienna, Georgia, deep in South Georgia and had been kicked out of college in his younger years. He picked up a job as Carter's chief driver in Carter's failed try for governor in 1966 and stayed with him for his second, and successful, campaign for governor in 1970. Carter named Powell his press secretary, and thus at twenty-six, Powell became Carter's second-closet assistant, next only to Hamilton Jordan, another young south Georgian.

During Carter's ascent to president and his administration, the *New York Times* called Powell the most influential press secretary in US history, and *Time* magazine wrote that "he was the most popular and trusted press secretary ever to match wits and wisecracks with the White House press corps."

However, things were not always smooth between Powell and the press, and he later wrote a rather bitter book called *The Other Side of the Story*, in which he accused the most prominent media outlets "of arrogance and biased behavior," detailing specific cases. One reviewer called the book "savage" but admitted that many of Powell's points were valid. Powell had stayed in Washington and excelled as a columnist and then a TV commentator and lecturer. In an odd matching, he then joined Sheila Tate, who was a former press secretary to Nancy Reagan, to form Powell Tate, which had quickly become one of the largest PR firms in Washington.

Powell knew the communications field had changed in the years since Carter's candidacy, and it had been pretty scary then. Television had placed government leaders in a different dimension. In its first 150 years, most Americans never actually saw a president in person or even a congressman or senator. Now they were nightly visitors in their living room; lobbyists jammed the halls of the capital. Between 1985 and 1992, the number of fax machines in the country jumped from five hundred thousand to four million.

With the sudden attention from the debate, Franklin needed a fast influx of skilled hands, and he wasn't sure how that would fit with his tightly knit campaign plan.

Powell took his call, and his first question was "How's Hardy doing?"

"He is a Godsend. I don't know how you knew what he'd be," Franklin said, "but we haven't collected a dollar in campaign funds, and we need at least three people who know how to work that end. I'm terrible at asking for money. I couldn't even ask merchants to pay for their newspaper ads."

"Get me an idea of who all you need and call me back in the morning," Powell said. "Also tell Hardy to call me. He'll know some of the people you need."

"Well, definitely the money types, and an office manager, an advance man, and maybe a speechwriter. I've been writing them all, and I've got five promised next week."

Franklin looked at his schedule and decided they'd go to Lebanon, a town of ten thousand on the Vermont border, but a quick drive from Concord on I-89. The contact had promised a crowd of sixty-plus. Franklin was also ready to escape the flurry of attention, calls, and applications now coming in for jobs. He had a talk he felt would be appropriate for a smaller town in a relatively rural area, and he and Hardy had not spent any time in the Lebanon area. They stopped at a few townships on the way to touch base with the town councilman.

Chapter Seven

THE ENDURING DEBATE

America needs a government of constant progress along liberal lines. America requires that this progress be sane and that this progress be honest. America calls for government with a soul.
—Franklin D. Roosevelt, speech in Oklahoma City, July 9, 1938

I n Lebanon, the crowd was again mostly middle-aged men, who looked like Republicans. Franklin had gotten to the point where he could tell. But they were friendly, and he hoped they were open to an argument about what government meant to them.

"A few months ago," Franklin began, "a letter came to one of his newspapers from a man who could find little good about the United States of America.

"'I am weary! I am incensed! I am old!' the letter read, 'and I am not willing to go even one more dollar in national debt. It is time for all of us to stand up, act maturely, face the music and put a stop to this absolutely ridiculous habit of adding debt so that politically parasitic personalities can get another dollar. We cannot afford it. We don't need it, it is unconsciousable and is unsustainable. Is that plain enough, and I shall say it again? Yes, the government may shut down. Yes, the Social Security checks may not be delivered. My own existence may have to change. I may have to cook squirrels on an open fire, live in a tent, wear the same clothes every day, but I have been there before. I can do it again. But something drastic has to be done. Sacrifice should be the order of the day, and everybody should be called on to tighten their belt and trim the national debt.

"'We have seen vast and grandiose programs bleed the very life out of our citizens. We have watched the redistribution of wealth until all sensibility has left the scene. We have a foreign policy that begs for mega dollars leading to unprecedented tax levels and the raising of debt limits each year. Call me irrational or out of orbit, but I sense there are throngs of people who feel the same way.'"

Franklin paused. "That is an actual letter my newspaper received from a seventy-two-year-old man who is a retired minister, and I fear there are a lot of Americans who have a tendency to feel as he does, and I'm not just talking about Paul Tsongas." Franklin hoped the audience caught his little joke, but only a few scattered chuckles followed. He feared some of them agreed with the letter writer.

"I never met the writer of this letter, but I knew people like him who weren't quite as 'out of orbit,' as he phrased it. What he was really saying was that he didn't want one more dollar of his tax money used to help feed poor people and especially poor black people. His resentment against welfare was actually resentment against blacks, whom he would like to have still been slaves. That sounds harsh, but his letter is beyond harsh, and too many Americans give credibility to that kind of thinking." Franklin realized he was on dangerous ground. The latent resentment against welfare was deep-seated and was based on resentment against poor people in general, black and white.

Undaunted, Franklin went on to make his main point. The United States is not a poor nation that must ignore its needs and its poorer citizens in order to survive. The more he thought about it, the more emotional he became although he kept his voice at a controlled level.

"There are more millionaires in the US today than ever in its history, and they have a greater percentage of the national income. None of them are having to tighten their belts, but there are plenty of Americans who are having to tighten their belts. Thankfully, no one is having to cook squirrels or wear the same clothes every day. The US is first and foremost the richest nation in history, and in the year 1991, it stands as an example for all the other nations on the globe. We must not forget those dominant truths as we strive toward a better life for all us, and not just the wealthy.

"This letter writer is clearly paranoid, but there are echoes of his grim philosophy in Mr. Tsongas's campaign in New Hampshire today and in the naysayers through the years who have opposed progressive measures and a higher standard of living.

"That is the major reason I decided to run for president despite the odds against me. I felt that Americans like this letter writer needed to be called to task and told in no uncertain words that he is wrong. We don't need sacrifice and sackcloth. We need boldness and vision and the willingness to look at our history and recognize how the Founding Fathers took a leap forward despite their weaknesses, how generations since have looked at their challenges and determined to meet and conquer them, not shrink from them on the excuse we were too poor and too divided in purpose.

"Some of you may have seen the candidates' debate yesterday, and I will repeat to you what I said then: I believe all this for the best of all possible reasons—because it is true."

Hardy applauded despite himself, and a number of others joined in. He'd never seen Franklin speak as convincingly or confidently. He was miles ahead of where he'd been a month earlier.

"With your patience, I'd like to read an article from the December 1939 *Readers Digest*, which shows how enduring and deep is the dispute which we still face today. Magazines are my favorite antique, and I found this old copy of the *Digest* in an antique shop. The cover price in 1939 was 25 cents, but the price as an antique was $2.50, a bargain for a look at what people were thinking, reading, and anticipating in one of the truly pivotal years of the twentieth century, with World War II breaking out months earlier, and the US finally rising from nearly ten years of the Great Depression. In the years since this *Readers Digest* was published, the world has undergone more changes than any other half century of history, but in reading the articles from December 1939, you find a ring of familiarity in the hopes, fears, and solutions that the writers expressed.

"The lead article was by Wendell L. Willkie, described as a prominent businessman, who within a few months would become the 1940 Republican candidate for president against Democrat Franklin D. Roosevelt's bid for an unprecedented third term.

"Willkie was writing about the nation's continuing economic problems, which included high unemployment. 'The solution has been in our hands,' Willkie wrote. 'Industry needs a great deal of additional capital, and, there should be no difficulty in getting that capital as soon as American investors are reassured as to the future of free private enterprise. In promoting recovery, the chief emphasis has been placed on what the government should do: we have had colossal expenditures for "priming the pump" and a colossal tax program to pay for these expenditures... The greatest threat to the American system today comes from the effort to restrict free enterprise, and only such enterprise can make economic recovery possible.'

"In essence, Willkie was presenting a 1930s version of supply-side economics, and his words could have been suitable for a speech by Ronald Reagan or Jack Kemp.

"For balance, the second article in that issue of the *Digest* was a defense of President Roosevelt's policies by Elmer Davis, a prominent radio commentator and author. Davis contended that Roosevelt and the New Deal, while not fully successful in curing the Depression, had been good for big businessmen, such as Willkie, who were its fiercest critics.

"Davis wrote that it was big business which had actually come up with the idea of government interference in the natural economic processes, by asking for loans and subsidies to businesses and farmers in distress.

"So long as government advanced funds only to the rich, or businesses and farmers, it looked like a happy inspiration, but most businessmen lost faith in it when it was extended to the poor. So they began to complain against government spending and the consequent deficits.

"'By 1938, the US Chamber of Commerce,' Davis wrote, 'was calling for "a balanced budget,"' but also a reduction in "excessive and hampering taxes," a position remarkably similar to the 1980s.

"'Experts are still debating the reasons for the collapse of Coolidge prosperity,' Davis continued, 'but one fact is clear: many industries were producing more than they could sell, and they could not sell because not enough people had money to buy them. Mr. Roosevelt has been trying to give more purchasing power to more people.' End of article.

"The debate hasn't changed much in fifty years," Franklin said, "and Davis fairly stated the consumer-side economic theory, which has prevailed for most of the years since he penned those words. But overshadowing the economy in that month of 1939 was the outbreak of war in Europe, and the question of whether the US would become involved."

"An article by Hugh Johnson, a retired general and former head of the National Recovery Administration, NRA, was entitled, 'Could Hitler Invade America?'

"General Johnson wrote, 'The correct answer to that question depends on our getting in, or staying out of, the new world war. If we get in it is doubtful whether either our free economic system or our democratic political system will survive the necessary war dictatorship.'

"Well, we had to get in and, happily, General Johnson, who was a failure as head of the NRA, was wrong again. But the most errant prediction in that issue was contained in an article by a Catholic priest defending his church's stand against birth control. 'Birth control as now practiced is bound to bring about a notable decline in the population,' he wrote. 'Statisticians predict that in twenty or thirty years our nation will cease to grow and begin to decline unless there occurs a widespread change in the attitude toward birth control.'

"Actually, the world's population has tripled during the years since even though birth control, through the use of the pill, which came into general acceptance in 1960s, has become widespread.

"Another article dealt with small businesses that had been started and had prospered despite the Depression. In 1937, Margaret Rudkin began baking a special bread to feed her sickly son back to health. Friends who tasted the bread asked her why she didn't try and sell it. Mrs. Rudkin's family needed money, so she began baking the bread for sale in the nearby towns. By late 1939, she had created a business that was selling twenty-five thousand loaves of bread a week. She named the bread for the farm on which the family lived in Connecticut—Pepperidge Farms, and of course, the business expanded to become one of the largest food companies of 1982.

"And then finally, this passage from an article entitled 'No Age Is Golden.'

"'In times like these, legends of golden ages have a particular appeal...of simpler times and ways, of years when faithful toil never went unrewarded, when the domestic and public virtues flourished unimpaired and universal contentment was expressed on every face. They are like a middle-aged man's memories of his youth, which he sees through a kind of golden twilight.'

"In times like these, 1991, such legends also have appeal...legends of a simpler time, say, like December 1939, with World War II just beginning, before the Nuclear Age, before hyperinflation, before Vietnam, before Watergate, before the baby boom, before the civil rights revolution and school integration, before the pill...before the *Readers Digest* accepted advertising.

"But as you glance through the articles, written by people at the time, not by historians looking back, you realize that people in the Computer Age are still arguing about many of the same things that divided them in prenuclear times. The United States is up to the challenges of the twenty-first century just as it was of the twentieth century and the nineteenth century and the eighteenth century, and don't let anyone tell you it's not. President Bush says we have the will but not the wallet to meet the challenges, but that's exactly backwards. We have the biggest wallet of any nation in history. The question is whether our leaders have the will, as George Washington did at Valley Forge, as Jefferson did when he approved the Louisiana Purchase, as Lincoln did at Gettysburg, as Franklin Roosevelt did in expanding the government to meet the needs of all the states and all the people and then summoned the Free World to defend every nation threatened by the desert of tyranny.

"The challenges today are also the opportunities for an even greater tomorrow. Dare we not meet them? I believe we certainly will, and I am asking the voters of New Hampshire to put me on the path to help lead the march forward!"

The applause was broad but tepid. Franklin had hoped to arouse more sparks, but he did notice that Hardy looked pleased. He shook a lot of hands and was told to come back before the primary.

As they left the meeting, Hardy told him he thought it was a great speech for a civic group and presented a lot of food for thought. He said he never heard Jimmy Carter make a better one but that Franklin needed to smile more.

"I'm just not a smiler," Franklin admitted. "My face doesn't contort that way, so I haven't had much practice, but I'll try to do better."

They headed back to Concord. "The hard part begins now," Hardy said. "I recall when Carter began to get more attention, people came out of the bushes offering advice, wanting consulting jobs. Can you handle that?"

Franklin wasn't sure. He supervised a maximum of fifty people on some of his newspapers plus smaller staffs on other newspapers throughout his small chain. He never liked staff conflict or suffered disapproval well. "We'll see," he said. "I already feel the change, which obviously we needed. Attention is the essential ingredient of being a political candidate, but I'll miss our tight little group."

"Me too," Hardy agreed. "Carter changed when the attention increased. He got where he didn't trust the media and was always unhappy with his speechwriters. He depended a lot on Jody, Hamilton, and his wife, which reminds me, when is your wife coming up?"

"Soon, I'm trying to decide if I should officially announce I'm a candidate...and where to do it."

"By the way I talked to Jody this morning, and he'll be sending some people for your approval. They should be in Concord tomorrow. I know a couple of them. You should like them."

They picked up local newspapers as they passed through the small towns and were pleased to see that Burkhart was getting news releases in many of them. In Lebanon, they had gotten a reporter-photographer to take a photo of them with the club president and gave him a tape of the speech.

"In talking about the Depression years, I don't think I've gotten around to the most important pop culture element," Franklin said.

"What was that?"

"The music. The 1930s and 1940s were the greatest years ever for pop music. Today a lot of the music of those years are standards, which means they have been played ever since. Tell me one song from the last twenty years you still hear today, except maybe a Beatles song."

"Everybody thinks the music of their teen years was the best ever," Hardy remarked.

"That's true, but the music of my younger years really was the best. It included the big band era, swing and jazz eras, sentiment and crazy songs like 'Pistol-Packing Mama.' You could understand the words and most of the songs were reassuring and just plain easy listening, as they are called today."

"They are also called elevator music," Hardy felt obliged to note.

"I never heard any of them on an elevator, but I heard them constantly on the radio and jukeboxes. They brightened the mood for nearly thirty years of economic hard times, war, and life's usual struggles. The people who grew up listening to them became the greatest generation, built the industrial arsenal that won World War II, and many of them fought and died in the war. The music certainly helped. And what a unique time it was for songwriters such as Rodgers and Hart, and later Rodgers and Hammerstein, Cole Porter, Irving Berlin, Georgia's Johnny Mercer, Harold Arlen, and of course, the big band leaders such as Tommy and Jimmy Dorsey, Glenn Miller, Charlie Spivak, and many others. I got to hear some of those bands in person when they played for dances at the University of Georgia in the forties and early fifties. During the thirties, they had to travel from one town to another every night, playing for small dances and spreading the music of the day. Even with the economy in the tank, many people still danced and sang, and they had great tunes and uplifting words to sing.

"From 1930 into the 1950s, nearly every teenager tuned in the radio and then the TV, to your *Hit Parade*, which played the ten most popular songs of the week as selected by surveys of record sales, radio requests, and jukebox plays. I can still recall the lyrics to a lot of those songs fifty years later.

"They were the soundtrack that made you forget radio reports of how many soldiers had been killed on the Russian front that day, or how many coal miners were on strike, or how many people were looking for work. People listened for the music…and the music was great and usually romantic."

"The beat was awfully slow," Hardy said. "You could go to sleep on some of those songs. Even Frank Sinatra chanted some of his songs."

"But so many lyrics reflected the times and what Americans were experiencing, such as *Saturday night is the loneliest night in the week, cause that's the night my baby and I used to dance cheek to cheek; thanks for the memories,'* which Bob Hope sang in a 1938 movie and adopted for the theme song in all his radio, TV, and tour performances, changing the words to fit the occasions at the locations; but do you know what the very first no. 1 song on the *Hit Parade* was in 1930?"

"*'Yankee Doodle Dandy*?'" Hardy guessed.

"Close, but it was *'Happy Days Are Here Again,'* which Democrats adopted as their theme song in Franklin Roosevelt's first presidential campaign in 1932. I'll mention just two other songs written in the 1930s but which became most popular in 1940s, *'As Time Goes By,'* the song which is the theme in the classic movie *Casablanca* in 1943 but was first heard in 1933, and *'I'll be Seeing You,'* which dominated the *Hit Parade* in 1944 but first came out in 1938. It was the song for its time, and touches on so many simple sentimental points. *'I'll be seeing you in all the old familiar places that this heart of mine embraces, all day through. In that small café, the park across the way, the children's carousel, the chestnut tree, the wishing well.'*"

"You really are incredible," Hardy said. "How do you remember all this?"

"I have a memory for trivials, but I can't remember numbers, and I almost forgot to recall the role movies played in the music. Movies had lots of fistfights and violence, but they also had lots of music and dancing. Fred Astaire and Ginger Rogers set the pace in a series of movies in the 1930s with music by Berlin, Gershwin, and Porter, including *Top Hat, The Gay Divorcee*, and seven others. They were nearly always dressed in tuxedo and gowns, and the furnishings were the latest art decor, giving their movies a look of elegance and casual wealth. Astaire and Rogers were incredible, especially Astaire, whose every movement, dancing or walking, seemed graceful. Then there was Eleanor Powell and her beautiful legs, which flashed across the screen in sexy dances while she displayed an unchanging but innocent smile. She was a favorite of the studio president, the legendary Lewis B. Mayer, and there was a well-documented rumor that he took her out on a date, and when it was time to go home, he began trying to embrace and kiss her, and she pushed him away and said, 'Mr. Mayer, you sit right over there, and I'll sit here, and you won't have to see me to the door.' They never dated again, but Eleanor kept dancing into the 1940s. She was the greatest female tap dancer ever."

"Actually I saw her in an old movie on TV," Hardy said. "You're right, she had great legs and showed them off to the hilt. They were kind of like Susie's legs."

"I guess you could say that, but not around Susie, she's still sensitive about things like that."

"Oh, one thing more about old movies and music. In *Casablanca*, Bogart never says 'Play it again, Sam,' that was the name of a play Woody Allen wrote years later about the movie. What Bogart said was 'You played it for her, play it for me. Play *As Time Goes By*, and as Sam plays the song, Bogart, in a drunken haze, recalls the romantic days he and Bergman spent in Paris during the time just before the Germans invaded and they were separated by the war. *Casablanca* is remembered best for its dramatic phrases, such as 'Round up the usual suspects' and 'We'll always have Paris,' and 'Here's looking at you, kid,' but *As Time Goes By* was the catalyst and one of the most influential songs of the war years."

"Sing it again for me, Mr. Franklin." Hardy laughed.

"Well, if you insist. *You must remember this, a kiss is still a kiss, a sigh is still a sigh, the fundamental things of life as time goes by...*"

They were back in Concord by then and went by the office, which they found had been expanded, as Franklin had approved.

Burkhart and Susie had done their usual competent job, and there were several strangers present. They were people Jody Powell had sent from Washington. Two of them were assistants for the fund-raising. Another was the prospective office manager and another was a reporter. Interviewing and hiring new employees had never been Franklin's favorite task. He'd been fortunate on his newspapers to hire a few very talented writers from other papers and to inherit others from newspapers he bought. He'd had a couple of business managers who turned out to be thieves, which disturbed him greatly because he had liked them. But there were also employees whom he felt made his newspapers the valuable commodities they became in the newspaper market of the 1970s and 1980s.

He glanced over the resumes and asked Charlie and Susie to handle the details. The fund-raisers were given the two new offices, and Charlie and the office manager and news writer shared a large suite, with Hardy and Susie. The campaign was moving from Wolfeboro to Concord. Franklin took a private office.

Phones and a mailbox in Concord had been arranged. The office manager had also installed cable TV and gotten four TV sets. He and Franklin sat down and reviewed the expenses and plans for the operation. "You don't really have a viable campaign now," the manager, whose name was Phil Sutton, told Franklin bluntly. "How much do you want to spend...and are you serious?"

Sutton had worked with Jody on several campaigns and one presidential campaign. He was from New York, which was probably good, Franklin thought, and had handled several congressional races there.

"Work with Hardy on transportation and with Charlie on contacts and New Hampshire plans," Franklin told him. "Give Susie any financial needs and receipts, and show me any news releases. Also give me a list of what you feel we need and what steps we need to take before the next polls and debate. Let's get a file of news releases from the other candidates, okay."

"What about the fund-raising?"

"I'll prepare the first letters and have them tomorrow so they can be sent out to possible supporters in Georgia and other likely

Democratic donors. I'll have a special letter for voters in New Hampshire. They are the key to my whole campaign. If I can make a good showing or maybe even win in New Hampshire, it'll be a new ball game, and we'll go on from there. If not, then I'll be ready to become a newspaper man again, only poorer."

The phone rang. Apparently, a forwarding number had been given to the phones in Wolfeboro. The caller was a club member who'd heard Franklin speak in Berlin. "I wanted to call and say how much I was impressed with your talk," he said. "In fact, I'd like to help you here in Berlin if you're looking for organizers."

"That's great," Franklin said. "I appreciate it greatly."

"I have some experience," he said. "I was an organizer for Ronald Reagan in 1980, and he carried the county by 3–1, but you're right. His supply-side economics haven't worked. It has shifted income from the middle class to the rich, and I also see now that he promoted resentment against the poor to sell his whole program. He talked about this fat woman in Chicago who lived high on the hog with welfare money, and that story sold me and a lot of others. You punctured it with that letter from the guy in South Georgia. Paul Tsongas is just selling a sanitized version. I know a lot of his supporters here in Berlin, and I believe they can be converted to Franklin supporters."

Franklin was elated. This was the first real offer of help he'd had for on-the-ground support.

Now he just needed more county organizers with this guy's viewpoint. He got his name, address, and email and gave it to the office manager. "Here's a start," Franklin told him, "and there aren't that many counties in New Hampshire."

Franklin then went in to talk with the fund-raisers. "I've got a letter for you to send out. You figure out how to get the right names and addresses. One letter will be to people in New Hampshire, and then we'll get up one for people who supported Carter and other Democrats through the years. Here's the pitch for New Hampshire.

"First, we want your vote. That's of main importance. We are running a self-financed campaign so far, but if the outlook continues to improve, we'll have to grow to meet the opportunity. This will still be a low-cost campaign compared to most. Unlike most candidates who promise they'll streamline government and cut costs and then pour millions, even billions, into costly and often foolish campaign expenses, we're not going to do that. We're going to run our campaign the way you'll want your government run—economically and effectively.

"So first, more than money, we want your vote for Thomas Alexander Franklin as the Democratic presidential candidate on Tuesday, February 18. But if you would like to help the campaign with a financial contribution, that will be appreciated in small amounts: ten dollars, twenty dollars, fifty dollars, and a few pictures of Ben Franklin that great New Englander, who was also the first real newspaperman, in fact, the first real American. His face is on the one-hundred-dollar bill, for those who might not know."

Franklin handed the letter to Lionel, the head fund-raiser, and told him to clean it up and let him know what he thought about it. Lionel looked skeptical. "We need to tell them what you're going to do for them," he suggested.

"Of course," Franklin said. "Get a copy of our last brochure. Stress the 50 percent cut in the payroll tax, opposition to NAFTA, repealing the 1986 income tax bill and making the income tax fairer to all taxpayers, substitute a demand-side economic system for supply-side to put more money in the pockets of consumers, improve relations with Russia so that their nuclear arms will not be scattered around to even less-responsible countries."

Lionel and his assistant, Sydney, read the points and seemed to like them. They smiled and walked away. Franklin thought they might be a fit. He wasn't sure about the campaign manager, who soon brought him several sheets of suggestions—expensive ones. "These other candidates have experienced consultants and scores of workers already out in the field. Clinton especially has an election-ready machine, and he's got all that charisma. Kerrey is a natural, war hero, senator, governor, and Tsongas has a head start," Sutton reported.

"You forgot Harkin and Brown," Franklin reminded him. "Get the office outfitted and running and one more office with maybe two employees in Portsmouth, and here's the name of a guy who wants to be our county coordinator in Berlin."

"Let me level with you," Sutton said. "Everybody said you were running a Model-T campaign and told me to at least try to move it up to a Ford Fairlane campaign, but a Model-A is about the best I can see at present."

Franklin was not offended. Actually he appreciated Sutton's honesty.

"You're right," he said, "but you have to also realize that we were considered a Model-T candidate until I squeezed into the debate, and then things moved at warp speed, and that was only two days ago."

Sutton seemed pleased at Franklin's realistic appraisal view of the campaign. "Also," he added, "you're bucking several tides. I was in the 1976 Carter campaign and what won for him was running against the federal government. You're actually running in favor of the federal government. I'm not sure things have changed that much in sixteen years. People still think the federal government is too big. Jimmy avoided definite positions on the issues and managed to keep his options open. I think that's how he won. He also smiled a lot, and I don't think I've seen you smile yet."

Franklin smiled, without showing his teeth. "Carter and I grew up just sixty miles from each other," he said, "but we are very different Georgians and very different candidates. I actually never forgave him for beating Carl Sanders in 1971. I thought Sanders was the best governor in my lifetime and should be the Georgian who would become president someday."

"And you're still criticizing Reagan, who is popular in New Hampshire," Sutton concluded.

Franklin looked at the schedule they'd been working on. "I tell you what, why don't you nail down about ten of these speaking requests and get the campaign more organized. But I'll handle the issues. If you don't like them, I'll understand, but the issues and my positions about them are more important to me than winning. I happen to think they are the positions that can win and should win. The country needs a change from the economy of the past twenty years," he finished, carefully including Carter's term in that period. "Hardy has a recording of my talk today, go listen to it, and we'll discuss the campaign tonight."

Franklin felt a little out of sorts when he realized he should be on a high. He was getting attention; even the other candidates were mentioning his name. Tsongas in particular was calling him irresponsible as well as an irrelevant outsider who'd come into New Hampshire to spread dangerous ideas.

His experience in business told him he needed someone with the background and contacts of Sutton, so he decided to make a better effort of connecting with him. He was concerned that the campaign had not made more contact with women, and he saw no women's groups in the list of speech requests. A call revived him. It was from a union leader in Manchester who wanted him to speak to another group there as soon as possible. He said his union was considering endorsing Franklin over Harkin because they thought he made a better case against NAFTA, explaining how it would take American jobs.

Franklin noticed one high school on the list, and it gave him an idea. He called Susie over and asked her if she had ever made a speech. "In high school, I spoke at sports banquets and in class recitals, and I was pretty good, if I do say so."

"I'll bet you were," Franklin exulted. "I'm going to get up a little speech I want you to do at this high school in Ossipee, it's not too far, and they probably remember you from basketball days, but not from later," he added.

"I've been there," she said. "I'll give it a try."

Franklin wrote a short speech, emphasizing a few campaign promises, then adding a special message from Susie. "This is a candidate who cares about individuals and looks at what they can become not what they are. I can testify to this personally. I was in a deep depression when I first met Mr. Franklin and actually didn't even like him. But he saw something in me he felt could be valuable in his campaign, and he gave me a new reason to live. I believe he can lift the entire country in the same way because he sees the slump it's in, both economically and spiritually, and that's why I'm out here talking for him, which I couldn't have imagined doing a few weeks ago."

Charlie went with Susie to the school, a small one with about one hundred students and staff on hand, and Susie got a great reception. Charlie recorded her remarks and wrote a story about their little excursion and how young she was. It was a great human interest story; he found an old picture of Susie from high school basketball days and took another one of her during her speech to go along with the story. He felt it would be published in many New Hampshire weeklies and some dailies.

Back in Concord Franklin and Sutton conferred, and Sutton had confirmed five speeches in the next four days. All of them were along New Hampshire's well-populated twelve-mile coastline.

Franklin and Hardy set out the next morning for Dover, then planned to go to Rochester, Durham, and wind up in Portsmouth for the night.

Chapter Eight

THE BEST WAY TO TAX

Government itself cannot close its eyes to the pollu-
tion of waters, to the erosion of soil, to the slashing of
forests, any more than it can close its eyes to the need
for slum clearance and schools and bridges.
—Franklin D. Roosevelt, address
at dedication of the Triborough Bridge,
New York City, July 11, 1936

I n late October, Portsmouth's beach season was well past, and
many of its oceanfront stores were closed. But the trees still had
a few bright leaves, and there were more restaurants than they'd
found in any other New Hampshire city. The population of more
than thirty thousand made it the state's fourth-largest city, with many
small towns nearby, including Durham, site of the largest University
of New Hampshire campus. Dartmouth, on the western border was
the largest and best-known college in New Hampshire.

Franklin liked Portsmouth and decided to make a major talk on
taxes there. It was a subject he felt he had a popular position on. A
crowd of about one hundred crowded into the hotel meeting room.
"All most people know about taxes is that they don't like them,"
Franklin opened, "and that's one of the problems in the US. People
who take the time to understand the tax system are the ones who
determine who gets taxed the most, and they make sure it isn't them.

"They start by telling the general population, including politicians, that the system is too complicated and needs to be simplified. That gets a receptive hearing, but their plan to simplify taxes always ends with the simplifiers paying less tax. The worst and most recent example is the 1986 tax revision bill, which was a deal made in hell by Republicans and Democrats and approved by a smiling President Reagan who couldn't have been more pleased. He had advocated a top marginal rate of 35 percent and found the congressional bill had reduced it to 28 percent, the lowest top rate since the 1920s.

"He happily signed the bill, recognizing it as the longest step toward a supply-side economy, which he had set out to create in 1981. The economy had responded by shrinking, with the budget deficit rising and jobs disappearing. That trend must be stopped, and it will require a massive effort and lots of people who are willing to look realistically at the tax system, plus people now making a fortune from the current system to give up some of their advantages, which may be pie-in-the-sky thinking.

"If you'll look at my campaign pamphlet, you'll see that the first promise is to cut the payroll tax from 7.2 percent to 3 percent, giving every wage earner an immediate tax break in their regular paycheck. The offset will be to extend the payroll tax on earned income from its current $60,000 a year, a figure set when the amount earned over that total was relatively small, to all earned income. Today millions of dollars paid to the highest earners escape any payroll tax at all, not to mention their incomes from dividends, interest, and other nonpayroll income, which also escape the payroll tax.

"That will be a significant start to making the system fairer and less burdensome on the middle and poorer-income groups. It would be the largest transfer of taxes from those incomes to upper incomes in the nation's history, and it would put more money in the pockets of your customers and of tourists.

"A next step will be to repeal most of the 1986 tax bill, starting with restoring the tax exemption on second or vacation homes, the results of which have been so punishing to New Hampshire.

"The nation's most successful years economically were when income taxes were most progressive, or graduated, which they no longer are. To use a familiar example, an all-star athlete who was scraping by on $1 million a year in 1980 and paying a top rate of 50 percent now pays a top rate of only 28 percent, and keep in mind that the top rate today is only paid on the amount of income over $180,000 a year, not one's entire income, a point many Americans don't realize and politicians never emphasize. The average top rate on middle income in 1980 was about 20 percent, which is what it still is today despite all the so-called tax cutting in the 1980s, but the rate on the richest Americans came down dramatically as their incomes went up.

"The number of tax brackets was reduced in the name of simplicity, but that made the system less progressive and less graduated as lower incomes were pushed into a higher bracket. All this is not easy to understand for most people, many of whom are shocked at the disparity in people's incomes and some who just plain don't believe it. I plan to keep talking about it. Because if the trend continues, the nation will return to the wealth extremes of the 1900s and the 1930s, which brought on the Great Depression.

"The simple fact is that middle- and lower-income Americans are paying a disproportionate amount of a growing tax bill. In 1943, to pay for World War II, the highest tax rate briefly rose to 89 percent, which seemed high, although it only affected amounts of income past very high overall sums. You may recall that President Reagan, then a movie actor, who were among the highest-paid Americans, said that a star wouldn't make but three movies a year because the income from a fourth would all be paid in income tax. That year, Reagan contended for the role of Rick in *Casablanca*, but for some reason he was passed over, and Humphrey Bogart got the role. Maybe it was because that would have been Reagan's fourth movie, and we can all be thankful for Bogart's classic turn in *Casablanca*.

"A progressive tax is the soundest, fairest tax yet devised, and it created the demand-side economy, which we need today. It's what has pulled the nation out of every economic downturn, including the Great Depression. It leaves more money to people who are the essential consumers and thus the real job creators. When there is a demand for products, the supply-side always responds with more production, which creates more jobs.

"Paul Tsongas, among others, is selling a warmed-over version of Reagan's supply-side economics, and we all know that warmed-over dishes are less tasty than the original. Tsongas has convinced me he's not Santa Claus, but I now recognize him as a tight-fisted version of Old Man Potter."

The first question was on a subject he hadn't touched on in his talks. How do you stand on abortion?

"As one of the other candidates has said, abortion should be safe, legal, and rare."

"So you're pro-choice?"

"Yes, but I'm certainly pro-life also. I think we need new terms for the debate."

"You've never been anything but a newspaper publisher, according to your brochure. What makes you think you could be a president?"

Franklin smiled.

"Well, I think being a newspaper publisher is pretty good preparation. You get experience in writing, business, selling, printing, getting to know the leaders in your community, state, and often nation. You also develop opinions on a lot of issues and research them. I was also president of two state press associations. That's kind of like saying all Bill Clinton has done is be governor of Arkansas, but I admit the fact that I'm not a politician in the accepted sense. The people have never elected me to anything. That's why I'm counting on New Hampshire voters so much, to prove voters will support me. To a great extent the people of New Hampshire will determine if I continue my campaign. That's why I want your votes more than your dollars. As my associate will tell you, we're running a very economical campaign, which is the way I'll run the government if given the chance."

The crowd was mostly younger businessmen, and Franklin managed to meet and talk with a number of them. He urged anyone who would like to help in his campaign to call one of the office numbers. He ran into a real estate agent who wanted to know if Franklin could use an office in Portsmouth. "That's a great idea," Franklin replied. They walked down the street where the agent had his own office with an empty adjacent space in the same building. "I'll let you have it for fifty dollars a month if you cut my payroll tax, and we can share my two assistants who handle the phones," the Realtor said.

"That's a deal," Franklin said and pulled out a fifty-dollar bill. "We'll be back and send more campaign material over."

Durham, where the university had its schools of agriculture, liberal arts, technology, and business, was nearby. It was a fairly large campus in a small city. Franklin stopped at the main building and asked to see the president, who happened to be in. "I'm planning to be on the Democratic presidential ballot in February," Franklin told him, "and I've lived in college communities for the past thirty years and been very involved in campus activities."

A bit surprised, the college president looked at the name tag Franklin still wore from the meeting. "I've heard about you," he said. "Saw one of your ads in our weekly newspaper and read an AP story about the candidate debate last week." Before Franklin left, he had arranged to come and speak at an assembly the next week and attend a football game.

He and Hardy made a couple of more stops in townships before heading to Portsmouth for the night. "How many townships have we been in?" Franklin asked.

"About eighty, I think, and Charlie and Susie have been in about sixty, which only leaves about sixty to go, if we make them all."

Franklin began talking about the pop culture of the Depression years again. "They were years of so much intellectual churn," he said. "*Intellectual* might not be the best word for all of it. For instance, there were the so-called pulp magazines. They thrived in the thirties and through the forties and were my favorite reading material as a teenager as well as giving me my start as a writer. There were dozens of these magazines, called pulps for the cheap paper they were printed on, except for the covers, which were slick paper with colorful depictions of the hero, the villain, and heroine in various states of duress and undress. The cover artists were actually very good, and some of the original covers sell for big money today, such as Virgil

Finlay, Frank Paul, and Hannes Bok. The magazines sold for ten cents to twenty cents with about 120 pages jammed with stories. There were westerns, detective, and jungle stories, including the early adventures of Tarzan, but my favorites were the science fiction, or SF, magazines. They were a genre unto themselves with a remarkable group of fans, who wrote letters that were more interesting than the stories, formed clubs, published what were called fanzines, and organized state and national conventions that are still being held today. The magazines paid about one to five cents a word for their fiction but during the Depression managed to attract an impressive list of authors, some of whom became famous later, such as Ray Bradbury and Leigh Brackett, a noted screen writer. To science-fiction fans, they were all great. As Isaac Asimov, author of the Foundation Series, later wrote, 'There was once a magic world that no one knew but us.' One of the best science fiction writers, L. Ron Hubbard, later founded a religion he called Dianetics and became best noted for that although he was often called a scam artist."

"So you didn't have TV, but you had Big Little Books, comic books, lots of other books, movie serials, and then pulp magazines during the war years."

"I thought they were exciting at the time," Franklin admitted. "I looked forward eagerly to the day a new comic book or science fiction magazine came out. Of course, there also was radio, a very important presence in our lives, not just for music, but also for news and entertainment and in my younger days for sports. One of the best memories I have of my father, who died when I was seventeen, was of us listening to Joe Louis's boxing matches when Louis was champion. We always pulled for his white opponent, even Max Schmelling, the German, who was the only white opponent who ever beat Louis. That was in 1936, before Louis became the champion. In the 1938 rematch, Louis knocked Schemelling out in the first round. The war had started by then, and a lot of Southerners were pulling for Louis that time. He went on to defend his title a record number of times, served in the Army during the war, and when he finally lost it, it was to another black boxer, Jersey Joe Walcott. Boxing was big time

THE LAST NEW DEALER

in those years. I don't even know who the heavyweight champion is today."

After dinner at the hotel, they decided to do their dog-and-pony karaoke show in the bar, which was quite large, no doubt for summer tourist crowds but half empty on this late October evening.

Franklin asked the singer if he knew Kenny Roger's "Lucille," and the crowd got into the chorus: By the time the singer got to "The Gambler," the crowd was louder and really into it. Franklin clapped for them and then announced that he was picking up the bill for the drinks. He introduced himself and explained that he'd be a candidate in the presidential primary and hoped they'd consider him. A few in the crowd had seen him in the debate, but not many had ever heard of him. The total bill was less than the price of five TV spots, and Franklin hoped paying it was legal for a candidate. The crowd was mostly young traveling businessmen, mainly from New Hampshire, but some from neighboring Maine, which Franklin was glad to see. The Maine caucus was scheduled less than a week after the New Hampshire primary.

"Not a bad day," Hardy remarked as they left, "plus great restaurants. I don't know how many votes you're winning, but this campaign is a lot more fun than Carter's were."

They returned to Concord the next morning to meet with Sutton, the campaign manager, and the other new people Jody had sent. Sutton was upbeat. "I've got coordinators in eight counties and ten cities," he reported. "It wasn't hard. A lot of them have seen your newspaper ads, and others were people you met in the townships. We're building a network, and they seem enthusiastic, especially about cutting the payroll tax. The union people I've talked to in Manchester and Nashua sounded very supportive although most of them are still leaning toward Harkin. There's also a groundswell of support for Clinton, but your attacks on Tsongas are having an effect. He's dropping."

Franklin suddenly had a better feeling toward Sutton. He apparently knew what he was doing. They talked a while, and Sutton related some experiences in the past, which included stints with Carter in 1980, a loss; then Mondale in 1984, another loss; and

Dukakis in 1988, his bitterest loss. He had worked with a few winners in state contests, but his main experience was with losers, just as Hardy's was. He obviously expected to be on the losing side with Franklin, but he admitted he needed a job when Jody Powell called him, and Franklin was paying him top dollar on the staff.

They compared dates for more appearances and several new debates that had been scheduled. A new poll would be out in a few days, and Sutton felt certain Franklin would be climbing.

Franklin called his contact in Little Rock. "What's the word down there?" he asked.

"The word is pussy," the reporter said. "No pun intended, but Clinton's good luck charm is petering out. The shoe is going to drop in a few weeks."

"That's very funny," Franklin said, "but he's gaining momentum here in New Hampshire. Are you seeing any polls down there?"

"Yes, the papers are following Clinton since he's the governor and he's leading. They show Tsongas and Kerrey running close behind, and your name usually shows up with about 8 or 9 percent, along with Harkin and Brown."

Franklin called his wife, Jean. "I want you and the children to come up here for Thanksgiving week," he said. "I need you all, and I think I'll officially announce that week. I'll get you rooms in Concord, and you can see what a New England winter is like."

Jean sounded surprised. "Are you really ready to make that commitment?" she asked. "You haven't even discussed it with me."

"I know, I'm sorry. We'll definitely discuss it before the official announcement. I want to make a few more speeches and see a couple of more polls, but things have been going surprisingly well."

After the call Franklin sat and pondered his strategy. He knew that the so-called pundits had decided that the nation's voters had become primarily economic conservatives and cultural liberals. He didn't believe it, and polls tended to back him up. He thought it was just the opposite. In the first place, less than half of the eligible Americans voted in the presidential elections and even less than half in the midterm elections that determined the House and Senate.

Most of the nonvoters were either poor, old, or disinterested because they didn't think elections affected their personal lives.

Low voting had always plagued US elections partly because that was the way the political leaders planned it. The Founding Fathers at first only wanted property owners to vote. Then they designed the electoral college to diminish the impact of popular votes for president, not to mention denying the vote completely to women until 1921, and most blacks until the 1940s. Then there was the tradition of holding Election Day on Tuesdays, usually a workday for most Americans. That tradition had persisted through the agriculture era, the industrial era, and into the computer era, even while other nations had long since moved elections to the weekend or specified holidays. Ironically, one of the few states that had moved its voting to Saturday was Louisiana, not otherwise known for encouraging democratic practices.

A few weeks before the 1988 election, an impartial polling group had asked voters what they thought Bush and Dukakis should concentrate on if elected. The leading priorities had little relationship to what the two candidates were saying in their speeches. Nearly 70 percent of those polled wanted the wealthy and big corporations to pay a larger share of the federal tax burden; 66 percent wanted the government to protect jobs with tough trade policies; 55 percent backed national health insurance.

Bush's best-known promise was "no new taxes," which meant nothing since it's how taxes are levied and on whom that makes the difference. Quite simply, government decides who pays the taxes and who gets the biggest share of the revenue from those taxes, and there was no doubt how that equation had been changed in 1980 and early '90s and who benefited. That was the message Franklin wanted to get out, and he felt he needed clearer ways to do it.

Tsongas, by contrast, seemed to be gaining support with the exact opposite message. Franklin was convinced that a lot of closet Republicans were supporting Tsongas, feeling that Bush would easily win the Republican primary. Oddly, however, Bush had drawn an opponent from his right, a position hard to locate, in Pat Buchanan, who was best known for his TV performances on CNN and as a speechwriter for Nixon. He was attacking Bush for being too liberal.

The people of New Hampshire were very proud and protective of the fact that the state has neither a state income tax nor a sales tax. Less publicized was that a third of the state's budget came from the federal government with other revenue from excise taxes on such items as motor fuel, alcohol, and tobacco products. A large share of revenue came from tourists in the form of taxes on rooms and meals and souvenir items. That revenue had been adversely affected by the economic slump and the rise in gasoline prices had cut down on tourism in general.

President Richard Nixon's revenue-sharing program with the states had helped many of them upgrade facilities, and New Hampshire had managed to maintain one of the best-funded public school systems among the fifty states.

Franklin wanted to remind them of all that without sounding like a public scold on the tax system, but it was hard. His instincts told him that the US tax system was the main problem that kept the economy from growing and was even infringing on that narrow path between the wilderness of chaos and the desert of tyranny.

The next day a new poll was published by the *Boston Globe*. It showed Franklin at 10 percent, still behind the leaders, Clinton, Tsongas, Kerrey, and Harkin, but in double figures and ahead of Brown and the lesser candidates. Tsongas had definitely slipped, and Kerrey and Harkin didn't seem to be moving.

Another debate was scheduled Friday, and Franklin had two major speeches the following week, one in Manchester and the other in Nashua. He also noted that Susie was filling more school engagements. Burkhart, who usually accompanied her, said she was getting good receptions.

New Hampshire was generally prosperous compared to Southern towns and cities, but Franklin now noticed appalling signs of poverty. It reminded him of an anecdote he meant to use about Edward the Duke of Wales, who later gave up the British crown to marry a divorced American. In evening dress, with red carnation, the youthful Edward was visiting the grim coal fields in the north of England where many miners were near to starving. "I'll show you misery," his driver said, stopping at a small cottage. Inside an old woman lay motionless. "Dead," croaked a child, "starved to death."

Prince Edward grew more and more upset. "This is ghastly," he exclaimed. "What caused all of this?"

"Management," his guide replied.

"Bad management?" the Duke asked.

"No," the guide replied. "Just hard management."

According to the article in *Time* magazine, Feb. 11, 1929, edition, the distraught Prince Edward was outraged. "I never knew things were so bad," he exclaimed. He left the mine and returned to his train, where after a night's sleep he sprang to his horse and kept a fox-hunting engagement, galloping off after a frightened red fox. But the incident left an impression on him. Later, during his brief reign as king, he denounced the royal sport of fox hunting.

The miners meanwhile remained hungry and haggard, but like true Englishmen, they fought valiantly a few years later to keep their island from falling to the Nazis and to maintain their freedom and their expensive system of royalty, which exists to this day.

The second debate was not an exciting affair. Most of the candidates repeated their talking points and the panel of questioners, selected from the network channels, didn't seem to grasp the issues. Tsongas continued his role as "a hard-nosed realist who felt the nation had to get spending under control." He repeated that he wasn't Santa Claus. Clinton wavered slightly on his middle-class tax cut, almost agreeing with Tsongas that spending needed to be cut. Kerrey kept promising a national health plan; Harkin stuck to his basic New Deal solutions; Brown suggested a national sales tax. Franklin had a hard time getting a word in, but he tried to make the most of his answers by saying that the federal government needed to loosen its belt rather than tightening it. The audience seemed impressed.

The media mainly ignored the Democratic debate and seemed more absorbed by the Bush-Buchanan battle on the Republican side. There were separate party primaries in New Hampshire with voters choosing which one to vote in.

Franklin desperately sought a chance to get in a question to Tsongas and caught a small opening near the end of the debate. "Mr. Tsongas," he asked, "we know you are a good and compassionate man who overcame grave health problems to make this campaign, but do you truly believe the federal government has no obligation to assist the poor in the country?"

"I resent that question," Tsongas answered sharply. "I've probably done a lot more to help the poor than you have or any of the other candidates. But the best way to help the poor is to get jobs for them, and my economic policies are the best way to build a job economy and provide better incomes for all in the long run."

Franklin couldn't believe his luck. That was the opening he'd been hoping for. "As the greatest New Dealer, Harry Hopkins reminded us years ago, people don't eat in the long run, they have to eat today and tomorrow," Franklin exclaimed with just the right touch of emotion.

Tsongas looked momentarily stricken. At that point, Harkin interjected, "Why didn't you support an increase in the food stamp program in your last Senate session?"

"Public doles have never gotten the country moving or helped move people off the welfare roles," Tsongas answered defiantly. "That's the kind of philosophy I'm trying to get the Democratic Party away from. It's a philosophy most Americans don't like, and we will keep on losing elections if we stay on the path Mr. Franklin and Senator Harkin support."

The moderator called time over for the debate. Franklin felt he had gotten in the sound bite people would remember. "People don't eat in the long run" was an old saying but still carried impact, and many of the younger media types and watchers probably hadn't heard it.

Harkin shook his hand later and said he had gotten tired of the self-righteous tone of Tsongas's attack on the New Deal.

Tsongas muttered that the requirement should be raised for which candidates were allowed in the debates.

Post-debate comments and polling indicated that no one won the debate, and the small audience had been bored, but the exchange between Franklin and Tsongas got attention in the morning's reviews. More exciting to Franklin was an invitation at the Concord office to a Democratic Party regional meeting in Boston in just two days. All the Democratic candidates had been invited but several had declined, and there was a spot open for a speaker if he'd come. Franklin immediately called the contact and accepted, even on the short notice. He was in no position to be choosey.

Chapter Nine

THE SPEECH IN BOSTON

In our personal ambitions we are individualists. But in our seeking for economic and political progress as a nation, we all go up, or else we all go down, as one people.

—Franklin D. Roosevelt, second inaugural address, January 20, 1937

Franklin met with Sutton and the office staffers and was told money was trickling in from the letters they'd sent out. It wasn't much, but the amount might pay the rent and some salaries. Franklin's $6 million was still the bulk of the funding and was holding up well.

He already had in mind the speech he'd give to the Democratic group in Boston. It was an opportunity for national attention plus some TV coverage by a Boston station, not to mention the Boston papers and the *New York Times*.

He and Hardy left that day, deciding to spend a night in Boston. On the way, they stopped at a few townships on the state border with Massachusetts, near Tsongas's hometown of Lowell, where he was especially well-known. The latest poll still showed him slightly in the lead, with Clinton closing fast.

The Boston meeting was in a large hall, not a hotel, although light sandwiches, coffee, and tea were available. The major candidates who were present were Tsongas, Brown, and Franklin, if he could now be granted that designation.

The crowd looked to be about two hundred, from throughout Massachusetts, according to the moderator, who praised the candidates for attending and noted that the major Democratic local leaders from Boston and its surrounding counties were on hand.

When his time came, Franklin started nervously. This was the most important speech of the campaign so far, he felt, more so even than the debates. He began by explaining why the 1992 election was so critical, not just for the nation, but for the entire world. "Make no mistake," he exclaimed with feeling, "this election is the best—and may be the last—opportunity to turn the nation away from the trickle-down economics of the Republican years and to help stabilize the nations of the former Soviet Union, which has disintegrated into fractious governments with no clear idea of which path they will take or what forces will gain control of Russia's nuclear arsenal, still the second largest in the world, with unknown fingers on the triggers." He noted that the former Yugoslavia was already torn asunder by war and destruction, and it was supposed to be one of the best of the Soviet satellites. "But we cannot help the world until the United States itself is on a sounder path with a growing economy and an outlook that promises solutions rather than problems," he continued. "After nearly twenty years of the supply-side economics mirage, surely the people are ready to hear a demand-side theory that not only helps individuals but will pay the way for nationwide progress.

"I'm from Georgia," he admitted, "as you might have guessed from my accent, and I bring you greetings from Jimmy Carter, who was a better president than he gets credit for. Unfortunately, he fell into the same trap other Democrats have, which was to abandon some of the better New Deal theories that pulled the country out of the Great Depression, rescued the world in World War II, then gave the nation its longest, strongest economic years. In the process, we created the broadest, most prosperous middle class of any nation in history, not to mention the strongest military and the foundation on which the entire world's economy now rests. That's the legacy of the New Deal.

"More people are rich in the United States than there were in the so-called Gilded Age. They just have to pay taxes. Far more people are in what we call the middle class, which is the greatest achievement of the Democratic Party, and make no mistake, it was Democrats who achieved that, usually against solid opposition from Republicans on everything from Social Security to minimum-wage laws, to going off the gold standard, to the GI bill, to home loan assistance, to food stamps, and to Medicare. You can look it up, as Casey Stengell used to say, and you'll find that Republicans fought all those programs at their birth, and almost killed some of them in their cradles. The Democrats who saved them and have extended them to include more and more Americans through the years deserve our homage and appreciation, but we must also recognize that their enemies are still in the field. The legislative battles today have their roots in the battles of the New Deal years, and the Republicans haven't given up. Indeed, they are stronger today than they were then, mainly because they have more money now and don't see the need to help the thousands of Americans who are still in need by today's standards."

The Democratic chairmen loved it. Many of them were on their feet, cheering and clapping, which they hadn't done for the other candidates. Franklin had given them the red meat of the New Deal they hadn't heard from Carter or Mondale and Dukakis and certainly not Tsongas or Kerrey or Brown.

Using one of his favorite quotations, usually credited to the Duke of Wellington in 1850, Franklin compared the world to the midnineteenth century when the Duke said, "What all the wise men said would happen, has not occurred, and what all the damn fools predicted has come to pass."

"That is the contrary nature of events," Franklin said, "but we have certain proof that supply-side economics don't work, except for leaving those of lesser income without optional money to spend, while the supply-siders have virtually stopped working because they can make more profits by selling their stock to each other and consolidating companies to eliminate competition.

"Theodore Roosevelt, nearly a century ago, condemned that practice as the very opposite of free enterprise or capitalism, and when companies consolidate, they seek to raise the big purchase price by cutting both the number of employees and their pay scale. Everybody loses except the executives and the big stockholders. The stockholders get richer, the brokers take their percentage, and the buyers and other deal makers divide the rest. Then it's on to the next deal while the displaced workers from the downsized companies scramble for jobs at Walmart or McDonald's."

Since he'd done the same thing with his newspaper, Franklin was on familiar, if uncomfortable ground. "Is that the kind of country we want? Is it the kind of country that can sustain the strongest economy and most prosperous middle class in the world and show other nations of the world the way to their own secure and prosperous future? Paul Tsongas must think so," Franklin stressed, "and the sad problem is that he really believes it and should be running on the Republican ticket. The demand-side economy needs more spending money, which is why my first pledge is to cut the payroll tax from 7.5 cents to 3 cents on the first dollar a worker earns and levy the tax on all earned income, which will be fairer and bring in more revenue to keep the Social Security system solvent for you and your children and grandchildren just as the system has helped your grandparents and parents and assured that the nation's elderly would not be the poorest segment of the population as they once were."

Franklin paused and said he'd take questions.

"I'm a Democrat," one man said, "but you're saying personal initiative and self-reliance didn't build this country and make it great, and we should depend on the government. We've seen how that policy has left the poor poorer and more dependent."

"Well, first my family didn't have much money. My father died when I was seventeen. I started a newspaper with a $2,000 loan when I was twenty-four. I then quit a good job in my late thirties to form an investors' group to buy a larger newspaper. I was lucky enough to build a multimillion dollar corporation, with personal initiative and self-reliance and with the money from advertisers who sold their products to thousands of people, who had not been as fortunate as

I was, but had enough spending money to buy the goods advertised and buy the paper and make it a financial success. A lot of that money came from federal government projects or from colleges, hospitals, local governments, and industries that provided arms for the military forces and built the planes and ships that were so successful in the Persian Gulf War.

"But when I drive through many towns today, small and big, I go off the main streets and explore the streets behind them, and too often the main streets are like a movie set and hidden behind them is the shabby real world of slum housing and junk-littered yards where the grass hasn't been cut in months. In every one of your hometowns, there are streets and neighborhoods that look like third world countries and not part of the richest nation in history, in which companies can spend millions buying out competitors and sending weapons to other countries so they can make war on each other and destroy what little civilization some of them have achieved. Iraq, for example, had moved closer to the twentieth century, and now, its electrical system, its roads, its dams, and many of its buildings that were among the oldest in the world have been reduced to rubble. It was mainly a mad dictator's fault, Saddam Hussein, but sadly he still rules over the rubble and over the thousands of Iraqis killed in the war and others of his own people who have been gassed to death in the months since."

"So you were against the Gulf War?" asked one man.

"I opposed it in my editorials leading up to the war, and despite the glorious victory and the small number of American casualties and the joyous parades and President Bush's 90 percent approval ratings, I still think it was a needless gamble with American lives, resources, and reputation. The fact that a terrible gamble turns out well doesn't make it any less of a terrible gamble, and it didn't turn out well for thousands of Iraqi civilians or the several hundred Americans who were killed."

Tsongas, when it came time for him to speak, was forceful even if misguided, in Franklin's view. "I've been in politics for a long time," he said, "and I've never lost an election. I understand when all the pollsters tell Democrats to support middle class tax cuts or other tax cuts, and when I say no, there has to be a purpose. I'm not suicidal, politically, and the purpose is when you talk to economists, men and women in business, most editorial writers, there is no call for middle class tax cuts. We have to take our money, the precious reserves we have, and put it into venture capital, into equity capital, not Head Start, and those kind of things... I would love to come out for middle class tax cuts. That's what my advisers are saying to me, but it's not good economics, and it seems to me if you are going to compete with George Bush in a sort of bidding war, we are not being responsible. I have to be the non-Santa Claus alternative to what's going on." Franklin decided Tsongas needed a better speechwriter as well as a better message. Even in his home territory, Tsongas got little applause.

Returning to Concord, Hardy played a tape of Franklin's speech for the rest of the staff. They were all impressed, even Sutton, who remained dubious about Franklin's message. Susie loved it, of course. She had become a real fan and made a copy to use as part of her own presentations. She had three more talks scheduled for the week, including to two large women's groups.

They all sat down and studied the schedule for the next few weeks. Franklin realized the days of leisurely rides through the state were over. Most of the leaves had fallen, leaving a much bleaker landscape. What was brighter was the political landscape. Calls were coming in for more interviews, including one on WMUR-TV, the only regular channel station in New Hampshire. Franklin, who once owned and operated a cable system in Athens, also made sure the cable systems were contacted since they reached many homes in the states that didn't have regular TV.

He continued to provide ads for the weekly schedules he set up in September and which would run until January, with a different message each week. Charlie and the writer sent by Jody were getting out the ads and also news releases and photos to the weekly newspapers, most of which used them, especially of Susie.

Franklin felt his next important speech would be the one at the University of New Hampshire. He gave it special attention, with emphasis on his opposition to the war against Iraq and the possibility of its dire consequences.

With the war having been such an enormous television and public relations success, few voices were raised against it, and it was almost forgotten that the Senate vote supporting President Bush's pursuit of the war was only 52–47, with a relatively close margin in the House.

Franklin was pleased that his friend, Senator Sam Nunn of Georgia, had led the opposition. Nunn, considered one of the Senate's leading defense policy experts, supported continued economic sanctions against Iraq but a delay in granting war powers to the president. His position was based on both knowledge and conviction and provided cover for other Democratic senators to vote no.

George Will, one of the most thoughtful and widely published conservative columnists, predicted that the war would be disastrous for the United States in the long run, even if victorious.

Another surprising opponent was Ross Perot, the Texas billionaire, who would later play such a prominent role in the 1992 election. He was already making frequent appearances on the Larry King TV show, which eventually led to a declaration of his candidacy for president as a third-party candidate. His solution for the problem of Iraq's invasion of tiny Kuwait was to "put the leaders of all of those Arab nations in a tent and let them come out with a solution." His suggestion was an idiom he would make famous later in the campaign. Franklin opened his speech with a quotation.

"The great French philosopher Voltaire said, 'History is the patter of silken slippers descending the stairs and the thunder of hobnail boots moving up.' I believe Voltaire was right, but in the year 1992, the United States has the historic opportunity to change that enduring condition of mankind. We can reduce the hordes of men in hobnail boots and increase the number of people in silken slippers, and we dare not ignore the unique time and chance.

"But the thirst for war, and an easy victory, had been too great. President Bush had depicted the commitment as a matter of honor for the US to make good on his promise that Saddam's invasion of Kuwait 'would not stand.' It was surprising, in fact, that the Senate and House votes were so close.

"As in so many cases in the past, once the dogs of war are loosed, there can be no turning back. The war's financial cost was not even placed in the budget, and the deficit hawks overlooked it. The war was quite expensive, but the victory and its acclaim by the population, especially TV viewers, appeared worth the price. Only 250 Americans were reported to have been killed in the one hundred hours the war lasted, although thousands of Iraqis were killed and much of the country laid waste by bombing attacks.

"Kuwait was liberated, and then suddenly the war stopped, with Saddam still in power and much of his military machine intact. His threats of germ warfare and other types of mass weapons were never seen and much of his air force escaped by simply flying to Iran for the duration."

Franklin tried to determine the mood of his potential college audience. Was this a subject that really summoned their deepest feelings? The Vietnam War had been a live subject for students of twenty and thirty years earlier, but there was no shooting war in 1991, no threat of the draft. Franklin was not sure what their most defining concern was in the 1990s.

The auditorium at the university was half filled for Franklin's talk, which he considered pretty good. His name was still not an attraction, especially for young people. A professor introduced him, mainly emphasizing his background as a newspaper publisher and as a candidate who had never before run for or held public office. That actually got a round of applause. Franklin opened by explaining the reasons he opposed the war and how the outcome had left many unresolved problems. "The US proved its superiority, but the match was comparable to the University of New Hampshire playing the Chicago Bears in football, although I suspect New Hampshire would put up a better fight," he suggested.

He cited the efforts for a peaceful settlement and Saddam's stubborn refusal to back off his conquest of Kuwait. "He apparently never believed the US would resort to military action. He got a rude awakening last year on the night of January 17. US planes based in Saudi Arabia bombed Baghdad, and the first attacks knocked out the telephone exchange and thirty-four other designated targets in the first hour. Iraq had been reduced from a second to a third world country again in just hours. CNN was the only news network with correspondents in Baghdad and provided dramatic coverage of the US attack. Iraqi antiaircraft defense was totally ineffective, mainly disabled by laser-guided bombs dropped by a fleet of pilotless decoys.

"CNN sent out immediate and spectacular images of the tracers and bombs igniting the night sky. It was war such had never been seen during the Vietnam War, and it thrilled an audience eager and hungry for a visible triumph. American pilots performed to perfection, with no midair collisions despite all the supersonic planes whizzing around. It was revealed later that Saddam Hussein, the main target of the attack, was in an earthquake-proof anti-nuclear bunker deep beneath the destruction on the ground. It had been built for him by a Swedish company for the purpose of holding hostages as a shield against an aerial bombardment.

"In the next few days, 95,000 tons of bombs were dropped on Iraq, while a global TV audience watched in awe at the display of US technology. The press corps was kept in Riyadh, Saudi Arabia, and given periodic briefings of how effective the attacks were and were shown video taken by cameras on the guns. Saddam had some crazy idea of luring the western troops into a bloody ground warfare, but his large tank corps and suicide attacks never took place. The land battle in Iraq lasted less than four days, although Iraq had claimed troop strength of 545,000 against only 258,000 for the US-led forces. The carpet bombing and other strategic attacks had settled the issue. One British officer commented that 'not since Hiroshima have there been so many bodies on the ground.' Nearly all the bodies were Iraqis. The US and its allies reported a total death toll of only 250. The loss of Iraqi lives was never reliably known, but its military deaths alone were put at more than 100,000.

"The Iraqis surrendered en masse and Hussein ordered all of his troops out of Kuwait. The troops of the US coalition were at the gates of Baghdad when the order was given for them to go no further. The basic mission had been accomplished. Kuwait was freed, and Saddam had been exposed as a second-rate Mussolini, instead of Hitler.

"General Norman Schwarzkopf, who led the US forces, proved an efficient organizer but complained after the war that he had been deprived of final success. Saddam was still in power, and although weakened, his troops were able to defeat an uprising by Kurds in the northern part of the country a few months later, using the poison gas mercifully missing against the US forces, probably in fear of a nuclear response."

It has been argued since, Franklin explained, that the US did not want to completely overthrow Saddam because he still was seen as the main opponent to the strongest foe in the area, which was the Islamic state of Iran. The US had helped build the Iraqi military during its ten-year war with Iran, which basically gave Iraq an advantage.

"Saddam was—and is—an extremely evil and dangerous ruler, especially to his own people. The crown prince of Kuwait, who had been in exile in London, has returned and restored royal authority with no provisions for free elections in Kuwait. He now presides over a nation left in ruins by the Iraqis, including the destruction of its oil wells, the main source of its national income, only 2 percent of which is sold to the US. The justifiable glory of the Iraqi venture must not blind us to the stern enemies still in the field, some of whom carry briefcases instead of rifles and may not be as obliging as Saddam's paper tigers.

"George Will wrote recently that the awesome military force demonstrated in Iraq 'is not irrelevant to the same efforts against the threats to America's problems on the home front, such as inadequate schools, scandalous numbers of children in poverty, money spent wildly in excess of revenues on weapons that turn out not to be so smart.'

"Will was trying to explain to conservatives the paradox of their convictions that a strong federal government is necessary for waging war but must be kept weak and under suspicion when dealing with domestic problems. As he mentioned in his column, more Americans were killed by gunfire on the streets of United States during the forty-three days of Desert Storm than were killed in the war.

"Those of us who opposed the war and have been concerned at what comes next in the Middle East feel the chill wind of desperation in the face of 90 percent approval ratings for President Bush, higher than any president has received in modern polling, but I am reminded of what a great philosopher said when told that you can't argue with success, 'on the contrary, success is exactly what must be argued with lest it become accepted wisdom with no basis except its success in a certain situation.'"

The applause was generous, but Franklin felt he had gone too long about the enormity of the US onslaught. He was trying to make the point to the students and professors that war can be terribly destructive without being an enduring solution.

Questions followed, including the obvious one, What would he have done to persuade Saddam to get his forces out of Kuwait after the United States had put its honor on the line?

"More sanctions and negotiations were already having an effect," he answered. "That is a slower, less satisfying solution, but the stakes were not great enough for us to have put our honor on the line. The Iraqis who trashed Kuwait as they fled were guilty of reprehensible behavior, but they can point to their devastated country as evidence that brutality comes in various forms, including impersonal bombs dropped from planes flying far above the bloody results on the ground. The United States proved its military might in a convincing manner for those who have less faith in US military development and skill than I do. As for Saddam, he unfortunately seems to still be in control with no fear of being overthrown. Perhaps the generals who must overthrow him are the same ones who planned the strategy for the mother of all wars."

A number of younger professors came by to meet and talk with Franklin after the talk. They were almost uniformly supportive and appreciative of the graphic nature of the presentation. More than the students, they were from the Vietnam era, still hardened by their resentment of that war. Franklin was glad they did not know how strongly he had supported the Vietnam commitment and still did. He felt it was a major factor in the Cold War, and that while it did not save South Vietnam, it demonstrated the US resolve to see the overall struggle through to its eventual end and kept nations such as Indonesia, Pakistan, the Philippines, and even India from coming under Communist control. After Vietnam, the wave of Communism in Asia definitely subsided, except in Vietnam itself, and stayed in retreat.

The journalism professors asked Franklin if he could speak to their classes while he was visiting, and he accepted. He also met and talked with the president again and the other vice presidents. Hardy had accompanied him and gotten the speech on tape. "You were great again," he said enthusiastically. "We need to get this in other colleges, maybe even Dartmouth or Harvard." Franklin arranged to attend the next football game.

They took a meandering way back to Concord, stopping in Dover and Rochester. Franklin talked to the newspaper publisher in Dover and placed an ad for the next six weeks although he felt the price was high, but only three months remained before the primary. He hoped some contributions would start to come in and decided he'd send a letter to prospective donors nationwide.

At the Concord headquarters, there were good reports, including a little money coming in. Sutton was pleased with most of his county coordinators. He felt more of them needed offices and office help in the large towns. Franklin told him to make the arrangements, especially for Manchester, the state's largest city.

Stories on his speech in Boston had appeared in both the Boston papers and in the *New York Times*. Charlie had also gotten a version in many New Hampshire papers. Franklin told Sutton of their reception at the University and said he thought that would also get good coverage. A reporter from the Portsmouth newspaper had been there and he'd give a copy to the Dover paper, along with the ad. It was an area of the state Franklin felt he needed more exposure.

He had a chance to talk privately with Susie and told her how proud he was of her efforts, which Charlie had raved about. "It's great," Susie exclaimed. "I was very nervous in my first speeches, but now I look forward to them, and the people have been awesome. Some of them remember me from my basketball-playing days, either having seen me in person or read about me. Not a single one has mentioned my senior year except to say they heard I was injured."

She smiled that startling smile that lit up the room and exclaimed, "I'm still a star in their eyes...and I owe it all to you."

"No," Franklin objected, "you owe it to yourself, with the strength of will you've shown and the basketball ability you always had. Actually you've made me a star. Nobody knew my name in most of these places a month ago. I do have an idea I'd like to discuss."

"Sure," Susie said.

"It involves LaConia High. Are you still sensitive about how you were treated there? I know you haven't been back."

Susie looked concerned. "I don't know," she said. "Some of that pain is still with me...but you know, it might do me good to go back and face it."

Franklin knew she was a trooper, but he also knew how painful the memory was of her last game and days at LaConia but thought his idea might help Susie and the campaign. "I'd like to talk to the principal about me, my family, and you attending the big Thanksgiving football game at LaConia Field. There should be a big crowd, right."

"There always was," Susie assured him, "maybe ten thousand if the team was doing well, which it is this year. I've been following it, even though I don't know any students there now."

"The announcer for the game is the LaConia sports editor who first put me on your trail, and if the principal agrees, I'm going to ask the sports editor to introduce me and my family, who are coming up for the Thanksgiving holidays, and then you, of course, as the only student who ever led LaConia to a state sports championship."

Susie looked concerned for a moment. "What if they boo?" she said with a touch of fear. "What if it brings back a bad memory for them...of Susie Slutz?"

"I'm betting the memory it will bring back to the teachers and the older students are those championship games in 1987 and the only state sports championship trophy the school has in its trophy case. And it'll bring back memories of the special player and beautiful young girl who was most responsible for winning that trophy."

"Well, I'll talk to my mother about it. I'm looking forward to meeting your family."

"My youngest daughter is about your age," Franklin said, "and she's a huge sports fan, including girls' basketball. She'll be thrilled to meet you."

The game was about three weeks away, but Franklin felt if he could make the arrangements, the presentation he had in mind would be a real public relations triumph despite a few uncertainties about it. He talked to Sutton, who thought it was a great idea, and one he'd never seen a candidate try.

A call came in a few minutes later that Franklin and Sutton felt could be a real icebreaker. It was from Underwood, the state Democratic chairman, who wanted Franklin to appear with the other candidates before a gathering of all the county chairs at a meeting in Manchester. Franklin quickly accepted. Each candidate would have a chance to address the chairmen and then mix and mingle with them. Franklin, of course, had never met most of them. This was his chance.

A busy week followed as arrangements were finalized for the appearance of the Thanksgiving Day football game and for Franklin's family to come up for the holidays.

Chapter Ten

THE THIRD REVOLUTION

We are all bound together by hope of a common future rather than by reverence for a common past... For all our millions of square miles, for all our millions of people, there is a unity in language and speech, in law and in economics, in education and in general purpose which nowhere finds its match.
—*Franklin D. Roosevelt, address on the fiftieth anniversary of the Statute of Liberty, October 28, 1936*

Franklin looked over a fund-raising letter he'd dictated to Sutton. Dictating was something he seldom did and was not good at, but the letter had come out fairly well.

Basically, it was his message as an economic liberal and a cultural conservative, with his pledge to run an economical campaign with little money spent on expensive TV ads, high-priced consultants and pollsters, but mainly with the businesses and people in New Hampshire. Sutton recommended sending the letter to ten thousand identified Democratic 1988 voters throughout the nation. Donations of one hundred dollars and less were requested.

"We might get a 5 percent response," Sutton told him, "if we're lucky. A lot of candidates have their hands in the money pie," he explained, in addition to the six or so in the New Hampshire presidential primary. Franklin and Hardy spent a few days traveling around Nashua, with several talks to civic clubs and women's groups, which Sutton had managed to add on the schedule.

The appearance before the Democratic chairpersons was on the following Tuesday. Franklin decided that he'd bear down on being a good Democrat in the New Deal mode, although he knew some of them were about as Republican as Paul Tsongas. He asked Phil Sutton to accompany him, thinking Sutton could make some contacts that would help him in organizing.

Surprisingly, several of the presidential candidates didn't show up. Jerry Brown and Bob Kerrey were among the missing. That gave more time to the others, Clinton, Tsongas, Harkin, and Franklin.

Franklin opened with one of his standard statements. "Ronald Reagan and most Republicans say government is not the solution to our problem, that government is the problem. We must argue with that idea for a good and simple reason. It's wildly not true. Our best answer is that the people are the government, and government is the ultimate expression of our overall values and needs, including our desire for a free and fair economic system.

"If the US government was the problem, and not the answer, then the United States could not have survived the challenges of the past 250 years, during which nearly every other government system in the world has failed, now including our most recent and formidable opponent, the Soviet Union. A strong federal government has been the answer ever since thirteen small, scattered, and quarrelling British colonies managed to cooperate long enough to gain their independence from the world's mightiest empire at the time.

"Those colonies then cooperated in designing a constitution that united them into a single nation and made it secure enough to go into debt to make the Louisiana Purchase, which doubled its land area but left it with a fifteen-million-dollar debt, not small change in 1803, but which was paid off in fifteen years. Then it was strong enough to build the Erie Canal, connecting the Midwest and New York City, which became the most important port and financial center in the world. It became strong enough to provide land and assistance to railroad companies to link the east and west coast across two thousand miles of wilderness and desert…and then it was strong enough and dedicated enough to withstand a deadly and costly civil war to establish in blood the principle of a single nation. We have witnessed what disunity has done to so many other ambitious republics across the world, such as the ones in South America, in the Balkans, in Germany, and even in Great Britain, now divided from Ireland and almost from Scotland. Only the United States has held firm and enjoyed the growth and progress to make it the preeminent nation in the world.

"But I want to emphasize that there was a third revolution in this country that made that possible. We generally call it the New Deal. It was the brainchild of Democratic statesmen in the 1930s and was guided by such farsighted leaders as Franklin Roosevelt, Harry Truman, and later, Lyndon Johnson.

"Roosevelt was no intellectual or grand political philosopher. He simply sat in his confined, often lonely wheelchair and cobbled together an economic system that has worked to bring more people in the nation and to an extent the world out of poverty than any of the famous or infamous isms of his time, such as communism, fascism, socialism, or even unfettered capitalism. He was an Einstein of politics, and his formula was about as mysterious—but it worked—to move more poor people to middle class, more middle class to wealthy, and more millionaires to multimillionaires.

"As Democrats, we should not be reluctant to claim credit for victory in that third American revolution, which rescued the nation from its worst economic depression and laid the groundwork for the great nation of today. There are only a few absolute economic truths in the world, and one of them is that a broad middle class is essential for a prosperous nation. In the thirty years after World War II, the US had the broadest middle class of any national entity in history, but it is shrinking under current policies, and this election may be the last chance to shift gears into forward again."

Franklin paused for a smattering of applause. He was not a mesmerizing speaker, but his passion was improving. He realized that what he had just said was almost diametrically the opposite of what Tsongas had told them a few minutes earlier.

There were a few questions, mostly for Tsongas, who apparently knew many of the chairpeople, and some for Clinton, who was still leading in the polls. He looked confident and pleased; Tsongas looked worried. Franklin's attack on his basic beliefs were getting to him. He nodded briefly on leaving; Clinton and Harkin both stopped to chat. Clinton was charming as usual and wanted to know how Franklin felt he could get further without support from his home state of Georgia, which Clinton felt he had locked up.

"There's three months until this primary," Franklin answered. "I've come from nowhere to somewhere in two months, so who knows?"

Clinton put a large hand on his shoulder. "You've got guts," he said.

"We all do," Franklin said, "or we'd be sitting at home watching football games."

The Manchester newspaper had covered the meeting and put a story on an inside page the next day. It centered on Tsongas's call for "more sacrifice and a balanced budget" and indicated he seemed to capture the mood of the group to move the party further right. Franklin's review of Democratic policies and the role of the federal government through the years were dismissed in a short paragraph, and he knew that would be the story AP carried.

He thanked Underwood for the invitation. "Some of these guys are from Republican areas," Underwood explained, "and at the local level, they'll go with the prospective winners who'll be the most conservative Democrats. You and Harkin probably scared them."

"I haven't made it a secret that I'm running as a New Deal Democrat. What part of the New Deal would they like to repeal?"

Underwood laughed. "Just the high taxes," he admitted, "but none of the middle class benefits."

"I guessed as much. I think some of them got my message."

The trip was definitely worthwhile for Sutton. A congenial type, he had met several chairmen who agreed to help him form campaign groups in their districts, especially in the Nashua and Manchester areas. "They liked your talk," he told Franklin. "They don't hear that from the other candidates, and they think you're cutting into

Tsongas's support that was mainly based on his familiarity. They'd never really heard what he was saying before, and they didn't like it."

Back at the office, Franklin had a surprise call. It was from Kathleen Kelley in California. She'd been a reporter on the daily paper he owned and operated in Opelika, Alabama. He hadn't heard from her in years.

"Hi," she said, "I've been reading about you. I can't believe you're running for president. Do you need any help?"

"Kathleen, is that really you, Kathleen Kelly that youthful reporter who went on to become a political figure in Alabama?"

She laughed. "It's me," she said, "about twenty-five years older but still interested in politics." They chatted for a few minutes, and before he knew it, Franklin had offered her a job to come to New Hampshire as his communications director. She'd worked in TV and radio and been the assistant state director for information and tourism in Alabama after she left the Opelika paper. But that was just part of Kathleen's background, which would have made a fascinating novel itself. He had one of his notions about Kathleen when she was a beginning reporter. She had that star quality, different from Susie's, but definitely star. They talked it over, and she agreed to come and see him about a definite arrangement in early December.

Franklin put down the phone in some dismay. He hadn't talked to Kathleen in years, but their conversation sounded as if they'd talked last week. The salary would be high for his staff but still less than she was making in California. She was married but separated and wanted to get back to the southeast even if it was by way of New Hampshire.

Chapter Eleven

THE THANKSGIVING
FOOTBALL GAME

*The American people have a good habit—the habit
of accomplishing the impossible.*
   *—Franklin D. Roosevelt, address at
   Soldier Field, Chicago, October 28, 1944*

I t was past mid-November now, and Franklin didn't feel he was
getting his message out strongly enough. He had now placed
twelve columns as advertising messages in at least one copy of
nearly every weekly newspaper in the state and in several dailies. But
after years of writing columns, he was under no delusions about their
impact on voters, nor did he really have much faith in TV commercials. They just cost more. He and his associates had now been in
more than one hundred of the townships, in every county and most
of the cities. He was still making several speeches a week, but he
knew he wasn't seeing as many people as Bill Clinton, for example,
who had a far better organized campaign. At that moment, a newspaper was tossed on his desk. It was a recent *New York Times*, which had
a long story inside on his "Darkest Horse Campaign," including his
talks at the university on Iraq and the talk in Manchester. His spirits
lifted as he read the accounts. *This candidate is really saying something
different,* he thought, *and hey, that's me.* Soon he had three requests

for TV interviews, including one in Boston. Maybe they could lead to a national TV interview, he thought.

That night he gathered the entire small staff together for dinner in a dining room at the hotel. He thought a little camaraderie would be good for them, and he also wanted to review their plans for the next few weeks.

He decided to make his remarks very personal. "I've talked to Hardy a lot about how life was growing up during the 1930s. I'm sure Charlie has some memories of those years also although he grew up in New Hampshire, and I grew up in Georgia, which had been in a Depression ever since Oglethorpe landed in Savannah in 1733, so we didn't notice as much.

"Actually, the difference in living conditions in Georgia was whether you lived in a rural area or in an incorporated city. I was lucky enough to live in LaGrange, an incorporated city of about eighteen thousand and also the home of a large textile manufacturer, which meant that by 1930, the year I was born, we had electricity, indoor plumbing, paved streets, and were in walking distance of the downtown stores, with movie theater, the church, stores, and cafés. We did have to make fires in the fireplaces, which meant bringing in coal and wood, but compared to houses just a couple of miles away outside the city limits, the house I lived in was years ahead of those in the rural areas. Some of them didn't get electricity until the Rural Electrical Administration, REA, extended lines to rural areas in 1948, thirty years later.

"The house I lived in was small. I shared a bedroom with my grandmother most years, but it was only a block or two to the main business section. LaGrange had two ten-cent stores, Kress and McCrory's, two department stores, and several pharmacies. Of course, most important, it had three theaters, one of which was in easy walking distance of my house. I've told Hardy a lot of this and how being a kid in the 1930s wasn't too bad in a small town, even without TV and most of the time without a car. LaGrange was also lucky to have a Carnegie library, as they were called. They had been financed by Andrew Carnegie, the steel magnate.

"I was a reader, and there was a lot to read for kids in the thirties, such as the newspaper comic strips, Big Little Books, the Oz books, a new one every year, which was usually better than the original one. Also during most of 1930s, jobs were fairly easy to find in LaGrange, either from New Deal agencies such as the PWA, the WPA, and the TVA, or of course, the textile mills.

"The New Deal, which as I've explained, was the third American Revolution, after the original one and the Civil War, was not easy to enact or sell to the public. Americans were schooled in the philosophy of individual endeavor and private enterprise, and although the government had done a lot for people since the nation started, many people didn't realize it, just as they still don't. The New Deal was based on the philosophy that the government should assume responsibility for the welfare of all the people, not just for businesses, which it had always helped. Of course, this idea of a broader-based government found a more receptive audience in the 1930s, when nearly half the workforce was jobless, companies had lost much of their stock value, and many families, poor and rich, were moving from farms to urban areas, looking for work.

"That was the other huge transition taking place, the end of the Agrarian age. When Franklin Roosevelt became president in 1933, his administration launched programs that increased prices for farm products, even if it meant killing little pigs and plowing under crops. Banks were placed under stricter control, and a series of projects such as the Tennessee Valley Authority, were started to recover land and harness water power. One of the first groups to provide jobs for the young unemployed youths was the Civilian Conservation Corps, which hired them to restore forests and also to sweep leaves, for which they were criticized, but the result was not only jobs but a better countryside. Jack Hardy's father was a CCC worker, getting one dollar a day with two-thirds of his earnings sent home to help his family.

"I don't mean to belabor the point, but explaining the New Deal and what it meant to the nation and to the world is essential to my campaign. The reason I call myself a New Deal Democrat is because the New Deal wasn't just something that happened in the

1930s. It's still happening. It was a concept, a set of ideas, and more important, a set of ideals, that are alive and need to be extended to the problems we face today and to nations in the world that are in conditions worse than the US faced in the Great Depression. It was faith and hope that made the New Deal programs possible. They were not easy to sell in the depths of Depression. As I've said earlier, even Roosevelt, a Hudson River Valley aristocrat, was a reluctant New Dealer. Few of his close friends had the same instincts. He was called a traitor to his class, and I believe the conditions he saw in his visits to Warm Springs in rural Georgia, gave him a clearer picture of the despair many Americans faced. As a gentleman farmer at heart, he was especially concerned for people who depended on farming for their livelihood, and he was appalled at how most tenant farmers lived in Georgia. Most of them were Negroes and got little sympathy or help from the government. Farming in Georgia at that time mainly consisted of growing cotton, but cotton had been hit hard in the 1920s by an infestation of boll weevils, traveling from South America into Texas and then into middle Georgia, where Roosevelt visited.

"The stock market crash of 1929 didn't affect land-owning Georgians as badly because few of them owned stocks and bonds, but the decline in cotton farming and prices had cut land prices to seventy-five cents an acre. For the tenant farmers, who worked land for larger farmers and got a small amount of the earnings, if there were any earnings, life was even worse.

"Years later, a tenant farmer, born in 1930, same year as I was, wrote, 'There was no money at all. There were no school buses. I walked three miles to school on dirt roads. Everyone had privies in the backyard. My family was lucky because our well was on the back porch. Mama made cornbread, salted meat, and we ate biscuits three times a day. Rabbits were caught in traps around the house, so we ate a lot of fried rabbit.'

"A white farmer's child born about that time recalled slightly better conditions: 'You ate what you could grow. Corn was prepared a lot of different ways, and we had eggs, butter, and milk. We raised four or five hogs and salt cured one each year. For Christmas we children got an apple, an orange, raisins, and walnuts. I didn't even know what a dollar looked like till I was a teenager, but we did have running water from the branch.'

"It was that sort of life and culture that convinced Roosevelt the government had to create programs to help poorer Americans have better lives. Those programs, under the overall name of the New Deal, rescued the capitalist system, not to mention creating better lifestyles for all Americans, and eventually creating a nation strong enough to prevail over older nations such as Germany and Japan, who had a head start on industrial development."

Most of his small group had finished their meals and drinks, but they had been attentive. Even though they were basically Democrats, they had never grasped the full difference in Democrats and Republicans and what the New Deal had meant for the country. Franklin wanted them informed to the point they would convey his policies as effectively as he did, or even better since they were younger. Even Charlie, about his age, was a recent convert from Republican philosophy.

The early effects of Roosevelt's programs were remarkable, Franklin continued. By 1934, the stock market had recovered half of its 1929 value; agriculture was emerging from a years-long Depression. Employment rose significantly, but as the economy recovered, opposition to the New Deal arose among business leaders, who complained that too much power was being concentrated in the federal government. They charged that some New Deal programs were "socialistic and undermined free enterprise, democracy and personal choice." In particular they complained that the federal debt had increased dramatically under Roosevelt and that spending should be reduced.

Roosevelt was not immune to the criticism. He was a politician and had actually spoken out against deficit spending by the Herbert Hoover administration. So in his 1937–1938 federal budget, he recommended a reduction in spending. WPA projects were put on hold and its payroll reduced accordingly; pump priming from other government funds were also reduced. By December, the stock market wiped out all the gains it had made since 1935. At the same time the Social Security tax on payrolls had gone into effect, taking $2 billion a year out of the consumer economy. From Labor Day until Christmas 1937, employment dropped by two million workers, bringing on cries of a Roosevelt depression from most of the same people who had urged him to cut spending.

"The president called Congress into special session, but it adjourned without passing any of the measures he recommended. Republicans, with the support of southern Democrats, who had always been leery of the New Deal, sensed a chance to strike back at its most costly programs, which were the very ones that had brought the nation out of the Great Depression.

"It's late, so I think I'll say to be continued and tell you later how the mightiest New Dealer of them all helped Roosevelt rescue the nation from its economic retreat."

They all retired, and Franklin and Hardy conferred on a pre-Thanksgiving trip he wanted to make to the western part of the state and then into Vermont.

"You were in great storytelling mood tonight," Hardy said. "Where do you get all of that stuff?"

"From books. More books were written about the Roosevelt administration and the New Deal than any period in US history. You just have to look for the good parts, which aren't as well-known."

"And who was this mightiest New Dealer of all?" Hardy asked.

Franklin smiled enigmatically. "Wait till next week. I don't want to tell the story but once."

They left early the next morning and took I-89 to Lebanon, stopping on the way in several townships they'd missed earlier. In Lebanon, a town of about ten thousand, they tracked down the Democratic chairman they'd met earlier at the meeting in Concord and gave him some more campaign brochures. He was noncommittal on his support but still seemed open if Franklin became a serious contender. Franklin said he understood but asked him to look at the polls near Primary Day.

From there they proceeded to Randolph, Vermont, some fifty miles north in what was known as the White River Valley. Franklin wanted to visit the weekly newspaper editor there, whom he had long admired. He'd never met him but had picked up a Vermont magazine on one of his tours of New England, which featured an article about the editor. Franklin had called ahead to make sure the editor, Dick Drysdale, would be available, and they found him doing what he usually was doing, putting together the week's edition of the *White River Valley Herald*. It was Vermont's second-largest weekly in circulation. Drysdale had bought it from his father when he was twenty-six.

"You're doing what I did for most of my early career," Franklin told him, "putting out a newspaper. I never found anything I'd rather do."

They chatted for a while about the newspaper business. Drysdale's paper covered fifteen towns in the area around Randolph. What had impressed Franklin about Drysdale was the philosophy he had expressed in the magazine article.

"I think of the *White River Herald* as something that has tied the region together and connected groups of people within the towns," he had written. The *Herald* functioned not as a watchdog or mover-and-shaker but as a facilitator, communicator, and neighbor.

That was generally Franklin's own view of newspapers. He had never been a strong crusader although he had taken clear positions usually trying to do what Drysdale had expressed: helping to create communities, which would see the newspaper as the link that bound the people to common interests. "We must have realistic assessments of our problems," Drysdale had written in that five-year-old article, "and suggest solutions with respect to all the players involved. That is the kind of climate a newspaper should create."

"I think you were on to something," Franklin told him, "and that's still the role weekly newspapers can play into the digital future."

Franklin said he'd like to run one of his ads in the White River Herald for five weeks and included some points Drysdale had made in his article. "I've met a good many people running for office and they're not rascals. In general they are fine folks, with a sincere interest in improving the lives of Vermonters. Insulting politicians is an amusing game as long as we are not serious about it, but in the long run if we lose respect for our citizen politicians and the political process we won't have any of them to kick around anymore. And we need them. The trouble with newspaper conglomerates is that they have no knowledge of the product and the community. When a plastics company in Central Vermont is purchased by a big firm, which is then gobbled up by an oil company, how much interest will the resulting parent company have in producing plastics in Vermont? How much interest will that company have in the long-term future of the little firm in Vermont or its workers or the small community which depends on it for employment? How much adversity will it tolerate, how many ads will it run?" Drysdale had written.

"On the Falkland Islands War: A single hostile action, the sinking of the General Belgamo [a British ship] has already cost a number of lives equal to the entire populations of the Falkland Islands. This startling fact demonstrates how in this era of enormous weaponry the weapons of war are grotesquely out of scale with its purposes. A war costing hundreds of deaths and millions of dollars, fought over an inhospitable home for 1800 sheep herders is going to make all the participants look tragically foolish in the history books."

These ideas expressed by a weekly editor in Vermont so clearly expressed Franklin's own views that he had reprinted them in his papers, feeling that he could not improve on them. The observation on the Falklands predated and reflected his own view of the much costlier war in the Persian Gulf. Sadly, he noted, history had been kinder to the culprits than Drysdale expected. Britain's Margaret Thatcher became the most popular prime minister since Winston Churchill, perhaps more popular since he lost his next election. Who really controls the Falklands today, he wondered.

"These are great editorials," he told Drysdale, "with more perspective than anything I saw in the large dailies and written, I'm sure, with the pressure of getting out the week's edition."

"Well," Drysdale remarked, "I'm appreciative of that kind of praise, which is seldom given from such a knowledgeable source. What is it you want?"

Franklin chuckled. "A nice editorial on my views would be helpful, if you are so inclined, and then some support for my candidacy in the Vermont primary if I'm still in the race. Also any advice you'd like to lend."

"That's cheap enough," Drysdale said, "plus, I appreciate the ads. Let's be in touch closer to the primary, and I'll do what I can. Here's the name of a fellow you should contact in Vermont. He's the congressman from Burlington, Bernie Sanders. I think he'll support you, and he's very popular statewide, even though he calls himself a Socialist."

Franklin winced. "I've been called that myself, but you mean he'd actually run as a Socialist?"

"Yes, but he always wins. Here's his card."

Hardy arranged to get Drysdale's paper at the Concord offices and send him future speeches. As they left, Franklin felt gratified at the time spent. He always enjoyed talking to other newspapermen, and Drysdale was a likable one.

Hardy wasn't driving especially fast, and Franklin realized he had questions that were bothering him. "You keep talking about supply-economics and demand-side economics, but the other Democrats aren't saying much about either of them, and I'm not sure the people understand what you are talking about. Is the difference that important?"

"Absolutely," Franklin answered emphatically. "As I've said, supply-economics was a theory developed by the Republicans as an excuse to cut taxes even deeper on the highest earners. Basically, supply-side is the ability of the rich to produce more products and put them out for sale. Demand-side is the ability of more consumers to buy the products the supply side provides. Of the two, the demand siders are the most important because when people don't buy things because they don't have enough spending money, the supply-siders are left with a lot of products they can't sell, and subsequently they close some of their plants, and a lot of workers are left with no jobs.

"A great early example in the US of both the most successful supply-sider, who later became a good example of a demand-sider, was Henry Ford, an automobile mechanic who probably didn't think much about his economic philosophy but faithfully fulfilled it. His first automobile company went broke because Ford spent too much time tinkering with design and mechanical techniques. Ford recognized his problems and came up with a plan to build each car as a unified machine and each one unchanged from start to finished car. He called it the Model T, and it was built by an assembly line. The first Model T in 1908 sold for $850, which was about a third of the price of other cars then on the market. The surge of income from sales allowed Ford to build a new factory, with all the innovations he had developed for the Model T. In the new factory, with the assembly line concept, a Model T could be assembled in ninety-three minutes. In the old plant, it had required twelve hours.

"With the assembly line process, the price of a new Model T soon dropped to $300, putting it in range of millions of more customers. Until the Model T, owning a car in the US was a luxury, limited mainly to the wealthy, and most of the producers, such as Ford's stockholders in his original company, were committed to the idea of a car designed to the buyer's exact demands. Ford had argued with his own shareholders, who still wanted to make luxury, more expensive models. He was convinced that his single model, in any color you wanted as long as it was black, was the way to increase the use and ownership of cars, and he was right. He was the ultimate supply-sider. By 1920, half of all cars in the US were Model Ts. Ford and his stockholders were making so much money they didn't know what to do with it. But they had put the nation on wheels, generating the need for paved highways, and all the other changes in people's habits and needs as cars replaced horses and buggies.

"Ford had happy workers because they believed in him, and he went on the floor to talk and encourage them, but the average pay was only $2.30 a day for most of them. Also, the turnover was greater than Ford believed practical for good production. The assembly line process required dedicated workers.

"So in 1913, Ford became the first great demand-side economist when he doubled the hourly wage at all his plants from $2.30 to $5.00 a day. He said he wanted the workers building his cars to be able to afford to buy one. His decision alarmed the business community, which operated on the theory that labor costs should be kept as low as possible, while keeping prices as high as the market would tolerate. Ford was called a traitor to his class, as Franklin Roosevelt would be called thirty years later when he enacted a minimum wage for most workers. The Wall Street Journal, then as now the mouthpiece for business and the Republican Party went further, calling Ford's actions blatantly immoral and an economic crime.

"But it worked. Other businesses were forced to raise their wages to compete. In helping the working class to become demand-siders, Henry Ford pioneered mass consumption in the US, which is how it became the driving economic force in the world."

"So old Henry Ford was a friend of the working man," Hardy remarked skeptically. "I always thought of him as a billionaire who was part of the Gilded Age."

"No, he actually played a role in bringing the Gilded Age to an end. An anecdote told about his grandson, Henry Ford II, who thirty years later became president of the Ford Company, illustrates a significant reason why the economy is not working as well today," Franklin explained. "Ford II was showing Walter Reuther, head of the autoworkers, through his new and modernized plant, and he pointed to a large computer. 'You see that machine, Walter,' Ford reportedly said. 'It can do the work of one hundred of your workers.'

"'Maybe so,' Reuther replied, 'but how many Fords can it buy?'

Franklin looked at Hardy solemnly. "That sums up the problem plaguing much of US business today. How many Fords can people buy who can't find jobs, or whose wages have been cut to compete with workers in countries such as China or the Philippines or even Mexico?"

"And a lot of them decided to buy Toyotas and Volkswagens," Hardy said bitterly. "Americans have become convinced that foreign cars are cheaper and better made. Do you think that's true?"

"Well, I never bought any cars except Fords, Chevrolets, or Plymouths, or other models from their plants, and I sure can't complain about my Lincolns. I look on buying from US-based companies as a form of patriotism, but apparently a lot of Americans don't feel that way."

The next day was a very special one for Franklin. He had not seen his family for nearly two months, the longest period he and wife, Jean, had been separated in their thirty-eight-year marriage. He was also particularly anxious to see his five-year-old granddaughter and two-year-old grandson, whom he was sure had become amazing little people in the past three months.

Franklin, Hardy, and Susie went to the Manchester airport to greet them and make introductions. Altogether there were Jean; son Tim and his wife; daughter April, her husband, and the two grandchildren; and his youngest daughter, Lara. The kids were delighted to see the light snow that had fallen the night before, and they all exclaimed over the view of New Hampshire as they flew in from New York. Franklin turned the younger members of the family over to Hardy and Susie, while he and Jean took a second car to Concord, where he had rooms for all at the motel.

"You still look great," he told his wife, who was sixty-two but didn't look a day over forty-five. She still kept her hair as black as it was when they first met and her complexion had always been as smooth and soft as a young girl's. He was very proud of her and glad to have her presence. "So much has happened," Franklin said. "Incredibly, I'm in the race and haven't spent much money yet."

"That reminds me," Jean said worriedly, "will we have any personal money left after the campaign and you go back to being an unemployed newspaperman?"

Franklin grimaced. "Now, you've got to enjoy the adventure. We've had a lot of them, and they all turned out pretty well." He reminded her that they were flat broke the week after they got married and had to pay for the ceremony and reception from their own salaries, which were eighty dollars and eighty-five dollars a week at the time, hers the largest. "This is our greatest adventure ever, and it's a comfortable one," he stressed, remembering he and Hardy's discussion about adventure being "discomfort viewed from a distance."

None of the children had ever been to New England, and they all found it enchanting but cold. "It's really cold," their granddaughter, Kristen, murmured as they unloaded at the motel. Actually it was only thirty degrees, not much colder than some November days in Georgia, but Franklin was concerned about the football game temperature, although the game was due to start at 11:00 a.m., so the crowd could get home for Thanksgiving Day dinner.

The big Thanksgiving Day football game was not as prevalent as it had been a few years earlier, but LaConia and nearby Franklin, of all places, played their final game each year on that day, and this year's game between the two old rivals was supposed to be a good one and would decide the region championship. That worked out perfectly for Franklin's plans, and the sports editor, who was also the game announcer, was agreeable to the role he'd play.

The family had a big dinner at the motel that night and Franklin caught up on events in Georgia. He and Jean had attended the first two University of Georgia games in early September, and the team was having a good season.

Charlie joined them the next morning and took some members on a short tour of the area before the game. Franklin arranged with the LaConia principal for seats on the second row at midfield. The stadium was not large, with most of the seats on the LaConia side and only bleachers on the visitors' side, which were all filled. Franklin, the opponent, was only twenty miles away.

Franklin had gone over the proposed half-time program with the band leader, the two principals, and the sports editor / announcer but had not told any of his group what was planned. The game was closely contested throughout the first half with LaConia scoring on a ten-yard pass for a 7–0 halftime lead.

After the bands performed, the announcer said a special presentation would be made on the near sideline and asked for the crowd to quiet down. He invited Franklin, his group, and school officials to come down from the stands.

"We are pleased to have with us this afternoon some distinguished visitors from Georgia," he said, "including Thomas Alexander Franklin, who assures me he has no connection to Franklin High nor any relationship he knows to Benjamin Franklin, although he considers old Ben to have been the greatest Founding Father. He will be a candidate for the presidential nomination in the Democratic primary in February. But he is with us today not as a candidate but to make a presentation to a young lady most of us remember and who is now a valuable assistant in his candidacy for president. His family is also here from Georgia to celebrate Thanksgiving in New Hampshire, and I hope you can meet them after the game."

Susie looked a little apprehensive, but Hardy patted her on the back and whispered this was all good. "Our honoree is the former LaConia High student who led the school to the only state sports championship in its long history—Ms. Susie Schultz, who was named the most valuable player in the 1987 Girls basketball tournament and was voted the school's outstanding student-athlete in 1988…let's give her a big hand for making all LaConia students and alumni champions for a season."

The announcer had calibrated the announcement just right, and the crowd rose to its feet cheering, even the ones on the Franklin side, as Susie, looking stunned, finally stood and waved. Her mother, also present, was weeping visibly, and Franklin, Hardy, and Charlie felt a few tears trickle down their cheeks. The principal then presented Susie with the trophy she hadn't received three years earlier.

Incredibly it all came together, and Susie realized that what these younger students and their parents remembered about her was her remarkable feats on the basketball court and in the classroom.

As they left the field, Susie's mother grasped Franklin's hand and whispered, "I can't ever thank you enough for what you've meant to Susie. Her life is totally changed, and she's as dedicated in this campaign as she used to be on the basketball court. It's been a miracle. Today was just the cream on the cake. For a long time I thought Susie was totally lost. You found her."

"No," Franklin said gently. "She found herself. She'd just been hiding like most of us do sometimes."

The temperature actually warmed up a degree or two in the second half, and LaConia won the game 13–7 with a late touchdown, making it a great Thanksgiving Day for the school, the town, for the Franklin campaign, and Susie. "Okay, gather your coats, we've got another big stop tonight in Concord," Franklin said. That was a Thanksgiving feast for the city's poorer residents, sponsored each year by area merchants. Franklin had made a $5,000 donation, which got his name high on the list of sponsors. He figured he was the biggest sponsor, which was fine with him. There was a large crowd of townspeople, some poor, some just coming by to eat and paying their own way. There was turkey and all the trimmings, and Franklin, his family, and campaign workers met and mixed with several hundred, passing out brochures and urging them to vote in the primary, preferably for Franklin. A lot of photos were taken.

Back at the motel bar, the visitors got to hear some campaign war stories. Jean said she couldn't believe the reception they'd gotten, and the children were all excited when the snow began to fall again.

Charlie sent a photo and article about the halftime events to all the weeklies in the state. He felt a lot of them would need items for their large post-Thanksgiving Day editions.

Franklin was pleased the next day to see that the Concord paper carried photos of him and his two grandchildren at the turkey dinner. Both five-year-old Kristen and two-year-old Stephen were very photogenic. The *Manchester Leader Tribune* carried a short article about the game on the sports page, as he expected, but nothing else.

But there was nothing at all about the other candidates in the papers he saw that day while all the other dailies carried a photo and article about the award to Susie. "Where are the other candidates?" he asked Phil Sutton.

"Probably making phone calls asking for money," he replied briskly.

"Okay, we'll send out another mailing this week, concentrating on New York, with a copy of that talk I made last week to the Democratic chairs."

"I'd say send one hundred thousand at least with a little design and photos, which is going to cost a lot," Sutton said.

"Let's do it," Franklin said. "I've got some unique ideas for December."

Chapter Twelve

THE ANNOUNCEMENT

*The royalists of the economic order have conceded
that political freedom was the business of the government, but they have maintained that economic
slavery was nobody's business.*
— *Franklin D. Roosevelt,*
Democratic Convention, June 1936

T he family stayed through Sunday, with a trip to Boston for
some shopping, but the big event was on Saturday afternoon, when Franklin decided to make a formal announcement of his candidacy. He wanted all the family around for that but
still kept it low-key. He chose Concord over going back to Georgia
because he still felt his showing in New Hampshire would decide the
game and thought a victory there was possible, depending on what
the other candidates did.

He discussed the idea of a public announcement of the candidacy with Phil Sutton, who thought it was a good idea. "You've been
running for more than two months," he said, "and an announcement
will make it sound as if you're really serious and give some credence
to the folks working for you."

On Friday they'd contacted his friend who was editor of the
Atlanta newspapers and another friend who was publisher of the

Columbus newspaper. Those were the largest papers in Georgia, with Atlanta the largest in the southeast.

Franklin also talked to his media friends in Athens, his current hometown, about sending a reporter and photographer to cover the announcement. All of them were willing but a little surprised. He assured them the campaign would pay expenses when allowed. Atlanta rejected the expenses offer, but Athens and Columbus accepted with conditions. The announcement was scheduled for 2:00 p.m. Saturday. Charlie was getting the word out in New Hampshire, and despite the short notice and post-Thanksgiving weekend, a goodly group of media people committed.

Franklin spent Friday putting together his announcement and calling a few reporters he'd met recently in Boston, Nashua, and at several TV stations and cable services. He especially wanted coverage in Portsmouth with its connections in Maine.

"We probably should have planned this earlier," Sutton decided, "but it needs to be done and preferably with all of your family on hand. There may not be much of a crowd."

But as with other poorly planned events of the campaign, this one turned out surprisingly well. The announcement ceremony was held on the state capitol grounds in Concord. The day was cold but clear, and all the media people and several friends from Georgia showed up. Also on hand were lots of Christmas shoppers in Concord who came by to see what the excitement was about. Franklin was surrounded on a small platform by family and staff, and he knew that the narrow lens of the TV cameras and the close focus of newspaper cameras would make the crowd appear much larger.

The visitors from Georgia made him a bit self-conscious. Most of them didn't know he was actually running. Only his closest acquaintances had followed news of his venture into New Hampshire. The Georgia media, especially Atlanta, were not only shocked but a little disgruntled that a colleague rather than a politician was suddenly part of a story, and they were just officially finding out about it. Franklin asked Charlie to introduce him since he was his most obvious New Hampshire connection and had heard him make the most recent campaign speeches.

"I appreciate all of you being here today," Franklin began hesitantly. "I've actually been campaigning for more than two months, feeling my way along to see if it made any sense for me to become a full-fledged candidate in the presidential primary in February. This week we decided it was only fair to tell all the people in New Hampshire who we've met and have voiced their interest that they aren't wasting their time and interest. So today, I'm formally announcing that I will enter my name for the Democratic primary ballot on February 18, and if the voters of New Hampshire give me a vote of confidence, the campaign will move on and upward, going to Georgia just three weeks later for the primary there."

Applause and cheers greeted the announcement, and Franklin put his arm around Jean and the grandchildren for a few shots he thought would play well. He outlined the basic campaign promises he'd been making: cutting the payroll tax, repealing the 1986 income tax bill, opposing NAFTA, assisting Russia in its transition from Communism to democracy, and generally seeking peaceful solutions to global disputes. He also promised to raise the minimum wage, linking it to the cost of living and letting New Deal principles guide him in making the economy stronger and expanding the middle class. Those were simple and brief talking points he felt would get across to the small audience and could be absorbed by the media people on hand. The day was too cold for a long speech, especially for the visitors from Georgia. But he felt compelled to explain why he had become a candidate.

"This year offers a unique opportunity in all of history to develop and promote the means for peace and prosperity not just for the United States but for the entire world, and the United States must lead. Never has one nation been so dominant in military power and economic power as the United States is today. That is both a great achievement and a great responsibility and, most of all, an opportunity we dare not ignore. What we do in the next four years could decide the fate of the world for the next one hundred years. I had heard no candidate clearly extolling that opportunity, that challenge, and I hope more of them will do so rather than being caught up in the narrow confines of budget-balancing and minor disputes between midget nations with midget leaders, such as Saddam Hussein."

Charlie handed Franklin a sheet of paper. It was a news release just off the wire. Franklin held up his arms and asked for attention. "I've just been given the latest primary poll figures which will be released for Sunday's newspaper and newscasts, and for the first time, they show Thomas A. Franklin in double numbers at 14 percent, behind Clinton, Tsongas, and Kerrey, but ahead of Harkin, Brown, and the rest of the field."

A loud cheer went up from the crowd, especially the small contingent of campaign employees. The media reps from Georgia looked mystified. "After today, Franklin's figures should go up more," Charlie announced, "and there are still nearly three months until the primary."

Franklin walked with some of his friends from Georgia to catch a plane back to Atlanta. The family stayed over until Sunday, giving him a chance to discuss with them setting up campaign offices in Athens, Columbus, and Atlanta. Son, Tim, and youngest daughter, Lara, were both out of college and still working for the newspaper company, which had now been sold. Middle daughter, April, had her hands full with two young children but agreed to see what she could do about an Atlanta office since she lived in the suburbs. Sutton talked to all of them about the mechanics of getting started. He was glad to see some activity planned beyond New Hampshire.

The official announcement of Franklin's candidacy had gotten good publicity, with the Boston newspapers and the *New York Times* carrying articles and photos and the publicity in Georgia newspapers better than he expected. Suddenly, he was considered a candidate to be contended with, but the other candidates didn't exactly know how to contend with him. He could no longer be ignored but was too elusive and unknown to make a traditional target. The worst thing that could be said about him was obvious: he was not a politician, which wasn't all bad, and he had no record. But he had written hundreds of columns and editorials on a broad range of issues over the past forty years, and opponents had begun to search those for damaging statements they were sure he'd put in print or uttered.

196

The following day, the small staff increased to six with a couple of professionals sent by Jody Powell. Also, just in the time of need, Kathleen Kelley arrived. She was ready to go to work, and she made an immediate impression at the Concord office. Now in her early forties, Kathleen was impossible to ignore. She still was drop-dead beautiful, with a great figure, jet-black hair, and flirtatious manner. But she had matured while maintaining an easy and engaging manner. He scanned her résumé and saw that she had worked both on newspapers and in TV in California, including a stint as a producer. She had also continued to be involved in political campaigns as she was in Alabama. Franklin introduced her to Sutton as someone who could help immediately, and Sutton was smitten by her, as most males were. Franklin noticed that her résumé didn't include some of the most interesting aspects of her career, but he already knew them.

He sat reminiscing about the first time he met Kathleen. She was still a college student working part-time at the Opelika newspaper when he bought it and became the publisher.

Assertive and imaginative, she just needed a little polish in her writing, but she soon became the star reporter. Her first big story was covering a scandal involving the county sheriff, who was popular but indicted and forced to resign. The paper's coverage just a few weeks after Franklin took over gave the paper an immediate surge in circulation and prestige. He had already completely redesigned the old-fashioned makeup, shifted from a wire-story-dominated page 1 to local and state news and revamped the feature section. Most importantly, he had brought a young sportswriter from the Columbus newspaper to become the sports editor and transformed the sports section into one that would be the chief source of print information on the nearby college football team at Auburn. Franklin considered Opelika and Auburn as one community. They bordered each other but had separate governments and identities, which was a problem during the entire ten years he operated the paper. As one entity, they were a metro area of nearly sixty thousand; separately they were two small towns, one industrial, the other a college community. In unity they formed the base for a quickly growing newspaper in circulation and advertising.

Kathleen was a native of the area and familiar with both towns and the college. He explained to her the situation in Concord and told her to mainly work with Sutton on publicity and contacts.

"You haven't changed a bit," she told him. "Still unorganized but with the overall goal firmly in sight."

"You haven't changed either," Franklin said. "I thought by now you'd be married with a couple of kids."

"Actually I am, but it's a long story. I'll tell you when it's time," she said.

Franklin and the staff were surprised and elated by the new poll numbers. "It's early, but you and Clinton are the only candidates with a percentage going up," Sutton said. "Tsongas and Kerrey are stalled, and the others actually lost a point or so."

Busy as they were, Franklin gathered the staff members for a late dinner Monday evening to explain why the New Deal faltered in 1937–1938 and how Roosevelt rescued it in the nick of time, with the help of the mightiest New Dealer of them all, the one he had hinted at in an earlier meeting.

Trouble for the New Deal arose first from its very success. By early 1936, the economy was recovering noticeably. The stock market was up, unemployment was down. By spring of 1937, the nation's industrial output finally pulled ahead of the 1929 levels. Opponents of the New Deal programs began loudly calling for a pullback, especially in public spending, and increases in the federal deficit. Roosevelt, even in the wake of his 61 percent popular victory in the 1936 election, was not immune to the criticism. Deep in his Hudson River Valley heart, he still yearned for balanced budgets and a more traditional approach to the economy.

Roosevelt's liberal advisers, headed by Harry Hopkins and Harold Ickes, argued what appeared to be obvious: the recovery had been achieved mainly by federal spending, which had been feeding the economy. The reality was that many people were still out of work or had low-paying jobs, and the construction industry was still sluggish outside the projects fueled by federal funds.

Roosevelt ignored a report that showed reducing the New Deal medicine would stall the economic recovery. He approved a statement in mid-1937 that the government would cut spending in an effort to balance the budget.

Franklin paused in his presentation and explained that he was reviewing events in 1937 to demonstrate how difficult it was to change political thinking even by a president as influential as Roosevelt and in a time when the nation was still emerging from its worst depression.

Secretary Ickes charged in a speech that "America's sixty richest families have resumed the efforts of the power of money against the power of the democratic instinct. As long as federal funds were used to bolster banks and businesses, there were no complaints. It was only when funds were channeled to help poorer Americans that the New Deal programs came under attack," Ickes exclaimed.

These were the early battles in the enduring dispute that continues to this very day. Roosevelt finally came to the conclusion that some large businesses had "gone on strike against the government" to thwart the New Deal. This was a theory later used in a different context by Ayn Rand in *Atlas Shrugged*, her epic book supporting unfettered capitalism, which has become a bible for today's conservatives.

"By early 1938, the Roosevelt Recession, as his opponents called it, had reduced the economy in some areas to depression levels again. Most painful, newspapers in Germany were gloating over that country's growing economy under dictator Adolph Hitler, while the US was struggling again, placing the blame on the inefficiency of democracy."

Franklin paused and told the group the bar was still open for anyone who wanted a drink. "I'd like to continue for a while because I feel it is important that you all understand the challenges the nation faced in 1937, just as it does in 1992, and the importance of dealing with the challenge." A few staffers did order drinks, and Franklin got a glass of White Zinfandel for himself.

When he resumed, Franklin reiterated that while the New Deal had planted the seeds for a different way of looking at the government's economic and cultural problems, the roots were still in shallow ground, and the opposition was growing. The banking system had been saved, the level of industrial output had risen, but the stock market had slipped back; only half as many people were unemployed as in 1932, which still left thousands in need, or as Roosevelt dramatically phrased it in his second inaugural address: "I still see one-third of the nation ill-clad, ill-nourished, and ill-housed." He was mainly talking about the Southern states, having witnessed firsthand and close up the abject poverty and living conditions in the Georgia counties around Warm Springs.

Now, in early 1938, conditions were growing worse, and his advisers were divided over whether more of the New Deal medicine was the right remedy. In an extended stay in Warm Springs that spring, Roosevelt made up his mind, and in the relative seclusion of the Little White House in Georgia, he outlined immediate steps to reverse the course and to preserve the concepts of the New Deal, which were to be even more essential a few years later in providing the funding for the massive effort required to win World War II and then later the funds for the Marshall Plan to finance the rebuilding of Europe after the war and to pay for the interstate highway system and other postwar projects in the United States.

"So 1938 was a critical test of Roosevelt and his eventual goals, even when he was hesitant and uncertain that the people and especially Congress would follow him. In those 1938 spring weeks at Warm Springs, he was at a crossroad, and he took the path less traveled by in the poetic words of Robert Frost, which was the path of more spending and ignoring the deficit.

"The stock market had fallen again in early March and Harry Hopkins and his chief assistant, Aubrey Williams, a Georgian, hurried to Warm Springs with a new spending plan. Roosevelt told them he was ready to spend again. Secretary Morgenthau, still opposed, told his staff that Hopkins had 'swamped Roosevelt during that week in Warm Springs.' The result was that on April 14, the president approved $3.7 billion in federal funds for Hopkins's WPA and Ickes's PWA, two similar but slightly different agencies, which put unemployed people to work on projects the nation truly needed, many of which are still used today, fifty years later.

"At the same time Congress began to enforce antitrust laws more stringently to prohibit monopolies that were raising prices and eliminating jobs, just as buyouts and mergers have done in the 1970s.

"The New Deal medicine quickly worked its cure again. The economy began to perk up, but it was too late to save the Democrats from a resounding defeat in the midterm congressional elections of 1938. Republicans picked up 81 seats in the 431-seat House and 8 seats in the 96-seat Senate. Democrats still held large majorities in both houses due to their sweeps in 1932 and 1936, but Congress was now dominated by Republicans and Democratic delegations from the twelve states that had formed the Confederacy. Many of the Southerners had never been enthusiastic about the New Deal, and there was lingering resentment against Roosevelt's attempt to 'pack' the Supreme Court in 1937 after it had declared several important aspects of the New Deal unconstitutional.

"So from high tide after the 1936 elections, the New Deal was at low tide after the 1938 elections with one very crucial piece of legislation still unapproved and its concept still in jeopardy. The crucial New Deal bill which had not passed was the Wage and Hour Law, which had originally been part of the National Recovery Act that was thrown out by the Supreme Court. The Wage and Hour Bill was introduced in May 1937 by Hugo Black, a senator from Alabama who would soon be named to the Supreme Court. The bill was bitterly opposed by most Southerners, who feared it would eliminate the differential in wages paid in Southern states and the higher wages usually paid in states outside the South. That differential had been a major asset for Southern states in persuading industry to move from Northern states. South Carolina's Senator Cotton Ed Smith, facing a hard reelection fight in 1938, proclaimed that 'one can see the main object of this bill is to overcome the splendid gifts of God to the South,' by which he apparently meant the means to pay less for labor, much of it done by former slaves who had been paid nothing as recently as eighty years earlier.

"The bill narrowly passed the Senate, supported by some Northern Republicans, who realized the Southerners were right. The North was at a disadvantage in low-wage industries. The House was more adamant against the bill, and oddly, labor unions opposed it, along with the Southerners, because they didn't want the government setting wage scales. The margin was close, and a turning point came on May 3, 1938, when Claude Pepper, a supporter of the wage bill, defeated an opponent by a resounding margin in a Florida primary. Pepper's vote was expected to give the bill a majority in the House, and many former opponents rushed to join him. The bill was approved on May 24, although with many weakening amendments. It established a minimum wage of twenty-five cents an hour for most workers and a forty-hour workweek, with overtime after that. Weak as it finally emerged, the bill increased pay for millions of workers, including all textile mill employees, leather workers, then based mostly in Northern states (except for a large leather plant in Buford, Georgia, which had weathered the Depression better than the rest of the state)."

Chapter Thirteen

THE MIGHTIEST NEW DEALER

I call myself a little left of center.
—Franklin D. Roosevelt, press
conference, May 30, 1944

"T he Wage and Hour Bill was the last gasp of the original New Deal, but its guidelines, concepts, and mainly its demonstration of how national unity under leadership from Washington could move the nation in a different direction were crucial for its greatest test of all: World War II, which was already exploding in the wings," Franklin emphasized to his group of campaigners.

"Okay," Hardy interrupted him. "But who was this mightiest New Dealer? Was it Harry Hopkins or Roosevelt himself?"

Franklin smiled. "No, it was someone mightier than either of them. The mightiest New Dealer was Superman, who first appeared in the June 1938 edition of Action Comics, just in time to give the New Deal a jolt when it seemed to be sagging. Although Superman was a comic strip and a fictional character, from his first adventures, it was very clear he was a New Dealer. Let me quickly admit as a child I was not aware of Superman's political leanings; it was years later in Larry Tye's brilliant book on Superman that Superman's political role became clear. Tye wrote, Superman never revealed how he voted, but during the Great Depression, he was a New Dealer, hell-bent on truth and justice. He was just the crime fighter needed to take on Al Capone and the robber barons. In his very first episode, he tackled a wife beater, saved an innocent girl from being executed, and in subsequent editions, he exposed a mutinous arms manufacturer, then an unscrupulous coal mine operator and a crooked football coach. He never read them their rights. He was a superpowered friend of the average Joe, and the rich SOBs got a boot in the rear. Those were the lessons that Depression-era America wanted to hear. They were the very lessons that Roosevelt preached in his fireside chats, but where the president spoke soothingly, Superman was neither kind nor gentle with those he considered wrongdoers.

"I'd never comprehended that side of Superman in my comic book reading days, but after seeing Tye's rendition, I went back and read reprint editions of the early Superman stories and discovered exactly what he meant. In fact, there was a caption on the title page of each Superman strip for years that described Superman as 'faster than a bullet, leaping over skyscrapers, lifting huge weights, possessing an impenetrable skin...these are the assets of Superman, champion of the helpless and oppressed in his unceasing battle against evil and injustice.'

"That caption captured the essence of the early Superman strips and, more precisely of Jerry Siegel, the young writer who created Superman in his teens but was unable to get him in print for six years. Siegel was not an artist, but he got together with another teenager in their hometown of Cleveland, Ohio, who was an artist, and the team of Jerry Siegel and Joe Shuster finally got their brainchild in print after six years of rejection. In those years, the successful comic strips were the ones in newspapers, such as Dick Tracy, Little Orphan Annie, Flash Gordon, and Buck Rogers. That was where the money was.

"Comic books as we came to know them hardly existed before Superman. There were a few that were mainly reprints from the newspapers, but only a handful were original comic strips. In fact, Superman's first comic book appearance was a collection of strips designed for a newspaper, which had to be cut and stripped together into a comic book format.

"Finally two publishers of girly magazines took a chance on Superman as the lead feature in their first venture into comic books. They were so uncertain of its success that they only printed 200,000 copies. In a couple of weeks, vendors sold 130,000, or 64 percent of them, when 30 percent was considered a success. The publishers were still unsure that Superman was the reason for the sales, and they used a reserve of old covers already on hand for the next nine monthly editions of Action Comics before putting Superman on the cover permanently in the eleventh edition.

"They should have known before then. Sales had kept climbing, and the first-year anniversary edition, Action Comics No. 13, sold 725,000 copies, on its way to an eventual monthly sale of nearly 2 million. By then Siegel and Shuster were also producing a daily comic strip, a bimonthly edition with four Superman stories, plus writing and drawing other strips for the DC comics chain. Joe Shuster had always been troubled with poor eyesight, and he drew his strips only about two inches from his eyes. Siegel was also stretched too thin. Shuster's last cover for Action was the twenty-fifth, and there is no record of him drawing another one although his style was evident. After that he concentrated on the daily strip.

"Siegel had to turn over some of the writing to his assistants, and the changes showed. The New Dealer Superman of the first two years slowly changed into the more fantasized hero who fought brilliant scientists such as Luthor and fantasy-world villains. Superman began avoiding such common foes as real-world bad guys who dominated his first two years. The timing was right as the Depression had abated, and world war was the gravest threat.

"In those early issues of Actions Comics, Superman was poorly drawn from a technical standpoint with faces often barely discernable, but Shuster always gave his panels a distinct impression of fast-moving action. Superman never seemed to be in repose. Lois Lane was surprisingly sexy for the comic books with skirt slightly above her knees and shapely legs.

"In one of the earliest Superman episodes, he kidnaps the leaders of two warring armies and brings them together in a field. 'What do you want with us?' one leader demands. 'I've decided to end this war by having the two of you fight it out between yourselves,' Superman answers. 'Go ahead, start fighting, or I'll clean up on both of you.' 'But why would we fight?' the other leader asks. 'We're not angry at each other.' 'Then why are your armies fighting?' Superman demands. 'I don't know. Can you tell me?' one leader asked the other. 'No, can you?' the other replies. 'Gentleman, it's obvious to me you've been fighting only to promote the sale of munitions,' Superman says. 'Why not shake hands and make up?'

"This episode is simplistic, of course, but it aptly demonstrated the folly of war for young readers and how national leaders send thousands to their death against an enemy they neither understand nor hate and would not throw a fist at if they had to fight each other personally."

"Jerry Siegel, who was about twenty-four when he wrote this story, showed his depth of comprehension, just as he did in other scripts, which were deeper than Superman's incredible exploits.

"In recalling the pop culture of the Depression years and my own childhood—the Big Little Books, the newspaper funnies, the movie serials—I'd have to say that for a short period of years, comic books had the greatest impact of all. In small-town Georgia, we read and then traded comic books every day. They just cost a dime, but a dime was still a dime in the late 1930s, which could buy a bag of candy or a movie pass, and I imagine in the large cities, comic books were even more of a factor in what could lighten up a child's dreary everyday life.

"Whatever lessons they taught, good and bad, for the greatest generation, comic books were part of what made that generation great and helped it through a pre-TV age when money was scarce."

"I remember seeing Superman in the movies," one of the young fund-raisers commented, "but never read a Superman comic book."

"Not surprising," Franklin said. "Those comic characters from the 1940s have had remarkable staying power in various forms. My own favorite was Batman, who came out about a year after Superman. The comic book industry had been ignited by Superman, but it was Batman who became the model for the many masked crime fighters who followed. The first year of his adventures were even more poorly drawn than Superman, but Bob Kane, the artist, improved quickly and demonstrated a knack for portraying dark, shadowy, eye-catching backgrounds and quirky habits by his characters that were unique among comic illustrators. Although Bob Kane was the only credit that ever appeared on a Batman title page, Kane did not write any of the stories. They were the work of Bill Finger, another teenager. Finger was the master storyteller among early comic book writers. His plots were worthy of A. Conan Doyle, and his villains were the most memorable of that era, as proven again in the biggest grossing movie of 1989, which had Batman battling the Joker in the bleak city of Gotham, which Kane created sixty years ago.

"Batman never sold quite as well as Superman but came close. One character, Captain Marvel, actually did outsell Superman for a few months during World War II. All of the comic books, even the lamest, made money for their publishers. My favorites, after Batman, which I bought regularly into my teens, were the Fiction House comic books, Jumbo, Jungle, Fight, and Planet. As the names indicate, all except Jumbo were devoted to specific subjects. They each contained eight or nine stories in the sixty-four-page editions and gave you the most for the dime, although never developing a widely popular masked or super hero. Fiction House's most popular character was a woman, Sheena, Queen of the Jungle, obviously based on Tarzan and a remarkably durable character who ran monthly for years despite the limited area of her adventures, which was the jungles of Africa. Sheena and the other Fiction House strips were mainly drawn at the studio of Will Eisner and Sol Iger, who were actually better artists than those at Detective, DC.

"Eisner-Iger became best known for its 'good girl' art during World War II with Sheena setting the pace for a myriad of lightly clad bosomy beauties from the jungle to the most distant and coldest planets of the universe. Honestly, I hardly noticed their sexiness. Fight Comics had a series on famous boxers going back to John L. Sullivan and including Gentleman Jim Corbett, Bob Fitsimmons, Jack Johnson, Jack Dempsey, Gene Tunney, and others, which were educational in a time when boxing was still a huge sport, especially on radio."

"Did girls read comic books?" Susie asked.

"Actually, they did, but not as much as boys did. A survey in the early forties claimed that a third of comic book readers were girls, and then Wonder Woman made her debut in the January 1942 Sensation Comics and set a pattern for more female heroines in lead roles. Lois Lane, in Superman, and the Catwoman in Batman, and a number of other prominent females attracted some female readers, but I believe mostly males.

"An interesting point about Sheena was she had a male companion known only as Bob, but he always was dressed in normal male clothing, even including boots, instead of a loincloth such as Tarzan ran around in, and as Sheena did, although her loincloth covered more than Jane's in Tarzan. Bob also carried a rifle and never swung through the trees on vines."

Franklin surveyed the sleepy-looking group, who had remained attentive. "Mainly we must remember that persuading people to adopt new ideas, even for their own good, is never easy, and even Franklin Roosevelt had to overcome great obstacles but always found his true center in creating a foundation which maintained his New Deal concepts not just during his presidency but for years to come.

"Superman came along at a critical time, 1938, and set off a publishing boom that boosted the economy and brought thousands of young readers into the magazine market. Of all the pop culture fads of the Depression years, comic books made the strongest impression on me, and the characters have proven remarkably durable.

"But the dominant period of comic books was short, from the debut of Superman in mid-1938 until the end of World War II seven years later. Even in those years, comic books had to contend with the wartime paper shortage going from their original sixty-four-page standard size to fifty-six pages by 1943 and to forty-eight pages by 1945, which remained the size for years.

"The Golden Age was over, but copies of the ten-cent comic books that survived from those years grew in value, and collectors today pay thousands of dollars for well-preserved copies. Like most kids, I didn't take care of my copies, and others were lost or discarded through the years, but I did hold on to the first copy of Batman, which an aunt bought for me one Saturday night in 1940 for 0.10 cents. I've turned down offers of $2,000 or more for it."

"Why are they worth so much today?" Hardy asked.

"Original copies are scarce. Comic books were fragile, and the publishing companies ground up thousands of returns unaware they'll ever be worth even a dime. Collectors are just crazy in all fields. Poor Vincent van Gogh, the artist, died penniless, but one of his original paintings sold for $3 million last year."

"We've got a plane to catch at eleven tomorrow morning," Jean said, "and you need to be talking politics by then to somebody. By the way, I know where that first issue of Batman is, in a cellophane bag. We might need to sell it before this campaign is over." Everyone laughed, but not too heartily.

Franklin saw his family off the next day and went to the office, where he found a number of requests for appearances. "Activity is good," Phil Sutton told him, "and here's a request you'll like. It's from Dartmouth University for a talk to a large group of faculty and students next week. They particular want you to talk about your theory of demand-side economics, which they've never heard of."

"That's great. I need to talk about that, but it's not a subject that seems to keep an audience awake."

The staff was still excited about the latest polling results, which showed Franklin in the higher tier of candidates, but still a good bit behind Clinton, the leader, and Tsongas, who was dropping. Franklin had moved even with Kerrey and Harkin, both of whom were stalled.

The next day he and Hardy were on their rounds, heading for Plymouth again and some townships they had missed. On this trip, Franklin also decided to cross into Maine and place a few ads aimed at the Maine caucuses. He hoped to make contacts with publishers to help him on the strategy for caucuses, which were different from the primaries. A lot fewer voters were involved, but they were usually the people most interested in politics and therefore easier to identify and reach.

"Tell me a story," Hardy said. "They make the driving easier."

"Well, I was talking about my comic book years last night. They are still vivid in my memory. As I think I've mentioned, my father was a traveling salesman who went to small stores in the area to sell them orders from a wholesaler in LaGrange. He often came home very late at night, and I waited to see him before going to sleep. I'd worriedly look out the window the next morning, and his car still wouldn't be there, which meant he hadn't come home at all. I knew my father drank a lot, but I never asked where he was those nights or how he afforded them. And then one day he came home and told my mother and I that we were moving to Columbus and had to leave the next day.

"I was devastated since I'd never known any home except LaGrange. All my school years had been at one school. All my friends and acquaintances were there in the neighborhood, and I was so close to downtown and its stores, the theater, the church. But my mother was even more unreasonable. She seldom left her bed in those days and hadn't been out of the house in months and then only briefly. She was, for all purposes, a shut-in. She cried and screamed and claimed she was dying—not an infrequent claim—and my father was the maddest I'd ever seen him. He was always a quiet man, his emotions in check whenever I saw him. But not that day. I learned later that he had lost his job earlier in the month but had managed to get a similar job in Columbus and had arranged for my mother, grandmother, and me to live with two aunts and an uncle who'd moved to Columbus a few years earlier. 'We've got to go,' he exclaimed loudly. 'Start packing.'

"I couldn't bear the thought of going to the school to get my things and saying goodbye to my friends and teachers. I was sure I'd break down crying, so my father said he'd go for me. He told me the teacher said she probably would have cried too. So the next day we all got in the company car he had, and he drove the familiar fifty miles south to Columbus. I didn't see LaGrange again for more than ten years, when I stopped there on the way home from college."

"My family never moved from Hickory," Hardy said, "but I can imagine how bad that must have been."

"I actually never got over it, in a way. That's one reason I kept looking for small cities to live in and ended up in Athens, which had the added attraction of being where I went to college. The school I attended in Columbus was also within walking distance. It had been built in 1892. It's still in use, I think, one of the oldest schools in Georgia. I joined a fifth-grade class in October, so I was definitely the new kid in class. We lived in a large apartment house built in the 1900s as some rich family's home, but Columbus was filling up by October 1940 with soldiers and their families moving to Fort Benning, which became the largest infantry school in the world during World War II. There were two apartments on the second floor and large four bedroom apartment on the first floor, which was the one my aunts and uncle had rented. My mother, father, and I had one small room on the first floor, and my grandmother moved into the room with one of my aunts. During the war, we actually rented out two of the other rooms and a bathroom to army couples. You talk about a house with a lot of people in it, that was it, but I lay on my cot in the corner of the room with my mother and father and lost myself in my comic books and fantasies. It sounds bad today, but I don't remember it being that bad. There weren't as many children in the neighborhood as in LaGrange, however, and town was about a five-block walk, still not far, and by then I was riding a bicycle, and there was a lot more town. I think my father's weekly income got up to forty dollars a week during the war, enough to give me a dollar's allowance, which was still enough for two movies, a comic book, popcorn, and a bag of lemon drops every week."

Hardy looked at him quizzically. "How did you get from there to being a millionaire newspaper publisher?"

"Dreaming, also known as fantasizing. That's most important. Plus a lot of luck. Sometimes I did think it was just a dream not really happening to me."

"Kind of like this presidential campaign, huh?"

"Yeah, but I've thought and read about it for years."

"Well, we're sure going to need a lot of that luck, and soon," Hardy commented.

"My contact in Little Rock says to just hang in. Luck is on the way."

A couple of days later, they were on the road to Dartmouth College, chartered in 1769, one of the ten oldest colleges in the nation. Its reputation outweighed its relatively small size, but Franklin felt a speech there would gain him a measure of recognition he still lacked. As far as he knew, none of the other candidates had spoken at Dartmouth. Its location in Hanover was a short drive on I-89 from Concord. Susie and Charlie accompanied them complete with brochures and copies of a few columns.

Dartmouth's most famous alumnus was Daniel Webster, a senator and orator of the 1800s, who had represented Dartmouth in a case before the US Supreme Court when the state of New Hampshire sought to revoke Dartmouth's original charter from England's King George III and make it a state university. The court ruled that the charter was "forever," and Dartmouth remained an independent liberal arts institution for men only. The decision was acclaimed as an important step in protecting the right of private property and encouraging the development of free enterprise ventures. Most colleges at that time were affiliated and funded by religious denominations.

Having been given the subject of demand-side economics, Franklin approached the occasion with enthusiasm. In fact, he had gotten some credit for originating the term, which never became as familiar as supply-side economics, its opposite theory.

The lecture hall was large, and at least one hundred students and faculty appeared to have gathered there. Franklin began by acknowledging his appreciation to speak at a forum as prestigious as Dartmouth. Then briefly he explained that demand-side economics was simply the idea of providing enough money to the general population so they could not only pay for the essentials of daily life but also have discretionary income to buy other products and thus create a market that would encourage the supply-side to produce more products and employ more people. "There's nothing mysterious or complicated about it," he exclaimed. "It is the economic system that has built the United States, usually with help from the federal government and has pulled the nation out of all its recessions and depressions, including the Great Depression. As a consequence, a greater number of people enjoy a good livelihood and have attained the status we call the middle class.

"No nation has attained such a vigorous middle class as the United States, but statistics, the facts on the ground, show that middle class growth has retreated in the last ten years and desperately needs a political leadership that sounds a certain trumpet."

Franklin was quoting from one of his own columns, but he'd stumbled across an even stronger argument from the most prominent economic theorist in history—Adam Smith. Smith was an eighteenth-century Scottish philosopher whose book *The Wealth of Nations* was the source of modern capitalism. Smith is widely considered the greatest exponent of the free market. "Certainly, Smith's *Wealth of Nations* celebrates the free markets, but Smith also believed consumers should be the chief beneficiaries of the free market, even more than businesses," Franklin told his audience.

"Smith wrote very clearly on that point when he stated, 'Consumption is the sole end and purpose of all production, and the interests of the producer ought to be attended to only so far as it may be necessary for promoting the interest of consumers.'

"That part of Smith's philosophy is seldom emphasized, but it is the very essence of demand-side economics. Smith goes on to write in *Wealth of Nations*: 'This is precisely what the existing British system has failed to do. It puts the interest of producers and merchants ahead of that of the consumers, who want low prices and a steady supply of goods. Merchants often prefer the opposite.' He acknowledged that it is in the interest of every man to live as much at ease as he can so merchants have encouraged policies that benefit them more than consumers. He notes that while businessmen often complain of high costs for operation, they say little about high profits.

"These quotes are directly from Smith's *Wealth of Nations*, as recorded in Arthur Herman's book *How the Scots Invented the Modern World*, which I strongly recommend. Smith, in an earlier book, complained that excess concentration on commerce contracted the minds of men, causing neglect of education for other pursuits. Education deserves the most serious attention of government, he wrote. In fact, the only function Smith actually recommends for a civic institution is the creation of an education system.

"Realize, of course, that Smith was writing in Scotland more than two centuries ago, and his theory of free markets was influenced by the restraints he saw placed on it by the control of monarchs and other tyrants. He felt it was time for rulers to learn from their mistakes and let commercial society follow its own course.

"But there were limits, Smith felt, and it is those limits that are ignored by the supply-side economists of the past fifteen years in the United States. The other prominent economist I've recently studied is generally regarded as the father of an active government role in the economy. That is Maynard Keynes, who lived not far from where Smith had lived two centuries earlier. In his most significant book *The General Theory of Employment, Interest, and Money*, Keynes wrote, 'The engine of economic growth is not investment by the few but consumption by the many.'

"That is almost the exact opposite of the supply-side theory promoted by George Gilder in the 1970s in his book *How the World Works*, which mainly calls for lower taxes on so-called job creators, which Gilder sees as the wealthy and business owners.

"That theory, as David Stockman, President Reagan's first director of the budget, admitted in a series of articles in *Atlantic* magazine, was primarily an argument for reducing taxes on the wealthy while reducing services and other functions of the federal government. It was the so-called starve-the-government formula supported mainly by opponents of any government assistance. But as Stockman details at some length in his book *The Triumph of Politics*, Congress slashed taxes, mainly in the higher income brackets, but balked at cutting much spending, resulting in increasing the federal budget deficit more during the Reagan years from 1981 to 1991 than the combined deficits of all the years from George Washington's first deficit to pay for the troops who fought the Revolution until Reagan took office. You can look it up, because most Americans don't even like to admit it because the economy boomed during those years, and why shouldn't it have, since as Senator Lloyd Bentsen dramatically proclaimed in his 1988 debate with Dan Quayle, 'If you let me write two hundred billion dollars in hot checks every year, I could give you an illusion of prosperity too.'"

Most of the students present recalled that exchange since they'd been in high school at the time.

"That was Keynesian economic theory at its core, although Reagan wouldn't have admitted it or perhaps didn't even recognize it. By pouring billions of federal dollars into defense spending, he was stimulating the economy as Keynes suggested. And it worked. The money went to workers on defense projects and to military personnel stationed at US bases, and the result was an increase in their spending money, which stimulated the overall economy and pulled the nation out of its economic slump while interest rates stabilized. At the same time, the price of gasoline began to drop, after a temporary increase caused by Carter's decontrol, which Reagan accelerated.

"By the mid-1980s, it was 'morning in America' again, as Reagan proclaimed. Demand-side economics had worked again. As Paul Krugman, the economist, wrote in the *New York Times*, 'Economists have to face up to the inconvenient truth that Keynesian economics remains the best framework we have for making sense of recessions and depressions. This will be very hard for people who have giggled and whispered about Keynes.'"

Franklin called for a break to allow questions. A professor rather harshly told him that this was a college business class and that Franklin had wandered too far into the political arena.

"I'm sorry," Franklin answered, "but economics today is a political matter. The overall task of government is deciding from whom it gets its revenue and to whom that revenue is distributed. That's true for federal, state, and local governments. Virtually every decision goes back to that simple question, who pays and who benefits. Supply-side economic theory claims that if you reduce taxes on the wealthy and on business that they will use the money to create more jobs, but that hasn't been the case. Demand-side economics simply claims that if consumers have more money, they will buy more products which in turn enriches the supply-side. That has worked well in the United States."

A student asked, "Well, where is the money going that companies have gotten from the large tax cuts if not back into the economy or to expand its plants and add more products, thus creating more jobs and higher pay?"

"That's where the money should have gone," Franklin answered. "That's the expected trickle-down theory, but in recent years, too much of that money has gone into buying each other's stock, which has been more profitable for the stockholders and less risky. I know, I did it myself as a newspaper publisher. Look at the enormous sums spent by companies to buy other companies, usually their competitors, and the result is almost invariably a reduction in the workforce of the buyer and also the seller to finance the payments for the sale. The price of a large company's stock has become the controlling factor of management today, not quality of the product or even the amount of sales. It's the price of its stock that determines value and management's success or failure. That's why a manager willing to lay off thousands of workers for a short-term bump in earnings gets a huge bonus, plus he can then sell the company for a higher price per share of stock."

"You sound pessimistic about the way the system is working," a student said. "Is this trend inevitable, and doesn't it help the job-creators in an indirect way?"

"The real job creators are consumers," Franklin repeated emphatically. "Their purchases comprise 70 percent of the gross national income, and when those purchases increase, jobs increase for businesses. When consumption declines, business declines, and so do jobs. I was a newspaper publisher for thirty years, and I could tell how business was doing by the amount of advertising in our newspapers. The more business, the more advertising. Although we'd tell merchants they needed to advertise more when business was bad, that seldom worked. They advertised when business was good and provided them with enough money to advertise."

"So demand-side economics kept newspapers going, which sold you on the idea," one student interjected.

"Yes, but it keeps most businesses going, which is the idea. The Declaration of Independence suggests government's functions are to protect the individual's life, liberty, and pursuit of happiness, but the New Deal, 250 years later, expanded the government's role to being a provider of happiness, defined as material well-being. That is why I've called the New Deal the nation's third revolution, along with the revolution against Great Britain and the Civil War. It was an economic revolution, relatively bloodless but far-reaching and just as liberating. It produced the great American middle class, which as I mentioned is now shrinking."

Franklin closed, and there was smattering of applause. Several students and professors stopped to ask him questions or make comments. One young man with a pad and pencil asked if he could chat with him a few minutes. He was planning to write a thesis on the subject and wanted specific information on how to find the quotations from Keynes and Adam Smith.

"Be sure and send me a copy," Franklin told him. "I'd like to know more about it myself."

A reporter from the *Boston Globe* also stopped to talk and get some points for a column in the *Globe* that might be picked for the *New York Times* as an op-ed piece.

Susie was surrounded by a group of young men who seemed to profess interest in the subject but seemed more interested in Susie. As Franklin, Susie, and Hardy were driving back to Concord, Franklin asked her if she'd met any nice young men at Dartmouth.

"Men are usually nice when you first meet them," Susie said. "It's later you find out what they really are."

"Susie, you still sound bitter," Franklin said gently. "Your whole world is in a different place today."

"I know, working in this campaign has been better than winning the state championship, but I'm still not ready to start dating again. I haven't had a date in more than three years."

"That's a shame for you and some great young men," Franklin said. "You'll find one you can trust."

"First, I've got to be sure I can trust myself," Susie said, "but I'm getting there."

In Concord they found that Kathleen Kelley was already making an impression. Phil Sutton had taken her under his wing and was giving her the grim details of what a thin campaign they were running. Kathleen was laughing. "That's Mr. Franklin," she said.

"He was always looking for corners to cut. He wouldn't hire a new reporter unless there was a vacant desk."

"Kathleen, you're as pretty as you were twenty years ago," Franklin told her, "and just as sassy I bet."

"You've got more gray hair and still have that worried look you had when you first walked in the office at Opelika," she said, "although I know you're a rich publisher now."

Franklin smiled. "Yeah, but I'm running for president for some reason, and the odds are longer than they were for changing that newspaper into a valuable property."

"Well, when you sold it ten years later, it was about the best newspaper in Alabama," Kathleen told the group, "and I'll never forget the cast of characters you had to work with during those years.... including me."

"Maybe you especially," Franklin said. "But those characters were a mix that produced a remarkable newspaper product."

Kathleen smiled at him mischievously. "They had a remarkable leader," she said. "He never seemed to be doing anything much, but he was the puppet master pulling the right strings. I realized that early on, and my experiences in the years since have made me even more impressed with how you turned that newspaper around and turned us all around, like me for instance. I could hardly write a sentence or imagine a story until you came. That's why I wanted to come join this campaign."

Phil Sutton was delighted. "Kathleen has been involved with several campaigns in California and is great at interviewing and organizing TV shots," he gushed. "How did you find her?"

Franklin thought about that for a long minute, his mind drifting back through the years to the first time he ever saw her. She was a college intern who had a knack for getting good interviews, and Franklin already had an idea for an interview opportunity that would challenge the best of reporters.

The group of investors Franklin put together to buy the newspaper in Opelika had gotten up about $500,000 as a down payment and another $500,000 in noncompete payments over ten years, which was a deal in those days when large corporation were beginning to see newspapers as the kind of moneymakers that would increase the price of their stock. The *Opelika Daily News* was the smallest daily in Alabama, with a paid circulation of about five thousand and a gross income of less than $400,000 a year and no stated profit. Four of the seven stockholders worked on the newspaper, with the publisher being paid $180 a week and the other three even less. They divided up any profits at the end of the year, but that wasn't on the books.

Franklin, with his longtime desire to run his own newspaper, persuaded the investors to buy it for a million dollars, which sounded like a lot of money to the owners who were struggling with the finances and with each other over management policies. Franklin, at the time, was editor of the daily newspaper in Columbus, about thirty miles away but across the state border in Georgia. He had read the little Opelika paper for years. It was near a college town, Auburn, site of Auburn University, which adjoined Opelika although they had developed into rival cities. Opelika was the more populous and was the main shopping district for both cities plus the surrounding area. Like LaGrange and Columbus, it had been a textile mill town for years but had lately attracted several other industries, including a large Uniroyal tire plant that employed several thousands.

In the meantime, Auburn University had grown to more than fifteen thousand on-campus students, the most of any college in Alabama and had also won a national championship in football in 1957, so football was very big at Auburn, which fit well with Franklin's plans to expand and improve the newspaper. In the first few months, he changed the name from the *Opelika Daily News* to the *Opelika-Auburn News*, irritating some of the staff members, including the former owners, who still lived in Opelika and had virtually ignored Auburn in the newspaper and as a market for subscribers and advertising.

The next big step was adding a Sunday edition to the existing five-day schedule, which meant that some employees had to work on Saturday nights for the first time in their lives. Several of them balked, including the old stockholders, long accustomed to a leisurely Monday to Friday schedule of six- to eight-page editions with maybe twelve to sixteen on Wednesdays. The content relied heavily on the Associated Press wire, with few local stories on the front page. Sports coverage was confined to AP stories and coverage of the white high school in Opelika. The paper also relied on AP wire photo for its artwork. Local photos were scarce and usually routine group shots sent in by clubs or individuals.

Franklin started by revamping the feature and comic pages, adding new features and strips he'd carefully selected in his years as an editor and comic fan. But the biggest change was in the news columns, which suddenly became virtually all local with AP stories relegated to summaries and inside pages. He had persuaded one of the sportswriters on the Columbus paper to come with him to Opelika as sports editor, which gave the sports coverage a quick infusion of both quantity and quality. Franklin's plan with the Sunday edition was to emphasize Auburn and other college football games, usually played on Saturdays and therefore available for early and large coverage in the Sunday edition, which he didn't send to press until the last college score was in on Saturday night. In the early years, Franklin was usually in the office from 8:00 a.m. Saturday, getting together the Friday night high school coverage, which ran in the Sunday edition, to 12:00 or 1:00 a.m. Sunday, putting out the college pages. He also often attended Auburn home games, sometimes covering them. It was a grueling workday, but he wanted a hand in making the Sunday edition successful. It was the key to the newspaper's growth, he believed. He enjoyed the challenge, but it finally took a toll on his nerves. He was also putting together most of the daily editions plus writing regular columns and supervising the staff.

Kathleen and the younger members of the staff, several of them Auburn students as she was, responded well. Some older members of the staff refused to work on Saturday nights, and Franklin had to bring in new employees for the tougher jobs, such as operating the press, which was the next to final production step, usually well past midnight. Then, of course, there was the inserting of sections and the delivery to carriers.

The emphasis on Auburn football worked. It helped that quarterback Pat Sullivan and wide receiver Terry Beasley made their varsity debut on the Saturday before the first Sunday edition. They went on to two of the most exciting careers in college football, and Auburn was a consistent winner for the next three years, with the *Opelika-Auburn News* providing blanket coverage in photos, statistics, and articles, outshining the several competing papers which came into the area. On Sunday morning, newspapers from Columbus, Birmingham, Montgomery, and Atlanta were all on newsstands in Auburn and Opelika, and all those larger dailies also offered home delivery service to the East Alabama area. It was a competitive situation unique in the state, because Opelika-Auburn was only twenty miles from the Georgia state line and was also in the Central Time Zone, giving Franklin's paper an extra hour to wait for the latest reports.

Franklin was worried about what would happen to the Sunday edition when the football season ended. High school and college games had filled the edition. Would there be enough local news to maintain the Sunday paper's appeal?

Alabama politics had been even more bizarre than usual in 1966. Governor George Wallace wanted to run for a second consecutive term, which was prohibited by the state constitution. After a bitter but failed battle in the legislature to change the constitution, Wallace announced that this wife, Lurleen, would be a candidate in his place, and if she was elected, he'd be her chief adviser. The idea was dismissed at first. While an admirable woman and mother, Lurleen was totally unpolitical, had never run for or held any public position, and had not been very active in her husband's campaigns. She was also recovering from cancer, but run she did, against a formidable field which included former governor John Patterson, who had defeated Wallace in 1958, causing Wallace to vow he'd never be "out-segged again," meaning no candidate would be stronger for racial segregation than he was.

Lurleen, with Wallace making speeches for her, got his revenge on Patterson and won the election. Meanwhile, Wallace was getting ready to run for president in 1968. He'd won several primaries in 1964, and in 1968, he not only won primaries but got 14 percent of the popular vote in the general election and carried five states in that year's presidential election. Republican Richard Nixon narrowly defeated Hubert Humphrey to win the election, and most political observers concluded Wallace took more votes from Nixon than from Humphrey. It was the election that gave birth to the Republican strategy in every election since.

In the meantime, Lurleen had died in office of cancer and been succeeded by Albert Brewer, a back bench state senator Wallace had plucked out to run for lieutenant governor.

So for Christmas 1969, Franklin had the idea of sending Kathleen to Montgomery to do a story for the Sunday-before-Christmas edition on Wallace and his three children on their first Christmas after Lurleen's death. He couldn't believe the larger papers didn't think of it, but Kathleen was eager for the opportunity, and a trip to Wallace's home was arranged a few days before Christmas. It turned out spectacularly in more ways than one. She got the story and several Christmas photos of Wallace and the children for the front-page layout that gave that Sunday edition a special appeal that even the football editions had lacked. Franklin felt it established the *O-A News*, as most people now called the paper, as a factor in the crowded market.

Then, a few weeks later, Kathleen came into Franklin's office, closed the door behind her, and pulled a chair up close. "You'll never guess who came over to see me this weekend," she whispered. She lived in a mobile home park her mother operated.

"No way I would guess," Franklin admitted, since he knew Kathleen had a wide variety of male friends, including one of his partners in the newspaper.

"George Wallace," she exclaimed. "He'd called me several times since the story and photos came out, and last Saturday he called and wanted to come visit me at the mobile home. I could hardly believe it."

Neither could Franklin, although he recognized that Kathleen was deadly serious. Among other things, Wallace was planning to run for governor again in May 1970 against Albert Brewer, who had proven to be an exceptional governor in the months since he succeeded Lurleen, and early polls actually showed him leading Wallace.

"What did he want?" Franklin asked dumbfoundedly and rather naively.

"He wants me to be one of his girlfriends," Kathleen answered. "He's hoping to get married again before the election, and I'm in the running."

"You must be kidding. You're at least twenty-five years younger than he is."

Kathleen laughed. "I'm going to play along," she said. "Who knows? He's a perfect gentleman, and we really just talked."

That was the part of her life that wasn't in Kathleen's résumé, and there was more.

The Brewer-Wallace primary proved to be one of the closest and roughest in Alabama history. Brewer led in the first primary but failed to get a majority as several other candidates were in the race. In the runoff, Wallace bore down on racial issues and wasn't out-segged by the more moderate Brewer, who had allowed court-ordered integration after the passage of civil rights legislation in Congress. Wallace won the runoff and was elected governor to another term in 1971, his fourth straight in reality.

In the meantime, Kathleen had continued a relationship with him. Franklin never pressed her for details, but a fellow employee had visited her mobile home and reported that it was filled with Wallace photos and other Wallace campaign material.

Then, soon after the primary, Wallace announced his marriage to Cornelia Folsom, niece of former governor Big Jim Folsom, for whom Wallace had been the state campaign manager in the first of Folsom's two elections. Cornelia was an attractive woman in her midthirties who had once been a performer in the famous Wakiki Springs, Florida, Water Ski show. Her mother, Ruby, was a familiar personality in state political circles, having been Big Jim's capital hostess early in his first term before he remarried.

Kathleen told Franklin in one of their private office talks that she was not surprised or upset at Wallace's marriage. "He told me it was going to happen but that I could count on a state position when he's inaugurated," she confided.

"You're incredible," Franklin said. "What are you, twenty-four years old and just a reporter on a struggling small newspaper?"

Kathleen gave him one of her beguiling smiles. "You made it possible. Who else would have sent me on that Christmas assignment and edited the story and selected the photos, I might add?"

A few months later when Wallace became governor, one of his first appointments was Kathleen Kelly as assistant director of tourism and publicity, a fairly prominent position and a surprise choice to nearly everyone, even including Franklin, who still had trouble believing he was losing a good reporter in such a remarkable way.

It all turned out well, except for Wallace, whose ambition still wasn't satisfied. Two years later, after a successful year as governor, he ran for president again and was stronger than in 1968, winning several early primaries that actually gave him a lead in delegates going into the Maryland primary. Then, while he was campaigning in Baltimore, he was shot in the back by a would-be assassin, who was immediately caught, but Wallace was seriously wounded. There was a dramatic photo of him with wife, Cornelia, lying across his fallen body to shield him from further bullets. He won the Maryland primary a few days later but had to suspend his campaign to recover from his wounds. He never fully recovered although he went on to win two more terms as governor and lived to be seventy-four.

Kathleen in the meantime did a competent job with the state, writing speeches for Wallace and traveling to many tourism events, where she was an effective representative. She had also become a girlfriend of the youthful state attorney general, twenty-nine-year-old Bill Baxley, also elected in 1970. Where did she meet him? Incredibly, it was while he was campaigning in 1970 and came by the Opelika-Auburn newspaper office for an interview. Franklin was very impressed by the young man and called Kathleen over to conduct a full interview. She and Baxley became friends, and when they both went to Montgomery after the election, they began a relationship. Baxley was unmarried at the time and had a reputation as a gambler and heavy drinker, although his problem actually was that one drink or two was too much. But he was a courageous attorney general, taking on cases neglected for years, and was a racial moderate for an Alabama politician in those days. He was reelected to a second term in 1974 and ran for governor in a crowded field in 1978 but lost to former Auburn football All-American Fob James, who'd never run for or held a political office before.

By then Baxley and Kathleen had parted ways. She returned to reporting and eventually moved to California. Baxley stayed in politics and was elected lieutenant governor but then lost another bid for governor.

Franklin had related part of Kathleen's story to Hardy as they drove to a speaking engagement in Keene. "She must have been a hellava interviewer," Hardy said incredulously.

"That's why I think she can help us. I might get her to interview you about the campaigns you worked with Carter and how they differ from this one," Franklin suggested seriously.

Hardy chuckled. "I'm game," he said. "She still looks great. Must have been sensational back in the early seventies."

"More mature now, and actually more attractive in a way."

Chapter Fourteen

THOSE FACELESS MEN

*These Republican leaders have not been content
with attacks on me, or my wife, or on my sons. No,
not content with that, they now include my little
dog, Fala. I am accustomed to hearing malicious
falsehoods about myself. But I think I have a right to
resent, to object to libelous statements about my dog.*
—*Franklin D. Roosevelt, campaign
dinner address, September 23, 1944*

They arrived in Keene, a town of nearly twenty thousand, with a newspaper of about twelve thousand circulation, which covered the southwest corner of New Hampshire. Keene was one of the places near substantial granite deposits, from which the state got its nickname, the Granite State, but its main products by 1991 were poultry and vegetables. This would be Franklin's first major appearance in Keene, and he had decided to bear down on his differences with Paul Tsongas, who had a strong following in the area.

The newspaper editor who was a friend of Burkhart introduced him. Franklin discussed his economic views and expressed how important it was to get New Hampshire and the nation's economy moving again. "This is no time for uncertainty on the government's part," he explained. "More money must be put into consumer hands so they can spend it with your advertisers and other businesses. There is more money in the United States today than ever in its history, so don't let people like Paul Tsongas poor-mouth you and tell you middle-class and poorer Americans need to tighten their belts. They have already tightened them to the pinching point, while wealthier taxpayers have had to let their belts out just to accommodate their wallets.

"Tsongas wants to continue that trend, and it doesn't work for the vast majority of people. The recession continues, and we've found in the past that lean times can become a habit. We must not allow this one to become a habit. It must be dealt with by the next president immediately. We must get money into the wallets of all Americans, and my proposal to reduce the payroll tax from 7.5 to 3 percent will do that with your next paycheck, but it should be only a beginning."

Franklin got warm applause from the crowd of about sixty, most of whom were small business owners. He then invited questions, and the first one was on a subject he'd been hoping someone would come up with.

"How do you stand on capital punishment?" was the question. It was of immediate interest in the primary since Bill Clinton was facing a decision as governor of Arkansas in the next few weeks on whether to commute the execution of a convicted murderer of a police officer.

"I believe the justice system needs a death sentence as its ultimate punishment," Franklin replied, "but it should be used sparingly and reserved for crimes which are either heinous or aimed at the entire government structure instead of just one person. By that standard, I would probably commute the death sentence of the man in Arkansas. I don't know all the circumstances, as Governor Clinton does, but from what I do know, he doesn't meet my requirements for the death sentence. What are they? A serial killer proven and convicted, anyone else who has committed more than one murder and seems inclined to commit others, and most importantly, anyone who kills or attempts to kill a representative of the federal or state government or is a serious candidate for office, which is an attack not only on that individual but on the many people he or she represents and who was chosen to make decisions that affect the people of a city, state, or nation. Obviously, that would include the assassination or attempted assassination of a president or serious candidate for the presidency.

"Senator Ted Kennedy, who should know, once referred to the frustration of 'faceless men who emerge from obscurity' and in the space of few seconds change the course of history with the enormity of one violent act.

"Those who are inclined to commit such acts should know they will pay with their lives not eventually but almost immediately, as the assassins of four US presidents did, and the attempted assassin of another did. But in recent years, including 1981, when President Reagan was almost assassinated, that penalty has not been levied.

"We need to give these people clear and unforgettable faces, and we need to give them the death sentence as a warning to others that they cannot escape the supreme penalty when they attack the state or its representatives.

"One problem today is that after every assassination or attempt, there is an effort to find scapegoats almost as soon as the sound of gunfire fades. The key figure, the shooter, is often neglected or even forgotten. He or she needs to be tried and executed, within weeks if possible.

"Senator Kennedy was speaking about such faceless men as Lee Harvey Oswald, Sirhan, and James Earl Ray, but he might also have recalled such names as Charles Guiteau, Leon Czolgosz, Gieuseppe Zangara, and John Wilkes Booth, the assassins of presidents Lincoln, McKinley, Garfield, and Mayor Cermak of Chicago, who was standing in front of Franklin Roosevelt in 1933 when Zangara fired a shot, which had it not hit Cermek would have hit Roosevelt and would have changed the history of not only the nation but the world.

"Actually, the assassinations or attempts all changed history. Jack Ruby, another faceless man, saved the government the burden of trying and executing Oswald. In fact, Oswald could well be alive today, living off the very government which he violently attacked on November 22, 1963, had Ruby not acted as judge, jury, and executioner.

"Of course, several of the assassins or near assassins are doing just that, still living off the government although their deeds were as potentially dangerous to the state as those that succeeded. Most recently, of course, there is John W. Hinckley, who shot and seriously wounded President Reagan and his press secretary. He needs to be held responsible. He needs to be executed. Hinckley was literally caught with the smoking gun. Whatever motives or twisted thinking prompted him to act, he is the central figure, as he undoubtedly hoped to be, and he should be dealt with accordingly.

"Guiteau, who killed President James Garfield in 1881, was quickly tried and hanged. Czolgosz, who killed President William McKinley, was tried and executed within two months. Oswald, of course, was shot to death by Jack Ruby. Oswald's madness launched a dark age of the American spirit, eroding the national confidence to the point where our leadership in the rest of the world was damaged. Hinckley is in prison, and conceivably, he and the two women who aimed guns at President Ford could all be free and on the streets again at relatively young ages. Each of them should have been dealt with as Guiteau, Czolgosz, and Zangara were.

"What those assassins and would-be assassins committed far transcends murder or attempted murder. Their real target was the democratic process by which this nation selects its political leaders. They sought to nullify the votes and efforts of millions of Americans with the single vote of a deadly bullet, substituting the tyranny of violence for the constitutional votes of the citizens.

"Assassins influence political leadership in too many nations of the world, and in Africa, sometimes the assassin even becomes the new leader. Most emphatically, that is abhorrent to the American system. If our nation is at fault in the frequent assassination attempts on its chief executives, it is because of its attributes rather than its flaws. Those attributes include a broad degree of personal freedom and open access to governmental leaders.

"This nation, its history and principles, all reject every aspect of the assassin's role. Indeed, the presidential assassins arrived at their tragic encounters precisely because they turned away from their nation and sought to reduce its system to the disorder and turmoil still prevalent where the democratic process breaks down.

"I remember vividly the orgy of witch-hunting which followed the assassination of President Kennedy. In fact, years later, it has not completely abated, and Hinckley's attempt to kill President Reagan will feed the fires anew for those who overlook the real culprit in their zeal to condemn the United States, its customs, its heritage, its way of life, or some innate evil they perceive as the perpetrator of violence in this and other countries.

"We have learned little since Kennedy's assassination. We do not even tell would-be assassins that the price of their madness will be their life, not a long, smug sojourn in a comfortable prison environment.

"Instead, too many Americans point at political adversaries or the nation as a whole, thus assuring that other troubled minds will find solace in their ugly fantasies and tell themselves it is not their own sinister nature but the nation's which encourages their infamy.

"Some words from the late senator Albert Gore of Tennessee, a staunch supporter and friend of President Kennedy, are as appropriate today as they were when he spoke them in the aftermath of Kennedy's assassination.

"'I accept no blame for what this demented man, Oswald, did,' said Senator Gore. 'I feel no sense of guilt. It is an injustice to our millions of people of good will, including the thousands of hospitable, cheering people in Dallas, to accuse them of murderous guilt. I reject that guilt for myself and all people. This was the act of one madman.' Amen!

"Like Gore, we must remember that the chief culprit is the one who pulls the trigger. The faceless men really do have faces, and they are the faces of civilization's enemies, in the gravest form."

Franklin hadn't intended to talk about capital punishment, but he was glad he did. Most of his content was from a column he'd written after the attempt on Reagan. The group had responded well, and a couple of members told him and Hardy they'd help organize the Keene area for him. "It's strong for Tsongas but that's only because they've seen him so often and feel like he's a fellow New Englander.

They don't know what he stands for," one man told them as he glanced over some of Franklin's pamphlets. "We'd like to get you down here again before the primary."

On the way back to Concord, they stopped at two more townships. "That's 187," Hardy said. "I don't know if we can find the other 15."

"You're right," Franklin agreed. "We'll concentrate on the cities, but I do want to go back to Dixville Notch."

Back at the office, they found Phil Sutton in a gloomy mood. "Since you won't hire a pollster, we're having to depend on getting our information from our opponents and independent polls," he groused, "but overall the results are encouraging. Tsongas is dropping. Kerrey and Harkin and Brown are barely moving. Clinton's steadily climbing. He's got money, organization, and that smell of victory about him."

"What about me?" Franklin asked.

"You are in the mix behind Clinton and Tsongas, not dropping but not rising much either. Plus, money is slow coming in. A lot of people still don't take your candidacy seriously."

"Understandable," Franklin conceded, "but we're about to hit them with some holiday specials, and wait for the sky to fall on Clinton."

"What's that?" Sutton wanted to know.

"I'm not sure, but my source in Little Rock says it'll be soon," Franklin answered.

They were joined by two of the fund-raisers. "We need to do a mass mailing in New Hampshire again," one of them said, "and this time we need to ask for their vote but also point out that to compete with the sums of money being spent by the other candidates that we also need some dollars. The letter can point out, accurately, that we are spending nearly all our money in New Hampshire in small-town newspapers, for printing material and for campaign staff in the state. But the primary is now only eight weeks away, and we are being trounced in the money game."

"For instance, how many people have you personally asked for money?" one man interceded. That was a sore point with Sutton and other staffers. Franklin had to admit he hadn't asked anyone for money. "Okay," he said, "let's do another mailing and add a couple of more staff to the fund-raising."

Sutton agreed heartily. The lead fund-raisers voiced relief. "One person we'd like to add," he implored, "is Kathleen Kelly. She says she had experience fund-raising with the Wallace presidential campaign, and she gets attention when we call on potential donors."

"I'll say," said the other one. "And no wonder. I get a hard-on just looking at her."

"Hell," added the other fund-raiser, "I nearly cream my pants when she crosses her legs."

Franklin frowned at the two men whom he had not talked with much. "Guys, you might keep those thoughts to yourselves. After all, she's in her midforties."

"So are we," the fund-raiser said, "and remember, the forties are the new thirties."

"Susie is twenty years younger, and she has the same effect on me," the other fund-raiser said.

"Well, I sure as hell wouldn't kick either one of them out of bed," the younger one commented.

Charlie and Susie came over with a stack of mail, grinning like Cheshire cats.

"You're going to love this invitation," Susie said. "Can you guess where it's from?"

"A big donor wants me to meet with him?"

"Much better," she replied. "It's from a vice president at Harvard, asking you to speak to an assembly there the Monday before Christmas."

That was good news. Franklin felt a speech at Harvard would attract the attention necessary to be considered a top-tier contender and give him the national attention he'd gotten only sporadically. "They want you to talk about foreign affairs," Susie said, "especially your ideas about Russia after the breakup of the Soviet Union."

"That's great. Confirm the date, and you and Charlie plan to go with Hardy and me."

Susie broke into her biggest Christmas-tree smile.

"Wow," she exclaimed, "I never thought I'd get to Harvard. It doesn't even have a woman's basketball team."

"But first, you and Charlie sit down and help me get up this proposal for all the weekly newspapers in New Hampshire to run as full pages of advertising the week before and week after Christmas Day. Usually those are slow periods for advertising, especially the week after, so we'll offer a package, both pages for a combined half price.

"Here's the first column. It's a Christmas column I wrote years ago, but I think it reflects a nostalgic and imaginative image of me as a teenager and also depicts the nation right after World War II. I've made a few changes, but otherwise send it out as is, with a caption that this holiday story is as a message from the Franklin for President Campaign." He turned to Sutton. "Okay," Franklin said, "here's the new letter to send out: 'The Franklin for President Campaign wishes you Merry Christmas and asks you to consider a vote for him in the February 18 Democratic primary.' If there's room left on the page, add our office phone number and address and a list of goals, although I doubt there will be room for those. A colorful Christmas border would be better." He'd already told Charlie to hire another former New Hampshire publisher whose paper had been sold and who was available. Like Charlie, he'd been president of the New Hampshire Press Association.

"Here's the page I want to run on the Thursday before New Year's Eve. That should be an easy sell. It's usually a really slow week.

"The headline can be 'The Songs You Were Singing to Your Best Beau or Girlfriend on New Year's Eve for the Past 50 Years'... and if you'd like to hear one of them this week, call your local radio stations and request they play it. I don't know what kind of response this will get, but it's possible we can get several hundred people calling radio stations and mentioning our campaign. Be sure to put at the bottom of that page, 'This list of favorite songs through the years is brought to you by the Franklin for President Primary Campaign.'

Here's the list from a book called *The Song Is Familiar*, compiled by Elston Brooks for *Variety* and *Billboard* magazine:

1930—"Happy Days Are Here Again" (picked up in 1932 by the Democrats as their theme song).

1931—"Goodnight Sweetheart" (still the perennial last-dance song).

1932—"A Shanty in Old Shantytown."

1933—"Stormy Weather."

1934—"Smoke Gets in Your Eyes."

1935—"Cheek to Cheek."

1936—"The Way You Look Tonight."

1937—"That Old Feeling."

1938—"Thanks for the Memories."

1939—"Over the Rainbow" and "Deep Purple."

1940—"I'll Never Smile Again."

1941—"I Hear a Rhapsody."

1942—"White Christmas" (set a record to that point as no. 1 on *Hit Parade* for ten straight weeks.)

1943—"You'll Never Know."

1944—"I'll Be Seeing You."

1945—"Don't Fence Me In."

1946—"The Gypsy" and "Oh, What It Seemed to Be."

1947—"Peg O My Heart" (which was written in 1913) and "For Sentimental Reasons."

1948—"It's Magic" and "A Tree in the Meadow."

1949—"Some Enchanted Evening."

1950—"My Foolish Heart."

1951—"Too Young" (twelve weeks as no. 1) and "Because of You" (eleven weeks as no. 1).

1952—"You Belong to Me."

1953—"Song from Moulin Rouge" (this was a pivotal year for popular music because there was a noticeable decline in the sentimental ballad which had dominated the lists for more than 20 years, signaling the revolution which would occur two years later with the breakthrough of rock 'n' roll).

1954—"Hey There" and "Little Things Mean a Lot."

1955—"Yellow Rose of Texas" and "Ballad of Davy Crockett" (which were both no. 1 for nine weeks, but the song that put the big beat on the charts for the first time and ushered in the new era of popular music was "Rock Around the Clock," which was no. 1 for only two weeks. "Rock Around the Clock" was the background theme music for the movie *Blackboard Jungle*, which showed the nation another side of the Little Red School House).

In the fifty years from 1930 to 1980, the halfway point of 1955 was the year which altered the nation's music tastes in several important ways.

Another popular song of that period was "The Song Has Ended but the Melody Lingers On." But as the rock era rolled in, the melodies were mainly lost and no longer lingered.

Franklin left it to Sutton and the former New Hampshire publishers to get the space and contact the radio stations about cooperating, promising them all a round of paid ad spots.

In his speech at Harvard, Franklin spoke mainly about war. "General William T. Sherman is famous for saying 'War is hell' but was more eloquent than that on other occasions. His description that I prefer is 'War is cruelty, and you cannot refine it.'

"That goes to the crux of the matter. People are always trying to justify war in terms of patriotism, bravery, and other euphemisms that try to refine it when it is still about killing people, destroying their homes, their cities, their livelihoods, their food, often their children. War is cruelty at its most extreme, as Gen. Sherman described it…and you cannot refine it."

Franklin paused and hoped he had at least gotten the group's attention. "But today, in this year of 1991, as I have tried to emphasize in my campaign, the world has a unique opportunity to change the age-old method of settling disputes by killing each other…and the opportunity to build a foundation for peace that will at least prevent a war between nuclear powers and at best can discourage smaller wars by persuasion or sometime minimum force as an alternative that seems more desirable to the would-be combatants than war. This is a great opportunity, one in a thousand years, but it faces centuries of good and bad governments preferring war instead of peace, just as the US did earlier this year in Iraq. As the most dominant and powerful nation, not just in the world today, but in all of history, the US must lead the way, must become the foremost proponent of settling disputes without killing each other and vandalizing nations that are trying to emerge into the nineteenth century, much less the twentieth. In the long, bloody history of mankind, we have made incredible progress toward conquering such enduring enemies as starvation, diseases, and natural disasters, and yet the twentieth century has seen more people die as a result of war than any century."

Franklin was properly impressed with Harvard. Several US presidents had studied there. A group of about two hundred students and professors were on hand and looked fairly happy to have a guest speaker. Franklin repeated his usual statement that the United States was the strongest, most prosperous nation in history and should not have to resort to war to have its way, right or wrong (but usually right) in global affairs.

"The United States today has the opportunity because of its dominance to lead the world to a surer, more civilized way of existence.

But the world will not wait on us. Action by the US is needed immediately to assure that Russia becomes a stabilizing partner rather than a suspicious or even military enemy again. We are already seeing the tragic results of the division of Yugoslavia into warring factions. The same could happen if Russia and other former Soviet allies become warring factions which would have nuclear weapons.

"The opportunity for assuring a broad and lasting peace is at hand, but so is the chance of spreading anarchy. Our first goal, I believe, must be to seek a tentative alliance with Russia, the other major nuclear power in the world. Despite our differences during the Cold War, they were settled with little loss of lives or actually without a shot fired in anger between the two major contenders. While both sides engaged in limited warfare through proxies for more than forty-five years, a general peace was maintained, and the US won its greatest victory, although there were few parades, no fireworks, no medals awarded. Those were reserved for an admittedly impressive spanking of a minor bully and his paper tiger army, which in ten years had been unable to defeat Iran, even with US help, it should be added. Such is the folly of warfare. Saddam was defeated, but he still controls Iraq, and he took the opportunity to slaughter hundreds of Kurds who opposed him, and he has thus emerged more secure as Iraq's dictator.

"Before continuing, I'd like to introduce my campaign assistant, Susie Schultz. She has been speaking to groups in New Hampshire, and I've asked her to relate how we first met, she as a waitress, I as a customer at a small motel café."

Susie, adorned in her most fetching sleeveless blue dress, stood up to her full five feet, eleven inches and smiled and got an appreciative round of applause from the mostly male audience. She had improved her speaking poise considerably in appearances at small New Hampshire settings, but this was her most challenging event.

"Well, I was taking an order from Mr. Franklin at this restaurant, and he asked for french fries, and I told him we didn't serve those anymore, but we had freedom fries, which were the same thing. He asked why the name change, and I told him the manager had adopted the custom after the Iraq War, when the French refused to help us against Saddam Hussein, seemingly because the French were afraid to fight. So he told me the story of how Germans had driven French troops backward for more than two hundred miles to the outskirts of Paris in the first month of World War I, and the French had been unable to even slow down the German advance, until at the Marne River, the French troops suddenly turned and started fighting, eventually forcing the Germans to retreat.

"The German commander, Alexander von Kluck, wrote later, 'The reason that transcends all others for the German failure at the Marne was the extraordinary attitude of the French soldiers; that men will stand and let themselves be killed where they stand is a well-known fact and is counted on in every plan of battle. But for men who have retreated for 20 days, sleeping on the ground and half dead from fatigue should be able to take up their rifles and counterattack when the bugle sounds, that is something on which we had not counted. It was a possibility not studied in our war academy.'

"Mr. Franklin said he still wanted some french fries, and I served them to him and thanked him for the history lesson, which was my tip for the night," Susie concluded to a round of applause.

Franklin took the podium again and pointed out there was a tragic sequel to the phenomenal example of French bravery and determination. "The German drive was stopped some miles from its destination. Paris was saved, but the war continued. The two warring armies dug hundreds of trenches only a few yards from each other and continued to fight for four more years over just a few yards of dirt that came to be called No Man's Land. According to Barbara Tuchman's great book, *The Guns of August*, the trenches ran from Switzerland to the English Channel across French and Belgian territory, creating a setting for human attrition that sucked up lives at a rate of five thousand and sometimes fifty thousand a day and eventually bringing into the conflict nearly every nation in the world, including in April 1917, the United States. US troops joined the French and British along that long bloody string of trenches known as the Western Front, and that finally persuaded the Germans to surrender.

"That was the price for bravery by the French, but it was still bravery that needs to be remembered. Only twenty-two years later a generation of German troops marched around the same stretch of France virtually unhindered and that time continued into Paris. Now, ironically, fifty years later, with West and East Germany united, Germany is again the dominant nation on the European continent but presumably a potential and valuable ally of the United States in assuring that Europe will never again attempt to commit suicide as it did twice in the twentieth century.

"The moral of this story is that the results of war are unpredictable except that they will bring death and destruction. It also demonstrates why in this most optimum time of opportunity, we must not allow the chance and circumstances for a durable peace elude us.

"Powerful nations are the only ones that can demand and enforce conditions for peace, which is why the United States has the greatest responsibility, so I certainly do not want the United States to become weaker militarily, only more dedicated to maintaining order and peace.

"Many Americans still don't seem to realize that we won the Cold War, a conflict longer than the two world wars combined, but we must now organize the peace, which the victors in those previous wars were unable or unwilling to do. The US has the advantage today of having no powerful partner in the victory as it had in World War I, when the interests of Great Britain, France, and others had to be accommodated, or after World War II, when the Soviet Union was already looming as an adversary. Today we have no equal partners who must be placated. We can decide the shape of the peace. But we must also recognize that Russia is no longer the Soviet Empire with which we contended for nearly half a century. It is, however, the second-largest nuclear power in the world, and its weaknesses as a government could be more dangerous to us today than its former strength.

"From all indications, its leadership is unsteady and its direction uncertain. Gorbachev, who played such a crucial role in ending the old regime, is now ostracized by the former Communist rulers and mistrusted by Boris Yeltsin and the party that has organized around him. Of course, there is still a large Communist contingent, anxious to regain control. Yeltsin is erratic and reportedly a heavy drinker, and beyond Gorbachev and Yeltsin, there is no leader of national prominence. The US must help them find one, and there is no time to lose. Yugoslavia's example is a terrible warning of how unchallenged outlaw leaders can wreck the peace and the chance for orderly solutions.

"The US State Department is undoubtedly still full of cold war warriors, who will find it difficult to accept Russia as a possible partner, even though Russia can be our most useful partner. That will not be an easy transition, either for political leaders or for the people, who for years have looked on the Russians as our worst adversary. But we forgave the Japanese and the Germans and actually worked to rebuild their countries and their economies after they committed far more heinous atrocities against us than the Russians. In fact, to my knowledge, in the Cold War period, I don't recall the US and the Soviet Union ever exchanging shots in anger. Our proxies did, of course, and let me stress that I supported both our Korean and Vietnam missions. I feel they were both essential steps along the path to ultimate victory in the Cold War, even though Vietnam did not end as we wished. US troops never lost a battle while they were engaged there, and the resolve the US demonstrated at a critical time in the Far East almost certainly prevented Indonesia from coming under Communist control, and possibly India and Pakistan."

Franklin paused. "That may be too much to digest in one sitting, but it is critical, I feel, that this year's presidential candidates delineate clearly the conditions and path the nation must pursue to seize this historic opportunity for a broad and lasting peace. Thank you for your attention."

Franklin received a strong applause, and he felt that he had gotten a degree of passion into his words that he often could not muster.

"We have many questions," said the vice president who'd invited him, "but I think it will be best if they are submitted in writing since time is short. We would appreciate you answering them in writing when you have the opportunity."

"That will be fine," Franklin said, "but I would like to take a few questions about my campaign, which several students have asked me about at an earlier talk."

"Are you raising enough money to keep competing?" one student asked.

"Well, no," Franklin answered, "but Ms. Shultz is passing out envelopes which can be used to send us help if anyone should like."

"Has a newspaper publisher ever been elected president?"

"Only one. Warren G. Harding, in 1920, with the largest popular plurality to that time. Harding, as you probably know, died two years into his term of causes still being debated. He was a handsome man but was hurt by rumors of adultery in and out of the White House and of corruption by some officials in his administration. Historians have not been kind to him, ranking him as a failure among the presidents, but as Alice Roosevelt Longworth so famously described him, 'He was not a bad man, he was just a slob.'

"Ironically, his Democratic opponent in 1920, who lost so badly, was also a newspaper publisher, a far more successful one than Harding. James M. Cox, also of Ohio, got out of politics and built one of the nation's great newspaper chains, which include *The Atlanta Journal* and *Constitution* as well as many TV stations. His children and grandchildren are among the richest Americans today. His running mate in the 1920 election, a young New Yorker, who had been undersecretary of the Navy under President Woodrow Wilson, also did well. His name, of course, was Franklin D. Roosevelt, who survived not only the crushing defeat to Harding but overcame a crippling attack of polio that hit him two years later to become the greatest president of the twentieth century."

The students and most professors cheered that final summary by Franklin but were clearly ready to make their next class. Franklin lingered to talk with reporters from the Harvard campus newspaper, the *Boston Globe*, and the *Manchester Union-Leader*, which had not previously written about him at any length.

The *Union-Leader* reporter seemed incredulous that Franklin would propose any kind of alliance with Russia. "Can we trust them?" he asked.

"We have the bigger stick," Franklin replied, "so the question is, can they trust us? But someone has to trust someone to assure that our great victory in the Cold War does not turn into the chaos that would inevitably result in small conflicts, which we are less able to handle than a large conflict."

"You were great," Susie, Charlie, and Hardy assured him as they left.

"Not everybody is going to cotton to some of those ideas," Charlie added, "but at least you gave them a lot to think about."

"By the way, wasn't Susie great for an all-star basketball player who had never made a political speech until a few weeks ago," Franklin commented.

"She sure was," Charlie agreed. "I'm so proud of her."

The speech at Harvard earned Franklin a strong response. The *Boston Globe* and *New York Times* both carried articles about it. So did the Manchester daily and other New Hampshire dailies. Charlie prepared a story and photo which he sent to every weekly in the state, and he anticipated many would use them in one of the December editions, which were enlarged by Christmas advertising and thus had more news space to fill.

On December 20 had come the political event Franklin and the other candidates had been anxiously awaiting. Governor Mario Cuomo of New York decided not to run for president in the New Hampshire primary. The day was the last in which a candidate could qualify for the primary, and Cuomo supporters chartered a plane to bring him from Albany to Concord in order to sign up at the last minute. He was involved in the closing days of the state assembly, which had still not approved his budget for the next year. He had earlier claimed he couldn't commit to the presidential race until the budget was passed. Supporters thought he'd left the door open slightly. But they were wrong. Cuomo didn't get on the plane, and the deadline passed.

If Cuomo had earlier expressed his intention to run, Franklin wouldn't have been in the race. Like many Americans, he had looked on Cuomo as another Roosevelt ever since his speech to the 1984 Democratic convention. Cuomo had been elected governor of New York three times. He was an involved and competent administrator as well as an inspiring speaker and writer. He expressed progressive views but had appeal to moderates. He'd been the obvious leader for the nomination in 1988, far more favored and popular than Michael Dukakis. But Cuomo never even ventured to the starting gate. He seemed certain for 1992, safely elected to a third term as governor. He overshadowed the field of candidates who were running. All of them, including Franklin, knew there was a stature gap they could not close against Cuomo. All of them were running on the chance that once more the Hamlet of Albany would shy from the conflict.

A few days before the deadline, Cuomo said that announcing for president might actually hurt him in the battle over the New York budget. "If opponents are doing this to prevent me from running for president, they would no longer have that motive if I announced I'm a candidate."

But the budget bill battle always seemed like a straw man. Cuomo was not like candidates such as Tsongas, Kerrey, Clinton or Harkin, and certainly not Franklin. He was a celebrity whose campaign from the start would have enormous attention from the press, plenty of money, and a ready-made group of supporters in nearly every state. He would almost be a shoo-in, the other candidates felt, but they hung in on that chance he might not run.

On December 19, he told reporters, "The deadline for running for president is tomorrow. I wouldn't pocket veto the presidency." He conferred with his son, Andrew, then wrote two statements, one that he'd be a candidate, the other that he wouldn't. On the morning of December 20, dozens of reporters and cameramen congregated at the state house in Concord, where Cuomo's $1,000 filing fee and declaration of candidacy had to be delivered in person by 5:00 p.m. Legally, Cuomo could have faxed his declaration. A signed check had been given to one of his supporters to present, but Cuomo and his supporters felt that would be seen as arrogance in a state that was not kind to arrogant candidates, and at least eight candidates were pleading for their votes in person. Actually twenty-nine Democrats and nineteen Republicans had filed to be on the February 18 presidential ballot. Harkin and Kerrey filed on the final day, although they had been campaigning for months.

CNN kept showing a picture of a plane poised on the tarmac in Albany waiting for Cuomo and his party. The candidate was to be flown to Manchester then driven the eighteen miles to Concord. Among the anxious TV watchers were Franklin and his small campaign staff. They were all still exultant over Franklin's appearance at Harvard but realized that a Cuomo candidacy would quickly overshadow the results. Then at 3:00 p.m., Cuomo called reporters to a meeting and told them since the state budget was still undecided that it was his responsibility as governor to deal with this extraordinarily severe problem. "Were it not, I would travel to New Hampshire today and file my name as a candidate in its presidential primary. That was my hope, and I prepared for it, but it seems to me I cannot turn my attention to New Hampshire while this threat hangs over the heads of New Yorkers, who I have sworn to put first."

Cuomo noted that he might have entered the race at a later date but that he was accepting the "deadline Democratic Party chairman, Ron Brown, had set to get Cuomo and everybody else out of the way and concentrate on the field that we have."

The most logical explanation for Cuomo's decision against running was that he had always been a provincial New Yorker whose interests were in New York, and his emotional commitment was there. He had little enthusiasm for the difficult and distant rounds of running for president or even the nomination. At base, he simply just didn't want to be president that much, and those who do have to exert every effort toward that goal. "I was always afraid of people who had too great a hunger for it," he said later. He indicated that the presidency should seek the man, not the man seek the presidency. That was a popular theory and perhaps a sound one, but in the late twentieth century, it had become implausible. Even Franklin liked the theory. He just didn't see any men the presidency was seeking with the possible exception of Cuomo.

Franklin and Sutton sat and discussed the new playing field. "Money that's been on the sidelines will begin flowing now," Sutton said, "and we need to get some of it, and I'm not sure we will. The other candidates are already running multistate campaigns with active fund-raisers in numerous states. We're in effect running a one-state campaign with a presence in Georgia, I guess. We've got to expand and fast."

Franklin looked skeptical. "My idea all along," he explained, "was to come into New Hampshire with the kind of effort we've made here and try to win this first primary, which would give me the attention and name recognition to move forward. We've made a few inroads in Maine, which will have a caucus a few days after the New Hampshire primary. I see a chance of winning that. Then comes South Carolina and then Georgia, both of which are states that offer us opportunity. If we can do well in those four states in the first weeks of the campaign, I'll be somebody, maybe even the favorite. So let's not worry about the rest of the country yet. Actually I've been wondering what the other candidates were doing here in New Hampshire. I haven't seen much of them."

"They are organizing in other states," Sutton said bluntly, preparing for the long haul. "If we don't win here in New Hampshire, we're finished. You've done a hellava job for an unknown, but Clinton,

Tsongas, and Kerrey are still leading you in the polls and we're nearly at Christmas break."

"I've been planning the Christmas season strategy for weeks, long before you came on board. First I've invited my family up for the holidays. They should be in tomorrow. I thought we'd all go Christmas shopping in New Hampshire stores, mostly in Concord and Manchester, with photos and stories. A special Christmas column I wrote years ago will be running in all the newspapers in the state, which certainly got the attention of the publishers and I hope some readers and advertisers. And you'll be glad to know Charlie has worked out a deal with the state's only TV station, plus several cable channels to carry a commercial for me eight times during the week before Christmas.

"Our campaign is also going to sponsor a three-hour presentation of the movie *It's a Wonderful Life* on WMNH, which hasn't shown it since NBC got the rights to carry it exclusively on its stations. WMNH can carry it as a paid advertisement, with the explanation that it is being brought to the viewers in New Hampshire courtesy of the Franklin for President Presidential Campaign. The movie will run on the Sunday before Christmas with five commercial breaks."

"Where are the commercials? Who made them?"

"I did, several weeks ago. The main commercial, which will run the most during the week, is an excerpt from the movie in which Jimmy Stewart in the role of George Bailey tells Lionel Barrymore as Old Man Potter the need for better access to housing for the people of Bedford Falls. It is a powerful explanation of my own feelings, expressed as only Jimmy Stewart could, and we'll plug the movie during the earlier commercials. I'm counting on this to have a strong impact.

"Then the week before New Year's, we'll be running a full page in all New Hampshire papers listing the no. 1 pop songs from 1930 to 1955 with readers urged to call their favorite radio station and request a playing of their favorite song, from whatever year."

"This all sounds expensive," Sutton commented. "But we've got a lot of money saved up from penny-pinching and not running any

TV or sending out mailings or doing other things candidates usually do, like fund-raising."

Franklin smiled and slapped Sutton on the shoulder. "This Christmas blitz is going to be aimed at older voters, many of them Republicans who may not usually vote for Democrats. It will also reach a lot of Tsongas voters who may just be supporting the most familiar name."

Sutton didn't look convinced, but he was pleased they were finally getting some exposure on TV, even if it was in a forty-five-year-old movie that he figured most people had seen several times.

Sutton was anxious to see the spot commercial that was going to run. As it happened, Charlie had a copy he'd picked up that morning from the station in Manchester where it'd been made. Sutton already had projection equipment in the office and was looking at some of the commercials the opponents were running. "Set it up," said Charlie. "It's scheduled to start running on December 23 and run for eight times a day through the 29th. We got the last four days at an after-Christmas cut-rate and in primetime."

Sutton put the commercial in his projector and got it running:

The scene was the meeting of the Bailey Bros. stockholders soon after George's father died. They were discussing whether to try and keep the company going. Old Man Potter, the richest man in town, was a board member of Bailey Brothers. He made a motion that the company be closed. "I say this institution is not necessary for this town, and it should be dissolved and its assets and liabilities turned over to the receiver."

One director objected, but another seconded Potter's motion, and the chairman asked George (Jimmy Stewart) and his uncle Billy to leave while the directors discussed the motion. "I would say it was Peter Bailey's faith and devotion that was responsible for this organization," the chairman said. Potter spoke up at this point. "I'll go further...Peter Bailey was no businessman. That's what killed him. Oh, I don't mean any disrespect to him, God rest his soul. He was a man with high ideals, so called, but ideals without common sense can ruin this town. You take this loan to Ernie Bishop. I know the bank turned down a loan to Bishop, but he comes here and we're building him a house worth $5,000. Why?"

George, still standing at the door about to leave, interrupts. "Well, I handled that loan, Mr. Potter. You have all the papers, his salary, his insurance. I can personally vouch for his character."

"Oh," says Potter sarcastically, "a friend of yours?"

"Yes, sir," answers George.

"You see," says Potter, "if you shoot pool with some employee here, you can come here and borrow money. What does that get us but a discontented, lazy rabble instead of a thrifty working class, and all because of a few starry-eyed dreamers like Peter Bailey who stir them up and fill their heads with a lot of impossible ideas. Now, I say—"

"Just a minute, now hold on," George says suddenly. "You're right when you say my father was no businessman...but neither you or anyone else can say anything about his character...and he did help a few people get out of your slums, and what's wrong with that? Why...you're all businessmen here. Doesn't it make them better citizens? Doesn't it make them better customers? What did you say just a minute ago? They should wait and save their money before they even think of a decent home. Wait? Wait for what? Until their children grow up and leave and until they're so old and broken down that they... Do you know how long it takes a working man to save $5,000? Just remember this, Mr. Potter, this rabble you're talking about, they do most of the working and paying and living and dying in this town. Is it too much to ask that they live in a house with a couple of decent rooms and a bath? My father didn't think so."

The excerpt from the movie ends at that point, and an announcer comes on and says, "Neither does Thomas A. Franklin, who's running for president in the February Democratic Primary."

"That movie scene with Jimmy Stewart and Lionel Barrymore in the great movie *It's a Wonderful Life* took place in the year 1927 a few years before the Great Depression, but in a nation that still had a small middle class and a struggling lower class, which at the time usually did not have a home of their own," Franklin explained to Sutton. "If you listen carefully to that exchange, it makes the case for the coming of the New Deal and of its goals to raise living conditions and the hopes of all Americans. I don't know who wrote those lines. Frank Capra, the producer, gets credit for the movie, and he did write much of it."

Actually, according to books about the movie, there were many scripts, most of which Capra discarded. Many of them were far different than the final draft. That version was mainly Capra's with the help of a husband-wife team, Albert Hackett and Frances Goodrich, who have never gotten much credit. Capra, Stewart, and the picture were all nominated for Academy Awards but failed to win, which was a disappointment that troubled Capra the rest of his long life. As he said once, "I thought *Wonderful Life* was the best movie I had ever made." He won three other Academy Awards. "In fact, I thought it was the best movie anybody had ever made."

Following the excerpt, the announcer goes on to say that Thomas Franklin believes the nation should fulfill George Bailey's promise of easier home loans but that in the past twenty years, the progress of the middle class had stalled under Republican administrations, in better housing, better incomes and better public facilities.

"As George asked, don't better living conditions make people better workers, better customers. More than fifty years later, those words ring just as true, and we have the evidence in the great nation which the United States has become." End of commercial.

"*It's a Wonderful Life* is first of all about homes and how important they are to creating a comfortable and secure middle class. And I feel that message comes across in this commercial," Franklin explained to the group watching the commercial.

Sutton rubbed his chin. "When you isolated those few minutes from the rest of the movie, they do have an impact that I never noticed before."

"I think having Jimmy Stewart present your message is brilliant," said Charlie. "So much better than an unknown announcer no one knows."

"Or me," Franklin added with a chuckle.

"But you had this idea," Hardy said, "and I've never seen a better political commercial."

"How did you get all the clearances?" Sutton wondered.

"Mainly through Jeanne Basinger, a movie historian, who compiled a book on the making of the movie. I also worked with the NBC station in Boston, which will be carrying the movie and a schedule of the spots, which were very costly by our standards but were part of the price for the rights."

"I think it was awesome," Susie said. "I've actually only seen the movie once, when I was a child, but I'm going to watch it again this year. Are you supposed to cry at the end?"

"Nearly everyone does," Franklin said. "I saw it first when I was just seventeen, and my eyes still tear up at the end and in the drugstore scene, when George is a teenager. Watch for that, it's terrific."

Hardy came over and shook hands. "I went through two campaigns with Carter, and I never heard him as convincing as you were at the end of that TV spot. I wanted to tell you that."

"That means a lot," Franklin said, "but he had a much better smile."

Franklin told Sutton to call the New Hampshire TV station and make sure they had all the spots scheduled for after Christmas and to find out how much another group of spots in those post-Christmas days would cost. "Get figures on nine a day for three days at the end of December. I've got an idea for a follow-up."

Franklin's family arrived the next day to spend the rest of Christmas week with the campaign. None of them, including Franklin himself, had ever seen a real white Christmas, and New Hampshire came through beautifully with a heavy sprinkling of snow on December 23.

Franklin had a suite for them at the Wayfarer. The five-year-old and two-year-old were especially delighted, and Charlie got some great photos of them. So did Susie, who had taken to photography as well as writing.

Franklin and Jean visited for a while to catch up on things, and then they all went shopping in Manchester, taking the opportunity to meet and greet as many local residents as possible, most of whom seemed to enjoy the break from their shopping.

Tsongas had been running TV spots of himself swimming. It was obviously an effort to show that he had completely recovered from his bout with cancer, and it was also eye-catching. The spot had started around Thanksgiving and had given Tsongas a lead in the polls over both Kerrey, who was second, and Clinton, who dropped to third. A new factor in the voting mix was Pat Buchanan, the cherubic TV commentator and columnist who was a hard-right conservative and had decided to run in the Republican primary against Bush, accusing Bush of being too soft on conservative issues. Bush himself was still on the sidelines, but Buchanan was getting attention, to some extent away from the Democratic contest.

Tsongas was still denying that he was Santa Claus, a peculiar point to make in the Christmas season, but it suited his theme that he was the candidate telling Americans the unvarnished facts that the nation had a budget deficit that would become worse if taxes were cut for the middle class.

Franklin thought it was a poor strategy, but it was obviously popular with some New Hampshire voters who were apparently impressed by Tsongas's sincerity and courage.

Franklin and his family attended a Christmas music program at the Baptist Church in Concord and then a midnight Mass at the Episcopal Church. On Christmas Day, they went to the Baptist Church in Manchester, trying to be friendly but not too conspicuous. They were introduced at all the churches as visitors from Georgia. At the Baptist Church, several members recalled Carter's visits sixteen years earlier.

Kathleen joined them for the afternoon and reminisced with them about their days in Opelika and Auburn. She had attended church with Jack Hardy at his invitation she said, and they had also had dinner together. "I think I'll interview him tomorrow about the Carter campaign," she mused.

Franklin met with Sutton and a TV announcer the next morning to prepare the following commercial for the post-Christmas days: "We hope all our viewers enjoyed the special presentation of the movie *It's a Wonderful Life* on WMNH, which was made possible by the support of the Franklin for President Campaign. Due to copyright restrictions, it has not been shown for several years on this station. Mr. Franklin does want to state that any resemblance in the words spoken by Old Man Potter and Paul Tsongas are purely coincidental and were not intended to reflect on Mr. Tsongas's campaign. We hope you will vote for Thomas A. Franklin in the Democratic Primary on February 18."

Sutton liked the commercial although he didn't altogether understand it. Franklin liked it a lot. It was about as negative as he wanted to get, but he felt Tsongas had it coming. Potter and Tsongas had both promoted that fashionable Republican philosophy that money is good for rich people but makes poor people discontented.

Franklin liked the commercial so much that he used it in a series of quarter-page ads in place of the full-page column he'd originally planned.

Campaigning in all camps slacked off the week between Christmas and New Year's. Franklin was pleased to have another invitation to speak to a labor gathering in Manchester just after New Year's Day and he was doing two TV interviews in the slow week, both on Boston stations.

He and Sutton had also hit on the idea of sending Susie and Kathleen to small radio stations in New Hampshire with a prepared list of questions for the announcers, who usually were not familiar with the campaign or the issues. The two women also had a list of prepared answers. It was a tactic that Jimmy and Rosalyn Carter had used to their advantage in the 1978 campaign.

Chapter Fifteen

ENCOUNTER WITH HILLARY

*The American people are quite competent to judge
a political party that works both sides of the street.
—Franklin D. Roosevelt, campaign
speech in Boston, November 1944*

Franklin and Jean were having breakfast in the hotel on her last day before returning to Georgia with family when an attractive woman approached them. "May I join you?" she asked. Franklin quickly assured her they'd be delighted.

"I'm Hillary Clinton," she said. "I'd been hoping for an opportunity to meet the Franklins. You're making quite a splash for a newcomer to politics."

"Well, thank you, Hillary," Franklin stammered. He was still overimpressed with famous people, and Hillary Clinton was already definitely famous.

"That commercial with Jimmy Stewart was brilliant," she said. "Our tracking poll shows it helped push you into second place, just behind Bill. Who came up with it?"

"Well, I guess the main credit should go to Frank Capra," Franklin said modestly. "I haven't got a good tracking service, but that is good news.

Hillary looked at Jean. "So this is your first campaign, how do you like it?"

Jean shyly admitted she had not been as involved as most political wives and had spent most of the time in Georgia. "I guess it's old hat to you."

"It should be, but it really isn't. This is my first presidential campaign with my husband as the candidate, and it's a huge difference than running for governor. Our first campaign together was George McGovern's in 1972, when Bill and I were still law students at Yale. We went down to Arkansas to support McGovern against Nixon, and Arkansas definitely wasn't McGovern country."

Franklin smiled. "I well remember," he said. "It was hard to find McGovern country since Nixon carried every state except Massachusetts."

"The next year Bill ran against a longtime Republican congressman in Arkansas who was considered unbeatable…and he was, but Bill came surprisingly close, and suddenly he was the rising Democratic star in Arkansas politics. We'd married by then, and I became a real Arkansan, although as you may remember, I famously—at least in Arkansas—didn't change my last name. Bill was elected state attorney general in 1976 and two years later in 1978 was elected as the nation's youngest governor. Two years after that, he became the nation's youngest former governor when he was beaten by a Republican in the general election."

"That must have been an exhausting start to your marriage," Franklin remarked. "Four elections in the first six years."

Hillary laughed her familiar full-throated laugh. "And I also had a baby that year," she noted, looking at Jean. "You have three children, I believe. That must be great."

"And two grandchildren," Jean added. "They are all around here somewhere."

"These early campaigns were just warm-ups. Arkansas elects its governor for only a two-year term, so Bill had to run again in 1984, 1986, and 1988, before the state constitution changed to provide four-year terms. He was elected to a four-year term in 1990 and promised to serve the full four years. But then he toured the state, asking if he should run for president, and most people told him to go ahead. We looked at the field and decided this was the year, no offense to you, since you were not exactly on the horizon. We worried that Cuomo would get in, and when he didn't, we decided we'd made the right decision. But believe me, you should have run for governor or even mayor before tackling president. Whatever made you do that?"

"The truth is that I didn't want to be a governor or a mayor. I would have been lousy in either job. I wanted to be president, and at sixty-one years old, I didn't have time to work my way up the political ladder. I'd just as soon have stayed a newspaper publisher."

"Well, you are certainly bold, and it takes that, but if I had to bet, I'd say you'll be a newspaper publisher again this time next year."

Franklin accepted that good-naturedly and noted that Bill might have the chance to finish up his current term as governor next year.

"Touché," Hillary said. "Seriously, Bill and I have been impressed with what you've done and with some of the issues you've raised. I read a summary of your speech on foreign policy at Harvard, and you are so right. This is the year the US needs to improve relations with Russia and Cuba, but I'm not sure the people are ready to hear that. We find that the prevailing sentiment seems to be, 'We beat those Communist heathens, and we need to keep stomping on them.'"

Franklin nodded grimly. "You're right. but we must challenge that attitude. In many ways, a weak Russia is more dangerous than a strong Russia, and it still has the second-largest nuclear arsenal except that now it is scattered over thousands of miles and the borders of uncertain minor governments."

Hillary nodded. "That's right," she said, "but it may take time to bring the people around to the place they are willing to trust Communists."

"Of course, but it took a miracle to persuade Americans to spend the money to rebuild Germany and Japan after World War II, and they had been far more brutal enemies than Russia has ever been. Russia was actually our essential ally in World War II. Its armies decimated the Germans before the US had to invade Europe."

Hillary seemed impressed. "I wish Bill was here. He must have been called to another appointment, but I'm sure going to tell him about our conversation."

"We met Bill in Atlanta earlier this year at an event Governor Zell Miller held for him. He has great charisma."

Jean chimed in. "I was as impressed by him as any governor I've met...since Carl Sanders."

"As I'm sure you and Bill found in your Arkansas campaigns, most people remain cloistered in the villages of their doubts and fears, barricaded behind strong opinions and weak information. They will not be easily changed by pragmatism or contrary evidence from their prior conviction," Franklin offered.

"Say, that's real good," Hillary exclaimed. "Who said that?"

Franklin laughed. "I wrote it in a column several years ago, and I've never been able to find a source for attribution. So I guess I said it."

"Say it again," Hillary said, as she pulled out a pad and a pencil.

Almost embarrassed, Franklin repeated the phrases: "People remain cloistered in the villages of their doubts and fears, barricaded behind strong opinions and weak information, and they are reluctant to accept contrary evidence."

"Do you write most of your speeches?"

"I have been, but it's getting tedious, although not as tedious as writing three editorials and a column every day as a newspaper editor."

They shook hands all around. "I'm so glad I ran into you," Hillary said. "Let's talk again. We all have an exciting and challenging six weeks ahead."

She couldn't know how exciting or testing for both her and Bill.

"I really liked her," Jean commented after she left. "She's much warmer than I thought. She and Bill make a great team."

"Both are very smart too. She talked about their going to Arkansas to campaign for McGovern. The story is that it was their last quarter of law school at Yale, and they missed nearly the entire quarter but then returned and aced their finals. Hillary then went on to serve as a legal assistant to the committee considering the impeachment of President Nixon, who resigned before the committee acted, but it was an early encounter Hillary had with history."

"So what are we doing running for president against a couple like that?" Jean wondered.

"Discipline," Franklin answered. "Bill's discipline, which is erratic, but not Hillary's. She's dedicated to the goal, which is to make Bill president, and maybe later herself."

"Do you really believe that?"

"Well, you know what their enemies say, eight years of Bill, then eight years of Hillary. I'm not sure she shouldn't be first. According to their biographies, Hillary was the driving force in Bill's second term as governor when he came back from defeat. She took a leave of absence from the Rose Law Firm and organized 25 hearings to promote a program for higher school standards. At the time, physics was not taught in most of the 182 school districts. Foreign languages were not taught in 180 districts. In Bill's second term, legislation was approved after a hard and complicated battle that also included a teachers' test requirement. Bill became known as the Education Governor, and that cleared the way for his subsequent victories. Hillary was the catalyst. She's tough."

Despite the approval ratings of 70 to 90 percent for Bush after the Iraq war, biographies say Hillary never wavered in her belief that 1992 was the right year for Bill to run. "Clinton said later, I've got to give her credit. She thought in 1988 that the US still had a reasonably good economy, and the consequences of Reaganomics were not fully apparent to the voters, but by 1992, they would be. She always believed that she's been right."

That was also what Thomas Franklin thought. More than any reason, he felt the economy was the straw which would break the back of Bush's popularity and that the Democrat who stressed that could defeat him.

Meanwhile, Tsongas was still playing his "no Santa Claus" role, telling his listeners that the only way to save the nation was by cutting its spending, no tax breaks to poor families, and making other sacrifices, such as paying a higher tax on gasoline, which Franklin thought was insane, not to mention unfair.

The spot commercial comparing Tsongas to Old Man Potter began to run a few days before Christmas, and the staff picked up an immediate impact, including a response from the Tsongas campaign, which charged that it was a cheap trick and irresponsible but didn't quarrel with the details.

The family went back to Georgia for New Year's Day, so Franklin invited the staff members to a New Year's Eve dinner at the Wayfarer. Susie couldn't come because she had a date with one of the students from Harvard who had heard her speak. He lived in Portsmouth and had earlier asked her to an event at the college. Susie nervously told Franklin about it. "It'll be my first date in nearly three years," she said worriedly. "What do you think?"

"I think you'll be fine and that he is a very lucky young man to have such a pretty and intelligent girl as a date," Franklin assured her.

The other staff members gathered for the New Year's Eve party in a private room at the hotel, and several toasts were given to the coming year, 1992, in which Thomas Alexander Franklin would be elected president of the United States of America.

Jack Hardy and Kathleen Kelly were present as a couple, which surprised Franklin. They were very different people, but two of his favorites, both unattached and about the same age.

Sutton reported on the campaign. "Believe it or not," he said, "but the best report we now have from polls shows Franklin is ahead of Tsongas 22 to 20 percent with Clinton moving up to about 30 percent and the rest below 20 percent, including Kerrey and Harkin at about 16 percent."

A round of applause followed Sutton's report. "There's still a large undecided vote, of course, and on the Republican side, Pat Buchanan has surprising numbers against Bush, who has still not been to New Hampshire. He's expected early in January, and when he comes, it will be in force. Our problem is how to head off Clinton, who is obviously getting a lot of votes that could be Franklin's. They are both Southerners and considered cultural conservatives. Actually, except for Harkin, they are the only ones calling for higher taxes on the rich, but Clinton has the organization, the money, the media momentum, and frankly he's the best speaker with the most charisma, not to mention he's been elected five times as a governor."

Franklin asked to speak. "You're right, and as it happens, I had a talk with, would you believe, Hillary Clinton this morning. She sees the race as you described it, but my source in Little Rock tells me Clinton's past is about to catch up with him, and we should sit tight."

Franklin carefully had two glasses of wine. He noticed that Hardy had more than usual. The others had larger amounts, but 1992 arrived right on time at midnight, and everyone was still relatively sober and in a celebrating mood. Kathleen and Hardy embraced but barely kissed. She came over and gave Franklin a peck on the cheek. "Do you realize we all may be celebrating next New Year's Eve in the White House?" she exulted.

"There will have to be a lot of victory celebrations between now and then," Franklin reminded her.

At the office the next day, one of the new receptionists had more cheering news. "Radio stations are getting the first responses from the favorite songs advertisements," she said. "We haven't heard from the whole state, but smaller stations are reporting dozens of calls. The most requests so far are for 'I'll Be Seeing You,' 'Heartbreak Hotel,' and 'Little Things Mean a Lot.' I never even heard of that song."

"You're too young," Franklin said. "It was popular in the 1950s, about the time Jean and I were first dating."

He began preparing his speech to the labor unions in Manchester. He was planning to bear down again on his basic theme, which was how the nation had been developed with government spending and the progressive income tax system.

A large crowd was on hand at the labor hall. Hardy and Susie accompanied him. "As I've said," Franklin began, "the New Deal was America's third revolution, the first being the creation of the nation after breaking with Britain, the second being the Civil War, the final and most dramatic period of the New Deal was World War II. With the pressure from the imperatives of the war, Roosevelt was able to turn up spending on New Deal programs to the level which was always needed to lift the national economy totally out of its doldrums. There was also the flood of new job seekers from the countryside as the agrarian age ended and thousands who had previously worked on small farms and large ones found that better tractors and other machinery were replacing labor previously needed to plant and bring in the crops. Potential new workers crowded into the big cities.

"The movement of black farm workers from Southern states was an unprecedented population and racial shift. The automobile also transformed the labor market, creating jobs and reducing the travel between jobs and workers. In addition, even before World War II, women began to enter the labor force in greater numbers and at lower salaries than male workers in most cases.

"The New Deal had laid the foundation for the precedent of federal spending, but the war created the urgency. As the war spread, President Roosevelt demanded larger and larger production quotas to make the United States 'the great arsenal of democracy.' Then came the Japanese attack on Pearl Harbor, December 7, 1941. President Roosevelt had even more cause to challenge the private sector to accelerate its production, creating jobs and paying higher wages, which in turn provided more tax revenue the government needed to pay for the war.

"It was more of the medicine spooned out by the New Deal but now in amounts that reached the deepest ailments of the Depression and ushered in the industrial age to replace the agrarian age.

"Four weeks after Pearl Harbor, Roosevelt outlined to Congress and the nation the efforts and the price to be paid for victory. 'We must raise our sights on the production lines,' he pronounced, 'and let no man say it cannot be done.' He then announced production goals for 1942: 60,000 airplanes, 45,000 tanks, and 6 million tons of merchant shipping. The figures were staggering compared to the industrial production that then existed. The totals meant a plane every four minutes by 1943, a tank every seven minutes, 630 vessels every day. Even Harry Hopkins, the straw boss of the WPA and PWAs, who had achieved so much in such a short time during the 1930s, questioned Roosevelt's demands to reach so high. Roosevelt's reply, according to several books, was 'The production people can do it if they really try.' He was asking Americans to equal the war output that Germany and Japan had spent years building up from 1933 to 1940."

Chapter Sixteen

CLINTON'S PAST CATCHES UP

When people carelessly deride political parties, they overlook the fact that the party system of government is one of the greatest methods of unification and of teaching people to think in common terms of our civilization.
—Franklin D. Roosevelt, address at Jefferson Day dinner, St. Paul, Minnesota, April 18, 1932

Franklin, sensing a unique opportunity to reach his labor union audience, decided to elaborate on how Roosevelt achieved this almost impossible progress. "It was Roosevelt, rather than the business leaders who envisioned the country's latent potential if the government furnished the money," he continued. "Gone was his dithering of the mid-1930s about balancing the budget. It was full-throttle Keynesian economics. First, however, much of the private sector effort had to be converted to the tools and needs of war. In early 1942, the sale of automobiles was halted to consumers by government decree, and the inventory on hand at dealers was delivered to the lend-lease program for Great Britain and Russia, with the remainder rationed to police, firemen, doctors, and others considered essential to the public's health and safety. Nearly the entire manufacturing facilities of the auto industry were converted to armaments programs. In the process, four hundred thousand employees of car dealers were suddenly laid off, as forty thousand dealers closed. But jobs were waiting in the new defense facilities, springing up throughout the nation, not to mention the armed services. Older industries converted to meet the demands and furnish the jobs. A former corset factory was making grenades, a pinball machine maker began turning out armor-piercing bullets. In total, it was the greatest expansion of production in US history, or probably in any nation.

"It is important to remember and honor this home-front effort because its performance, much of it with union labor, was nearly as important in winning the war as the performance of soldiers on the battle front who depended on the home front workers who met Roosevelt's challenges.

"Of course, the sudden shortage of consumer items drove up their prices, and on January 30, 1942, Roosevelt signed an emergency price control bill that imposed ceilings on a range of consumer items. Rationing was instituted for gasoline, shoes, sugar, and silk stockings. For some reason, store-bought bread was not sliced, and since I lived on sandwiches in my childhood years, I felt that having to slice my bread off the loaf was a burden. Also, mayonnaise was rationed, but my grandmother came up with homemade mayonnaise, which was actually better than the bought kind.

"Some Americans complained about the restrictions and the controls, but I mainly remember that no bombs were ever dropped on the United States, no tanks ran through our towns, no deadly battles were fought on American soil. We watched the turmoil and mayhem in the movie newsreels and heard bad news on radio, of which there was plenty in those fateful years, so slicing bread seemed a trivial price to pay. The comic books cut back from sixty-four to fifty-six and then to forty-eight pages and eventually went up to twelve cents a copy.

"But the economic depression had been dealt its death blow, and the momentum from the war-fueled economy would carry over to a prosperous postwar period unlike any the nation had experienced.

"The fact to remember is that the wartime economy was the New Deal on steroids, and although it took the war to finally bury the Depression, it was the precedent and foundation laid by the New

Deal that produced the modern United States and, in many ways, the modern world.

"So where did the money suddenly come from? It had been such an issue before the war. Well, of course, it came from the spenders who suddenly had some discretionary income, but first it came from a vastly expanded and progressive income tax system, which rose as high as 89 percent on the very highest income during the closing year of the war.

"The struggle over who pays taxes and who benefits from the revenue continues, of course, and that conflict even persisted in the pressure of war, as many Republicans argued for sales or consumption taxes rather than higher income taxes on the wealthier. But Roosevelt saw higher income taxes as both needed for revenue and also as a curb on inflation, which partly stemmed from people who suddenly had more money and could pay higher prices for items, driving up the price for others.

"In the face of opposition, President Roosevelt stubbornly held to his belief throughout the war that wartime taxation be fair and redistributive. The conservative coalition of some Southern Democrats and most Republicans in Congress consistently sought to substitute the regressive sales tax as they still do fifty years later. The government was able to finance about 40 percent of the total war expense through higher taxation and borrowed most of the remainder, raising the national debt from 43 percent of the Gross National Product in 1941 to 127 percent in 1946. The economy held, and we are still paying off some of that debt, and as a taxpayer in 1991, I am proud that a small part of my taxes pays the debt for assuring victory in World War II. Most importantly, as a lesson for today's economy, let's keep in mind that the deficit as a percent of the GNP in 1992 will be about 20 percent compared to 127 percent in 1946. The fearmongers and naysayers have never been right about the present or the future, and that is why the United States is the richest and most powerful nation in history and why Franklin D. Roosevelt was the indispensable leader of the 1930s and 1940s. His vision still touches every phase of our national life to this very day."

The union members gave Franklin an ovation and hurrahs as he explained with figures and facts a theory which they felt in their hearts but had seldom received such a reaffirmation from their politicians.

"This is why we must keep the federal government strong and respected," Franklin added, "at a time when it is belittled and even ridiculed by a portion of the population that has little faith and less information on how the nation got to its present status."

Franklin paused to make sure he had the emotional tremor in his voice to complete the point. "We are in a time again when we must not let fearmongers and naysayers distract us from the proven pathway to further greatness, both for the nation and for the world. As Eleanor Roosevelt told the 1940 Democratic convention, this is 'no ordinary time.' It is a time of historic opportunity but also of daunting challenges. More money is available in the nation today than ever before. There are more billionaires today than there were millionaires a few years ago, and the number multiplies yearly. But in this richest of nations, there are still many pockets of poverty. In many small towns I drive through, I need only turn and go a few blocks off the main street and I find that Main Street is like a movie set and behind it is the real town of slum houses, unpainted stores, and idle youths with too much time on their hands and too little hope in their hearts. Unions helped lift much of the nation to a middle class status and beyond, but the US is beginning to fray around the edges, even here in New Hampshire, which has one of the broadest middle class societies.

"I think the cause is so-called supply-side economics, which enriches the supply-side but tells consumers on the demand-side to fend for themselves. That is not the philosophy which built the nation. It is the philosophy you hear from Paul Tsongas, who apparently has never accepted the New Deal. Today's middle class is under attack, and the battle is being lost year by year, and that is why this election year, 1992, is so critical in launching a counterattack, as the United States did against the Axis powers in 1942, when the Axis were on the ascendency and seemed certain of victory.

"The counter attack must start in union halls and must be conveyed to the people who can help reverse the trend and restore the economy to the path it followed so successfully from World War II to the 1970s. This is the year that trickle-down economics must give way to trickle-up economics. Another four years of Republican control may drive a nail in the coffin of the New Deal ideas that lifted us out of Depression, won World War II, and built the unprecedented postwar boom."

Franklin had painted a gloomier picture than he intended, but in his heart, he truly did feel that the hour was late to affirm the goals of the New Deal and to "dispel the cloud of gloom and doom that had enveloped so much of the nation!"

The labor leaders gave Franklin another round of applause and a standing ovation as he finished, and many came forward to shake his hand and speak with him. "We must get this speech out to all our members in New Hampshire," said the leader who had invited him. "Many of them are still for Harkin, but I truly believe you are the better bet. He has never presented our case so well and forcefully."

"Well, thanks, I appreciate that," Franklin replied. "I admire Senator Harkin, but I think he needs to broaden his message, as I've tried to do. I feel it's important this message gets a strong vote of support here in New Hampshire to provide an example to all the states that demand-side economics is the answer to our problems and that supply-side economics is simply transferring more money from the working people to the wealthy, the so-called job creators, who are just buying up their competitors instead of creating new jobs."

"That's it. Keep saying that. Harkin hasn't put it in those words. Be sure we get a full copy of this talk and we'll get it to every union hall in the state."

"Do you have any connections in Maine?" Franklin asked.

"A few. It's not a strong union state, but there are pockets where we can influence caucuses."

"They'll be meeting just a few days after the New Hampshire primary, and any support I can get there will be a great help. How about Georgia, it's the next big primary?"

"That's your home state," the union leader said. "Are you worried about it?

"Well, yes, Georgia is a state in political transition, and there are several Georgias—the Atlanta area and the rural areas, the white and the black, the suburbs and the coast. I've written editorials there for forty years, some for Republicans, some for Democrats. I worked to create a two-party system, which meant backing Republicans. I was also a Goldwater supporter in 1964 and a supporter of Bo Callaway for governor in 1966, when he had the chance to be the first Republican governor of Georgia in modern times. He was running against Lester Maddox, the guy who chased blacks out of his restaurants with a pistol and ax handles and was actually a little crazy. Callaway won narrowly in the popular vote but failed to get a majority because of a write-in vote for Democrat Ellis Arnall, and the US Supreme Court upheld an 1824 Georgia law that sent the election to the General Assembly, which was heavily Democratic and elected Maddox. That's how complicated it was, but that was twenty-five years ago."

"But you did come back to the Democrats when Carter ran for president, right?"

"That's complicated too. I knew Carter but was never a big supporter for various reasons. How I do in Georgia will be decided here in New Hampshire and maybe in Maine. I'll need help here because my main positions are not ones that will be popular in Georgia. It voted heavily for Goldwater, then for native son Carter, but for Bush four years ago. It's become more conservative and more Republican."

The labor leader looked puzzled, but he was still enthusiastic. "You're right," he said. "For you it all depends on New Hampshire."

Hardy and Susie were busy passing out pamphlets and getting cards and names. "That was terrific," Susie exclaimed as they left. "I've got enough names to spend a week calling and setting up meetings where they'd like for me to talk to their wives and friends."

"You're getting better at projecting," Hardy said. "Carter never made a more effective appeal to a labor group."

As they drove back to Concord, Franklin sat in back with Susie so they could compose some notes. She looked happier than he'd ever seen her. "We missed you New Year's Eve," he said. "I hope every-thing went well."

Her eyes suddenly glistened. "Oh, Mr. Franklin"—which she still called him—"it was fabulous. That was the first real date I've had in nearly three years, and he's a true gentleman and a straight-A student at Harvard, can you believe it?"

"Your first date since the…problem?" Franklin asked hesitantly.

"Yes, but it was wonderful."

"Did he kiss you at midnight?"

"Yes, yes, and several other times. He even tongued me, and I tongued him back, and it was great. He didn't try to go further, and I certainly didn't, but I loved it."

Franklin was surprised at her candor but felt that it was part of her personal therapy from the time of rejection that had envel-oped her for so long. "We called that french kissing, when I was in college," Franklin related. "I later decided it was the best thing the French sent us since LaFayette."

"Better than french fries?" Susie asked coyly.

"Yeah, and not as many calories."

"I haven't felt this complete in my life," Susie said. "Not even when we won the state basketball championship. I really think we—you—are going to win the primary, and then who knows?"

"I'm glad you said 'we' because that is what it will take, and there probably need to be more of 'we' in the main offices." He decided it was time that he called L. Bradford Ashmore.

During Franklin's twenty-three years as a newspaper publisher, Ashmore had been his more valuable player. Brad, as everyone called him, was a force of nature. To begin with, he was six feet, eight inches tall. He was multitalented, loyal, tireless and relentless, and a bit untamed, but he made things happen, and he was the spark that the milder-mannered Franklin could use when needed. They were the pair that created the publishing company. Brad handled a lot and did not let other people's feelings get in his way at times. He carried the day by also being charming and helpful, and as mentioned, he was unfailingly loyal to Franklin, whom he always called Boss, a term Franklin did not actually like.

When they returned to the Concord office, he called Brad, who despite his varied talents was running a small gun and watch repair shop in Birmingham and had left the newspaper business after a series of publishing jobs that didn't work out. Brad had been working at the Opelika paper as a circulation carrier, inserter, and maintenance man when Franklin came to that paper as publisher, in 1969. He was also still a student at Auburn University. As usual, he was on the job when Franklin arrived on a Saturday afternoon, which was then an off day for the rest of the staff. As the only employee present, Brad helped Franklin unload the files and materials he had brought from his position as editor of the Columbus daily newspaper. Brad was loud, profane, and informative; Franklin immediately spotted him as someone who could help build the run-down, five-day-a-week daily newspaper into something better. That was an amazing bit of insight.

As a circulation district manager, Brad increased the paper's circulation in Auburn from a few hundred to more than six thousand in two years, which equaled the circulation in Opelika, where it had been operating for more than fifty years. Most importantly, Brad taught himself to be an ace photographer, beginning with football and later extending to the news and other action events. He had an able teacher in one of the other photographers, but his special talent was in catching the shot no one else got. His height helped and also his willingness to push ahead and order people to get in line for a photo shoot. He bought long-range lens (with permission) and learned to take live-action football shots from the press box, pioneering football action shots no other newspaper was getting. Photographs soon became the attribute that set the *Opelika-Auburn News* apart and provided the edge to surpass the several other dailies that circulated in the area.

Another factor in Brad's brilliance was a mild extravagance which Franklin allowed in pursuit of excellence. On Auburn football game days, Brad and other *O-A News* photographers would take up to one hundred or more photos of action, festivities, and reactions, many of which would be printed and placed on the wall of the office for Franklin and other editors to select the eight or nine to be used. That process resulted in dramatic examples of photography, which

Franklin delighted in. He felt that the future of small newspapers, and to some degree all newspapers, was staff-produced photos, both routine and dramatic. Previously the paper had mainly used AP wire photos, if any. Franklin dropped the AP photo service to force himself and the staff to rely on local staff photos and to a large extent on local or staff-produced articles.

Brad slowly became an excellent reporter, using the same traits that made him a great photographer. He got the story, and if it lacked polish, that could be fixed by the editor, usually Franklin. In those days, he was functioning as editor, publisher, and community representative.

In that first year, he also assembled a remarkable staff of young and seasoned employees, including three of the former owners, who proved invaluable. He raided the Columbus paper for a sports-writer and later the Columbus sports editor himself, who became his associate publisher; a circulation manager who joined with Brad in eventually expanding the circulation to twenty thousand and was also a valuable sports reporter and contact in the nearby community known as the Valley. It was another textile center, which actually had more mills than Columbus, LaGrange, or Opelika. Only the textile complex in North Carolina had more textile workers than the Chattahoochee Valley, which was the name usually given to the area from LaGrange to Columbus to the Valley and Opelika-Auburn.

But what really linked the communities around Opelika was allegiance to Auburn University football, which in that first year of the Sunday edition had the exciting combination of Pat Sullivan at quarterback and Terry Beasley as his receiver. Both made All-American as sophomores and led Auburn to an 8–3 season, including beating archrival Alabama, coached by the legendary Paul "Bear" Bryant.

Franklin's stockholders kept helping him get loans to finance the newspaper's growth, and the income was also increasing, doubling in that first year. Franklin, with a wife and three young children, was feeling the responsibility, and he had never suffered harsh criticism well, of which there was always some in the newspaper business. He thought the people there should be satisfied with having a much-improved newspaper, but that isn't the way the world works in the newspaper business or in politics.

Franklin also had to make the transition from being a dedicated University of Georgia fan to being a dedicated Auburn fan plus living in Alabama instead of Georgia, where he had lived all his previous years. To make sure he kept his Georgia connections, he soon bought five weekly newspapers in South Georgia, about fifty miles below Opelika, and composed and printed them in the Opelika plant. They gave him a reason to attend both Georgia and Alabama Press Association meetings, and eventually he served as president of both of them, his only real claim to any political experience.

Brad answered his call from New Hampshire. "I thought you'd never call," he said. "I've been reading about you, and I heard you already got Kathleen up there. I haven't seen her in twenty years… and I'd like to."

"She's still a good looker and smarter than ever. You can help us. Our chance in the primary is looking better. When can you come?"

"How about next week?"

"Great, call this number in Concord and talk to Phil Sutton, who'll get you a plane, a car, and a place to live. And bring your winter clothes. It's cold, and the ground is covered with snow."

Reports on Franklin's talk to the labor union in Manchester were mostly good and generated requests for several more talks, plus there were two debates in the first two weeks of January. He also did interviews on a Maine TV station and another with WMUR in New Hampshire. In the interviews, he tried to get in his main themes of lower payroll taxes, a demand-side economy, and better relations with Russia. "The middle class in the US is struggling because most of its families haven't had a pay raise in twenty years, while the stock market has soared along with pay for CEOs and so-called money managers on Wall Street," he stressed.

He also threw in that he would oppose NAFTA. The announcer hadn't asked, but Franklin urged him to ask the other candidates about NAFTA. He wasn't sure the announcers knew what NAFTA was, and he didn't have time to explain.

There were two debates during this period, but they were mostly uneventful. Franklin was invited but got minimum attention from the moderators or the other candidates, who had apparently decided that ignoring him was the best strategy despite his climb in the polls.

Clinton and Harkin were the friendliest candidates. Kerrey and Brown acknowledged him but had little else to say. Tsongas was clearly cool and looked at him with obvious disdain. Tsongas's consultants told Hardy and Burkhart that the senator was angry and resentful over the commercials comparing him with Old Man Potter. He also recognized that Franklin was taking votes away from his earlier lead.

In the debate, Franklin had little chance of outtalking more seasoned debaters such as Clinton, Harkin, Brown, and Kerrey, while Tsongas stuck to his standard story of sacrifice to reduce the budget deficit and put the nation's economy on a pay-as-you-go path.

When he got a chance to speak, Franklin thanked the voters for giving his dark horse candidacy a chance and urged them to look at the issues as well as the background of the candidates. "You can make a real difference for the nation by voting for me," he concluded.

His office was still getting response from radio stations requesting favorite songs of the past, most of them older voters; the other ads were also getting some response. Clinton was the only candidate using much TV, and he did have offices in most cities, plus the highly regarded consultant team of Carville, Begala, and George Stephanopoulos, who were his chief spokesmen.

On January 16, Franklin received a call from his contact in Little Rock. "It's about to happen," he said. "The newspapers here are carrying a story tomorrow based on a report in the tabloid National Star that a former Little Rock TV newswoman is claiming she had a twelve-year affair with Bill Clinton and has decided to come forward with her story because Clinton 'is lying to the American people and telling me to lie about it too. I'm sick of the deceit and of all the lies. The truth is I loved him, and we did have an affair.' There's lot more detail, some of it lurid," the caller said. "I'll fax you a copy of our edition, and you can probably get a copy of *The Star* in Concord."

Franklin put the phone down and remarked shakily, "This sounds like the break we've been waiting for—and actually have counted on—about Clinton. His reputation had caught up with him." Franklin wasn't waiting to get a copy of *The Star*. He called Sutton in and told him about the story and told him to get a copy of *The Star* in Manchester or Boston or wherever, and to order as many copies as possible.

He looked at the latest summary of polls they had accumulated. Clinton was clearly in front with nearly 30 percent, Tsongas trailing at 22 percent, and he and Kerrey varying between 20 and 18 percent, depending on the poll. The trend was down for Tsongas and up for he and Kerrey before the last debate. Incredibly, he realized he might be leading in another week. He had dreamed about the possibility but felt his own shortcomings as well as his lack of political background were insurmountable.

Hardy and Burkhart came in with big smiles. Hardy had gotten the news from a friend in Jody Powell's office. "Can you believe it?" he shouted. "What will all those people in those townships we visited think about Clinton now?"

"Who knows?" Franklin said warily. "We haven't seen the story, and *The Star* is not exactly a gold-standard source. Get CNN on TV and let's see if they are reporting it."

CNN wasn't carrying it yet. Soon a copy of the article was faxed from Little Rock. Franklin and the others gathered around a table to read it. The boxcar headline across two pages read, "My 12-Year Affair with Bill Clinton—Nightclub Singer Jennifer Flowers Breaks Her Silence to Tell All."

Headlines in smaller type took up half the first page: "They made love all over her apartment…not just in the bedroom but on the floor, in the kitchen, on the couch, even in the shower; he begged her to have sex in the governor's mansion. He talked about leaving his wife for her but he was too ambitious to risk his political career with a divorce. He cried when she told him their affair was over in 1989."

The article went into intimate details such as Clinton "would come to her apartment and tumble into bed. He stayed four hours and we made love several times that night."

There were four photos of Jennifer Flowers, showing her to be an attractive blonde in her midthirties. In the lengthy (for *The Star*) article, Flowers told of losing her job as a nightclub singer after a lawsuit was filed by Larry Nichols in the fall of 1990, charging Clinton with using taxpayer money to conduct illicit affairs. The suit named five women, including Flowers. Nichols had been fired from his state job, and the Arkansas press did not believe his charges had any credence. But Flowers said she was getting anonymous calls and had lost a second job because of the publicity. Then Clinton called her, she related, and told her he was going to run for president and warned that their relationship would be scrutinized again. "Just deny everything," he said. "They don't have any proof, and if you say it's not true, they can't prove a thing."

"A lot of people will hate me for this, and to tell the truth, I'm sick at my stomach when I imagine what Bill thinks," Flowers was quoted.

More damaging to Clinton was a sidebar article entitled "The Bill Clinton Love Tapes." Flowers had recorded their telephone conversations in recent months because friends told her she needed to protect herself. She had a press conference scheduled for Monday January 20, at which she planned to play the tapes for a press conference live on CNN.

Franklin shook his head as he read the tabloid's articles. The details were incredible, and the tapes promised even more. Phil Sutton looked elated. "For a lot less, Hart had to withdraw from the 1988 primary, and that was just four years ago."

"What do you think?" Franklin asked Kathleen.

"Wallace never had to deal with anything like this," she said. "He wasn't married when he was seeing me and several other women, one of which he did marry, of course, and there was never any mention of his going with other women in the media, even during the campaign against Brewer, which was a cruel one in most other ways."

Franklin recalled Big Jim Folsom's second campaign in 1946, when Folsom was a widower for a while. During the campaign, Folsom liked to tell the story that his opponents had used every trick to defeat him. "They even sent this pretty little girl up to my hotel room," he'd say, "and when they use that kind of bait, they'll catch Big Jim every time." He always got a big laugh because he had a reputation as a buffoon, but he also married soon after.

"We need to hear what Clinton says about all this and what happens next," Franklin said. He also had an idea but worried about it backfiring. He immediately called Brad Ashmore, who was scheduled to leave for New Hampshire the next day. He told Brad about the Clinton article and told him to rent a truck for the trip and round up about ten thousand copies of *The Star* and bring them to New Hampshire. "We need a lot of people in the state to know this story," Franklin said judiciously. Ashmore knew more about distributing newspapers than anyone. Franklin suggested he call *The Star*'s nearest printing plant or get all the copies he could find in Birmingham and the cities between there and New Hampshire. Franklin felt they could give copies to outlets and let them furnish them free to customers. He realized ten thousand was a lot but thought the papers would be better than any type of mailing they could get up.

This story was obviously a game-changer, but Franklin knew the Clintons well enough by now that he didn't think they'd back off. Clinton had the best consultants, and he had Hillary, who was really the key. Gary Hart's wife, in 1988, had not supported him very convincingly. She clearly gave the impression that she was distressed and believed he had betrayed her. That doomed his presidential hopes.

Franklin figured Hillary would be different, but it was too early to know what approach the Clintons would take. For another day, the Clinton operation managed to keep a lid on the story, but by the third day, the story had jumped from a suspect tabloid to Fox News Network and then to newspapers and TV stations throughout the world.

Clinton called the allegations "an old story, complete trash from a tabloid that says there are people who have cows' heads." But *The*

New York Daily News published it all. "Clinton is running for president, let's put it out there for him to react," its story concluded.

At an airport, a reporter bluntly asked Clinton if he had committed adultery. "If I had, I wouldn't tell you," Clinton answered angrily.

Then came the TV debate of the candidates on WMNR. Cokie Roberts, a respected commentator and daughter of a congressman, asked Clinton to comment on "concern by members of your party that the Republicans will come forward and find someone who will confirm these allegations of womanizing."

That question put the issue in the media mainstream. Clinton replied that Republicans had been trying for years to use the rumors against him, and they were all "a pack of lies."

The next day, *The Star* published the edition that had been faxed to Franklin's office, and it included details of fifteen recorded phone conversations between Clinton and Jennifer Flowers. They had not been widely publicized until then.

The recorded conversations were no surprise, however; Clinton had already acknowledged earlier that he knew Flowers and had helped her get a job with a state agency after she told him of her firing due to the rumors about them. On the tape, Clinton's voice is heard telling Flowers, "There's nothing they can do if everybody is on record denying it. They don't have pictures. If no one says anything, they don't have anything."

Clinton and his main consultants were now being followed by a gang of media people, and even the *New York Times* had finally carried an eight-inch story on an inside page, giving legitimacy to the tabloid report. Clinton had another big problem that day. He had to be in Little Rock for a final decision on a capital punishment appeal of a convicted murderer.

Ironically, media members following Clinton lost his vehicle in a snowstorm between Cleveland and Manchester, where Clinton boarded a plane to fly back to Little Rock for the execution case. Meanwhile, the popular news show *Nightline with Ted Koppel* had decided to devote its entire time period to the Clinton story, although ABC had chosen not to carry the details on its nightly news programs. Nightline was to be an analysis about the ethics of running the story in the first place, but the result was to put the story more fully into the news stream, sort of by the back door.

When the Clintons themselves weren't available, ABC settled for Mandy Grunwald, who had joined the Clinton consulting group; Larry Sabato, a professor who had written the book *Feeding Frenzy*, about campaign rumors and scandals; and Jonathan Alter, a media critic for *Newsweek*.

Grunwald gave a powerful performance, accusing Koppel of ignoring the real issues in the campaign and using his program to publicize unsubstantiated charges from a tabloid. "You're letting *The Star* set the agenda for you...and I find that troubling," she charged.

Koppel had been accused of conveying a know-it-all attitude to his guests, and many viewers were smugly satisfied at Grunwald's attack on him, to the point that they overlooked the real point of the program, which were Flowers' phone calls and charges against Clinton. He had, in effect, avoided another bullet.

Franklin and staff watched the program in dismay, shocked that Koppel had not confirmed the charges more effectively. Requests for Clinton appearances were pouring in for the weekend, which also happened to be the weekend of that year's football Super Bowl.

The other primary candidates weren't completely forgotten, but mostly they were asked for their reaction to the Clinton revelations. Franklin said quite frankly that he was disturbed and even if the allegations were not fully verified, they had cast a shadow on the contest that needed to be considered. "I'm surprised that the governor of Arkansas had so much time to talk to Ms. Flowers on the phone, although according to him, she was a casual acquaintance," Franklin commented.

The offer that the Clintons decided to accept on TV was from *60 Minutes*, the top-rated talk show on TV. This would be a thirty-minute segment to follow the regular sixty-minute program, which was scheduled on CBS after the Super Bowl. With carryover from the Super Bowl, usually the most watched event of the year, and the normal *60 Minutes* audience, the Clintons' appearance was likely to be the most watched news event in TV history—how bad could that be, Clinton's advisers decided.

Franklin and staff watched with intense interest and then fleeting disappointment. The moderator, Steve Kroft, had not pinned Clinton down on any specific acts of misbehavior, nor had he gotten Clinton to totally disavow Jennifer Flowers as a paranoid liar who concocted from thin air the detailed accounts of a lengthy affair.

As expected, Bill and Hillary tried to keep the emphasis on their marriage and devotion to each other, and they gave a convincing performance. Bill did admit that he had been responsible for "causing pain in my marriage," but he balked at a specific question about committing adultery. "I think most Americans who are watching tonight will know what we're saying, and they'll feel that we have been more than candid."

Hillary broke in. "I don't think being any more specific about what's happened in the privacy of our life together is relevant to anybody besides us."

Later when Kroft said, "Most Americans would agree that it's admirable that you've stayed together, worked out your problems, and seemed to have reached some sort of arrangement and understanding." Clinton broke in strongly in what was his most effective minute in the interview.

"Wait a minute, wait a minute. You're looking at two people who love each other. This is not an arrangement or understanding, this is a marriage. That's a very different thing."

Hillary then added the most memorable lines in in the interview. "I'm not sitting here like some little woman standing by my man like Tammy Wynette"—referring to Wynette's current popular song, "Stand by Your Man"—"I'm here because I love and respect him, and I honor what he's been through and what we've been through together. And you know, if that's not enough for people, then heck, don't vote for him."

Franklin was especially impressed by Hillary's simple plea: "Then heck, don't vote for him." Franklin had a feeling that was what a lot of people would do: not vote for him, but he wasn't sure. More than half the voters had probably watched the *60 Minutes* segment, and most of them certainly knew Bill Clinton's wife was standing by him.

The surprising news in the Franklin campaign office on Monday was that there was a new leader in the New Hampshire primary field, and his name was Thomas Alexander Franklin. He had eased ahead of both Clinton and Tsongas, with Clinton slipping to a third, closely followed by Kerrey, who seemed to be inheriting some of Clinton's falloff. Harkin and Brown also increased their support, but Franklin had a solid three-point lead over Tsongas and Clinton, who were virtually tied.

"Clinton definitely took a blow, no pun intended," Sutton remarked. He and Franklin surmised that Franklin benefited as expected from his first TV spots, the sponsoring of the *It's a Wonderful Life*, showing and the coverage of his speeches at Harvard and the Labor Union hall.

"Don't forget, Hardy and I have been in 120 townships, and Charlie and Susie have been in most of the others. Small groups add up in polling," Franklin reminded Sutton.

"Brad called," Sutton said. "He's got a truckload of ten thousand copies of last week's *Star*. He also rounded up some people willing to help him distribute them. He's planning to offer a bunch to every grocery story and curb market and restaurant that will take them, concentrating on the Manchester-Nashua areas, which is where 70 percent, maybe 80 percent of the Democrats live."

"Good, people who saw the *60 Minute* program need a chance to see Jennifer's side of the story."

Charlie was preparing a news release on the new tracking poll. "Can we use these figures?" he asked. "This isn't our tracking poll."

"Let's see what the papers use in the morning and quote their stories to verify and substantiate the polls. We want the headlines on Tuesday to read, 'Franklin Now in First Place,'" Sutton said.

In the national polls, Franklin figured he'd still be in third place at best, but he was now definitely a player and was trying to get accustomed to the feeling. He'd never really felt like a winner in his whole life, despite his other successes. He still recalled the day in early grammar school when that feeling took root. There were about thirty children in his class, and the teacher asked all of them to sing the note "Ahhh." On that slim evidence, she then separated the class into bluebirds and redbirds in order to assign them to music class. Bluebirds were the ones whose "Ahs" sounded best to her, and redbirds were the ones with the sourest notes. Franklin was among the redbirds. Ever after, deep in his psyche, he'd always remained a redbird. People like the Clintons were bluebirds.

The primary now loomed only three weeks away, and he had several speech options. He decided one would be at the University of New Hampshire in Dover and one in Berlin, a city of nearly twenty thousand, where he had spoken early in the campaign. He also planned a late trip to Dixville Notch.

Brad had quickly made himself useful after distributing the copies of *The Star* by helping Charlie with contacts at newspapers, both in New Hampshire and southern Maine. Fund-raising got a real shot in the arm with the news that Franklin was now in the lead.

Franklin felt it was time to try an idea from Carter's campaign he had pondered but didn't feel would work earlier. He called his longtime friend Milton Jones in Columbus, Georgia, who was close to Jimmy Carter and helped Carter in his first presidential campaign. The idea was Hamilton Jordan's. He and his wife persuaded about one hundred of Carter's Georgia neighbors and other supporters to go to New Hampshire in January for door-to-door contacts, asking people to support their friend and former governor for president. The group became known as the Peanut Brigade and was given major credit for Carter's upset primary victory in New Hampshire and later in several other primary states. Jones had been one of the leaders. Franklin asked him if he'd try again, although he wasn't sure there were one hundred people willing to do that for him, plus those who came for Carter were now sixteen years older. But Milton actually recalled the venture as "a lot of fun" even though the weather had been punishing. "If you can get the group together and come the first week in February, I can promise better weather," Franklin told him, and also a small stipend for everyone, which Carter hadn't provided.

"That's not much notice, but I'll check around and let you know," Jones said.

For the trip to Dover, Franklin took Brad and Susie. He wanted some creative photos, and he knew Brad was the person who could get them. Susie was always a big hit at colleges and had become efficient at getting names and addresses.

All the buzz was still about Clinton and the *National Star* revelations. Two references to other candidates on the tapes had proven most embarrassing to Clinton. On one, he tells Jennifer that "Bob Kerrey is single so nobody cares who he's screwing." On another tape, the voice that sounds clearly like Clinton refers to Mario Cuomo as "a mean son of a bitch." Jennifer suggests that Cuomo may have Mafia connections, and Clinton replied, "Well, he acts like one." As everyone knew, Cuomo was especially sensitive about talk that Italian Americans were associated with criminal activities. "I meant simply," Clinton explained to reporters that Cuomo was a tough and worthy opponent. He said he tried to call Cuomo and apologize, but Cuomo later said Clinton never reached him. A headline in one New York paper read, "Clinton Talks Like Bigot."

Tracking polls by the middle of the week showed Clinton's support leveling off but at a lower level. The execution he allowed in Arkansas seemed to help more than hurt since Clinton strongly supported capital punishment and was emphasizing law and order in a year when that was a popular issue.

For his speech at the university, Franklin decided on a subject he had long pondered and had written about in many columns, which was simply how difficult it has been throughout history for nations to sustain stable and democratic governments. The best and almost only outstanding example was the United States of America, and it has survived a few bumps in the road, including, Franklin felt, at the present time when so many Americans were blaming the government for any and all troubles.

A good crowd of students and faculty members greeted them in the main auditorium. Brad took several photos of Franklin mingling with the students and shaking hands with the president and other university officials.

"I'd like to talk a few minutes about democracy with a little *d*," Franklin began. "The dictionary defines *democracy* simply as government by all the people, usually through elected representatives, with equality of rights in society.

"In one of my earliest editorials, I wrote that 'democracy is the narrow path between the wilderness of chaos on the left and the desert of tyranny on the right.' And it must be stressed how indeed narrow that path is and why so few governments have been able to follow it without straying into the wilderness or more often into the desert because people will always choose tyranny over chaos if a choice must be made. They may prefer freedom, but they will not willingly tolerate life without a degree of order and direction. The United States has been one of the few nations to navigate the path for so long a period and with such a diverse and fractious population, assembled from dozens of nations, with a wide variety of languages, cultures, races, and religions. The United States is a veritable miracle of government, achieved without any allegiance to a long-established royalty, such as Great Britain, to an emperor as Japan has, or under the heel of stern dictators, which so many nations have accepted in the place of disorder. US voters can change its officials peacefully while the government itself is maintained as it has been for 250 years, often challenged, once almost fatally in the Civil War, but surviving as the best hope of its own people and as an example to other nations.

"In the days leading up to the Civil War, a great Georgian, arguing against his state's secession from the Union, said to the convention which was to decide the State's path, 'What better government can we find in all the world, why should we risk our state's future in the uncertainty of breaking the bonds with the nation our forefathers founded and have nurtured and which we in the South have played so large a role in building?' The speaker was Alexander Stephens, who would lose his effort to keep Georgia from seceding and then become vice president of the Confederate states. That is how powerful the lure of the wilderness is even to the wisest of men."

Franklin paused, as Brad snapped several photos of his arm-waving speaking style, which was Franklin's main concession to the theatrics of a speaker. "I'm told by advisers that the nation is in an antigovernment mood, especially the federal government, but I do not intend to contribute to that mood, and I join with Alexander

Stephens in asking, 'Where in all of history can we find a better government?'

"Today the United States has more opportunities and challenges than any nation has ever possessed. It is the surviving superpower in the world, but it has only 6 percent of the population and even less of the geographic area. It is essential that our power be used to not only promote more democracy but to promote more civilization, which is a prerequisite for real democracy.

"Millions of people, including some in our own country, still go to bed hungry every night; millions still use outdoor privies and have no access to even rudimentary plumbing and modern sanitary facilities or clean water. Millions, in fact, still live in conditions common four hundred years ago, subject to diseases modern medicine has long since found a cure for, suffering from extreme heat or punishing cold without modern appliances or the means of improving their conditions. Even worse, millions of them still live in the midst of war and looting and other man-made disasters that make nature's disasters seem mild. So what has our great and powerful United States done to assure that the ocean in which we are all adrift will not one day engulf even so formidable a yacht as our own nation?

"Unfortunately, when nations desperate for the tools to make their people more secure and comfortable ask for our help, we send them bombs and planes and other instruments of destruction instead of commodes and ovens and bathtubs or medical equipment to make their lives better, and of course, it is because what their leaders ask for are the weapons of war rather than the tools of civilization. Most recently we taught Iraq a lesson by bombing its infrastructure back to conditions the Babylonians were facing in the world's earliest civilization. The country was laid waste, but Saddam Hussein still rules and is stronger than ever, having killed off his main opposition, the Kurds.

"But if the strongest nation is tempted to use the power of war to solve problems against contemptible bullies, can we expect better of weaker nations? Can we expect to promote peace along roads strewn with rotting bodies and destroyed buildings?"

Franklin got a good round of applause, and Brad took a number of photos of him with students and faculty members. Susie got names and addresses and promised to send copies of the photos. Nearly all the students were from New Hampshire. One professor approached Franklin and shook his hand with enthusiasm. "I was going to vote for Harkin," he said, "but I'm switching to you, and I'd like to help you organize a group in my hometown of Plymouth. There is a small college there, and I'll take copies of your speech and distribute them to friends."

Franklin was elated. This was the kind of help he needed in these closing days, and Plymouth was a town where he'd gotten little support.

After the talk, Franklin, Brad, and Susie toured the campus with Brad taking photos of Franklin at several sites and at a basketball game Franklin managed to work in. He also got some shots of Susie with a couple of players and of the coach with Franklin, who asked the coach about the season and told him he'd like to attend the next game. The coach admitted he was a Republican and would probably vote for Buchanan in the primary and Bush in the general election. "I understand," Franklin told him, "but if you know any Democrats, remember me to them for the primary."

The game itself had been a downer for New Hampshire as it lost 72–45. The Republican coach looked despondent. "To win, you need players who are agile, mobile, and hostile," he told Franklin. "We don't have enough of them." Franklin did carry away one good memory of the game. As the score mounted against New Hampshire, the cheerleaders led the crowd in a chant he'd never heard but greatly enjoyed. "That's all right, that's okay, they'll all work for us someday," the cheerleaders chanted of the opponent's taller, huskier players.

While in the vicinity, the trio visited Portsmouth and talked to an editor about doing a photo layout and article on Franklin's visit to the university. He looked at the photos, took the students' names, and promised to use them in a Sunday layout. By design, they'd gotten photos of several students from Portsmouth and nearby Kittery, as well as Dover.

Back in Concord, Brad and Susie collaborated on a story and sidebar which was given to the Concord newspaper, which also agreed to carry a page of photos, with an emphasis on the basketball team, which had several players from the Concord area.

In the meantime, Bill Clinton was involved in another public relations crisis of national proportion, which Sutton thought would hurt him worse than Jennifer Flowers. It involved his draft status during the Vietnam War. Like many men of his age, he had not served in the military during that long conflict. In addition, Clinton had actively opposed the Vietnam commitment and joined a demonstration against the war during his Rhodes Scholar year in England.

This time the story broke in the respected *Wall Street Journal*, not a suspect weekly tabloid. An army recruiter in Arkansas was quoted as saying Clinton had signed up for the ROTC program at the university "and was able to manipulate things so that he didn't have to go in."

The situation was much more complicated than that, and Clinton professed to be shocked since the same recruiter had consistently said through the years that Clinton had acted properly in regard to his draft status. He had a deferment while in college and then registered for the draft and drew a high number that was never called. Charges that he dodged the draft had been raised as early as his first run for governor in 1978. "They were false then and are false now," Clinton said. To make things worse for Clinton, he was suffering from a severe cold and sore throat and he wanted to spend the last weekend before the primary in Little Rock.

But the draft story had become another media "feeding frenzy." This time Clinton did appear on *Nightline*. Ted Koppel read a letter Clinton had written to the draft board when he was twenty-three. The letter had mysteriously turned up in the past week. Clinton admitted that he had written the letter and listened intently as Koppel read it on live TV. "That letter confirms everything I've said for the past eighteen years," Clinton exclaimed. He had opposed the US commitment in Vietnam and came to believe the draft itself was illegitimate. "No government rooted in parliamentary democracy should have the power to force its citizens to fight and kill and die in a war they may oppose, a war which even possibly may be wrong and does not immediately involve the peace and freedom of the nation," Clinton had written.

Clinton, of course, was expressing the feelings of many in his generation, including nearly all the young Republican politicians who also avoided service in Vietnam. An exception, of course, was President Bush himself, who served with distinction in World War II. On the Democratic side, Bob Kerrey had served in Vietnam and lost part of his leg. Harkin had been in the Navy.

And then there was Franklin himself, who was not a military veteran. He had been only fourteen when World War II ended, in college during most of the Korean War, and then had received a deferment as his mother's only surviving child after his father died when he was seventeen.

The draft story hit Clinton's staff harder than it did Clinton. "When will it be time to quit?" a staffer was quoted. "When Hillary says it's time," another staffer answered, and he knew that time wasn't imminent.

The final weekend of the New Hampshire primary campaign had several other surprising moments, and all in all, it was the most dramatic primary in the nation's history. Clinton, recovering from his cold, made an impassioned speech in Dover just a few hours before his appearance on *Nightline,* and it possibly fired him up for TV. He pointed out that politics and public service are the work of his life and that his dreams for the country were his "vision thing." He recalled that Bush had been resurrected politically by his 1988 New Hampshire primary victory after running third in the Iowa caucus a week earlier. Clinton claimed Bush had spent only three hours in the state during his term, mostly on his way to and from Kennebunkport, "while your unemployment and food stamp rates tripled. They say I'm on the ropes, but I'm going to give you this election back, and if you'll give it to me. I won't be like George Bush. I'll never forget you gave me a second chance, and I'll be with you till the last dog dies."

Franklin and his staff had watched *Nightline* with great interest and studied the many commentaries on the primary, most of which concentrated on Clinton and his Job-like catastrophes. Franklin was trying to stay focused on his own campaign. In the latest tracking poll, he was still leading Tsongas with Clinton falling further behind and Kerrey climbing. The big event still ahead before the voters got their say was a CNN debate on Sunday night.

Musing on Clinton's last remark about "being with you till the last dog dies," Franklin asked Hardy if that sounded like a threat or a promise.

"He sounds like he's in a fighting mood," Hardy said. "I recall the closing days of the 1980 presidential campaign. Carter was in a bleak mood, but he held out hope until that last weekend when the Iranians rejected the final opportunity to release the hostages, only to release them as soon as Carter was no longer president."

"I remember," Franklin said. "I thought that it was the decisive setback for Carter. The final margin made it seem that he didn't have a chance from the start, and he actually had been a pretty good president."

The week had been mostly upbeat for the Franklin campaign. His speech and visit at the University of New Hampshire had gotten the notices they'd hoped, with a full-page of photos and an article in the Portsmouth and Concord daily papers and photos and stories in many of the other papers. But most exciting was the visit of the newly organized Peanut Brigade from Georgia.

Milton Jones had called a few days after Franklin contacted him and reported he had gotten up about fifty people willing to spend six days in New Hampshire in the first week of February. Several of them were veterans of the trips for Carter sixteen years earlier, and Jody Powell had offered advice to Hardy and Charlie on organizing the walking routes and pinpointing the houses where Democrat voters lived. They decided to concentrate only on the cities of Manchester, Nashua, Concord, Portsmouth, and Keene.

The group flew in on a Monday and left on Thursday, but Franklin had a chance to visit with all of them, most of whom he knew. The majority were from Columbus, Athens, and North Atlanta. They found fairly good weather and went door to door as they had done for Carter, saying they were friends of Franklin and recommended him to the people of New Hampshire. They also left pamphlets and copies of Franklin's columns and other information. Franklin was surprised at the number of families the group managed to contact.

Franklin had been toying with an offbeat promotion idea for several days in January. It would be expensive and could even backfire, but he needed something to give his campaign a real jolt, and he thought this might do it. In mid-January, President Bush had made his first campaign trip to New Hampshire. Local Republican leaders were pleased and relieved since Bush had been under attack not only by the Democratic candidates but also by the upstart campaign of Pat Buchanan, running against Bush in the Republican primary and making some inroads. But the president was obviously annoyed by having to take to the campaign trail instead of running the country from the Oval Office. In a speech to Republicans, he said, "I've known the economy is in a freefall. Maybe I haven't conveyed that as well as I should...but there are some fundamentals that are pretty darn good." Later, in a speech at Dover, Bush said he was tired "of these carping little liberal Democrats jumping all over my you-know-what." He wasn't going to buy some fancy quick-fix, and when someone asked him about Pat Buchanan's no-tax pledge, he reacted angrily, saying what was needed was a pledge to elect more Republicans. Bush then displayed his penchant for uttering inane references by adding, "Whatever my burdens, I feel blessed, so don't cry for me, Argentina." The phase was from a song in the popular play *Evita*.

Franklin decided that plea needed some emphasis, and his idea was to organize a rally in Manchester and invite the star of *Evita* who sang that song, "Don't Cry for Me Argentina," to come and perform it in Manchester's largest auditorium.

The idea was audacious, so he explained it to Sutton, who looked dubious but recognized the potential for drawing a crowd, which still wasn't easy for Franklin.

Franklin told Sutton to offer the singer up to $2,000 plus expenses for a one-night performance and to send out invitations to all the women's clubs and high schools in the Manchester and Nashua areas. Admission was to be free. The biggest site they could find was the high school auditorium in Manchester. Since they were playing strictly in the dark, they had no idea how many people to expect. "Make the arrangements," Franklin told Sutton, and get some invitations out that will just say that a Broadway star will be present and singing her popular songs from a current hit show. Any political talk will be kept short.

Incredibly, the plan developed as outlined. The star was willing to come with her manager and attendants, and the price was right. She felt it would be good publicity for the play, which had been running for months and was in need of a late boost.

The date was a Wednesday night in the second week of February, which suited Franklin since the Peanut Brigaders from Georgia would be in New Hampshire and could attend and fill out the crowd if necessary. Franklin conveyed the news to Milton Jones, who thought it would help him recruit a few more Brigaders.

The star's performance occurred during the furor over Bill Clinton and at least for one night took the spotlight off Clinton. Franklin introduced her and explained she had come to dedicate a song to President Bush. He then played a recording of the speech in which Bush exclaimed, "Don't cry for me, Argentina."

"Here's someone who can make the president's request more eloquently," Franklin said in introducing Lily Pons, "straight from the Broadway hit *Evita*."

The invitations and other publicity had produced a crowd that filled the auditorium of about two thousand seats, making it the largest crowd of the Franklin campaign. Ms. Pons sang with force and sparkle and did several encores of other songs from *Evita* and two encores of "Don't Cry for Me." She got a standing ovation, and then Franklin thanked her for coming and reminded the audience Primary Day was just two weeks away, and he hoped they would remember him.

Overall the night went well, and Franklin felt it would appeal to people who didn't like Bush, but he worried the stunt would make him look like he was trying to ridicule the president. But it succeeded in putting the spotlight on him in the newspapers the next day and even on a couple of Boston TV stations. The Manchester daily had covered the event and had a story and photos on an inside page the next day. Concord and Nashua papers both played it on page one with photos of Franklin greeting Ms. Pons.

Sutton thought it was a home run and hoped they could do it again before the primary, perhaps in Maine. The visitors from Georgia were duly impressed and set out on their rounds the next day with a surer step. "This is more fun than the Carter trips," Milton Jones admitted, "but we haven't talked to as many residents. A lot of them are undecided now and transfixed by the Clinton stories."

With two more days to go, Jones figured they'd see about five thousand people in the four communities, which Franklin thought was good. He was just glad they were ahead of the Arkansas Travelers, who were due in the state the following week.

The Concord daily and even the *Manchester Union Leader* covered the Peanut Brigade with reminisces of the original Brigade who came for Carter. Jones summed up their efforts in a talk with Franklin in the motel restaurant. "One thing the newspapers and some of the people didn't remember was that Carter won the primaries but lost New Hampshire in the general elections in both 1976 and 1980. Ford beat him by 190,000 to 145,600, and Reagan won New Hampshire 221,706 to 108,800 more than 2–1," Jones recalled.

"Carter did win the New Hampshire primary in 1976," Franklin stressed. "The primary will be good enough for me."

"Well, we did meet a few old friends, but I got the impression most of them aren't eager for another unknown Georgian as their president. You've done a good job of getting better-known, and that's shown by your poll showings…if you can believe primary polls. Will you have any money left after this adventure? Our motel bill is more than Carter spent on the Peanut Brigade altogether in 1976."

"We're okay. What I'm concerned about is Georgia in a few weeks. What do you hear down there?"

"Clinton has a lot of support and is spending a lot of money. But if you do well here, all bets are off. Many Georgians think of you as a Republican, but these campaign talks I've read sound almost too liberal for Georgia."

"I know, but if you can do any organization down there for me, I'd appreciate it. Keep in touch with me and Phil Sutton, and thanks again for getting the Brigade together."

The Brigade was remembered fondly by some New Hampshirites, and their successors were invaluable in putting Franklin's name before more people on a personal basis.

A few days after the Peanut Brigade left, a group of Clinton's Arkansas Travelers arrived to work for their friend and five-time governor. There were already many so-called Friends of Bill in the state and also all over the country, cultivated by Bill and Hillary at Yale, where he was president of his senior class as well as Wellesley, where she had been the student body president. They had also made many contacts in his travels as chairman of the Democratic Senatorial campaign in 1986 and as chairman of the Democratic leadership group, the centrist group designed to dilute the party's liberal reputation, personified by Dukakis, Mondale, and Cuomo, had he run, and indeed of Franklin D. Roosevelt and Lyndon B. Johnson. Franklin and Harkin were carrying that banner in 1992, which could be detrimental at times, but Franklin was determined to keep FDR's legacy alive and vibrant.

In the second week of February, Franklin had scheduled a talk in Berlin, the largest city in the northeast quadrant and in the White Mountains, not far from Dixville Notch, where Franklin planned to visit once more.

A good group was on hand in Berlin, and Franklin reminded them Berlin was one of the first cities he had visited. He spoke of Berlin's importance as a pulp and lumber center and noted that the oldest ski club in the United States had been founded there in 1892. He then gave one of his standard talks with particular emphasis on reducing the payroll tax and repeal or revision of the 1986 tax bill, most particularly its treatment of taxation on second homes, which he had been told was a hot issue in that area of New Hampshire. He also promised to do all possible to preserve the face of the Old Man of the Mountain on Profile Mountain, a popular tourist attraction. Erosion was still eating away at its attachment to the side of the mountain.

In closing, Franklin stressed that the primary was only days away, and he described the candidates from whom the voters had to choose: "I openly admit that I'm a New Deal Democrat and proud of it and believe our federal government, whatever its faults, has proven to be the best form of government ever devised. Paul Tsongas is a good man, but he should be running on the Republican ticket. His policies are more trickle-down economics, which we've tried for too long, and not much has trickled from the richest Americans. It's mostly been a case of money flooding into higher incomes with little left trickling from those hands. Bill Clinton, you've probably heard of him, he's been governor of Arkansas for twelve years, and that's where he should stay. Tom Harkin is a good senator, and if you can't vote for me, I recommend him, but he is needed in the Senate. Bob Kerrey is an admirable American, wounded in Vietnam, but his policies belong to his state of Nebraska. He voted for the 1986 tax bill and supports NAFTA and does not have a clear program for improving the economy. Jerry Brown ran for president twice before and got nowhere either time. The last time he was a candidate in California, he was soundly defeated in a bid for the US Senate.

"I admit I'm a businessman who has never run for public office, but I think being a newspaper publisher and editor and running a business that produced a number of newspapers for forty years is a useful background for president, better, in fact, than being the governor of the same small state, over and over." He had tried out those lines in speeches to business groups and decided they went over pretty well, although he'd been reluctant to criticize his opponents, and they had mainly not criticized him, apparently hoping by ignoring him he would fade away. But he was expecting criticism in the last debate now that he was leading in the polls.

Charlie knew some of the Berlin group and mingled with them and got a few promises of support. "You still need to smile more," Hardy told Franklin as they left. "People like good smiles."

"I know," Franklin said, "but I haven't got one. Don't know why, but my face just doesn't work that way. I think it's from something deep inside me. Some people can light up a room, like Susie, some turn the lights down, like me."

They proceeded up to Dixville Notch and fortunately found the lady who had helped them nearly three months earlier. She greeted them happily and said she was hearing more about Franklin's candidacy now. "You've come a long way," she exclaimed, "from that day in September, when frankly I thought you were off your rocker."

Franklin smiled his wan smile. "You were nearly right, but I still want to make sure I carry Dixville Notch. How does that look?"

"This fellow Buchanan is getting some support on the Republican side, but I think you're okay on the Democratic side. Tsongas has been once, but Clinton, Kerrey, and Brown hadn't been seen."

"Okay, it's important that I be in the lead when that first-in-the-state return comes in from Dixville Notch. It will be reported, and in the past I've noticed that the early leader, even with just a handful of votes, often never loses the lead."

"Well, you should get twelve votes at least," she said, "and that's a good return from Dixville Notch."

Franklin hugged her and promised he'd be back in the general election.

"Oh, by the way," she called as they left, "we don't get cable TV up here, but we can get WMUR, and we loved *It's a Wonderful Life*, which some of us had never seen. It cinched votes for Franklin."

"Sutton won't like the amount of time we've spent up here to get twelve votes," Hardy mumbled.

The staff had been increased for the final weekend, and more money was coming in. Brad and Hardy were working on a get-the-voters to the polls effort, a tactic Franklin had first observed in Phenix City, when the so-called "machine" ran the county and always got officials elected who would overlook their illegal activities. On Election Day, a number of drivers would be hired to go around and pick up voters and take them to the polls, usually on the promise of voting for the machine candidates. Often a few dollars exchanged hands before the voters entered the booths. The tactic was very useful among older residents without transportation, who lived in public housing apartments or even the slums.

Brad had used the same tactic in Opelika and Auburn, and Hardy had experience with it in the Carter campaigns, which refined ways for identifying the voters, but it was essentially the same old system of hiring the right drivers and directing them to sites where your most likely voters lived.

Franklin had sent Susie up to the Bar Harbor, Maine area where she lived and worked during the years away from New Hampshire. She found acquaintances and former employees who were glad to see her in her new role as a key figure in a presidential campaign. She distributed pamphlets and made contacts for a one-week rush campaign in Maine if Franklin won in New Hampshire. Its caucuses were only six days later.

Then, there was the NBC-TV debate on Sunday night, the last joint appearance of the candidates before the Tuesday primary. Among the moderators was Bernard Shaw, famous for his on-the-scene reporting of the war in Iraq and for asking Michael Dukakis in a 1988 debate how he would react to the rape and murder of his wife. Dukakis was understandably surprised by the question and hesitated before explaining that he had always opposed the death penalty but would obviously want the culprit captured and brought to justice. It was a perfectly reasonable answer, to a totally irrelevant question, but the incident plagued Dukakis for the rest of the campaign because it coincided with the Republican claim that he was "soft on crime."

Another moderator was Ken Bode, whom the Clinton team thought was obsessed with why Governor Clinton had gotten a state job for Jennifer Flowers, which was actually a legitimate concern that Clinton had not fully explained.

According to later accounts of Clinton's preparation for the debate, his handlers had overprepared him for questions about Flowers and his draft problems, and oddly, the subjects didn't come up.

In the days leading up to the debate, Tsongas had almost disappeared, making only a few public appearances. Rumors naturally surfaced that something was wrong with Tsongas, maybe even a recurrence of his cancer. But happily that wasn't the problem. Tsongas had a bad eye infection, caused by a flying wood chip which struck him while he was touring a pulp mill. By the time of the CNN debate, both of his eyes were infected and swollen, and he was in serious pain. His advisers decided the best solution was a pair of glasses which could cover his swollen eyes. But Tsongas hated the glasses, and they made him self-conscious, according to later accounts.

During his reduced schedule, Tsongas had actually moved up in the polls and was just slightly behind Franklin and further ahead of Clinton and Kerrey. The numbers were still close and within the margin of error as the final weekend loomed. Franklin believed Tsongas was picking up voters deserting Clinton.

So the debate ensued, Clinton nervously expecting the worst, Tsongas in his new glasses, Franklin an unlikely and shaky leader, and the others hoping for a big knockout question or answer. But none of that happened. The moderators at first questioned Tsongas about his support of nuclear power, which was no longer a cutting issue in New Hampshire. Kerrey had long since lost momentum on his main issue of health-care insurance after it was revealed that he did not provide health insurance for his own employees in his restaurant chain. Tsongas, eyeglasses and all, stuck to his role as "pro-business, pro-growth."

"There are some Democrats who find my economic ideas hard to take. But my job is to turn this economy around," he claimed. Tsongas had gotten to the point where his opponents referred to him as St. Paul.

Harkin was his usual boisterous self, but there was a hint of pending defeat in his tone.

As usual Franklin didn't get much notice. The moderators seemed to feel he was still a fringe candidate. But toward the end, Jack Germond, a newspaper columnist, asked him, if he was having serious surgery, would he want a doctor who had never performed an operation before.

Franklin got the implication. "Of course not," he answered. "Nor would I want anyone else on this stage to perform the operation. This is not a contest to select a competent surgeon. We are running for the executive job of president of the United States, and I do have experience in a career of forty years as an editor and publisher of newspapers, during which I have written hundreds of commentaries on local, state, national, and international issues, have been involved with civic, state, and federal government, in dozens of communities, have never missed making a payroll, and have employed and supervised hundreds of employees from top journalists to salesmen to circulation carriers to press operators and compositors, men and women. I've never operated on anyone, and I dare say nobody else in the race has, but I feel my career has well prepared me for the one job we are all pursuing."

It was Franklin's longest answer of the night. He had finessed many of the issues he considered dull or that frankly he didn't know much about. He said he was not only asking for the votes of the people of New Hampshire but that his first goal would be to deserve their vote.

"A president is more than a political leader for the nation. He is also the moral and civic leader, a combination of responsibilities few other nations ask of their elected officials. I will strive to honor all of those functions."

That last description was clearly aimed at Clinton, but Franklin hoped it was broad enough that few noticed.

Kerrey had not been especially outspoken, but he still looked good, and he had the credentials, but in one of those mysterious quirks of political alchemy, he hadn't connected with the New Hampshire voters. It was revealed later that he hated raising funds, and his campaign had never built the financial support that Clinton had, and he hadn't self-funded as Franklin did.

Faced with the interruption of his lifelong dream, Clinton, Hillary, and his staff put on a full-court press in the final days of the campaign. An estimated seven hundred Arkansas Travelers flooded the state. They distributed twenty thousand videos of Clinton speaking. He did two live paid TV call-in shows and many other TV commercials. Later it was reported that the Clinton campaign spent $1 million in February on his sprint to the finish.

Franklin, however, held on to the lead in the polls. The early reactions from the debate were favorable. "You certainly didn't hurt yourself," Sutton told him. Tsongas had predictably done poorly, but

Jack Germond, the columnist, for some reason, declared Tsongas the winner in an instant analysis. Later polls returned a mixed verdict, and one poll found that Franklin's closing statement made him the winner. More importantly, the tracking polls still had Franklin leading late Sunday night, with Tsongas, Clinton, and Kerrey in a virtual three-way tie about three points behind him.

Franklin, along with Burkhart and Susie, went to church Sunday in Conway, where Burkhart was a member. Franklin had spent a lot of time in Carroll County, and he hoped the attention would pay off with a good vote on Tuesday.

Franklin had two more speeches on Monday, one to a group in Portsmouth of mostly business leaders and then a night visit Monday in Manchester with labor leaders who had become his most reliable campaign workers, a fact he found ironic considering his nonsupport of unions in the past. The main reason, he decided, was his attacks on Tsongas, who became more of a Republican as the campaign went on.

Tsongas still repeated that the Cold War was over, and Japan won, which Franklin found ludicrous. In the debate, Franklin had chided Tsongas about his economic positions and noted that he was reciting the Republican dogma that poor people should tighten their belts, while rich people filled their wallet. Sutton had liked that line so much that he got a short radio commercial made for use Monday afternoon and night. The stations were jammed with commercials, but he found some afternoon drive-time left, and the message was powerful: "Paul Tsongas wants poor people to tighten their belts and rich people to fill their wallets."

It was one of the few statements from the debate that broke the lengthy answers on complex issues. There was never a mention of Jennifer Flowers or Clinton's draft problems. The moderators apparently had been scolded on letting the campaign descend into tabloid journalism, although that was what the audience was expecting and which the Clinton advisers prepared for. It never came. Franklin's advisers were exuberant after the debate. Not only had Franklin not hurt himself, but none of the other candidates had helped themselves, which should leave the polls as they were.

They were surprised that Jerry Brown bore down on his proposal for a flat income tax, or even a national sales tax to replace all the other taxes, which would have been another windfall for higher-income earners. Kerrey stressed his plan for a national health insurance, to be financed by an increase in the payroll tax. Harkin called for a one-third reduction in defense spending with the money switched to social programs. "They create jobs too," he pointed out. Clinton called for a cut in middle-income taxes, but the amount he mentioned was $359 a year, which Tsongas charged would be of little help to most families but would add to the huge federal deficit, which Franklin considered a bogus issue.

On Monday, Hardy, Susie, Charlie, and Susie's new boyfriend from Harvard accompanied him to a noon speech in Nashua. He was pleased to have a Harvard man along. He had volunteered and told Susie he'd like to work on Primary Day. He was from Nashua and had played football at the high school. His name was Jayson Folkes.

Franklin decided he'd make a final case for what he considered the most important issue the next president would face. He knew the group was mostly informed Democrats, and he had to give them a reason to pick him from the others.

"I'm going to talk about a subject we haven't discussed enough in this campaign," he began, "the subject of war or peace. The subject has hung like a cloud of doom over the world for fifty years, which is whether there would be a nuclear conflict between the US and Russia, and what kind of world would survive such a conflict, if any. Then one day last year, the Berlin Wall fell, and no one tried to hold it up. Then the Soviet Union's government began to fall apart, and its internal weaknesses were revealed in all their hollow fallacies. Then the Soviet Union itself began to disintegrate as its Communist satellites fell away, all throwing off Communist domination.

"The Cold War was over, and the United States won, and don't let anyone tell you differently. Paul Tsongas says a great many foolish things, but nothing so foolish as 'the cold war is over and Japan won.' That's dumber than saying he's not Santa Claus. He proves that every time he tells people that, all they can expect at Christmas is a lump of coal—unless they are in that elite group of Americans he calls *job creators*. I'll tell you who are the real job creators. They are the millions of American consumers who buy the products and perform the labor that produces those products, and in both income and wages, they have been shortchanged for nearly twenty years, and that's why the economy is struggling today.

"But back to war and peace. This generation has a historic opportunity to establish a foundation for an enduring peace. An all-powerful government can ensure a peaceful world if that is its goal and it has the vision to see beyond the petty arguments that have pitted tribe against tribe, village against village, city against city, and nation against nation since the time of the cavemen.

"And today, 1992, the opportunity is at hand. Down the long dark corridors of mankind's existence, there has never been such an opportunity, and we dare not let it escape. The first step, however, will be one of the most difficult. Russia is coming apart and is groping for new leadership and new direction. It still has the second-largest nuclear arsenal in the world, which is a very dangerous arsenal indeed even if inferior to ours.

"We can't fully determine what path Russia's government will take or which path its people will want or demand, but we must try. We already have the example of Yugoslavia, which after losing the hard rule of Communism has broken into several warring nations, with many lives already lost and the peace of the entire Balkans in jeopardy.

"Fortunately, there are already respected national leaders who see the opportunity for the US and the danger in not acting. Last year, Senator Sam Nunn of Georgia, a Democrat, and Senator Richard Lugar of Indiana, a Republican, introduced a bill in Congress which would have been unthinkable just a few months earlier. The bill would authorize US assistance, including financial aid to help locate and safeguard nuclear weapons and materials stockpiled across Russia and in its former satellite nations. Their bill is called the Nuclear Threat Reduction Act of 1991. It would seek to provide a unified control over what are now parts of a nuclear arsenal controlled by national leaders who may see no compelling reasons not to use them, even if it means their destruction. Think of the example of Saddam

Hussein, if he had access to a nuclear weapon, or any number of other half-crazed dictators in control of weak and rebellious countries in which chaos is the rule rather than the exception.

"What Nunn and Lugar recognized was that the longtime theory of mutual-assured destruction, which was credited with holding the peace together between the US and Russia, is no longer valid—if it ever was, in fact—and that the US and Russia must work together to prevent the occurrence of a Dr. Strangelove incident, and if you've never seen that movie, I recommend it, especially to any who feel Russia's weakness is enough to forget about nuclear destruction."

Franklin saw that he had captured the audience's attention, and he moved to his main point in closing. "What this means is the US needs to work with Russia on many problems and perhaps even seek an alliance that will be strong enough to deter small wars and big wars. There is still China, of course, huge in population but weak in modern progress and certainly a concern for the future.

"The United States is strong enough that we can trust any nation, because they know that our goodwill is their best chance for growth and stability. I thank you for your attention. I have wanted to get this message out, and this is my last speech of the campaign, and I am depending on the votes of people like you to tell me if I should go forward with this message and campaign to other states and to the nation. The vote tomorrow will tell me how to proceed. The decision is in your hands and the hands of all the Democratic voters of New Hampshire and, I hope, a few Republicans who cross over."

Still ahead was an evening meeting with labor leaders in Manchester, just a few miles away. He was hoping to recruit some drivers for Brad and Hardy's get-voters to the polls effort. He had called Brad and told him to meet them at the union hall.

They had a useful hour or two in casual conversations with the union leaders, no formal speech, just fellowship and ideas for getting out a maximum vote. New Hampshire's uncertain February weather was always a scary factor for the first primary in a presidential year. Its occasional heavy snowfalls could cut the turnout in half, while a sunny day could bring out an extra few thousand voters.

After meeting with the labor leaders, Franklin invited all his campaign workers to the hotel bar where he had first energized the room with a rendition of "The Gambler." There was a large crowd, including many media people there for the big Primary Day on Tuesday. Franklin decided he wouldn't offer drinks to this crowd, but the singer was glad to get them going on a few Kenny Rogers songs and then introduced Franklin as one of the candidates which brought a jam of reporters to his table. Everybody got interviewed, from Susie, always a favorite; to Brad, looming over everyone; to Kathleen, with her long experience in politics, good looks, and Southern charm; to Charlie with his New Hampshire lore and memory of other Primary Days; to Jack Hardy, whom a few reporters recalled from the Jimmy Carter days

"Don't count your money while you're sitting at the table, there'll be time enough for counting when the dealing's done," the crowd sang with particular gusto. Franklin took the microphone and added in a hoarse voice, "Tonight the dealing's done, so make sure your vote is counted tomorrow."

Chapter Seventeen

THE GOLDEN STALLION

Liberty requires the opportunity to make a living—a living decent according to the standard of the time, a living which gives a man not only enough to live on, but something to live for.
—*Franklin D. Roosevelt, acceptance speech at the Democratic National Convention, Philadelphia, June 27, 1936*

B ack in his room he called wife, Jean, who was flying up the next morning with their children to be with him on Primary night. "Are you nervous?" Jean asked.

"More like numb," Franklin answered. "Ready to get the counting done. I'll have Hardy meet you at the airport. I'll be out making visits to the polls."

Meanwhile in the other camps, there was also apprehension. Clinton's impressive staff of consultants thought he could win, but as one of them remarked, "If this Jennifer Flowers thing hadn't happened, he would have won by a landslide." He was still ahead in endorsements, money, and certainly in name recognition, although a lot of that was negative.

On Sunday night, the polls showed Kerrey closing in on the three leaders. "He's 'a definite third,' one adviser predicted, maybe a second if it snows." It didn't snow on Primary Day, and the turnout was heavy in both Democratic and Republican primaries.

Sutton had obtained a suite at the Holiday Inn for the Franklins and the TV-watching crowd. It was a fairly new inn, and they would be sharing the premises with both the Kerrey and Jerry Brown campaigns and also the Pat Buchanan campaign.

The first return was from Dixville Notch and had come earlier in the afternoon. It showed 11 votes for Franklin, 5 for Clinton, and the rest scattered among the other Democrats. Bush led on the Republican ballot with 8 votes to Buchanan's 6.

"Well, we're ahead," Franklin exclaimed, as he clapped Hardy on the back. "I told you those two long trips to Dixville Notch would pay off."

Franklin had stayed in Concord on Primary Day but moved around the streets, shaking hands and telling people their support would send a message to the entire nation that a nonpolitician could win a primary and have the opportunity to inject New Hampshire views into the Washington scene. On Monday, the staff had sent postcards to every registered Democratic voter, reminding them that the day of reckoning was finally at hand. Franklin also hoped to pick up votes from Republicans who appreciated his views on foreign policy. The impressive total for Buchanan was a sign that President Bush's popularity had definitely fallen since the Gulf War aftermath of glorious victory.

The last polls had provided a hint of what might occur. Franklin still led slightly, with Tsongas second, but slipping, and Clinton coming on strong.

He ran into Susie at one of the polling places, where she was cheerfully talking up voters standing in long lines. "Let's take a break and get a sandwich for lunch," he suggested, and she readily agreed. "I've been out since just after dawn," she said. "It's cold, but it hasn't snowed, and the streets are pretty clear."

"Was the Dole campaign much like this?"

"I don't remember this much excitement," she said, "but there were fewer candidates who had a chance. It was mainly between Dole and Bush. I was working for Dole, as I told you, but I really didn't know much about what either of them stood for. I remember that Dole got very upset when Bush called him a tax collector for the Great Society."

"I appreciate you—and also Jayson—out working for me today. He's taken to politics, hasn't he?"

"He liked your speech at Harvard, and I guess he also likes working with me."

Franklin gave her his best smile, which wasn't much. "Things are doing well with the two of you, I assume?"

"Yes," Susie said. "We've liked each other's company, and then we french kiss," she added mischievously, "but he's a perfect gentleman, and I'm a perfect lady, and that's as far as things go."

"That's great. Tonight will determine what's going to happen to the campaign. I'll have to map a new plan. I only had a strategy for New Hampshire."

"I've been up in Maine a few days," Susie reminded him, "and I believe you can do well there. The other candidates aren't visible, and whoever comes out of New Hampshire as a winner will have tremendous momentum. Sutton and I already have a tentative speech for you with a labor group in Augusta next week, win or lose."

Franklin went back to the motel to check the latest returns. He decided he looked too tired to impress any voters, and he wanted to visit with his wife and children who had come up that morning and were out campaigning with Brad and Kathleen. Brad was getting some photos in case of victory, or defeat, for that matter. Sutton had also booked them into several radio stations. Son Tim had a deep and impressive voice and daughter Lara in particular was a good social mixer.

The polls closed at 7:00 p.m., but some exit polls results were already counted. Buchanan's strong showing against Bush still attracted the most media attention, which bothered the newspaperman in Franklin. Everyone knew that Buchanan wouldn't be around long. Of course, they didn't think he would be either, and the exit polls showed Tsongas and Clinton leading for the Democrats.

But then the actual vote count began trickling in. By 8:00 p.m., the Democratic field was a tight race among Tsongas, Clinton,

Franklin, and Kerrey. Franklin still couldn't understand how any Democrat had voted for Tsongas. He was so obviously campaigning as a Republican, and the suspicion was that he was getting a lot of Republican votes in the more conservative northern counties.

Soon a crowd had gathered in the large barroom of the hotel, and Franklin, his family, and several staffers retreated to his suite, with a promise to be back when the returns were clearer. Franklin was pleased to see in the early returns that he had the most votes in Carroll County, about 40 percent. Tsongas was losing his lead, and Clinton had stalled. The Berlin area gave Franklin a boost, as did LaConia and the city of Franklin, which were early urban areas to report.

The majority of late votes would come from Concord and the area south of Concord. That included counties nearest to Tsongas's home areas of Lowell, Massachusetts, and he briefly moved into the lead but was not getting the total from there that had been expected.

As the returns began pouring in from Manchester, Nashua, Portsmouth, and Dover the huge dimensions of the total began to take shape, with all the candidates getting a share, including Brown and Harkin, who moved into four figures.

Franklin and Jean watched with mixed emotions. Jean still hadn't crossed the emotional gap to being a real contender's wife. Franklin thought about the nearly two hundred townships he'd visited, the various stunts he'd tried, and the help he'd gotten from Charlie, in particular, and all the others.

Tsongas's total passed thirty thousand by 9:00 p.m., and that was with most of the Massachusetts border counties in. Clinton was close behind at twenty-eight thousand. But Franklin was hanging in at twenty-six thousand with the suburbs of the larger cities still not in, plus some scattered rural areas.

At 9:30 p.m., the Manchester city vote was completed, and the big surprise was that it gave Franklin a lead over all the candidates and actually put him in the overall state lead at thirty-seven thousand.

The Franklin crowd was first stunned and then started cheering.

Kathleen gave Franklin a warm hug and kiss on the cheek. She'd known him the longest except for his family, and like them she was having trouble believing the returns. "You were always kind of shy, actually," she said, "not at all like Wallace and Baxley."

Hardy had tears in his eyes. "This is better than Carter's first victory here," he said, "and my first victory in a long, long time. Don Quixote, you've caught the dragon."

"It was a windmill," Franklin corrected with a laugh. Charlie hugged him and said he'd seen a lot of New Hampshire primaries, but this one was the best ever.

Sutton was breaking out champagne when Franklin reminded him there were still nearly 25 percent of the votes out, and the margins were close. "Just got a report form Nashua," Sutton said, "and you are even with Clinton there and beating Tsongas handily. It looks like a squeaker for you over Clinton in a solid second, Tsongas third, and the rest of the field way back, including Kerrey with just 18,000, Harkin has about 17,000 and Brown is pulling about 13,000. The effort for write-ins for Cuomo got only 6,699 votes, compared to 1,433 write-ins for Bush, and 1,228 for Buchanan."

By 10:00 p.m. 95 percent of the votes were in, and the spinning was going strong in the room with reporters and consultants. Clinton's savvy advisers had gotten an early jump by getting Clinton on TV early and thanking New Hampshire voters for making him "the comeback kid." The phrase struck a chord with the media, and Clinton made a second-place finish sound like a victory, even though he trailed Franklin by 3,700 popular votes.

Clinton considered whether he should call Franklin and congratulate him on his victory. Hillary vetoed the idea. "We're the ones declaring victory," she said. "Franklin's still an unknown candidate to most of the nation. Tsongas got less than 30 percent of the vote in the state next to his home. You're the only candidate with a truly national campaign. Franklin or Tsongas probably couldn't name ten people in South Dakota or anywhere else."

"Franklin can name ten in Georgia, which is the next big primary state," Clinton said grimly.

The crush of media people in the Holiday Inn lobby was unbelievable by ten o'clock, and Franklin's manager urged him to come down and make his victory speech. He had been in his room working on it. He felt this was a special moment, not only for his campaign but for the American political process.

He and Jean emerged in the ballroom waving and smiling, accompanied by their children. Applause and cheers greeted them. The noise was almost deafening. The children seemed to enjoy it, accustomed as they were to rock music, but it definitely affected Franklin, who had never liked loud noises. He tried to put his notes together while acknowledging the crowd. He let it go on for a while because he knew it made for great TV and radio and was a sign to the general public that the night's leader was standing at the podium.

As the noise subsided, Franklin looked out at the crowd with disbelieving eyes. "I came to New Hampshire less than six months ago as a stranger," he began softly, "not knowing a single person in the state. I was the darkest of dark horses in the presidential primaries, but tonight the voters of New Hampshire have made me a golden stallion."

That line brought a new round of cheers.

"But let me stress," Franklin continued, "that this is not my victory, it is a victory for the political process and for the message which I attempted to present to the people of New Hampshire, and in that sense, it is truly a victory for the people of New Hampshire, who have demonstrated to the nation that politics is not a rigged game and that a candidate can win without spending millions of dollars and can come into a hotly contested race and get the most votes if his message touches the needs and desires of the people.

"That is the real lesson of this night, and it was delivered by the voters of New Hampshire. That is my most cherished satisfaction, and of course, I cannot adequately express my appreciation for the more than 38,000 who had enough faith to vote for this darkest horse. I also want to recognize the role that all the candidates played in the primary. They make the political process possible in this country, their willingness to spend the money, the time, and the emotional energy is essential for democracy, and every candidate in this race can be proud tonight of the support he received. The race was close and a relatively few votes would have produced a different result. But when you think about it, the Kentucky Derby is close, just a few seconds difference, but we mainly remember the winner, not the runners-up, and I hope that you will remember me as this campaign can now go on. The voters of New Hampshire have made that feasible. You have sent a message to the people of the United States that Thomas Alexander Franklin is a candidate worthy of their attention and that his message is one they need to hear."

Franklin paused to collect his thoughts as the noise became deafening again. He felt a sense of achievement he had never felt in his life, and he wasn't sure how he would handle it. He finally felt like a bluebird.

"The basic message was not complicated," he continued. "First it was that the nation needs to end its experiment with supply-side economics, which has shifted the burden of taxation from wealthier Americans to middle-income Americans and even to the poorest Americans. The evidence is all around us. Consumption is down because middle-income Americans no longer have the discretionary income to make the purchases that generate the supply-side. The consumers are the real job creators in the economy, and they have been short-changed during the past twenty years by the continued shift of the tax burden from the rich to the middle class; whose wages have been stagnant while the highest earners have seen their incomes rise to unprecedented levels. The robber barons of the 1890s were pikers compared to today's CEOs, performers such as athletes, and rock stars and actors. This economy is out of joint, and the people of New Hampshire have sent that message to the rest of the nation tonight. And beginning tomorrow morning, I plan to carry that message to the people of Maine, who will be holding their presidential caucuses next Monday. This is a short time, but the voters of Maine now have the example of the voters of New Hampshire, and I'm sure they'll hear it.

"The other message I tried to convey in my campaign was that the nation and the world have a unique and historic opportunity to lay the foundation for a durable peace in a world which almost destroyed itself in this century. Today one nation stands alone as the most powerful in military power and in economic strength and thus bears an enormous responsibility with its unprecedented position to reach out to former enemies such as Russia and to set parameters for irresponsible leaders such as Saddam Hussein.

"It's certainly true we won a great victory over Iraq and showed the world how powerful our military strength can be, but the price of that victory has yet to be fully totaled, and the ugly fact is that Saddam is still in power. War is often that way, even at its best. And we have the chance to finally look to solutions that do not involve killing a country's young men and destroying its buildings and peoples' homes and its infrastructure, which require years to build but can be wiped out in a few seconds.

"These are not always the most popular or fashionable positions, but they are the ones I stressed, and I commend the voters of New Hampshire for ignoring the weaknesses of the messenger and accepting the strengths of the message. This has been a great night for the democratic process and for the nation. Thank you and I hope to see you again in the fall election."

"That was powerful," Sutton told Franklin as they left the ballroom. "It should overshadow Clinton's claim as the 'comeback kid.'"

"Phil, here's what we need to do as soon as possible. Get a radio commercial out of that talk's basics and run about a two-minute spot on as many Maine stations as you can contact tomorrow. The Maine caucuses are Monday, and we don't have many identified supporters there."

Franklin called Burkhart over and asked if he could contact the publishers he knew in Maine and get some of them to represent him at the caucuses. He also gave Burkhart a rough sketch of a half page ad and told him to put it in all the Sunday papers in Maine and any weeklies that didn't go to press before the caucuses. "This will cost a few dollars," Burkhart remarked.

"Well, the campaign will surely be getting a few dollars, or more, after tonight," Franklin assured him. "Either that or we'll get some new fund-raisers."

He called Kathleen over and gave her an idea for a half page ad thanking the voters of New Hampshire for making him "A golden stallion" and sending a message to the nation that they liked his ideas.

Franklin joined Jean in their room, and they looked at each other in dismay. "I'm not sure I'm ready to be a politician's wife," she admitted. "That crowd tonight was exhilarating but exhausting. And this was just New Hampshire."

Franklin gave her a big hug. "We've been in a lot of adventures together," he reminded her, "some of them scary. I guess this is the scariest, but at least we've still got money in the savings account and prospective jobs. There were times when we didn't have either one."

"We were younger," she mentioned.

Actually health was an issue that worried Franklin. When he had operated the daily newspaper in Alabama, he had begun having panic attacks and trouble with breathing, usually at deadline time. He took Valium, the new tension pill, and managed to get through, but it was a major reason he sold the paper when a great offer came in. He needed to ease the tension, but he kept on challenging the odds on deal after deal, and none of them without their doubts and pitfalls. He had realized his luck would run out eventually, but he took his boldest plunge yet at sixty-one, running for president.

The next few days were a taste of what winning candidates face, especially candidates who have not won anything before and the media know little about. Fortunately, Sutton had lined up some extra help in case they won and was thus able to handle the crush of attention that descended on their relatively small office in Concord. Franklin also called Jody Powell and asked him if he could come to Maine for a few days to help them organize, especially with Georgia coming up just one week later. Franklin had an uneasy feeling about his home state. Too many people there knew he wasn't presidential material and that he was actually still a redbird who had bluffed his way through, still an introvert who faked his performance as an extrovert when the occasion demanded. Jean was similar, sweet and friendly but not engaging and outgoing. But she truly cared about people and had looked after members of her family, old and young, all her adult life.

Franklin's speech on Wednesday night would be in Augusta, the capital of Maine. There are not any large cities in Maine, the largest being Portland with about eighty thousand people but an urban area of about one hundred thousand, including Biddeford. Augusta had only twenty-five thousand. Overall, Maine had nearly one million more people than New Hampshire, but they were mostly in a quadrant just south of the New Hampshire border.

Franklin felt a quick journey through those communities would attract exposure for a number of precinct captains who would control the caucus voting. He already had accepted engagements in Brunswick, site of Bowdoin College; Lewiston, which was nearby; and Bath, a city of just over ten thousand, but the name appealed to him, and it was also nearby.

The chief opponent in Maine, of course, was Tsongas, still playing on his regional identity. Clinton had chosen not to make a strong effort in Maine, but Jerry Brown did and proved surprisingly strong. He had organized the environmental activists in that state. Tsongas was still known as a nuclear energy supporter, a subject Franklin had not actively dealt with. In fact, he was trying to decide the best approach to his audience in Augusta. Hardy accompanied him and suggested he give his talk about the narrow path between tyranny and democracy, but Franklin wondered if that was too esoteric. He had only a few opportunities to make a strong impression in Maine, and he remembered a story about the Civil War he thought might be an icebreaker with the flinty Mainelanders.

A large group greeted him enthusiastically in Augusta. He realized again how important were the few thousand voters in New Hampshire that put him in first place. The headlines and the newscasts had called him the winner, which was true, but he had always thought winners should get a clear majority of the votes. He had 38 percent, but in the arithmetic of the primaries, that was a winning total because he led. Ironically, he recalled that was about the percentage with which Abraham Lincoln won the 1860 presidential election.

Chapter Eighteen

A GETTYSBURG STORY

We are stricken by no plague of locusts. Plenty is at our doorstep, but a generous use of it languishes in the very sight of the supply.
—*Franklin D. Roosevelt,*
First Inauguration address

"Thank you, thank you," Franklin said to the crowd in Augusta, Maine. "I'm so pleased we scheduled this talk before I knew whether I'd come as a rejected intruder or as a legitimate candidate who deserved your time, and now I can also say I deserve your consideration and your votes in the caucuses on Monday.

"First, I'd like to stress how proud I am to be a citizen of the United States of America and thus eligible to seek its highest political office, and I'd like to thank a special group of courageous men from the state of Maine for making that possible.

"Even as a child, growing up in LaGrange, Georgia, I instinctively was glad that the United States won the Civil War, which means I was glad the Confederacy had lost. That was not a popular or fashionable view in Georgia, then or even now, but it made sense to my child's mind, and it certainly makes sense to my adult mind. The Civil War, as Lincoln stated, was the great test of whether a nation, so constituted, that is, based on rule by the people, and encompassing a vast area with many different peoples and viewpoints, could long endure.

"The United States has evolved through three revolutions to eventually become the strongest, greatest nation in all history, the one that stands alone today as the best example of democracy but also as the example other nations can follow to their own better fates.

"The first revolution, of course, was against England, which delivered the chance for independence, and that revolution continued through the uncertain years under the Articles of Confederation and the adoption of the Constitution. I would even include the Louisiana Purchase in that revolution because it resulted from France's own conflict with England, and it doubled the geographic size of the newly born United States.

"The second revolution was the Civil War, when eleven states attempted to break away from the federal government and establish a competing nation. Had they succeeded, the outcome would likely have been years of minor and major conflicts, not to mention two weaker nations instead of one strong one, which flourished into the power that helped win two world wars and the one in which I am proud to be a citizen today. I must say that I am also glad to be a Georgian, but I thank God that Abraham Lincoln and other political leaders in the Union were steadfast in recognizing that what made the United States great then and now, was the united strength of all its people and their resources, both north, south, east, and west. It is the distinction that separates our country from other ambitious nations, which were fractious, constantly remaking themselves, even Great Britain, which can only persuade part of Ireland to come into its fold and needs a royal head of state, a king or queen, to hold it together.

"The third revolution was the New Deal, which Maine was less enthusiastic about at first, but I'll get to that later. The Civil War was absolutely essential to the ongoing of the democratic experience, and the war's outcome was seriously in doubt from the beginning and never so much as one July day in 1863 when a Confederate Army under Robert E. Lee had invaded the Union states and penetrated into the middle of Pennsylvania near the little town of Gettysburg.

"One of the most crucial players in that epic battle of Gettysburg, which many historians believe decided the final outcome, was Joseph Chamberlain, a young colonel from Maine, and his Twentieth Maine regiment of tough fishermen and lumberjacks who had learned how to fight. An Alabama brigade, led by Colonel William Oates, had gained the high ground on what was to become the legendary Big Round Top, a mountain that overlooked the Gettysburg battlefield. Oates of Alabama from his vantage point could see the sites where both sides were gathering. For the rest of his life, Oates believed he held the key to Confederate victory at Gettysburg. He just needed to get some artillery on top of Big Round Top, and he would have what he called a Gibraltar—'I could have held against ten times the army I faced.'

"But as his men began their descent to lower ground, a group of federal troops, including Chamberlain's twentieth Maine brigade, emerged from the rocks below on Little Round Top Mountain. Chamberlain told his men, 'You are to hold this ground at all cost.'

"No sooner had Chamberlain's soldiers put their backs to the rocks behind them than the Confederates appeared on their way to Little Round Top. During the next hour and a half, one of the fiercest and most decisive battles of the entire war raged along the mountainous path from Big Round Top to Little Round Top. From behind their rocks, the Maine soldiers fired and sent the Confederate line staggering back 'like a man trying to walk against a strong wind,' as Colonel Oates later described it. But he rallied his troops, and they tried another charge around Chamberlain's left flank, again and again, wrote Captain Howard Prince of the Twentieth Maine, their charges continued, beaten off by an ever-thinning line. 'At times I saw around me more of the enemy than of my own men,' wrote Captain Prince. But doggedly the Twentieth Maine clung to the position, blocking the Confederates.

"Soon, Chamberlain's men were down to their last cartridges, the dead all around them and the Confederates preparing for another charge. Chamberlain decided they would fix their bayonets and charge first. Some of the men protested, but then one jumped out in front of the line, and Chamberlain, with sword drawn, led the regiment head on into the surprised Confederate troops, who stopped and then stumbled backwards. To their rear they suddenly ran into other federal troops who finally arrived from nearby.

"The Twentieth Maine had held its line at the loss of 130 of its 336 soldiers, but its delay of the Confederate takeover of Little Round Top had given the federal troops time to surround the two mountains and make possible the victory at Gettysburg on the third day of the battle. Colonel Chamberlain was awarded the Medal of Honor for his performance.

"Gettysburg is usually regarded as the battle which ended any thoughts by General Lee and other Confederate leaders that they could make a successful invasion of the North. Lee had hoped the deep invasion of Pennsylvania would encourage Northern opponents of the war to argue more convincingly for a negotiated peace that would allow the Southern states to secede without further fighting and, in effect, divide the nation. He also felt that winning the Battle of Gettysburg was essential in persuading England and France to recognize the Confederacy.

"The battle was very close, and there were a number of critical turning points, including Lee's third-day decision to charge the Union lines across a wide open field. But the Twentieth Maine, under Chamberlain, had thwarted the opportunity the Confederate troops had for success on the second day at Gettysburg. Chamberlain returned to Brunswick after the war and became President of Bowdoin College and then served as Maine's governor from 1867 to 1871."

While not a roof-raiser, Franklin's dramatic history lesson got a warm response, and the reporters present were anxious for more details on Joshua Chamberlain for which Franklin referred them to their files or history books.

Franklin had a call from Sutton, who related that he had arranged for a Friday appearance in Portland by Lily Pons, the Broadway star who had sung "Don't Cry for Me, Argentina" to such a big gathering in Manchester. "I thought you'd like the idea, and we don't have much time, so I went ahead. She said she'd come for just another $1,000. Said she had a good time last month and got great publicity."

"You did good," Franklin assured him. "I actually meant to make that suggestion. Also, get Kathleen to make up a half-page ad of headlines for the Wednesday papers about the victory in New Hampshire. Get Brad to help her put it in as many different papers as possible, and be sure to get the ad in the Sunday edition of the *Maine Sunday Telegram*, which is the Portland paper and has something like 130,000 circulation on the weekend, and in the Bangor weekend edition, which has 87,000 circulation and covers most of the Northern part of the state."

"Don't forget the TV and radio stations. They are stronger than the one in New Hampshire."

"Got 'em covered," Franklin assured him. "Am going to Portland tomorrow for a TV interview and then to Bangor on Friday. Also have talks in Brunswick and Bath tomorrow, and I'll plan to be at the Lily Pons concert Friday."

He spoke briefly with Kathleen about the page of headlines. He told her to be sure and get the Boston and *New York Times* pages as well as New Hampshire's and Maine's. "I'd also like to see how the Georgia papers played it," he added.

That night, Franklin, Hardy, and Charlie got a hotel room in Brunswick and found that it had a lively bar as befitted the city with the oldest college in Maine. After dinner they tried their singing routine, using "The Gambler" again and worried that its popularity might not have reached Maine. They needn't have worried. The crowd of mostly students loved it and also joined a lusty chorus of "Lucille" and "Coward of the County."

The next day Franklin found another large crowd of students and professors in the main college auditorium and gave them essentially the same talk about Joshua Chamberlain, Bowdoin's former president. He added a local angle Franklin thought might be of some interest.

In college, Franklin had been a member of the Chi Psi social fraternity. He had always been fascinated by the colleges where Chi Psi had started in the 1840s, as one of the oldest men's collegiate fraternal groups. The first three chapters had been at Union College in

New York, Middlebury in Vermont, and at Bowdoin in Brunswick, Maine.

"So I've always felt a special tie to Bowdoin," he explained, "and made sure to visit here a few years ago when I was on a tour of New England. The Chi Psi chapter here was the first one established after Chi Psi's legendary founder, Phillip Spencer, was hanged for mutiny on a US naval vessel, giving the fraternity a martyr and a great closing line for the fraternity song, 'Humanity received a blow the day that Phillip Spencer died.'" There were a few Chi Psis in the crowd who took up the refrain and got the crowd in a mood to hear the Chamberlain story.

Surprisingly, there were many who didn't know much about the man who was their distinguished former college president and state governor.

"Charlie, are we going to be able to get an ad in those Sunday editions?" Franklin said.

"Yeah, they'll be expensive, but nearly every home in Maine gets a Sunday paper. It's a tradition especially on long winter days in February."

"Great. Sutton says money is beginning to come in, and if we should lead in Maine, there'll be an avalanche of it."

The Broadway star came to sing "Don't Cry for Me, Argentina," and Franklin played the recording of President Bush's speech with the reference although he worried how that would go over in Maine, where Bush had a second home in Kennebunkport and a long association with the state.

But the auditorium was larger than the one in Manchester, and it was filled to capacity. The event seemed to go over as well as it had earlier, and it was well-covered by the TV outlets in Maine and by reporters and cameramen for the Sunday newspaper editions.

Saturday was a slow day, mainly devoted to calling people Charlie knew in Maine or ones that Sutton had uncovered as uncommitted for the caucuses. Then Sunday morning, the two big circulation papers from Portland and Bangor hit nearly every home in the state, and they had a couple of pleasant surprises.

Portland's front page had a photo of Franklin singing along with Pons "Don't Cry for Me," with a sidebar story on the campaign and the event. After all, it had taken place in Portland and was probably the biggest campaign event there of the year.

The Bangor coverage wasn't bad considering he hadn't been there in person. It carried an AP story on his speech and another AP article on Lily Pons's appearance, plus, of course, both papers had gotten in the advertising page of headlines on the New Hampshire victory. Franklin thought Kathleen and Charlie had done a good job of finding the best headlines, as nearly as good as he might have done, which he immodestly considered a high standard. He wasn't sure how good a politician he was, but he thought he was a pretty good newspaperman.

In its Sunday edition, the Portland paper had gone into its file copies and history books and compiled a page of photos of Governor Chamberlain, accompanied by a résumé of his time as governor and as president of Bowdoin College. An article on Franklin's speech had been held over to Sunday and ran as a sidebar, which Franklin felt made it more effective. As a candidate and a longtime Sunday newspaper reader, he was elated.

The caucuses were the following day, and the Franklin team scattered throughout Maine to make late contacts. Susie went to Bar Harbor to make sure her relatives and acquaintances had the right information and were going to the caucuses. Franklin retreated to the hotel and greeted well wishes and late deciders. Brad had come up to join Hardy in a ride-to-the-polls effort that was considerably smaller than in New Hampshire, but surprisingly, in the three large cities, it worked well as a lot of people needed transportation.

Franklin didn't know what to expect and the TV networks seemed equally puzzled. The vote total from caucuses came in at a veritable crawl. Then to top that, the returns only point toward a later election that will actually decide the delegates. But from a public momentum standpoint, the leader in the caucuses can be proclaimed a winner.

As in New Hampshire, the candidate with the most votes in the scattered popular vote returns was Thomas Alexander Franklin, with

32 percent, to Brown's 24 percent, Tsongas's 20 percent, Clinton 12 percent, and the others trailing. Some returns were still coming in, but the order of finish seemed set.

At the motel in Portland, Franklin and his crew celebrated again, and Franklin gave a TV interview that stressed there was still a long road ahead, but he liked the TV headlines that read "Franklin Wins Again" and figured that would be the headline in the next day's papers. Two in a row in alien territory for a Georgia boy, with the Georgia primary looming ahead in just a week. It was incredible.

Tsongas finished third again in a neighboring state, and that had definitely thrown a cold blanket on his chances; Clinton's second place in New Hampshire had kept him in contention, and he and Kerrey, Hardin, and Tsongas all had reason to hope for better results in some of the small states ahead where they had some presence and Franklin had little to none.

Chapter Nineteen

CHALLENGE IN GEORGIA

We know that equality of individual ability has never existed and never will, but we do insist that equality of opportunity still must be sought. We know that equality of local justice is, alas, not yet an established fact; but also is a goal we must and do seek.

—Franklin D. Roosevelt, address on the centennial of Arkansas' admission into the Union, Little Rock, Arkansas, June 10, 1936

After nearly six months away from home, Franklin felt almost reluctant to leave the frosty states in which he had arrived in September as an unknown candidate, the darkest of dark horses, and now leaving in late February as a legitimate candidate for president. He gathered his belongings, including a number of treasured souvenirs and loaded up the car he had rented for the trip home. Hardy rented a car and was going to follow close-by on the one-thousand-mile trip to Athens. Not only did Franklin still dislike flying, but he felt a few days listening to the radio on the road would give him a chance to see that stretch of the country close up, maybe even tell a few people he was running for president.

Other staff members were flying to Atlanta to organize a suite of offices in north metro Atlanta, which Sutton had rented on a month-to-month basis. Nothing was still that certain in Franklin's mind about either the Georgia primary or what was to follow. He knew Clinton had a strong foothold in Georgia and was still backed by Governor Zell Miller and the state's most prominent black leaders. Also, Clinton had the campaign team of Carville and Begala, who were credited with Miller's victory for governor in 1990. Unlike New Hampshire and Maine, Georgia was a large state geographically, the largest east of the Mississippi River, in fact, and the 1990 census had found it to be the ninth most populous state, with nine million people, up from just twentieth in 1950. The Atlanta metropolitan area was the main reason, the rest of the state having actually lost population while Atlanta soared to nearly 5.5 million, counting outlying counties.

The new Georgians had also changed politics in the state. Georgia gave John F. Kennedy his largest vote majority in any state in 1960 and had never voted for a Republican candidate in its history until 1964, when Barry Goldwater defeated the incumbent president, Democrat Lyndon Johnson. In 1968 Georgia had given a plurality to George Wallace of Alabama running on the states' rights ticket and then in 1972 a solid majority to Republican Richard M. Nixon.

Native son Jimmy Carter carried the state in 1976 and 1980, but Georgia was back in the Republican column in 1984 for Reagan and in 1988 for George Bush. Clearly it had become a Republican stronghold, and no one knew that better than Franklin, who had operated a newspaper in some twenty-five Georgia counties. But a primary was a different animal. Clinton was suspected of liberal leanings by Georgians, and the actual favorite of the majority seemed to be Pat Buchanan.

On his drive home, Franklin thought about all that and plotted his strategy. He did have some advantages in Georgia, and he sure didn't plan to make that speech about Joseph Chamberlain and his heroic stand at Gettysburg. Otherwise he didn't plan to alter his message from its basic economic liberalism and cultural conservatism, which he felt most white Georgians still preferred when they could get past the racial question. Nearly all black Georgians voted solidly Democratic.

Franklin and Hardy met near the North Carolina border to assess their plans. It was already Thursday, and the primary was the following Tuesday. Franklin had called Sutton and arranged for a country band to tour the state with him from Friday to Monday. He decided to improvise the rest of the weekend as events dictated. He and Hardy then continued their slow drive down I-85, stopping occasionally to have a snack together and make a few calls. There were a lot of easy listening radio stations along the way, and Franklin also spent time planning his speeches and debate strategy. After the busy months in New England, he realized that the introvert inside of him was reveling in the solitary drive. He had always been something of a loner, sometimes by design, more often by the simple fact that he had no one to talk to. Both he and wife, Jean, were only children. She had two close cousins, but he had never been close to any of his cousins. He had to pinch himself occasionally to realize that this lonely guy was suddenly the leading Democratic candidate for president, at least that was what the headline said on a newspaper he bought as he crossed the Georgia line. It was a weekly paper in Hartwell, part of a group whose owner ironically lived next door to him in Athens, indicating his many close connections in Georgia.

He called Jean and told her he'd be home in about an hour, and they could have supper together. The familiar interstate signs now passed swiftly—Lavonia, Jefferson, Commerce, Watkinsville, and finally Athens, site of the University of Georgia and the home he had built there three years earlier after selling his newspapers in suburban Atlanta. He had arranged for Susie Schultz to stay at his home in a part of the house originally built for Jean's elderly mother, who had lived with them until her death. Susie and his younger daughter were about the same age, and he thought it would be a good idea to have one key campaigner close at hand.

As a city, Athens had many charms. He had now seen several Ivy League campuses, and he still considered UGA's north campus the most collegiate scene he knew. Compared to the colleges and cities in New England, Athens was young. The oldest building on the university campus had been built in 1803, and many of the larger campus buildings were actually WPA projects built during the 1930s and

'40s. But one site at Georgia was hard to equal on any campus: that was Sanford Stadium, home of the football Bulldogs, erected in 1928 in a shallow valley surrounded by trees but with views of the entire campus from most of its now eighty thousand seats.

Athens itself was built on a series of hills and was old for a Georgia city, founded before the university and still having many homes built before or shortly after the Civil War. Several of these large homes had been bought and preserved by the thirty-five fraternities and sororities on campus. Milledge Avenue, where many of them were located, was one of Georgia's most impressive streets and was located on one of the hills that overlooked the campus, with steep streets leading down to the campus at several points.

Franklin knew he was prejudiced, but since the first time he visited Athens as a high school senior attending a high school press association meeting, he'd planned to attend the university and then move there and live if he ever had the opportunity. It took years, but he finally got back in 1989.

It was hardly the Athens where he had attended college in the immediate postwar years, nearly half a century earlier, but it was close. The downtown section and the older part of the campus were familiar enough for him to find his way around, but enrollment had grown from six thousand to thirty thousand in the ensuing years with the necessary changes in housing and buildings. The old homes still lined Milledge, and the magazine shop was still on the same downtown corner. The old country lodge that was the site of so many parties still stood about two miles from the main campus.

Franklin's house was a model he had selected with a turret wing on the front, containing a room for his daughter and an extra room and bath on the first level, where Susie was to stay.

After greeting everyone, he began making phone calls. The first call went to former president Jimmy Carter. "Mr. President?" Franklin said. "Have you got a minute?"

"Tom, I'm so glad to hear from you," he answered. "Take it from one who knows, winning the New Hampshire primary is a good sign."

"I know, I've been using your 1976 strategy and even have Jack Hardy, one of your drivers that year. He's been great!"

"I remember Jack," Carter said. "You'll have to tell me about all that happened in New Hampshire. I found it a fascinating state."

"I'll do that, but I'd like to ask a favor first. As you know, the Georgia primary is almost on us, and I've got a lot of ground to cover before Tuesday."

"Oh, you don't have to worry about Georgia, everyone in Georgia knows Thomas Franklin."

"That's what worries me," Franklin chuckled, "but what I wanted to ask is if you would introduce me at a rally in Columbus Saturday night."

Carter hesitated a moment. "Tom, I'd love to," he finally said, "but the debate Sunday night is being held at the Carter Center, and I'm the host to all the candidates, and I feel it would be awkward for me to show favoritism to any one of them."

"I understand," Franklin quickly agreed, "but keep me in mind for future occasions, okay?"

"I will," Carter agreed. "I think you've made all Georgians proud, and nothing would please me more than for another Georgian to be elected president. Maybe you can do better than I did."

"You were great, Mr. President. By the way, we used your idea of the Peanut Brigade in our campaign, and it made a difference."

"I read about that," Carter said, "and I also appreciate the kind things you said about me."

Franklin then called his next choice for a Columbus introduction, none other than Milton Jones, who had led the Brigade to New Hampshire for him. Jones wasn't a former president, but he had been a state senator, a member of the Board of Regents, and was a great speaker. He called Milton, who was agreeable to the task and figured it wouldn't hurt his own political future.

The State Democratic Convention was Friday night, so that was taken care of. Franklin then called his favorite governor, Carl Sanders, whom Carter had beaten when he sought a second term in 1970. Sanders was the governor Franklin had thought could be president someday, and he still held a slight grudge against Carter for denying him that chance.

"Governor, how are you? This is Thomas Franklin," he greeted Sanders, who now lived in Atlanta, although he was originally from Augusta.

"Tom, you're a miracle worker," Sanders exclaimed. "What made you ever think you could win a primary in New Hampshire and in Maine."

"Dreaming," Franklin replied honestly. "You were always my favorite politician, and you'd have won by bigger margins. That field was weak, and then Clinton got hit with two bombshells a week before the primary. The real miracle is that he still finished second. He's tough."

"I know him," Sanders said. "Governor Miller thinks he has things in place for Clinton to win Georgia next Tuesday."

"What do you think?"

"Clinton is a guy with five bullet holes in him who just keeps walking, but I don't think he can keep it up. You've got a better chance than he has."

"Great, what I'd like to ask you is if you would appear with me at a rally in Atlanta Saturday afternoon and introduce me? We're trying to get a football stadium outside the downtown area to avoid the traffic."

Sanders agreed after a little hesitation. "I haven't been in politics for a while," he said.

"A lot of Georgians, mainly including me, think you were the governor who showed us the path to growth and prosperity. Those skyscraper hotels, the colleges, the Braves, the Falcons, and the Hawks are all your legacies."

"It's kind of you to say."

"I'll have someone pick up you and Betty about 12:30, the festivities will start at 2:00 p.m. with our country band and Brenda Lee of DeKalb County singing. Look forward to seeing you."

The debate was scheduled Sunday night, and Franklin had an ambitious and bold plan for Monday night in Athens at Sanford Stadium.

The next morning, Friday, he and Susie and Hardy drove to Atlanta and met the bus and the three-piece band. Sutton had arranged for a mid-Georgia tour. Franklin also asked Kathleen to come along, giving him a Southern beauty and a New England beauty to distribute paraphernalia and charm the residents along the way. He and Hardy sat together, and Franklin gave him a running history of the communities on the route. The tour began in Jonesboro, about twenty miles south of Atlanta, where Franklin had operated a daily newspaper for several years and been a frequent visitor. It was the county seat of Clayton, one of the five metro Atlanta counties which had soared in population. It was also the site of the Hartsfield-Atlanta Airport, which had become the busiest airport in the nation and was arguably the main reason for Atlanta's growth and importance as a convention and business center. It had certainly sparked the growth of the skyscraper hotels, which had changed the city's skyline and provided the basis for its surprise selection as the site of the 1996 Centennial Olympic Games.

Jonesboro was a small town, however. Its moment in history had been 150 years earlier when General Sherman's troops made their circle around Atlanta with Jonesboro being the most southerly point.

The bus proceeded to McDonough, south on I-75, with another stop and introduction by its state senator who had become a friend of Franklin's during a court battle to keep a small college open in the next town along the way, which was Forsyth. Jean Franklin had attended college at the all-girls Baptist college there, then known as Bessie Tift but it was now just Tift College. A couple of years earlier, Tom and Jean had become involved in an effort to keep Tift open after its trustees voted to merge it with Mercer University, a larger Baptist college in nearby Macon. The dispute went all the way to the Georgia Supreme Court, which ruled the merger was illegal and not in the best interest of the two schools. Franklin, who was selected as chair of the proposed board if Tift remained separate, wryly remarked there were two ways the court battle could have turned out. One we would lose, or worse, we might have won. He had serious doubts that Tift could continue on its own, although it had a large campus, with attractive buildings impressively in view to passersby on I-85.

Next came Macon, the city at the very center of Georgia and its fifth largest. Franklin's connections there were also strong; he had cousins who lived there or nearby, and his book on Georgia newspapers, *The Last Linotype*, had been printed by Mercer University Press, requiring many trips to Macon in the mideighties.

The bus stopped at the large mall in Macon, and after the band played a couple of numbers, Franklin made the basic speech he'd been using at all the stops. It stressed his idea for reducing the payroll tax to three cents on the first dollar of wages while raising the total amount taxed. He reminded the crowd that this would give immediate relief to the lowest earners and would make the levy fairer by extending it to all taxpayers instead of just to those making less than $60,000. He also explained that it would help smaller businesses by lowering the amount of payroll tax they had to match since few of them had employees who made more than the $60,000.

"In effect, this would shift a large share of the federal tax burden from the poorest Americans workers to the richest. It's long overdue, and it's doable because it will be hard to argue that it would not be fairer. It's the first step toward transforming the US to a demand-side economy from the so-called supply-side economy, which has left middle- and lower-income Americans struggling during the past sixteen years, especially in Georgia."

The concept was difficult to explain because the Social Security deduction had always been sold to the people as an investment in their future rather than a tax. That was the theory in the 1930s, but it had, in effect, become an unfair income tax. Social Security payments and other benefits from the system were obviously essential to the nation's well-being, but the method of financing was unfair, and Franklin had been against it for years, as had many liberals in Congress. President Bush's argument against it was simply "Let's not fool with the Social Security system." But the latest tax data showed that many lower-income families now paid more in payroll taxes than they did in regular income taxes, and even for median family incomes, the Social Security, or payroll, tax averaged $2,018 compared to an income tax of $2,704 for a total of $4.722 on an average income of $28,230. Combined with user fees and state taxes, plus a sales tax in many states, there had been no gain in purchasing power for middle- and lower-income families in nearly twenty years. Franklin felt that was obviously the chief reason for the current recession and for the decline in middle income. Meanwhile, the after-tax income for the wealthier was mushrooming due to the tax revisions of the 1980s.

This was the economic dilemma brought on by Reagan's supply-side economics, but it didn't fit well on a bumper sticker, and even in more affluent New Hampshire, the message had not been an easy sell. In Georgia, it should have been, but Georgians had a deep-seated disdain for all government and taxes despite getting far more in revenue from the federal government each year than the total amount Georgians paid in federal taxes.

The cut in the payroll tax was the factor Franklin emphasized, but the rest of the message seemed to be lost on crowds of mostly rural Georgians who had come to Macon to shop for the day. The traveling band and bus did attract attention, however, and Susie and Kathleen were always crowd pleasers with their charm and looks. "You've got a pair of really good attention-grabbers in those two girls," one band member whispered to Franklin.

The bus rolled on as Franklin nervously looked at his watch. He had to be back in Atlanta for the State Democratic Convention and a speech by 7:00 p.m., and Friday afternoon traffic would be a challenge. He sat beside Susie and asked her impressions of Georgia and the South so far. She had never been south of Boston before this trip.

"First, it's really warm," she said. "I've never known any seventy-degree days in early March. But it's great, much more comfortable than thirty-five with a good wind and little sun. And then the people all talk so slow, slower than you," she added with a grin. "You've picked up your speech a lot in six months." She looked through the windows at the mall crowds as they were leaving Macon. "And of course, I've never seen so many black people. There are hardly in New Hampshire and Maine. Too cold, I guess, so maybe they are smart to stay south. Also, the towns look shabbier than in New England, but everyone has been friendly and cheerful, and most of them say they'll vote for you or Pat Buchanan. Clinton isn't mentioned much.

"I loved Forsyth and the Tift campus. Jean told me about going to school there and the tough restrictions on the girls. She said they had to walk blocks to church every Sunday morning in high heels. But I'd say she came out well. She reminds me of you a lot."

"Yeah, they say opposites attract, but Jean and I were almost boringly similar: both lower to middle class, both only children, college graduates at a time when few women were college graduates, both fatherless from our teen years, both Baptist. We met at Baptist Training Union. Both shy and relatively quiet. Both bookish and semismart but not brilliant by any means; then we got married and had the national average of three children. We were the model atomic family of the 1950s, except when you look deeper, we really weren't. Shortly after we got married, both of our mothers and Jean's grandmother came to live with us, two of them semi-invalids. Jean had to look after them and then the three children, and I worked very long hours at the daily newspaper with a low salary and few days off. Jean actually made more than I did as a home economist for the Georgia Power Company when we married, but she gave up her job when our first child was born. She later took a job at the hospital for $50 a week, low even in 1960. I finally got up to about $220 a week, but into our thirties, we lived a fairly frugal life, but still middle class. Things were just cheaper then, although not as cheap as during the Depression. A movie ticket had tripled to a dollar."

"Both of your mothers and a grandmother lived with you. That was hard wasn't it, especially for Jean."

"Everybody told us they didn't see how we did it, but they didn't know the half of it. Jean's grandmother was confined to a wheelchair, and as I told you earlier, my mother was a neurotic semi-invalid who hardly ever left her bed. But Jean's mother worked all those years, so we could afford a maid to help look after Jean's grandmother and my mother, plus I had two childless aunts in town who loved me dearly and helped in so many ways."

Susie gave him a look of slight awe. "No wonder you're cool," she said.

"Jean was the one who had the hardest role. She's tougher than she looks, but we always made plenty of time together with frequent movies, short trips with the children, and lots of adventures in the newspaper business, including a couple of newspaper conventions each year."

The bus had reached Perry by then, another city where Franklin had owned the newspaper for a time. A good crowd was there, and Franklin greeted a number of former employees and acquaintances, including Sam Nunn's law partner, who was from Perry. The bus continued on down I-75 to Cordele, where his talk was brief. Cordele had the smallest daily in Georgia. Franklin had once tried to buy it for some reason but fortunately without success. He would have disliked the situation, and twenty years later, the county had fewer people and stores than it had then.

The bus continued through Americus and Plains, home of Jimmy Carter, whom Franklin knew was already in Atlanta for the State Convention. He visited briefly with the owner of the newspaper and then went to the small airport, where he had arranged for a plane to pick he and the women up and fly them to the airport in DeKalb County near Atlanta.

If he was uncomfortable in large jets, he was really a bare-knuckled passenger in small planes, his main experience in them having been when he flew with Fob James, as a candidate for governor during his Alabama days. James, a former Auburn football star, lived in Opelika, and he won the race to become the only person not named Wallace to be elected governor of Alabama in a period of twenty-two years.

The view of the Atlanta area at Friday rush hour traffic was daunting and made landing in the small airport in DeKalb County seem even more of a good idea. Brad Ashmore met them and drove them to the World Congress Center in the middle of the city of Atlanta for the Democratic convention with an expected three thousand in attendance. The Congress Center was another reason Atlanta had become such a popular convention spot. It was huge, with ample space for displaying equipment and products and seating even more than three thousand in its main banquet hall.

Of the presidential candidates, Clinton, Kerrey, Tsongas, and Brown were all present, with Franklin joining them late.

During Franklin's relatively leisurely trip from New England after the busy week in Maine, which brought him the cherished headline "Franklin Wins Again" in both newspapers and on television, the other candidates had been bashing each other in Maryland and western states where they felt their chances were better. Clinton was depending on the strong support of Governor Miller in Georgia and endorsements from such leaders as US Representative John Lewis and Atlanta mayor Maynard Jackson. Kerrey had the support of Max Cleland, Georgia's secretary of state, who had lost an arm and both legs in Vietnam and had been President Jimmy Carter's director of veterans' affair.

Franklin had chosen not to contest the other states at stake on that Tuesday, which included Utah, Colorado, Idaho, Washington State, and Massachusetts. There were a lot of delegates in those states, but the prospects appeared to be that the other candidates would divide them and Franklin had not been to any of them. Georgia was the one where he and Clinton, still the runner-up in delegates, would be most clearly matched against each other.

Franklin arrived at the Congress Center with a large amount of apprehension and a small amount of preparation for what was supposed to be a relatively short speech, considering how many candidates and other dignitaries were on hand, including of course, Governor Zell Miller.

The candidates spoke in alphabetical order, which meant Clinton went first. He was at his charismatic best and in recent talks had been calling Tsongas a closet Republican, in language similar to that Franklin had used in New Hampshire.

Kerrey had done Franklin a favor in an early speech in Georgia by flatly stating: "Bill Clinton should not be the nominee of our party because he cannot win in November. He is going to be opened up like a soft peanut by the Republicans." That phrase stuck in people's mind and damaged Clinton and, by reflection, Kerrey. Earlier, Kerrey had defended Clinton on the draft evasion issue, and many in the media accused him of now criticizing Clinton because he was running behind. Kerrey, rather reasonably, argued that he was criticizing Clinton for never admitting responsibility. He added at the convention, 'it's a shame that men and women who went to Vietnam and suffered when they came home and now all of a sudden all the sympathy in this campaign is flowing to somebody who didn't go."

Clinton, having been advised that Franklin was closing in on him in the Georgia polls decided to level his main criticism at Franklin, one of the few times in the campaign he'd even mentioned Franklin's name.

"I'm happy to see Mr. Franklin here at this Democrat event," Clinton said. "I understand he has been seen only at Republican events, and in fact, editorially supported Richard Nixon for president in his newspapers in both 1960 and 1968; Barry Goldwater in 1964; Gerald Ford in 1972, against fellow Georgian and Democrat Jimmy Carter, and Ronald Reagan in 1980 against Carter again. He attended the national Republican Convention in 1964 and 1968 with the Georgia Republican delegates."

Clinton went on to extoll his own loyalty to the party and all its candidates, while continuing to go after Franklin's admittedly checkered career of supporting Republicans in Georgia, including Bo Callaway for Congress in 1964 and for governor in 1966. "The only Republican I can think of with a clear record in Georgia is General Tecumseh Sherman," Clinton concluded with a flourish.

Franklin rose to speak next amid cheers and catcalls. His reception was not assuring, but he smiled bravely. "I knew someone was reading those editorial columns I wrote twenty and thirty years ago," he commented to a round of laughter, that helped break the tension.

"First, you have to realize I have been writing my thoughts on paper for people to read and examine since I was sixteen years old, and then I was editor of the student newspaper at my alma mater, the great University of Georgia, the best newspaper I have ever worked on." If there was any subject Franklin thought he knew a lot about, it was the State of Georgia, with all its flaws and assets.

"I told audiences in New England that I was proud to be a Georgian, proud to be a Southerner, but even prouder to be an American, and I've made my campaign about the importance in this election—and in all of our elections—to demonstrate that the American system of government is the best system men have devised, and we must work even harder to maintain it in the face of those who would damage it and divide us.

"Since I began writing opinions, that has been my first goal and incentive, to keep the incredibly rare system we call democracy alive and well in this nation, which has always been democracy's great hope, and today, in the year 1992, is more essential than ever as the example other nations look to.

"From the Revolutionary War, through the frontier years, through the supreme test of our Civil War, through the Great Depression and World War II, our nation has emerged stronger after each challenge until today the United States stands as the most powerful nation in all of history.

"That is both a distinct privilege and a great challenge. We have survived, but we have always faced obstacles on that narrow path between the desert of tyranny on one side and the wilderness of chaos on the other. Few nations have been able to keep their balance on that narrow path, and that is the path I have advocated in local, state, and national elections, choosing the candidate and party that seemed to me to offer the surest guidance.

"My first editorial campaign, in the *Red and Black*, the student newspaper, and later in the Columbus newspapers, was against the county unit system, which was the very unfair and undemocratic method by which Georgia then elected most of its public officials, including the governor. In 1954, the governor elected under that system received just 34 percent of the popular votes cast. What the system did was award unit votes from each of Georgia's 159 counties, but there were only three levels—six votes for the 5 largest counties, four votes for the next 16 largest, and two each for the other 137 counties.

"A candidate could win one hundred thousand votes in a large county such as Fulton or DeKalb, and another candidate could get one thousand votes in three smaller counties and have the same weight on the outcome of the election. The system was based loosely on the electoral college, which elects presidents but was much more extreme and unfair—although I also oppose the electoral college method—but the county system effectively disenfranchised the vast majority of Georgians, and its main defender was the state Democrat party, which held all the statewide offices and most of the lesser offices.

"So yes, in opposing the county unit system, I opposed its main defenders. In addition, there were seldom, if ever, any contests for the top offices between the two parties. Georgia, from the Civil War until recently, was strictly a one-party state, that party being the Democrats, and the Democratic candidate was the only choice a voter had for governor or any other major office. I felt a choice was needed, so I worked and editorialized for a two-party system that would give Georgians a choice. In presidential elections, for instance, because of the electoral college, every vote from Georgia for more than one hundred years was cast for the Democratic candidate. No candidate for either party ever set foot in Georgia during those years to campaign or spent a dollar for advertising because the outcome was known before the candidates were even selected. The only time a Democratic presidential candidate got less than 70 percent of the popular vote was in 1928, when the Democratic nominee was Alfred Smith, a Catholic. During Franklin Roosevelt's four elections, Georgia was his most loyal state. In 1960, Democrat John F. Kennedy won by a larger majority of the popular votes in Georgia than he did in Massachusetts, which was ironic since he was a Catholic like Al Smith, just thirty-two years earlier. Goldwater broke the one-party mold in 1964, to become the first Republican to ever carry Georgia, and yes, I supported him because I felt it was the chance to finally establish a basis for a real two-party system in the state.

"In 1966, the Democrats nominated Lester Maddox as their candidate for governor, and yes, I supported and voted for Bo Callaway the Republican, who received the most popular votes but lacked a clear majority by a few thousand votes. The final outcome went to the General Assembly because of an 1824 law that required a gubernatorial candidate to have more than 50 percent of the popular votes in the general election but not in party primaries.

"Callaway would have been Georgia's first Republican governor, instead the heavily Democratic Assembly elected Maddox, an Atlanta fried chicken restaurant owner, who had never held any public office and was best known for having chased Negroes out of his restaurant with a pistol when they tried to integrate it in 1964. He also sold ax handles to his white customers with the implied message that they could be used by whites to defend themselves. So yes, I worked for Bo Callaway in that election and would again under the circumstances. Would Mr. Clinton have done otherwise? I assume in those years he was supporting Orval Faubus for governor of Arkansas." Faubus was the governor who had blocked school integration until federal troops were sent by President Eisenhower to escort black students to the high school.

"I moved to Alabama for business reasons and spent the next twenty years working to defeat George Wallace in gubernatorial elections and in his presidential campaigns. I supported Nixon in 1972, but I was also one of the first editors to write that Nixon had known in advance about the Watergate break-in and should be held accountable. But no one seemed to care. Most voters were determined that year to vote against the long-haired hippies who were disrupting college campuses and causing riots and generally wreaking havoc in the nation, and chaos is the most certain condition people will not tolerate. Nixon carried forty-nine states, all but Massachusetts, even though I believe most people already believed he was involved in the Watergate scandals. I was one of the earliest editors to call for his resignation and for the resignation of Vice President Spiro T. Agnew. Whatever his faults, Gerald Ford brought a certain and necessary legitimacy to the presidency when it was seriously threatened.

"But in 1992, I have declared that I am running as a Franklin Roosevelt New Deal Democrat, which is what I have always been at heart, and which the country desperately needs at this time. My positions today are consistent with my positions through the years. I am for democracy in its most feasible, possible form, with an equal vote for each citizen, fair elections, and a choice between two final candidates for the highest offices, including the presidency.

"Years ago in Georgia, people told me Georgia would never give up the county unit system and that I was wasting time writing against it. But when the federal courts ruled the system unconstitutional in 1963, the people of Georgia accepted the decision, and I've heard few people say they'd want it to return.

"A two-party system has come into being, and Georgians now have a choice. It's a mixed blessing because the Republican party in many ways is the old Talmadge machine in updated clothes, and my choice today is definitely the Democratic Party of Zell Miller, Sam Nunn, Max Cleland, Andrew Young, Jimmy Carter, Joe Frank Harris, George Busbee, and Carl Sanders, who have led Georgia to its best days and to become the most progressive state in the South.

"Thanks in particular to Governor Sanders, Georgia is the only Southern state that has all three major sports teams with the National League baseball champion Braves, NFL football with the Falcons, and NBA basketball with the Hawks.

"I stand before you as a native Georgian who has written a history of its newspapers, has traveled and worked in nearly every corner, and has carried its message of excellence to New England, where two states chose me to carry the Democratic banner as their presidential candidate this year, but they will count as little if the state I love best and know best and want to help the most does not support me in Tuesday's primary. In those states, I told of the benefits Roosevelt's New Deal brought to the nation, and I will say that no state benefited more from the New Deal programs than Georgia, which was Roosevelt's second home and where he saw the needs and the answers for many of his programs. Those needs and the importance of those programs must have renewal and continued support in 1992, and only a strong Democratic president can assure that. The nation's middle class must not recede any further. Four more years of Bush-Reagan policies will erode the middle class to a point not seen since the Great Depression. My promise is to reverse that trend, and I ask you to join the people of New Hampshire and Maine to give me the opportunity."

Franklin received a resounding ovation, and some of the other candidates even applauded. "I would also like to recognize the Georgians who worked to bring the 1996 Centennial Olympic Games to Atlanta, and I hope to be here as your president to welcome the world to Georgia, along with Georgia's governor, for whom I will be voting to serve a second term in 1994," Franklin added.

Franklin got another rousing ovation, including from Governor Miller and others on the stage. Out of the corner of his eye, he saw Jean and Hardy, who was driving for her that night, and they looked excited, with big smiles.

The remaining candidates made their talks, Kerrey and Tsongas, but Clinton and Franklin had been the main attractions.

Tsongas was understandably subdued. A few hours earlier, he was upset by a headline in that day's Atlanta newspaper which quoted Lieutenant Governor Pierre Howard, a Clinton supporter, as saying, "Tsongas is not Greek for Bubba." Tsongas was still sensitive to Greek references, which had started early in the campaign, when people were asking if they really wanted another Greek from Massachusetts as a candidate, after Michael Dukakis flamed out in 1988. Tsongas saw the headline as his consultants were getting him ready to cross the street to the Congress Center with three thousand Georgia Democrats waiting for their first look at him, and he was suddenly furious. "They're saying my father and mother are scum," he was quoted as telling his consultants, who were trying to calm him down and explain that Howard had used the reference in his own political campaign by joking that "Pierre was French for Bubba." Tsongas didn't appreciate the joke, and he felt he already faced a hostile audience in Georgians, suspicious of candidates from the North in general.

In his speech, he stuck to his story that Americans needed to tighten their belts. "He got scattered applause. Some in the audience were closet Republicans and probably liked his message, but it ran counter to Democratic conventional wisdom and certainly to Franklin's thinking. Tsongas knew that a victory in Georgia was beyond his reach.

As Franklin was making his way through the crowd, he felt a tap on his shoulder and turned to find it was Hillary Clinton. "Bill threw you a hard curveball, and you knocked it out of the park," she said with a slight smile. "I still think we'll win Georgia, but you've made it a race."

"Actually Zell Miller has made it a race," Franklin said, "but I appreciate your comments. There were a lot of things I wrote in editorials that could have hurt me more. As they say, doctors bury their mistakes, editors print theirs."

Franklin also exchanged greetings with Bill, who came over to join them, tall, smiling and looking confident. "You did good," he said. "I like a lot of your ideas."

After a fitful night's sleep, Franklin was up early the next morning to catch the bus for another quick tour, this time through the counties north and west of Atlanta, ending that evening in Columbus, his longtime home. First stop was Marietta in Cobb County. It was exploding with growth and had been the site during the Civil War of the Battle of Lookout Mountain, a late Confederate victory which temporarily delayed General Sherman's drive on Atlanta. Franklin had Susie, Kathleen, and Brad along for this trip. Sutton had arranged several greeting groups along the way, and the country band attracted a crowd in the Marietta Square. Susie and Kathleen were always popular, and the crowd was friendly. Franklin made a special point in his talk of the opportunity the United States had at this time in history to work for peace on a worldwide basis. "Our strength gives us the chance to be both bold and generous," he pointed out. "Russia's weakness is an opportunity but also a danger if it begins to break up as Yugoslavia is doing. We won't know who would gain control of their nuclear arsenal."

He sat with Susie again to get her impressions of Georgia and the South. "Educational," she said. "I'd never seen slums like the ones in Atlanta. But the city overall is tremendous. It's a city in a forest and so unlike the rest of Georgia. I'm also surprised at all the monuments and historic plaques about the Civil War. Nearly every street is named for a Confederate general. Stone Mountain was awesome, especially the engraving on the side of Confederate leaders. I'd never even heard of General Jackson."

"That's old Stonewall. He was killed in the 1863 Battle of Chancellorsville, by friendly fire from his own troops. The war might have lasted longer and taken even more lives if Jackson had lived. He was a military genius. So was Lee, which also prolonged the war. Lee is a strange paradox, but don't tell a Southerner that. Most think he was a saint. I never did. He was commander of the federal West Point Military Academy before the war, and Lincoln offered him command of the Union forces before Virginia seceded. He declined, claiming first allegiance to his state, but deep down he was also a supporter of slavery. He told Lincoln when he resigned his federal commission that he would never again raise his sword except in defense of Virginia, and oddly enough, to my knowledge, he never led a battle in any Southern state except Virginia. His greatest battles were the two invasions of the North, which ended at Antietam and Gettysburg, both in Union states."

"I've learned more history on this trip than I did in twelve years of school," Susie remarked.

"Have you learned some about Alabama from Kathleen?" Franklin asked.

Susie laughed. "I'll say. She's a blast and such an interesting life. She's a real pro at some of this campaign stuff, and her stories about George Wallace and Bill Baxley and their Alabama campaigns are hard to believe. But you know, Kathleen and Brad and Rheta Grimsley Johnson, the syndicated columnist, whom I met yesterday in Atlanta, all have something in common. They give you credit for the opportunities and the confidence that brought out the best in them. It was like that with me, I told them. I'd still be waiting tables if it were not for you."

"That would be a waste," Franklin said, "but you and the rest all had the ability and the personality to take advantage of the opportunities."

"But you saw that star quality, as you told me, and were willing to nourish it. I think that might be a real asset for a president of the US."

The bus moved on to Cartersville. The band played, and Franklin gave a brief address and reminded people to vote on Tuesday. Franklin was concerned that the turnout would be low. Governor Miller had the legislature move the primary date up by a full week to March 3, with the intention of helping Clinton get a victory before Super Tuesday the following week. That was before Franklin became a factor. Miller had a longtime commitment to Clinton, whom he had met as a governor and had attended many events with him in the past year. He had also been instrumental in getting the Clinton campaign team of Carville and Bagala. Miller had then lined up the prominent black leaders in Georgia, who had helped him in his 1990 campaign.

The bus continued to Rome, one of the larger cities in that section of Georgia. Franklin gave a slightly longer speech there, recalling that the rise in hostility to the federal government had been encouraged by the Republicans. They had even tried to reduce popular programs such as Richard Nixon's revenue sharing program with cities and states, which had provided funds for many needed projects such as hospitals, libraries, and schools. Discretionary domestic spending by the government had declined from 22 percent of federal outlays in 1980 to 15 percent by 1989, according to the latest figure, Franklin pointed out.

"Local governments are being asked to foot more of the bill for infrastructure at the same time they are facing more demand for services. But the Republican administrations keep cutting taxes on the highest wage earners, which in effect shifts the burden to the lower-wage earners and means city and county services are underfunded."

As the bus moved back through Cobb County, Franklin told Susie of the most famous lynching to take place in Georgia. The site was on the route. "There were many lynchings in the years from 1895 to 1946, most of them lynching of Negroes, sometimes in pairs or groups. Seldom was anybody arrested or charged in court for being in a lynch mob. So-called anti-lynching bills were introduced in Congress every year, including Roosevelt's terms as president, but the bloc of Southern legislators was too large and held too many key chairmanships for the anti-lynching bills to pass.

"But rather oddly, the most famous lynching was of a white man, and the decisive testimony against him was by a Negro, who almost certainly was the real culprit. The victim's name was Leo Frank. Have you ever heard of the case?"

"I don't think so."

"Well, it had far-reaching effects. Frank was a Jew from Brooklyn whose family owned a pencil factory in Atlanta. He was the manager. It employed many people, including some underaged by today's standards. One of them was a thirteen-year-old girl named Mary Phagan, whose murdered body was found in the plant in April 1913. She had been strangled to death, and only a handful of people were at the plant that day because it was a holiday period. She reportedly had gone to get her weekly check from Frank, who was the last person to report seeing her alive. He was only thirty-one and was a well-known citizen in the Atlanta community, but in addition to prejudice against blacks, there was also an undercurrent of anti-Semitism in Atlanta at the time, not to mention against Northerners in general. Suspicion immediately centered on Frank as the murderer. Then Jim Conley, a Negro janitor at the pencil plant, told police he saw Frank with the body of the girl, and Frank had asked him to help dispose of her.

"For some reason, and this is the only recorded case in the South, the authorities chose to believe a black man over the denials of Frank, a white man. This became the most hotly debated issue in Georgia. Atlanta had three separately owned daily newspapers at the time, and one was *The Georgian*, owned by Randolph Hearst, then at the height of his power, when his newspapers were pioneering sensational reporting that attracted readership. The Leo Frank case was a natural for such daily headlines in a period before radio or TV, which created an atmosphere of tension Atlanta had seldom seen.

"Based mainly on Conley's testimony, and a puzzling reticence on Frank's part to defend his own case, a jury found Frank guilty of murdering Mary Phagan and sentenced him to be executed by hanging. The verdict set off a new round of turmoil and heated dispute, which was covered not only by the Atlanta newspapers but also by the national press, including the several dailies in New York City at that time. John Slaton, the Georgia governor, was besieged by requests to either pardon Frank, order a new trial, or at least commute his death sentence. Finally, after carefully reviewing the case, Slaton commuted the death sentence. Suddenly, Slaton himself became the target of demonstrations and calls for his resignation. Mobs of protestors marched to the governor's mansion, and some had to be dispersed by police but Slaton held to his decision. Like many students of the case, he did not feel the evidence against Frank was conclusive enough.

"Then one night a few weeks after Governor Slaton's decision, a group of Georgians, most of them from Marietta, where Mary Phagan lived, drove to Milledgeville, where Frank was being held in prison, broke into the prison, obviously with some collusion, seized Frank, and took him back to Marietta with them, where they hanged him in the spot we passed a few minutes ago. His dead body was photographed and distributed, which was the custom after lynchings in those days. The state and much of the nation was stunned by the act, and it inflamed emotions on both sides. No one in the lynching party was ever arrested or charged although many of them were recognized as well-known citizens and were identified years later in several books written about the case.

"The Frank lynching led the Jewish community in the country to form the B'nai B'rith society to combat anti-Semitism in the entire nation, but on the other side, it inspired the revival of the Ku Klux Klan, both in Georgia, at a cross burning on Stone Mountain, and then throughout the nation, even in states where there had been little Klan activity in the past.

"By 1923 there were reported to be five million Klan members, among them a couple of Georgia governors; Hugo Black, a US senator from Alabama who would be Franklin Roosevelt's first appointment to the Supreme Court in 1937, and Robert Byrd of West Virginia, who was the Senate Democratic majority leader for many years.

"In the 1980s, fairly recently, Frank was given a posthumous pardon based on a review of the case and one new witness, who testified that he saw Jim Conley kill Mary Phagan."

"What a terrible story," Susie exclaimed. "I've always thought of Georgia as the most tolerant and progressive Southern state."

"Me too," Franklin agreed, "and overall it probably is, but it has had many dark chapters, most of them related to race, but some just pure meanness and cruelty. Georgia and Virginia were the sites of the most violent and memorable battles during the Civil War, and the time of the Leo Frank case was just fifty years after Appomattox and the Confederate surrender, at least by its troops. Feelings remained hard and the so-called Lost Cause was at its peak of popularity in the early twentieth century.

"This country has an obligation to its own people and to the people of the nations that look to the United States as their model to meet the needs that only the federal government can or will provide, such as good, safe highways, better schools, and the funds to cities and counties for law enforcement and fire departments and updated water systems. Much of the opposition to federal programs still stem from the scars of the Civil War not just in the South but also in the arguments the Republicans use against federal spending. That resentment to the government can usually be traced back to divisions and feelings left by the Civil War."

Chapter Twenty

HIS OLD HOMETOWNS

*Inside the polling booth every American man and
woman stands as the equal of every other American
man and woman.*
　　　　*—Franklin D. Roosevelt, campaign address
　　　in Worcester, Massachusetts, October 21, 1936*

"Georgia is so big," Susie said. "I'm looking at this map,
and we've been traveling for two days and haven't
been east or south of Macon or up in the mountains,
which look interesting, or to Savannah and the Golden Isles I've read
so much about."

"It may be the wrong approach," Franklin said, "but I'm going
to my old hometowns or places where I'm not as well-known or have
never owned newspapers. We'll get to Savannah and the Golden Isles,
I promise, and also the mountains. "Until recently not many people
lived in the mountain counties, but they began to attract families a
few years ago and get lots of tourist travel in the fall. You'll have to
come back this fall and see what real college football is like, maybe
that Harvard man will bring you. You are still seeing him, aren't you?"

"Oh yes," Susie answered quickly, "and he wants to help on the
campaign when he gets out of college for the summer, which should
be in about four weeks."

"Who would have thought a few months ago you'd be going with a Harvard man, and I'd be the leading candidate for the Democratic nomination for president?"

Susie laughed. "Is it real?" she asked. "Can it last?"

Franklin looked noncommittal. His experience in life was that both the good times and bad times have a time limit. "By the way, you've never mentioned your father. Would I be inquiring too much to ask what happened to him?"

"No," Susie said. "There's not much to it. He left my mother when I was only two years old, and neither of us has heard from him again. His relatives tell mother that he's alive and well and living in the Midwest and hasn't married again. Technically, they are still married. But she's an independent sort and just went to work as an accountant to support us all these years. That's how I learned how to handle office work. I was pretty smart in school, and by the time I was in fifth grade, I was also the tallest girl in school, which made me feel awkward and gawky, not to mention being taller than most of the boys, but it obviously made me a good basketball player...that and having a sharp shooting eye. Mother bought a goal and put it in the backyard, and I practiced for hours from the time I could push the ball toward the goal." She looked out at the passing landscape with a sad expression. "I changed schools to have a better chance to play top-class basketball, and so I didn't have many friends in high school. Then suddenly I became the school basketball star, and it was hard to handle all the kids who wanted to be friends, especially boys.

"I was aloof in my first years at high school. My junior year was great, of course, when we won the state championship and I was voted the most valuable player. That meant so much because I still didn't have close friends since I lived in another county."

"Your father doesn't know what an outstanding daughter he has?" Franklin asked.

"I don't guess so...and of course, in those bad years of mine, I wasn't very outstanding." She looked up at Franklin and broke into her Christmas tree smile. "These past few months have been the best in my life," she exclaimed. "I've met so many interesting people, been so many places… It's been so inspiring as well as educational, and of course," she added almost shyly, "it's all because of you."

"No, as I told you once, it's because of you. You were there all along and just had to find yourself again."

The bus had come to a stop in Carrollton, almost at the Alabama line. "Believe it or not," Franklin told her, "I closed a deal on a newspaper at that coffee shop across the street. I remember it vividly because it was the day after President Nixon resigned, and as we signed the contracts, we were watching Gerald Ford's opening speech as president on TV. It was August 9, 1974. The paper was a small weekly in Fairburn, which is about thirty miles from downtown Atlanta. It soon merged with that daily in Jonesboro I told you about, and from then on I concentrated on business in Georgia."

"How did you keep up with all those different newspapers?"

"Not too well sometimes, plus I kept living in Alabama for fifteen more years."

Franklin greeted the newspaper publisher he'd been telling Susie about, and they briefly discussed the political situation. "You can count on my vote Tuesday," the publisher told him, "but I don't know about November, Bush has been pretty good for the newspaper business."

"I'll be better," Franklin said. "I want to get more money into the hands of your advertisers' customers so the advertisers will have more to spend on advertising. Consumers are being squeezed by high prices and low pay."

Brad came and sat in a seat in front of them. "You've got another winner here, Boss," he said, nodding toward Susie.

"I found her in a restaurant. Remember I always told you former waitresses would make good ad reps."

"She's told me about some of her waitress days," Brad said, "and I think what has impressed her most about Georgia is how many Waffle Houses there are."

"They're everywhere," Susie said. "At every interstate intersection, and then in every little town off the interstate."

"They are sort of like doughnut shops in New England," Franklin observed. "I was impressed by how many doughnut shops are there."

The bus pulled into LaGrange, the city where Franklin had spent his first ten years and the town he still treasured in his memories, despite some hardships and disappointments there. "During the 1930s, the years of the Great Depression, LaGrange was one of the best places in Georgia to be," he told Susie.

A small crowd had gathered at the town square, which Franklin considered one of the most interesting town squares in the country. When he was in first grade, the teacher had taken the class to the square to see a procession of cars, which included this large car with a man waving his hat to the crowd. He was President Franklin Delano Roosevelt, and the sight remained in Franklin's memory. The jaunty smile, the top hat, the thrill of having the president visit during one of his weeks at Warm Springs, about thirty-five miles away. At the time, the county courthouse occupied most of the square, but just a few weeks later, in one of several mysterious fires that occurred in LaGrange over a ten-year period, the courthouse burned to the ground one night. For several years the square was simply a well-tended piece of ground in the middle of town until someone had the bright idea of putting a fountain with a stream of water shooting up in the middle of the square, giving LaGrange one of the most attractive squares in the state. Then later, the president of LaGrange College arranged to acquire a statute of General LaFayette, the French military leader who was one of George Washington's generals against British forces during the American Revolution. LaFayette, who was only twenty-three when he came to America to help Washington, returned to France in time to participate in its revolution and to write its Declarations of Freedom after the overthrow of King Louis XVI.

Years later, then in his seventies, LaFayette returned to the United States for a tour of the country he had helped gain its independence. One leg of his tour took him through the middle of Georgia, through Milledgeville, Barnesville, and the area which was to become the site for LaGrange. He remarked to a friend that the land in that area reminded him very much of his own estate in France, which was called LaGrange. And so the town was built and named for LaFayette's estate. His statute was placed in the middle of the square, along with the fountain. A church was at one corner, and on another corner was the city's largest store, Mansour's. On another corner was an early LaGrange hotel. The movie theater was just down the street, and Franklin had lived just three short blocks away on Broome Street, the only street by that name he ever encountered.

He reviewed some of LaGrange's history for the crowd and even recalled the fires which over a short period destroyed two blocks of the downtown business section, the courthouse, the elementary school Franklin attended, and the high school. Then strangely, the fires stopped, and LaGrange continued much as it was in his childhood, mainly dependent on Callaway Mills for its jobs and still having many of the advantages other small towns did not have in the 1930s, such as electricity, indoor toilets, running water, convenient shopping, and relatively good schools.

To make the point of how much the New Deal had meant for LaGrange, Franklin related again how his family had to buy his schoolbooks for the first grade, and then as he entered the second grade, the teacher presented every student with nicely covered books stamped "Courtesy of the State of Georgia, E. D. Rivers, governor."

Franklin always felt that Georgia's early adoption of free textbooks for its schoolchildren had given Georgia an advantage that put it ahead of other Southern states in education. Alabama, for example, did not provide free textbooks until 1966, when Governor George Wallace, at the peak of his political power as a defender of segregation, pushed a free textbook bill through the legislature, which former governor Big Jim Folsom had been unable to do, although it was his idea.

"To the people of LaGrange, I will promise if you help me become the Democratic candidate for president, LaGrange will become better known than Plains, Georgia, and may even get another industry," Franklin promised.

That line brought wild applause. Despite the many gifts from the Callaway Company to the city, most people in LaGrange always

believed that Callaway kept out other industries for fear of competition for workers and agitation for higher wages. Textile mills furnished jobs, but they were hard jobs, and pay was low, and it had
only been in recent time that the mills were air conditioned.

But as in New England, textile plants were on the decline, along
with the many jobs they provided in poorer areas. Southern cities
such as LaGrange were particularly hard hit by the supply-side views
of Reagan and the other economic conservatives who saw the global
economy as the controlling factor in business decisions, even if it
meant loss of jobs in the United States. As with the push for NAFTA,
they argued that consumer goods would be cheaper and better jobs
would be created in the coming electronic world. But on the ground,
the theory was further enriching the highest-paid sectors of the
nation and leaving many workers in poorer areas on the sidelines.

Calls for smaller federal government and states' rights and
"local decision-making" had become so fashionable, especially in the
South, that some vital programs and activities had been allotted to
local governments, which simply abandoned them altogether. That,
indeed, was to some extent the aim of the conservative movement.
Any vocal criticism of the obvious economic disparity was met with
cries of class warfare.

Even conservatives had begun to question the Reagan-Bush
economy's failure to provide better balance in living conditions and
more equitable rewards for the efforts of the poorest Americans.
Franklin had tried to make that his dominant message, and he
repeated it in LaGrange, his original hometown, which was a
Republican stronghold.

The myth of the classless society was dear to leaders such as
President Bush, who proclaimed that there were no classes in
America and that everyone, rich and poor, had a common interest
in the so-called global economy. But Franklin had read one poll that
showed 84 percent of US citizens supported a surtax on millionaires
and called the current system unfair and out of proportion. That
poll was an exception. Most polls were ambivalent. Franklin felt that
was because everybody wanted to be rich, and nobody wanted to
be poor, and that attitude subconsciously persuaded people to favor

the rich over the poor on questions that were depicted as "class warfare." Another politician who argued that point was Senator Bernie Sanders, the self-proclaimed Socialist who was running for the Senate and had helped Franklin in Vermont.

Franklin made his points in LaGrange to great applause, but he sensed the underlying discomfort in a town that was still a "company town" although Callaway textile mills had long since been sold to Milliken in North Carolina and the workforce sharply reduced.

Brad looked at him with a scowl. "You're letting your compassion overcome your politics," he advised, referring to Franklin's long-time description of himself as "a compassionate conservative," a term Franklin first used in 1960, long before the current president Bush revived it.

"I know," Franklin said, "but this may be the last election to draw the lines. The middle class is definitely slipping past the point where its voice can be heard or even when it can muster an effective voice. The old dogma of self-reliance at any cost has a powerful appeal and is so American sounding. The wealthy love the line and so do a lot of poorer Americans."

"What about blacks?" Susie inquired. "Aren't they poorer on the whole than even the poorest whites?"

"Yes, but poorer whites have seldom been willing to support programs to help blacks in the South, even if it also helped them. Race runs very deep. The New Deal succeeded because the economic situation was so desperate, but some were still suspicious of Yankee solutions. While many common childhood diseases were debilitating Georgia and other Southern states, the Rockefeller Foundation sponsored a program to inoculate children free of charge to lessen the effects of such diseases as smallpox, mumps, diphtheria, measles, and chicken pox. The programs were often administered through school systems if there were any, but for years, many Southern communities rejected the inoculations for fear they were plots to poison their children. Fortunately for me, LaGrange had begun to allow inoculations and vaccinations by the time I was in grade school. I had nearly every one of those diseases, but all of mine were mild cases because of the inoculations."

Franklin had visited LaGrange often in recent years, and he had told others in his small campaign group LaGrange had a special place in his heart, but he had no illusions about how popular he'd be there on Primary Day. LaGrange had become a Republican stronghold and the Callaway family was the leading Republican family in the state. Franklin had been one of Bo Callaway's staunchest supporters when Bo ran for Congress in 1964 (successfully) and for governor in 1966, when he won by a plurality but lost on that obscure 1824 law that required an absolute majority in the election. Callaway had carried all of Georgia's largest counties but had lost in most of the smaller ones. Republicans challenged the state law all the way to the US Supreme Court, which by a 5–4 vote upheld the 1824 law. The deciding vote was from Justice Hugo Black of Alabama, considered one of the court's most liberal members in many respects but who, in effect, voted for the ax-handle restaurant owner who had closed his restaurant rather than serve blacks.

"When I was growing up here, the divisions by class were very defined," Franklin explained to Susie. "First, there were the Callaways and then there were the rest of us, who were roughly divided into the upper middle class, consisting of doctors and lawyers, the next tier, which were Callaway executives and the business owners and a few educators. Next was the lower middle class, which was rather large, consisting of families like mine, although my father earned only $20 a week, then there were the mill workers, who most of us considered the poorer class even though they were not any poorer than the lower middle class, but they worked in the mills, which carried a certain stigma. They were known as lint heads. Then, there were the Negroes, nearly a third of the population, who were the poorest of all, and I hardly ever saw any of them. They not only didn't go to school with whites, they didn't go to church with them, and they were not frequently seen in the downtown stores. I assumed they had a little business district of their own in some part of town I never visited. The only black person I saw regularly was our maid. There weren't even any blacks in the movies I saw except an occasional servant, and I never remember a single black character in the comic books. Although we knew there were many black cowboys in the Old West."

Susie admitted that she hadn't realized how racially segregated the South had been.

"Class division was even worse in Columbus," Franklin said. "Many more rich and many more poor. And in 1992, I fear the country is sliding back to a society more broadly separated by economic class with the middle class losing ground at the top and accepting a level below where it's been since World War II."

The crowd gathered around the great square with the shooting fountain and statue of LaFayette holding the documents of the principles for freedom he had published after the French Revolution.

Brad came over and stood behind him. "Boss, remember the day we came here and took a picture of the square for the cover of *Georgia Journal*. I don't think I've ever been colder. It must have been about twenty-four, and you wanted every corner around the square to show in the photo."

"And you got it," Franklin reminded him. "And I do remember how cold it was."

"That doesn't sound very cold to me," Susie said.

"You weren't there," Brad remarked.

The article was about a couple who owned a newspaper in Barnesville and had just bought and remodeled a house that LaFayette supposedly stayed in during that visit to Georgia in 1824. There was a historic marker at the house, but who knew. The roads through Georgia were so bad then that LaFayette had a terrible time getting to his ultimate destination, which was Mobile in Alabama, then still owned by the French.

In Columbus that night, Franklin had asked his friend Milton Jones and Mort Harris, a prominent lawyer, to introduce him.

He called out the name of many friends in the town and recalled his grade school and high school days in Columbus, not to mention his twenty years on the daily newspaper. All in all it was a friendly crowd, and he gave them his speech about how important the nation's role was in the world of 1992.

"What we must now be is the greatest force for peace just as we were the greatest major force in winning three world wars, and I'm counting the Cold War, which in many ways was our greatest victory and which provides us with such an unprecedented opportunity to establish decades of peace. But I want to stress that we will need every member of our military to maintain that peace as we needed them to wage the wars. There will be some shuffling around, but I project that Fort Benning, the army base near Columbus, will be as important ten years from now and into the future as it was as the largest infantry school in the world in the past fifty years."

This was a theme Franklin had been developing but had not talked much about. He had seen Columbus grow from about the size of LaGrange to become Georgia's second-largest city in the 1990 census. Fort Benning had been the main factor in the growth, and the textile industry continued an essential role until about 1970, when exports and automation caught up with it.

Columbus was obviously facing some economic challenges, and further reductions at Fort Benning would undermine its growth. Franklin wanted to assure the people of his longest hometown that a vote for him as president would be a vote for a surer future for Columbus.

A strong point he made was that he would support raising the minimum wage, and that would include the minimum wage for military personnel to make their jobs more attractive and more useful. "Soldiers are trained for valuable tasks at home as well as on battlefields," he said. "Too many skillful and inventive men and women do not have the chance to use the full range of their skills learned in military service."

A good crowd was on hand, drawn partially by the band and familiarity with Franklin. The media people crowded around and wanted to know more about his plans for expanding the military role beyond preparing for war. "The short answer is to be better prepared for peace and make peace a more desirable goal for smaller nations than killing and blowing up buildings and killing each other's people.

"An example today of what must be done is to stop the genocide in the former Yugoslavia, which has divided into warring camps since Tito's death and the collapse of the Communist government. Thousands have already been killed on both sides, and some NATO troops sent in to restore order have been captured and killed. The main fighting seems to be between the Serbians, who are mostly Muslims and the Slavs, who are mostly Christian. The Serbs appear to be the aggressors and have superior military equipment.

"This is a situation where cooperation with Russia in a US-Russia alliance could be most helpful. NATO is ineffective, and the US does not want to send ground troops. Russia backs the Serbs, and I suppose we favor the Muslim Slavs, but the fighting is growing worse, and the longer it goes on, the harder it will be to contain it. That will be the first foreign engagement a new administration must deal with, but the best way will be to make it part of the overall approach to a foreign policy that is a quest for peace. The US is strong, but it can be most effective when it finds allies on both sides of disputes."

Mort Harris, a high school classmate of Franklin's, was a tax lawyer who had been pleased and impressed with Franklin's call for a more progressive and fairer tax system. Harris had done a great deal of research on "the widening gap," as he called it "between the rich and the poor," and termed it "a political, economic, and moral dilemma for America."

He gave Franklin the latest figures he had compiled on the problem, which Harris said would keep growing unless immediate changes were made in the income tax system. In his introduction, Harris stressed that Franklin was the only candidate calling for significant changes in the tax system.

In his address, Franklin noted the nearness of Columbus to Warm Springs, where Roosevelt had spent so many days and where he had recognized the problems of poorer Americans he had never seen in New York.

"Roosevelt's New Deal is the chief theme of my campaign," Franklin said, "and no state's people benefited more from the New Deal than Georgia, even though Governor Eugene Talmadge opposed nearly every early program, and many other Georgians grudgingly accepted the ones that had a degree of federal control.

"Part of that control was federal insistence that Negroes share in the benefits, although they never shared fully, due to reluctance on the part of local officials to include them in all the programs. That included Georgia congressmen."

Franklin was no ardent integrationist, partly because of the disruption for both races of forced integration, as opposed to ending discrimination and building a stronger economy for blacks. The South has always lived on "half a loaf," he often said, and blacks got the crumbs.

Franklin and his family spent the night in Columbus with friends and attended the First Baptist Church Sunday morning. He had joined that church when he was eleven years old; he and Jean had met there and were married there. Although he was not a regular churchgoer now, he had served First Baptist Columbus as a Sunday school teacher, director of the Training Union, and had been elected a deacon when he was only thirty-four.

The only televised debate in Georgia among the Democratic candidates was on Sunday night at the Carter Center in Atlanta, which was one of the most ambitious presidential centers yet built. Many national and world leaders came there to meet with Carter, and Carter used the center as his base for traveling throughout the world, organizing health facilities and programs and acting as an observer and supervisor of elections in nations striving to be born. By nearly every measure, Carter was the most active and effective former US president. He had been only fifty-seven when he was defeated for reelection, and with wife, Rosalyn, he set a course to build better relations and improve living conditions in the third world.

The debate included only four candidates in person, as Senator Harkin had chosen not to compete in Georgia, and Senator Kerrey participated from a studio in Colorado, where he was campaigning. The three moderators were all Atlanta TV or newspaper reporters. Franklin knew them casually and was not impressed by any of them. They were Dick Williams, a *Journal-Constitution* columnist and former TV commentator; Bill Nigurt; a WSB-TV political reporter; and Cynthia Tucker, the youthful editorial page editor of *The Constitution*, who had attended and graduated from Auburn while Franklin was publisher and editor of the daily paper in Opelika-Auburn, but their paths had never crossed.

Based on the debates thus far, Franklin did not expect much fireworks. The Jennifer Flowers exposé had seemed to have run its

353

heated course, but Clinton's draft story was still a prominent issue. Those had dominated the campaign in the past three weeks but oddly enough did not come up in the Georgia debate, at least from the moderators, who had apparently been lectured on the need to make duller issues the focus of the debate and leave stories of more interest to the tabloids and TV.

The first question to all the candidates was how they planned to create more jobs that paid middle-class wages. Each candidate was given forty-five seconds to answer.

Jerry Brown had the first shot, and he began by saying it was impossible to give an answer in forty-five seconds. He thus suggested eliminating all current federal taxes and replacing them with a flat income tax on everyone. This was also a favorite tax plan of Republicans, which they praised for its simplicity, usually neglecting to mention it would further shift the tax responsibility from wealthier Americans to the poorest or, more specifically, to consumers. It was the ultimate supply-side dream, except for its close cousin, the national sales tax, which would be even more regressive.

Clinton was at his most charming and stuck to his promise of middle class tax cut and a tax rebate to the poorest families.

Senator Kerrey reminded the audience that the Cold War was over, and the United States needed to revise its trade policies with Japan and the European Union.

Franklin, the last to answer, repeated his message that Tsongas was advocating a "warmed-over" supply-side economics and that the original version had brought on the "sour economy" the nation was now experiencing plus reducing the middle class, "which was the nation's great achievement since World War II."

Dick Williams, the most conservative member of the moderators, referring mainly to Clinton's call for a middle class tax cut, gave a short speech: "At the 1984 Democratic Convention, Walter Mondale said he was going to raise taxes and many people said that his campaign was dead in the water from that moment on. One of the cornerstones of your campaign is a middle class tax cut, and yet you are getting an extremely strong challenge from Paul Tsongas, who says that you want to be Santa Claus. Tsongas says 'no tax cuts' and that you are 'pandering to win votes' and that he senses the mood of the public is that they are buying Tsongas's ideas."

Clinton defended his tax cut plan and pointed out that Tsongas had recommended an across-the-board cut in capital gains taxes. "I think that's very wrong," Clinton said strongly. "So the question is not whether to give the middle class a tax cut, it's whether the cut goes to the middle class or to people investing in stock. Who gets the cut?"

Franklin finally was given a chance to speak. "Mr. Clinton is quite right in his answer. He just doesn't go far enough. I disagree with the original premise, however. Mondale lost for many reasons in 1984, and it's never wise to be quite so frank with the public about taxes. Mr. Tsongas is, in effect, running on a Republican platform this year, the one that always wants to cut taxes for the wealthiest and raise taxes on the poorest. And there was no sign of support for that in the first two primaries, both in his backyard. I won by advocating almost exactly the opposite of his message."

Kerrey got his word in by long distance from Denver by saying he supported a middle-class tax cut but suggested the first priority must be to create more and better jobs to rebuild our technology industry and establish a national health insurance program.

Tsongas stuck to his guns on more austerity for the middle class. "I know that's not what pollsters are telling us to say, but when I say no, I'm not being suicidal politically. When you talk to economists or men and women in business or to editorial writers, there is not one call for middle-class tax cuts. We must take our money, our precious reserves, and put them into venture capital, equity capital, and things like that."

"May I have a word?" Franklin asked. "I'm both a business-man and an editor and not only support a middle-class cut tax but a complete revision of the tax code to restore it to some semblance of what it was before Congress adopted so-called supply-side econom-ics. My first proposal in this campaign was, and still is, is to reduce the payroll tax by 50 percent and extend it to all earned income. That would be a fairer tax and would shift the burden from the lowest-paid workers to the highest-paid ones. I'd like to hear a comment on that idea from all the other candidates and especially Mr. Tsongas. That change alone would put millions of dollars in the pockets of workers who must spend every dollar they earn, and they are the cornerstone of a demand-side economy, which has rescued the nation from every economic slump and will rescue it this time if we can get the supply-siders out of government, and certainly not elect any more like Paul Tsongas."

Franklin's answer drew a response from the audience, but it wasn't what the moderators wanted to talk about. Kerrey was asked about his support of universal health care.

"We must shift to a premium-based system and to a tax-based system," he said. "My proposal would allow us to focus on job training and education just as the Japanese and Germans do, and say to workers, don't worry about both your job and your health care."

Given a chance to speak, Franklin said he admittedly didn't understand any of the health-care proposals. "The one system most Americans do understand and support is Medicare. It has proven its value and its basic simplicity. And I would say to the candidates, especially Mr. Tsongas, who has repeatedly told us that Japan won the Cold War, that you cannot compare the United States economy with Japan's because for years the US has covered the bulk of Japan's defense expenses, not to mention keeping thousands of troops in Germany and Korea."

"Since Mr. Franklin is mainly for the old Democratic solutions of more taxes, more government, and more controls, I suppose he's for letting the federal government take over the health industry," Tsongas said with a smirk.

"That's what Jerry Brown is actually proposing in his single-payer tax system, with the single payer being the federal government," Kerrey interjected. "There would have to be a big change in the public attitude for the nation to adopt that sort of system, which is similar to Canada's."

Tsongas commented, "As wonderful as the Canadian system is, if I had been in Canada when I got cancer, I would not be here today. So there's a limit to my enthusiasm to how much I can embrace it."

Jerry Brown explained his case for a single payer: "If you created a universal system, with a single payer, so that we're all in the same boat, whether it's the president, a veteran, or a poor person or anyone in the middle, we'd all be part of a universal system... Today, it's frightening, with 1,500 different insurance companies trying to make a profit in delivering the whole fragmented system unify it as they do in Canada with a single payer, and I believe you can allocate money in the proper way to ensure that every American has a basic level of care, including long-term care."

Tsongas was given a chance to comment further on a health-care plan, which he had proposed. "You've got two mandates: one, everybody gets insurance, and two, you don't bankrupt the country. Giving care to everyone is the easy part. How you contain the cost is the difficult part."

"Wow! How long did it take him to figure that out?" Franklin asked.

But Tsongas went on with another two-parter: "On containing cost, there are two choices: one, government is efficient. If you believe that, we have counseling available for you after the program. The other choice is the use of the marketplace, where companies compete against each other so that it is in the self-interest of them to bring those costs down and so they reach the best doctors, the most efficient doctors, the best hospitals. I am very wary of a program that says people like me, a cancer survivor, is going to have to wait. No thanks, I'd still rather be here."

Kerrey, who had made health-care insurance his main campaign focus leveled his remarks at Tsongas. "I must disagree with Paul Tsongas, by the way, about Medicare and Social Security. They are both more efficient, in fact, than the private sector has been. And the government runs them."

Franklin also tried to get a word in on Tsongas's statement about the government. "It's ridiculous," he said strongly, "sort of like that Japan won the Cold War just as one example. As a director of several private companies, I'm sure he's familiar with the fact that the private sector providers put their executives on income contracts in the millions of dollars plus retirement plans and dismissal plans that pay executives huge amounts for years after they are fired or retired. The only way those companies save money is by paying nurses and other employees as little as possible and almost kicking patients out of the hospital within two or three days. Private companies, quite frankly, can get away with things the government would never do. I'm speaking as someone who greatly admires and respects physicians and hospitals and all aspects of the American medical care system, which has saved my life and so millions of others that would have been lost in earlier years.

"But many of the hospitals I see today look like expensive temples as well as places of healing, and I don't know any starving doctors or hospital executives. Doctors deserve every penny they earn, but I'm not sure that medical facility owners and managers deserve the salaries they get today, much of it made possible because the government foots the bill for so many patients who were totally on charity or simply couldn't pay their bills before Medicare and Medicaid. These programs have made our health care better and also greatly increased money for expansion and improvements by providers of health care."

"Mr. Franklin and I have found a great deal to disagree about during this campaign," Tsongas said. "His ideas always lean toward pure Socialism, which would eliminate jobs, cripple companies, and he now even attacks our health-care industry, which is the finest in the world."

"I haven't denied I am running as a Franklin Roosevelt New Deal Democrat," Franklin said, "and if you look back at some of his critics, they used the same words Mr. Tsongas just did, including when Roosevelt tried to add a health-care plan to the first Social Security Bill enacted in 1935, and fifty-eight years later, we hear most of the same arguments.

"Mr. Kerrey has made health care his primary issue, and I commend him for that, but looking back at the history of attempts to reform it, I am not hopeful, which is why first priority should be to make the tax systems fairer for the many Americans who are paying a disproportionate amount compared to their income so they will have more dollars for all their needs, including health care."

The debate which had been fairly civil suddenly changed to rancorous. Tsongas tried a ploy to direct criticism away from his Republican views. "I would like to ask Governor Clinton, Bill, this campaign in the last couple of weeks has become nasty. The fact is what's happening between us, and really all of us, really only serves George Bush, and I called on Ron Brown, the Democratic Party chairman, the other day to get us altogether and agree we won't mention each other in ads and that we stop the attacks and focus our attention on George Bush. I will make a pledge that all of my ads will deal with substance and what I stand for, and I would ask all you to do the same."

Clinton replied, "Well, you said that very carefully so that you can say anything you want as long as you don't use my name. I ran a commercial comparing our positions, using your words from 'A Call to Economic Arms.' That was not a negative ad. I think the people are entitled to know what the differences are between us."

Jerry Brown broke in. "I've been reading your booklet too. You've got some things in there about tax credits for research and development, weakening the antitrust laws, removing company directors. What is the silver bullet in your call to economic arms that's going to stimulate the economy, when we've been doing all those things for the last ten years?"

"There is no silver bullet," Tsongas admitted. "This is real life, the real world. I'm a real estate developer, and you learn something along the way. You learn that you can't build a building if you can't fill it. I'm also a director of seven companies, from large to struggling start-ups. There's no venture capital out there. The Japanese take these companies and grow them, they build them. In this country, they are starving out there. Talk to any small businessmen. What do they want? Credit, capital, a trained workforce. Those are the forces that drive an economy. Those are the silver bullets that drive an economy. There's no magic. Just hard work, like how we built this country in the first place."

Franklin asked if he might add to that. "I'm a small businessman, and I'm not a director of any company except mine. But I can tell you what I want are more customers—customers who have money to spend on the products we advertise. Customers don't have enough money today because of policies Republicans have enacted and which Senator Tsongas has supported and still supports, which are supply economics. What's the difference in his policies and the ones George Bush and the Republicans have used for twelve years?"

Tsongas replied with a sneer. "I don't think Mr. Franklin deserves an answer."

In closing statements, Kerrey decided to identify himself with the antigovernment candidates despite his strong support for better health care.

"My fundamental principle is that the federal government has gotten too big. I believe democracy works bests at the local level, and I intend to seek full funding of Head Start. It's a community-based program. My health-care proposal takes the federal government out of the picture and puts power in the hands of the states to make the decisions about how they are going to manage health care. It reduces the size of the federal government. I am committed not to just reduce the federal deficit but to distribute decisions back to the local level."

Dick Williams, the chief moderator, turning to Franklin, said, "Tom, I've read your editorials off and on for several years, and you've changed your positions enough that I'm not sure where you stand today. Basically tonight I gather that you believe a larger federal government would be the best way to solve problems. Is that correct?"

"Well, Dick. I've also read you for several years, and I know where you stand. You're a conservative Republican who doesn't think the federal government has done anything right but cut taxes on the wealthiest Americans. Yes, I do believe in a strong central federal government, the government that in 1775 persuaded thirteen scattered, quarrelling colonies to get together long enough to throw off the control of the strongest empire in the world at the time. The government that then created a new nation under a constitution, a nation strong enough virtually at its birth to take the bold step of making the Louisiana Purchase, which doubled the land area of the nation. A government strong enough to build the St. Lawrence waterway, joining the East coast to the Great Lakes and creating the foundation for the most successful economic power in the new industrial age. A government strong enough to prevail in a massive civil war to assure all the states remained a unified country, rather than breaking away for their own purposes, in that case to maintain human slavery. A nation strong enough to rise from the ashes of that war to become the decisive factor in winning two world wars in the twentieth century and, when suddenly gripped by economic disaster, had the determination and the vision to not only overcome its immediate economic doldrums but to enact programs and laws that would improve life for future generations.

"Yes, I believe that the strength of a strong federal government made most of that possible and will continue its excellence against the challenges of the future. I believe it, and I believe it for the best of all possible reasons—because it is true!"

Franklin recalled how that last sentence had electrified the crowd in the first New Hampshire debate, and he decided to try it on Georgians, even though he knew a lot of them disliked the federal government, for one main reason: it had forced racial integration on them. He decided to take a chance and remind them of all the good things the government had made possible.

The debate crowd gave him a rousing ovation, greatly upsetting the other candidates, especially Tsongas, and annoying the moderator, who looked daggers at Franklin and admonished the crowd against any further demonstrations. After the debate ended, Franklin greeted a few old friends and gave the media all the time they wanted. He was pleased with the attention by the three main TV stations in Atlanta and by the newspaper reporters, of which there were several who had never been very friendly in his publishing days.

Two very important people who stopped to see him were Bill and Hillary Clinton. "I'm supposed to win this primary," Bill said. "I need it, and Governor Miller and James Carville told me there was nothing to worry about. But you have a home court advantage, and I always knew that, and tonight you and I both put Tsongas in his place. I may be looking at a strong second."

Hillary smiled. "You were great," she said. "I mean that, but where do you go from here? We're organized in every state, including

Florida and Texas. I haven't seen much evidence of Thomas Franklin there."

Franklin returned their smiles. "I'm just worried about Georgia right now," he said. "Tuesday could be the last Primary Day for me."

"You have to look ahead," Hillary advised. "That is, if you really want to win the nomination."

"Probably not as much as you do. You and Bill have been planning this campaign a long time. I just started a few months ago. You've got Friends of Bill—and Hillary—all over the country. I'm not sure I have many right here in Georgia."

Hillary looked puzzled. "Our polls show you have a lot," she said. "If Zell Miller was not on board with us, you'd win in a walk. You've got something the other candidates don't have. You understand how much the economy needs help and how important it is to get help. Even Bill has had trouble making that point compelling. He's just coming around to realizing how much Tsongas sounds like a Republican. You're going to see him attacking Tsongas a lot more in the rest of the states. You've had a great influence on him."

"Thanks," Franklin said, adding with a smile. "Flattery will get you a long way with me. I obviously have low self-esteem, but so did a lot of presidents, including Abraham Lincoln."

"Where did you get that line about 'I believe it for the best of all possible reasons—because it is true'?"

"I think one of the Founding Fathers used it in arguing about the Constitution, but I've never been able to reference it. So I guess I invented it. If you find out who said it first, let me know."

Hillary gave him a pat on the shoulder. "See you at the polls," she said. "We're not contesting South Carolina, but we'll be in Florida."

The next day was the last campaign day before the Georgia primary. Franklin had thought long and hard about his strategy. He finally decided to send Brad, Kathleen, and the band bus to Augusta, Savannah, and down the East Coast to the Golden Isles. They had plenty of pamphlets and other literature to pass out, plus both Brad and Kathleen were effective surrogates and familiar with the Georgia coast. He outlined an ambitious itinerary for them and made them promise to be in Athens by 7:00 p.m. for the final preprimary event at Sanford Stadium, home of the Georgia Bulldogs, which seated ninety thousand. The event had been publicized with newspaper ads, radio spots, and on cable TV of the area.

He decided he and Jack Hardy and Susie Schultz would travel together through the middle of Georgia, east and southeast of Atlanta, and meet up with the others in Athens.

Leaving Atlanta, they went first to Conyers in Rockdale County, where Franklin had owned the daily paper for sixteen years. He had sold it just recently, in fact, as he dissolved his publishing company, and he was still close to many of the people who worked there. He had converted the *Rockdale Citizen* from a weekly to a five-time daily a few months after buying it, betting on the remarkable growth the county was experiencing, and its twenty-five-mile distance from the center of Atlanta. Conventional wisdom at the time was that suburban newspapers could only be subsidiaries of the large city dailies, but the Rockdale Citizen had become an ABC-audited ten-thousand circulation daily, which was a higher circulation than the combined total of the two Atlanta dailies in Rockdale County. At the time, Rockdale was nearly all-white, and it had only one municipality, Conyers, which was an important asset for a small suburban daily.

The *Citizen* pioneered a number of suburban paper attractions. It carried only local news stories on its front page, with national, state, and international roundups on page 2. It also carried only locally produced photos except for an occasional mugshot.

Franklin thought it was the best newspaper he ever had, even including the daily in Opelika. The staff was bright and hardworking. Most of them had worked at the weekly paper, including the publisher, who was the daughter of the former owner. Franklin named her the publisher and asked her to begin writing a column and editorials, which she had not previously done. She turned out to be excellent at the task. She had actually been born in Rockdale, a rarity in those days since Rockdale had less than seven thousand people as recently as 1930. I-20, one of the three interstate highways in the Atlanta area, passed through Rockdale in early 1960, and the population had jumped to eighty thousand in the 1990 census. It was also the second smallest of Georgia's 159 counties in land area, next only to Clarke (Athens), site of the university.

During the years he was expanding his newspaper company, Franklin looked for weekly papers in Georgia that might be converted to dailies. He studied the maps and the population trends and then visited them if there seemed a possibility of buying the paper. He already owned the Jonesboro paper, which was about thirty miles southeast of Conyers and twenty miles north of Henry County, which also had a weekly his company owned. On a trip to Jonesboro one day, he passed a crossroad with a sign that pointed south to McDonough in Henry and east to Conyers in Rockdale, and on a notion, he took the turn to Conyers, a town he had only passed by on the interstate. He stopped to visit the newspaper publisher, who was from a longtime Rockdale family and had launched the *Citizen* thirty years earlier against a weekly published in nearby Covington. The *Rockdale Citizen* had driven two weeklies from the market, including the *Rockdale Solid South*, whose publisher was the founding president of the Georgia Press Association, which Franklin would serve as president during its one hundredth anniversary year, in 1985–1986.

Franklin wanted Hardy and Susie to meet some of the people at the *Rockdale Citizen* and also see its so-called Olde Town. "I had many good times here," he told them, "although I never actually lived here. Ashmore was a regular visitor as my right-hand employee and supervised installation of a new press and starting daily delivery."

The *Citizen* had a unique office, which was right on Main Street, and consisted of two Williamsburg-style houses which had been joined together next to a third house, which was moved to make room for a parking lot. "Not too convenient," Franklin admitted, but a lot of good newspapers have been put out here. The *Citizen* was not actually sensational, but the editors sought out intriguing local stories and played them with large headlines, and its daily street sales confirmed the formula. The *Citizen* was seldom dull, which too many newspapers were, Franklin felt, including some of his other ones. He had early on installed equipment for full-color photos and the photographers took advantage with outstanding color shots for his relatively small papers. Rockdale was politically a Democratic county, and the *Citizen* publisher assured Franklin he should do well in the primary.

After a tour of the building and visits with his former employees, Franklin and his companions moved on to Covington, a larger city than Conyers, with several pre-Civil War mansions still in use. "I wanted you to see these," he told Susie. "Sherman's army didn't burn everything along the march to the sea, which followed this route. The story is that he had a friend in this town and told his soldiers they could loot but not to burn. It's been great for twentieth-century tourism. Conyers was too small to have mansions. It got its name from the abundance of rock in its soil, which also made it poor for farming."

From Rockdale they swung through Gwinnett, Forsyth, and Hall counties. Gwinnett had soared from twenty-seven thousand population in 1930 to almost two hundred thousand in 1990, and neighboring Forsyth has grown from twelve thousand in 1960 to nearly fifty thousand by 1990."

"Gosh, Forsyth must have had a big industry move-in," Susie said.

"No, it had something better. An all-white population. Gwinnett, by contrast, has an interstate and many industries did move there," Franklin explained. "It's large in area for a Georgia county and convenient to Atlanta and Lake Lanier, but Forsyth has neither an interstate nor any large industry. Its strong attraction was no black residents, and I mean none at all—until about three years ago, and even today Forsyth's population is 97 percent white, and its public schools are almost 100 percent white. Forsyth's racial breakdown came to wide attention on a weekend in January 1987, when Hosea Williams, one of Martin Luther King's chief lieutenants, led two marches from Atlanta to Forsyth County to dramatize the county's 'whites only' reputation. The marches were a big news event, but the National Guard had to be called in to deal with violent clashes that broke out between the marchers and counterdemonstrators. Oprah Winfrey took notice and broadcast her TV show live from Forsyth County that week.

"After order was restored, a flood of white residents began moving to Forsyth County. I guess it could have been a coincidence, but not likely, and today Forsyth's population is double what it was that fateful weekend, but it still has only a handful of black citizens."

"Sounds like the place to live," Hardy interjected with a grim chuckle.

"But what happened to the blacks who once lived there?" Susie asked. "Surely there were some."

"There were," Franklin agreed. "Accounts written or collected after the events recounted what was called the racial cleansing of Forsyth County. The story was not widely known until the marches to the county led by Hosea Williams and the TV show by Oprah Winfrey."

As they drove through Cumming, the Forsyth county seat, which for years was just a crossroads with a small grocery store but now was a growing small city, Susie looked out her window intensely. "You're right," she said. "I don't see any blacks, it's almost like being back in New Hampshire."

"What happened," Franklin explained, "was in 1912, an eighteen-year-old white girl, reportedly one of the prettiest in Forsyth County, was found nearly beaten to death on a path outside Cumming. By the next day, the sheriff had arrested three black suspects. A crowd of whites stormed the jail and seized one of the three, who supposedly had confessed, and he was hanged that night. In 1911, lynchings were not uncommon in Georgia, as I mentioned, and the body was displayed on the courthouse lawn as an example of quick and brutal justice. That seemed to calm the passions roused by the attack on the girl, but a few weeks later, she died of her injuries. On the day of her funeral, as the story goes, 'all hell broke loose' in Forsyth County that night, and white men on horseback rode out to the little cluster of houses along the river, where the county's approximately 1,200 blacks lived, and told them to load up and get out of Forsyth County before the next sundown. By the end of the month, all of the blacks were gone, leaving their houses, schools, churches, and even the harvest in the fields.

"For years, Forsyth remained all white. Neither stores nor industries were encouraged to come there, and blacks were even afraid to drive through after several incidents when cars were stopped and told to detour. Soon any whites in Forsyth who objected moved away, and there was no one left to protest the past, the present, or the future, until Hosea's march into the county on that 1987 weekend. After that, whites began moving into Forsyth's booming residential districts, but few blacks.

"Forsyth is actually an example of what many neighborhoods in the South have become since school integration was ordered, just without the background and the violence, but there are many school districts as racially segregated as Forsyth County."

"That's a terrible story," Susie said. "What's going to happen?"

"We'll all become little New Hampshire," Hardy joked, "and all the blacks will move to Boston and New York."

"Progress is slow, but there are ways to improve relations. The first way is for more blacks to become middle class. I guess you played against black girls in state tournaments, didn't you?" Franklin asked.

"Yes, and they were all very good, very quick and fast. But usually I was taller. Don't let anybody ever tell you that height isn't the most important asset in basketball, especially at the grade and high school levels."

"The reason school integration was so hard for many Southerners to accept was not only were they reluctant to send their children to the same schools with blacks but blacks quickly began to dominate high school sports. Whites no longer saw their children or their children's friends on the football field or the basketball court. I'm convinced that a major reason for the quick growth of private schools for whites, all of which almost immediately fielded sports teams—with nearly all white players—was the desire to see their kids competing."

"You make the situation sound so hopeless. All the people I've met in the South have been so nice," Susie said.

"You're a pretty white girl, even with a New England accent. That makes a difference. But whites and blacks are divided by more than the color of their skin. Almost as important is the economic factor. They can't, and the government can't, do much about their skin, but the government can do more about their economic status, and I believe that is the ultimate solution. A black person with money or even a good job is looked on entirely differently. Usually he lives in a better house, drives a better car, and wears nicer clothes. The government has tried many programs and laws to improve the status of blacks, but their economic status is the key, and it has not been boldly addressed. Many minorities came to the United States poor and have become rich or well off, and their children and grandchildren are even richer. Consider the millions of immigrants that came during the 1880s to 1920s. They virtually took over many industries in the country because they were entrepreneurs who created and bought businesses and usually made sure their relatives were involved so that their extended families shared in the growth and wealth. A more recent example are the Indians from India who got into the motel and hotel business. How many motels do you go in that are operated by Indians? Most of them, but how many do you go in that are operated or owned by blacks? Not many. Another example are the Koreans who have come to the US in recent years and are the main operators of curb markets and convenience stores. Being an entrepreneur is the best way to accumulate money, and we have not encouraged or made it as easy for blacks to become entrepreneurs, as Indians, Koreans, and some poor whites have done, including this one."

"You haven't talked much about that," Susie mentioned.

"Not precisely, but part of what I mean by a demand-side economy is getting more money into people's hands so they can buy things and help small businesses get started. Today we've squeezed the money out of consumers with this unrealistic allegiance to supply-side economics. That's got to be changed for all Americans to prosper, whatever their color, background, or social status. There's more money in the nation than ever. It's just being stuffed into too few pockets."

By this time, they were in the city of Buford, site of the Buford Dam, and which at one time had the largest shoe and saddle manufacturing plant in the South. Many of those plants had moved to Georgia from New Hampshire and other New England states, but

Buford's leather plant was now as empty as New Hampshire's, as the leather makers moved on to other countries, always in pursuit of cheaper labor.

As they passed through Buford, Franklin pointed to two large buildings that once held the leather business at its peak. On one corner in Buford was a statute of two men putting a leather saddle on Trigger, the horse of western movie star Roy Rogers; Trigger's had been made in Buford.

"Buford was lucky, as was Georgia," Franklin explained. "See this big dam we're passing over and that lake that looks like it runs into the horizon. About the time the leather, shoe, and saddle business were fading away, some influential Georgia politicians—all Democrats, of course—persuaded the federal government to build a dam right here at Buford on the Chattahoochee River. It was authorized by Congress in 1946 as part of the vast development of the nation's waterways after World War II. Now, as you can imagine, the war had left Congress facing a huge, long-term budget deficit and lots of projects that had been put off during the war. So waterway development was first sold as a defense measure, since defense was still the surest way to get funding through Congress.

"Waterway development was also seen by visionaries as a means for more electric power production, better flood control, and assuring clean water sources. Later, lakes for recreation, boating, fishing, and other water activities became huge sources of tourism.

"Buford Dam was not a priority in the 1946 bill, and its first appropriation was only $750,000. Its journey through the congressional funding process was fraught with pitfalls, both financial and political. But both of Georgia's US senators at the time, Richard Russell and Walter George, favored the dam projects, and they had considerable influence because of their seniority and closeness to President Harry Truman and their earlier relationship with President Roosevelt, who died the year before the Waterway legislation was introduced. Obviously the projects were an extension of the New Deal, a first cousin to the Tennessee Valley Authority and another step by the federal government in making life better for poorer states.

"Buford Dam's fate still hung in the balance even after the groundbreaking on March 1, 1950. Republicans had won a majority in the House in the 1946 elections, and in June 1951, the House Appropriations Committee refused to approve more money for the fledgling project. The essential person who rescued the project was Atlanta Mayor William Hartsfield, who argued that the dam was necessary to provide a water source for the rapidly growing Atlanta area. Approval finally came and the government began acquiring the rights to fifty-six thousand acres of land in the area. Seven hundred families had to be relocated, some unwillingly, although most of them were paid more per acre than they could have gotten otherwise. Total price for the land was $19 million, not an insignificant sum in the 1950s.

"When completed the Buford Dam was a $1 billion project but its impact on Georgia, especially the Atlanta area, has been indispensable. On the day Buford Dam was dedicated in 1956 and the Lake Lanier basin began to fill with water, Georgia's population was about four million. Metro Atlanta was less than a million. Georgia was twentieth among the states in population. Today Georgia is pushing ten million in population, ninth-highest state in the nation. Atlanta is among the ten largest metro areas in the country with five million.

"A lot of factors contributed to the growth, but the building of Buford Dam must rank with the development of Hartsfield Airport as the two major reasons, with Mayor Hartsfield heavily involved in both. No one would question the importance or value of Buford Dam today, but an honest question is, would today's Congress have approved funds for the project? Every county around Buford Dam is now represented in Congress by a Republican, and the voters in the area voted heavily for Republican George Bush in the 1988 presidential election. Forsyth County, which borders Lake Lanier, is not only Georgia's fastest growing, it has also become the most faithfully Republican.

"In 1946 the US was still financially strapped from World War II and the Korean War. Its budget deficit was larger than today. But both Republican and Democratic Congresses and presidents supported the waterways projects, and their vision has been proven many times over. Buford Dam's potential for providing a water supply to Atlanta's growing population becomes more important every year."

Susie looked out over the broad expanse of Lake Lanier. "So this was another gift from the New Deal," she exclaimed. "It's a gift that keeps on giving. Who is it named for?"

"A poet, Sidney Lanier, who died in 1872, but among other great poems his greatest was *The Song of the Chattahoochee*, which forecast the river's value in years to come."

They had reached Gainesville by then and stopped for lunch. Gainesville was the largest city on their itinerary. "This is the chicken capital of the world," Franklin explained. "I mean, more chicks are hatched here than anywhere in the world, and chickens are now Georgia's largest agricultural product."

"Plus there's nothing like a good fried chicken or a Chic-Fil-A sandwich," Hardy added.

"What's a Chic-Fil-A sandwich?" Susie asked.

"It's made from boneless chicken and was developed right here in Georgia. Try one," Hardy advised.

Susie ordered one with french fries. "Will freedom fries be all right?" the waitress asked.

Susie smiled broadly. "I was a waitress myself," she said, "and when I asked that question, I got a history lesson and a whole new career. Just make it french fries."

They made a couple of more stops and arrived in Athens about five o'clock with the big event at Sanford Stadium set for seven. One stop was at the Holiday Inn for the girls to change clothes. They'd been in their traveling jeans and jackets all day, and Franklin had called ahead to order some new red blouses and black skirts for them to wear to the rally at Sanford Stadium. He met Phil Sutton in the lobby to check on the program, which was to be an all-star show of personalities and entertainers from the area, including Kenny Rogers, who had a home a few miles outside Athens and had agreed to lead the crowd in singing "The Gambler" and "Lucille." Other scheduled speakers were Michael Stipe, the lead singer for the rock band R. E. M., who lived in Athens; Gwen O'Looney, the mayor of Athens; Michael Thurmond, the first black state legislator from Athens and now the state secretary of labor; Herschel Walker, Georgia's great All-American football player; Dr. Charles Knapp, the university president; and the main speaker and star of the show, Lewis Grizzard, newspaper columnist, humorist, and the author of eighteen best-selling books. Grizzard usually got $20,000 for a performance but had agreed to appear for the rally because Franklin had hired him as a sportswriter when Grizzard was just seventeen. In the past few years, Grizzard, in the words of his Atlanta newspaper editor, Jim Minter, had become "the hottest thing on southern newsprint." His columns appeared in four hundred newspapers across the country and he had recently added a country music show to his performances.

"Everyone has confirmed," Sutton reported, "and we should have the biggest crowd of the campaign."

Kathleen and Susie came out in their new outfits, and they looked stunning. Kathleen with her early forties figure, as striking as it had been twenty years ago. Susie, with her early twenties figure, alluring arms and legs, and Christmas tree smile. Their red blouses fit snugly around their shapely bosoms, and the short black shirts displayed their legs at just the right point. Franklin was very proud of both of them in many ways and knew they'd be a hit with the many students there, male and female.

The lower seats of the stadium were nearly full when Franklin got the show going by introducing Kenny Rogers. "This campaign has revived my career," Rogers told the crowd. "I've never had as many requests from New Hampshire and Maine as I've had the past few months."

The crowd joined him in a round of songs, and then Franklin introduced the speakers, all of whom were advised to speak not more than five minutes except for Grizzard, whom Franklin gave a slightly longer introduction. Grizzard lived in Atlanta and was a die-hard Bulldog fan, but he had been a bit of a problem to persuade to appear at Franklin's rally. At heart, and in his columns, Grizzard depicted himself as a "good ole boy" Southerner who still worshipped Robert E. Lee and his Confederate heritage as well as being a conservative in politics and culture.

In an era of political correctness, the one-time sportswriter was the most politically incorrect celebrity in the four hundred newspapers that carried his column. At forty-five, he had become almost a mythic figure, whose very name evoked acclaim or rage, especially in Georgia.

By 1992, Grizzard had attained a level of celebrity few journalists achieved, although by then he was far more than a journalist, more than an editor, more than a writer of best-selling books, more than a highly paid after-dinner speaker. He was a full-fledged corporation with an official fan club, a traveling road show, and frequent TV appearances, including on the Johnny Carson show. Grizzard's visibility in the role of professional Southerner placed him at the vortex of the South's cultural paradox, which looks back fondly at its rather sordid past which Grizzard tends to ennoble while pursuing a very different lifestyle which in many ways he is a blatant exemplar.

Grizzard was at once an apparent redneck espousing the principles of God, family, and country but in real life he was a literary rarity, plays golf three hundred days a year, is a member of three golf clubs, seldom attends church, opposes any kind of gun control and never hunts, is thrice divorced, and pro-choice on birth control.

His books have sold more copies than any other Georgia writer, except Margaret Mitchell, who wrote only one book, *Gone with the Wind*, and possibly Erskine Caldwell, who was born in Moreland, where Grizzard grew up some twenty-five years later.

The subject of most of his writings, especially his sixteen books, is himself. He regularly exposes his innermost thoughts and personal life, real and imagined. Few writers have ever written so thoroughly and without qualms about their personal problems and the people in their lives as Grizzard had. His life has few corners to explore because he has explored them all in print in his imaginatively named books such as *They Tore Out My Heart and Stomped That Sucker Flat*, *If Love Was Oil I'd Be about a Quart Low*, *Elvis Is Dead and I Don't Feel Too Good Myself*, *My Daddy Was a Pistol and I'm a Son of a Gun*, *I Took a Lickin, and Kept on Tickin*, and *If I Ever Get Back to Georgia I'm Gonna Nail My Feet to the Ground!*

It takes a unique writer to humorously portray the pain, worry, and agony of three heart operations, but Grizzard did it following the operations to replace a faulty valve in his heart, present at birth. There are few more poignant portrayals in modern nonfiction of a marriage breakup than Grizzard's understated but heartrending account of his second wife's departure in his 1990 book *If I Ever Got Back to Georgia*. There are no portrayals of a wayward father so devastatingly but compassionately rendered as Grizzard's recollections in *My Father Was a Pistol*.

Yet Grizzard never had a book reviewed in the *New York Times*; he remains outside the circle of writers such as Garrison Keillar and Art Buchwald or similar writers whom he has long surpassed in both quality and quantity not to mention money.

Despite the widespread publications of his column and his book sales, he is not a familiar celebrity outside the South, but Franklin knew he could draw a great crowd in Georgia, despite their differences in political philosophy. They went a long way back and had several connections.

Grizzard had been born in 1946 in the hospital at Fort Benning about the time Franklin was beginning his career on the Columbus newspaper as a copyboy and part-time proofreader. Both of them had roots in Newnan and Coweta County, and both spent four years at the University of Georgia as journalism majors. But their paths crossed most fatefully in 1965 when Franklin was editor of the Columbus morning paper but had decided to help start a newspaper in Athens. He felt the existing daily was a poor example of a newspaper for the hometown of the state's largest institution of higher learning, and it was widely known that the paper was going to be sold within a year. So Franklin, always the entrepreneur, but one without any money at the time, approached the owner of a small weekly shopper in Athens, and the owner of one of the Columbus radio stations with the idea of starting a newspaper in Athens, and thus be in position to make a bid for the existing paper when it came up for sale.

Remarkably, the trio, only one of which had access to much money, the radio station owner, agreed on a plan for the venture, mainly designed by Franklin. As they plotted, Franklin suggested that their first step should be to hire the older paper's sports editor, who seemed to be its best asset, and sports was of crucial importance in Athens.

So after ordering a press, the next step was a call to Wade Saye, sports editor of *The Banner-Herald*, which dated back to 1832 and was one of the state's oldest newspapers. It was not a terrible newspaper, but it relied heavily on Associated Press stories, including its sports coverage and seldom ran local photos. The Atlanta newspaper at that time had arguably the best Sunday sports section in the nation and each week sent staff writers to nearly all big games in the South and two or three to Georgia and Georgia Tech games.

Saye agreed to come for a raise from $150 a week to $170 a week but only if he could bring along an intern who was still a student at the university. Franklin thought that was a good deal and didn't even know the intern was Lewis Grizzard.

Franklin's family situation persuaded him that he couldn't leave Columbus at the time, but Glenn Vaughn, who also was an editor at the Columbus paper, was glad to take his place and go to Athens, which turned out to be the second best thing that happened for the fledgling venture, Grizzard being the first.

The newspaper, called *The Athens Daily News*, started in late June 1966 and immediately became a readership success if not a commercial one. Vaughn and wife, Nancy, were innovative and hardworking and built a strong editorial staff to go with Saye and Grizzard. Grizzard later wrote that his two and a half years on *The Daily News* were the most fun he ever had in the newspaper business. So when Franklin asked him to come and talk at his rally, he couldn't refuse.

Grizzard started out by saying that he had originally planned to vote for Pat Buchanan in the Republican primary that day. "I was convinced that if Buchanan needed to, he'd go to Congress and pull a knife on somebody to get something done. I like him, and I felt if we're going to have a columnist run the country and I can't get elected, it might as well be Buchanan. But then Franklin came along, and he actually won a primary in New Hampshire, of all places. I didn't know he even knew where New Hampshire was. Then I remember that's how Carter got his start, and decided another Georgian as president wouldn't be bad. When Carter was president, he invited me to the White House, and Willie Nelson sang as the entertainment, Franklin has promised an invitation and he's going to have Kenny, Conway Twitty, and George T. Jones. That sold me although I'm still a hard-case conservative. Once when I spoke at a Baptist Church, they told me I could say anything I wanted to as long as I didn't dance. In those days, Baptists looked on dancing as a moral sin and threw out members caught in the act—of dancing, that is. Franklin told me I could say anything I wanted as long as I didn't say I was going to vote for Buchanan in the primary, and I'm not. I'm going to vote for Thomas Alexander Franklin.

"I was for that trickle-down tax policy because I liked that Republican claim that nobody poor ever gave me a job! Franklin convinced me that wasn't true, that he and Glenn and the other folks who started the Athens Daily News were not only poor, they owed money.

"But I'm against welfare in any form because the dole has never worked in any society. I'd go back to the FDR programs to create jobs for people if it was nothing but cleaning up New York City. That would take a million people and would be five years of work right there, just cleaning up that one city...

"I just finished my new book. It's an attack on political correctness and the speech police. I'm calling it *I Haven't Understood Anything Since 1962* and *Other Nekkid Truths*. It's all original stuff, never been in any columns. I don't think there's anything in it the Journal-Constitution would run.

"So I'm planning to vote for Franklin even though he's a bleeding heart liberal. I was invited to the Reagan White House once, and they had things on my plate I couldn't even identify and then a cello player came out but if you've heard one cello player, you've heard them all. I liked Carter's party a lot better, and I'm looking forward to Franklin's.

"The most consistent thing I've found in life is the Waffle House. The food and service are always the same—great. I like the

T-bone steak and the sausage and cheese sandwich with a few pickles thrown in.

"I need to tell you something about my father, who was a veteran of both World War II and Korea. He could walk in a room and just take it over. He had that kind of personality. If he met you once, maybe three years later on a cold October night you'd get a call from him, and he'd be stranded somewhere and needed $20. He was taken prisoner in Korea, and he came back all messed up. He was a bender drinker. He didn't drink socially, but every five or six weeks he'd go somewhere and be drunk for three days.

"In conclusion I want to say that I'm for women's lib, even though I've been accused of being antifeminist. Hell, I've freed three women myself," referring to his three ex-wives.

Grizzard left the platform to a rousing applause and the little band played "Precious Memories" for him.

Franklin came to the microphone. "Is everybody having fun?" he asked. The crowd, which had grown steadily during the performances, shouted back, "Yeah, Go Dawgs."

"Good, so now we'll get to a little serious business, but I'll keep it brief. A lot of my acquaintances here have asked me why in the world I'm running for president. 'You couldn't even get elected president of your fraternity,' one old brother told me and barely got accepted in the first place, so I've thought I'd boil it down to the basics. You see, the American economy is like a lot of those steak sandwiches Lewis was talking about. The US has more steak sandwiches for its people than any country in history, and some of them are whoppers, then they go down to medium-sized ones, and then to small ones. Finally, there are just a few sandwiches left, and they have to be divided among the people still left. The T-bones are long gone to the big eaters, and the cheese and sausage are barely enough to taste. People are cutting up the pickles to eat and a few bread crumbs are on the floor for the people at the end of the line.

"What's been happening in our nation—and to an even greater extent in the world, of course—is there are still a lot of T-bone steak sandwiches, more than ever, in fact, but a lot of sausage sandwiches are getting scarcer, and then for some people there are only the crumbs on the floor. Meanwhile the people eating the T-bone leave meat on the bone, which is thrown to the dogs, and the pickles on their plates are brushed aside because they don't eat pickles.

"That's a simple example, but it's the basic dilemma in the nation and the world today. There's more money, more food, more of everything, but too many people in the world aren't getting a pauper's share.

"And as Lewis also said, it's not as if there isn't plenty of work to do. Franklin Roosevelt's CCC boys were accused of being paid to rake leaves, which they did plenty of, but they did a lot more too, not to say that raking leaves wasn't important. They saved the soil and planted thousands of trees that prevented dust storms such as the ones that covered the country in 1933. They built parks and playgrounds and cleared ground for hundreds of roads. To see other results of FDR programs, look around you from this stadium at the buildings on the UGA campus. When I first came here as a student in 1947, half of the new buildings had been built by the WPA, and even today it is federal funds that finance many university programs that would not exist otherwise. But all those expenditures not only provided jobs, they were investments in the nation's future and the university's future, and we are enjoying the benefits today.

"That's why I'm running for president, to remind people of the debt we owe the past and the vision we must have for the future, not just for the United States, but all the world. These are beliefs I grew up with in Georgia and reaffirmed here at the university. I hope all of you will give these ideas the vote of confidence the people of New Hampshire and Maine did, and use your primary vote to encourage the ideas presented by the candidates as well as the candidates themselves. Many of you know me and never suspected me of being a presidential candidate. So I ask you to look at the ideas and judge them, not me as a person. I believe they deserve your support tomorrow."

Suddenly, Sutton appeared on the platform and handed Franklin a note. He read it quickly, as an incredulous look crossed his face. "Everybody wait a minute," he implored loudly over the microphone. "We have another guest who wants to speak, and I think everyone here will want to hear him. Nobody leave…the dealing isn't done."

Walking toward Franklin was a tall black man who had gotten the second-highest number of votes in the Democratic primaries in 1988—the Reverend Jesse Jackson. Franklin greeted Jackson with a firm handshake and hug. He had only met him once, a few days earlier, when he and Sutton talked to Jackson and Bert Lance, who had been close to Jackson during the Carter campaign.

"Welcome, Reverend Jackson, we're so glad to have you at this event. I think all of you know Reverend Jackson," he said to the applauding crowd, "a great American and a great Democrat."

"Thank you," Jackson waved to the thousands who were nearly all standing and applauding as many of them had supported him in previous elections and still held him in awe, both the whites and the blacks, plus the many university students on hand.

"I felt that I had to come here tonight and say a few words about this candidate, Thomas Alexander Franklin, and about the primary tomorrow," Jackson said in his unmistakable voice. "I've kept quiet until now, but this man has convinced me to come forth and put my hand on him and urge all of you to support him tomorrow."

Franklin stood there stunned, and he could see Sutton out of the corner of his eye virtually jumping up and down. Their earlier talk with Jackson and Lance had not been encouraging. But now, in this most dramatic of venues, with full media attention, Jackson was giving Franklin his most important endorsement of the campaign. The excited crowd echoed Franklin's exultant feeling.

"What convinced me to do this," Jackson explained, "was Mr. Franklin's speech here about the many people in the US and in the world who only have the crumbs that fall from the table, and how as a people and a government, we must find ways to give more people a chance at a bite of the whole sandwich, even if some of the heavyweights have to give up a small bite. Too many Americans are being left with the crumbs, or even less, that's what I have been trying to preach in my campaigns, and I never heard it expressed so well as Mr. Franklin did. He put the words right out there where the simplest person could understand them, and feel ashamed as well as determined to do more…more…more…and the first thing to do is vote for this man in the Georgia primary tomorrow, and I'll also say in the South Carolina primary this Saturday."

To roars of applause and cheers, Jackson waved to the crowd and gave Franklin a big hug. "That's all I wanted to say, and I'm glad to get in these words. It's been a long night, but an important night."

Franklin, still a bit stunned by the surprising turn of events, glanced over at his closest cohorts: Hardy, Susie, Kathleen, Sutton, and Ashmore. Jean had joined him on the stage earlier.

Kathleen and Susie, who had been on the road all day, were weeping, as if suddenly realizing that the weary miles and handshaking had been worthwhile. Hardy and Ashmore were still applauding and giving each other high-fives.

Franklin finally called for attention and asked Kenny Rogers to come back on stage and lead one more chorus of "The Gambler." The words had never sounded so meaningful. "Don't count your money while you're sitting at the table, there'll be time enough for counting when the dealing's done."

"And we're still dealing!" Franklin shouted as the crowd slowly left the stadium as well as most of the media, who had a great story and were on a short deadline.

Some seventy miles away, another group of political consultants were watching the proceedings in open-mouth silence with a hint of despair thrown in. That was Bill Clinton's high-powered group of James Carville, Paul Begala, George Stephanopoulos, Frank Greer, and Stan Greenberg, any of whom were getting a higher salary than Franklin's group combined.

They had planned on Georgia as the firewall for Clinton, which would give him momentum over the other candidates going into South Carolina on Saturday and then Super Tuesday a week later. Georgia governor Zell Miller had used political muscle to move the primary date up a week so that Clinton could get an easy victory. The Clinton team had concluded in recent days that victory wouldn't be easy. There would be no knockout, but they still counted on leading the field, given Clinton's support not only by Governor Miller but also by Maynard Jackson, Atlanta's first black mayor, Andrew Young, Carter's UN ambassador, and other black leaders.

But after the New Hampshire campaign and Franklin's emergence as a factor, they realized that even a lead in Franklin's home state would be hard to achieve, and they sat stunned by Jesse Jackson's announcement. They were now wondering if it wouldn't be Franklin who scored the knockout.

There were three other primaries that day, in Maryland, Minnesota, and Colorado, none of which looked hopeful for Clinton, even though Franklin was not even contending in those states. Georgia was the big prize of the day and would deliver the verdict that dominated the TV report and the headlines, and all of a sudden, Georgia looked like a surprise ambush for Clinton.

Clinton and Hillary came into the room of consultants from their adjoining suite, and Clinton reluctantly accepted the blame for Jackson's endorsement of Franklin. "It was the open mike incident," he admitted. A few days earlier in a TV studio for a round of interviews, Clinton heard a false rumor that Jackson was going to support Tom Harkin in the Southern primaries. His reaction, in front of an open microphone, was a tantrum in which he charged Jackson with "a dirty, double-crossing, backstabbing thing to do. For him to do this to me is an act of absolute dishonor." The explosion was familiar to his consultants, and it passed quickly, but his words were caught on the microphone, and the Tsongas campaign had used them in a radio commercial on Georgia and South Carolina radio stations aimed at black listeners.

The radio ad said, "Clinton didn't wait for all the facts, he just attacked, calling Jackson a backstabbing double-crosser. Paul Tsongas doesn't go around attacking respected national leaders like Jesse Jackson. Paul Tsongas wants to create new jobs. Help elect a president who respects your community, who knows what dignity means for all Americans."

Franklin's campaign declined to run a similar commercial, but quietly Sutton arranged for some of the time purchased on black stations for Franklin to carry the commercial by the Tsongas people instead.

In the debate, Tsongas had called for an end to negative advertising. When criticized for the commercial he was running on Clinton's outburst, Tsongas responded that he "responded the way they responded to me."

Jackson had earlier stayed out of the dispute. He met with Clinton shortly after the outburst and said the incident was behind them and stuck to his earlier refusal to endorse any of the candidates before the Georgia primary. He apparently changed his mind before Monday night with an impact that all observers expected to change the primary's outcome.

The Clinton brain trust was baffled, but Clinton and Hillary quickly rallied them to go out on Primary Day and take full advantage of the ground game Miller's support had given them in Georgia and to emphasize the personal contact Clinton had made with so many Georgians, even stressing to some that Clinton would not be a tool of Jackson, whom many white Georgians intensely disliked.

Chapter Twenty-One

PRIMARY DAY IN GEORGIA

Our Constitution is so simple and practical that it is possible always to meet extraordinary needs. That is why it has proved the most enduring political mechanism the modern world has produced.
—*Franklin D. Roosevelt, first inaugural address, March 4, 1933*

A beautiful March day dawned for the primary, a slight nip of winter still in the air and both parties putting in more money than had ever been spent in a Georgia campaign.

Pat Buchanan traveled many of the same roads Franklin had, also in a bus, which ironically had been used by George Bush in his campaign four years earlier. Crisscrossing Georgia, Buchanan relentlessly criticized Washington and the party bigwigs who ran the government. He actually had lived in Washington most of his life and worked for three presidents, Nixon, Ford, and Reagan. Those who knew him from his columns and his appearances on TV saw an able, articulate man with a quick smile who seemed not to take himself too seriously. But his message to rural Georgians was a hard-core appeal to those who still resented having to give up segregation, and there were plenty of them. "If you speak out against the agenda of the civil rights crowd that want racial quotas, they call you a racist," he told the crowds to cheers of support. He sounded a lot like George

Wallace twenty-four years earlier, Franklin thought. But like Wallace, Buchanan had a way of speaking in cloaked appeals, as Wallace had in 1968 when he carried five states in the general election as a third-party candidate.

Buchanan didn't shy away from calling the late Martin Luther King Jr. "a flawed leader because of sexual flings and leftist leanings." He also belittled Vice President Dan Quayle, one of his Republican opponents, but said he wouldn't go too far because he might "be accused of child abuse."

Clinton himself was also out campaigning on Primary Day, in an airplane, flying from one metropolitan area to another and greeting crowds at airports. As they had two weeks earlier in New Hampshire after the Jennifer Flowers revelations, Bill and Hillary bore down hard and had the Arkansas Travelers on hand to help them again. Georgia was a different situation than New Hampshire, however, three times as large and four times more populous. In addition, Bill's voice had faded to a whisper as he continued to battle his sore throat and allergies. Hillary, however, was an eager surrogate, who told audiences that Bill Clinton was the only Democratic candidate with a real national campaign and the only one who could go the distance to the convention and then defeat George Bush. "These other candidates are good men, but they are pretenders for president. Bill Clinton has been a governor for twelve years, he has dealt with the most difficult legislative body in the country, knows every governor and senator in the nation, and he has prepared for this job all his life. He has taken more abuse than any candidate in history and has survived and is tougher for it. He is the only proven legitimate candidate in this primary."

Hillary was effective and clearly recognized that Clinton was fighting for his candidacy in Georgia. He needed first place but could survive with a strong second. Third place would be a death rattle.

The money the Clinton campaign was spending was evident in the radio and TV commercials it continued to run on Primary Day and the efforts to get blacks to the polls in Atlanta, DeKalb, and Clayton counties.

Tsongas, Kerrey, and Brown had not given up and made evident efforts, but the obvious campaign momentum was with Tom Franklin, with his explosive campaign finale in his native state, where he had to overcome many handicaps, not the least of which was his own personality. Symptoms of the struggle to be an extrovert occasionally surfaced in the form of panic attacks, which he had suffered during his years of getting newspapers to press on deadline, or the inability to speak in public, a fear he had finally conquered but not easily. He wondered if anyone ever did even as he watched men like Bill Clinton or the other candidates seem to effortlessly spout hundreds of words. And now, on this early spring day, he was on his way to the campaign's Atlanta headquarters, weary but expectant of a victory that would make him the leading Democrat candidate for president of the United States.

Most of his associates were on the road that day, carrying voters to the polls. He decided to take a helicopter ride to the Atlanta hotel, where he and his family would watch the returns come in. He asked Susie to come along with him so she could see Athens and parts of Georgia from the air.

As they flew over Athens, Franklin pointed to the unusual double-barrel cannon in front of City Hall. "It was created during the Civil War and is the only one in existence. The inventor's idea was to have both barrels loaded and fired at the same time toward the enemy linked together by a stretch of chain which would cut down several soldiers at a time. But in practice, the balls always left the cannons a few seconds apart and would fly off in different directions. So the double-barrel cannon was never fired in actual battle and it has sat there near City Hall for 130 years, a major tourist attraction but basically a meaningless one."

"A lot of tourist attractions are," Susie said brightly. "No one is really sure the pilgrims landed on that rock in Plymouth that's designated Plymouth Rock."

"You can get a great view of the stadium over there. It sits in a valley, which is why so many campus buildings can be seen from its seats. The oldest building on campus, Old College, was built in 1803, which would make it practically new at some of the colleges

385

in New England, and then there was a surge of building after the Civil War in that area called the Old Campus. But like most colleges, UGA didn't even have one thousand students until after World War I, when the agricultural school expanded, and women were first admitted. Enrollment went to about three thousand just before World War II started. Then you see all those buildings that make up most of the main campus today. They were all here when I got here as a student in 1947 and they all were WPA projects but built in the classical style, the English building, the mathematics building, the fine arts auditorium, the biology building, and most important to me, the commerce-journalism building, which had large murals on the wall, painted by WPA workers, portraying scenes from the Depression era. I actually never knew what they were until I was out of college."

They flew over Milledge Avenue, where most of the fraternity and sorority houses were located, many of them huge Colonial houses that had outgrown their use for individual family use in the modern age and had been preserved for the Greek groups which needed multiple rooms and baths.

"It's a beautiful campus," Susie agreed, "much better than Dartmouth or even Harvard."

"You're right, but don't tell that to your New England friends. They'll just think you don't appreciate the better things of life."

"There's Lake Lanier," Susie exclaimed a few minutes later, "and Stone Mountain. I must climb it one day. There are bigger mountains in New Hampshire but none of all stone."

The helicopter landed in a field near the Peachtree Plaza Hotel, where the night's watch party was scheduled. They had avoided Atlanta's midmorning traffic jam. There were contacts to make and other work to do at headquarters.

The Peachtree Plaza was about seventeen years old and at twenty-five floors was the tallest building in Atlanta. It was also one of the most striking buildings, all glass walls you could see through from inside but not from the outside. Its glass elevators were also on the outside walls and provided an exciting ride from the bottom floor to top floor, which was topped by a large dome that served as a dining room. "It's not the Ritz Plaza," Franklin observed. "It's better."

Atlanta's hotel boom from 1970 to 1980, along with the expansion of the airport, was what made it the commercial capital of the southeast and the third most popular convention site in the country. The airport was annually the first or second busiest in the United States, alternating with Chicago's O'Hare.

"I had no idea Atlanta was so huge," Susie admitted. "I still thought of Georgia as the state in our schoolbooks, rural with Atlanta still rebuilding from the fire in *Gone with the Wind*."

Franklin chuckled. "It was never that bad. Actually the first skyscraper period was in the 1920s, and after that, not much was built until the boom of the 1960s. The airport and Buford Dam were the catalyst, plus three interstate highways from Eisenhower's highway program of the 1950s, perhaps the largest federal domestic project ever conceived, and the essential next step. He was a Republican, of course, but was greatly influenced by the New Deal, and also the autobahn he saw in Europe which Hilter had built in the 1930s.

"Hitler was one of history's most evil villains, but his ruthlessness got a lot of things done. What's remarkable about Franklin Roosevelt and the New Deal was that they got so much done without the force and control of a dictator. And most important, the New Deal projects and programs are still helping people in 1992, while Hitler's programs led to the ultimate destruction of a historic country. That is the lesson we must keep uppermost in our minds."

"You've done a good job of making that clear in your speeches and columns," Susie assured him.

"I don't know," Franklin mused, "I often wonder if I'm getting through. Then something happens like Jesse Jackson coming to endorse me because of that speech on the crumbs that so much of mankind still has to live on."

"That was so dramatic," Susie exclaimed. "I've heard Jackson speak on TV, but I didn't even know we were in touch with him."

"I hardly did. Bert Lance was the main connection. He was one of Carter's most important friends but got into trouble over some banking regulations after he became Carter's director of the budget in Washington and had to resign. He kept close ties with Jackson and was looking for a candidate in 1992. I knew him slightly and talked with him when I decided to go to New Hampshire. That primary unlocked so many doors for me."

"And now today," Susie said, "a lot more doors should open."

"You're right," Franklin said, "and I must decide how many of them I'm up to going through."

"Oh, don't say that. You should be favored in Florida next week, and if we win there, gosh, who's to stop us?"

Franklin thought the most likely person was himself. He still had many fears to overcome and some health worries.

At the hotel they were surprised to find Charlie Burkhart, who had flown down from New Hampshire to be there for the expected victory party.

"Charlie, I'm so glad you made it," Franklin greeted him. "I told Sutton to try and get in touch with you. I wouldn't be here if it wasn't for you."

"It's my first trip to the South," Charlie said. "Atlanta is fabulous, Sherman did a poor job of burning it."

"He just burned the outdated part," Franklin said. "It was sort of an early version of urban renewal. A lot of industrious Georgians built a new city, helped, I might add, by a lot of so-called carpet-baggers who wanted to get in on a good thing. Susie will have to give you a guided tour. She's learned a lot about it this week."

In a suite reserved on the fifteenth floor, Franklin made calls to some campaign supporters in several counties, asking if there was anything he should do.

"Yes," said several of them. "Get on the radio and tell people to be sure and vote. The lines at the polls are unprecedented for a primary, and they close at 7:00 p.m. Hardy and Ashmore have done a good job of getting likely supporters to the polls, but there are some black areas we've hardly touched."

Franklin called Bert Lance, who was in Atlanta working with Hardy on getting out the vote. He and Lance reviewed the areas that seemed to be lagging, and Lance promised to get some of Jackson's people on the phones, calling and driving buses to pick up possible voters at housing projects.

Early information from the rural areas was encouraging. On the Democratic side, Franklin and Clinton were splitting the votes, while Buchanan and Bush were getting a large number of votes for the Republican side, most of which Franklin figured would have gone to Tsongas otherwise. On the Democratic ballot, Tsongas was barely scratching, but Kerrey was running stronger than expected. The huge Atlanta metro vote always was the last to report.

Totals were coming in from the smaller metro areas, like Savannah, Augusta, Columbus, and Macon. Franklin led in all of them but not by much. Clinton was close behind, and Kerrey got about 10 percent of the Democrat votes. Buchanan was about even with Bush in the Republican totals, which gave Franklin the overall state lead in number of votes with 30 percent of the Democratic total to 25 percent for Clinton.

Franklin's followers in the Peachtree Plaza were cheered by the fact that he was still leading at 9:00 p.m. as the suburban Atlanta votes began trickling in.

Sutton came in with news that there were still long lines at traditionally black voting precincts in DeKalb and Fulton counties. Franklin was particularly pleased with the results from Columbus, where he got 40 percent of the total; and Rockdale, where he got 50 percent; and Athens-Clarke, which usually cast a large Democratic vote, where he got 60 percent. It made him feel good beyond the vote returns. The Atlanta newspapers had actually endorsed Tsongas, contending that his tough-love message of less spending was the only way to reduce the deficit and boost the economy. That hurt Franklin's feelings because he was a faithful reader of the Atlanta dailies, and during his time as president of the Georgia Press Association, he had always taken their side when many of the small newspapers opposed them. Franklin recognized that the Atlanta papers were not only the most influential papers in the state but also contributed the largest amount of dues to the GPA and having a member of their staff on the GPA board gave the organization an invaluable access to Atlanta advertisers and leaders.

Editorials still carried weight with voters, he believed, and politicians welcomed their endorsements and support even if they wouldn't admit it openly and still put all of their money in TV, radio, and mail outs. Franklin, as in New Hampshire and Maine, had spent most of his advertising dollars in Georgia newspapers, in Georgia's 159 counties and numerous cities. It must have worked, he felt, as he watched his lead hold and slightly grow in the state as a whole. When the Atlanta metro counties finally counted nearly all their votes, Franklin had more than 30 percent of the Democratic votes, to 24 percent for Clinton, 15 percent for Tsongas, 15 percent for Kerrey, and 8 percent for Brown, the rest scattered. Bush finally pulled ahead of Buchanan with 62 percent to 38 percent, almost the same margin he won in New Hampshire.

At 9:00 p.m. CBS-TV declared Franklin the winner in Georgia, or more precisely the leader, as Franklin interpreted it, but he knew the headlines and TV reports would declare him the winner because he received the most votes. He hoped the media wouldn't notice that in his home state he only got 30 percent of the Democratic votes and less than that of the total votes. But what the news media liked was a leader, a winner, to make their reports more dramatic. Franklin had always frowned on that interpretation, but he tried to feel jubilant. Kathleen came over to him and said, "Look happier, this is your breakthrough victory. Get ready for all the attention you are about to get."

"You too," Franklin told her. "You went through this with Wallace a time or two, so help me talk to the media. You know what to say."

He was analyzing the vote totals in his own mind. Georgia was a large and diverse state, he realized, and he felt that Jackson's late endorsement had pushed him to the forefront with black voters. On the other hand, Miller had lost support by his strong stand for removing the Confederate battle flag from the Georgia state flag, and that indirectly hurt Clinton, which was ironic since Franklin had advocated removing the battle flag longer than Miller and was probably more passionate about it. He felt it was long past time for the southern states to downgrade their Confederate symbols. South Carolina still flew the battle flag over its state capital, and thousands of cars in the South had battle flags on their bumpers, and in Georgia, the battle flag dominated the state flag. Miller had made an impassioned speech for its removal at that year's General Assembly session but never got the flag to a vote because it was apparent it would lose.

Franklin joined the celebration. In a crowded field of both parties, he had received a plurality of the voters in a pivotal state, giving him the most delegates for the nomination at that time.

He tried to take calls while dealing with many requests, but the demand was too much, so he decided to just talk to reporters from TV, radio, and newspapers who were on the scene in person. He stressed that his home state roots and longtime presence in certain counties had pulled him through, and a glance at the returns confirmed that. He had a clear majority of the voters in Columbus-Muscogee and the adjoining counties and a majority in Clayton County in the Atlanta Metro area, where his newspaper partnership with Jim Wood had undoubtedly helped. Jim was the majority owner of the paper there and had also been elected to two terms in the General Assembly. Wood's political gimmick was a tomato sandwich luncheon every year, with no alcoholic beverages. Wood had also been the Democratic candidate for Congress against Newt Gingrich when Gingrich ran in that district in 1992 after the redistricting, but Wood lost to Gingrich, who was already a five-term congressman.

There were long faces at the Clinton election party. Early on they had considered Georgia their firewall before the major tests on Super Tuesday, which was coming up two weeks later. They couldn't believe they had lost to Franklin, who had never won a real election, lacked charisma in their eyes, not to mention an organization and professional consultants like the team of Carville and Begala. But Carville put his finger on their worst Georgia problem. "It was that damned open mic blast at Jackson," he fumed. "Plus Governor Miller's organization was handicapped by the Jennifer Flowers and draft evasion stories. We're lucky to have finished second again, which means we're still in there. In fact, Kerrey's poor showing may be the most significant result of this primary."

In the meantime, Franklin got through to Jackson on the phone and thanked him again for his endorsement and asked if he would make some commercials for the South Carolina primary, which was coming up in just four days. They agreed to meet Wednesday and talk about that. Spotting Charlie Burkhart in the crowd, Franklin called him over and asked if he would help get some thank-you ads in the Georgia newspapers and some ads in the South Carolina dailies touting the victories in the primaries with a plea to support a Southern candidate on Primary Day.

When he and Sutton had a chance to confer, they agreed that their spending splurge during the last days of the campaign had been a key factor in emerging as the Georgia leader. Franklin had approved buying an entire prime time hour on Atlanta's fourth most watched TV station for the Monday night event at Sanford Stadium, with accompanying short advance commercials urging watchers to tune in and a list of the expected speakers and performers, including Kenny Rogers, Michael Stipe, and Lewis Grizzard, not even knowing that a surprise speaker would be Jesse Jackson. The station extended time to make sure Jackson was on air live and in primetime.

The other stations picked up much of the program in their 11:00 p.m. newscasts and again on election morning. The Atlanta newspapers also bannered the story and had a number of photos and excerpts from the speeches, especially Jackson's. It was a boffo Primary Eve explosion and undoubtedly helped spur the record turnout of voters.

Susie finally got to Franklin and gave him a big hug. "You had more friends in Georgia than you thought," she exclaimed.

"Talk to some of those reporters," Franklin told her. "They'll like you, and I can't get to them all. Tell them about the basketball tournaments."

Franklin took a congratulations call from Clinton, who was gracious, and then got one from Governor Zell Miller, who was also gracious and said if he had known Franklin was serious about running that he would have supported him. "But you've still got a long way to go, and Clinton's organization and money will begin to weigh in next Tuesday."

"I'm still for you and hope you can get the flag changed," Franklin told him. "I know that hurt you and Clinton today."

"You got it," Miller agreed. "But I loved the show at Sanford. You had some of my favorite singers, including Alan Jackson from Newnan, singing 'Here in the Real World,' the big hit this year."

"It's my favorite country song," Franklin said, "even ahead of 'The Gambler.'" Miller was known as a big country music fan.

"Here in the Real World" seemed very appropriate for the week's outcome, Franklin felt, but he still wondered what the real world was in politics for 1992. To most of the country, he was still a virtual unknown although he realized his name would be familiar after this night.

Suddenly he noticed Brad Ashmore's six-feet-eight-inch figure move into view, followed closely by Jack Hardy. "Where have y'all been?" Franklin asked. "You're missing the excitement."

"We've been at polling places where hundreds of voters were still standing in line," Brad answered. "The Miller people were in charge of most of those polls, and they closed them early, figuring most of the late voters were for Franklin."

Franklin smiled tightly. "That's the way the Founding Fathers planned it," he said. "Look at the Constitution. It was designed to limit voting. In the first draft, only white male property owners were eligible to vote. That was modified slightly, but the Founders meant for only the handful of electors in the electoral college to choose the president, not the people at large. They felt only the wealthier, most educated citizens should make that choice, and they had some good reasons. In the early United States, information was scarce, communication was slow and uncertain, and the majority of people couldn't even read. We think democracy is a hit-and-miss situation today, but then it was mainly a miss, and the writers of the Constitution knew it. We think about slaves not being able to vote until the Fourteenth Amendment in 1867, but no women, white and black, could vote for sixty more years until 1921, when the Nineteenth Amendment was passed. So that was 133 years after the Constitution was adopted before women could vote. Democracy has been a slow and tedious process, and it's still imperfect."

"Well, these people wanted to vote, and they were willing to wait in the cold, some for hours because of the slow process, and then the doors were shut in their faces," Ashmore complained loudly.

"But we're ahead," Franklin pointed out, "and I think a big reason is because you and Hardy and the rest of your crew got a lot of late voters to the polls. You should feel good about it."

Brad put his arms around Franklin, "How about you, Boss?" he asked. "How does it feel to be in the lead for the Democratic presidential nomination?"

"I'm appreciative…and apprehensive. Look at the county-by-county totals. Clayton County and Rockdale and Henry, where you worked so much, gave us a clear majority, and in the end that made the difference."

"You didn't do too badly in Athens," Hardy chimed in.

"There are a lot of educated people there," Franklin chuckled, "but what's interesting is that I got a plurality in so many two-unit counties, as we used to call them, and which I wrote against so long as being unfair. We might have won a majority just based on the two-unit county vote. Go join the party, you've earned a good time."

Kathleen came up at that time with several reporters. "They've been asking me about my days working for George C. Wallace," she said brightly, "and how you compared to him."

"I hope you told them I'm no George Wallace, in any way, including as a political candidate," Franklin said with a grimace.

"I did, there couldn't be two more different men. Wallace was a pure—or sometimes an impure—politician. You are still basically a newspaper publisher, reserved and concerned. Wallace was magnetic, of course, the best politician I've ever known. He had a rough kind of charisma, pugnacious rather than charming, but he was someone you didn't forget."

"You're right," Franklin agreed. "He was relentless. I didn't even know him well, but he'd often call me at home to ask about some issue or tell me some idea he was pursuing and we'd talk for thirty minutes."

The reporters were inquisitive about Kathleen's role with Wallace. "I got my first job out of college as a reporter on Mr.

Franklin's newspaper in Opelika," she explained, "and he sent me to interview Wallace and his family and take photos of them on their first Christmas after his wife Lurleen died. Mr. Franklin ran a big front page layout on it in the paper, and Wallace liked it a lot. I did some other articles on him when he ran for governor in 1970, and after he was elected, he asked me to be the assistant state director of tourism and publicity."

"And he married again during that time," one of the reporters mentioned.

"Yes, to Big Jim Folsom's niece, who had been a performer in the Cypress Garden Water Ski Show in Florida. She made a wonderful first lady for Alabama."

"And you kept working with Wallace?"

"Well, I kept working for the state and would write speeches and publicity for him as governor. It was a great job. I got to go to tourism shows all over the country promoting Alabama, and when he began running for president, I was a speechwriter and advance person for the campaign. It was a good experience for helping Mr. Franklin."

"What did you think of Wallace as a person?" one reporter asked.

"He was always nice and respectful to me," Kathleen replied, "and the people around him were fiercely loyal. But as I said, he was pugnacious. He was only about five feet, seven inches tall and was a lightweight boxing champion in his college days, and he always gave the impression of being a former boxer in his manner and personality, and it helped him. He was obviously driven in his political ambitions, and I guess he'd be described as a racist today, but he didn't dislike black people. He always treated them with respect, and I never saw him mistreat one. He just didn't think racial integration would work for the good of either whites or blacks, and he didn't think they would ever be socially compatible on a broad scale, and if you look around, you'll see he was right. Where blacks have succeeded is when they have moved into the middle class and gotten good jobs and basically become like middle-class whites, but there still isn't near enough of that, in Georgia, Alabama, or California."

"Kathleen, we appreciate your time," one reporter said. "You're quite a philosopher as well as a political adviser. Do you think Mr. Franklin has a chance to be the Democratic candidate?"

Kathleen paused a long time. "You want an honest opinion?" she asked. "I'm for him because he's the most considerate man I've ever known, especially as a boss, but that's also his handicap. He may be too nice, and he hates to tell people what to do. He wants to just ask them, and I've seldom seen him lose his temper with anyone. Plus it is agonizing for him to fire somebody unless he has a clear and obvious reason. Wallace, for example, was much harder and a dynamic leader. I was still working with him the day he was shot in May 1972. He recovered, but he was never the same again."

Franklin was being asked to make a victory statement. To a round of cheers, he took the microphone and thanked all the supporters in the crowd and in the campaign. He particularly thanked the publishers and editors of the small papers in Georgia who had supported him.

He paid special attention to the Columbus supporters whom Milton Jones had organized and brought to New Hampshire, and he also mentioned former governors Joe Frank Harris, Jimmy Carter, and Carl Sanders as mentors and supporters and again said he planned to vote for Zell Miller for reelection in 1994.

"And, of course," he concluded, "a special thanks to the Reverend Jesse Jackson, whose endorsement meant so much to me, and who I feel has many years of valuable service to give to the country."

He mentioned all his opponents by name and noted that each of them had won support in his home state, which was a tribute to their perseverance and their contribution to making democracy work.

"You can't have a democracy without candidates willing to make the sacrifices that give the voters a valid choice. In Georgia today, in both party primaries, the voters were given a variety of good choices, a sign of vitality in our system, and don't forget it. It's the best system devised for electing governments, and those who constantly criticize it and complain are eroding the foundation for a free and democratic nation. We must never destroy the imperfect society we have in pursuit of the perfect society no nation has yet come up with. Freedom, as I've often said, is the narrow path between the desert of tyranny on one side and the chaos of anarchy on the other. And few nations have been able to tread that narrow path. It has been difficult for the United States, and today we have the chance to lead many nations down that path who have never followed it for long. Let's make that the goal for 1992 onward into the twenty-first century."

It had also been Primary Day in other states although Georgia had the spotlight. Paul Tsongas quietly picked up the electors in three states, Maryland, Utah, and Washington; Jerry Brown had edged out Clinton in Colorado even though Clinton had the support of the governor as he had in Georgia; Kerrey won in North Dakota the week before. Harkin was shut out and was on the brink of ending his candidacy.

Early the next morning, Franklin got in touch with Jesse Jackson. They arranged to rendezvous at a small café in North Georgia on the South Carolina border, where they hoped they could avoid the media. It worked. Hardy drove Franklin there, and Jackson arrived with only two aides. "Thanks to your help, I obviously have momentum for the South Carolina primary on Saturday," Franklin told him. "I've made arrangements to put some ads in the daily papers, too late for the weeklies, and gotten time for commercials and one speech on TV channels in Columbia, Charleston, and Greenville. But I want your advice on what to say and do, I hardly have any other contacts or organization in the state."

"Well, give that speech about the crumbs from the sandwiches left on the floor for the poor and run it on TV if you can. It touches a lot of voters in South Carolina, especially black voters who will make up half the votes in the Democratic primary. My backers can assure that many, if I get the word out, but I need to know more about your ideas for the presidency."

"The first proposal I made in New Hampshire, and which I pushed in Georgia, was to reduce the payroll tax by transferring most of it from the lowest paychecks to the highest. That tax is 7 percent on the first dollar a worker earns and zero on every dollar a person makes over $60,000 a year, shifting that tax to all earned income instead of the first $60,000 will be the largest transfer of the tax burden from low income to higher incomes in the nation's history. And it should be easier to get through Congress than other tax changes. Next will be attempts to restore the tax brackets to what they were before Reagan changed them to favor the highest earners.

"I've emphasized the unfairness of Reagonomics and the need for tax revision that will leave consumers with money they need for discretionary spending and give the economy the lift it needs to create more jobs. That will be very important here in South Carolina, where a lot of jobs have located in auto plants to make up for all the jobs lost in textiles and agriculture.

"Also we must make sure food stamp programs are maintained at their current levels and not cut as the Republicans want to do. Those programs not only help poor families get enough to eat, they help farmers, large and small grocery stores, and the economy in general. Yet they are under attack as wasteful welfare, a term that needs to be redefined and appreciated for the good it does for millions of families, not condemned as a dole, which it isn't. Most funds for Aid to Dependent Children and food stamps, which are the programs usually labeled as welfare, go immediately back into the overall economy as well as giving recipients a better life. That message still hasn't gotten out enough. South Carolina is probably a state that benefits the most from those programs, but a lot of whites, and some black, voters still resent welfare, and you know why. Republicans have associated it mainly with the black population when actually whites benefit the most."

Jackson sat there nodding. "All that's been said before," he noted. "And we still get the crumbs. That was what I got in 1984 and 1988 after winning a lot of Democratic Primary vote. I think I got the most votes in 1988."

"That's mainly what I wanted to talk to you about this morning," Franklin said. "Next to the economy, my main goal is to use this special moment in history when the US is in such a powerful position to assure peace, for the smaller nations that keep wasting their scarce resources on killing each other in pointless wars. So my idea is to create a new cabinet position answerable only to the president to be known as the Secretary of Peace. We have secretaries of Defense, Army, Navy, Air Forces and once had a Secretary of War. A designated Secretary of Peace will send a signal to our military officers and other leaders that peace is a truly important priority on the national agenda, not just a pretty word to be cast aside at the first affront to someone's pride.

"For this position, the nation will need someone who has symbolized and worked with other national leaders for peaceful solutions throughout his career and who knows the leaders of countries that are considered both our friends and sometimes our enemies, who can sit down and talk with them as someone they trust and believe in."

Franklin paused a minute for emphasis and to catch his breath. "The perfect person for that job, I feel, is you, Jesse Jackson. You know Saddam Hussein. You know Fidel Castro. You know many of the African and Asian leaders who are at war or threatening to be. You are almost the indispensable person to be the first Secretary of Peace. And the results I believe could be historic for millions of people."

Jackson smiled and sat back in his chair. "You're laying it on mighty thick, but I appreciate it," he said. "I think the idea is a great one, and I have talked to a lot of those leaders, and some of them are inclined toward cooperating with us than fighting with us. We destroyed Iraq, and where did it get us? We've starved Cuba for thirty years, and the people there hate us for it. They don't blame Castro, and they are getting desperate." Jackson looked solemn for a minute, then asked, "But our political leaders say no candidates can carry Florida if he suggests reconciliation with Castro."

"I'm going to argue with that idea before the Florida primary next week," Franklin said, "in strong and definite terms. Thirty years is long enough for us to keep two such natural allies from coming together economically, culturally, and in baseball, I might add. From an economic standpoint, it would give Florida an enormous boost. What if Georgia and Florida were not in the same nation, as Florida and Cuba aren't."

Jackson stood up. "You're right. I like your ideas, and the time is short to get some action going on that primary Saturday.

I'll do the commercials this afternoon in Columbia if you make the arrangements."

Franklin grabbed his hand and shook it vigorously. "My staff isn't very large as you know. But a fellow named Phil Sutton will be calling you within the hour, and you can think about what you'd like to say, which I'm sure will be better than anything we could write for you."

"You know," Jesse said slowly, "you just might be the candidate we've been waiting for."

Franklin felt that tightening in his chest, and his heart picked up several beats. He recalled the line from Shakespeare which seemed to fit the situation: "The world is out of joint, O cursed spite, that 'ere I was born to set it right."

"Could you help get up a crowd for an event Friday night?" Franklin asked him. "We'll have you speak and then I'll make a speech, mainly about creating jobs?"

"Okay, in Greenville, I know just the place. It'll be a crowd that should be voting in the Democratic Primary."

As Franklin and Hardy drove back to the office in Atlanta, Hardy still wanted to know more about the Great Depression years. "So much interesting happened in those years you never hear about. You make it sound like the folks during the Depression, with the help of the New Deal, saved the country and had a lot of fun doing it."

"I wouldn't say a lot of fun, but fun was cheaper in those days and not as demanding. One person who helped the country get through it was a curly haired little girl named Shirley Temple, who between 1935 and 1940 was the top box office draw at the movies. I've mentioned how movies, or the picture show, as we called it, was so important during the Depression. For children, they were usually just a dime and a nickel for a bag of popcorn, and in the late 1930s, many theaters were the only air-conditioned buildings in town, which in the South during the summer was almost worth the price of admission even without the movie. Shirley Temple movies were incredibly popular, but by the time she was a teenager, she was washed up. In later years she became a Republican, and Nixon and

Ford named her their chief greeter at White House events. In fact, I got to meet her when Jean and I went to the White House state dinner for President William Tolbert of Liberia during Ford's term as president. It was the only White House dinner I ever attended, and it was great. My wife sat by David Gergen, who was a Ford consultant, and I sat by Pete Rozelle, who was commissioner of the National Football League. Shirley was just about my age, so she was in her midfifties by then but had matured into a beautiful woman, although she never made a movie to my knowledge after her teen years. Her last movie was with Ronald Reagan, of all people."

Hardy looked at him quizzically. "We're a long way from Wolfeboro, aren't we? Makes me feel a little like the first Carter campaign, but it's so different. Not nearly as many people, not nearly as much stress, but that feeling of expectancy is definitely rising in the staff we have. We just need more."

"I know," Franklin admitted, "and we've spent a ton of money in the last week. I hope some is coming in after that lead in Georgia because I'm committing a lot this weekend in South Carolina. Then, next week is Florida...I don't know if we'll have enough to compete. It's a big state and very expensive. No one TV station covers a large part of it, and there are dozens of newspapers."

"But you're in the lead now, with two big primary victories, plus a third one likely Saturday."

"Yeah, but Florida's the big ball game, and we hardly have a campaign staff there."

They arrived back at the Atlanta headquarters and found Sutton fretting about the same thing: nothing going in Florida. He was making the arrangements for the short campaign in South Carolina, however. "Let's send Kathleen down there and at least get a presence in the big cities. How's the money holding out?" Franklin asked.

Sutton looked glum. "It's coming in, but your original investment is about gone. That last week in Georgia cost a lot, but it was worth it. Most campaigns would give their left ball to be in your position."

"Get those commercials with Jackson on the air in South Carolina, and I'm going to air a speech to white voters Friday night.

My guess is that most whites will be voting in the Republican primary, which will be good for us."

Kathleen happened by, and Franklin asked her into his office to chat. "You know Florida," he said, "so we'll get you some resources to go down there and set up offices at least in Tallahassee, Jacksonville, Orlando, Fort Lauderdale, Tampa, St. Petersburg, and Sarasota."

"Sounds like fun," she said. "I've always loved Florida during spring holidays."

"I may let Hardy go with you. The two of you are working together well right now, aren't you?"

"I'd say so," Kathleen answered with a smirk, "but probably short term. By the way, I have a copy of a really, really tough ad from one of the campaigns I worked on in Alabama with Bill Baxley. It makes this campaign look like a lovefest."

She pushed the sheet of paper toward him. Some of the words in it were not unfamiliar to him. He had been a Fob James supporter against Attorney General Bill Baxley for governor of Alabama in 1978, but he'd always thought Baxley was the best politician in the state outside Wallace, and he also liked Baxley's liberal tendencies in a state where they were dangerous politically. But James was from his hometown of Opelika, and they shared many friends. He didn't think the James campaign had used the ad she showed him against Baxley, but some of the points had been used. The ad read as follows:

Did you know Bill Baxley has

1. been arrested for public drunkenness and indecent exposure;
2. named his son after a Mafia leader;
3. transported his mistress in a state car;
4. gambled extensively in Las Vegas;
5. been drunk while presiding over the Senate;
6. had the Lieutenant Governor's Office pay for his mistress's hotel rooms;
7. promised to raise your taxes;

8. said he wants Alabama to be the most liberal state in the South; and
9. had venereal disease several times.

Is this the type of man you want to be governor? Pd. Political advertisement by Conservatives and Christians against tax increases.

—Dothan, Alabama

"That's tough," Franklin agreed. "Alabama campaigns were always tough. I suppose this ad was for the campaign when Baxley ran for governor after being elected lieutenant governor in 1986."

"I think so," said Kathleen. "I dated Bill when we were both in Montgomery during the Wallace term in the early 1970s and Bill was the attorney general. He was only thirty, you know, younger even than Bill Clinton when he was elected Arkansas attorney general. Baxley knew I'd been Wallace's girlfriend briefly, and he was actually trying to settle down. Bill wasn't really a big drinker, but he just couldn't take but a few drinks without passing out. I was gone when he ran for governor the second time, but the fact is most of those points are true. The one falsehood, I'd say, is that he had venereal diseases. I certainly never heard that. He was a gambler, however, and he wanted to make Alabama more liberal and raise taxes, and he was arrested for drunkenness and indecent exposure when he was a student at the University of Alabama. You may recall we published that in the Opelika paper. and you still endorsed him for attorney general."

"And he was a good one," Franklin added, "taking on cases that had been pending for years and needed to be resolved. He prosecuted the men accused of bombing the Birmingham Church, where three children were killed."

Kathleen winced. "I recognized all the good points about Bill," she said. "Doesn't he remind you of one of your opponents?"

"At least one and some former presidents," Franklin admitted. "Although Baxley's list of sins is more colorful. I noticed his worst sin to the group that ran this ad was that he wanted to raise their taxes."

Alabama had the lowest state tax structure of the fifty states, mainly because its property taxes were so low. Even Wallace couldn't get them raised at the peak of his national popularity.

"What's funny," Kathleen remarked, "is I think Baxley got reelected."

"So has Clinton, six times as governor. There's a lot of forgiveness for sins in the Southern culture…but not for raising taxes."

Hardy came in at that time and Franklin discussed the foray into Florida with him. "By the way, who were those two men who followed us to the café this morning? I saw you talking to them after breakfast."

Hardy laughed. "You're in the big-time now," he said. "They were secret service agents who've been assigned to watch you because you're the leading Democratic candidate. They'll be around from now on."

"We led them on a merry chase this morning," Franklin noted. "They must have thought I was trying to shake them."

"Well, they weren't amused," Hardy said. "They asked me to provide an itinerary for each day from now on, which will mean more planning than you've ever done. But at least I'll know where we're going."

Franklin frowned. He preferred the flexibility, and that had served him well. He glanced at the map of Florida on the wall. He first visited Florida when he was eleven, and his uncle and aunt took him to Daytona Beach on a summer vacation, the first time he'd been out of Georgia or had ever seen the ocean. He'd gone back many summers since and knew how big and complex Florida was.

"I'll have a plan for next week," he promised. His priority was to get a speech ready for the Friday night meeting Jackson was arranging at the largest black church in Greenville. He talked to Hardy about going on to Florida with Kathleen and then asked Susie and Brad to accompany him to the South Carolina event.

Jackson was as good as his word. The church was overflowing by 7:00 p.m., and there were media people from three TV stations and all the major South Carolina newspapers. It was Franklin's one chance to make a meaningful impression before the Saturday voting.

He looked out into the sea of virtually all black faces. Most of them had come straight from work, and they were dressed in various attire, from fancy suits and ties to their work clothes.

He greeted them and then asked them to join him in a little experiment. "Tomorrow is a crucial day in this election year," he said. "So I want you all to bow your heads and close your eyes. Then will everyone who still lives in a house without indoor toilet facilities please raise your hand. No one will see you but me, so don't be embarrassed. It's important for me to know."

The crowd followed his request for the most part. A few hands were raised, but not all that many.

"Thank you," Franklin said. "My first promise to every citizen of the United States if I should become president is to see that everyone has a house with indoor plumbing. It is unseemly that in 1992, in a city like Greenville, South Carolina, that there are still people living in what might be described as third world conditions. The United States is the richest nation in history. Indoor plumbing has been known for years. It is a protection against disease and discomfort and the best way to assure sanitary living conditions for people, and there are ways to provide it for every citizen. And then the US must take the lead in assuring sanitary conditions for the nearly 50 percent of the world's population, who still don't have indoor toilets, running water, stoves for cooking, tubs to bathe in, washing machines and dryers to keep their clothes clean.

"These are the basics of civilized life in 1992, and there are millions of people in the world without any of them, and sadly there are some families and homes right here in Greenville that do not have them. Yet when other nations ask the US for assistance, we usually send them guns and bombs and planes and weapons instead of commodes and washing machines. I made this speech at Harvard University a few weeks ago, and the campus newspaper headlined its report: 'Send Commodes, Not Bombs.' To our states, Washington must also use that philosophy and tell states to use federal money to end more of their third world living conditions before they build more football or baseball stadiums."

The crowd applauded wildly with shouts of praise. Franklin had managed to achieve the cadence black speakers could do so well. He wasn't as good at it, but he tried.

"To reach the goals of better living conditions for all Americans, we must dig up so-called Reaganomics and supply-side economics by the deepest roots. It is a formula for empowering the wealthy and diminishing the middle class and further impoverishing the poorer. It is not a secret. It is as simple as 2 plus 2 equals 4. There is more money in our country today than ever in its history, but too much of it has gone into too few pockets, and the trickle-down theory has not worked. It has never worked. Those who have benefited so well have used the money to buy each other's stock and buy out their competitors, reducing competition and raising prices for consumer goods or, even worse, moving their operations to other countries where the wage scales are much lower, sometimes as low as a few dollars a day. A bill now before Congress, known as NAFTA, will speed up that process as more companies move to Mexico, while the lower prices of food from the US will force many Mexican farms out of business and send their laborers clamoring to the borders of the US as illegal immigrants.

"We must restore demand-side economics in this nation so that the consumers will have enough income to pay for US-made products and improve both their lives and the overall economy. That was the strategy that built this country, and don't let anyone tell you different The real job creators are the masses of people who use their income to buy the products workers like those in South Carolina make.

"Ronald Reagan said many ridiculous things, but the most ridiculous was 'Government is not the solution, government is the problem'. The next most ridiculous was 'We launched a war on poverty, and poverty won.' Don't believe that. Government has been the answer ever since George Washington needed more food for his troops that won the Revolutionary War; since Thomas Jefferson needed the money to make the Louisiana Purchase and double the land area of the young United States; since Abraham Lincoln needed the money and the troops to put down rebellion by states that wanted to keep human slavery; by Franklin Roosevelt when he needed support to lift the nation out of its worst depression and build the foundation for the modern nation that stands today.

"Give me your votes tomorrow and I promise to start working toward those goals. True, I don't have the political experience some of the other candidates have, which means that I don't know these things can't be done. I haven't been governor of a state for ten years that is still one of the poorest states in the nation. I daresay Arkansas has more families without indoor toilets than South Carolina. I haven't heard Bill Clinton talk about improving that situation. Paul Tsongas admits he's not Santa Claus, what he is, is a Republican with a sack of coal.

"I've lived next door to South Carolina all my life. I know its history, and frankly, some of it is not pretty. But white or black, all South Carolinians like to eat. As I said in a talk last week, South Carolina and other Southern states have been left with half a loaf for both races to survive on for too many years, and it is only the crumbs that are left for the poorest among us, which too often are the black citizens. My first proposal to Congress will be to cut payroll taxes so that all workers will immediately see more money in their paycheck. That can be done, and the difference can be made up by the thousands of earners who now pay next to zero in payroll taxes. Did you know that? Did you know that if you make more than $60,000 a year, you don't pay any payroll tax over that amount while the minimum wage worker pays 7 percent on his first dollar? Is that fair? No. Is it class warfare? Yes, and the richer class has won. It's common sense for all Americans to share the tax burden of the payroll tax which supports Social Security funds that keep many elderly citizens from becoming destitute and a burden on society and on themselves.

"Let's not be content with the crumbs in South Carolina anymore," Franklin called out, "and let's start tomorrow by sending a message to the nation just as the people of New Hampshire and Georgia have done that demand-side economics is the answer, not supply-side."

Jesse Jackson came to the podium as Franklin concluded and raised his arm. "This is the man I endorsed in Georgia," he said. "Did I make the right decision?"

The crowd responded with shouts and applause. "Well, let's get everybody out to vote tomorrow," Jackson implored.

Franklin went through the crowd, shaking hands and getting some information on people who would need transportation. He left most of that to Brad, who was with him, and Susie, who was doing her usual job of making people smile.

She came over to Franklin and gave him a big hug. "You were great again tonight. More passionate than I've ever heard you. By the time you get to be president, you'll have it down pat."

Franklin smiled indulgently. "It's still a long way," he said.

"I've talked to more black folks tonight than ever in my life," Susie said. "They were all so nice and polite, and I even got where I could understand most of them," she added in her Yankee accent.

Voting in South Carolina began nearly the next morning. Brad had called in and said the ground game was going well, but they didn't have enough volunteers. Also he missed Hardy who was in Florida with Kathleen.

Chapter Twenty-Two

ANOTHER FACELESS MAN

The Presidency is not merely an administrative office. It is preeminently a place of moral leadership. All our great Presidents were leaders of thought at times when certain historic ideas in the life of the nation had to be clarified.

Franklin D. Roosevelt, the New York Times *Magazine, September 11, 1932.*

F ranklin spent the day making calls to Florida and talking to Sutton about engagements there the next few days. The primary, along with several other Southern primaries, plus Texas on Tuesday, March 10, was just days away.

The South Carolina vote was heavy. Franklin easily won the Democratic plurality at 40 percent with Clinton getting 30 percent and the rest scattered. Bush, in the Republican primary, got the most votes overall, which didn't surprise anybody.

For the Clinton brain trust, South Carolina was a jolt, if not a surprise. But the main effect was to make them increase their efforts in Florida, Texas, and the other Super Tuesday states. Also, in Illinois and Michigan, which were to follow a week later. In those states, Franklin was not even in the ring.

Hillary Clinton, according to later accounts, was the main person keeping that campaign's spirits up. She felt the consultants were out of touch, and she could see the appeal of Franklin to the Southern audiences. He was Southern, and his message was about the South's real problem, which was economic. "He's telling blacks they aren't discriminated against just because of their color but also because so many of them are poor," she told the Clinton consultants.

Kerrey seemed energized by his third-place finish in Georgia. Tsongas was on the ropes but making a big effort in Florida, where Clinton was charging Tsongas wanted to cut Social Security benefits, a sensitive issue in the state's heavy retirement areas.

Clinton was still being dogged by personal questions however. He lost his patience with one persistent reporter in Florida and told her that a publication had gone so far as to run through a list of his personal phone calls and called every name asking why he had called. "How would you like that?" he asked the reporter.

"Well," she answered, "I'm not running for president."

The good news for Clinton was that polls showed him ahead in Florida, Texas, Tennessee, and Mississippi.

Franklin still led in the overall delegate count after South Carolina, but he saw little light on Super Tuesday. Clinton had money and organization and a friendly message.

Franklin decided to concentrate on Florida and bear down on his proposal for normalizing relations with Cuba. That's been called the third rail of politics in Florida, but Franklin wasn't so sure. It had once been an emotional issue with the immigrants from Cuba in South Florida who were getting older, and polls indicated their children and grandchildren didn't feel as strongly about the matter. After thirty years, Franklin thought most Americans, including most Floridians, were ready to try something new, especially Democratic voters, and he needed a blockbuster issue that would get attention in a short campaign.

He and Brad and Susie flew to Orlando to meet Hardy and Kathleen and any other supporters they had picked up in the past few days. Hardy had rented a nice suite of offices there, and they had set up phones and made contact with the Florida Press Association and radio stations, especially in North Florida, which bordered Georgia and Alabama.

"I've got a message that should be popular in a lot of Florida," Franklin told Susie. "Social Security and interstate highways are the two programs that built the Florida economy, not to mention the space program, all federal-funded projects. Florida was largely a swamp where few people lived until about 120 years ago. The many retirees who live mainly on Social Security are especially good prospects. He felt deeply and rightly so, and they were likely voters in the Democratic primary. The Cuban die-hards were mostly Republicans, anyway, he'd guess.

Florida was indeed a miracle of growth. The 1870 census found only 180,000 people living there, although it likely did not count Indians. Ironically Florida was one of the earliest areas settled by Europeans. The Spanish established a colony there in 1565, at St. Augustine, which claims to be the oldest city in the United States and also boasts of what is called the fountain of youth for which its founder, Ponce de Leon, was looking when he established the small colony there, more than sixty years before the pilgrims settled in Massachusetts.

The Spanish, French, and English controlled the area Americans know as Florida until 1819, when England ceded it to the United States, which then obtained the rest of the area north and west of the Florida isthmus.

Henry Flagler, a partner of John Rockefeller, had become a hotel and railroad millionaire and became fascinated with Florida's potential in the 1880s. Flagler built the first railroad from the north through the heart of the United States to northern Florida. It eventually went all the way to Key West, bringing an inpouring of tourists to Florida's warmer climate and beaches. It was already one of the fastest-growing states in the early 1950s, when the government established Cape Canaveral, its first space launch site, and sent the first American into space from Canaveral in 1961.

Shortly after that, Walt Disney chose a site near Orlando for his largest theme park, Disney World, and by 1990, Florida's population had reached nearly twenty million, making it the fourth most populous state. The highest geographic point in Florida is only 345 feet, one of the lowest in the United States, but it does have the nation's largest swamp, the Everglades, which cover nearly 20 percent of its inland area.

"The real problem for a campaign like ours," Franklin was telling Ashmore and Susie, "is that Florida's primary is March 10, leaving only one weekend after the South Carolina primary."

"But we're really on a roll," Brad commented, "where are we going after Florida?"

"Let's carry Florida, and that should tell us."

In Orlando, Franklin found few happy campers at the campaign headquarters. Sutton gave him the harsh facts. Money was finally coming in from his victories in Georgia and South Carolina, but there had been no big bundle. Most large donors still couldn't believe in his chances despite his primary victories.

Sutton had staffed enough offices in Florida for the semblance of a ground game and had managed to arrange for public appearances in Orlando on Sunday night and another in Miami on Monday afternoon.

"That gives us a chance," Franklin said. "Plus we have radio and newspaper ads in a lot of places around Jacksonville, Tallahassee, and Pensacola where a lot of the people are transplanted Georgians and Alabamans who may have at least heard of me."

For Orlando, Franklin had prepared an exclusive speech about his background as a science fiction writer. His only published fiction story, in fact, was a science-fiction short story in Planet Stories, and he'd had many letters published in science-fiction magazines of the early postwar era.

At the Orlando event, he appeared with Brad and Susie, both impressive personages, and delivered a strong argument for continuing and expanding the federal space program, which provided hundreds of jobs in central Florida.

"My favorite comic heroes as a child were Buck Rogers and Flash Gordon," he opened his talk, "and then as a teenager, I became an ardent science-fiction fan. SF fans were a small but passionate group in my teenage years, writing letters, stories, and even publishing their own fanzines, as they were called. Isaac Asimov, the most famous science-fiction writer, wrote of SF fans, 'There was once a magic world that no one knew but us.' He was talking about the magic world of the future, which reached from Earth to the furthest parts of the universe. We always believed men would walk on the moon and perhaps on the stars.

"Then, along came Cape Canaveral, not to mention the Russians, and showed the way to the future we had dreamed about. Unfortunately, the moon was barren and airless and unlivable as we suspected, but the scientific advances developed by the space programs have helped pave the way to the Computer Age and its miracles and right here in central Florida is where Americans gathered to develop the means to rocket men into space, to look back at the earth as a beautiful ball in the far distance and to recognize the unlimited possibilities humanity has. And those limits are just beginning to be explored. The space program was the federal government's greatest development of the 1960s, as the interstate highways were in the 1950s, and World War II was in the 1940s, and as the early New Deal programs were for the 1930s.

"Now we are moving to the computer age and can only guess what programs will fuel its economy and energies, but one thing is sure, it will be conceived and financed by the combined determination and resources of the United States, as one nation, willing to put its money and efforts into its hope and promises and not be afraid of such paper tigers as the national debt. That sort of fear would have killed the space program in its infancy. It would have made Thomas Jefferson afraid to make the Louisiana Purchase. It would have tempted Abraham Lincoln to tell the seceding states 'Go your way, and see how well you fare without the great United States government to build your dams, your railroads and to protect all of your rights.'"

The crowd in Orlando was responding well, and Franklin was pleased to see many TV cameras and eager reporters who needed a new angle for their next article.

"Imagine what Florida was and would be if it had not remained part of the United States and of the tourists its connection to the other states provide. Its land was mainly suitable for raising fruit, but not the kind of products people then considered crucial to their food supply or manufacturing needs. It was remote and accessible to other states mainly by water. Now Florida is one of the most prosperous states, one of the most visited, one of the most desirable for retirees, one of the most pleasant in which to live for any age. I mention all this to emphasize again how important a strong central government is for all states, even the one most different and distant from the others, such as Florida is.

"So ask the other candidates what their plans are for the space program or if they even have any plans for it. I pledge to you I do, both for Florida's sake and most important for the future's sake."

"Good job, Boss," Brad told him as they made their way through the crowd.

Back in Orlando, Sutton had good news. Their best access to the polling being done in Florida showed Franklin was in the ball game, competing strongly with Clinton. Tsongas was not doing well, despite significant effort in money and organization. Clinton had again accused Tsongas of wanting to cut Medicare and reducing taxes for millionaires and corporations as Reagan had done. That was similar to the charges Franklin had been making against Tsongas, but Clinton increased the tempo and put his own stamp on one particular criticism. "Tsongas says the nation can no longer sacrifice fairness to growth. It won't work, it's not America," Clinton claimed hoarsely.

Some reports quoted Clinton as saying "It isn't American," a crucial difference, at least to Tsongas. When he arrived in Florida, Tsongas immediately attacked Clinton for the use of the term "not American," charging it was a code way of saying that Tsongas was different because he was ethnic. "Let me say to Bill Clinton, there are a lot of people in this country that came from ethnic stock, and we are Americans."

He then added he would be referring to Clinton as Panda Bear from now on, and he held up a big fuzzy bear doll he had picked up on the way. "He'll say or do anything to get votes."

Franklin was surprised but gratified that his two opponents had become so contentious with each other. Looking at the polls Sutton compiled, he noticed Kerrey moving up and Brown hanging in, but he and Clinton were the clear leaders with Tsongas losing altitude.

And that was without much of an organization or any campaigning in the state.

Susie was telling Sutton that Franklin's Orlando speech would dominate the Monday news cycle, and they needed to get segments of the speech on radio commercials if possible. Sutton was worried about the speech he knew Franklin was planning to make in Miami the next day. He had read parts of it, and like most political consultants, he felt an outright call for a better relationship with Castro's Cuba would alienate too many Cubans in the Miami area. He shared his concern with Franklin, who told him that it would be an important economic step for Florida as well as the right way for the United States to demonstrate a path for better relations by all nations. Word had gotten out about the speech, and a large crowd was expected at the midtown venue.

Susie and Brad accompanied Franklin to the speech, and indeed, there was a large crowd, one of the largest Franklin had drawn. He was pleased since the primary was on Tuesday, he had only a few more engagements scheduled that evening and on Primary Day. He also noticed an unusual number of TV camera crews on hand.

He was introduced by a Florida congressman he had met a few days earlier who heard him speak in Orlando and liked his progressive views. "The part about the New Deal and the Space Program will be very popular in this area. There is also a lot of opposition to the NAFTA treaty. Among the Cuban population, there is still deep resentment against Castro, but the younger Cubans would like to see a settlement. No politician has been willing or brave enough to say it—until you."

Franklin opened his speech with his reminiscence of vacations in Florida, especially one to Miami just after the Eden Roc and Fontainebleau Hotels had opened with Count Basie as the entertainment at the Fontainebleau. He also recalled his experiences as an editor covering the 1968 Republican convention, which nominated Richard Nixon for president and was basically held on an island off Miami to discourage demonstrators.

"What a wonderful opportunity beckons the US in this year of 1992," he exclaimed. "The US is not only the strongest nation in history, economically and militarily, it is now reaching for the stars, and a rocket was launched from Cape Kennedy that carried another man to the moon. Surely there has never been such an opportune time to look for solutions to past problems rather than let old grievances blind us to the role of peacemaker for all nations. It will not be an easy role, but the opportunity comes so seldom that we dare not turn away from it. Already we are seeing the divisions and dangers as the Soviet Union dissolves with a variety of hands gaining access to nuclear buttons. The Cold War is not only over, but we must put its divisions behind us and seek an alliance with the emerging non-Communist Russia that will keep peace there and protect the world in general from its still deadly nuclear arsenal despite its current weakness in most other respects.

"And the US must set an example for smaller nations by demonstrating our own willingness to heal old wounds and accept new directions. One of the most grievous and long-lasting is the US division from Cuba, a nation so close to us that it could well have been the forty-ninth state rather than an adversary which harms both Cuba and the United States."

Franklin paused as there was a mixed reaction from the crowd. No candidate for president had talked to them that way since the Cuban revolution in 1959. Reviewing some Cuban history, Franklin pointed out that Cuba was Christopher Columbus's first landing site in what became North America, and Columbus claimed it for Spain. It became Spain's richest colony in the New World but was in constant attack from raiders such as the Dutch, the French, and the British, all of whom coveted the island for their own growing American empires.

"Spain finally gained full control in 1763, nearly 280 years after Columbus arrived, but Spain did not treat its colonists well, and in addition, Cuba was one of the few places in North America where slavery was still legal. The other slave areas at that time were the southern states of the US. In fact, the states that seceded in 1861 had long eyed Cuba as a possible new slave state for the US. It was a rich agricultural state, with sugar cane being the largest crop and tobacco its second most important crop.

"Cuba's slaves revolted against Spanish rule regularly through the years and in 1868, after the end of the Civil War in the US and the freeing of its slaves, a ten-year revolt was launched that resulted in the abolishing of slavery in Cuba and a promise of improved conditions by the Spanish.

"As most of you know, the US declared war on Spain in 1898 and gained control of Cuba, which it then granted independence. But Cuba could not sustain a democratic government for long, going through a series of dictators, but remaining an ally of the US, including during World War II, when several US naval bases were established, notably Guantanamo Bay. Then the dictator, Fulgencio Batista, was overthrown by a revolt led by Fidel Castro in 1959, and it has controlled Cuba for thirty-three years, the longest period of the same government since the US ousted the Spanish in 1898.

"They haven't been good years economically. Sugar production has fallen. Most consumer items are old and inadequate. The once-flourishing tourist business has disappeared. There are food shortages. For years Cuba depended on subsidies from the Soviet Union, but those have now stopped. Once on the verge of becoming a first or second world nation, Cuba has fallen back to almost a third world nation. That is not only sad for its people, it is unnecessary. In fact, it is a tragedy, not just for Cuba, but all of Latin America, for which Cuba once lighted the way…and I must add for its closest neighbor, the United States, and especially Florida."

There was scattered applause and even a few shouts of "Right on."

"The burning issue before us is, should this continue? Should Cuba and the United States continue to be estranged like a couple who were married for years but have refused to face realistically the factors that divide them and continue to ignore the many good reasons they could reconcile?

"I hope you'll pardon this rather lengthy history lesson, but I understand history is not a frequent subject in Cuban schools today, and I thought it was worth recalling that Christopher Columbus first landed in North America on the coast of Cuba. I thought it was worth recalling the determination of the people who have inhabited

Cuba and struggled through the centuries for control of their own government, against Spain, France, Great Britain, and to an extent even the US, but perhaps most often and importantly against themselves. The slaves rose up and fought and gained their freedom.

"These are facts not generally known in the US, or even in Cuba. It is a great and inspiring history, and it is not at an end. Columbus called Cuba the loveliest land that human eyes have beheld, and it was known in the last century as the Pearl of the Antilles."

The crowd had remained attentive through Franklin's lengthy history lesson. What he was trying to do was stir former Cubans' love of their native land and understand why it was important to their own lives and to others to mediate divisions with the United States. He realized that Castro and the Communist rulers were the main culprits, but even they were subject to public pressure.

"As I often said during this campaign, democracy is the narrow path between the desert of tyranny and the wilderness of chaos. Cuba has tried to trod that path, but usually has lost its way in the wilderness, and the people have sought the certainty of the desert of tyranny, which people throughout history have done when faced with that choice.

"But there are side paths back to the main path, out of the desert but short of chaos. If I should be elected president of the US, I will make it a priority to lead Cuba on one of those paths and see that the United States meets them halfway or more. My goal will be peace and a better life. Looking at Cuba's history, you can understand why so many people have accepted the relative certainty of the Castro regime for thirty-three years—the longest period of stability, however bitter, most of them have known rather than plunge the country into further chaos, which was the case for so long.

"This is not to excuse the harshness or the predations of the Castro regime, it is only to admit it has lasted more than thirty years. Surely, many people must fear what will happen if the Castro government is overthrown or collapses tomorrow. What would follow? Would it be a new war, more death and destruction, ending with another dictator, perhaps better but possibly worse than Castro?

"Give me your votes tomorrow if you can believe in a better future and a renewed relationship between Cuba and the US. We have been stuck in the present deadlock for too long, which starves people, deprives families of modern conveniences, blocks the natural contacts between Cubans in the US and their relatives and friends in Cuba. I believe that reconciliation is the course many Cubans prefer, and that is why I decided to make this plea tonight."

Franklin waved and held up his hands to the crowd as many of them cheered and applauded, while a good many others booed and shook their fists. It was a disconcerting and unsettling reception. Susie grabbed his hand. "Where did you learn all that about Cuba?" she asked with one of her best Christmas tree smiles. "It was incredible."

"From my trusty friend, the *World Book Encyclopedia*," he answered and then turned his head slightly as he heard what sounded like two gunshots in the distance. Something lightly brushed his cheek, and when he put his finger to his cheek, he felt a trickle of blood. Then Brad roughly pulled him to the ground and lay on top of him. "Someone's shooting at us!" Brad shouted as two more shots sounded. Franklin lay on the ground with Brad on him, and he could see little, but he sensed turmoil all around as the crowd scattered in disarray. He reached for his cheek again, but there was only a smear of blood, and his cheek seemed to have a slight nick, but around him he could see a great deal of blood, apparently from a woman lying nearby. Her chest was gushing blood, and she had apparently been hit by the bullet that missed him. With a terrible sinking feeling, he suddenly realized the woman was Susie. "Brad, let me up," he implored. "That's Susie. She was hit."

"The EMTs are almost here," Brad said. "They'll get the blood stopped and take her to the hospital."

There was a commotion in the crowd not far from them and a man screaming as he struggled with the secret service men and then the police. His hand still held a high-powered pistol, but the secret service man had pinned his arm behind him and shook the pistol loose in a few seconds. "Don't look, Boss," Brad advised. "They're getting Susie to an ambulance, and she's unconscious I think."

Police had now gathered around Franklin and Brad, advising them to stay where they were until they made sure there were no more gunmen in the vicinity.

A man came and grabbed Franklin's hand. "That was the most reasonable account of our situation I've heard," he said. "I'm a Cuban refugee, and I want Cuba to be the Jewel of the Antilles again."

Other people were patting Franklin on the back and telling him what a great appeal he'd made to the common sense of Cubans. Then one lady sobbed, "This had to happen."

Policemen and the secret service agents took Franklin and Brad to a car and told them Susie was on her way to the hospital with two doctors in attendance. "Did you see her? What did they say about her?" Franklin asked impatiently.

"The bullet hit her in the chest," the secret agent said. "It was a large bullet that exploded on contact. It was meant for your head… and it doesn't look good, but doctors can work miracles today."

Franklin nodded and uttered a prayer. He did not pray often these days, but if ever he needed a favor from the Almighty, he needed it now. He thought about Susie. She had been through so much, and finally she was happy, so alive, so bright, so full of energy for the next task, with a boyfriend who seemed a good match. It wasn't fair. She couldn't die. She was just beginning to live.

Then for an instant he thought about his campaign and the next day's primary. He knew what Susie would be saying. "Don't give up, win this one for me." She had believed in him, one of the first people who actually thought he could win in New Hampshire, and even in the nation. She'd heard most of his speeches, read most of his columns. Surely she would survive, but it didn't sound good. He thought about her mother and a few tears formed in his eyes although he hardly ever cried.

The police carried Franklin and Brad to the hospital, avoiding the crush of news media anxious to get a statement from him. Franklin rushed in and sought the doctor that had come to the scene of the shooting. The doctor's face was blank. "How is she?" Franklin asked frantically.

"I'm sorry. Didn't they tell you? Ms. Schultz expired on the way to the hospital. The bullet pierced her heart. She was dead when she got here."

Brad was weeping by then. He was emotional like most big guys. Franklin just stood there unbelieving, trying to assemble his thoughts.

He glanced up at the TV on the hospital wall and saw his own face at the scene of the speech. The police there were interviewing a young man who was still struggling with one of them. He apparently was the shooter. He looked defiant and kept shouting, "No deals with Cuba's freedom!" His eyes, from what Franklin could see, were the eyes of the dedicated zealot whose only thoughts were of their twisted passions.

Franklin asked the secret service man to get the rest of the group together at the hotel and told the doctor to get the body ready to send to New Hampshire. He planned to put Charlie in charge of those arrangements. The primary suddenly seemed unimportant, but he knew it wasn't. It wouldn't be to Susie, and it wasn't to the thousands of voters who had supported him, including the thousands in Florida that day. The secret service man took him and Brad back to the hotel. "I'm sorry," the agent said. "I saw the man across the street raise his hand with something in it, but by the time I sprinted over there, he had fired three shots, and I tackled him. He must have been about thirty yards from you and Susie."

"Ronald Reagan's agents were almost standing next to him and still let John Hinckley shoot him and three other people," Franklin said consolingly.

Sutton had rented a motel suite for the Primary Night watch party. Franklin was trying to think of the people he needed to call immediately. One was Susie's mother, and for the life of him he couldn't remember her name and number. Brad was scrambling to find it. It was funny how little details like that annoyed him. Charlie would have it, but by then Mrs. Schultz would likely have seen it on TV.

At the hotel they found Charlie, Hardy, Kathleen, Sutton, and several other campaign workers.

Franklin got the number and immediately called Susie's mother. When she answered, her voice was shaky. She'd already heard the news. It was all over TV, even in New Hampshire, perhaps especially in New Hampshire, which was Susie's home.

"I can't tell you how shaken and sorry I am about this," Franklin told her. "I loved Susie like a daughter myself, if that's possible. The six months I knew her will be among the most precious in my life's memories. I felt I knew her much longer. She was a courageous, smart, and beautiful young lady."

Mrs. Schultz fought back her tears. "She loved what she was doing with you," she said. "She felt it was the most important part of her life, and she gave you credit for bringing her out of her long depression. She'd finally begin to live again...and these last six months meant so much to her... For her sake, keep going," Mrs. Schultz said. Franklin handed the phone to Charlie, telling him to work with Mrs. Schultz on the funeral arrangements and have the campaign pay for all of them.

He turned to Sutton and the others. They had mixed expressions. All were crestfallen about Susie, of course, but they were still part of a campaign team, and they sensed a good chance to win an important victory in Florida the next day. "We need to get our ground game organized tonight," Sutton said. "I've already called Jody Powell and got some names of people who helped Carter, and the wheels are rolling. The most important cogs, of course, are Ashmore and Hardy. Are your heads on straight?" he asked them.

"Barely," said Hardy, "but you're right. If we get enough people to the polls tomorrow, we'll win. This is the biggest story in Florida since the last hurricane."

"I'm ready, Boss," Brad added. "I know how much winning meant to Susie."

"Kathleen, you stay with me and get a few more girls over to help us handle the press and make statements. And, Brad, I almost forgot. Print some great photos you made of Susie at events in New Hampshire, Georgia, and especially in the last few days in Orlando and Miami and get them to AP, the *Boston Globe*, and the big Florida dailies. Charlie can help you."

By now their telephone numbers were in the media domain, and there were virtually dozens of calls waiting. Kathleen began taking as many as she could with six other girls whom Sutton had hired for Primary Night.

"The chief reporter from the *Miami Herald* is on this phone and desperately wants to talk to you," Kathleen said.

Franklin took the call. "What was she like?" the female reporter asked. "We've got the details on the events and the shooter. But we don't really have much about the victim."

"Okay, get the receiver comfortable in your ear and I'm going to tell you a remarkable story," Franklin said. "I met her about six months ago, when she was waiting tables at a small motel in Wolfeboro, New Hampshire. Yes, that's Wolfeboro, w-o-l-f-e-b-o-r-o. It's the county seat of Carroll County and was Susie's hometown. I ordered a hamburger and french fries, and she asked me if freedom fries would be okay because that was what the management called fries after the French didn't help the US in the war against Saddam."

"What?" the reporter asked. "She wouldn't serve you french fries?"

"No, they called them freedom fries, and so I gave her a short lecture on how gallantly the French had fought against the Germans in World War I, and I finally got the hamburger and fries." Franklin wondered how all this sounded, but he could hear her typing furiously.

And so he went on to tell the story of how he discovered that the waitress had been an All-state girls basketball player who missed the winning shot in the state championship game because she was pregnant and then was suspended from school before finishing her senior year and left the area and lived with relatives in Maine for two years before coming back and taking a job as a waitress.

"Wait a minute," the reporter stopped him. "Are you telling me this Susie Schultz who was one of your main campaign assistants for president was a waitress just six months ago?"

"Yes, and an incredible one at that. She's always been a star. She was the Most Valuable girls' basketball player in the state when her team won the New Hampshire state championship in her junior year and was an A-plus student in shorthand, typing, and her high school business course."

Franklin filled the reporter in on more details, including the boyfriend Susie had met at Harvard on one of their campaign visits and her role in the campaign thus far.

"Is this all true?" the reporter asked skeptically. "And then she gets killed…at what…twenty-two by an assassin who was shooting at you? What a story. I mean, I'm sorry, of course, but well…. What a story."

"You get it down and call me if you need any more details. Charlie Burkhart is also here and can give you more information. And please get this on your wire to AP, the *Boston Globe* and *New York Times*, and to the Atlanta papers and to the *Concord Monitor* in New Hampshire. As an old journalist, I can tell you it's a great one, although incredibly tragic."

"You're right. I got it all. I haven't got much time to deadline… but thank you…I'll probably be calling you back."

Franklin hung up and began taking other calls. The TV crews and scores of reporters were in the lobby, and he agreed to see them in thirty minutes.

First he took calls from Jimmy Carter, Zell Miller, and surprisingly from Hillary Clinton. "Bill's too hoarse to talk," she explained, "but we're glad you're all right."

Franklin held back a small sob. "Not all right exactly. I knew this was a tough business, but I didn't realize it would be this tough. We'll probably suspend our campaign after tomorrow, at least for a few days until Susie's funeral, and after that, we haven't planned ahead. This was like George Stephanopoulos being shot in your campaign except Susie was prettier and probably nicer."

Hillary couldn't restrain a chuckle. "I hope you go on," she finally said. "Your ideas have brought a different dimension to the campaign. I really mean that."

Another urgent call was waiting for him, and he immediately knew he'd better take it. It was his wife, Jean. Franklin knew that he was all right and sometimes he'd forget that Jean couldn't know that, even with the reports telling her he was.

"Jean," Franklin exclaimed. "I'm okay. It's been a madhouse here. You can't imagine. I'm glad you aren't here. You'd hate it."

She was sobbing on the phone. He couldn't tell if she was because he'd delayed calling her or because of Susie's death.

"How close did that bullet come to you?" Jean wanted to know.

"Pretty close. It nicked my cheek as it sped by and left a slight abrasion, hardly any blood...and then it hit Susie in the heart. She was standing about a foot behind me. I've talked to her mother and been trying to figure how to proceed from here. The funeral will be in Wolfeboro, probably Sunday, and I want you and the children to come up, so start planning that. I'm suspending the campaign for a week after tomorrow. I'm operating on pure adrenaline now, but my nerves are holding up. I'm taking an extra Valium a day. But how are you?"

"Distraught, of course. Why did you get into this? It's about to break your heart."

"It already has," Franklin admitted. "Susie had meant so much to me and to herself. Why don't you fly to Miami tomorrow for Primary Night...and to comfort me. April or Lara should be able to come with you...and Tim also, if he can arrange it. The outlook for the primary is all mixed up now, but given the publicity of the shooting, I could do pretty well...maybe even win."

"Oh, great," Jean said. "And then what, another primary, another ordeal?"

"Will you come on to Miami tomorrow? We're all at the Fontainebleau, where you and I stayed in 1956, when it was brand-new. It still looks great."

"I'll try," she said hesitantly.

"Good, I'll have Sutton make the arrangements and call you back in about an hour. I love you."

He realized Jean had reluctantly gone along with this most unlikely adventure of his, although they had experienced several newspaper ventures that were pretty scary. A reporter from the *Miami Herald* was on the phone and wanted to tell Franklin about the shooter's confession and what the charges were likely to be.

"The guy's a real nutcase," the reporter said. "He's not only an anti-Castro zealot, he's against government in general and is borderline anarchist. His name is Luis Gomez. He says he first noticed your talks about the evils of anarchy, which was why he went to the speech today. His family fled Cuba after Castro took over and his father had all his land confiscated. That had been gnawing at him for fifteen years—he's thirty-five years old—and then he began reading a lot of anarchist literature from the days when anarchists regularly assassinated government leaders, finally including President William McKinley in 1901." McKinley's assassin was captured on the spot and is the only potential US presidential assassin to make a lengthy statement to the police about his action.

"I done my duty," he wrote in his confession. "He [McKinley] was an enemy of the good working people." He told reporters that he had heard Emma Goldman, a Communist, lecture, and her doctrine was that all rulers should be exterminated. "That set me to thinking until my head nearly split open... McKinley was going around the country shouting prosperity when there is no prosperity for the poor man... I don't believe we should have any ruler, and it is right to kill them. I know other men who believe what I did was a good thing to kill the president and have no rulers. I don't believe in voting, it is against my principles. I am an anarchist, I don't believe in marriage. I believe in free love."

Leon Dzolgosz, the assassin of President McKinley, was hurriedly tried and executed by electrocution on October 29, 1901, just six weeks after he killed McKinley. The example of swift justice must have had some beneficial effect as there were no more assassinations of a US president until November 22, 1963, more than sixty years later, when President Kennedy was shot.

McKinley had been the third US president assassinated in a span of just thirty-five years from Lincoln in 1865, to Garfield in 1881, and then McKinley in 1901. Attempts were made on both Roosevelts. Theodore, when he was a third-party candidate in 1912, and most ominously on Franklin Roosevelt in February 1933 in Miami, shortly before he was to be inaugurated for the first time. The attempt on FDR was eerily similar to the attempt on Thomas

Franklin. FDR was also speaking in Miami Park when a man named Joseph Zangara jumped onto a bench and, drawing a small revolver, fired five shots at Roosevelt from about ten yards away.

A woman jostled Zangara's arm, and all the shots missed Roosevelt but one shot hit Chicago Mayor Anton Cermak, who was standing next to him. In an early demonstration of his ability to maintain calm in times of crises and make the right decisions, Roosevelt ordered secret service agents to put Cermak in his car and rush him to the hospital.

Four others were wounded by Zangara's shots and Roosevelt also ordered that they be assisted and carried to hospitals. All but Mayor Cermak were not wounded seriously, but Cermak died a few days later.

In less than a month, Zangara was tried, convicted, and executed just as McKinley's assassin had been thirty-one years earlier. Also, as in McKinley's case, there was no suspicion of elaborate plots or sinister intentions other than the shooter's own twisted mind. In an interview with the press, Zangara said he hated all presidents and like McKinley's assassin had been motivated by anarchist propaganda he had read or heard.

The public, already badly shaken by the ongoing economic depression, seemed to feel the assassin's real target was their faith in the future. The fact that Roosevelt was spared, together with his courage and concern for Cermak after the threat to his own life, actually bolstered national morale at a time when it was at low ebb.

As for Roosevelt, his chief adviser at the time, Raymond Moley, an important co-creator of the New Deal, wrote that later that evening Roosevelt showed no sign of shock. "His view of the incident was fatalistic, and he did not tighten security around him, including the suggested placement of a high wire fence around the Little White House in Warm Springs, where he was obviously more vulnerable."

Zangara's act was the last in a series of assassinations of government figures in the years from 1880 to 1933, most of them instigated by anarchist teachings, speeches, and writing. Most disastrous in its results was the assassination of the Austrian archduke in June 1914, which is generally blamed for igniting World War I in which millions were killed and the seeds of World War II were planted. The killer, Gavrilo Princip, a Serbian rebel, died in prison three years later.

John Wilkes Booth, who shot and killed Abraham Lincoln in 1865, the first time an American president was assassinated was an exception to the anarchist rule in some respects. Booth was motivated by his hatred of Lincoln personally and of his own obsession with Confederate secession. Had he killed Lincoln a year earlier or even two weeks earlier, before Lee's surrender at Appomattox, his act could have prolonged or even affected the outcome of the Civil War, with enormous consequences to the nation's history.

All lives are precious, of course, but some are obviously more valuable to the overall flow of history. Assassins are not only attacking the individuals but the very basis of democracy and government; most of them have admitted they wanted to interrupt the orderly exercise of a civil society, which is why they were so dangerous and their actions so disruptive. Lincoln's assassination, even as the war was ending, had dire effects on the post-Civil War period and left a nation in a disrupted condition for years. His successor, Andrew Johnson, was a Southerner, distrusted by the Republican Congress, and with good reason. The healing of the war's wounds was prolonged by Booth's action.

The assassination of James Garfield in 1881, and of McKinley, were less disruptive, but both dramatically changed the course of events; Garfield was succeeded by the little-known Chester Arthur, who was considered an opponent to Garfield's plans for civil service reform in the government.

Theodore Roosevelt, who succeeded McKinley as president, urged that teaching sedition and advocacy of assassination should be made an offense against international law, like piracy, so that the federal government would have the authority to deal with them. Against strong objections that such laws violated traditional American rights, Congress adhered to Theodore Roosevelt's pleas and amended the Immigration Act in 1903 to exclude persons believing in opposition to organized government.

The amendment should have kept Zangara from his deadly day in Miami or Lee Harvey Oswald from his perch in the warehouse in Dallas on November 22, 1963, or John Hinckley from the Washington sidewalk where he shot at Reagan, or Luis Gomez from the Miami Park. Gomez was not only shooting at Thomas Franklin and Susie Schultz but at the orderly performance of democratic government, which he, like the earlier assassins, wanted to destroy.

The policeman told Franklin that Gomez, the shooter, expressed regret that he had killed the girl instead of Franklin but that he felt she was equally guilty because she was holding an elect-Franklin sign and was supportive of what Franklin was saying. Gomez admitted he brought the pistol to the rally with the idea of shooting Franklin but hesitated until he heard Franklin make the statement that a worse government might succeed Castro if he were overthrown. "Nothing would be worse than Castro," Gomez contended, "not even a battle for control with more killing and destruction. That argument has been used to keep Castro in power all these years. When Franklin said that, I raised the gun and fired. The US must keep pressure on Castro or he will never change."

Franklin felt remorse that he had used those words in light of the consequences but he had believed them and still did. A slow and deliberate move toward independence for Cuba was much less destructive and surer than an attempt to overthrow a regime in power for more than thirty years.

The policeman said Lopez would be charged with murder and held in Florida. Franklin expressed the view that he had advocated in several speeches and columns which was that persons who attack the process of democracy, such as assassins or attempted assassins of public figures, should always receive the death penalty. He noted that Florida had been one of the most active states in executing criminals, some who had committed murder in minor robberies or gang fights. "All lives are precious," he said, "but some are more valuable to the cause of law and order. That's why I don't support the death penalty for simpler crimes."

The policeman was skeptical. "That's a hard sell," he said. "I'm for executing anyone who takes another person's life."

Franklin didn't wish to debate the subject at that time and had many calls on hold. He took as many as he could, finally begging off the others and getting the supporters in the hotel suite together to plan for the next few days. They were all enthusiastic about his chances in the primary and were already at work on the so-called ground game, which mainly included getting voters to the polls. A very despairing Jack Hardy and Brad Ashmore would lead the effort again.

Sutton had brought in a number of helpers to make phone calls. Deep down Sutton knew that their best chance was the enormous wave of emotion and publicity about the shooting and sympathy for Susie's death. He was already seeing TV descriptions of Susie's life with photos Brad had supplied of her on the campaign trail and other photos the stations had obtained of her in her basketball days.

Franklin, no sound sleeper on the best of nights, got very little that night, and he hoped Hardy and Brad slept better but doubted it. He planned a light Primary Day, staying in the hotel and making a few calls. He had already announced that the campaign would be suspended until after Susie's funeral.

As expected, the early morning newscasts and other programs were dominated by the assassination attempt, as were the morning editions of all the daily newspapers in Florida, and in most of the nation, he imagined. The attention seemed certain to drive up voter turnout, mostly in favor of Franklin. The other candidates, including Clinton, seemed uncertain how to proceed, but Clinton's forces were not holding back on getting out voters they believed would support him. Neither was Tsongas, who had been enraged by Clinton's accusation he wanted to reduce Medicare payments. Brown was making a spirited effort to remain viable in the race, and Kerrey, riding on the continued respect for him, was expected to get a respectable vote.

Franklin talked to Susie's mother again and assured her the campaign would take care of all expenses for the funeral and for her to make the arrangements.

He'd gotten a call from Jean, and she and his son and two daughters were flying to Miami that afternoon from Atlanta and should arrive by 6:00 p.m. in time for the first returns. Sutton had rented the main Fontainebleau ballroom and expected a large crowd, including many people from Georgia.

Chapter Twenty-Three

THE DARKLING PLAIN

*The loneliest feeling in the world is when you think
you are leading the parade and turn to find that no
one is following you. No president who badly mis-
guesses public opinion will last very long.*
—*Franklin D. Roosevelt, recalled
by his Secretary of Labor Frances Perkins,
interview, University of Illinois, 1958*

Franklin and his family with a few advisers hunkered down in
the main suite with three TV sets and several telephones. He
was uncertain how the events of the week would play out, but
the early returns showed a definite trend in his favor.

As the night wore on, Franklin held the lead among Democrats
while most of the heavily Cuban vote in the Miami area was going to
Bush or Buchanan, as he had expected. Long lines slowed the counting as the vote was the heaviest ever for a Florida primary. By 9:00
p.m., the outcome was certain, however. Franklin was building a large
margin in the Tampa-St. Petersburg area and in the Orlando, Cape
Kennedy area. Clinton seemed to be strongest in northern Florida,
part of which was in the Central Time Zone, with polls closing later.
Franklin was pleased that he did get a good vote in part of the Miami
Metro area, despite, or because of, his stand for improving relations

with Cuba. Tsongas was running last among the Democrats, behind Brown, who was making a surprisingly good showing.

By 10:00 p.m., Jack Hardy was ready to lead the crowd in a chorus of "The Gambler." Everyone was counting their money before the "dealing was done."

By 10:30 p.m., Franklin was clearly the leader among the Democrats with nearly 50 percent of the total, while Bush easily beat Buchanan in the Republican primary. Franklin emerged with the most votes overall; Clinton was second with 25 percent of the Democrats, and slightly more popular votes than Bush, who had a wide majority in the heavily Cuban precincts of Miami and its environs.

But the returns from all the Super Tuesday states raised the Clinton campaign to a new level. He was second in Florida but first in Texas, the other large state in the day's primaries, and led in six smaller other states, including Tennessee, Mississippi, and Arkansas. At the end of the night, his total delegate count had surpassed Franklin's.

Tsongas survived Super Tuesday, with leads in Massachusetts, Rhode Island, and Delaware. But the big story on TV and in the next day's newspapers was Franklin's winning margin in Florida. His supporters celebrated, but Franklin was not in a celebratory mood. "The memory of Susie Schultz won this primary," he told his circle of friends and family. "That was way too high a price to pay."

He did manage to speak to the crowd, thanking them for their support and announcing he was suspending his campaign until Susie's funeral on Sunday. He paid tribute to her and also revealed what he knew about the shooter, which was that he was upset by Franklin's remarks about the consequences of a Castro overthrow in Cuba, but also resented organized government in general. "He was an advocate of chaos, as have been all presidential assassins, and those types are the greatest threat to stable government in all nations."

Franklin took his usual Valium pill and considered taking two. He expected another difficult night sleeping and was not surprised as his mind kept racing and his stomach tightened. If this was what victory felt like, he wondered what defeat was like, but in his heart he knew. He'd had plenty of experience with disappointment and defeat, not including the present week. He led in Florida, but Susie was still dead.

He heard from Mrs. Schultz the next day. Arrangements for the funeral had been made for 2:00 p.m. Sunday at the small church she and Charlie Burkhart attended in Wolfeboro. Reservations had been made at the small motel for Franklin's family and other associates, the place where he had first met Susie.

Franklin and Sutton scanned the newspaper headlines and watched the early morning TV news programs. The assassination story was still dominating the day, reporters at the *Boston Globe* and in Miami had done compelling sidebars on Susie's life; the *New York Times* headlined Franklin's lead in Florida on page 1 with sidebars on his call for renewed relations with Cuba and a sidebar inside on Susie's life with photos.

Projections on the election and the primary outcomes focused on Bush's clear victory over Buchanan's challenge, and the close struggle between Franklin and Clinton for the Democratic nomination. There was also an article about Franklin shutting down his campaign for the next week.

Franklin went through the round of calls and TV interviews and then begged off for a little rest and plans to get back to New Hampshire. He wanted to be there to see Susie's relatives and friends and again thank the supporters whom he felt gave him the endorsement he needed for the subsequent victories, and their implied support of his positions in favor of a strong federal government, the importance of the New Deal, and the urgency for the United States to lead the way for peaceful relations among all nations.

He was disappointed that the message had not received more notice in some of the states Clinton won, but he realized that he'd spent too little time and money in those states. That was also the problem that faced him in the primaries just ahead. Clinton was a clear favorite in Illinois and Michigan, and Franklin felt any effort in those states would be wasted.

Later in the day, he and Sutton looked at the primary map and the delegate count and not incidentally at the bank account. "The money's getting low," Sutton admitted, "and I don't know what to expect from this victory in Florida. It should help, but suspending your campaign for a week is sending a negative message."

Franklin looked down. He realized it was, but he felt that it was the right thing to do. "Pay off the people in Florida," he told Sutton, "and let me think about the next step. The funeral for Susie will be Sunday in Wolfeboro. Get the word out." For Franklin, all the joy was gone out of the campaign. Susie had been its spark plug.

Nationally, Franklin's lead in Florida gave his numbers a boost, but overall he fell further behind Clinton in number of delegates due to Clinton's showing in the other states, especially Texas. Harkin had dropped out, but Brown and Tsongas were still in contending positions. Tsongas was counting on Connecticut coming up in a week, but Brown was making a sustained effort there. Franklin had not established a base there except for the fallout from his showing in other New England states. He had won Vermont's small primary, thanks to the visit to the publisher in Randolph, which gave him three New England states, all relatively small in delegate count, but still important.

Franklin and Jean sat in their room to discuss the future of the campaign and their lives. "How are you feeling?" Franklin asked her tentatively.

"Weary," Jean replied, "and overwhelmed. What matters is how do you feel?"

"I think I've accomplished a lot," he said. "Not just leading in several primaries, but getting out the points I've been writing about for so many years, which could have never had the exposure or attention a political campaign gives them. I could have kept on writing day after day, dropping rocks into the well, and as I've said, never hearing the splash. In a campaign, you hear the splash. I'm just sorry one of the splashes had to prove fatal to Susie."

"I'm sorry too," Jean consolingly agreed. "But what I keep thinking is that it was supposed to be you. There are plenty of other people out there who don't like what you're saying, and the next one may be a better shot. That's what I worry about. Also, how's our money holding out?"

"After today, it'll be fine, I believe. I've got to call some people. I haven't done many personal appeals, and I was never bashful about asking people to give me money to buy newspapers...well, maybe a little...but I usually got the money."

"You've always done what you wanted to," Jean said rather spitefully. "It's worked sometimes. Most times, in fact. So do what you feel is right, for you and I guess for the country."

Franklin touched her hand gently. They didn't have any money when they got married, had paid for their own wedding, and took a New Orleans' honeymoon on advertising trade outs. They were in their forties before they could really feel financially comfortable, but then Franklin's newspaper buying ventures kept them in a constant state of uncertainty. Franklin knew that unlike Hillary Clinton, Jean had never yearned for political fame or power, and he had never expected it. He couldn't even get elected his homeroom representative in high school.

The following day, they all gathered and got a plane to Atlanta, on the way to Manchester and then to Wolfeboro by car. Franklin picked up as many papers as he could at the airports. He was pleased to see an editorial column by Gene Patterson in the St. Pete Times, praising him and basically endorsing him. Patterson was a former editor of the Atlanta Constitution, a Pulitzer Prize-winning columnist and now publisher of the *St. Pete Times*.

In Atlanta, Franklin was rewarded with big spreads in the Atlanta newspapers, which had not always been kind to him. As many Georgia papers as he had worked on, he had never worked for the Atlanta papers, turning down a fifty dollars a week offer just out of college to go with the Columbus paper at that same salary.

In Wolfeboro, Franklin called a meeting of his chief advisers and supporters, including Sutton, Brad, Burkhart, Hardy, Kathleen, Jean, and a couple of office managers.

"The next major primary is in Connecticut," Franklin explained. "We're all here in New Hampshire for a few days, so my plan is for us to begin working Connecticut with some newspaper and radio ads and try to get a few speaking engagements. Since I'm second in number of delegates, that shouldn't be too hard. Most importantly, the New York state primary is the week after that, and I want to make a real push in New York, where I should have some latent support, which will be energized by any kind of success in Connecticut.

"So that's it. We put everything into Connecticut and New York and then see where we stand. If we can carry New York, it will give me enough delegates overall to have a real impact at the convention, even if not enough to win."

Sutton nodded his head. "That's a reasonable goal," he said, "and a doable one. New York will be expensive, of course, and Clinton is sure to make his strongest campaign there, with plenty of money and support by people who think he looks like a winner. Brown will be the other significant contender. I think Tsongas is out of gas and money. Cuomo is still a possibility if it looks like a deadlocked convention, which could happen if you carry New York."

"Sounds exciting," Kathleen chimed in. Hardy looked weary and worried. Brad was always up for a challenge, as were Sutton and the others.

"Okay, you can begin laying some groundwork in Connecticut. I'm still going to take a few days off until the funeral, but I'll be writing speeches and columns designed for Connecticut and New York."

Jean tugged on his arm. "What about me?" she asked.

"Why don't you and the children stay for the funeral and then a few days in New York? Then if you like, you all can campaign in New York with me?"

Jean nodded somberly. "I want to be with you. I know the last few days have been tough."

In the little motel at Wolfeboro where he had started six months earlier, Franklin spent the next two days writing and making calls and watching the other candidates on TV. Mrs. Schultz asked him to speak at Susie's funeral, and he consented, having heard too many preachers speak at funerals and deliver short sermons with little relevance or mention of the deceased. Susie had not been a member of the church.

The main funeral service was held inside the church building since Sunday was a cold, late winter day in Wolfeboro. Among the many people showing up for the service was a man who introduced himself to Franklin as Susie's father. He was a tall, handsome man who looked forlorn and sad. "I hadn't seen Susie since she was a small child," he admitted. "Obviously, I wasn't a good father, but I followed her career and sent money to her mother when I could. I understand you meant a lot to Susie and helped her find an important role in life. I appreciate that."

Franklin smiled tightly. "Thank you. She was a wonderful woman with a bright future. Whatever your role in her life, your genes helped produce a woman who excelled at everything she did. Her mother could use a helpful hand now."

The man grasped Franklin's hand and thanked him again for what he'd done for Susie. Franklin thought grimly, *Yes, but I also got her killed.* Susie's friend from Harvard was also there. He spoke with her mother and shook hands with Franklin but choked up when he tried to speak.

Franklin gave a heartfelt tribute at the service. "I could talk for an hour about my six months of knowing Susan Ann Schultz," he said, "but I've written a longer tribute, and I hope all of you will pick up a copy of at the back of the church. It tells of how Susie excelled at nearly everything in her life. She did her homework, respected her teachers, and was usually the best student in her class. When she began playing basketball in the fifth grade, her height gave her an advantage, but her determination and diligence made her an all-star. By the time she was a freshman in high school, she was on the first string and obviously an all-star in the making. As a sophomore, she led her team to the state finals and to the state championship as a junior, when she was named the Most Valuable Player in the tournament.

"But Susie was so much more than a basketball star. She was the best typist in her high school class, selected the prettiest girl and Homecoming Queen. The school employed her as an office secretary.

"Then came a dark period in Susie's life, when she failed to make the winning shot in the state finals of her senior year, lost a baby, and was suspended from school before graduation. She went through a terrible time of depression, became a waitress in another state, but within months, she was the best waitress the motel had ever had. But what's most outstanding about Susie Schultz is that she emerged from that deep night of her soul with her confidence restored and became one of the most effective members of the longest, short presidential campaign, helping the candidate defeat far better-known and financed candidates in four straight primaries. She was an essential player in every one of those campaigns, with her intelligence, her personality, her beauty, and most important, her belief in the principles the candidate was talking about. She typed speeches and campaign literature, distributing it and welcoming supporters, who enjoyed her attention and competence. Let us all be thankful she passed our way and revere her memory even as we mourn her loss. The shooter meant to kill me and I agonize each day that the bullet hit Susie, but as Solomon wrote in the Holy Bible: 'Not always is the race to the swift or victory in battle to the strong, for time and chance happeneth to us all...' Susie was swift and strong, but chance happened to her as it does to all, but her example even in death has lifted the entire nation to a better understanding of the danger we all face from these faceless zealots who have killed such vital persons in our lives as Martin Luther King, John Kennedy, Bobby Kennedy, and almost Gerald Ford and Ronald Reagan...and Susie Schultz. Like all of them, she made a valuable contribution to those who knew her and to her nation. May God rest her soul, Amen."

The shivering crowd, many of them from places where March did not have such wintry conditions, gratefully moved on. Jean touched his hand, tears streaming from her eyes. "You did good," she said. Mrs. Schultz also hugged him but could not speak. Charlie and Hardy came to him, and both uttered the same thought. "We must go on for her."

The minister came by. "That was touching," he told Franklin, then fixed him with a serious expression. "Did she know Jesus?" he asked.

"She never mentioned him," Franklin answered bluntly, "but I'm sure he knew her and was proud of her."

As they returned to the motel, Franklin asked Jean if she remembered when they had stayed at this same motel seven years earlier. "Vaguely," she said. "It seems so long ago, but I remember the other people on the tour, about forty of them, I think, mostly from Georgia. It was a great trip, and we haven't kept in touch with any of them. They were mostly older than we were at that time, into their sixties and even seventies. We were the youngsters in the group."

"I was remembering the tour took us on a cruise on Lake Winnipesaukee, which is just across the highway. The cruise was about two hours, and we got a great view of the autumn foliage and the White Mountains to the north. But when we got back to shore, there were boys hawking newspapers with extra on the front page and big headlines. Naturally, I was interested and bought a copy. The extra was about the assassination of Egypt's president, Anwar Sadat. I had written about him the week before we left on the tour. Sadat was one of the most courageous advocates for peace in our time."

The paper told of him being shot many times as he was reviewing a parade by soldiers who felt he had betrayed the Arabs in their battle against Israel. Sadat had taken the first step toward trying to make peace with Israel after nearly forty years of strife and warfare following the establishment of Israel under a UN mandate in part of land that had previously been Arab Palestine. The Arabs in the surrounding nations, including Egypt, immediately launched a war to drive the Jewish settlers out and refused to accept Israel as a legitimate nation. President Harry Truman immediately recognized Israel, however, and that gave it the basis to establish a government and a strong military, with plenty of help from the United States.

But there was no peace. In 1956, the Arab nations again tried to force the Israelis out of the slice of Palestine they had been given to establish the state of Israel, but the Israelis prevailed again. In 1967, another war broke out, and this time the Israelis won more decisively, taking over additional land from the Arab nations. In each of the Arab-Israeli wars, Egypt had been the largest nation on the Arab side. But in 1977, Sadat, who had become Egypt's leader after the death of Gamal Nasser, suddenly flew to Jerusalem, asking to speak to the Israeli National Assembly. It was a surprising and daring move on Sadat's part, encouraged by US president Jimmy Carter, who was determined to make a new and serious effort to bring about a settlement of the constant conflict in the Biblical lands of the Middle East.

A Bible scholar, he had written a book on the subject, entitled *The Blood of Abraham*, suggesting a path to a durable peace.

Sadat's brave gesture of personally going to Jerusalem gained little in the way of Israeli acceptance but caused him to be ostracized in the Arab world, no doubt sowing the seeds of hatred that would take his life in 1981. But with constant prodding by President Carter, Sadat had continued a search for an accord between Egypt and Israel. Carter also persisted, and in the summer of 1978, he managed to get Begin and Sadat together with him for a lengthy conference at Camp David, the presidential retreat in Maryland. Through fourteen hot summer days, the three leaders and their aides struggled over a settlement they all would support. Begin was the most resistant, Carter the most determined not to leave Camp David without an agreement. Finally, a rough outline was agreed on, with some items left to be decided. The Camp David Accords were Carter's finest hours as president but oddly he got little credit for overcoming the great odds against a settlement, which both the Israeli government and most Arab governments opposed, not to mention the large and powerful Jewish community in the United States, who felt Carter was giving too much to the Arabs and never forgave him, one reason for his defeat for reelection in 1980. Ironically both Sadat and Begin won Nobel Peace prizes for that year, but Carter didn't, although he had clearly been the lead peacemaker. His omission was never explained satisfactorily, and the Prize would have been an asset in the 1980 election. [He was finally awarded the Nobel Peace Prize twenty-four years later in 2002]. Egypt and Israel have never engaged each other in war since the Camp David Accords.

Sadat was one of the unique peacemakers, but sadly, the war makers often prevail, at least in the short run. In the long run, the treaty produced with such pain and determination at Camp David, survived, providing a victory of sorts for the Jewish rabbi, who promised that the peacemakers would inherit the earth.

At the hotel, Franklin and Sutton went over plans for the campaign in Connecticut. Some money had come in after the Florida primary, but Sutton wanted Franklin to make calls to potential large contributors in New York, assuring them that he would be campaigning there and make a concerted effort. Sutton also said that the publicity from Susie's death had carried over into Connecticut and New York, giving them a base there despite the lack of organizing and advertising. "We can make a showing," he told Franklin, "and the votes are going to be divided four ways. Tsongas has a following in Connecticut and could be a significant factor. Brown is making a push there, and I understand he has a growing organization. Of course, Clinton is the big factor. He is also heavily favored in Illinois and Michigan next week, and you won't even be on the ballot."

For some reason Franklin had never got around to filing in those states. He partly blamed Sutton, but he knew Sutton had been carrying a heavy load. He told him to hire some more help for New York and Connecticut and set up several major rallies in Connecticut. "Maybe we can get Lily Pons to sing again."

He told Jean and the children they were on their own the next few days for some touring.

Franklin tried to call Jack Hardy but got no answer. He did get Charlie Burkhart and asked him to carry Jean and the children to Hartford, Connecticut, and rent an office for a week. "I'll come on down later with Hardy. You haven't seen him today, have you?"

"No," Charlie said. "He's usually right around the hotel, but I haven't seen him since the day of Susie's funeral. By the way, Kathleen's here and says she needs to talk to you."

"Okay, you go to Hartford with Jean and call me when you get set up."

He met Kathleen in the restaurant for a very late breakfast. She looked tired and anxious. "We haven't talked much about my life in California," she began. "I went out there about eighteen years ago. I worked in TV and politics and then settled down to a regular TV job and also got married."

"That is big news," Franklin admitted. "I can't believe you hadn't told me."

"Well, we're separated now, but I also have two daughters, four-teen and twelve." She laughed. "I think I decided to join your cam-paign as a lark from normal life, and let me say, it's been great, better than any campaigns with Wallace or Baxley or as a director of the

Publicity and Tourism Department…except of course the assassination attempt…and Susie's death. She reminded me of my daughters, and I really came to care about her."

"I suppose Jack Hardy knows all about this," Franklin said.

"Yes, we've talked about it. I was always upfront with him about the fact that I'm still married and have two children. But he said he'd been with other married women and was even married to one himself. But what I wanted to tell you is…my twelve-year-old daughter called me last night and desperately wants me to come home. So does the older one. They are at an age they need their mother… and frankly, I need them. So I told her I'd be back to California this weekend."

There were tears in her eyes, and she didn't look like the confident, cheerful Kathleen he'd always known. "I know this is a bad time for you, but after your victory in Florida, there will be loads of eager consultants and writers and all sorts of campaign aides wanting to get on your ship. They'll all have more experience than me and can help you in New York and later…if there is a later."

"I understand," Franklin assured her. "I just appreciate the time you did come. It was a great help, and…and it was so good to see you after all these years…more than twenty it's been, I guess."

"Can I be blunt without upsetting you?" she asked.

"Yeah, please do, I'm accustomed to that."

"You gave me my first real job, but more important, you believed in me and gave me creative ideas like that Christmas Eve visit with Wallace and so many others. You helped me recognize that I was more than just a pretty face and body, and I needed that reassurance at that time. Even Wallace never gave me that. But I've noticed through the years that when the going got tough, you got going." She reached over and grasped his hand. "Please don't take that as a criticism. Most of us would have done the same thing. I've followed your career from when you were that young, nervous publisher in Opelika until today, when you're a leading candidate for president. You've been marvelous at building things and giving people opportunities, but then one day you tell them…. 'Good luck, I'm on my way to another project.'"

Franklin winced a little, but he knew it was the truth. His dedication and emotions had a time limit, and he could see that Kathleen thought his limit for politics was on the clock.

"You're right," he said. "Unlike my favorite hero, George Bailey, when the Old Man Potters of the world come to me and offer to buy me out, I've usually said, 'I'll take the money and get out of town.' In Opelika, for example, and at other times, I was mentally and physically exhausted. I tried to do too much…put the paper out, run the newsroom, oversee the business and advertising, buy the equipment and be the front man in the community, not to mention writing columns and covering a lot of Auburn football games and dealing with all the brilliant but sometimes difficult staff members, like you."

Kathleen laughed. "You always seemed so cool and unconcerned, but I thought you were trying too hard. You did a wonderful job, and I can see that same attitude in this presidential campaign. Nobody can do it all. How many speeches have you written? Who's your main consultant? Sutton? He's pretty good, but he's never run a presidential campaign, has he?"

"I think he ran a campaign for a mayor one time."

"And Hardy, he seems to have been your right-hand man."

"That's right, since the first day in New Hampshire. And where is he today? I haven't seen him since the funeral. Have you talked to him?"

"Yes, I talked to him that night and explained why I was going back to California."

"How did he take it?" Franklin asked with a mounting degree of concern.

"Not well," Kathleen admitted. "He said he loved me, that I was the first woman he'd really loved since his divorce and that he needed me. That was the sure tip-off to me that I was doing the right thing to leave. I like Jack, but we are very different types. It would have never worked, and I also had my daughters to think of, not to speak of still having a legal husband. I tried to let him down easy, that this is best for him in the long run. He's wounded and said he was a recovering alcoholic, which I didn't know. He's another one you've rescued from depression, but I wasn't sure how he'd handle another political defeat, especially after Susie's death. I happened to be on the campaign with Wallace when he was shot, and now almost you. My girls read about it, and that was one reason they got concerned about me. I was still fairly close to Wallace after he was shot by that guy in Maryland. Wallace kept on running and getting elected, but he was never the same after the shooting, and he was a lot tougher than you."

"Kathleen, you're a great lady, and I honestly think you belong back with your daughters…and maybe your husband."

"I love you, Thomas Alexander Franklin. I'll always be proud to tell people that I worked for you." She kissed him on the cheek. "I haven't heard from Jack since our conversation two days ago," she said. "Find him, he may be on a bender."

"Goodbye and good luck," Franklin said warmly. Do you have any ideas where Jack might be?"

"I really don't. We'd only been to a few places here in New Hampshire, and he had no acquaintances except in the campaign. I'm sorry. He somewhat reminded me of Bill Baxley, but without the good looks and political savvy. Bill always turned up in a day or two."

Chapter Twenty-Four

HERE IN THE REAL WORLD

We may make mistakes—but they must never be mistakes which result from faintness of heart or abandonment of moral principle.
—Franklin D. Roosevelt, fourth inaugural address, January 30, 1945

Wolfeboro was not an easy place to get lost but Hardy's car was also missing. In the nearly eight months since they began their quixotic political journey, there had been hardly a waking moment when Franklin did not know where Hardy was. He spent most of the day calling possible contacts, including Brad, who had gone on to Connecticut, but to no avail. He constantly checked his own phone and the various offices. No one had seen Hardy since the funeral.

Franklin wrote some passages for a speech and did some paperwork and then decided to drive around the area in one of the rental cars. The March evening was getting very cold for a Georgia boy, but the car heater worked well, and the radio picked up both news and a country music station, of all things. The news reported on the pending entry into the presidential contest of Ross Perot, the eccentric multimillionaire whom a lot of people had suddenly decided should be president. Perot was frequently on the Larry King TV show and was fond of sounding like an intellectual hillbilly, but there seemed no good reason for him to run. He had never sought or held political offices. His views were mainly those of hard-right Republicans except that he had opposed the war in Iran and opposed the NAFTA treaty, two views he shared with Franklin. He was fanatically against the federal government and deficit spending.

Franklin switched to the country music station and picked up a tune that was currently popular. It rang a bell. It was a song he and Hardy had played several times one night at a bar in Concord, and it summoned up memories as well as fitting the situation.

Franklin decided to go to Concord, which was only about twenty miles away. The night was getting colder but dry. He found the hotel bar where he and Hardy had stayed that night. As he entered, he heard the closing strings of that song, sung by Alan Jackson of Newnan, Georgia, Franklin's birthplace. It had been the chosen song of the year in country music. Franklin loved it and so had Hardy. Jackson was softly singing the final verse as Franklin's eyes scanned the tables. "And, darlin', it's sad but true, the one thing I've learned from you is how the boy don't always get the girl, here in the real world."

At a booth in the very back of the room, Franklin found Hardy. Hardy looked up at him. "Where are we going next?" he asked in a shaky voice. He smelled of alcohol, and he had a two-day stubble but otherwise sounded and looked himself.

Franklin sat down. "Are you okay?" he asked.

"I guess you could describe me that way, but with an asterisk. I came over here to have a beer sometime yesterday, and then I had a few more. Then I had a few shots of Old Grandad and went to sleep. As benders go, it wasn't much, but I just couldn't get going. I kept meaning to call you or someone, but I was ashamed. If you hadn't found me, I'd have come on back tonight...I guess."

"I talked to Kathleen," Franklin told him. "She wanted to go back to California and her daughters, and she wasn't sure how long this campaign will last. I think she sensed an ultimate defeat, and she wasn't sure you were up to that. I guess you told her about the many losers you'd worked for, including Carter's 1980 race."

"Yeah, I was worried about that too, but whatever happens, this has been a blast. Those victories in New Hampshire, Maine, and Georgia were better than any I'd ever known, even Carter's first campaign. Florida was good too, of course, but I kept thinking of Susie. I thought Kathleen could comfort me, but she wasn't really my answer. How about putting another quarter in the machine and play Alan Jackson one more time?"

"Okay, and I'll have a glass of wine while you drink a strong cup of coffee."

Several other people in the bar applauded as the song began: *"Cowboys don't cry and heroes don't die, good always wins again and again, and love is a sweet dream that always comes true, oh if life was like the movies, we'd never be blue. But here in the real world it's not that easy you see, cause when hearts get broken it's real tears that fall. I gave you my love, but that wasn't enough to hold your heart when things got tough, and tonight on that silver screen, it'll end like it should, two lovers will make it through like I hoped we would. But here in the real world it's not that easy you see, because when hearts get broken, it's real tears that fall."*

Hardy's head nodded. "But to quote another recently popular ballad, 'I wouldn't have missed it for the world, wouldn't have missed loving you girl,'" he recited. "I think I should I go to the men's room."

"Good idea," Franklin said. "We sometimes forget that our bodies are really just a complicated plumbing system designed by the master plumber, and when the plumbing works well, we're okay, and when it doesn't, we're in trouble. Hard liquor isn't good for the plumbing."

"I've learned that over and over. It helped me go sober. I won't forget again."

Hardy returned and still looked despondent. "Kathleen was something else," he said. "The best I've ever had by far, and she'll be hard to forget."

Franklin summoned a happy saying from another old movie. "Well," he told Hardy, "you and Kathleen will always have Wolfeboro."

"That's right," Hardy said as he broke into a big grin. "We'll always have Wolfeboro, and frankly that will be better than Paris was for Bogart and Bergman. I always thought Bergman looked like a cold fish, and Kathleen was hot as a firecracker." He paused at the memory. "And we'll always have Wolfeboro."

Franklin drove back to the hotel in Wolfeboro and told Hardy to follow him. Jean and the family were still there and seemed to be packing. She looked at Franklin plaintively. "We had a nice ride," she said, "but you know, I think you will be better off if we go back home. Don't you?"

Franklin was taken aback but not really surprised. He and Jean had a strong bond, but he knew this campaign was straining it. Jean went on, "We're not good campaigners, and April needs to get back to her children, so does Tim. But we'll do what you say."

"But reluctantly?" Franklin asked. He smiled and hugged her. "I need you," he said, "but the next few weeks will be hard and harried...so you're probably right. I might even feel better if you are all back at home. You don't really like being a presidential candidate's wife, do you?"

"I like being your wife, and I liked being a newspaper publisher's wife, but you're right, a presidential candidate's wife might be a bridge too far for a shy Baptist girl who went to an all-girls Baptist college, was an only child with a lonely childhood, and was extremely sheltered from the world. A lot of the people who've worked for you here said you rescued them from ordinary lives and guided them to being more inspired, creative people. I'm your most unlikely creation, but all I ever wanted was to be a housewife with children and have a caring husband. I got that, and you deserve the credit. But you were always looking for something else, some adventure, something to prove you were a bluebird, not a redbird, as that long-ago teacher had labeled you."

"You're right," Franklin agreed. "You go on back home, and I'll see this through the New York primary. There are things no other candidate has been willing to tell the people. Maybe they don't want to know. But the country is on a path toward an economic past, which might have been all right for the eighteenth century but isn't for the late-twentieth century and certainly not for the twenty-first century. We've become a more balanced nation, with more rich, more middle class, fewer poor, but the balance still needs adjusting. The US is the greatest nation in history, and it created the most prosperous, broadest middle class, and that is its secret, the reason it has survived as a democratic government when so many other nations failed, and even the best like Great Britain depended on such medieval crutches as royalty to maintain its unity. Now, at the dawn of the twenty-first century, we have the opportunity to guide the rest of the world to the economic and governmental freedoms we've achieved but which are declining in our own country."

Jean gave him a big hug. "You're wonderful," she said. "You would make a great president. I'm just not sure I'm up to being a president's wife."

"Don't undersell yourself, but you and the children go on home and get some rest from the campaign. I know who I want my wife to be for sure, and the presidency is a shifting goal. Take the car Hardy and I were in and drive to the Manchester airport. I just need to see if I can win New York, Franklin Roosevelt's state. And I'll try to keep a little money for us to live on. But I do think I've made a difference, which is hard to do just writing editorials. You've got to get into the arena, as Theodore Roosevelt once said."

Jean and the children left the next afternoon, and Franklin and Hardy took the Lincoln Town Car and set out for Hartford on I-91.

"Okay," Hardy said, "tell me about the last great New Deal program you were talking about."

"Well, it was the GI Bill, adopted in 1944, and so we usually don't think of it in connection with New Deal programs, but next to Social Security, the GI Bill has meant more for the country and the world than any other New Deal program. It transformed the US into the nation it is today, better educated, better prepared for the post-agrarian age, and for the post-industrial age. From the GI Bill came the raw material for the space age, the computer age, and millions of people sitting in stadiums watching football games played by students who might never have gotten into college but are now making millions of dollars a year."

"The GI Bill did all that?"

"That and much more. You hear about all these experiments government pays for, like how many ants make an anthill? Most of those are for academic programs where the experiments are performed or the papers written on the subjects. They finance the publish-or-perish system in academia.

"In the closing days of World War II, President Roosevelt was still trying to get programs through a reluctant Congress that would enhance the benefits of the New Deal. Congress had a majority of Democratic members, but the real majority was composed of Republicans and conservative white Southerners, who also controlled most chairmanships. They had gone along with costly programs to wage the war and fund the military industries, but they were balking at further expenditures, even Roosevelt's Senate majority leader, Alben Barkley of Kentucky, who resigned in a fit of anger when Roosevelt vetoed a tax bill which he denounced as 'a bill providing relief not for the needy but for the greedy.' The bill was partly designed to finance what Roosevelt had introduced as the second Bill of Rights, including 'the right to a job that pays enough for adequate food and clothing and recreation; the right of farmers to a decent living; the right of businessmen to be free of unfair competition and non-monopolistic practices; the right of every family to a decent home; the right to adequate medical care; the right to protection from the economic fears of old age, sickness, accident or unemployment; and the right to a good education.'

"All of that was a large dose for Congress to swallow, and some of those rights are still being debated—and denied—to this very year. But Roosevelt plunged ahead first with a bill to raise the Social Security tax, which was then just 1 percent. The Senate rejected the proposal 48 to 17.

"Not only was Roosevelt facing a Congress in which his proposals lacked support, but 1944 was an election year. Republicans had gained seats in the past three elections but were still numerically in the minority due to Democratic gains in 1932 and 1936, plus the solid South, although many Southerners were reluctant New Dealers.

"Roosevelt then sought a tax increase that would raise revenues by $10 billion. Congress passed a bill raising them by only $2 billion, and it was Roosevelt's veto of that bill which caused Barkley to resign and turned more Democrats against him. The Senate quickly overrode the veto and reelected Barkley to the leadership.

"Defeated and angry, Roosevelt was also anxiously awaiting the uncertainties of the D-Day invasion of France in June and beginning to suffer health frailties, which would take his life in less than a year. He then put forward a proposal giving men and women serving in the Armed Forces the right to an absentee ballot, which he had long advocated but been thwarted by a reluctant Congress, many of whom felt Roosevelt would get the majority of the military votes in the 1944 presidential election.

"In April, Congress passed the much-amended measure, which Roosevelt called that fool bill, but he signed it because it did allow for ballots to 112,000 military personnel. As it happened, the congressional battles over the bill and the resultant delays and attempts to block any military voting publicized the issue to the point where 4 million soldiers cast absentee ballots, most of them for the president, helping him win a fourth term in November 1944."

"That is a story you've never told me. I was eligible for the GI Bill but never took advantage of it," Hardy muttered.

"Roosevelt dropped several proposals from his new Bill of Rights but not the GI Bill, because he knew Congress would be hesitant to oppose a bill specifically designed to help service men and women. In January, he requested that the American Legion sponsor the bill. It was the beginning of federal aid directly for education, although limited at the time to veterans.

"The bill included an array of economic benefits to veterans such as tuition for college, the most enduring part; and helping buy homes at a low interest rate. A significant aspect of the bill was that it included black as well as white members of the military.

"A New Deal measure to its teeth, it was seen by the Republicans as more social planning and opening the way to federal funding for education, previously funded mainly by the states. But the GI Bill ignited an unprecedented increase in college enrollment, construction, and faculty, not to mention sports. Before World War II, the University of Georgia had never had more than 3,500 students, and that only was briefly in the late 1930s when women finally began to attend in significant number.

"By 1948, when the GI Bill had made it possible for thousands of veterans to afford college, the enrollment at Georgia was 8,000, and other colleges reflected a similar increase. The enrollments were followed by larger investments by the states in dormitories, buildings, and salaries. Education became a part of the postwar economic boom that has kept on growing as the children of the GI generation also expected to attend college and more and more women enrolled.

"In a fireside chat, Roosevelt declared, 'The men and women serving in the armed forces must not be demobilized into an environment of inflation and unemployment.'

"During the debate on the GI Bill, Roosevelt stayed on the sidelines and let the American Legion and other veteran groups take credit for approval of what was one of the most ambitious and enduring New Deal measures and one Roosevelt had planned for several years. During his visits to Warm Springs, he had been struck by the low level of education in Georgia, with nearly all state funds directed to schools with all white students. In those segregated days, he had wanted to include national health care in the Social Security program but felt that would defeat the entire proposal since it would mean integration of hospitals and hospital rooms.

"That Roosevelt was able to carry to success the GI Bill was one of his most remarkable feats, considering the makeup of Congress and the declining nature of his health, not to mention the constant demands of his leadership in those crucial final days of World War II."

On June 6, 1944, the Allies invaded continental Europe, the first successful invasion of continental Europe across the English Channel since William the Conqueror's famed invasion of Great Britain in 1066 from the French side to the British coast, an entirely different feat.

When Roosevelt first launched the New Deal in 1933, a prominent British statesman, then out of office, remarked, "Roosevelt is an explorer who has embarked on a voyage as uncertain as that of Columbus, and upon a quest which conceivably could be as important as the discovery of the New World. The courage, the power and the scale of Roosevelt's effort, must enlist the ardent sympathy of every nation and his success cannot fail to lift the whole world into the sunlight of an easier and more genial age." So wrote Winston Churchill in 1933 in a prediction of the New Deal others were slow to see at that time.

"In 1944, Roosevelt was putting his final achievements of the New Deal in place while overseeing the success of the Allied armies against the Germans, Japanese, and their allies, and also dealing with the early problems of the Cold War with Soviet Russia, whose armies now controlled more of Europe than Germany's ever did," Franklin concluded.

Franklin and Hardy were nearing Hartford, Connecticut. Sutton had arranged for Franklin to speak at a large meeting of businessmen. It would be Franklin's only speech of any importance in Connecticut, and he had been making notes right until the time they arrived at the hotel.

"This better be good," Hardy said as they entered. "We don't have much of a ground game here, and I understand that Tsongas, Clinton, and Brown are all making a strong effort, but you have a publicity advantage from Florida."

The crowd was a large one but did not look friendly. "I'm going to talk about taxes today," Franklin began, "a subject most people don't like to talk about. All they know is they don't like to pay them. But taxes need to be talked about, and they need to be paid. The real question that is endlessly debated and decided, by people who don't mind talking about taxes, is who pays the money and who gets most of it. I'd like to remind you that on this day, March 8, 1992, the United States Treasury has more money and better credit than any nation in history. We are not only rich but the challenges before us are less daunting than they have been in many years. The Cold War is over, and contrary to what Paul Tsongas says, the United States won. If you don't believe it, ask a Russian. Just don't ask a Republican because they are still trying to figure how to run for president without having the Communist menace to blame everything on.

"The US has the money, the power, and the governmental model to mold a new world out of the clashing ideologies and warring powers of the old world, and we dare not turn away from the historic opportunity. But as I said to begin with, we must discuss taxes openly and with a reasonable temper because that is how the nation gets its revenues, both to use and to invest. The Founding Fathers who composed the most remarkable document since the Magna Carta did not deal in depth with the question of taxation. In their time, such wealth as there was, was based on land and slaves and later on tariffs levied by the federal government on goods coming into the US from other countries and significantly on alcoholic beverages.

"In fact, at one time, taxes on alcohol provided one-third of the national income. It was the dependence on alcohol for revenue that prompted the passage of Prohibition in conjunction with passage in 1916 of the Sixteenth Amendment, which provided for a tax on income which had previously been ruled unconstitutional by the Supreme Court. Ironically, the two amendments were considered dependent on each other with income replacing alcohol as a major revenue source, but most people didn't like either one. Salaried income was becoming the basis of wealth rather than land. The agrarian society was passing, and the industrial age actually was concentrating more wealth in a few families and industries, which resulted in the so-called roaring twenties. Only a relatively few Americans were roaring. Most of the nation was still emerging from the agrarian age with a middle class that lived at what we would consider almost poverty level today. There were not nearly as many products to buy, of course, or other ways to spend disposable income. The men usually worked eight to ten hour days, six days a week, and women at home worked nearly all the time without the help of the modern appliances and conveniences we have today. In a twinkling-of-an-eye as history counts years, the modern age overtook us; the New Deal saved us from the challenges of the Great Depression, and gave more Americans a chance to be financially stable and more productive.

"The progressive feature of the income tax which levies the tax on incomes according to a person's amount of income was essential and was mainly developed during the Depression years under the leadership of Roosevelt to hold down inflation and later to finance the industrial and military buildup to win World War II.

"When the income tax amendment was approved, the United States was a relatively small but ambitious power among the older nations of the world. In the seventy-six years since, the rich have gotten richer, the broadest middle class in history has been created and the poor have been elevated from grinding poverty, while the nation has become the richest, most powerful nation in history. What's not to like?"

Franklin paused to look around the room. He realized there were a lot of Republicans in the group who thought they were paying too much in taxes and who didn't like the government taking any of the money they were making, especially to give it to other nations or to spend it on welfare programs that didn't benefit them directly.

"The benefits of this rich society we live in must be shared to an extent to keep our own wheels rolling," Franklin emphasized. "The richest person in this room depends on the roads built by the government; on the economy which has grown so that people have enough money to buy the products it produces; when natural disaster strikes, the first call state officials make is usually to the federal government to come and help repair the damages and give people refuge from the storm, physically and financially.

"The armed forces, which stand guard at the gates of our freedom. The police and other first responders and other workers who make life comfortable and worth living deserve fair salaries for maintaining the physical foundations of our society so it can make the deals that provide the money. As in all of the nation's achievements, it is all the people and states working together that have assured stability and progress.

"On the matter of taxes, it makes little sense for the government to take its largest bite from workers and families who have the least, leaving them with less to live on and, in some cases, survive on when nearly all of the money they get goes directly back into the economy at local stores. I was a small businessman for forty years, and while I didn't like to pay taxes, I hated even worse not having enough customers or advertisers in my papers not selling enough of what they advertised. The US is a consumer-driven economy, and in the past sixteen years, consumers haven't had enough money to buy the goods they need, which is why the economy is in a continued slump. There are many reasons for this, automation has eliminated jobs that aren't coming back, cities have seen their industries suddenly close down or move their operation overseas, other businesses or industries have been sold and consolidated with former competitors with the owner realizing millions from the sell-outs and the buyers eliminating jobs.

"The result has been a sharp decline of small stores and sometimes the large stores that those laid-off workers supported with their purchases. I don't think this has affected Connecticut as much as states in the Midwest and the Southeast, but the impact is felt nationwide. The tax system has been taking money in taxes from the lowest earners and leaving more and more to the highest earners who don't buy as many consumer products. These are not fashionable facts to present or politically helpful, but the figures and the sad condition of many families and communities are obvious. The total amount of money collected in taxes over the past twenty years as a percentage of the Gross National Product varied very little. It is still about 20 to 22 percent, but the sources of the tax revenue have changed drastically. Millions of more dollars have come from the consumer class while millions less have come from the so-called investor class. That's what happened to many small businesses that depended on the average consumers who spent most of their income on life's necessities such as food, clothes, and housing. Much of that money has been diverted to people or companies who spent it on buying up other companies, then cutting their payrolls or moving them overseas. Much of the illusions that the war on poverty would solve all the nation's problems was based on a belief that the problems resided in the personal weaknesses of the poor themselves, but those solutions overlooked the people who already were working at jobs then available, which needed doing and were essential to the communities where the poor lived and were usually society's unpleasant jobs and paid very little. But the real problem was erosion of the jobs in plants that went overseas or were eliminated by technology.

"The income tax was based on the graduated or progressive system, which worked well for the nation and for most of its citizens for nearly fifty years but which has gone askew in the past twenty years. As William Greider so methodically points out in his book *Who Will Tell the People*, the tax revenue collected from the richest 1 percent of Americans dropped by 36 percent since 1977 as Congress has revised the tax code several times, always in favor of the wealthy, while the tax on families in the middle of the income ladder have dropped only 7 percent.

"Greider wrote that both Democrats and Republicans in Congress have been responsible for the widening gap in the tax burden, designing it after the one favored by Andrew Mellon, the very wealthy Secretary of the Treasury under Calvin Coolidge, in the 1920s. Mellon's goal was to eliminate the graduated tax system altogether and replace it either with a flat tax or a consumption tax, which would be the same for all consumers whatever their income or means. If that sounds familiar, it is because the so-called 'fair tax' being promoted by Republicans today is nothing but a sales tax on all Americans, and the flat tax, most recently advocated by Steven Forbes, when he ran for president, would, in effect, put everyone in the same tax bracket, whether they earned $10,000 or $1 million a year.

"Doonesbury the comic strip demonstrated it simply and effectively in a cartoon showing a man and wife talking seriously with Forbes. The man says, 'We pay 16 percent now but would pay more under your plan while you would pay less.' 'Well, yes,' Forbes says, 'there would have to be some sacrifices.'

"That cartoon illustrated better than pages of tax arguments how tax revisions through the years has been sold to the public on the idea that the next revision would simplify their tax returns by reducing the number of brackets. Actually, the more brackets, the fairer or more progressive the income tax becomes!

"Mellon, in the 1920s, explained it in blunter language than today's politicians would venture. 'The prosperity of the lower and middle classes depends upon the good fortune and light taxes on the rich,' he stated candidly, and that argument became the basis of supply-economics and the trickle-down system. If the US is to remain stable and the beacon of fairness and prosperity to the world, that trend must be reversed," Franklin concluded with a flourish.

He received only a light applause from the large group of mostly businessmen and Republicans and he was afraid the populist message on taxes had not earned him many votes. But he glimpsed two reporters who recorded the speech, one from the local Hartford Courier and the other from the *Boston Globe*. He hoped they would publicize the message he was trying to convey. There was also a TV reporter and a cameraman there, who asked him to talk with them afterward. A few men came by and congratulated him on his talk. One man was a union leader who asked him if he could give the same talk to a large union meeting scheduled that night. "I'll do it," Franklin said. That would give him two appearances in Connecticut before the primary vote and an audience that might be open to his arguments. He even had thought of some useful additions.

After talking with the reporter, Franklin and Hardy drove over to the newspaper office to place a large ad in the Sunday paper, which would come out two days before the primary.

Hardy looked at him warily. "I've never heard you bear down on the tax system that much," he said.

"You missed some of my columns," Franklin said, "plus I felt there were a lot of high earners in that audience who didn't appreciate how much they have benefited in the past few years."

The union meeting was at 7:00 p.m., so they stopped at a hotel to rest. Franklin polished up the speech and added several proposals he'd push if elected president. "The first speech and column I made in my New Hampshire campaign was to cut the payroll tax on all workers from 7 to 3 cents a dollar, more than 60 percent, and make up the difference by raising the lid on income subject to the payroll tax, which was then about $60,000 a year. Everyone would get a cut, and even the few people who make more than that would get the cut on their first $60,000, even though they would pay more on the amount over that. Most important, the minimum wage earner would get a cut on the first dollar he or she earned.

"Speaking of the minimum wage, it should be raised immediately and tied to the annual cost of living. The minimum wage in 1940 was 50 cents an hour and is only $4.50 today, while the maximum wage paid to CEOs, ballplayers, and other performers has gone up by huge percentages."

He planned to add those promises plus his plan to increase the number of income tax brackets, if he could explain the changes clearly.

The number of brackets was the key to making the income tax as fair on higher incomes as it is on lower incomes, a point never understood by most taxpayers who are constantly belabored with the importance of simplifying the code by reducing the number of brackets. Too many people had bought into that solution, which actually helps only the wealthy. The fewer brackets the less overall tax they paid. At one time during the 1930s, Congress had approved a code which had a top bracket of income that affected only one taxpayer in the entire country: John D. Rockefeller, and he didn't complain because he was still the richest American.

Franklin also added an emphasis on his opposition to the NAFTA treaty. "It is a bill that makes it easier and more profitable for US companies to move their operations to Mexico. In turn, that makes it easier for those companies to compete with companies still in the US by cutting their prices on the products they make in Mexico. There was a company in my hometown of Columbus, Georgia, which moved operations to Mexico so it could cut the price of its product by just 10 percent to beat the price of its US competitors. It had been in Columbus for a century, its parent company was one of the oldest manufacturing companies in Columbus. Wasn't there some other way they could have made that cut and stayed in the US?

"Make no mistake, NAFTA is harmful, and no one has explained clearly where the good jobs are coming from to replace the ones lost. The most likely result is that cheaper US farm products going to Mexico will cut into agriculture employment in Mexico and create more Mexican immigrants to the US seeking jobs."

This speech got a rousing reception at the labor leaders meeting plus promises to distribute copies throughout the state before the primary. Franklin and Hardy stayed overnight in Hartford and went by the newspaper office to proofread the ad for Sunday. Franklin also bought a small ad for the Monday edition urging people to vote for him on Tuesday, and they made contacts with a couple of radio stations for spot commercials on Sunday and Monday.

They then proceeded to New York City, where Sutton had set up the campaign's most impressive headquarters, and also hired several additional campaign workers. Sutton was in an enthusiastic mood. "We're in play in Connecticut," he said, "and I'm getting good reports today about your talks in Hartford. The paper and TV station there both gave you good exposure. Your call for tax reform was on page 1, and a TV reporter was at the union meeting and got passages of your talks on the 11:00 p.m. news, including the statement that NAFTA is harm. You must use that phrase more in New York."

Sutton then introduced the consultants he had hired for New York, or at least the highest paid. They were Jeremiah Jones, Joe Jacura, and Bennie Friedman. Jacura and Friedman had worked with Dukakis when he won New York in 1988, and Jones had been a consultant to Jesse Jackson and had talked with Jackson after Franklin's South Carolina victory. He felt Franklin had a good chance to win a large number of black votes in New York.

"We've got offices set up in eight cities," Sutton said, "which is not a lot in New York but give us a footprint. Clinton, Brown, and Tsongas all have more, of course. About all New Yorkers know about you is that you were shot at and missed in Miami."

"They know I'm a Roosevelt New Deal Democrat, don't they?" Franklin asked.

"Most of them don't know what the New Deal was and a lot of them don't know Franklin Roosevelt from Theodore Roosevelt if they have heard of either of them. Clinton and Brown have been out in the city for weeks. Clinton is very strong. The other thing they know about you is that you're from Georgia, just like Jimmy Carter, and Carter has fallen badly in favor since his presidency. Oddly, his efforts in behalf of the Israeli-Egyptian peace treaty, which has proven far more helpful to Israel through the years, was not popular among New York's Jewish population, confirming the old adage that no good deed goes unpunished. Ted Kennedy defeated Carter 59–41 percent in the Democratic primary in 1980 and twelve years later, New Yorkers are still wary of a candidate from Georgia. Carter, in a book, described New York as a state with a habit of sucking at the federal budget tit more than any other state in the union."

Franklin was a great admirer of New York, however, not only as the home state of Franklin Roosevelt, but as the state which also makes the largest financial contribution to the federal government and was the most important state, starting with Alexander Hamilton, in creating a strong central government.

The expanded campaign staff was working hard in New York. Then on Tuesday, the Connecticut votes came in. The result was a four-way battle among Franklin, Clinton, Brown, and Tsongas that see-sawed back and forth throughout the evening with Brown showing surprising strength. Clinton had made the mistake of taking a few days off to go to Little Rock for a round of golf at an all-white country club, which hurt him with the black vote. But toward ten o'clock, the group gathered around the TVs in Franklin's headquarters and were overcome with emotion not felt since the Florida results. Franklin edged ahead as the final returns came in. Obviously bolstered by a strong union vote in Hartford and a surprise showing in New Haven, site of Yale University, trailing only Clinton who had once been Yale's student body president.

"You still got a sympathy vote from Susie's death in Florida," Sutton speculated. "She was from New England and had gotten publicity in Connecticut when she was a basketball star."

"Those late speeches didn't hurt either," Hardy interjected. "The papers and TV had been full of coverage on Primary Day."

The margin was close, but Franklin was "the winner," edging Clinton by several thousand votes. Brown and Tsongas were close behind. Tsongas had announced he was suspending his candidacy before the votes, but his familiarity as a neighbor from Massachusetts carried him to nearly 20 percent of the total vote. Brown was the main surprise with 24 percent of the total while Clinton came in with 25 percent, to Franklin's 28 percent.

Brown immediately proclaimed that the race was now between him and Clinton. Like all the candidates, he still looked on Franklin as a phantom who would eventually disappear, but Connecticut was a jolt to both he and Clinton. They consoled themselves with the thought that if Tsongas had totally withdrawn, they would have been the leaders.

The reality was that going into New York, Clinton and Franklin had accumulated the most delegates, as Clinton had carried all the Super Tuesday states except Florida and then led in Michigan and Illinois.

Clinton now depicted both Brown and Franklin as "spoilers, whose continued candidacies were only helping President Bush in the general election." Brown had responded airily, "What is this, the politburo? I'm not the spoiler. Slick Willie is the spoiler. If he gets the nomination, he is going to ruin the whole Democratic Party."

Franklin didn't respond except to remind voters that he and Clinton had won the most primaries and had the most delegates, and New York could well determine the nominee.

Chapter Twenty-Five

WHAT WOULD FDR SAY TODAY

*We can never insure one hundred percent of the pop-
ulation against one hundred percent of the hazards
of life, but we have tried to frame a law which will
give some measure of protection against the loss of a
job and against a poverty-ridden old age.*
—Franklin D. Roosevelt,
presidential statement signing the Social
Security Act, August 14, 1935

The New York media gave the Connecticut primary a big play
the next day, and Franklin's new consultants felt his plurality was great impetus for the New York primary, which was
three weeks away. By now, Clinton and Brown, the better-known
candidates, were slashing away at each other. The New York media
was especially centered on the scandals and missteps that seemed to
follow Clinton around and had for years. He was running in his
fourteenth consecutive campaign, starting with his long shot bid
for an Arkansas congressional seat in 1974, which he narrowly lost,
establishing him at twenty-six as the brightest newcomer in Arkansas
politics. He ran again in 1976, winning the state attorney general's race, and then two years later he won his first term as governor,
becoming the nation's youngest governor at thirty-one. Arkansas had
gubernatorial races every two years, and in 1982, Clinton became the

nation's youngest ex-governor, losing to the Republican candidate after a hectic first term.

Clinton was crushed by his defeat but undeterred from his lifelong goal of political success. Significantly, Hillary began calling herself Hillary Clinton instead of Hillary Rodham. With the name change, her influence in the governor's office actually increased. She led Clinton's education reform initiative, while becoming one of the state's best-known lawyers, a point that bothered some voters.

Reflecting on elections he'd been involved in, Jacura complained that politicians underestimated the power of women. "They've got half the money in the country and all of the pussy," he joked.

Franklin allowed himself a half smile. He'd never heard that observation before and thought it was clever but a trifle sexist. Jacura noticed his discomfort. He'd been told that Franklin was a real prude, and he thought he needed to get over it before hitting the sidewalks of New York.

Fortunately, a trickle of money turned into a strong current after the Connecticut primary, replenishing Franklin's shrinking financial resources. He knew Clinton and Brown considered New York their Armageddon and would be putting all their resources and efforts into winning or leading in the state.

He decided to make as many speeches and distribute as much literature as possible. He felt a lot of New Yorkers would be favorable to his New Deal approach, such as a lower payroll tax, more income tax brackets to close the gap between the percentage paid by the lower earners and highest earners, a single-payer health insurance plan, and ending the long deadlock with Cuba and restoring the once friendly relationship and working to build an alliance with Russia.

As Franklin began to make his way through the groups and clubs Sutton had scheduled, he also mentioned his ideas for a cabinet post for a secretary of peace, which had not seemed to stir much reaction.

Then at a meeting in Greenwich Village, he was asked his opinion on allowing gays to join the armed services without restrictions.

"By 'gays' I assume you mean homosexuals," he said carefully. "I don't know of any laws that keep them from serving now, but I believe the military chiefs of staff, the Senate chairmen of the various services, and the secretaries of the services are in a better position to examine and make decisions on that matter, and as president, I would follow their advice."

There was visible disapproval from many in the group. Franklin was repeating the position he had consistently taken when the subject had come up. He knew that Clinton had danced around the subject but not definitely ruled out presidential support.

"What about same-sex marriage?" another man asked in a high-pitched voice.

"For centuries, in all societies and religions, marriage has been considered a relationship between a man and woman," Franklin answered. "It is the foundation of the family and for the perpetuation of the human race. I favor providing all rights to cohabiting adults, but as I said, every authority I know of long ago decided that legal marriage is a relationship between a man and a woman, and I believe that is certainly the opinion of the vast majority of the American people. Also, of course, two members of the same sex can't produce children."

There were some disgruntled sounds of disapproval, but they were definitely in the minority.

That was not the last time Franklin encountered the question of same-sex marriage or gays in the military, which seemed to be a first concern of the homosexual lobby. He had been told it was large and vocal in New York. Clinton had said he'd consider the issue, and to his advisers' surprise, the statement had not become an issue in the primaries as none of his other opponents openly opposed it nor made it an issue. Franklin, however, was the only one who had stated clearly that such a decision should be made by the chiefs of staff or senatorial chairmen.

As they left the meeting, Hardy said, "You were pretty tough on the queers in there."

Franklin quickly corrected him. "That's a term I've never used, not as a kid or a teenager. I always considered it derogatory and belittling. I also try to avoid using 'gay' because I still feel it is a perfectly good description of what the dictionary defines as 'light-hearted, mirthful' and only as a slang term for homosexual, same as 'queer.' 'Queer,' is defined in the dictionary as 'strange, odd, out of sorts, or homosexual.'

"I've never understood how such a good word as 'gay' got hijacked from regular use to mean homosexual instead of 'Our hearts were young and gay' or the *Gay Divorcee*, which was one of Astaire-Rogers' first and best movies in the mid-1930s."

"I'm with you," Hardy said, "but the consultants aren't going to like it."

Franklin shrugged it off. He was finding a warm reception for his advocacy of better relations with Cuba and steps toward an alliance with Russia, as well as his economic proposals.

He was still looking back at Clinton's election record with amazement and appreciation. If anyone could be called a professional campaigner, it was Clinton. Franklin didn't recall another politician with such a lengthy record of success, except maybe another former Arkansas governor, Orval Faubus, who was governor for twelve consecutive years in the 1950s and 1960s, after calling out the National Guard to block school integration in September 1957, resulting in US troops being sent to the state. Clinton himself was just entering public school in those days, but that was the history of politics in Arkansas. Faubus' long tenure had mostly been wiped from people's memory.

Franklin planned his biggest New York event in Hyde Park at FDR's museum, with a speech on what Roosevelt would be advocating if he was running for president in 1992. He told Sutton to spend what he needed to assure a large crowd on the Saturday before the primary. He also invited the Broadway star of *Evita* to sing "Don't Cry for Me, Argentina," after playing the recording of Bush's speech with that phrase in it from the New Hampshire campaign.

Franklin persuaded one of Roosevelt's granddaughters, whom he had met at a Warm Springs commemoration, to introduce him. Ironically, she had been stricken with polio just a few years before the Salk vaccine was perfected in 1957, which had virtually eliminated polio as a health threat not only in the United States but throughout the world. The research that produced the vaccine had been largely financed by the March of Dimes in Roosevelt's memory and by the Warm Springs Foundation, which continued to be the largest treatment center for polio victims in the world.

At a black church, Franklin gave a talk he had made at a New Hampshire church on Jesus telling Peter three times to "feed my sheep." He stressed his theory that blacks were not only discriminated because of their color but also because they were generally poor and that he hoped to encourage more black entrepreneurships, which was the surest path to higher income and at which they lagged behind such latecomers to the United States as Koreans and Indians from India, who had virtually taken over the motel industry through family connections and diligent work.

He realized that his editorials and columns would present a mixed record on such subjects as school integration and busing. He had actually felt schools were not the best place to begin forced integration and that the result would be the abandoning of public schools by many white families. Franklin had sent all his children and grandchildren to public schools, but in many systems, especially in the larger ones in the North and Midwest, the public school systems had become as racially segregated in 1992 as they were before the Supreme Court decisions that ruled school segregation unconstitutional. The result was certainly mixed as support for public schools by the many influential white families declined, and school officials were left to deal with problems that were more extensive than their resources.

Public schools in such cities as Baltimore, Atlanta, Detroit, and Chicago, not to mention most of New York City, had returned to segregated enrollments, and while a segment of middle-class blacks benefited, a large number of poorer blacks had actually seen their education opportunities decline. That was not a popular subject in New York, but it was a serious and ongoing problem that Franklin felt needed to be admitted and faced.

In the campaign, Jerry Brown was encountering problems with the large Jewish vote. Desperately trying to attract the black vote, Brown had proclaimed that Jesse Jackson would be his first choice for vice president, but Jackson had fallen out of favor with Jewish voters because of his connections with the Nation of Islam and the Reverend Farrakhan, both openly anti-Israel. Jackson had also referred in his 1984 campaign to New York as "Hymietown." The prospect of Jackson as vice president was one that turned many Jewish voters off for a variety of reasons and struck others as unabashed pandering to the black vote.

But Brown's worst burden was his support of a sales tax or a flat tax, which was broadly condemned, not just by his opponents, but by most of the media and by most New York Democratic leaders such as Senator Daniel Moynihan, who said it could destroy Social Security and Medicare.

Opposition ads depicted the flat or sales tax as a "gift to the rich," which Franklin fully agreed with. He had opposed such taxes his entire newspaper career and, of course, in all of his speeches and columns during the campaign. He felt, with some justification, that he was one of the most effective supporters of transferring the tax burden from the lowest earners to the highest earners, a cause he had continually supported long before Brown, a supposed liberal, began promoting the sales tax in the primaries.

Republicans had been supporting a consumer tax ever since the income tax began climbing in the 1920s. Mellon, while serving as secretary of the treasury, finally got the sales tax to a vote in the Republican-dominated senate in 1926 where it was handily defeated despite support from some conservative Democrats. It had never emerged as serious legislation since although as recently as 1990, it was being pushed by Southern legislators under the name of "a fair tax," a term made popular by Georgia representative John Linder and a radio talk show host in Atlanta by the name of Neal Boortz, who wrote a couple of books on the subject.

The event at Hyde Park turned out well, a beautiful spring Saturday, a crowd from throughout Upper New York plus many from New York City. Lily Pons got an appreciative applause when she sang "Don't Cry for Me, Argentina." "We're sending a recording of that to President Bush to play on the morning of November 7, Franklin told the crowd to laughter and cheers. Several speakers spoke before Franklin, including former governor Carl Sanders, who had come up from Georgia; Senator Sam Nunn of Georgia, and Representative Elliott Levitas of DeKalb County, a longtime congressman from the district served by Franklin's main newspaper.

"On this land, and in that house," Franklin said, "is where the Third American Revolution was born and nurtured and, in many ways, it was the most important revolution. The first was fought to throw off British control and for the colonies to unite into a new country, an idea planted at a meeting in Albany, New York, in 1754, organized by who else but Benjamin Franklin—no kinship I know of. Franklin was the first American who recognized that only through unity could the scattered, small, and quarrelsome English colonies succeed and prosper. The immediate concern was encroachment by French settlers to the north and by Indians in the lands, where the English were pushing westward. The French and Indian War had pitted those two forces against the English colonies. It was at this time that Franklin, already a successful newspaper publisher, printed the famous Unite or Die Cartoon, believed to be the first editorial cartoon, showing a snake, cut into thirteen pieces from its head to tail, with each piece named for one of the thirteen English colonies.

"Benjamin Franklin outlined a plan for unifying behind one central government, mainly for defense purposes. Seven colonies sent representatives to the Albany meeting, and those delegates approved Franklin's plan, which contained many features later included in the US Constitution, composed some thirty-three years later. But in 1754 the other colonies failed to ratify the actions of the Albany Convention, and the colonies continued on their separate ways. But Franklin and his supporters had defined the path to the future, and to the first American Revolution.

"That revolution period actually spread over several years, including the formation of the first Continental Congress, the Declaration of Independence, the Revolutionary War, the Articles of Confederation, the adoption of the US Constitution, formation of the first federal government headed by George Washington, and several years later of the Louisiana Purchase in 1803, which created the huge land mass that has become the United States. Each step along the way was bold and revolutionary and required the same vision that produced the latter two great revolutions. In each revolution, the walls of ignorance and fear which trapped other countries and other generations had to be scaled or torn away. And in each revolution, New York and New Yorkers played an essential role.

"As the nation moved from the Colonial period and the Agrarian Age, New York became the model and the driving force in creating the industrial society. One of the first great cooperative state and national projects, funded with money from the entire nation, was the Erie Canal, which connected New York's port with the Great Lakes area and made the fledging United States one of the leading nations in the world in trade and development. It was an early example of state and federal cooperation, with private input, that has fueled most of the giant steps toward becoming the great nation of 1992.

"As the US grew and prospered, it was still divided and weakened by the unresolved dilemma that baffled both the men who wrote the Declaration and the group that formulated the Constitution, the question of human slavery, so prevalent in the Southern states and a major economic factor for the entire nation. By 1850, the US was one of the few nations in the western world that still sanctioned slavery. As Thomas Jefferson had predicted, slavery was like a cowbell in the night, which would finally ring one day and call the nation to a fateful showdown. Throughout the early part of the eighteenth century, the conflict on slavery was held at bay, but in 1860, the reckoning was finally at hand, not only to resolve the problem of slavery, but to determine what kind of nation had been founded in 1788—one nation, indivisible or merely a loose collection of states which could be broken apart when one or more states could not concur with the others. It was the issue that had first brought Benjamin Franklin's group to Albany, New York, in 1754, the issue which had been the most challenging decision for the fifty-five men who produced the Constitution and had been the issue Alexander Hamilton and George Washington had fought and insisted on to win the first revolution. Even old Andrew Jackson, so belligerent and cantankerous on many subjects, is best known for his famous toast: 'Our federal union. May it always be preserved.'

"The Republican Party, formed just eleven years earlier, was expected to offer the main opposition in 1860 to the dominant Democratic Party of the president, James Buchanan, which was still dominated by the slave states. In 1857, the US Supreme Court's infamous Dred Scott decision had declared that slaves were legal property and not subject to interference by the federal government. The Democratic Party split into Southern and Northern wings in the summer of 1860, which gave the Republicans a sure path to victory in the presidential race since the electoral vote would be split three or four ways. The leading Republican candidate for president as the campaign began was a New Yorker, US Senator William Seward. Seward was well-known, a strong speaker, and while he was anti-slavery, he was not an abolitionist, which made him more acceptable to the slave states, although their leaders all vowed to oppose any Republican. But then Seward delivered a compelling speech against the Dred Scott decision which left no doubt as to how he stood against extending slavery to territories in the west and accused Supreme Court Chief Justice Roger Taney of being in collusion with President Buchanan.

"Taney was so infuriated that he said he would not administer the oath of office to Seward if he should be elected president. Later Seward delivered his most famous speech in which he declared there is an irrepressible conflict on the subject of slavery, and that the United States must, sooner or later, become entirely a slaveholding nation, or entirely a free-labor nation.

"Seward had now become the leader of his party and also of the anti-slavery forces in the nation, which made him vulnerable at the nominating convention which wanted a candidate less divisive and controversial.

"Ironically, they settled on Abraham Lincoln, a one-term congressman from Illinois who had won praise in 1858 for his senatorial campaign debates with the Democratic presidential candidate, Steven Douglas. Lincoln had declared that the nation could not survive half-free and half-slave, but he was considered less objectionable to the South than the better-known Seward.

"At the convention in the summer of 1860, Seward led on the first ballot with 173 delegates to 102 for Lincoln. But the tide turned, partly due to the opposition to Seward by the influential newspaper publisher Horace Greeley, who had turned against Seward over a trifling grievance. The hearts of most of the delegates were still with Seward, but they became convinced by his enemies that he could not win a single Southern state. Ironically, neither did Lincoln, although he did win an electoral majority. The popular votes split four ways, with Lincoln getting only 39 percent of the popular vote in the general population.

"Seward went on to serve as Lincoln's secretary of state with great distinction and was the target of an assassin on the same night Lincoln was assassinated. Seward was badly wounded but recovered his health enough to oversee the purchase of Alaska from Russia, thus attaining the territory which would become the nation's valuable forty-ninth state.

"History does not reveal its alternatives, of course, which may be just as well, but in retrospect, it is interesting to contemplate the fate of the nation if Seward had maintained his delegate lead at the 1860 Republican convention and become president instead of Abraham Lincoln. My own conclusion is that while Lincoln proved a historic leader, that Seward as president would have been a stronger hand, the war would have been shorter, the union would have been preserved, the slaves would have been freed and fewer northerners and southerners would have lost their lives.

"In a speech to Congress in February of 1860, Seward used much of the language Lincoln had made famous after his election. They were of similar mind and of similar sentiment in keeping the union insoluble, despite the disunion then threatened over the issue of slavery."

"The Republican Party in the north does not seek to force our system on the South," Seward proclaimed. "You are sovereign on the subject of slavery within your own borders, nor do we harbor any ulterior motive to introduce Negro sovereignty...the bonds of the union are not simply its written contracts or roads or train tracks and trade routes that facilitate commerce and social contact...the strongest bonds are the millions of contented, happy human hearts linked by affection to their democratic government, the first and the only such government that has ever existed, which takes heed always of their wants."

That speech of Seward's received wide praise and acceptance. Even Frederick Douglas, a Negro leader of the abolitionist movement, called it a masterly effort to reassure the timid wing of his party. Seward is the ablest man in his party and deserved its presidential nomination, Douglas said.

"That was a sentiment widely held by most Republicans at the time. They felt Seward's previously harsh words such as irrepressible conflict had been softened to make him acceptable as a candidate. Actually, Seward's convention supporters became over-confident but his several enemies, most importantly Greeley, remained adamantly against him, and the dark horse Lincoln slowly gained support until the convention, held in his home state of Illinois, nominated him. He was less experienced than Seward, who was a former New York governor, emotionally less prepared for the tribulations that lay ahead for the next president, but Lincoln did keep the union together, and with the Gettysburg Address, gave it a new identity and more defined mission.

"President and General US Grant perhaps summed up the Civil War best for both sides when he remarked of Confederates: 'Never have so many fought so nobly for such an ignoble cause.'

"Thus, the second great revolution that created the United States resulted in a strengthening of original bonds between the states, assuring that it would remain one nation, not scattered provinces such as Europe, Latin America, and nearly every other large territory had become.

"The third revolution, of course, began here at Hyde Park, in the mind, imagination, vision, and humanity of a man whose legs were crippled to the point that he could not walk or stand alone without help. Many people never knew how crippled Franklin Roosevelt really was, because he never accepted or looked the part. And certainly he never acted the part. He summoned the rest of the nation to stand up and follow him out of the chaos of the economic depths into which it had fallen as he became its president, and then summoned the Free World to march with him in defeating the most serious threat to the whole world's freedom. That is Franklin Roosevelt's legacy to us today, one that marks him, in my mind, as the greatest American president, and indeed as one of the greatest leaders of all times.

"I say this to you, not because he was a New Yorker, but because he was an American, as were the other leaders I have mentioned today. I hope you will forgive me this history recital, but New York history is the story of the United States and how it came to its present eminence as the towering national entity in the world.

"New York provides the example for progress in so many fields—commerce, industry, retailing, entertainment, the arts, the theater, and in absorbing the diversity of nationalities, cultures, languages, and races into its great melting pot. New York is the example that shows the entire country what can be achieved. Yes, I love New York and have enormous regard for the role its people have played in the development not just of the United States but of the world.

"But I come today to speak of what Franklin Roosevelt would think and plan if he was running for president in 1992. He would see not only the tall buildings but also the blocks of slums, the hungry and homeless, living on the streets, the tottering infrastructure, the worn-out taxicabs, and he would be appalled that such conditions still exist in the nation he raised from the Depression and showed a path to a better way of life seventy years ago.

"In his second inaugural speech, Roosevelt said, 'I see one-third of a nation ill-housed, ill-clad, ill-nourished.' Would he see a nation much different today? The United States had about 130 million people during his second term, and today it has more than 300 million. Can we say that a third of them still do not answer to that description? When you walk down the alleyways of New York City, you will find them. They live in the richest nation in history and thus enjoy many of its benefits but many are like beggars in velvet, left behind in too many ways, some without modern plumbing or indoor heat or the necessities for health maintenance; some sleeping in buildings overrun with rats, their children ill-housed, ill-clothed, and ill-nourished just as they were in Roosevelt's day.

"President Ronald Reagan infamously proclaimed that 'we declared a war on poverty and poverty won.' But it was not victory by poverty, it was a surrender by political leaders—such as Ronald Reagan. They withdrew from the battle.

"I believe Franklin Roosevelt would declare a renewed war on poverty. When he was inaugurated president in 1933, the United States was not a rich nation in comparison with some others. It became a great nation when the New Deal programs created jobs and built schools and then finally engineered the great economic engine that produced the arms, the planes, the tanks, and the armies that won World War II. The nation met that challenge because President Roosevelt set impossible goals for the people and the nation's industries, and they met those goals, courageously and magnificently, even though many leaders said the goals were impossible. The man who could not walk without help never believed that, and the nation emerged to take its place as the leader among nations and become the drum major for the future."

Franklin paused to let a wave of applause subside and collect his thoughts for the major point of his talk, which was Roosevelt's support of a fair and progressive tax system to finance the kind of government necessary to meet the needs of a growing nation and fulfill its responsibilities to the rest of the world.

"Taxes were not prominent on the early New Deal agenda since Roosevelt realized they were likely to encounter the strongest opposition, and he was right. It was not until June 1935 that he sent Congress a package of bills which were labeled 'the second hundred days' and were in many ways more far-reaching than the first one hundred days. Their effect on the nation then and to this very day was historic.

"The tax proposals included a steeply graduated individual income tax to replace the tax that brought in very little revenue because individual incomes were so low, a tax on inheritances and a corporation income tax scaled to the size of a corporation's gross income.

"This was the first New Deal proposal that reached directly into the pockets of the wealthy and the outcry was louder than had greeted any of the other New Deal measures, many of which had helped bolster the economy and actually benefited businessmen as much or more than the workers and consumers.

"William Randolph Hearst, whose support had pushed Roosevelt over the top for the 1932 Democratic nomination, directed his editors to use the phrase 'soak the rich' in all references to the tax measures and use the words 'raw deal' instead of 'new deal' when writing of Roosevelt's overall plans. The labels stuck, in a broad range of criticisms.

"Actually the tax proposals were in part an answer to Roosevelt's increasing criticism by left-wing politicians, mainly Louisiana's Huey Long, who had announced he would run as a third party candidate for president in 1936 on a platform of income redistribution. Hearing Roosevelt's tax message, Long, then a US senator, shouted 'Amen.' Roosevelt had actually advocated such tax changes while he was governor of New York, so his 1935 plan should not have been a surprise.

"Roosevelt vowed to keep Congress in session all summer in 1935 until it acted on the tax measures and the rest of the Second New Deal. Many parts of the tax bill were amended or eliminated, and what finally emerged did little to restructure wealth, but a precedent had been set and a model designed to make the income tax more progressive and that continued through the war years and afterward. In 1960, the tax on income above $450,000 a year was still 70 percent. That affected only a handful of wage earners, but imagine how much revenue such a tax would bring in from the multimillion dollar incomes of 1992. I'm not suggesting that, just mentioning how much Americans paid in the past to finance a government that performed the functions that laid the foundation for today's progress and benefits.

"In May of 1935, the President also proposed, and Congress passed, a bill creating the Rural Electrification Administration, REA. At that time, nine of every ten farms did not have access to electricity, which as I've mentioned in many speeches divided the nation into city dwellers and country dwellers. Every city's lighted streets ended at the city limits, wrote one public power advocate, and beyond lies darkness. I was fortunate to grow up in a small Georgia town in the 1930s, which had electricity all my life, and I could see what a different world the area was outside the city limits. No other single development of the New Deal affected the lives of more Americans than the REA, and yet today sixty years later, there are still some areas in rural states without electricity and there are millions of people around the world without what most Americans consider a basic necessity. In those countries, women are especially deprived as they still cook as their grandmothers did, wash clothes by hand, dry them by the winds, have no vacuum cleaners or refrigerators or sewing machines. There are many women who live and work like the peasants of the pre-industrial age in our own country and there are millions in other countries and when their government asks for our help we send them guns and arms instead of toilets and washing machines.

"What a difference it would make in the lives of those people, and probably in their politics and the way they look at America, especially women and children, and even the men, if they would consent to give up their war games and accept peaceful goods rather than killing machines.

"Franklin D. Roosevelt ignored the voices of dissent and ridicule in the 1930s and those who called him a Communist and worse because he recognized the people's needs and acted to help them. Thank God, such a leader was in that position in those critical years when other nations were looking to dictators such as Hitler, or descending further into poverty and despair such as India, China, and most of Africa.

"In a nation much richer than it was in the 1930s, would Roosevelt demand any less? Would he be content to still tolerate squalor in our streets amid the shining towers of our wealth? He would be distressed, I believe, but not surprised. He had to exert every political trick and plea to get social security and other redistributive measures approved in a nation virtually on its economic knees. He knew the difficulties but he ignored the obstacles and plunged ahead and we are so much the better for it.

"Roosevelt would be pleased if he were running this year to behold the progress made on his ideas for national health care, such as Medicare and Medicaid, Head Start, and federal funds to education, all approved in Lyndon Johnson's war on poverty, but he would be disappointed and challenged by the failure to make health care truly national by approving a single-payer plan financed by a slight adjustment to the payroll tax on higher incomes, which pay so little today toward Social Security or Medicare or Medicaid. I believe Roosevelt would call for another War on Poverty just as he called for the nation to commit to the war on the Axis powers in World War II, and as President Eisenhower did to finance the interstate highway system and as President John Kennedy did to finance the space program that sent men to the moon.

"In his greatest speech, the one to the Democratic convention in 1936, Roosevelt declared, 'Governments can err, presidents make mistakes, but better the occasional faults of a government that lives in a spirit of charity than the consistent omissions of a government frozen in the ice of its own indifference.'"

The crowd rose to its feet at the famous lines with which Roosevelt had defined the fight he was waging for the people's cause. Franklin went on to say there were predictions that Roosevelt would not be reelected in 1936 and that Democrats would be punished in Congress for the New Deal programs adopted in his first term. But on Election Day 1936, he won the largest popular vote majority of any president since James Monroe in 1820, carrying forty-six of the forty-eight states, while a record number of Democratic congressmen were elected.

"That was the reward for bold actions and straight talk that have been missing from our debates in recent years and which need to be renewed as Roosevelt and Johnson renewed them in 1936 and 1964 and swept to unprecedented victories."

Franklin had finished with a flourish and hoped he hadn't talked too long but the setting and the occasion had inspired him. He also noted an unusual number of media, print and electronic, scribbling away and taking many photographs.

Hardy, Brad, and Charlie all greeted him enthusiastically. "Boss, that was great," Brad exulted. "Who knew you were such a New Yorker?"

"I wasn't just pandering, as Tsongas might charge. I really believe that New York was the engine for the phenomenal progress this country has made, giving the central government the strength and ideas it needed to scale the heights of its opportunities."

"I like that phrase," Charlie said. "Let me be sure and get it in a news release." An attractive young lady stopped to talk with Franklin. She was obviously a reporter, and she also wanted to ask if he needed any campaign workers. She knew he had lost his most important consultant in the assassination incident. She looked familiar and Franklin realized she was Joan Walsh, a commentator he had seen on network TV and who had greatly impressed him. He gave her a card and told her he'd love to talk to her but wasn't sure he could match her salary. "I'll call," she said. "I think you're right about so many things that aren't being told the people and I'd like to help you tell them."

"Great, be sure and call. I can't think of anyone better to tell them than an attractive TV commentator."

On the way back to the office, Hardy asked if he really meant that William Seward might have been a better president than Abraham Lincoln.

"Well, Lincoln has become our most revered political figure, and with justification, but he had the least public experience of any candidate who had ever been president—until I announced—one two-year term in Congress some ten years before he was elected president. Seward, by contrast, had been both a governor of New York, the largest state, and its US senator for ten years at the time of the 1860 convention. He was widely considered as the leading Republican in the nation and the clear favorite for the presidential nomination, which he expected until the emergence of Lincoln just before the convention. Seward swallowed his disappointment, however, and became Lincoln's most valuable ally as Secretary of State and a frequent collaborator on Lincoln's speeches. He was widely credited with preventing any foreign nations from recognizing the

Confederacy, especially Great Britain, whose recognition could have changed the outcome of the war.

"Lincoln, despite his steadfast support against secession had little leadership experience and nothing like the recognition that Seward enjoyed among other political leaders. Seward's proven leadership could have shortened the war by two years and saved many lives as well as leaving the nation less torn asunder. He apparently lost the nomination because of his more adamant opposition to slavery, which was the basis for the formation of the Republican Party in 1854. Seward deserves a higher place in US history than he receives. Unfortunately his name is best known for the phrase Seward's Folly, which was widely used to describe his purchase of Alaska while secretary of state, a deal eventually comparable to the purchase of Manhattan Island from Indians for a few strands of beads."

"By the way," said Charlie, "you might go easier on that adulation for Franklin Roosevelt. He's not remembered that fondly by everybody, if he's remembered at all." Charlie had been born in Maine, one of the two states that didn't vote for Roosevelt in 1936.

"I realize that," Franklin admitted. "That's why I keep talking about him. The political differences in the US today in many respects, are still over the politics and direction that Roosevelt determined. Even the words today are similar to the words used against him and are still repeated by opponents of what the New Deal accomplished. The debate actually goes back to the Constitutional Convention, and if I can say anything to tip the scales toward remembering that it was Roosevelt and his supporters who forced the nation onto the path toward a stronger central government that is aware and cares about responsibilities that only it can achieve, then my campaign will not have been in vain.

"Roosevelt was the leader who assured the direction to that path. There were many who helped him, of course, for the job was momentous and the opposition powerful and unbending. Perhaps only in a time such as the Great Depression, and then World War II, could anyone have transformed the US into the modest welfare state and the industrial powerhouse that it has become."

"The country was stronger than one man," Charlie protested. "I'm trying to think of some Republicans I supported in my early years who I felt were better choices than Roosevelt."

"There weren't any," Franklin said flatly. "I've looked through the history books for one and could only find Republicans who were either outright isolationist on the war or wanted to go back to Calvin Coolidge's policies to cure the Depression, or were a mixture of both. The best they could come up with to run against Roosevelt in 1940 when there was even opposition from some Democrats against him for breaking the so-called third term precedent was Wendell Willkie, a utility company executive, who had been a Democrat and only turned against Roosevelt when he tried to take away some of the tax advantages that utility companies enjoyed in those days. Wilkie had never been elected to a political office, kind of like me. He was foisted on the Republicans mainly by Henry Luce and his *Time-Life* magazines because the party machinery couldn't come up with a candidate from its congressional or government ranks."

"I recall that Willkie was no isolationist," Charlie put in.

"That was his saving grace and why he got the nomination. Even most of the Republican leaders realized that Hitler's Germany, then dominant in Europe and seemingly unstoppable, had to be opposed. But Willkie was ready to join in repealing much of the New Deal. He did better in the general election than Alf Landon in 1936, but Roosevelt still won 57 percent of the popular vote and defeated Willkie 449 to 82 in the electoral vote. He won that year although every former Democratic candidate for president spoke out against him, including Al Smith. The opposition labeled him a Communist, and the votes were sharply divided along economic lines. Roosevelt won an estimated 75 percent of voters who paid nothing in rent but only 40 percent of people whose average monthly rent was $65 or higher. He carried every large city while Willkie won in the country and smaller towns, a pattern that hasn't changed much in seventy years.

"I believe he is the Roosevelt who belongs on Mount Rushmore, rather than Theodore, but there is little chance that Franklin's image will ever join him. His supporters were numerous, but his opponents are more implacable and their memories are long. The best evidence is that one of the first measures approved by the Republicans in Congress when they finally obtained the majority in 1947, just two years after Roosevelt's death, was a constitutional amendment stating that no person shall be elected to the office of president more than twice, and no person who has held the office more than two years of a term to which another person was elected shall be elected more than once. The amendment was approved before some of the new Republicans had found their seats in quite clearly a burst of stored up rage and resentment against the man who had been elected president four times. But it was a mischievous action, the first Constitutional amendment since 1933, and the only one approved by Congress until 1960, a total period of nearly thirty years.

"If the amendment had been in force in 1940, when Roosevelt was elected to a third term, or in 1944, when he was elected to a fourth term, it is difficult to imagine who would have emerged to replace him in those most critical years for the nation, and indeed for the world. The Republicans were down to Willkie, who would have died in his first term in 1943, and later Thomas E. Dewey, a youthful governor of New York, with no foreign policy experience. The Democrats also had no viable alternatives. Jim Farley wanted to run in 1940, but he had mainly been a political fund-raiser. John Garner was too old and not a real New Dealer. Henry Wallace, who became Roosevelt's running mate for vice president in 1940, was widely viewed as a Communist sympathizer and failed badly when he ran as a third-party candidate in 1948. Roosevelt was the indispensable candidate and if the Twenty-Second Amendment had been in force the outcome is distressing to contemplate.

"In the years since, ironically, the only two likely third-term candidates were two Republicans, Dwight Eisenhower in 1960 and Ronald Reagan in 1988, so perhaps the nation owes those angry Republicans of 1947 a debt of gratitude. The amendment easily obtained the necessary margins in the House and Senate, went to the states, and was approved by the necessary two-thirds majority by March 1951, just four years later. So I'll keep talking about Roosevelt and hope some other candidate will join me. I haven't heard any stand up for the New Deal as strongly as it deserves."

"Well," said Hardy, "They've probably read the polls, which say the country wants less government, lower taxes, and a balanced budget."

Franklin smiled ruefully. "Andrew Mellon couldn't have asked for better polls. In fact, he was getting similar results when Roosevelt won by such large margins. In 1932, they were only polling people who had telephones or cars. They missed most of Roosevelt's voters."

"Maybe today they aren't polling people who still don't have indoor toilets." Brad laughed. "Or who have only one car and a twenty-inch TV set."

"Or who have never heard of Thomas Franklin," threw in Jack Hardy.

Chapter Twenty-Six

A WALK IN CENTRAL PARK

Here is my principle: Taxes should be levied according to ability to pay. That is the only American principle.

—Franklin D. Roosevelt, address at
Worcester, Massachusetts, October 21, 1936

They were back to the New York office by then and got a warm greeting from Sutton. "Your speech was carried live on one TV station," he told Franklin. "I saw it and thought it was powerful if a trifle long and a little hard on rich people, which makes it tough to raise money from them."

"Speaking of money, have we got any left?" Franklin asked.

"We are spending faster, but I expect a big collection after that speech. What other states are we going to make an effort in?"

"Let's look at what's left," Franklin said, pulling out his list of the primaries and caucuses. "For some strange reason, Democrats have scheduled six primaries on March 13. The only candidate who has had an active campaign in all of them is Clinton although the names of all the serious candidates are on the ballots."

"They set up this to sift out the riff raff candidates who don't have much money or organization," Sutton remarked, "and that could include us."

Brad begged to differ. "We've got a good chance in New York," he said, "and that's the one that counts most."

"Wisconsin looks promising," Franklin suggested. "Carter won it in 1976, and it was the state that gave him the momentum for the nomination. Also the Peanut Brigade was very active there, and we may be able to get some of them back this year."

"What about the New York campaign?" Sutton asked.

"Let's get some TV spots with segments from that Hyde Park speech and also medium-sized ads in selected weeklies in upper New York. I'll keep making appearances in the New York City suburbs, with a few visits to Wisconsin if we decide there's a chance to make a decent showing there. By the way, a woman named Joan Walsh will be calling you. She's a regular on TV and in some magazines and wants to help. She'll be a great asset, I think, and give us some valuable exposure as well as a bit of credence with the New York media."

"I've heard of her," Sutton said. "Can we afford her?"

"I think so. She may just take a short leave from her regular job."

Franklin then called Milton Jones in Columbus to ask whether he could get some Peanut Brigaders for a week in Wisconsin. Milton was enthusiastic. "We had a great time in Wisconsin in 1976," he said, "but that was sixteen years ago and Billy was a big hit, but I don't think he'll come this year. I'll see what I can do."

Sutton lined up a major appearance for Franklin in Milwaukee for the next week, and Franklin shuffled through his speeches for one he'd been wanting to make. He'd once considered Wisconsin a progressive state, which had been a strong supporter of New Deal ideas, but Reagan carried it handily in 1980 and 1984, and Bush had beaten Dukakis there in 1988.

Franklin knew what he wanted to emphasize but needed new ways of saying it. He realized he was sounding too downbeat. "Our income tax has been skewered from the rich to the middle class and the focus must be changed if the middle class prospers as it did in the years before 1970," he told Hardy on their flight to Milwaukee. "That needs to be recognized before the gap between the rich and top middle class becomes too wide to ever deal with. That is why this election, in the year 1992, is so critical to changing the economy to one that raises taxes on the richest Americans while shifting that money to the middle income. It will be the essential step in restoring a demand-side economy."

On the way to the meeting site they stopped at the newspaper office where a meeting with the editorial board had been arranged. The editors asked reasonable questions. Franklin emphasized what a unique moment in history this was, with Russia enfeebled, and its satellites, including Cuba, in need of help. In the Middle East, Iran and Iraq were exhausted from their ten-year war, plus Iraq was now shattered by the one-hundred-hour war with the United States. "We need to seek peaceful settlements in that area and hope it spreads to the rest of the Middle East." The editors told him that Clinton appeared very strong. "I know that," Franklin replied with a wan smile. "So did Udall against Carter in 1976."

At the meeting site, Franklin was greeted by a fairly large group of businessmen who looked prosperous. Not the best audience for the message he brought. "Today we live in a time not unlike the so-called Gilded Age, which was anything but gilded except for families like the Vanderbilts and the Rockefellers," Franklin began. "I was standing a few months ago in the Grand Ballroom of Biltmore, the grandest of the mansions built by the billionaires of that day. It was a monument to the extravagance, bad taste and supply-side economies of the nineteenth century. In itself, it illustrated how the US economy was changed during the New Deal, and changed in large measure because of the graduated income tax.

"Biltmore was constructed in 1895, as the country home of George Vanderbilt, a grandson of Cornelius Vanderbilt, who had accumulated one of the nation's largest fortunes. He started at sixteen, operating a small ferryboat between Staten Island and New York City. He competed with his business rivals by improving service and using daring, sometimes unfair, business tactics. But his big breakthrough came by way of a government contract, as has been the case for many wealthy families. His company was chosen to transport provisions for forts along New York Harbor during the war of 1812. By 1850 Vanderbilt had become the major steamship owner in the United States, hence his nickname Commodore. Soon he moved into the growing railroad industry, and by 1873 he owned railroads that reached as far west as Chicago.

"His grandson, George, devoted most of his inheritance to building Biltmore, a house that could rival the castles and palaces he had seen on his travels in Europe. Fortunately for North Carolina, he found in its mountains and climate the ideal spot for his dream. He bought one hundred thousand acres of land near Asheville, at the foot of the Blue Ridge Mountains, and for five years in the 1890s a veritable army of workers labored to produce the house, the gardens and pathways that became Biltmore.

"As a home it left something to be desired, being too drafty, inconvenient to town, the driveway was three miles long, and with enormous heating and cooling problems. But as a tourist attraction for post-World War II Americans, and an economic engine for the Asheville area, Biltmore has been an uncontested success, and at $12 a tourist the descendants of its builder, George, who still own Biltmore, may eventually recover the cost.

"The ballroom alone is larger than the average $100,000 house of today. Several mobile homes could be anchored in the dining room, and I was especially impressed with its libraries, which had shelves and shelves of neatly bound books. I had to wonder what they all could contain and if many of them had ever been opened.

"During the nineteen years, 1895–1914, that George Vanderbilt, his wife, and one child lived there, some eighty servants were required to maintain the house, cook the meals, and keep the grounds and gardens. Many of the servants lived at Biltmore, either in the below-ground level or in a dormitory-like arrangement on the fourth floor, from which they had the best view of the surrounding mountains.

"Vanderbilt died in 1914 of an appendectomy at the age of fifty-two. His grandson writes in a book about the estate, 'World War I reared its ugly head, income and inheritance taxes took their place in America's lives and fortunes.' Even a family as rich as the Vanderbilts could no longer afford a palace. Mrs. Vanderbilt moved out in 1929 and the house became a private corporation in 1932, so it could be opened to the public.

"Biltmore is assuredly worth visiting, but I would hated to have lived there. Like the Taj Mahal, the pyramids, and other of mankind's remarkable monuments, it was built to satisfy one man's pride and ego and in the late nineteenth century there were a few men and families in the United States with access to the sums of money that could buy them whatever extravagance their hearts desired. That was possible because there was no tax on the huge fortunes they accumulated. Adoption of the income tax amendment in 1913 was one of the truly pivotal events in US history, ranking alongside the Declaration of Independence, the Bill of Rights, and the Fourteenth Amendment in determining the kind of nation that would follow.

"The income tax was very light in its early years, and payroll deduction of the tax did not begin until 1943. There have been abuses and there have been injustices in the tax, but it has been the essential change that made possible the middle class and greatly broadened taxes on the affluent class, reducing some large fortunes but increasing many small fortunes. It also made it possible for the federal government to deal with the challenges of the Great Depression and World War II, while still allowing the maximum degree of individual liberty.

"The Vanderbilts may not be able to afford palaces today, but their descendants are still very well off and are still able to practice free enterprise in a free economy and in a society which provides consumers with more buying power. Where there were only a handful of affluent families in the nineteenth century, there are thousands today and millions of other Americans enjoy a standard of living virtually unknown in most of the world.

"Taxes are the price of civilization, as Justice Oliver Wendell Holmes once said, and they are also the price of maintaining civil order and discouraging revolution, two objectives which should be dear to those who call themselves conservatives and who enjoy more than the normal comforts and rewards of living in the United States.

"Despite the pressing problems of a diverse population, and the increasing intrusion of a troubled external world, the United States is a much more stable nation today than it was in 1913, when the income tax was adopted. The income tax is an important reason why and when considering the alternatives so visible in other countries, most Americans would have to conclude that their taxes buy a pretty good bargain.

"The rich are richer, the middle class has risen to unprecedented levels, until the last few years, the poor are not as poor, the governments at all levels have more revenue for the valuable and various services they provide, so what's not to like about the income tax system, unless you want to build a mansion that will be a tourist site fifty years from now. Instead let's encourage more people to build livable, affordable homes for 1992, which many still don't have, right here near the center of our nation. The middle class is visibly declining, and with it the middle-class institutions such as department stores and other businesses, which it helped finance and sustain during the thirty years after World War II. The trend is unmistakable and the solutions are not difficult: we need a revised tax structure but certainly not the one the Congress approved in 1986, which worsened the problem.

"In Wisconsin, where the great progressive Senator Robert LaFollette pioneered consumer protection laws and direct primary voting as early as 1901, the simple fact is that his hopes and missions are still incomplete. That should inspire Wisconsinites of today to seek ways to fulfill his dreams. Instead I sense a retreat from the philosophy that has built the United States of 1992 at a time when opportunity beckons so invitingly for us to move while the opportunity is available and present and build an even better example for other nations.

"People come to the United States and expect to see the nation of Astaire-Rogers movies and TV commercials but too often are surrounded with scenes of poverty and of a nation they thought belonged in the third world. The ragged edges of our nation are too evident. We don't need to live in mansions, but no one deserves to live in slums either, with scarce food and sometimes unclean water, in the most prosperous nation in history."

This was a message Franklin had been delivering throughout the campaign, but he had heard few splashes in the well. No urgency. No rising momentum of support for what he was saying. Instead the questions were more often about the growing national debt, the need for balancing the budget, and the fear that inflation and high interest rates would return if the government tried to launch another all-out war on poverty. "It may take debt," he exclaimed. "The nation has made its greatest progress in times its debt was highest. It has survived without balancing the budget since George Washington begged Congress for shoes and jackets for his soldiers at Valley Forge."

Franklin reviewed the three great revolutions that he felt had created the nation: the Revolution and its aftermath, including the adoption of the Constitution, the Civil War and wave of development that followed, and "most importantly, the New Deal and its programs that laid the foundation for modern living conditions and prosperity."

"Wisconsin led the way for much of this progress," he concluded, "and I ask you today for your vote to be the next Democratic presidential candidate and launch another New Deal and renew with vigor our war on poverty, which was not lost, as Reagan claimed, but was abandoned by weaker champions."

Franklin became more forceful as he finished and gained some enthusiastic applause, which he hoped inspired the several media types to give his speech good play throughout the state. He realized he was an unknown quantity in Wisconsin and had little to lose by being aggressive in his views.

As they left, Hardy and Charlie were uncertain. "You should have saved that for a labor group," Charlie said.

"Remind me to give it at the next few New York City groups," Franklin said.

Back at their New York City headquarters, they found Sutton in a buoyant mood. "Reports are looking good," he said. "We got some TV spots made with Joan Walsh in them relating some of the points you've made in speeches, with the Statute of Liberty in the background as you suggested, and they look and sound great. They'll be running on select channels this weekend. Also you need to do some interview spots with Joan, clearly identifying her as a member of the campaign, not a regular reporter. That'll get attention."

"Sounds good," Franklin said, "I'm anxious to see them. What do the polls show?"

"A close race among you, Clinton, Brown and Tsongas, with Clinton slightly in the lead."

As the candidates became more involved in New York, Brown called Clinton "the scandal of the week candidate." The New York media, always inclined toward sex and the sordid side of politics, found in Clinton a source of constant delight. The popular Phil Donohue TV Show invited Clinton as a guest and Donohue wanted to talk about nothing but the Jennifer Flowers accusations. Clinton gave his usual response that his marriage had problems but was solid now. He and Hillary never separated, and they loved each other. When Donohue continued to badger him on personal matters, Clinton finally said, "I don't think any decent human being should have to put up with the kind of questions you're putting me through. If you keep it up, we're just going to sit here a long time in silence." The audience gave Clinton a huge applause. One member of the audience told a TV commentator, "I'm not even for Clinton but I think this is ridiculous." The audience cheered and applauded again. Clinton had turned the corner on the personal attacks and transformed himself into a victim.

"That was when his poll numbers began going up," Jacura noted. He was Franklin's main New York campaign director, and he wanted him out on the hustings every day meeting and speaking with certain groups. New York is so large that such appearances were mainly for the purpose of getting media attention, which Clinton and Brown were dominating. Brown's was not all positive. His flat tax proposal and his sales tax idea were both unpopular to most New York voters but he continued to pound them. Franklin's position in opposing them was strong and needed more emphasis, Jacura told him. Brown was also still hurt by embracing Jesse Jackson.

Tsongas, surprisingly, seemed to be a beneficiary of Brown's decline, but Franklin also picked up slightly. He had not made a hard bid for the Jewish vote, although stressing his support for the existence and security of Israel. He also stressed that Israel had some responsibility for preventing all-out war in the Middle East.

Donohue had another program which included Clinton, Brown and also Franklin, and the tone was elevated with the emphasis on the issues. Franklin took the most liberal view, repeating his example of the "big pie economy," which was leaving too few crumbs on the floor for the poorest American, not to mention the world as a whole. He kept stressing that Brown's plans would sweep up most of the crumbs as well as reduce the size of the pie.

Donohue did question Franklin on his lack of experience in government service, but Franklin parried him successfully by pointing to the emergence of Ross Perot as a serious presidential contender. "He has no political experience and his main issue is to reduce the deficit which would make the economy even worse," Franklin pointed out. "He's Jerry Brown without the political experience, and I don't know which is worse."

Donohue then switched to racial issues and mentioned that Franklin, in his editorials, had seemed to oppose integration in public schools. It was not a subject Franklin was completely comfortable with because the simple fact was that he really didn't believe forced integration of schools was the best answer to improving the lives of black children or white children. He had firsthand experience with the dilemma as a longtime Southern resident and an editorial writer during the period of the racial revolution from 1960 onward.

His children and grandchildren had all attended public schools, and his children were among the earliest to be integrated in the midsixties. As an editor and publisher in the cities where they lived, Franklin felt his family needed to set an example of support for public schools. In Opelika, two private schools had opened the first year of integration, and a significant number of children from the top white families left the public schools and transferred, including the children of some Auburn professors, who were usually supportive of school integration.

Franklin's children never had any trouble from the transition but school systems across the South, and in the large cities of the north slowly lost many of their best white students as their families either moved or sent their children to the new academies. The result was less financial support for public schools and eventually less fan support for their sports teams.

State financial support for schools, blacks and whites, had never been high on the list of priorities for Southern legislators. During slavery days, blacks were actually forbidden to learn to read, and after slavery was abolished, there were still many educational barriers to former slaves. Strict segregation of schools was certainly one of them. Thus the states had to build two systems, one for whites and another for blacks, from funds that had scarcely been sufficient for one system. In addition there was the task of providing two sets of teachers, with most black teachers and principals placed in all-black schools to handle students most in need of strong discipline and the best teaching. Predictably, the black teachers, who were products of schools, and sometimes churches, far inferior in background to white teachers and principals, lost their jobs. They had to adapt to teaching white students, who often knew more about the subject than they did.

To bake a pie you first need the right ingredients, and they were scarce in the early days of school integration in the South. But miraculously, for many schools the mixture worked. There was the expected grumbling, and even a few fights, but not nearly as many as anticipated. The children of both races proved more accepting of the situation than their parents. Many schools eased the transition by setting up separate classrooms for lower-performing and high-performing students, giving teachers a more cohesive group of students and making it possible for even poor students to attain status among their classmates. This system worked in smaller schools, especially where whites and blacks were about equal in number. Franklin's children attended a high school almost fifty-fifty in racial makeup, but had only a handful of blacks in their individual classes. This was a pattern in many Southern schools and was allowed despite the court-ordered "integration" of schools.

Franklin had always advocated that what blacks really needed was more access to money. Blacks are not segregated only because of their skin color, he argued, they are also segregated because they are generally poor. All that was too complicated, or even debatable, to explain in a political campaign. The conventional wisdom was that racial integration was right and proper and the best way for blacks to advance.

Racial equality will follow "economic equality," Franklin told one black church group, most of whom looked reasonably affluent and on the brink of creating a middle class of their own. But he could tell that was not the message most of them wanted to hear. "I'm the only candidate Democrat or Republican who will work to open more doors for blacks to the middle class," he proclaimed, "and that is the next and most important step toward equality, economic equality. You can never change your color but you can change your economic condition. Look at all the black athletes who are now millionaires and should own some of the teams they have made successful and which should be hiring back executives. But how many black owners or executives are there, compared to black players? About as many as there are white point guards and white defensive ends.

"It all starts with money, and that starts with making our tax system more equitable so that the $10 an hour worker is not paying the same percentage of his income, or even more, in taxes as his boss who makes $2,000 an hour. Sadly, that's the difference in many companies."

Franklin went to other black churches and also to union meetings and gave his message on income equality. The newspapers covered a few speeches, and portions of them were made into TV spots which Joan voiced beautifully and effectively. She was proving a great asset in New York and in raising the image of the campaign to a more serious level than it previously enjoyed.

Then another appearance with Phil Donohue for the three surviving Democratic candidates. Donohue laid off Clinton's personal problems this time, having found that his misadventures did not seem to have the same impact as Gary Hart's did in 1988. The big differences, Donahue believed, was the strong and unyielding support of Clinton by his wife, Hillary, compared to the tepid support by Hart's wife and Hart's less-than-convincing defense of his background. Clinton apparently had no shame, only defiance and determination. He was weathering that storm as well as the storm over his draft maneuvering.

Donohue did disagree with Jerry Brown's tax plan, explaining how it shifted the tax burden from high earners to lower earners. Clinton and Franklin both joined in enthusiastically but Donohue gave Clinton the most time. When he turned to Franklin he first asked about his statement on gays in the military and opposition to same sex marriage. Franklin stood his ground pointing out again that the chiefs of staff and other military leaders were more conversant on the subject and he would follow their advice. The other two candidates were less definite, both saying they'd take a look at the matter as president, and wouldn't rule it out.

Donohue then turned to Franklin's remarks on racial integration.

"You sound like you'd like to go back to the separate but equal argument which the courts have thrown out," he exclaimed.

"I'm for what will provide the best education for both black and white children," Franklin said, "assure them the best teachers, and maintain our communities, including those formed around public schools. That includes whole cities which have now fallen into disarray because their schools have."

"Do you blame black citizens for that?" Donohue asked.

"No, I blame the neglect of our political leaders who have refused the attention and the finances needed to deliver the services they promised partly because their funds from the federal government have been reduced by supply-side economics, which I consider the root of so much of our problems.

"We also have to accept the fact that the wide divides in family wealth between blacks and whites reflects generations of discrimination in asset building and will require more than a simple mixing of the races in schools to change. There is scarcely any effort to integrate churches, for instance, which are a cornerstone of social life for millions of whites and backs. There is a feeble effort to increase the number of technical schools for blacks, in which they show an aptitude and have successful working backgrounds in and where they can develop skills and opportunity for well-paying jobs. These less dramatic solutions are ones that can be effective and if they had been emphasized twenty years ago by now would provide the foundation for a sizable black middle class, and not just for blacks I might add, but also for the white working class which has been especially hard hit by the movement of lower-paying jobs overseas.

"In the cities where I grew up, the financial foundation was thousands of textile mill jobs that have disappeared, and nothing has replaced them. So it is not just blacks, but also the white working class for which a stronger job economy must be built."

Donohue wasn't too convinced by Franklin's arguments. He wanted ways to bring the races together as friends and neighbors. "You're still talking separate but equal," he concluded.

Oddly, Donohue did not pursue the "gays in the military" issue, and the four-way exchange among he and the candidates was subdued compared to his two-way exchange with Clinton. If anything, Franklin felt that Clinton was the winner as he got the most attention and the most air time and the most softball questions, apparently in an attempt to make up for the grilling on his sexual history which Donohue had dwelt on in the previous interviews.

Back at the offices, Sutton and the others told him he had done well, but Sutton was concerned about his position on racial matters. "That approach may be too subtle for most black audiences," he said. "It lacks the red meat approach they are used to hearing."

"Yeah," Franklin pointed out, "and look at the school systems that approach has gotten them in New York. A lot of blacks who were teachers and leaders in their communities lost their jobs and better incomes and the schools are still segregated."

"We've got some TV spots Joan has produced," Joe Jacura interjected, "with the Statute of Liberty in the background, and they're terrific."

Franklin watched the spots and agreed. Joan repeated his economic passages, and her delivery and personality put them across well. She looked like a slightly older version of Susie, with a better speaking voice and flashing eyes, combined with a fulsome figure that could be admired by both men and women, but especially men.

The New York media had also centered on Joan as their favorite Franklin surrogate to interview, both in person and on camera, for local and network programs. "She's been worth every dollar we're paying her," Sutton said, "but dollars are running short for the rest of this campaign. Spots on New York TV are expensive, and space is limited for the next few days. Clinton's people are breaking the bank for this primary and Brown is spending more than you'd think."

"What about Wisconsin?"

"It's almost an afterthought," Sutton admitted, "but what's helping us there are the Peanut Brigaders, who've come up from Georgia for the final week. Many of them are veterans from the 1976 and '80 campaigns and have experience with what they're doing."

Jack Hardy was listening nearby. "There's not as many this year, and they are sixteen to twenty years older," he commented. "Most of them don't know Franklin as well as they did Carter. After all, he had been the governor. Franklin lived in Alabama most of that time and was mainly a Republican in Georgia."

"That speech you made in Wisconsin got great coverage," Jacura put in, "and the labor people liked it a lot. They are out campaigning for you. They are all against NAFTA, and you're the only candidate riding that horse."

"Can we do a postcard mailing to identifiable Democrats in Wisconsin on the Monday before the primary?" Franklin asked.

"Yes,' said Sutton. "I think that will be more productive than a few TV commercials and reach voters in the rural areas who probably haven't even heard of you."

Meanwhile, Ross Perot's popularity kept growing. Franklin didn't like the idea of third-party candidates because there was no run-off provision in the electoral system. He felt the nation was better served to have its political battles settled within the two-party framework. The electoral college could produce a president who had won only a minority of the votes, which had happened with Abraham Lincoln, who got only 39 percent of the popular votes but a majority of the electoral votes.

In other nations, he had observed how minor parties could gain a niche and through deals with one of the larger parties could become the controlling force with a small minority of the overall votes. That made for divided government and sometimes chaos, and in the worst example, paved the way for the Nazi party under Hitler to finally become strong enough to elect Hitler as the premier. The Nazis never won a majority of the votes until Hitler ruthlessly outlawed the other parties and seized control of all governmental authority after the death of President Hindenburg in 1934 and the assassination of most other previous premiers.

Now, Ross Perot was gaining widespread support as a third-party candidate in the 1992 US election, and actually led President Bush and the perceived Democratic candidate, Clinton, in some opinion polls. That was scary, Franklin thought, not only for the future of the two party system, but for the country should Perot actually become the president.

George Stephanopoulos had rather accurately described Perot as "a weird little man who is a ventriloquist dummy for voter anger." A Texan, with a pronounced Texas accent, Perot was also a billionaire who could finance his own campaign and had attracted enthusiastic audiences through regular appearances on the Larry King TV show and other TV and radio talk venues. His strong conservative views attracted many other rich supporters who were urging him to run. He had played it coy until one night on Larry King he said he'd consider running if voters sent him $5 and a pledge to work for him. "I just want you to have some skin in the game," he explained "God bless all of you who've written and called me, now the shoe is on the other foot." He told King he expected everybody to fade away silently at that point. Instead there was an avalanche of calls and letters urging Perot to declare and run as a third party candidate.

The wave continued, and when Perot appeared on the Phil Donohue show just a few weeks later, eighteen thousand calls were attempted in one thirty-second period and a computerized call-in system had to be installed. The response was unprecedented in TV history. It seemed everyone in the country suddenly wanted Perot to be the president and "raise the hood" and work on the car as he put it. His kind words for Paul Tsongas were not surprising since their plans for the nation's problems were similar: harder lives for the poor, more money for the rich. In a book he later published, Perot made the case for his bitter-tasting medicine: cut spending by $416 billion a year, increase taxes by $312 billion, including raising the gasoline tax by fifty cents a gallon. Ironically his book was called *How We Can Take Back Our Country*. It was actually a formula for his main theme, which was how to balance the federal budget. Perot was much more dangerous than Tsongas. First, he had billions of dollars he said he'd spend on his campaign and his folksy manner and personal success appealed to a broad range of Americans.

As the New York and Wisconsin primaries drew closer, Franklin became more concerned with Perot's surprising strength in the polls. One of his appeals, of course, was that he was not a politician in a year when politicians were not in favor, not excepting the candidate from Georgia, who had never served a day as a public official, or even sought an office. He just wasn't as rich as Perot and their platforms were almost directly in conflict.

Perot, who had always been a Republican, would have seemed to be a staunch Bush supporter but Bush had angered him in a dispute over Perot's efforts to send hired military personnel to Vietnam to search for American POWs who had not been released. He also said he didn't think Bush understood business or had any interest in domestic affairs. Franklin finally decided Perot was a springtime diversion who would soon fade while he was facing the most challenging primary in the country.

On Sunday night, Franklin accepted an invitation to speak to a large group of New York Democrats and felt it was the opportunity to stress the importance of a functional two-party system which presented voters with a reasonable choice on Election Day, no matter how harsh or divisive the preliminaries had been.

A large crowd was present, and it included party leaders from around the state.

"The most critical issue the people have to settle in this election is the same one Lincoln mentioned in the Gettysburg Address," Franklin began. "He was faced with a country torn asunder by war because its essential bond had been broken, and the electoral system had failed to resolve its grievance in the 1860 election. The shadow over our nation today is not so deep or dangerous as the one Lincoln encountered but a shadow does exist, obscuring any other political considerations that now seem so important.

"The shadow persists and deepens because in all the oratory of the two conventions, and in all the columns and commentaries, little if any attention is given to that truly dominant and definitive question, that was first posed at the Constitutional Convention in the historic summer of 1787, which simply is: Can the democratic process of selecting our governments and officials continue to function in the United States or in any nation?

"If the answer to that question is no, and if you take seriously what many candidates say this year, a no answer is not unreasonable, then all the other questions which are seeking answers in this election become relatively unimportant.

"If the answer is yes, then it is time somebody starts saying a good word for politics, politicians, and the political process, because the impression that is displayed constantly and unchallenged to the American people is destroying the basic belief in the elective system, which must exist if our present form of government has any chance of success, much less of serving as an example to the rest of the world, and encouraging the spread of constitutional democracy to other nations.

"The evidence is clear that a lot of Americans have lost confidence in many of their political leaders, whatever the philosophy, competence, or performance of those leaders. It is a short step from there to a loss of confidence in the process that produced those leaders, which is a system that is not without flaws but is based on peaceful transfers of power, and free expression of views through the most extensive and intricate communications system in history.

"Do enough people really trust and believe in that system? Or would they prefer to swap it for some of the other types of government that espouse freedom and liberty in theory but are in essence smothering dictatorships?

"Iran is a recent and dramatic example of the substitution of a more brutal, dehumanizing tyranny for a government that whatever its faults, allowed enough freedom that actually eroded its own base of support.

"Few of us truly believe the hateful things said about opponents in political campaigns, but if enough Americans lose faith in both major parties, the nation and government are definitely in danger. That danger is propelled by two factors that were not as powerful during previous national crises, including that most severe of all US crises, the Civil War.

"The first factor is the impact of television's exposure of all the warts, in living color a few feet away from your very eyes and of our political leaders and the political process, which can appear downright ugly and repugnant on a noisy convention floor. Among the many things which Vietnam demonstrated was that it's tough for a nation to conduct a war that is beamed into its living rooms every night. Can the political process survive similar exposure?

"Secondly, the US population is becoming more and more Balkanized, hopelessly fragmented on issues which cannot attain total agreement in a nation as diverse and free as ours. Certainly I have learned that in my short time as a presidential candidate.

"The essence of democracy, of course, is respect and assimilation of all views, minority and majority, and that process has served the nation well. But the overriding question remains: Do enough Americans still believe democracy serves them well, and are they willing to abide the political system which is vital to democracy's survival?

"The alternative to the process is not just the loss of an election, or the dilution of a preferred privilege or delay in passage of a cherished program. The alternative is the loss of elected governments with enough authority to govern, and when those are the choices, tyranny or anarchy, tyranny always prevails."

"I view with alarm the turmoil and the ugliness of the political conventions. I wince at the demagoguery of Pat Buchanan or the paleness of a Bush, or the shrillness of the most narrow-gauged supporters of all the candidates, including my own at times.

"But then I think of the dark alleys where politics are determined in many nations, or the relentless firing squads in Iraq, and in Cuba during Castro's early days of power, of the savaged Cambodian villages and cities, of the uncertainty in so many of the newer nations, of the terrorism that has become the dominant factor in some nations.

"And then I appreciate how precious is the one vote we all have, how vital it is to the democratic process and how fragile is the freedom we take for granted...how valuable are all our flawed politicians from George Wallace to Jimmy Carter to Ronald Reagan to George Bush and Paul Tsongas. They all play a role in what makes the system work," he concluded.

For Monday Franklin planned a different type of campaigning. He asked Joan and Charlie to accompany him and they went on a walk through Rockefeller Square and later around Central Park. The idea was to speak with a variety of New Yorkers but mainly media types from the nearby newspaper offices and TV stations who would interview them and take photos. It would be a situation with Franklin answering questions and repeating some of his campaign slogans. In a place as large as Manhattan, he thought this might be the best way to spend the final day of campaigning. The other team members were out setting up travel arrangements to the polls in as many locations as practical with the race so close. With Joan along on the walk, it wasn't a problem attracting other reporters willing to answer or ask questions and being on TV.

Like Jimmy Carter, Franklin was not above committing adultery in his mind, although unlike Carter, he never expressed that view publicly, and he thought a nicely shaped female figure was God's most impressive creation.

As several media types began to follow them, Franklin offered brief statements:

"Elections should not only be the simple task of choosing between a Republican or Democrat but also to decide something about the nation's future. A poll taken after the 1988 presidential election asked voters what their most important priority was. The answers were surprising, and none of the priorities had been among the most discussed in the debates or the campaign. First, they wanted the wealthy and big corporations to pay the same percentage of their income in taxes as other Americans did, wanted to help the homeless find jobs and a decent living, tougher trade laws, long-term health insurance for everyone.

"Well down the list was Bush's famous pledge 'no new taxes.' Most people weren't sure which taxes he was talking about—income, sales, property, excise—and they also saw the statement as a cynical campaign statement, and it turns out they were right.

"The responses were regarded as an idle wish list, disconnected from what politicians were really considering. And today, in the primaries which absorb so much of our time, energy, and money, those basic priorities people support are seldom discussed.

"The winning strategies of the modern Republican Party is the path of George Wallace more than of Barry Goldwater. I know that's a shocking statement, but look at the states the Republicans now regularly win. They are the old Confederate states."

"How do you explain that the past two Democratic presidents have been from the South and two Southerners—you and Bill Clinton—have the most delegates for the 1992 Democratic nomination?" a reporter asked.

"Good question," Franklin replied. "I think most voters still recognize Democrats as the party that assures Social Security, Medicare, and other New Deal Programs, and Southern Democrats are more acceptable on other issues."

"What will be your first move on foreign affairs if you should be elected?" another reporter asked.

"Well, as I've said many times, it will be toward assuring an enduring and broad-based peace, which will require putting aside some long-held resentments and even hatreds from our past. But the US now finds itself as the most dominant power in the world since at least the Roman Empire, with the Soviet Union dissolving, Red China still a second-world country in many respects, the British Empire shrunken, no other powerful challengers in sight. But this rare moment in history will not last. We must move in meaningful ways to prove our right to leadership and our credibility as the world's major agent for peace as well as its strongest power.

"An immediate step, I believe, should be reaching out to Russia to assist in its transition from centuries of tyrannical government under Communism and earlier under the Czars. Russia and its former satellites still have the second-largest nuclear arsenal in the world, and it is imperative to help Russia become a more stable and democratic nation. Its current leaders seem open to that path, but they also face opposition in their own country and severe economic difficulties in transitioning from a Communist economy to something closer to a free market economy. They will need guidance and financial help and the crash course, which President Boris Yeltsin seems bent on may not be the best way. I'd gather our best experts on Russian society and its economy and send them there to discuss with Russian leaders what the better course will be. I think they will be amenable to such advice now.

"Also, we must look at our other recent adversaries and take steps to make them friends instead of enemies, such as Iraq, Iran, and especially Cuba, now in dire straits and near enough geographically to be our fifty-first state. If we were able to settle our grievances with Vietnam, and with Japan and Germany after World War II when they committed terrible atrocities against our nation and our soldiers, surely we can find grounds to move toward relations with these later foes, who are smaller and weaker and whose people are the real victims of their leaders."

The little crowd of media and Franklin supporters kept strolling through Rockefeller Square, picking up attention as they went. Franklin shook hands and chatted with individuals but mainly stayed on the lookout for cameramen and reporters. Joan Walsh stayed nearby, taking notes and passing out pamphlets. Hardy was also along doing the same. "This is fun," Joan exclaimed. "I think we're going to get some great coverage. Do you have any more gems of wisdom to toss out?"

"Plenty," Franklin replied. "And they may go down easier in small bites."

Soon they reached Times Square. Franklin looked around in awe at the newspaper buildings, some of them now abandoned. "This is where modern journalism was born," he commented, "and I fear for its future. We need a free and able press, but we still pay reporters and editors on a level with ditch diggers, only with better working conditions and usually more fun. Also, journalists are convinced that they have a role in maintaining an informed public and free expression."

"Do you believe that?" one reporter asked.

"Absolutely. Newspapers have their faults, some more than others, some are too dull and some are too loose with the truth, but I like what the French writer De Tocqueville wrote about newspapers after touring the United States in the mideighteenth century."

"What did De Tocqueville write?" asked one reporter with a dash of sarcasm in his voice. Franklin noticed from his name tag that he was from *The New York Daily News*, which still sold more single copies each day than any newspaper, most of them in New York.

"Discussing how democracy works in the United States, De Tocqueville observed that 'a newspaper can drop the same thought into a thousand minds at the same moment. A newspaper is an adviser that does not need to be sought but comes to you without distracting from private affairs. Newspapers therefore become more necessary as men become more equal individuals. To suppose that they only serve to protect freedom is to diminish their importance; they maintain civilization.'"

"Hey, that's good," one reporter said. "I've never heard that quotation."

"Too many people haven't," Franklin agreed. "I ran across it several years ago and used it on the title page of the history of Georgia Newspapers I published in 1985. I thought it would catch on, but people apparently don't read title pages closely, although every library and newspaper publisher in Georgia got a copy of that book."

"What was the main reason you decided to run for president?" a female reporter asked.

"It was the wide acceptance of supply side-economics as the solution to the nation's problems which was exactly the opposite of what the New Deal era taught us in recovering from the Great Depression and building the economic structure to win World War II, to build the interstate highway system, develop the space program, and I might add, conduct the war on poverty, much of which was successful, not to mention the ongoing Social Security System and Medicare. All of that was a product of a demand-side economy, which puts enough money into the pockets of more people so they can buy products which the so-called supply-side is glad to provide to customers.

"I believe the high inflation of the 1970s frightened Americans to the point that they were vulnerable to the supply-side argument that too much money in customers' hands was the cause of inflation and that it was better to concentrate money with those who owned most of the production and had most of the wealth. So taxes, which are the way the government can most effectively control the economy were shifted in unprecedented amounts from the richer tax payers to the middle income and lower earners, directly and indirectly.

"We can see the result best by comparing wages today with wages just twelve years ago in 1980. According to an economic study the average Fortune 500 corporation CEO's annual compensation is now more than four hundred times the wage of the company's average employee. The evidence clearly shows that the difference is huge and growing. The gap was estimated at 100 to 1 in 1990 and 42 to 1 in 1980, when supply-side began taking effect. Even at 42 to 1, the difference seemed ample incentive for an employee to work and aspire to something more. But there needs to be a reasonable balance that makes economic sense. The great economist Adam Smith's invisible hand may be invisible but even Smith himself wrote that the hand needed guidance.

"The president of the US has a salary of just $200,000 a year, which sets a standard for other government salaries. Executives paid so highly in the private sectors have to take a big reduction in pay to even become secretary of state, or much less other government jobs.

"I have been a small business owner and executive for nearly forty years, and I know the problems of both employees and employer. I am such a believer in the capitalist system that I became an entrepreneur in my early twenties on borrowed money. The capitalist system worked for me, and I want to see it continue working. But I believe we live in a 'demand side world' and that world is being turned upside down, and nobody running for president seemed sufficiently alarmed about it. The supply-side guru, Jude Warminski, wrote a book he called *The Way the World Works* in the late 1970s, and it became the economic guidebook for Jack Kemp and then Ronald Reagan and other supply-siders. But his ideas are not how the world really works and we're seeing the results in this economic ditch the nation is now in with the prospect of getting worse. That's why I decided to run for president because even a very dark horse president candidate can get more attention than some small-town editorial writer."

More cameras were now trained on him, and tape recorders were spinning. Charlie and Joan were nearby and taking notes for news releases.

"Why don't we hear more about demand-side economics?" the reporter from *USA Today* asked.

"Because you don't write about it, or try to explain it, and frankly it's just not the fashionable philosophy of the day. But it was the philosophy of the New Deal and Franklin Roosevelt and he was criticized every day in the press and by the Republicans as a would-be Socialist at best or Communist at worst. The high inflation and interest rates during the 1970s convinced too many Americans that we couldn't afford to take a chance on demand-side. But nearly all the inflation in the 1970s was caused by the unprecedented rise in gasoline prices. Today's US was built and grew on low oil prices."

"Are you going to stay in the race for president if you lose in New York?" one reporter wanted to know. It was a question Franklin had been asking himself.

"I'll let you know a day after the primary," Franklin promised. He was hoping that this day on the streets of New York and the subsequent coverage would give him the boost he needed to edge past Brown and maybe Clinton. A lot depended on how he was getting across, but he sensed he had struck a rich vein of response in an important audience: the news media in the nation's largest media market.

He and the others continued their walk, eventually getting to Central Park, where a large crowd had gathered. "Come around, everybody," Joan called out, waving her arms. Charlie found a loud speaker Franklin could use and he basically delivered the same talk he'd made to the media group, sprinkling in some proposals he'd made in his campaign, such as cutting the payroll tax and extending it to all salaried income instead of just a worker's first $60,000, adjusting the income tax brackets, so a plumber with a fairly good income wouldn't be put in the same tax bracket with a doctor or lawyer making more than $200,000 a year, or even worse, in a bracket with a CEO and Wall Street brokers and ballplayers who made in the millions The crowd grew to several hundred as he spoke and Joan and Charlie called for help and more pamphlets from the office.

When they got back to the office, the place was a madhouse of activity. Phones were ringing, and one secretary was actually gasping for breath. "I've got fifty people on hold," she said, "and have hung up on a hundred. The lines are completely blocked now."

Sutton appeared from an inner office and realized they were overwhelmed, but he was making arrangements to handle the overload and wanted to know where and how much Franklin wanted to be on TV that night and next morning. "I think I already have you booked on the key programs in prime time."

"How much money do we have left for spots altogether?" Franklin asked.

"Not enough for New York and Wisconsin."

Franklin pondered for a moment. "Well, saturate Wisconsin," he decided, "The money will go further and we need a lift in the rural areas there where we may have a chance to do well. It looks as if I'm going to get a lot of free TV and radio time in New York tonight if I can meet most of these requests."

He went into a private office and was surprised and delighted to find his wife, Jean, there. "I didn't know you were coming," he managed.

"Brad called me and said this was a night you needed me to be here, Tim and I chartered a private plane and flew up. I'm so glad I did. You look exhausted, but Sutton thinks the campaign is sky-high right now. I've called the other children and told them to be sure and watch all the news programs tonight. I can't get over how much difference there is in New Hampshire and New York. It's crazy."

Franklin bit his lip and felt a surge of panic in his chest. He grabbed her hand as he often had in the past when he had the unexpected panic attacks that had plagued him for years. The attacks were briefly disabling, making it hard to breathe or talk. They had started when he was a young journalist trying to get out his first personally-owned weekly newspaper and they had continued regularly when he became an everyday editor, meeting too many deadlines and feeling afraid he couldn't make the next one. Even at night they would sometimes hit him, making it hard to sleep. He was one of the first people, he thought, to take the anxiety pill Valium, when it first came out in 1957. He was still taking it forty-five years later, and he hurriedly took one now.

"Are you okay?" Jean asked.

"I think so," he murmured. "There's just so much to do and so little time."

"You've always tried to do too much yourself," Jean said. "That happened at nearly every newspaper you owned."

Franklin tried to get a deep breath, as his mother used to tell him she couldn't when he was a child. He knew Jean was right. He'd sold his early papers, including the Opelika-Auburn News because he felt his health was in danger and the panic attacks were making him miserable. But he fought them off and went on to new challenges and they subsided in number after he stepped away from the day-to-day task of putting the newspaper together, which was still what he liked to do. And he really liked running for president. What he didn't like he realized was dealing with so many people, not a good trait for an aspiring politician. As one doctor had told him, he was actually an introvert masquerading as an extrovert and the strain was wearing on his emotions as it had on Richard Nixon and others he suspected.

But the moments of panic soon passed and he put on his calm and collected demeanor which had gotten him through many deadline crises.

"I'm so glad you came," he told Jean again. "Where is Tim?"

"He went with Brad and some others to distribute papers and line up transportation to the polls tomorrow. That seems such a hopeless task in New York."

"You can be useful as well as ornamental," he told Jean. "Take some of these calls, tell them you're the candidate's wife and that he is the best husband you ever had and the smartest man you've ever known."

Jean looked panicked for a minute but quickly said she'd do it. "Tell Sutton to get you a phone and an assistant." Franklin felt she'd be a real trooper in the pinch. She always was.

The rest of the evening passed in a twinkling as immediate tasks presented themselves. They were getting regular reports from Wisconsin where Sutton had found a former Jimmy Carter campaign manager willing to try again. He was originally from Woodbury, Georgia and had known of Franklin for years. Brad had taken him under his wing for a few days and he became imbued with Brad's special enthusiasm. "I've never met anybody with such drive," he said of Brad.

Brad was now thirty-three years older than the brash young student who was a hard-driving circulation organizer when Franklin first met him and he had traveled some hard miles in the past three decades but he was still one of the most unforgettable characters Franklin had encountered. He still had that remarkable edge and personality that energized others as well as himself.

Franklin slept uneasily that night, glad that Jean was there beside him. He envied people like Jimmy Carter who he understood could fall asleep at any time and under any circumstance and Franklin Roosevelt, who despite his handicap and the weight of responsibilities could sleep for hours when he grew weary. That part of their personalities undoubtedly helped assure their success.

Primary Day in New York and Wisconsin passed in a blur. Franklin kept making calls and giving TV interviews, stressing his two main points; the need to get more money into the hands of consumers and the importance of pursuing better relations with all nations at this unique moment in history.

While others took reports from around the states in play Franklin and Jean settled down in their hotel suite with the TV sets tuned to the major networks plus CNN and the up and coming Fox News Network. Voting was heavy in both New York and Wisconsin, according to early reports, and at 6:00 p.m., there were still long lines at the polls despite predictions that voters were turned off by their ballot choices. Polls still showed Ross Perot climbing in a three-way race with the Democratic candidate and President Bush

Finally the day sputtered out, as all days do, no matter how momentous their events, and the actual returns began coming into the stations. The crowd at Franklin's headquarters was enthusiastic as the returns and exit polls showed him leading in both states. He could hardly believe it. He looked at Hardy who he'd invited to join him and Jean and several others and their eyes glazed over as they recalled the early autumn days in New Hampshire when such a night could not have been envisioned. Franklin felt a twinge in his heart wishing Susie could be there to share the victory, if it came, that she had done so much to launch.

"We're cooking," Joe Jacura exclaimed.

"Steady yourself down, there's still a lot of votes to be counted," Bernie Friedman reminded him. "Millions of them, in fact."

Jed Jones also added a note of caution. "Clinton is going to be very strong in the black vote," he predicted. "I can't count how many black churches he's been to and he's good in them."

Plus Clinton had hit a definite homerun with his offbeat performances no other candidate could carry off. His experience as a high school saxophone player was still paying off, so his handlers got him booked on the late night Arsenio Hall Show. Clinton donned dark shades and played a saxophone version of "Heartbreak Hotel." The performance entrenched his image as a cool "dude." It was ironic, Franklin thought that all of Clinton's many speeches probably did not win him as many votes as that saxophone number.

The returns kept coming in and Franklin still led. It was possible to see a double victory for him that would give him the advantage over Clinton in the remaining primaries. "You could actually be the president," Sutton said in an incredulous tone, a view he had never expressed publicly. Jean had a puzzled smile on her face. "Who will they get to be the president's wife?" she muttered quietly.

Hardy who was remembering the bitter end to Carter's 1980 campaign, and the twenty failed ventures he'd worked on since then was less exuberant. The years of losses had blunted his appetite for happy expectations. "It was hard getting our people to the polls," he commented. "We weren't organized for the traffic problems."

"Nobody is," said Bernie Friedman. "A lot of New Yorkers walk to the polls."

Franklin kept leading, and then suddenly he wasn't. A wave of votes came in from the Greenwich Village area, and he ran a poor third among them, behind Clinton and Brown.

"Those damn queers," Jacura yelped. "I knew they'd do us in... and it's happening."

"Steady yourself down," Friedman advised. "Franklin's *still* in second place."

But the tide had turned. The vote from the black precincts began to come in, and Clinton was easily outpolling Franklin in those returns. Tsongas was showing surprising strength in some suburban areas, pulling votes from both Brown and Franklin.

"It wasn't just the homosexual vote," Franklin said. "I believe I got as many votes as I might have lost on that issue. Just think how hard it is for a guy with a Southern drawl and a reserved personality to appeal to voters in New York."

"We're still in the game," Sutton pointed out, "still running second, and I want to hear from Wisconsin, where we're also a close second."

"Another problem," Jacura interjected, "was the emphasis you put on Franklin Roosevelt. He's not as popular in New York as he was fifty years ago. And actually he got only about 55 percent of the New York votes in the 1944 presidential race against Thomas Dewey, who was a forty-four-year-old nobody compared to Roosevelt, a three-term president, who was leading the nation to its greatest military victory."

Franklin grimaced at the thought. "You're right," he agreed. "Roosevelt actually never even carried his home county of Duchess in New York but he always carried Meriwether County in Georgia by more than 8 to 1. He deserved better in New York."

As the returns continued to come in Clinton's lead in New York grew and at 10:30 p.m. the networks projected Clinton would be the leader in the final count, with Franklin second, and Tsongas a surprising third, dealing a bitter blow to Brown, whose tax ideas were less popular even than Tsongas'.

The crowd was subdued but stayed late to see the final returns from Wisconsin which put Franklin in the lead around 2:00 a.m. "Just like Carter, in 1976," Hardy recalled with a smile. "The early edition of the daily newspapers that year had a headline that said 'Udall Upsets Carter' in Wisconsin, and when Carter finally pulled it out he got a publicity boost that was better than a simple victory."

The advisers looked anxiously at Franklin. New York was the first primary where he had made a serious effort and did not end up with the most votes.

"Where do we go from here?" Sutton asked softly.

"Let's talk about it tomorrow," Franklin decided. "We actually had a remarkable day today, considering the time and effort we spent or, more accurately, didn't spend here."

Franklin waited for the final results from Wisconsin, and this time it was Clinton who pulled out a narrow lead. Franklin realized his nerves were shot. He was also troubled by that fleeting remark Jean had made about the president's wife.

The next day they could examine the final count and analyze the results. The exit polls revealed that Clinton had won the black voters by a large margin and had done well in the homosexual precincts which were smaller and more difficult to measure.

Franklin ran well everywhere else, especially in the boroughs outside Manhattan and in upstate New York, with many voters apparently still familiar with his name because of the assassination attempt that killed Susie. He also did well with the labor votes as he had done in each state where his economic message got good exposure. The same factors bolstered him in Wisconsin and the late campaigning by the Peanut Brigaders apparently struck a nostalgic chord with some old Carter voters, but Clinton benefited from a heavy black vote in Milwaukee.

In the end, Clinton led in New York with 34 percent of the votes to Franklin's 30 percent, Brown's 24 percent, Tsongas' 12 percent, and the rest scattered. The breakdown in Wisconsin was similar, except that Franklin led.

The primaries ahead looked dismal for Franklin. His campaign had done little to make inroads anywhere else, and most important the original $6 million he'd put into the coffers was exhausted. "Contributions will be coming in this week," Sutton told him, "but we mainly need them to cover unpaid bills and"—swallowing hard—"unpaid salaries to employees."

Franklin patted him on the shoulder. "Don't worry, everybody's pay will be met, maybe with a little bonus. I've always managed when I sold papers to pay everybody off, and I never missed a payday. Let's have a meeting tomorrow afternoon and make some decisions."

Franklin had more trouble than usual sleeping that night. He tossed and turned for hours and when he looked at the clock it was 4:30 a.m. He decided that was long enough to lay awake so he quickly got out of bed, hoping not to arouse Jean, dressed, and decided to go down to the coffee shop for an early breakfast and morning paper.

The shop was almost empty with only one couple and two or three fellow insomniacs. There was a single waitress and cook in the back. Franklin decided to splurge. "I'll take an omelet, with bacon and toast," he said.

"You want fries with that?" the waitress asked.

"What kind do you serve?"

"French fries or hash browns."

"I'll have the hash browns," Franklin said with a slight smile.

He'd picked up a morning paper which had a front page story on the race for the Democratic nomination, mentioning that the next big primary was Pennsylvania with Clinton leading in the polls there and Brown and Franklin trailing.

The large lead headline and photo was on Clinton's lead in New York with a photo of him and Hillary celebrating. What a difference a few votes make Franklin thought, looking at the small headline and photo on the second-place candidate.

More alarming to him was an exit poll that claimed voters preferred Ross Perot to any of the candidates on the ballot. Perot was leading in other polls. A *Washington Post* poll on presidential preferences had Perot tied with Clinton at 23 percent while Bush was down to 21 percent.

A woman approached Franklin's table and asked if she could join him. The woman was Hillary Clinton. "Are you early or coming in late?" she asked.

"Up early, I couldn't sleep, which is a bad habit of mine."

"Mine too," Hillary said. "Bill can sleep like a log at any place."

"That's a great asset for a presidential candidate—or president. I heard that Jimmy Carter was that way. He could take a nap between campaign stops."

"But you have trouble sleeping at any time?" Hillary asked with genuine interest.

"Yeah, it's a hangover from my newspaper days," Franklin explained. "On afternoon papers, you had to be at work by about 6:30 a.m. On morning papers you went in about 3:00 p.m. and worked until about 2:00 a.m. Plus, I'm just naturally anxious."

"Bill was very upset that you finished so close to him in New York," Hillary confided. "He had worked New York long and hard, appeared on every TV and radio show, preached at forty black churches, and thought he'd win by an impressive margin. And then to make it worse you led in Wisconsin. We couldn't believe it."

"I was riding on Carter's surprising victory there in 1976 sixteen years ago. Some of his Peanut Brigaders from that year came up and campaigned for me in the last week. That and my opposition to NAFTA helped."

"That was it," Hillary agreed. "Bill's been hurt in every primary by his perceived support of NAFTA."

"Is it just a perception?" Franklin asked.

"Well, he could go either way. I don't think we realized how important the NAFTA issue was until the New Hampshire primary. Have you ever read Bill's campaign booklet *A Plan for America's Future?*"

Franklin nodded. He actually wasn't sure he had.

"His ideas for jump-starting the economy and helping the middle class are right out of the New Deal and not very different from the ones I've heard in your speeches."

"There are some differences and they are important ones," Franklin pointed out. "I'm an economic liberal, but a cultural conservative. I'm not sure where Bill falls in that spectrum."

"He's as good a Democrat as you can be today and get elected president. He wants to cut taxes on the middle class and pay for it with slight increases on upper income earners; he wants to guarantee health care for all citizens, to place medical clinics in public schools, give an income tax rebate to poor families with several children. He believes a revised health care system can save enough money to finance these programs because we spend so much today on excessive technology; prescription drug prices, which are higher than anywhere and plain billing fraud, which he estimates to be $75 billion of the government's total health care expenditures."

"He's right, I suppose," Franklin admitted. He almost added, I just wish he was a better person. "Not to rain on your parade," he finally said. "But a lot of presidents, including Franklin Roosevelt, tackled the health-care industry and came away empty."

Hillary looked disappointed. "You've been an honorable and worthy opponent," she said, "but you haven't mentioned health care in your talks and papers."

"We've got Medicare and Medicaid, thank goodness and Lyndon Johnson, but the next steps are going to be difficult. You have to remember those senators and representatives who must vote to change the health-care system face reelection every two years or every six years. I think we'd be better off trying to give people more tax breaks, especially the middle class, or either extending Medicare to cover more people. Medicare is popular and more important it's relatively simple. The people hate complex programs they don't understand and a health-care program that extends care to everybody sounds very complicated, not to mention expensive."

The small diner was beginning to fill up. Franklin looked around anxiously. "Keep your head down," he advised. "It would be a media sensation if we're seen talking together."

Hillary laughed. "You're right, but we're in a corner and I've got a head scarf. You're still not that recognizable. Let me finish my coffee. How do you think Pennsylvania looks in the primary?"

"Clinton is leading," Franklin admitted, "but we're making an effort and there are a lot of undecideds there." He didn't tell her that he had yet to make an appearance in the state, and the campaign's money and his personal money were running on empty. "I've been asked to speak to a meeting of Democratic county chairs a few days before the primary. I understand all the candidates will be at that meeting, which will be the most important one before the voting."

"Yeah," Hillary said. "Bill will be and probably Brown and Tsongas, maybe even Harkin, although he's officially out of the race. I hear it will be a daylong meeting with each candidate given about forty-five minutes to an hour to speak and take questions."

"I'll be there, then I'll decide where I'm going next which could be home. I've mentioned there is an overriding issue in this election which is the stability of the political system. As strong as the US is, the political infrastructure is fragile. There hasn't been a strong president since Johnson in mid-1966, more than twenty-five years ago. Jimmy Carter was a good man, but never had his own party with him in Congress. Reagan was strong for all the wrong reasons and Bush is obviously struggling today as Buchanan's strength shows in the primaries. Both parties are floundering, and the candidacy of Ross Perot is a serious threat to the system that has more or less survived and worked, sometimes uncertainly for more than two hundred years.

"But look at the four options the nation faces in this election. If the polls are even close to right today, Perot, a man without a party or any governmental experience, is leading. He could actually get enough electoral votes to win, which is unlikely but possible; secondly, he could get enough electoral votes to deny either of the major party candidates a majority, which would throw the election into the House of Representatives with an uncertain outcome, but a very certain crisis as the two sides fight to get votes from the candidate who comes in third. The other option is that Perot could draw enough votes from the Democratic candidate to allow Bush to win reelection with a weak plurality. All three of those possible outcomes are bad and two of them disastrous."

Hillary looked concerned. "You're right," she said. "That's why it is so important that Bill win a clear-cut victory."

"Or me," Franklin reminded her. "I still have a chance."

"That's right, and you are better than all three of those options, but you must admit you have even less political experience than Perot, have less money and he is apparently amassing a huge personal following, drawn from both parties and as you say, it is important to maintain the two-party system that has gotten us through every challenge but one, the Civil War, and I guess you could say the Republican Party pulled the nation through that crisis."

She finished her coffee and stood up. Hillary was not tall, but she was a formidable presence. "So what are you going to say at the meeting?"

Franklin smiled at her with sleepy eyes. "I'll have to sleep on it," he said. "What's Bill going to say? He needs to be more specific."

"He is specific," she protested. "He's the most effective Democratic speaker since Roosevelt, and he's going to win."

"You know, you should be the Clinton who is running for president," Franklin told her, "and I mean that."

She laughed her full-throated laugh. "You know what our enemies say, eight years of Bill then eight years of Hill, and they mean that as a threat not a compliment, but that's a long time to plan ahead."

"Well," Franklin advised, "I wish Bill would stop saying he's a 'new Democrat' so much, implying something was wrong with the Democrats of past and present, who made possible Social Security, Medicare, the Minimum Wage, food stamps, Head Start and dozens of other programs which have helped build the nation and the world, and have made most Americans better off. On nearly every progressive issue Democrats have had to fight an on-going battle against Republicans and against Democrats who often joined them in opposing progressive measures and some pseudo Democrats who want to repeal the twentieth century.

"Some so-called new Democrats sound too much like old Republicans who cater to the voter-blocs who are supported by millions of dollars and have opposed nearly all of the New Deal and been beholden to the richest Americans since the first term of Ulysses S. Grant."

Franklin looked at Hillary's lightly-lined face and contemplated all the election nights she'd been through. "For people like you and Bill, who seem to run in every election cycle, there will be a lot of victories along the road, but also some bitter defeats," he commented.

"We know all about defeats," Hillary said. "We learned when Bill was defeated for reelection after his first term as governor. I got blamed in part for not changing my last name from Rodham to Clinton, so I felt especially guilty, and we ran as Bill and Hillary Clinton the next election and won easily. It's odd what small things bother the voters."

"It wasn't a small thing," Franklin said. "Keeping your maiden name was an affront to what many people accept as the meaning of marriage. Frankly, it was a dumb thing to do, and indicates there may be other affronts to people you and Bill will miss in the coming years. You are two yuppies from Yale who've come a long way, but remember the roses still have thorns."

"That's good," Hillary said. "I'll remember that." Franklin decided to offer another of his favorite quotations.

"After the really bitter defeats, you might find some comfort in this passage from Ecclesiastes: The preacher says 'I saw under the sun that the race is not always to the swift, nor the battle to the strong, neither yet bread to the wise, nor riches to the men of understanding, nor yet favor to men of skill, for time and chance happeneth to them all.'"

Hillary was impressed. "What chapter and verse are those?" she asked, "We didn't spend much time on Ecclesiastes in Methodist Sunday School."

"Ecclesiastes 9:11. The whole chapter contains some of the finest wisdom in the Old Testament. Biblical scholars usually credit Solomon as the writer. He was supposedly the wisest man of biblical times, although he was unfaithful to his wife...or wives of which he supposedly had many."

"I do remember that," Hillary said, "and God punished him... or was that David? They both had large sexual appetites."

"That's right, but they were both great kings and great men of God, if the Bible is to be believed."

"Don't you believe it?" Hillary asked quickly.

"I think it was Napoleon who once said 'history is a myth agreed upon.' I'd say history and the Bible are myths we have faith in: Moses parted the Red Sea; David slew Goliath; Samson lost his strength when his hair was cut; Jonah was swallowed by a whale and lived to tell about it. We have to accept a lot on faith, such as Ross Perot is never going to be president of the United States."

"We can make that a reality," Hillary said. "You, Bill, and I. We can beat Perot and restore New Deal principles to the government and lay the foundation for years of peace."

"Tell your husband that and emphasize the part about principles. Tell him to follow the New Deal more than his New Covenant ideas, which are warmed over Republican solutions in more acceptable language. He talks too much about the success of people who have the most money and authority, and too little about the people who work hard forty to sixty hours a week and are told they are less worthy than the executive who puts in a few hours a day shuffling papers on his desk until it's time for a tax-free dinner."

"Bill believes all that," Hillary said.

She put a dollar on the table. "Let's work together to avoid an electoral disaster," she said. "I know you don't want that, and neither does the nation."

As she walked away Franklin looked around and decided no one had noticed them. Without her, he thought, Bill would be an also-ran. The Clintons were the kind of couple that when they arrive, the party begins, and when they leave the party begins to wind down. Jean and I are the kind of couple that might not even be invited, Franklin soberly thought.

Later that morning, he got together with Phil Sutton, Brad, and Hardy. Sutton had done some spade work in Pennsylvania. "We're running a weak second, possibly as low as fourth," Sutton said. "Tsongas has support there, mostly Republicans who don't like Bush or Buchanan. Clinton has devoted more time and money in Pennsylvania than he did in Wisconsin and has the governor and most county organizations in his corner...and did I mention we're nearly out of money."

"Thanks for the pep talk," Franklin said. "I'm getting my speech ready for the big meeting. Do you know the order the candidates will speak?"

"Yes," said Sutton. "You're last."

"Good, get a group of supporters to the meeting and please give Jean a ride. Hardy and I are going over today and spend the night. Get us a room at a hotel with a large bar."

The next day he and Hardy drove from New York City to Philadelphia, site of the meeting. "Do you know what you're going to say?" Hardy asked.

"Yes, I've thought a lot about it, and what's at stake, not just for our campaign, but for the nation, and, in fact, the world. That's what I've been talking about for the past eight months."

"I take it," Hardy said, "you're leading up to an excuse to endorse Bill Clinton, who we all recognize is an out and out sleaze ball and not even a very good Democrat."

"One reporter who followed Clinton throughout his political career describes him as perhaps the most personable, dynamic politician in the past quarter of a century," Franklin said. There must always be hope that the bearer of glad tidings knows what he wants to do and has some idea of how to go about doing it, despite personal frailties."

"Yeah," Hardy said. "How about Thomas Alexander Franklin?"

"And without the personal frailties," Franklin repeated.

He paused and looked out at the passing countryside. "I'm still open," he said, "but we must think of the outcome and whether it will help heal the national division. That is the most important issue of all."

"Clinton has lied to so many people," Hardy protested. "He has hardly anybody left to lie to."

Franklin swallowed hard. Hardy was right, some of the other leaders he'd mentioned, such as Roosevelt and Lincoln and Washington had not been serial liars even though like Clinton they were possible philanderers when sex was not nearly as easy or satisfying as it is in the twentieth century.

Franklin believed that soap and water had made men and women so much more sexually attractive to each other, and then the pill, developed only thirty years earlier had eliminated one of the barriers to sex, which had made both men and women hesitant for centuries. "And you have to admit sex is a powerful attraction and pleasant experience," he told Hardy. "Plus it is the act that prolongs humanity."

"Our president should be better than a male slut," Hardy protested.

Franklin frowned at Hardy's bluntness, even though he recognized its accuracy. It's just that men were seldom described that way. The accepted fact is that most men are always in heat, women aren't. A woman running for president with Clinton's resume of sexual adventures would be thought of as a slut, in Hardy's expression. So would have John F. Kennedy and perhaps others. Sex is much cleaner now, with soap and water, and less hazardous with the pill, even if not more chaste…or moral. "Even Jimmy Carter admitted he had lust in his heart," Franklin pointed out.

"Yeah, and it almost cost him the election," Hardy said.

"That's because people would rather be told a lie that comforts them than a truth that discomforts them," Franklin said. "Carter even threw in a few phrases like shacking up in that interview with *Playboy*, and that hit a lot of young people today right where they live, no pun intended."

Chapter Twenty-Seven

THE CHOSEN GENERATION

The first theory is that if we make the rich richer, somehow they will let a part of their prosperity trickle down to the rest of us. The second theory is if we make the average of mankind comfortable and secure, their prosperity will rise upward through the ranks.

—*Franklin D. Roosevelt, campaign address, Detroit, October 2, 1932*

A s they drove toward the meeting hall, Franklin remarked, "Whatever happens, we've had an exhilarating quixotic adventure,"

"But did we kill any dragons?" Hardy asked.

Franklin replied, "I think so. We helped keep Tsongas from dominating the Democratic primary with his pseudo-Republican philosophy and I like to think we influenced Bill Clinton to become more of an Old Democrat than a New Democrat, whatever that is."

"But you look worried," Hardy said as they arrived at the meeting hall.

"I've been looking at more reports on Ross Perot," Franklin said. "They are amazing and dismaying. He's almost a regular on the Larry King Show and is also on every other major radio or TV talk show. He's getting millions of dollars in TV time at no expense, and it's working for him. In some polls he's now running ahead of both Bush and Clinton."

"Well, as we know, the people are looking for an alternative to those two, including I might add, Thomas Alexander Franklin, who isn't doing too bad."

Franklin looked pained. "Perot's got a lot more money, a peculiar charisma and the confidence, all of which I lack. And thousands of phone calls come into the networks whenever he's on. I'm trying to figure what's he's saying that attracts so many of them."

Perot had apparently become convinced that a strong third-party candidate could win if he pulled popular votes from both Bush and the Democratic candidate, and that he could get enough of the electoral votes to at least throw the election to the House of Representatives where he felt he would be preferred to either major party candidate who came in second.

"Is he stronger than Wallace was?" Hardy asked.

"In a different way," Franklin answered. "He has a broader appeal and it's electoral votes that still elect presidents. He could get more electors than Wallace did if he just carries Texas."

Perot was on the ballot in every state, a feat of organization and popularity that proved his broad appeal. Could either Bush or Clinton have pulled that off? Other countries allowed several parties to enter candidates in the presidential election, but they also had a provision for a second round between the two leading candidates thus assuring a winner with a popular majority. The United States has no such provision, of course. Its winner can actually lose the popular vote and still become president through the electoral college. Franklin felt that flaw in the presidential election was a ticking time bomb that was sure to explode, creating a dangerous division in the nation. Three candidates with fewer popular votes than his main opponent had already been installed as president. Andrew Jackson, and Grover Cleveland all had more popular votes than the winners in those elections.

Thomas Franklin's entire campaign had been centered around the success of democracy in the United States, and to him success meant that its leader be elected by a majority of the voters, but

Franklin knew that in the case of the president, that wasn't always true. It was a terrible example to set for other nations, where the candidate with the most votes always won, or there was a runoff, or in some cases a revolution. In the US fraud wasn't even necessary. The system was a fraud in itself, Franklin reasoned.

He had written about the dangers and the unfairness of the electoral system in some of his first editorials for his college paper, *The Red and Black*. At that time, Georgia elected its governor and other state officials through the infamous county unit system, which gave voters in smaller countries one vote up to fifty times the strength of a voter in larger countries. "The courts had finally thrown out the county unit system which only applied to party primaries, but the electoral college survives, challenged but unchanged by courts, Congress or any prominent politician, despite its obvious perversion of democracy."

At least no third-party candidate had ever been elected, although Theodore Roosevelt, a past president, came close in 1912, running on the Bull Moose ticket against William Howard Taft, the Republican incumbent and Woodrow Wilson, the Democratic candidate, who won the first of two terms with only 42 percent of the popular votes.

But Perot seemed a real threat without a party behind him, and with his only real promise being to balance the budget at whatever loss for the best interest of the people. He was as folksy as the comedian, Will Rogers, and played on the broad anger that was easy to discern in the American public but difficult to define. "In his Texas drawl," he'd say, "it's time to take out the trash and clean out the barn." The American people were always eager for someone to "clean out the barn" or "drain the swamp" as another candidate put it in a future campaign.

Perot was never specific, but by late May, polls gave him 35 percent of the national vote, ahead of both Bush and Clinton with Clinton in third place.

For years Franklin had written against the electoral college and its potential for disaster to the method by which the United States determined its president. Now speaking to one of the largest crowds in the primary campaign, and possibly his last, Franklin decided to expound on his opposition to the electoral college. "As we were driving here," Franklin began, "there were radio reports about the high poll numbers of Ross Perot as a no-party candidate. That concerns me greatly, so I thought I'd say a few words about the danger that poses for our entire electoral system."

He reached out his arms to the several thousand people who seemed to be more attentive than usual. "As the world's most powerful nation, and most dedicated proponent of rule by the people, for the people, and of the people, the United States of America must be above reproach as an example of the system of government we call democracy. We must be the example to which other nations can point without reservation and emulate without regrets. We cannot sound an uncertain trumpet, either for our own citizens or the citizens of the many nations who look to the United States for leadership and as the model to which they aspire for their own government."

Franklin paused a moment to summon his confidence and energy. "Yet on the most important governmental office which the people are granted the right to determine, our system is flawed and outdated. We have come close to disaster on several occasions because of this plan, devised more than two hundred years ago for a handful of struggling states, scattered over a vast expanse of woods and rivers, when travel was difficult and communication scarce. I speak, of course, of the electoral college, which too many Americans think should play Notre Dame every year in football and be listed in the annual ratings of colleges and universities. It's not there, of course, and Notre Dame wouldn't stand a chance against it in any kind of contest, because it's still no. 1 in influence, durability and damage to the election system, undefeated, either in Congress, by the presidents or by the people, who would have to end it with a constitutional amendment.

"Electing the president through the Electoral College is like playing Russian roulette with the most powerful office in the world, and the loaded chamber is coming up one year. Every other democratic nation has a better way of naming its major leader. France allows a second or even third round of elections if no candidate gets an unchallenged majority. England allows the party which wins the most seats in Parliament to name its leader as Prime Minister. But the United States does not assure that its president has a majority of the popular votes, or even the most popular votes. That's one reason we have become divided politically and I'm not going to contribute to that potential disaster, which could send the 1992 election to a vote in the House, with each state having just one vote in a choice between the two leading candidates.

"So if elected president, I will propose and support an amendment to the constitution that stipulates a candidate for president must have the most popular votes as well as the most electoral votes, and if different candidates have those pluralities then a second election between the two of them be held within three weeks. This would give proper weight to both the states with their electoral votes and to the people with their popular votes, and a second round would produce a winner to which all citizens would feel they had a voice in electing. I urge that whoever is elected as next president summon the will and courage to propose such a constitutional change so that we will no longer play Russian roulette with our presidential choice and the vote cast in a state for one candidate will not in the electoral process actually be cast for the candidate he voted against if he or she lives in a state in which all the electors are cast for the other candidate, if he leads that state's popular votes."

Franklin had launched into an area that he had not even included in the written speech distributed to the media. But he felt it needed to be stressed in this crucial primary.

Franklin actually had come to the microphone, rather nervously. "What a crowd!" he exclaimed. "I campaigned for weeks in New Hampshire without seeing this many people. I appreciate the opportunity to speak to such a large and important group.

"Someone asked me if I was a little nervous. I've been tongue-tied before much-smaller groups than this. But I thought about the president I admire most and the one most of you probably most admire—Franklin D. Roosevelt. Roosevelt presented such a strong and vibrant personality, and looked so powerful from the waist up that many Americans never realized that he was not only crippled but that his legs were totally useless after his polio attack, which is worse than just being crippled.

"In his years as governor and president, there was only one recorded public incident of him actually falling and having to be helped to his feet before a large crowd. It happened right here in Philadelphia as he made his way through the crowd toward the podium at the 1936 National Convention. As he leaned over to greet a man in line one of his leg braces broke and he fell toward the floor, with some one hundred thousand in attendance and thousands more listening on the radio. He was caught by aides just before sprawling completely, but pages of the speech he was holding scattered!

"Two secret service men quickly lifted him but the pages of the speech were strewn widely. Roosevelt ordered his aides to 'clean me up' and retrieve the pages of the speech before they were trampled. Later that night, according to his biographers, Roosevelt told Grace Tully, one of his secretaries, 'I was the maddest white man you ever saw,' a phrase common in that time, which he uttered apparently unconscious of any racial connotation.

"Once at the podium, Roosevelt began hesitantly, still shuffling through the pages of his speech. There were no teleprompters at that time, of course. But as he continued his voice grew stronger and he delivered what is considered one of the greatest speeches of his presidency, including such great passages as, 'In this modern civilization economic royalists have carved new dynasties, new kingdoms, built on their control over material wealth. Against economic tyranny such as this, the American citizens can only appeal to the organized power of their federal government.' He concluded with his famous peroration, 'to some generations much is given, of other generations much is expected. This generation of Americans has a rendezvous with destiny.'"

"As he spoke those words in 1936, Roosevelt could not know what unique challenges were still to confront that generation, which he had to stand tall and boldly lead through to its greatest challenge. He never showed his withered pathetic legs to the public. They only saw his powerful personality. I thought of Roosevelt's example when coming here tonight and realized what he had to overcome when he made that speech!"

The crowd gave Franklin a warm applause at the end of the tribute to Roosevelt. Most of them had never heard of the 1936 incident. Then Franklin continued with a challenge to them: "I have often been asked why I decided to run for president this year, having no political experience, being virtually unknown outside my home state and not that well known there. The answer was difficult without sounding officious and putting myself in a place of importance that would seem ridiculous. But the simple truth is that I kept hearing attacks on the federal government of my nation—the greatest nation, the richest nation in all of history and most important, on its government which must be the model for all people seeking to establish a government answerable to voters but still strong enough to establish and maintain order and the rules of decorum which are under attack, fiercely and constantly not just from external enemies but also from unhappy thousands inside the nation itself.

"Ronald Reagan, a recent honored leader, said of the US government he led for two terms the government is not the answer, the government is the problem. He should have known better. Quite clearly, government is not the problem, it has been the answer ever since General George Washington could not get food and clothing for his ragtag army during the Revolution and recognized that only a united effort from all the colonies could assure independence from Great Britain.

"And then it was Thomas Jefferson, not the strongest proponent of a strong central government idea, who as the third US president, when the US was still a fragile and fledgling nation, deep in financial debt, who took the lead and approved the expenditure of $15 million, a sum equal at the time to an entire year's income for the young nation, to make the Louisiana Purchase and assure that the US would become the dominant nation in the Americas. Could any one state, or group of several states, have made such a commitment? Could any president not assured of financial support from all the states through a strong central government, have taken such a bold gamble?

"That has been the case throughout the years of US history, as the central government provided the land and much of the financing for the railroads across the vast, mainly barren area, between the Atlantic and Pacific oceans; approved the Homestead Act of 1862 to encourage families to move into frontier territory by giving them a plot of land they could own and develop. No other nation has ever grown so swiftly and so well as the United States of America.

"And, of course, there was its greatest test of survival as a nation and as an example of democracy, the Civil War, which at tragic cost in lives and destruction confirmed what the Founding Fathers and all US presidents had supported since 1788, which was that the states were one nation, indivisible.

"The dominant world power the US has become today was actually the result of three great revolutions: the first was the original revolution to become free from Great Britain, establish a constitutional government and to expand its borders; the second revolution was the Civil War, which assured the survival of that nation; and then the third was the New Deal, which created the modern nation that has extended promise and prosperity to a far greater number of the population than ever before, rescuing us from the worst economic depression in its history, providing the structure and programs to maintain such a nation, and equally important to demonstrate to the rest of the world the proper path to peace and prosperity.

"That is why this election is so important. Instead of boldness to carry out the unprecedented opportunity facing us I saw disunity and doubts about our own nation; then one day President Bush said, 'we have the will to move forward but not the wallet!' That's also exactly backwards. We have the largest wallet of any nation in history...a wallet immensely superior to the wallet with which Jefferson bought the Louisiana Purchase; a wallet much greater than Abraham Lincoln had when he summoned the people to a long and bloody war to secure survival of the Union; a wallet much fatter than during the Great Depression, or at the outset of World War II.

"No, what we had to meet all those challenges was not a big wallet but a big will, a will to build a larger, more secure country; to assure unity for that country, then to provide the means to emerge from the agrarian age and become the world's greatest industrial engine, while keeping our basic freedoms and protecting our citizens from the historic disorders of nature, such as floods, hurricanes and fires; then building an interstate highway to link the nation by car as well as train; dams to assure sufficient and safe water; a sewerage system to assure modern services to the most remote villages.

"And while doing all that our government also found enough in its wallet to send men to the moon and to win the Cold War against Russia without firing a shot or digging a lot of graves.

"This is the message I was not hearing in the political debates of today. Instead there were bitter complaints if a letter wasn't delivered on time for 5 cents, or that a remote road still wasn't paved and especially that taxes are too high.

"Polls taken in 1964 found that 62 percent of Americans trusted the government to do the right thing. The percentage had dropped to just 19 percent in polls taken last year after more than twenty years of government bashing led by Ronald Reagan and Republican supply siders who could not be satisfied with whatever amount of loot they were taking from the economy, and kept demanding more and threatening if they don't get more the nation will collapse. That has been their basic message since 1980 and it is still the message today, only with even less basis in reality. In simple terms the message is that tax cuts make rich people wiser while more money and security corrupts poor people, making them weaker, lazy and content with squalor and failure.

"Can we continue to sustain this great nation on that false philosophy? I say no, not in the late twentieth century when a demand-side economy should be sufficient for all citizens to share in the nation's abundance, and provides a reason for every American to get up in the morning and anticipate that day will be better than yesterday and that tomorrow will be even better."

Franklin paused for a moment hoping that his words were powerful enough to make an impact. They were not soothing or designed to elicit cheers and applause but they were words he once more wanted on the record of the campaign and in the coverage of the day's speeches.

"Franklin Roosevelt, in one of his most profound statements proclaimed, 'The test of our progress is not whether we add more to the abundance of those who have much, it is whether we provide enough for those who have too little.'

"He spoke those words in 1937. Some thirty years later, another great Democratic president, Lyndon Johnson, saw the nation still in need and declared a war on poverty. At the beginning of his term Ronald Reagan proclaimed we declared a war on poverty and poverty won. And he then proceeded to assure poverty's victory. But poverty had not won; the nation won many early battles and then retired from the field when the going got too expensive. Similar to President Bush, Lyndon Johnson's critics said the nation lacked the wallet to battle poverty while also waging a military mission in Vietnam. But as today, they had the wallet, they lacked the will. Today, there is no question we have the wallet but where can we find the will?

"That was the most remarkable characteristic of Franklin Roosevelt—his will. From the age of thirty-nine he had no legs to stand on. He could not walk across a room unaided, but he had a will few men have ever exhibited. He used his arms to pull up stairs. He ignored his handicaps to the extent that other people also ignored them, because all they saw in public was his indomitable will.

"And now in 1992, having vanquished our most dangerous external foe from the field, the US stands in the unique position of leading the people of this nation and all nations on a path to peace and prosperity unprecedented in history. We have the wallet and we have the power to enforce peace on reluctant nations, yet we are still tempted to wage war instead of wage peace. War is a tempting nectar while peace can be a warm glass of water; success in peace brings no medals, no parades no statutes of gallant heroes; peace only brings grey photos of men sitting around a table, signing papers and maybe shaking hands. But peace must be our goal, even in the face of such third world gangsters as Saddam Hussein. When faced by just a modicum of the power we could bring against him his army faded into the woodwork, leaving an estimated one hundred thousand Iraqi citizens as human sacrifices to Saddam's flawed ambitions. Fortunately, only about three hundred Americans died in the war, but those three hundred were someone's son, husband, brother, sister. Who knows that they did not include a great inventor, a great writer, or a great artist, or a great political leader?

"So we come today to our generation's challenges and opportunity. We are the children of what has been called the greatest generation, a generation that grew up during the Great Depression; came to adulthood just in time to fight and win history's most deadly and crucial war, and then built a postwar nation and world that prospered and patiently prevailed in the long Cold War with Communism, without a shot being fired at each other by the two main adversaries, the US and the Soviet Union, which finally collapsed in exhaustion and into obscurity.

"Now our generation has the opportunity to heal the world of its long devotion to conflict; to provide wider access to the daily comforts Americans take for granted, such as indoor plumbing, air-conditioning in the summer and forced air heat in the winter; the chance to provide a housewife in Angola with a washing machine and dryer; a child in Liberia with vaccinations. All the wonders that modern science and medicine have developed are possible for all peoples but nearly half the people in the world don't have access to them or perhaps even know they exist.

"An article on a speech I made at Harvard was headlined in the campus newspaper, 'send them commodes, not bombs.' That catches the essence and practicality of what I was trying to get across, which is that the US sends billions of dollars to nations to make more weapons to kill each other's people but few commodes or other ways to improve their daily living conditions. The shipments of armaments show that we have the wallet. The absence of products to make better lives rather than to take lives show that we do not have the will, or perhaps, the common sense.

"In that speech at the 1936 Democratic Convention, President Roosevelt concluded with his famous declaration that this generation of Americans has a rendezvous with destiny. But our generation, the children of the greatest, is the Chosen Generation in all of history to fulfill the dreams and hopes of all the generations that have gone before.

"The Greatest Generation needed great individual leaders and found them in Franklin Roosevelt, who rose on his withered legs and indomitable will to become the towering public figure of his time; and then other indispensable leaders such as Harry Truman, Dwight Eisenhower, George C. Marshall and in other countries, Winston Churchill and Konrad Adenauer.

"Our time and challenges need such leaders and let me say with all my heart how much I appreciate the support so many Americans have given me to be their presidential candidate. That support has been not only unexpected but almost miraculous and I would be remiss not to give those voters the credit they deserve for making it possible for me to stand before this gathering today to express my views to thousands of people who would never have read or heard them otherwise. That was my goal in this campaign, to stir interest and conversation about matters of public interest which I did not feel were receiving the attention they deserved.

"But my other goal was to assure that the American system of elections remained stable and in good working condition. As I mentioned earlier, it has been under attack from both left and right on the political scale and has arrived at a juncture where the two-party system itself is under threat. Looking at the fate of other nations which have fallen into the morass of multiple political parties offers little confidence that the United States with its many factions, races, ethnic groups and heartfelt beliefs could not fall into the same political chaos. Indeed, we suffered such a fate in the years leading to the Civil War when four sizable political forces split the national presidential votes and electors, none of which had close to a majority of votes. The largest had less than 40 percent of the popular votes and emerged as the winner, but with 11 states unwilling to acknowledge the winner. Many other national examples could be cited, including most ominously the 1933 example of Germany, then a floundering democracy, which became so divided, with its parliament split into so many parties that the relatively new and minor Nazi party, with a determined and charismatic leader, was able to elect that leader as prime minister, although neither he nor his party had ever gotten a majority of the nation's votes, or even a significant plurality.

"The US is far from that kind of breakdown, of course, but it is in a state of divisions where a three-way split among the popular votes and electoral votes could bring on a serious crisis, as occurred in 1824, the split among Andrew Jackson, John Quincy Adams, and Henry Clay, and the previously mentioned election of 1860, which precipitated the Civil War.

"As I have stated many times during this campaign the most important issue is not who wins but that the nation emerges stronger and united. The two-party system has its flaws but the nation is best served when it can resolve its choice of presidential candidates within the two-party system and present two candidates for the people to choose from in the November election. I sincerely believe that is more important this year than it has ever been. At the present time, the polls surprisingly show three candidates contending for the electoral votes, the incumbent president, an independent candidate, who has not been through the usual party nominating process, and the yet-to-be-selected Democratic candidate.

"For reasons I have expressed many times in this campaign I believe it is in the best interest of the people, the nation and the world that the Democratic candidate become president. That will fulfill my first priority in this election, which is the stability and longevity of our system of government. The man who must lead us will need to be of strong will, a good heart and stable health. He will need experience in the tasks of a governmental executive; he will need a network of friends across the nation to help him along the way; he will need determination and stamina and backbone to stand against the demands of both friends and foes. He will need to be someone of decisiveness who can make decisions and not look back with regret. He will need the self-confidence to pursue the job without fear and indecision that cripples him when he is the last and most important voice in the room."

Then, looking around the auditorium with a touch of anxiety in his manner, Franklin summed up his own decision. "When I look in the mirror each day I do not see that man. When I look in my heart I do not detect his presence; when I look in my soul, I do not find him there. So with great appreciation to you who have supported me I frankly tell you I'm not that man. Today, I am releasing my delegates to vote their choice as I will vote mine, which will be for William Jefferson Clinton, who I think comes closest to meeting those difficult requirements and who can gain the support of a majority of the electors and the popular votes against George W. Bush, a good man, but not the one I want to wake up on the day after the election and have as president for four more years, and against Ross Perot, who is a candidate without a party and without any political experience, and as far as I can tell has no business being president of the United States."

From the time he endorsed Clinton, the crowd began a low rumble which soon became a roar of cheers and applause. He stood there for nearly five minutes waiting for the tumult to subside then raised his hands for quiet so that he could get to the final sentence of his speech.

"My plea to you, especially to Mr. Clinton, is not to forget that we are the Chosen Generation, with the task and responsibility presented to no other generation in history, to pursue peace with as much courage as we have waged war, and as that headline read, to send commodes instead of bombs to the poor people of the world."

The crowd gave him a long standing ovation. Brad came over to put an arm around his shoulders. "Boss," he sobbed, "that was great, I haven't cried like this since the last time I saw '*It's a Wonderful Life.*'"

An aide to one of the other candidates was standing next to Jack Hardy. "You work with Franklin, don't you," he commented. "What a hell of a speech that was. Who wrote it?"

Hardy looked at him with a broad smile while tears trickled down his cheek. "The same guy who delivered it," Hardy proclaimed proudly, "the guy who should be the next president of the United States, Thomas Alexander Franklin, the last New Dealer."

Epilogue

THE COLLEGE THAT
KEEPS WINNING

*"You see things as they are and ask why? I dream
things that never were and ask why not?"*
                                    George Bernard Shaw

He heard a voice from far away calling loudly, "Mr. Franklin, Mr. Franklin, can you hear me? It's time to wake up." The voice persisted, calling his name again. Franklin was in the midst of a dream he wanted to see how ended. His mind was reluctant to let it go, but the voice kept calling. "Wake up, wake up."

Slowly he tried to make the transition from his dream to the fact that he was actually lying in a bed, looking up at a strange man standing over him, calling urgently and shaking his arm.

He decided the man must be a doctor and he felt the stress and pain of a body that had been battered and broken. He managed to open his eyes fully and behind the man he saw a person he recognized immediately. It was his wife, Jean. She had an anxious expression on her face, which was turning into a smile as he opened his eyes and forced his arm to reach for her hand. "Am I alive?" Franklin asked.

"Yes," said the doctor, "Alive and recovering. Do you remember what happened?"

Franklin tried to separate his long dream and the reality of what went before. "I remember too much," he murmured. "I'm trying to make sure what's real and what was in my dream." He looked at Jean. "Are you okay?" he asked.

"I am if you are," she answered. "You've been in a coma for a week."

"I'm okay," Franklin said. "I remember the rainstorm, sliding across the interstate and…then the campaign for president. I wanted to know who won…but then y'all woke me up. Who is the president?"

"George Bush," Jean told him. "He's running for reelection against Bill Clinton, that nice young man we met at one of Zell Miller's receptions. You remember I said he had a personality that was unforgettable, and I'm not easily impressed by politicians."

"Yes, I remember. You're hard to impress but Clinton impressed you." He looked at the doctor. "When can I get out of here?" he asked.

"If your mind keeps churning, I'd say in a few days, a week at the most. Your injuries are healing. Your head wound still needs watching."

"Actually, my brain feels great and is full of wild imaginings. It's almost like Dorothy waking up from her visit to Oz…or maybe George Bailey after his time with Clarence the angel who showed him what the world would have been if he'd never been born."

One question was uppermost in his mind. "Did you find the envelope in my coat pocket?" he asked Jean.

"Yes," she assured him. "I found it at the hospital and all the checks, papers and money were there. About $5 million, which I immediately deposited in the company's bank account and called John to find out where it came from. It's been collecting interest."

Franklin sat on the side of the bed. He felt fairly well despite some lingering aches and pains from the accident. His head was clearing quickly and his natural curiosity wanted to know what had happened in the past few days.

"I hope you saved the recent newspapers," Franklin said, "so I can catch up."

"I did. They're by your chair at home."

"First, let's get you up and start eating," the doctor said. "I think you've lost about twenty pounds."

"I've been trying to lose that twenty pounds for years." Franklin laughed.

As he slowly recovered over the next few weeks, Franklin had the opportunity to read and re-read some of the books he recognized as having influenced his dream about the presidential campaign.

He followed news of the current campaign closely. Ross Perot held a lead in the polls through the spring and early summer, even after Clinton clinched the Democratic nomination. The possibility of a failed popular election was definitely possible. Perot's erratic behavior remained a puzzle, but voters obviously wanted a choice other than the two major party candidates.

Perot was a reluctant campaigner and avoided open press conferences and when he finally held one he ripped open an issue that would haunt the early Clinton administration: gays in the military. Perot opened the door by saying he wouldn't appoint an openly gay person to his cabinet. Perot didn't like to discuss the subject and considered it irrelevant to the economy and the deficit. So he closed down the news conference abruptly and left, returning to his private campaign jet. Then amid claims that his daughters were going to be ridiculed in the press for various imagined reasons, Perot suddenly announced he was pulling out of the race just before the Democratic Convention opened in New York City.

He left thousands of campaign workers and possible voters in dismay and without a candidate. But the timing was incredibly favorable for Clinton, who was still coming in third in most nationwide polls behind Perot and Bush.

Perot claimed he withdrew because he did not want the election to be made by the House of Representatives, an outcome he felt would be disruptive for the nation. He said he had always felt he had to win a majority of the electoral votes in the general election to have a chance. Now, he said that didn't seem to be possible and he didn't want a failed election, which was news to his opponents and to Franklin, sitting at home watching the surprising developments.

The possibility of Perot's disruption of the election had been a major reason the candidate in his dream had withdrawn and endorsed Bill Clinton.

But Perot, always enigmatic, left the door open to reenter the race later. "I'm still in the stadium, I'm on the sidelines, but I am still here," he said.

Clinton was the huge beneficiary of Perot's withdrawal. He combined that with a star performance at the Democratic Convention followed by a bus tour with his running mate that covered several key states.

The bus tour carried Clinton to locations long neglected by national candidates in the larger states, and was somewhat similar to the New Hampshire campaign Thomas Franklin had conducted by car.

The Republicans cooperated at their convention. Sen. Phil Gramm was the keynote speaker and he was perhaps the strongest supply-wide economist in the Senate. His speech left no rock unturned in the dogma which Franklin had denounced in his phantom campaign and which Clinton was denouncing in his speeches.

Then Pat Buchanan, who had challenged Bush so surprisingly from the right in the primaries, gave another speech, aimed at the party's right wingers, in which he called for "a holy war for American souls" and took shots at Hillary Clinton as a radical feminist. The convention crowd chanted "four more years" which was exactly what a majority of voters had decided they didn't want.

Clinton's campaign team, watching on TV, could scarcely believe this turn of events. In his acceptance speech, Bush fell back on the Republican policies he once described as "voodoo economics," which was cutting taxes while lowering the federal deficit. Following the GOP Convention, Clinton gained a lead of twelve to fourteen points in the major polls with only six weeks left in the campaign.

But in late September, Perot announced he was getting back in the race. Incredibly, his name still appealed to thousands of voters. He came back with a different strategy, which he had designed on his own, without any consultants. Instead he put huge sums of money into TV segments of fifteen to thirty minutes instead of the thirty-second spots consultants usually preferred. He called them infomercials, with Perot himself as the spokesman and a series of easy-to-read charts illustrating his points. He thought people were tired of the same old commercials of candidates defining their pet issues. Perot was the producer, writer and star of his infomercials, and he stayed in his home city of Dallas, busy with these tasks rather than traveling all over the country as Bush and Clinton were still doing.

He did not make a personal appearance at one of his rallies until nine days before the election; he did participate in the three TV debates, however, and was judged to have won one of them and out-performed Bush in the two others.

On Election Day, the center held and Clinton was the winner, if you can call getting 42 percent of the popular votes winning. Bush got just 39 percent, a dramatic decline from his winning total of 53 percent four years earlier. His 39 million votes were the lowest percentage of the total for a major party candidate since 1912.

Perot's support turned out to be, in the old adage, a mile wide and an inch deep. He did receive nearly 20 percent of the total popular vote, but he failed to get any electoral votes, carrying not a single state, and not even coming close in most of them. George Wallace, running as a third-party candidate in 1968, had gotten only 14 percent of the total national popular vote but had carried five southern states with 46 electoral votes, coming closer to throwing that election into the House of Representatives than Perot would do in 1992.

Franklin now recovered from his injury, cast his vote for Clinton and attended one of Clinton's largest rallies at a football stadium in DeKalb County, Georgia where Clinton had a variety of Georgia personalities on hand to introduce him, including Gov. Zell Miller, Atlanta Mayor Maynard Jackson, Sen. Sam Nunn, and Rock Music Star Michael Stipe of R.E.M. Clinton carried Georgia by a narrow margin in November; Georgia had voted for Nixon in 1972; Reagan in 1984 and Bush in 1988. In the final count, Clinton's 42 percent of the national popular votes was the lowest percentage for a winning candidate since Woodrow Wilson's 43 percent in the three-way race with former President Theodore Roosevelt and incumbent President William Howard Taft in 1912. Bush's 39 percent and Perot's 20 percent combined for 59 percent overall against Clinton, but the alchemy of that creaking remnant of the eighteenth century, the electoral college, translated Clinton's lead into a virtual landslide of 370 electoral votes, more than Bush, Carter or Kennedy had accumulated in their winning campaigns. The College was to do much worse in the next few elections.

Analysts who looked deeper at the outcome recognized that Clinton had received no higher percentage of the popular votes than Dukakis in 1988 or Mondale in 1984. Nearly 60 percent of the voters had preferred someone else. But in the three-way race without a runoff provision, Clinton had the plurality if not a majority. Had a runoff been held, Bush would likely have inherited a majority of Perot voters and been reelected. A minority of the voters had prevailed again.

The 1992 outcome did illustrate a dangerous divide among the voters and Franklin looked on the outcome with concern but with the hope that Clinton would prove to be a better president than he expected, as he had expressed to Hillary in his dream.

That was not to be however, as Clinton, with his thin mandate, stumbled out of the gate making almost every misstep that confronted him. Immediately damaging was his response to early questions as to whether he would end all denial of homosexuals to the armed forces. As Franklin had tried to warn him, that was an issue with perilous consequences. Asked about this pledge, he said, "Yes, I want to." He quickly encountered serious opposition. The Senate Armed Forces Committee, chaired by Senator Sam Nunn, and the Chiefs of Staff, headed by General Colin Powell, then at the peak of his popularity as a Gulf War commander, were both opposed. Nunn made his opposition public, and more quietly so did the chiefs of staff, since constitutionally, the military services are under the command of the president.

Clinton hinted in a speech at the Naval Academy that any who objected to giving homosexuals the right to serve should resign their commissions. Nunn indicated that he would hold public hearings on the question, and Clinton was already on weak ground with the military over his draft status during the Vietnam War. Robert Byrd, the longest-serving Democratic senator, made the most forceful speech against Clinton's proposal. Byrd went back to the fall of the Roman Empire in his emotional appeal, blaming the empire's decline on the presence of male prostitutes in Ceasar's armies. "Remove not the ancient landmarks our fathers have set," Byrd pleaded. "It will lead to demands for same sex marriages and homosexuals in the Boy Scouts."

Clinton backed off but almost the entire first week of his administration was consumed with the so-called "gays in the military" issue. It concluded with a compromise put forward by Gen. Powell, which became the "don't ask, don't tell" policy that prevailed for several years but satisfied neither side of the debate. The issue faded but Democrats never fully recovered from the dispute as subsequent elections would show.

Then Clinton ran into controversy over his cabinet choices, which he had promised "would look like America." In that effort he put two women forward for attorney general and it was discovered that both of them had used illegal immigrants for house work. Both appointees had to withdraw. The third woman Clinton selected was Janet Reno who won approval but was a problem for him the next eight years.

Clinton plunged on through his cabinet appointments and encountered no more serious obstacles, although Franklin considered the cabinet mediocre except for Robert Reich, Clinton's old buddy from his Rhodes scholarship days in England. Reich, who was named Secretary of Commerce, was a true New Dealer and a clever one. But the strongest economic voices in the cabinet were former Texas Senator Lloyd Bentsen, a deficit hawk, and Wall Street banker Robert Rubin.

After a major battle in Congress the NAFTA Treaty was approved, with decisive support from Clinton and a majority of Republicans, but determined opposition from a majority of Democrats, many of whom never forgave Clinton for his support of NAFTA. Franklin continued to think it was a mistake although Clinton was praised widely for getting the treaty through Congress, and he expected more support from Republicans in the future. He never got it. In the next two bitter legislative battles he had little, if any, Republican support. First was the 1993 budget, which was painstakingly crafted, mainly by Clinton himself, to reduce the deficit while slightly raising the top income tax rate on the highest tax payers. The budget also included a five-cent increase in the gasoline tax, at the insistence of environmentalist champion Al Gore, the vice president, who said it would reduce the use of gasoline and pollution. But it also made it possible for Clinton's Republican opponents to point out that he had broken his promise not to raise taxes that affected the middle class. A gasoline tax, even a small one, proved another major blunder in Clinton's early months as president. The budget was approved with just a single vote in the House from a Republican, a woman from a closely-contested district in Pennsylvania, who never won another election.

Still, the overall bill, described by Republicans as the "largest tax increase in history" and a certain disaster for the economy, was absorbed into a rising GDP, bolstered by the spread of personal computers and the introduction of the Internet, a development primarily by the federal government by the way. During the next decade the 1994 budget bill would prove the key factor in an unprecedented economic boom, and the result in 1999, of an actual balanced federal budget, which after all the weeping and moaning about the national budget deficit, was hardly noticed on October 29, the day it was reported.

By then, however, Clinton and the Democrats had reaped the whirlwind of his early missteps. In the 1994 mid-term elections, Republicans won control of both the House and the Senate for only the second time in sixty-five years, interrupted briefly by the Republican victory in 1946.

Hillary had been put in charge of the Health Care bill, which was expected to be the hardest battle of 1994. It turned out not to be a battle at all because the bill that emerged from Hillary's efforts didn't even get enough support in Congress to make it to the floor for a full vote.

A broad crime control bill, dealing with the popular political issue of the year seemed assured of bi-partisan support, but Democrats added a provision that prohibited the sale of automatic machine guns, and Republicans refused to approve the bill unless that provision was removed. The crime bill, also opposed by the black caucus because of its tougher prison sentences, finally passed, with the sale of automatic weapons still permitted.

In that election, 53 Democrats lost their House seats, giving Republicans a majority they still held in 2016; Republicans gained nine seats in the Senate. The sweep also elevated many Republicans to control of state legislatures and governorships. Not a single Republicans incumbent was defeated. Such prominent Democrats as Mario Cuomo lost his bid for another term as governor of New York; Gov. Ann Richards lost reelection in Texas, beaten by George W. Bush, son of the man Clinton had defeated for president two years earlier. Even House Speaker Tom Foley lost. The 1994 outcome was a projection of what was to be the new vote distribution in US elections. Women voted for Democrats by a margin of 53 to 47, while men backed Republicans, 58 to 42, easily offsetting the margins of 91 percent of black voters and 60 percent of Hispanics for Democrats.

The route was broad and clear. Sitting in his den at home, Thomas Franklin studied the results sadly. Many of the political dangers in his dream had come true for the Democrats, who still didn't seem to realize that they had gotten on the unpopular side of too many issues. Democrats could take comfort in only one figure: only 40 percent of the eligible voters had cast a ballot, compared to 56 percent in the presidential election. This was also a pattern that would continue in the next mid-term elections.

Clinton won in 1996 with Perot again in the race as an independent against Clinton and Republican Robert Dole who was seventy-three at the time, making him the oldest major party candidate ever to run for president. Clinton won with 48 percent of the popular votes again missing a popular vote majority, which distressed him mightily.

Clinton's first term had started uncertainly, but his second term included one of the most emotional and bizarre years in the nation's history.

Early on, rumors were flying that Clinton was having an affair with an intern who was scarcely older than his daughter, Chelsea, 19. The rumors gained credence by the end of January 1997, and even so loyal a Clinton supporter as George Stephanopoulos said it would be difficult for Clinton to remain in the presidency, if the rumors were true.

But Clinton denied or sidestepped their magnitude. Actually, he simply lied, to his wife, to his cabinet, to the American people and to lawyers in court proceedings. As the prosecutor in the impeachment case brought against him in the House concluded: "He lied until there was nobody left to lie to."

During this time, Newt Gingrich, the Republican Speaker of the House also admitted to having an affair with a woman who later became his third wife. His chosen successor, Robert Livingston, incredibly also admitted to an extramarital relationship and both he and Gingrich resigned from Congress. But Clinton doggedly held on as president. His answer to whether he would resign was "Never." He weathered the storm of shameful details of making the oval office the scene of oral sex with the intern, Monica Lewinsky. He also had telephone sex conversations with Lewinsky, often late at night. Most of this was revealed in taped conversations with Lewinsky. As Sen. Lindsay Graham of South Carolina put it, "when someone calls you at 3a.m. you know they're up to no good."

Watching on his TV, Thomas Franklin was appalled by Clinton's reckless behavior, betraying not just his wife, but the millions of people who voted for him, not once, but twice. In a column very early in 1998, Franklin made the case that the honorable and best course for the party and the nation was for Clinton to resign, allowing Vice President Al Gore to become the incumbent president for the 2000 election.

The Republicans went ahead and impeached Clinton in the House where they had a clear majority on the grounds that he lied to a Grand Jury and committed acts violating his presidential oath.

But by the end of 1998, the public was sated with details of Clinton's transgressions and comforted by an economic boom, partially brought about by the Clinton budget of 1993, and resulting in the balanced federal budget of 1999, the first balanced budget since Johnson's administration.

The impeachment vote in the Senate, where conviction required a two-thirds majority, was easily in Clinton's favor and in effect gave him a new lease on the presidency.

That set the stage for the presidential election of 2000, which turned out to be the most controversial since 1876, and demonstrated once again the malignancy of the electoral college, designed for a nation of less than 10 million people, most of whom were not even expected to vote in presidential elections.

The 1876 presidential election was stolen, unfair and square, and so was the 2000 election in a time of supposedly more fairness. In 1876, just twelve years after the end of the Civil War, federal troops still controlled several southern states and most of their governmental functions. As the total popular votes mounted, one Republican observer noticed that the southern votes were going heavily to the Democratic candidate, Samuel Tilden of New York State. He also saw that four states were still not tabulated. They were Louisiana, South Carolina, Florida and Oregon. In the popular vote totals for the rest of the nation, the total by then was 4,224,000 for Tilden to only 4,036,672 for the Republican, Rutherford B. Hayes. Those four states finally submitted two sets of electoral totals, with both parties claiming victory. When the electoral college voters for all states met on December 6, it awarded all the contested electors to Republican Hayes, which gave him a total of 185 electors to Tilden's 184. Tilden had a substantial lead in the popular vote, due to his totals in the former Confederate states.

In January, Congress appointed a fifteen-man committee to decide which electoral votes should be awarded to Hayes and which to Tilden. The committee's decision was to be final. During its debate, tempers flared and members from both parties threatened to seize the government by force if they lost, raising fears that a resumption of the Civil War was possible, although not likely, considering the South's weakened condition. But days passed and the commission came to no acceptable decision; then just one day before the new president was to be inaugurated in March, southern members of Congress agreed to abide by the commission's recommendation. Actually a deal was made in secret between the southerners and Republican members of the committee for the Democrats to accept the decision in exchange for a promise by the Republicans to withdraw all federal troops from southern states and, in effect, end Reconstruction policies, which had resulted in former slaves winning several high political offices, and generally improving their status overall, such as being allowed to learn to read.

Hayes was awarded all the contested electors, giving him a one-vote victory over Tilden and the presidency. True to his word, President Hayes ordered all federal troops out of the southern states by April 10, 1877. He hoped that a coalition of black voters and Republicans would form a political majority in southern states, but that didn't happen. For more than one hundred years, the south was the Solid South, solid that is for Democratic political candidates. As soon as whites gained political control southern Democrats were put in power and virtually eliminated voting by blacks. Ironically when blacks regained their voting strength in the 1960s they became the most faithful voting bloc for Democrats. White southerners quickly proved that it was not party labels that mattered to them as much as skin color and economic status. By 1990, the South was almost as solidly Republican as it had been solidly Democratic.

In 1876, the centennial year of the Declaration of Independence, US voters had again been denied a fair and responsible election for president. The center didn't hold, and the system didn't work as it should have. The candidate with the most popular voters and by honest count, the most electoral votes, didn't win. It was a perversion of democracy.

In 2000, the stakes weren't quite as high and passions were not quite as hot as in 1876. But the outcome of the presidential election was even more confusing and wrongheaded than in 1876—and with everybody watching. Three cable news channels had joined the media circus by that year and elections were their meat and potatoes after Monica and the O.J. Simpson murder trial in 1984. Yet with so such blanket coverage they mostly missed or distorted the election's outcome.

As in 1876, the candidate with the most popular votes and arguably with the most electoral votes did not become president. As in 1876, the final verdict on the election was weeks in coming, finally being delivered by the Supreme Court in mid-December. And once again, it was the insidious electoral college which decided the winner.

The candidates were Democrat Al Gore, who had been Clinton's vice president for eight years and George W. Bush, son of President George H.W. Bush, whom Clinton defeated in 1996, for the Republicans.

The younger Bush had been elected governor of Texas in the Republican sweep of 1994 and Gore was the son of a longtime Tennessee senator, and had lived in Washington most of his life. Both were the equivalent of political royalty.

Polls indicated a close race that turned out to be right on the money. On Election Day, the networks whose main passion is to decide each state's winner, not tabulate the popular votes accurately or even pay attention to them, ended up that delirious night calling the election first for Bush and then for Gore. The problem, as it had been in 1876, was the Florida results, which basically showed Gore and Bush tied in the popular vote which would determine its electoral votes, and give one of the candidates an electoral majority.

There was no doubt who had the most popular votes nationwide. It was Gore, with a final count (some days later) of 51,003,694 to 50,459,211 for Bush, a lead of 459,000. There were also extenuating circumstances. Most important was third-party candidate Ralph Nader, running as the Green Party candidate, who got 2,324,410 votes nationwide, 97,400 of which were in Florida. Gore, of course, was an acclaimed environmentalist, who had written a book on the subject and would produce a prize winning movie on the environment. If any major presidential candidate ever deserved, and sought, the votes of environmentalists—it was Gore. So it's reasonable to assume that if Nader had not been on the ballot, or if there had been a runoff, Gore would have won the majority of Nader's Green Party votes, giving him a clear electoral majority.

Then, there was the "butterfly ballot" in Palm Beach County, Florida where the minor party candidate Pat Buchanan got several thousand votes which were clearly supposed to be cast for Gore, according to a later determination of poll officials and according to common political sense. Palm County voters were mainly retirees who voted heavily for Gore, except on the confusing ballots.

On top of that the entire vote count of Florida was being challenged by both parties and a recount was ordered by a federal court. The Florida secretary of state, a dedicated Bush supporter, had already declared Bush the winner as had the major networks at one point on Election Night. Thus, to the public the election had been decided, not by the vote count but by the TV networks.

At the end of the recount, Bush had a 350-vote lead over Gore, not counting the butterfly ballots or considering the 97,400 votes cast in Florida for the Green candidate Nader.

So by the narrow margin of a few hundred questionable votes Bush was declared the winner in Florida, giving him 271 electoral votes to Gore's 266.

A voting procedure designed in 1789 had decided the first election of the twenty-first century. Or was it still the twentieth. In any case, the winner was determined by laws and rules designed for a nation of 13 thinly populated states along the Atlantic coast, not for the nation of 330 million people, stretching from sea to shining sea, and supposedly the model for democracy in all the nations of the world.

Gore and the Democrats did not strongly contest the outcome. Gore had won the most popular votes but he was not exactly a popular candidate, being considered too stiff and dull. He had campaigned vigorously and all political reason seemed to be on his side, but he recognized that a long dispute over the presidency would further weaken faith in the elective process, which was already weakened by Clinton's misbehavior. Another factor may have been that his seemingly perfect marriage was under strain. He and his wife, Tipper, had been through three presidential campaigns, plus several senate campaigns by then. Tipper had always seemed to be the more popular partner. A perky, pretty blonde, she had first won notice with a campaign in the 1990s against lewd and obscene lyrics in pop music aimed at teenagers. At the time the Gores had four children in their teens and Tipper's campaign earned deserved acclaim, but its appeal was not strong in the so-called Democratic base. Still, compared to their running mate couple, Bill and Hillary Clinton, in the 1992 and 1996 campaigns the Gores seemed to have a sound marriage, with none of the drama and scandal associated with the Clintons.

While the Clintons survived the Monica Lewinsky affair, and Vice President Gore had faithfully supported him, Clinton's behavior left a shadow over the Democratic ticket in 2000. Gore himself was affected and could hardly bring himself to mention Clinton's name during the campaign although Clinton had left a growing economy, a relatively favorable foreign policy and a balanced budget that was projecting federal surpluses into the late 1990s. In fact, one of the issues in the campaign was what to do with the surplus money. Gore and others wanted to begin paying down the nation's deficit, but Republicans, who had complained so bitterly about the deficit wanted to cut taxes instead, especially for the highest earners.

The election verdict was finally settled by the Supreme Court in a one-vote margin that favored Bush. The nation, by then was weary of the long count and simply wanted a resolution. The public generally accepted the decision and Bush was sworn in as president in January.

The electoral process had failed again, badly, leaving the electoral college in place for a future disaster, which was not long in coming.

One victim of the election was the Gores' marriage. Even after Gore wrote a book he called, Joined at the Heart, about loving couples, he and Tipper suddenly announced their separation in 2010. Meanwhile, the Clintons' celebrated another anniversary and Hillary became a candidate for the Democratic presidential nomination in 2008.

She went into the primaries as a heavy favorite, but another unfair voting system foiled her candidacy. The first test that year, as usual, was the Iowa caucus, in which less than 30,000 actual voters took part in one of the most convoluted elective processes in the nation. On a cold January night, voters went to their nearest caucus site and divided into groups for the various candidates, which for the

Democrats were Hillary, Sen. Barack Obama and Sen. John Edwards of South Carolina. After hearing arguments for each candidate, the caucus-goers cast their votes. The result was very divided among the three candidates, with Obama getting about 38 percent, to Edwards' 32 percent and Hillary's 30 percent. The TV coverage and the next day's headlines seized on the phenomenon of Obama's narrow lead and favorite Hillary's third place finish. The handful of voters on a frigid Iowa night had set the tone for the primary season.

Hillary won the next week's New Hampshire primary by an impressive margin but the damage had been done. Obama kept winning low-vote caucuses while Hillary won the popular vote in the larger primaries, including Michigan and Florida, two of the most important states. But again a kink in the process robbed her of those votes when the party threw out the Michigan and Florida results because the states had voted "out of turn." Their votes would have given Hillary a lead and momentum at a decisive time.

Obama pulled ahead on the basis of caucus votes, and Edwards soon withdrew, giving Hillary an advantage in the later primaries, since she and Edwards were obviously splitting the white votes, and Obama, the first black candidate to have a valid shot at a presidential nomination, was sweeping the black vote. It was later revealed that Edwards was having an affair with one of his campaign workers, and she had his child later that year. The National Enquirer had the story but held it until after the campaign, hesitant to buck the tide of public disdain which had followed the exposits of Bill Clinton.

Barack Hussein Obama overcame the handicaps of his name and his unusual heritage as the son of a Kansas-born mother and a Kenyan father to become the Democratic candidate and then go on to win the presidency against Republican Sen. John McCain, a bona fide war hero. Obama entered office in 2009 with Democratic majorities in both the House and Senate but Republicans swore to make him a "one-term president" and his health care bill became the favored target of their opposition. Obama managed to get his health care bill through Congress after a bitter battle and many compromises, most of which favored the health insurance industry.

But the battle left the Democrats weakened for the mid-term elections of 2010, and they lost their majorities in both houses. As in the Clinton years, a Democratic president faced an implacable Congress and Republicans also won control of most state legislatures, which were to determine the districts for House seats after the 2010 census, guaranteeing Republicans a majority in the House for years to come.

By now, Thomas Franklin had sold his group of weekly newspapers in West Georgia but continued to write columns for several Georgia newspapers. He once more realized that the real opportunity to influence events was as a candidate or office-holder. He was especially distressed that the election process, which the candidate in his dream had supported so totally had failed so badly. But the worst was still to come in 2016.

In 2008, the nation had fallen into its worst economic decline since the Great Depression, which provided the way to victory for Obama. Bush was president at the time and his policies of tax cuts and supply-side economics had plowed the ground for what was called "the great recession." To many Americans it felt more like a second depression.

Obama proved to be a competent president, though never accepted by most Republicans and some independents as "one of us." Their campaign motto became "take back our country" and the inference was pretty clear. In the 2014 mid-terms, once more using the health care issue, the Republicans dominated elections to both houses of Congress, leaving Obama a weak hand, even though he won a second term as president in 2012, defeating Republican Mitt Romney, a former Massachusetts governor.

The years moved on. The recession, which started in September 2008 with the collapse of the Goldman Sachs Investment Company, continued. There was little to revive the economy as Republicans blocked most efforts to insert more money, citing the federal deficit as the reason, even after it balanced in 1999. Unemployment dropped to 6 percent by the end of 2016. But the total number of Americans actually employed stayed lower due to technology that replaced their jobs and companies that sought lower wage workers in other countries. Many companies actually considered themselves part of the global economy, not the American. They put their money in low or no-tax countries.

The US stock market soared, however, as companies became more profitable with much of their profits going to pay enormous salaries to their CEO and other executives, or to buy out their competition. Obama and the Democrats could do little to correct the imbalance and were further handicapped by the health care bill, passed in 2009, which was still a battle cry for the Republicans even though it had extended health insurance to millions of more Americans. Large companies, with their executives' highest salaries virtually untaxed, had used the money to become monopolies rather than job creators. The minimum wage had stalled at a 10-year low, compared to cost-of-living increases.

The 2016 presidential election promised relief from the deadlock in government and from Republican obstruction. Hillary Clinton was the favored nominee for the Democrats. She was arguably the most qualified candidate for president in the nation's history, having been First Lady for eight years, a US senator from New York for two terms, and Obama's Secretary of State in his first term. The Republicans had too many candidates, all of whom had some claim to consideration, except one. That was the billionaire realtor and former TV show host, Donald Trump, a public figure for twenty years, who had never sought or held a public office. His main public role in recent years had been leading a campaign to prove that President Obama had not been born in the United States and was therefore ineligible to be president. The campaign continued even after Obama's election, with Obama producing an official birth certificate from Hawaii, where he had been born. Trump denounced it as fake.

The Republicans were also having to defend Senate and House seats they had picked up in the mid-term elections of 2010 and even back to 1994. The 2016 election was the most media-centric election in history, beginning with the Iowa caucus and continuing to the final night of the campaign. The major polls all showed Clinton with a small but shrinking lead. Trump had proven a showman like no other candidate and Hillary Clinton was picked to pieces by large and small problems of her 30-year public career, including her husband's terms as president and Arkansas governor. Even the NAFTA treaty came back to haunt her. Bill's sexual adventures also hurt Hillary with woman voters who considered her "an enabler."

But there seemed no way she could lose. Trump was a three-time married confessed adulterer, tax manipulator and had been a Democrat most of his life. Thomas Franklin watched the campaign with dismay. Since his long dream nearly twenty years earlier he had been a regular dreamer, usually about small newspapers and the chance to buy or sell them or improve them. The dreams usually ended well but on the night of November 8, 2016, his dream kept on and became a nightmare. Jean finally shook him awake, "What's wrong, honey?" she asked, "You're talking in your sleep."

Franklin roused himself and was relieved that it had only been a dream. He had dreamed that Trump was elected president. When he turned off the TV and slipped into sleep the night before, the count was close, but New York and California still had not reported their final totals. They were expected to be strong for Hillary. But he had worried from the first state reports early in the evening. Trump had won Indiana and Kentucky by much larger margins than expected plus Republicans had easily won the Indiana Senate seat against a former Democratic governor and senator.

And it had happened! Trump won the most electoral votes, but he was losing the popular vote by the largest margin of any elected president in US history, some three million votes by count's end. But the electoral college was still in place despite its past disasters in 1824, 1860, 1876, 2000, and other elections, when the results were unfair and damaging.

The final popular presidential vote was 65,845,000 for Clinton and 62,980,600 for Trump. That was by far the largest popular vote difference between the electoral winner and electoral loser in the nation's history. The popular margin difference was more votes than were cast in the seven smallest sates.

But Trump and his supporters quickly took over the levers of power in the federal government and the people accepted the verdict, as they had accepted every electoral verdict, a tribute to respect for the constitutional process, but a failure to see the perverted process which the electoral college had become. Almost more distressing to Franklin was the results in congressional races, as the Democrats picked up only one seat in the Senate, when they had at least seven opportunities.

So the nation went into 2017 with Republicans controlling the presidency, the House, the Senate and the Supreme Court, and the Democrats so beaten and embarrassed that there was not a prominent leader left as a likely presidential candidate for 2020.

Trump defended his popular vote loss and the electoral college and claimed he would have campaigned differently if popular votes were to have been the deciding factor. But that was a bogus claim. He had lost his home state of New York by 4,547,000 to 2,819,000, or 59 percent for Hillary and 36 percent for Trump. He lost California by almost 2–1. A larger vote would most likely have expanded Hillary's popular margin, as many black voters who had supported Obama in 2008 and 2012 failed to vote in 2016.

Franklin felt great sorrow for Hillary as a person. She had not only been expected to win the presidency, but also to bring in a solid majority of Democrats in Congress. The baggage she and Bill had been accumulating for nearly thirty years finally proved too much. And at 69, her campaign had apparently ended the Clinton era in American politics, oddly unfulfilled. One factor that defeated her was the surprise popularity of Bernie Sanders in the primaries which left her weakened but at 74, Sanders was also no longer in position to be a future contender.

Franklin thought Hillary actually lost the election when she selected Virginia Senator Tim Kaine as her running mate. Kaine added little to the ticket and was not a strong campaigner. Trump had nailed him early when he said Kaine reminded him of a villain from the Batman movies. Hillary needed a Midwesterner as her running mate, which seemed important during the primary campaigns and proved decisive in the final election returns when she lost such usually reliable Democratic states as Michigan, Wisconsin, Ohio and Pennsylvania. A running mate from that critical area could have made the difference since Trump's margins were thin and those states had the decisive electoral votes. Any running mate should have been able to help her carry Virginia, because of the large number of federal employees living there.

Franklin comforted himself with one thought: Of the Republican candidates in the primaries, Trump was conceivably the most progressive, despite his many flaws. For much of his life, he'd been a Democrat, who came of age in the New Deal years. His true beliefs were difficult to decipher but in his private life he believed in spending money and had no fear of debt, having declared bankruptcy on some of his personal projects.

In the early days of his administration Trump repeated many promises but one promise stood out dramatically to Thomas Franklin: Trump pledged to ask for a trillion dollars to build and expand the US infrastructure, which had fallen into such disrepair, with many highways and bridges more than one hundred years old, and many office buildings and homes built for the nineteenth century or even the eighteenth. Trump was at heart a builder and the figure he proposed was the largest in US history, a trillion dollars, with a T.

That amount of money distributed into the federal budget, the budgets of the 50 states, and the budgets of many cities and counties would create thousands of jobs, put spending money in millions of wallets and create an economic boom comparable to the booms of World War II, the interstate highway system, the space programs and Reagan's military buildup.

The legacy of the New Deal lived on.

Photo by Pete McCommons

Millard B. Grimes has been a reporter, editor, and publisher on newspapers since his junior year in high school when he got a summer job as a proofreader for his hometown daily paper in Columbus, Georgia. A native Georgian, he graduated from the University of Georgia with a journalism degree in 1951 and then took a full-time job on the Columbus paper, where he was its front page editor when it won the Pulitzer Prize for Community Service in 1955. He became editor in chief of the Columbus morning newspaper in 1962 and wrote most of its editorials as well as a personal column for the next seven years. In 1969, he formed a group of investors to buy a small daily in Opelika, Alabama, and for the next forty years, headed a company that published some thirty daily and weekly newspapers in Georgia and Alabama, as well as two statewide magazines in Georgia, including Georgia Trend, the second-largest magazine in Georgia. He was an active observer of politics in both states, although never a candidate.

He did serve as president of the Georgia and Alabama Press Associations and was also president of the Magazine Association of Georgia. In 2007, he received the University of Georgia Grady College of Journalism's award for career achievement, and the journalism college's editing and reporting lab is named for him.

Grimes is married to the former Charlotte Sheridan, and they have three children, James Sheridan Grimes, Athens, Georgia; Kathy G. Garrett, Norcross, Georgia; and Laura G. Griner, Anderson, S.C.

Author's Note

The Last New Dealer is mainly a fictional account of the 1992 Democratic Presidential Party primaries, but it is also a very non-fictional account of how 13 small, scattered and quarreling British colonies along the unsettled North American coast developed into the most important nation in history.

I am indebted to many sources for the information, quotations and anecdotes, among the most important of which are those listed below:

Bartlett, Donald L. and Steele, James B. **America: Who Stole the Dream?**

Carter, Jimmy. **Keeping the Faith**

Carter, Jimmy. **Turning Point.**

Time-Life Books. **The History of the Civil War: Gettysburg.**

Edward Smith, Jean, **FDR.**

Germond, Jack and Witcover, Jules. **Mad as Hell: Revolt at the Ballot Box.**

Goldman, Peter and Mathews, Tom. **Quest for the Presidency**

Groom, Winston, **1942**

Hacker, Jacob S. and Pierson, Paul. **Winner-Take-All Politics**

Herman, Arthur. **How the Scots Invented the Modern World**

Jennings, Genelle. **Into the Jaws of Politics: The Charge of the Peanut Brigade**

Johnson, Haynes. **The Best of Times**

Kearns Goodwin, Doris. **No Ordinary Time**

Leuhtenburg, William. **Franklin Roosevelt and The New Deal**

Lippman Ted. **The Squire of Warm Springs**

McElvaine, Robert S. **The Great Depression**

McGregor, James. **The Lion and the Fox**

Miller, Zell. **Great Georgians**

Moore, Jim and Ihde, Rick. **Clinton, Young Man In a Hurry**

Phillips, Kevin. **The Politics of the Rich and Poor**

Tuchman, Barbara W. **The Guns of August**

Plus many more…

CPSIA information can be obtained
at www.ICGtesting.com
Printed in the USA
LVHW111300211220
674766LV00019B/88/J